W9-CFM-209

Power to Rise

THE STORY OF THE NATIONAL BALLET OF CANADA

18 FEB 98

DEAR SUZANNE,
WHAT AN INSPIRATION
YOU HAVE BEEN TO US.
THANK YOU.

James K

Power to Rise

THE STORY OF THE NATIONAL BALLET OF CANADA

James Neufeld

University of Toronto Press
Toronto Buffalo London

Published by University of Toronto Press Incorporated
Toronto Buffalo London
Printed in Canada
ISBN 0-8020-4109-4

Printed on acid-free paper 

Canadian Cataloguing in Publication Data

Neufeld, James E., 1944-
Power to rise

Includes bibliographical references and index.
ISBN 0-8020-4109-4

1. National Ballet of Canada - History.
I. Title.

GV1786.N3N48 1996 792.8'0971'09 C96-931624-0

Portions of chapter ten have appeared previously, in a different form, in the *Journal of Canadian Studies*.

Every effort has been made to identify and contact the copyright holders for the illustrative material in this volume. Upon notification, any credits will be corrected in subsequent editions.

University of Toronto Press acknowledges the financial assistance to its publishing program of the Canada Council and the Ontario Arts Council.

Publication of this book has been made possible, in part, by a generous grant from the McLean Foundation.

This book has been published with the help of a grant from the Canadian Federation for the Humanities, using funds provided by the Social Sciences and Humanities Research Council of Canada.

For the Artists of the Ballet

- and for A, K, and L

Contents

Acknowledgments ix

Prologue xi

CHAPTER ONE: They Were Going to Have a Company 1

CHAPTER TWO: An Okay Beginning 27

CHAPTER THREE: I Won in the First Few Years 49

CHAPTER FOUR: Not without Honour 77

CHAPTER FIVE: A Voice Crying in the Wilderness 111

CHAPTER SIX: I Don't Believe in a Flimsy *Sleeping Beauty* 139

CHAPTER SEVEN: A Ballet Company Is Not a School 167

CHAPTER EIGHT: Outspoken in Our Work and in Our Dancing 201

CHAPTER NINE: He Who Pays the Piper: Of Finances and Friends 229

CHAPTER TEN: Discovering the Centre 259

Appendices 289

- A/ National Ballet of Canada Itinerary 292
- B/ Concert Group Itinerary 333
- C/ Choreographic Workshops 336
- D/ Dancers of the National Ballet of Canada 338
- E/ Members of the Board, the National Ballet of Canada 342

Notes 346

Select Bibliography 358

Photo Credits 359

Index 361

Acknowledgments

A book like this could be completed only with the generous help and support of countless people and organizations — friends, family, colleagues, professionals in the dance field, libraries and archives, funding agencies, and the National Ballet itself. To all I owe an enormous debt of gratitude; from the earliest days, I have met with encouragement, support, and cooperation from all whose help was essential if the project was to become reality; many shared with me their personal recollections of the company; some showed me treasured scrapbooks and other memorabilia. The names of all these people are listed in the 'Note on Sources' preceding the endnotes.

Without the cooperation of Celia Franca, the company's founder, this project could not have proceeded. I am grateful to her for allowing me early access to most of her personal papers, housed in the National Archives of Canada, for welcoming me into her home so that I could record her recollections of the company, for responding to my many subsequent questions and requests for cooperation, and for trusting a dark horse to carry the story of her life's achievement forward to the Canadian public.

My greatest regret is that I began this project too late to be able to interview Erik Bruhn, but every other artistic director of the company, past and present, consented to be interviewed for the project. From the long list of those associated with the company who spoke with me, either on or off the record, I want to thank particularly Betty Oliphant, whose knowledge, candour, and perspective were essential to a well-balanced account of the company.

It was remarkable that the National Ballet of Canada would consent to be studied and scrutinized for an independent work of this nature, over which they retained no editorial control. From my first approach, Bob Johnston, the general manager, extended to me the kind of 'hands-off' cooperation that was crucial to my work, allowing me ready access to information without attempting to influence the final text in any way. Few other historians of an organization have enjoyed comparable assistance and independence. I thank Bob Johnston and the company administration for this extraordinary demonstration of confidence.

With this cooperation, my research assistant and I were able to work daily in the company's headquarters in the St Lawrence Hall in Toronto, were given full access to its irreplaceable archives, and were allowed to observe its day-to-day activities over the space of several years. To the many people who wondered about these strangers in their midst, and whose professional lives may have been disrupted by their presence, my thanks. I hope this record of your achievements will make up for any inconvenience.

The company's Publicity Department was unfailingly helpful and courteous in putting me in touch with valuable sources of information. Gregory Patterson, the publicity director at the time most of the research was undertaken, opened doors and made possible interviews which would never have taken place without his assistance. Julia Drake, his successor in the post, and Belinda Bale have also been extremely helpful.

The company's archives are a resource of immense significance to Canada's cultural and theatrical history. I was guided through their enormous holdings by the company's archivist, Assis Carreiro, who became an enthusiastic supporter of the project as well as a family friend, and, after her departure, by the current company archivist, Sharon Vanderlinde. Leslie Taschner and Su Lin Lee also answered innumerable archival questions.

My thanks also to the staff at the National Archives of Canada, especially to Anne Goddard, Paulette Dozois, and Roger Leblanc, who helped me gain access to Celia Franca's papers and to records of the Canada Council housed there; to Anne Yandle of the University of British Columbia Library Special Collections; to Annette Wengle at the Theatre Department of the Metropolitan Toronto Reference Library; to Jane Pritchard, archivist of Ballet Rambert and the English National Ballet, for making available documents in both collections relating to Celia Franca and to other early members of the National Ballet of Canada; to Cassie Burke, who allowed me to examine material relating to Erik Bruhn not yet transferred to the company's archives; to Kelly Rooney, at the Royal Winnipeg Ballet, who was patient and cheerful in helping me to obtain a necessary picture permission; to Joan Tanner and to John Fraser, for allowing me to use their essays on the National Ballet; and to Lawrence and Miriam Adams, who shared with me materials from the Dance Canada Danse collection, as well as their recollections as dancers with the company.

Two Leave Fellowships from the Social Sciences and Humanities Research Council of Canada made possible the initial research and writing for this book. Final publication of the text was supported by grants from the Canadian Federation for the Humanities and from the McLean Foundation. To all these organizations and agencies I express my thanks. My own employer, Trent University, cooperated fully in granting me the necessary leaves to complete the work. I am grateful for this cooperation and, in particular, to John Stubbs and Leonard Conolly for support and encouragement.

The staff at the University of Toronto Press, particularly Bill Harnum and Suzanne Rancourt, demonstrated their support by the care and expeditiousness with which they sped the text through to publication. Theresa Griffin copy-edited the complicated manuscript with meticulous attention to detail, against impossible deadlines.

Many friends helped in innumerable ways by expressing interest in the project and by extending their hospitality during my research travels. To John Wilkins, Carol MacKinnon, Chris Archibald, and Nancy Oldfield, all in Toronto; to Arthur and Marilyn Margon, in New York; to my brother-in-law, Bob Robertson, in Edmonton; to my aunt, the late Erna Wiens of Vancouver; to my parents, George and Schura Neufeld, and my brother, Philip Neufeld, in Ottawa, thank you. Leslie Getz and Leland Windreich shared their considerable knowledge of dance with me and became friends in the process. Mary McDonald, for many years the company's pianist, believed in the project from the outset and repeatedly buoyed me up with her faith and enthusiasm.

Power to Rise had an unusual genesis in that it was, from the beginning, a collaborative effort. Ramsay Derry, who edited the text, acted as consultant, adviser, and guide from the project's inception. His exacting creative standards, broad general knowledge, and knowledge of ballet in particular were invaluable throughout. V. John Lee, the book's designer, joined the team early on; his discriminating taste and keen eye defined and developed a design concept that did honour to the subject matter. Lynn Neufeld, my research assistant on the project, spent countless hours tracking down and compiling the statistics which appear in the book's appendices, and which I consulted at every stage of writing. The enthusiasm, help, and support of these three friends have made this book possible.

Finally, to Lynn, this time as my wife, and to my daughters, Katharine and Amy, whose lives have been disrupted by 'the book' for the past ten years, thank you. Without your help and your faith in me, I would never have begun.

Prologue

Long before I had any direct experience of it, ballet fascinated me. One of my early childhood recollections is of making a scrapbook with pictures of a ballerina dressed in white. Years later, looking through the archives of the National Ballet, I realized they were pictures of Celia Franca, in costume for Giselle.

I didn't see the real thing – a full-length ballet production, live, in a theatre – until I was nineteen years old. The National's brand new *Romeo and Juliet*, in 1964, swept me away, although I thought at the time that Franca's Lady Capulet was absurdly histrionic. Thirty years later, the detail of that evening has slipped from my memory, but the picture of Lady Capulet tearing her hair in grief is still vivid in my imagination. I realize now that Franca's performance embarrassed me then only because it exceeded the bounds of anything I had experienced. It became one of the things that fuelled my lifelong passion for dance, that brought me back to the theatre repeatedly, hoping to see enacted on the stage the dreams and emotions that underlie everyday existence.

Later, I encountered the works of Ben Jonson, the seventeenth-century English dramatist and poet who devoted much of his career to masques, curious amalgams of dance, music, poetry, and theatrical spectacle, created for the court of James I. A stanza in one of those masques struck me with special force.

For dancing is an exercise
Not only shows the mover's wit,
But maketh the beholder wise,
As he hath power to rise to it.

These words illuminated the passion for dance that has animated much of my life. Jonson proclaimed dance as a high ideal, one that united the dancer and the spectator, provided they had the power to rise to its challenge. I thought back on how long it had taken me to rise to the challenge of Franca's Lady Capulet, still living in my memory.

When I came to write this history of the National Ballet of Canada, Jonson's words remained my guide. I knew that, as an outsider, a beholder, I could not hope to provide an insider's view. The dancers' account is presented best by the dancers themselves, as Karen Kain has demonstrated most recently in her candid, moving autobiography. The beholder can tell different truths, however, can testify to the enduring value of the dances that exist only in the moment of performance, then vanish from sight. A chronicle of the company's activities, a reflection on its achievements and shortcomings, a tribute to such ephemeral creations, this book is above all a discharging of the beholder's duty. By recording, examining, and understanding the company's life, we who watch, like those who dance, may gain the power to rise and approach a fuller understanding of the delights and mysteries that dance can offer.

CHAPTER ONE

They Were Going to Have a Company

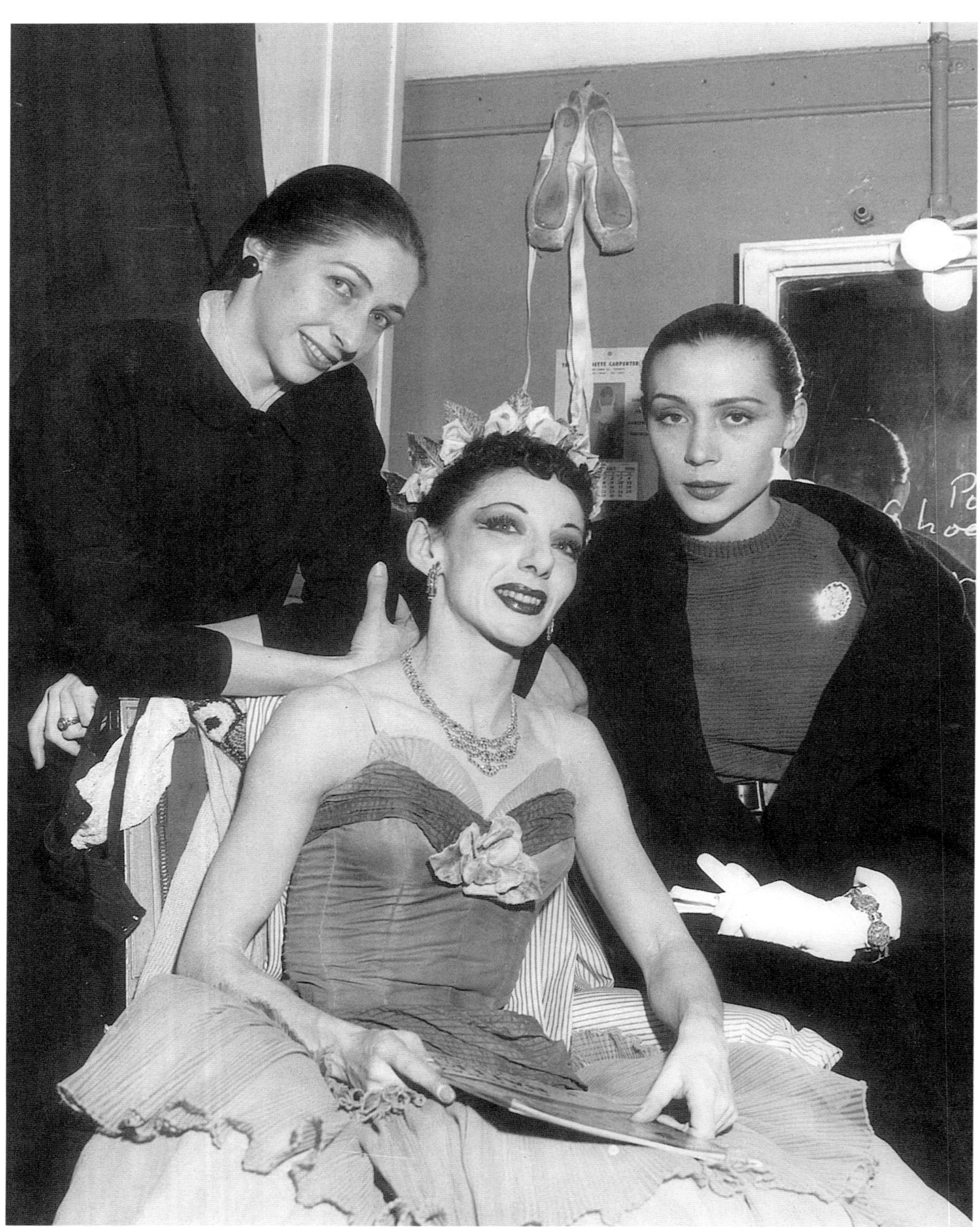

Ballet in Canada before the National Ballet of Canada

Opening night of Erik Bruhn's new production of *Coppélia* for the National Ballet of Canada. Some members of the audience in the O'Keefe Centre on that February night in 1975 could still recall with affection the company's first production of *Coppélia*, long a staple of the repertoire. It had last been seen at the Royal Alexandra Theatre twelve years previously, almost to the night. For those bent on pursuing this sentimental strain, tonight's opening night excitement was bittersweet. Celia Franca, choreographer of that first *Coppélia*, founder of the company, and *grande dame* of Canadian ballet, was no longer at the helm. She had resigned the artistic directorship of the National Ballet of Canada in favour of David Haber the previous July, just two years shy of the company's twenty-fifth anniversary. But such thoughts were undercurrents to the dominant nostalgia of the evening, for this *Coppélia* was dedicated to the three Toronto women who had brought the National Ballet of Canada into being. Their

OPPOSITE: Celia Franca, in costume for Offenbach in the Underworld, *with visiting Royal Ballet star Svetlana Beriosova (right), and Lois Smith (left), the rising star of Franca's company (ca. 1958).*

ABOVE: Though Kay Ambrose's designs were often criticized as fussy and elaborate, many observers considered Coppélia *(1952) one of her finest achievements. The Czardas, with Ray Moller (centre) and Lilian Jarvis (right).*

invitation to Celia Franca to come to Canada in 1951 and advise them on the prospects for a professional ballet company had led, by a sometimes perilous route, to the full panoply of this opening night, to this confident troupe of dancers, well known to its Canadian fans, experienced on the major stages of Europe and North America. A special program insert named them – Sydney Mulqueen, Pearl Whitehead, and Aileen Woods – for all to acknowledge as the founders, champions, and guiding spirits of the National Ballet.

And yet, the story of the National does not properly begin with them. Despite their pride of place in the received standard version of the founding, they were themselves responding to a combination of circumstances and a number of individual personalities which made their initiative possible, perhaps inevitable. The founding of the National was no isolated event, independent of the currents of the time. To discover why, and how, Mrs Mulqueen, Mrs Whitehead, and Mrs Woods issued their famous invitation in the first place, we need to take a few steps back in time, before the events of 1950 and 1951 which brought Celia Franca to Canada. We need to consider briefly the state of ballet as a popular art form after the Second World War as well as the climate for dance in pre–Canada-Council Canada.

All western ballet in the twentieth century begins with Serge Diaghilev, the Russian impresario who introduced the performers and repertoire of imperial St Petersburg to Paris, then to London and the rest of the western world. Once exiled from Russia, he turned his company into the cradle of the avant garde, nurturing the talents of choreographers, dancers, painters, and musicians in an outburst of creative energy that defined the artistic identity of the century. Stravinsky and Picasso were his collaborators. George Balanchine choreographed for him. And to him were drawn the aspiring dancers who, touched by his influence, would go out to embody their conceptions of the art he represented for them.

The Polish Marie Rambert and the Irish Ninette de Valois (born Edris Stannus) were two such pioneers. After working with Diaghilev in Paris, they settled in London and introduced ballet, as their experience with Diaghilev had revealed it to them, to the British public. Ballet in England had none of the tradition of royal patronage or public subsidy that had given the art a long life in Russia, France, and Scandinavia. Rambert, through her work at the Ballet Club in London's tiny Mercury Theatre, and through the formation of Ballet Rambert, de Valois, through her founding at the Sadler's Wells Theatre of the company that eventually became the Royal Ballet, established the art form in England. Through the 1930s and 1940s, these two women built, almost from scratch, a British version of ballet tradition that came to dominate the world's vision of ballet. The 1948 release of the movie *The Red Shoes*, starring the Sadler's Wells ballerina Moira Shearer, prepared the way for the Sadler's Wells' triumphant appearances at the Metropolitan Opera in New York in 1949. Ballet became redefined as one of Britain's cultural treasures, despite its arrival there a mere twenty years earlier.

Not everyone, however, agreed. George Balanchine made only a brief detour to England, where he worked in its popular musical theatre, the Cochran Revues and Sir Oswald Stoll's variety entertainments at the Coliseum. After moving to the United States, he founded first a school and then a company, the New York City Ballet, which also traced its roots to the Russian heritage as exemplified by Diaghilev. Balanchine, however, developed out of that common source a tradition of neoclassical, abstract ballet antithetically opposed to the ideals of British ballet. These large historical differences later became the source of conflicting views about the proper direction for the young National Ballet of Canada; the differences between de Valois and Balanchine touched even the Canadians' fate.

Diaghilev's dancers also taught. Enrico Cecchetti, the Italian expatriate who had made a brilliant dancing career in St Petersburg before becoming Diaghilev's ballet master, settled for a time in London, where he coached virtually every prominent dancer of the era. Through his teaching, and through the teaching of such pupils as Stanislas Idzikowski, the Cecchetti conception of style and the Cecchetti syllabus of movement for ballet became a living force in the creation of the British performance tradition. Established artists like Marie Rambert, developing ones like the young choreographer Antony Tudor, found in the Cecchetti tradition a strong basis for their art and communicated their respect to younger colleagues, aspiring youngsters like Celia Franca and Betty Oliphant. Far-flung as the world of professional ballet eventually became, one of the main branches of its tradition led inevitably back to London and the handful of dancers and choreographers who had come in direct contact with Diaghilev.

Franca's first Swan Lake *retained the role of Benno, the Prince's friend, seen here supporting Odette (Lois Smith) while Siegfried (David Adams) looks on.*

Prior to 1950, however, that tradition had virtually no foothold in Canada. Even the conception of dance as a profession must have seemed alien and exotic, frustratingly out of reach of the few who might have dreamed of it. Indeed, the desire to dance and the need to earn a living were mutually exclusive goals in the Canada of the late 1940s. The resultant conflict inevitably drove the talented and the ambitious away from their own country.[1] Paddy Stone, after a start in Winnipeg, went first to Broadway, then to London and a contract with the Sadler's Wells Theatre Ballet.[2] David Adams also left Winnipeg for study in England, where he eventually wound up as a dancer with the Metropolitan Ballet.[3] Lois Smith, on the west coast, had to supplement summer employment at Theatre under the Stars with work in San Francisco and Los Angeles as well as with American touring companies of Broadway musicals.[4] After initial studies in her native Ottawa, Patricia Wilde pursued an international career in Europe and the United States.[5] Patricia Drylie and Mildred Herman, both students of Boris Volkoff in Toronto, made careers in New York, Drylie with the Rockettes of Radio City Music Hall and Herman with Radio City Music Hall and Ballet Theatre. Under her stage name of Melissa Hayden, Herman enjoyed a long and distinguished career as a prominent member of the New York City Ballet and one of Balanchine's most popular ballerinas.[6] She returned to Canada in 1963 as an international celebrity, the first guest artist to be invited to dance with the National Ballet.[7]

Jury Gotshalks and Irene Apiné showed off their bravura style in the pas de deux from Don Quixote. *The outdoor setting suggests this photo may have been taken during the company's visit to Jacob's Pillow in Lee, Massachusetts, in August 1953.*

Hayden's experience provided the most conspicuous illustration of the problem that plagued dance teachers in Canada: the complete absence, within the country, of professional opportunities that would stimulate and retain their most promising students. Without such opportunity, without a tangible, professional goal for the serious student of dance, their teaching would forever be restricted to the beginners and the mediocre. As in so many areas of Canadian cultural life during this period, real promise in an individual conferred on her the dubious distinction of exile. To stay at home was to admit either cowardice or defeat. In commenting on the Third Annual Canadian Ballet Festival of 1950, Guy Glover, a National Film Board producer and prominent Canadian balletomane, lamented the fate of Jury Gotshalks and Irene Apiné, recently arrived in Canada and facing the dilemma head-on:

> *Here are two young dancers, with a formidable technical grounding, who attempt material which is technically beyond almost any other Canadian dancer, yet the relative isolation of their home-base* [Halifax], *the lack of frequent opportunity to dance before audiences, the lack of contact with a first-rate* maître de ballet, *are rapidly ruining them as dancers of top quality.*[8]

Such a climate could do little to sustain dancing or teaching at an advanced level.

But teachers there were, and not only of the small-town, ballet–tap–baton-twirling variety. In the 1930s, June Roper of Vancouver had placed ten of her students in Ballet Theatre and the two Ballets Russes companies of Colonel de Basil.[9] These touring companies, distant cousins of the earlier Diaghilev Ballets Russes, were among the chief popularizers of ballet for international audiences through this period. Few people realized that their 'Russian' ballerinas were often British, American, or Canadian dancers, recruited on the road and rechristened for their new profession. One of them, Roper's pupil Rosemary Deveson, later gave the young Lois Smith her first ballet instruction in studios on top of the Georgia Hotel in Vancouver.[10] In 1929, Boris Volkoff arrived in Toronto from Russia, by way of Shanghai and Chicago, and by 1930 he had established the dance studio which was to function until his death in 1974.[11] The British emigrants Gweneth Lloyd and Betty Farrally planted their flag in Winnipeg in 1938.[12] Out of their pioneering efforts sprang, in remarkably short order, the Winnipeg Ballet Club and then the Royal Winnipeg Ballet. The daring, resilience, and determination of its founders still characterize the company, whose demonstrated ability to adapt to changing circumstances has kept it a vital force in Canadian ballet and a significant rival to the National for the affections of the Canadian public. Betty Oliphant, a former student of Marie Rambert, destined to become the moving force behind the National Ballet School and acknowledged authority on dance education in Canada, arrived in Toronto in 1947 and quickly established her leading role in dance teaching circles. She assisted at the birth of the Canadian Dance Teachers Association, which emerged, with Toronto teacher Mildred Wickson as its first president, at the Second Annual Canadian Ballet Festival in Toronto in 1949.[13] Jury Gotshalks and Irene Apiné, after enduring the privations of enforced labour in Latvia, fled to Halifax and, in 1947, began teaching ballet through the Conservatory of Music, for want of any other established outlet.[14] By the late 1940s, the major players in the development of Canadian ballet were assembling, anxious to do something to create continuing opportunities for professional dance.

Some efforts had already been made. The Winnipeg Ballet, successor to the Winnipeg Ballet Club founded in 1938, offered sporadic performance opportunities to its dancers. But none of them was paid for dancing until 1949, and by 1951 the maximum honorarium for a dancer was a scant one hundred dollars a month for a nine-month season.[15] Boris Volkoff, in response to a request from Mr Mulqueen of the Sports Committee for Canada, had taken a group of dancers to compete in the *Tanzwettspiele* of the 1936 Berlin Olympics, where the essentially amateur troupe of his students had been well received in predominantly professional surroundings.[16] From that point on, the indefatigable Volkoff lost no opportunity to present his dancers whenever occasion warranted. His flamboyant Russian personality and vigorously athletic approach to style made him openly contemptuous of the emerging

In 1951, the British press covered Franca's departure from Waterloo station to conduct an eight-month ballet survey in Canada. 'Then I shall either return here or start the company,' Franca was quoted as saying.

British school of dancing, which he considered anaemic and prissy. From his Toronto teaching studios he took on any and all choreographic assignments, from promenade concerts to figure-skating shows, and during the 1940s he established himself as a dominant force in Toronto ballet circles. Despite efforts to raise funds for professional operation, however,[17] the Volkoff Canadian Ballet remained a non-professional enterprise, its dancers making their livings in other careers.[18]

But if the goal of full-time professional operation for their troupes eluded both Gweneth Lloyd and Boris Volkoff during this period, they did succeed in bringing together some of the far-flung amateur performing groups in the nation at the annual Canadian Ballet Festivals. These Festivals, the brainchild of Lloyd's Winnipeg associate David Yeddeau, created performance opportunities, public awareness, and a heightened sense of anticipation for the development of dance in Canada.[19] Between the first Festival, of 1948, in Winnipeg and the Montreal edition of 1950, a number of dreams had begun to form themselves into more or less concrete plans. As a result, Celia Franca, former dramatic ballerina of the Sadler's Wells Ballet and aspiring freelance choreographer, was a guest at the 1950 Festival, invited to judge the possibilities for forming a professional dance company on a national scale in Canada.

How exactly did she come to be there? Many people, over the years, have claimed at least partial credit for setting in motion the train of events that brought her. One of them, by Max Wyman's account, was Gweneth Lloyd herself,[20] who had left Winnipeg for Toronto in early October 1950 and quickly become deeply involved in the dance scene there. (The program for the Fourth Canadian Ballet Festival in 1952 lists Gweneth Lloyd, Celia Franca, and Betty Oliphant, all of Toronto, among the executive committee members of the Canadian Dance Teachers Association.)[21] Another was Boris Volkoff, who counted himself among the individuals consulted by Mrs Mulqueen, Mrs Whitehead, and Mrs Woods as to the feasibility of forming a professional ballet company in Canada.[22] Stewart James, who was eventually to make the first direct contact with Franca on behalf of the Canadian group, was another agitator for the cause. He had been trying to advance the Volkoff Canadian Ballet in the Far East as early as 1948 and 1949. In a letter commenting on his efforts, Volkoff stated that 'in order to be recognized and accepted as an essential part of our own National culture, we must be accepted elsewhere first.'[23] The same letter urged, however, that a decision to tour be held off until the spring of 1950, so that there would be 'ample time to discuss every angle and to perfect our plans.' Those plans had included a survey that James had done, on Volkoff's behalf, of the performance opportunities on the Ontario touring circuit.[24] Volkoff and James clearly had great hopes for the development of professional dance in Canada. James in his turn stressed the importance of Kay Ransom's contribution, as secretary of the Canadian Ballet Festival Association, to the dreams and plans. At the time of her death in 1977, he wrote in a letter to the Toronto *Globe and Mail*:

> *As the catalyst that brought together all the parts to make the National Ballet a reality, I, probably more than any one other person, know how it all actually came about. This last week saw the passing of one of the true heroes – though truly unsung – of the formation of the National Ballet and the development of dance in this country.*[25]

Janet Baldwin, a daughter of Toronto's upper middle class who studied dance with Volkoff and then married him and became his business associate in the studio, was a key player in the plans for the formation of a national company as well.[26] With a common goal, but with conflicting ideals and personal ambitions, these were the principal players whose active concern for the cause of dance in Canada eventually involved Mrs Mulqueen, Mrs Whitehead, and Mrs Woods in the project. Much later, Dame Ninette de Valois recalled the general climate of opinion in Canada at the time that her advice was solicited: 'I remember about the same time I made a lecture tour of Canada, and I got up against this proposition, that they were going to have a company, everywhere.'[27] Franca herself agrees that the three founders acted not as initial catalysts, but in response to a genuinely felt need and to specific pressures from the Canadian dance community.[28] The officially recognized founders of the National Ballet did not operate in isolation.

Nor was Franca's initial role entirely clear-cut. At the earliest stages of negotiations, she was apparently approached to be ballet mistress, not artistic director, of the fledgling enterprise. A handwritten sheet of paper, unsigned and undated but identified in a separate hand as 'from Stewart James,' exists in the National Ballet Archives. Addressed to Mrs Whitehead, it summarizes the state of negotiations with Franca at the time of writing. A portion of it is worth quoting.

> *Aprox Sept 20th I wrote to Miss Franca confirming my talks in London: –*
> *$60.00 per week per session of 1 year plus an option of 2nd & 3rd seasons. return fare London/Toronto/London to be Ballet Mistress and assistant to Artistic Director Position – She would like to know exact relation to Director and to dancers.*[29]

The terms of Franca's invitation clarified

According to this evidence, then, Franca was originally asked, by Volkoff's associate, Stewart James, to be ballet mistress for an artistic director whose identity is unspecified in the surviving documents. But on 19 October 1950, Aileen Woods wrote to Franca as follows:

> *We feel very strongly that this Professional Ballet Company would benefit greatly by hav-*

> *ing someone with your reputation and qualifications as its Producer and Director as well as being its Ballet Mistress. Can you possibly accept this further responsibility?*[30]

The invitation to Franca to serve as artistic director was thus clearly stated as early as October 1950, *before* her visit to the Third Canadian Ballet Festival in Montreal. It appears, however, to have been a revision of an earlier approach to her along somewhat different lines.

The background and precise sequence of events matter, because the date and contents of Aileen Woods' letter argue against an interpretation of early events that gained some currency in the 1960s. This version of the founding would have it that Franca accepted the offer to become ballet mistress for Volkoff's proposed company and then manoeuvred him out of the key position of artistic director after her arrival in Canada. Brian Macdonald implied as much in an address delivered in England and published in the British dance periodical the *Dancing Times* in April 1963.

> *Volkoff sent his company manager to England to study the administration of the Sadler's Wells Ballet, and while here the English dancer Celia Franca was recommended to him. She came out to see a ballet festival, decided to accept a job as ballet mistress for Volkoff, and settled in Canada in the spring of 1951. She met with Volkoff and his board of directors and, in the strange ways of ballet companies, emerged as artistic director of the National Ballet of Canada.*[31]

Macdonald, although a charter member of the company, would seem to be mistaken about the sequence of events. Whether or not Volkoff saw himself at this point as artistic director of a national company, Franca had in hand a clear offer of the position before her first trip to Canada. None of the documents surviving in the company's archives or in the Volkoff papers refers to the infant board of directors as Volkoff's board or to Volkoff as artistic director of the proposed company.

Volkoff and Lloyd inevitably felt passed over.

Today, long after the events in question, the motives and expectations of the key individuals are difficult to reconstruct. One hypothesis as to those motives, however, presents itself with considerable force. Both Boris Volkoff and Gweneth Lloyd had national aspirations which had received a degree of gratification through the medium of the first two Ballet Festivals. By late 1950, Gweneth Lloyd and David Yeddeau had left Winnipeg and relocated in Toronto, where the action was clearly going to be. (Lloyd had left Winnipeg for Toronto a scant two weeks before Aileen Woods' 19 October letter of invitation to Franca.) Was Lloyd hoping to become the founding artistic director of a new, national company? Despite Lloyd's statements to the contrary, it seems a reasonable enough assumption, and one to which Max Wyman lends some support in his history of the Royal Winnipeg Ballet.[32] But Boris Volkoff, with the help of Stewart James, had been moving in the same direction, as Macdonald suggested in his speech and as the initial invitation to Franca to serve as ballet mistress might argue. Franca herself acknowledges that James probably had Volkoff in mind as artistic director when he made the first overtures to her.[33]

If this hypothetical reconstruction of events holds true, then Volkoff and Lloyd, the two most prominent figures in the very small field of Canadian ballet in the 1940s, were on a collision course just at the time when some real progress towards a national company was finally being made; compromise, whether voluntary or imposed, was an absolute necessity. That compromise might take the form of a company structure which accommodated all the principal players. An undated, and clearly hypothetical, masthead for the proposed company, now in the National Ballet archives, lists the following personnel:

Artistic Director	*Celia Franca*
Resident Choreographer	*Boris Volkoff*
Artistic Consultant and Choreographer	*Gweneth Lloyd*
Stage Director and Company Manager	*David Yeddeau*
Business Manager	*Stewart James*
Wardrobe Mistress	*Janet Volkoff*[34]

The parity accorded to Gweneth Lloyd and Boris Volkoff under this scheme suggests a careful desire to offend neither party, with Franca handed the herculean task of mediating between the two – an uneasy triumvirate at best. Volkoff's own notes of 1964 hint at some such motive for this kind of compromise when they state: 'Neutrality was important and so my manager at that time was asked to go to London, England and search for such a person.'[35]

Two other factors must have tempered the ambitions of Lloyd and Volkoff. One, of course, was Franca's own unwillingness to act as ballet mistress for a person she had never met.[36] The second was the nature of de Valois' advice to the Toronto group, advice which stressed the desirability of heading the proposed company with a person of undisputed authority and an objective distance from the existing circumstances. As notes in the Aileen Woods papers state: 'Miss de V. heartily agreed that to bring in someone whose artistic ability was beyond question was a good idea.'[37] This advice is clearly echoed in a piece of correspondence with the Canadian Dance Teachers Association, dated 5 November 1950:

We were strongly advised in the field of ballet to bring someone from outside Canada, a

> *person with the highest recommendations, fullest qualifications and with undisputed professional knowledge and experience. This in the opinion of the Board will provide the stimulus that will make it possible to achieve the highest artistic standards.*[38]

Once de Valois had been consulted, the die was cast: a national company for Canada would not be headed by any of the teachers or coaches already working in the country. This decision may well have represented an implicit judgment by de Valois on existing standards. Given the politics of the situation, it also represented for the founders the least contentious solution to a delicate diplomatic problem.

In 1963, Sydney Mulqueen recorded her recollections of the sequence of events leading to the founding of the company. Her general account provides verification of some important points.

> *The founding of the National Ballet Company of Canada was first considered in 1950. At that time, numerous dance studios viewed with increasing alarm the rate at which their most promising pupils were leaving the country for professional employment elsewhere. Certain studios sent representatives to a group of Toronto women to learn whether some constructive move could be made to change this trend.*
>
> *A number of meetings were held and Miss Ninette de Valois, Director of the Sadler's Wells Ballet was consulted in England. Fortunately at the time Miss de Valois had under consideration a tour of Canada and promised to meet those interested in the problem during her visit. Before leaving England she stated that in her view Miss Celia Franca was the person best qualified to organize the Canadian project as its Artistic Director.*
>
> *Meanwhile the Toronto group had reached a basic decision in that the proposed organization should be founded and operated on a national basis and that it should draw its dancers from all sections of the country.*
>
> *During her visit to Toronto, Miss de Valois had a long and interesting meeting with the Toronto group, during which she gave them much valuable advice and confirmed her previous recommendation regarding Miss Franca.*[39]

This account suggests that de Valois' advice to the founding group was extensive and was taken seriously by them. In retrospect, the emphasis on 'a national basis' speaks volumes. A genuinely national company could not be a simple extension of the Volkoff Canadian Ballet or the Winnipeg Ballet. A genuinely national organization would have to try to overcome regional prejudices and preconceptions. An outsider might be better able to look beyond those regional allegiances than someone closely allied with the existing structures. Only by bringing in an outsider could the organizers hope to strike a balance between the aspirations of Volkoff and Lloyd, the two established figures of Canadian ballet.

The coalition of forces interested in promoting ballet in Canada managed to suppress its internal rivalries and operate harmoniously at the time of the Third Canadian Ballet Festival, to try to convince Celia Franca to come to Canada and take up the role of artistic director which had been offered to her. Years later Bernadette Carpenter, another early supporter of the cause, recalled some of the lobbying which took place in Montreal at that Festival.

> *After the opening night performance, our room was a hive of activity; each and every 'drop in' came with the hope we could interest Celia enough to stay to form a National Company. Into the early morning, a few die-hards lingered on, Anatole Chujoy, Mildred Wickson, Gweneth Lloyd, Janet Baldwin, and my husband, Don – each one of us hoping we were on the brink of a better future for young Canadian dancers.*[40]

Given the acrimony that was soon to develop, the degree of friendly cooperation suggested by this account is touching. The picture of a small, determined band of Canadian ballet enthusiasts (Anatole Chujoy, the visiting American critic, the only outsider present), united in their efforts to woo Franca and keep her in their midst, lingers in the memory as the unofficial counterpoise to the official account of formal invitation and response.

There was at least one other lobbying effort as well. David Adams had worked with Franca at both Sadler's Wells and the Metropolitan Ballet. By the fall of 1950, he had returned to Canada, and he was active at the Third Canadian Ballet Festival. He recalls a luncheon conversation with Franca during which he tried to convince her of the potential of young Canadian dancers, if they could only be given proper direction and professional performance opportunities. Adams' perspective on the situation was by now international. Franca herself has a dim recollection of Adams' writing to her from Canada, while she was still in England, urging her to consider the move.[41] She was thus being appealed to not only by complete strangers in a foreign land, but also by a recent professional associate. The small, interconnected world of postwar ballet had its representative, even in the far-flung outposts of the Commonwealth. Franca's decision to accept the Canadian offer (she had had similar ones, earlier in her career, from Australia and South Africa)[42] would extend that world and draw Canada decisively into its sphere of influence. The direction in which ballet in Canada was to develop hinged on one woman's response to a challenging invitation and a concerted effort to persuade her to accept it.

What made the matter so decisive, more so than the original issuers of the invitation can have realized, was the particular set of associations that Franca brought with her. If the original plan called for her simply to preside over a company in which the creative impetus would come from Volkoff and Lloyd, the proponents of that plan had not reckoned with the breadth of experience, strength of professional commitment, and sheer force of personality which supported Franca's skills as a teacher and producer of ballets. Despite her youth, she was a seasoned professional with fully formed artistic views, a daunting list of contacts in the world of ballet, and formidable reserves of will-power and artistic ambition. In choosing her, the original organizers of the company chose the militant champion of an entire tradition.

De Valois and her unqualified recommendation of Franca symbolized an important element of that tradition. Throughout her life, she remained unequivocal in her evaluation of the young Franca's particular gifts.

> *She was an extremely fine artist, very good in dramatic roles. I also saw her do an exceedingly interesting piece of choreography at Sadler's Wells when she was in the company. She had very strong artistic views and great integrity of purpose in all her work.*[43]

The National would trade on this recommendation for years, repeatedly quoting de Valois as saying that Franca was 'the finest dramatic dancer the Wells has ever had.'[44] Accurate though the quotation was, the emphasis on it did Franca a disservice. As the National's publicity kept recycling this endorsement, de Valois was becoming identified in the North American consciousness with the Royal Ballet.

Franca in a posed photo with one of the parts from the orchestral score for Dark Elegies. *She drew on her recollections of the ballet's first performances when she mounted it for the National's 1955–6 season.*

Memories of the barnstorming Sadler's Wells days faded quickly. By implication, then, Franca became associated with the Royal as well. But Franca had never danced with the Royal. She had left for Canada a full five years before the Sadler's Wells achieved establishment status by becoming the Royal Ballet. Her experience with British ballet's less establishment activities distanced her from the stodgy reputation the Royal gradually acquired, and gave her invaluable qualifications for the kind of pioneering that lay ahead of her. But the repeated use of de Valois' accolade obscured these facts.

Celia Franca had received her early professional experience with Ballet Rambert, which she joined while still a teenager. It was there that she encountered the work and personality of Antony Tudor, both as teacher[45] and as choreographer. There she served as one of the models on whom Tudor built *Dark Elegies*, in the first performance of which she danced at the Duchess Theatre, London, on 19 February 1937.[46] Other roles she danced with Ballet Rambert included the Woman in His Past (*Lilac Garden*) and the Chief Nymph in *L'Après-midi d'un Faune*, two works which would be significant in her Canadian career. At Ballet Rambert as well, she gained her first experience of the core works of the classical repertoire, adapted to the small stage of the Mercury Theatre.[47] After leaving Ballet Rambert, Franca danced very briefly with Mona Inglesby's International Ballet, where she learned Fokine's *Le Carnaval* from her teacher, Stanislas Idzikowski, who had taken over the role of Harlequin from its originator, the legendary Vaslav Nijinsky. In late 1941, she joined the Sadler's Wells Ballet, where she remained until 1946. As a principal with Sadler's Wells, she solidified her reputation as a dramatic dancer in roles like the Queen of the Wilis in *Giselle*, the Queen in *Hamlet*, and the Prostitute in *Miracle in the Gorbals*. The latter two were created for her by Robert Helpmann, the Australian dancer whose versatile career included choreography, dance (as one of Margot Fonteyn's great partners), acting, and, eventually, the artistic direction of the Australian Ballet.

In 1946 and 1947, Franca choreographed two original works, *Khadra* and *Bailemos*, for the Sadler's Wells Theatre Ballet, as the smaller touring company was called after the main company had made the move to Covent Garden. Alexander Grant, who would later succeed Franca as artistic director of the National, danced in *Khadra*,[48] with David Adams and John Cranko alternating in the role of the father;[49] Cranko and Kenneth MacMillan, both of whom were to develop into major choreographers of distinctly different styles, performed in *Bailemos*.[50] Franca then served briefly, in 1947, as a teacher with Ballet Jooss, the German company which had made its home in England since before the war. In the same year, she joined the Metropolitan Ballet as a leading dancer and ballet mistress.

That title fails to do justice to the variety of functions Franca performed in this fascinating company. In addition to dancing, teaching class, coaching, and taking rehearsals, she gained practical experience in such matters as casting, making up programs, checking the proofs, preparing for tours, and, as she later put it, 'just doing everything, really.'[51] During its brief life-span, the Metropolitan Ballet Company fostered an extraordinary array of international talent.[52] Here Franca worked closely with Nicholas Beriosoff, the custodian in the second half of the century of much of the Fokine repertoire, whose daughter, the fifteen-year-old Svetlana Beriosova, was one of the stars of the Metropolitan. Her haunting stage-presence and luminous face later made her one of the Royal Ballet's greatest dancers. With Beriosoff, the Metropolitan learned Fokine's Polovetsian Dances from *Prince Igor*,[53] which Franca would reproduce in the National's first season at Eaton Auditorium. John Lanchbery, later to become the principal conductor of the Royal Ballet, was the Metropolitan's conductor. Here Franca's path once again crossed that of David Adams. And here she first encountered the nineteen-year-old Erik Bruhn, who had broken with the rigid hierarchy of the Danish Ballet to gain some international experience. With him, she danced a pas de deux in Frank Staff's *The Lovers' Gallery*.[54] By 1950, when she was just twenty-nine years old, Celia Franca had a range of experience that extended well beyond the confines of the Sadler's Wells Ballet.[55] She knew the rough and tumble of professional dance from the ground up.

The significance of this background can scarcely be overemphasized. The major contacts on whom Franca would rely for repertoire included the likes of Tudor, Cranko, and Bruhn, individuals whose creative lives functioned largely outside the Sadler's Wells–Royal Ballet sphere of influence. Through Idzikowski, Rambert, and Tudor, she felt a clear connection with the Diaghilev tradition and with the stylistic principles of Enrico Cecchetti, its strongest proponent in the developing British school of dance. Her experience of the professional theatre, both in London and on tour, had formed in her, from a very early age, an uncompromising sense of professional standards and the behaviour appropriate to them. Her work as a choreographer, especially two original commissions for BBC-TV, then still in its infancy, had extended her range beyond the central classical repertoire and given her a glimpse of the possibilities of dance in a new medium. She was, in fact, a rarity: an experienced dancer with the skills and the ambition to look beyond her own performances to the entire artistic enterprise. Her range was not universal, but it was wide, and she had a well-defined conception of her own standards and goals.

Small wonder, then, that Franca, once she had arrived in Canada to set about the business of founding a company, chose to make her own alliances rather than fall in with Volkoff or Lloyd, with whom she had very little, professionally, in common. Lloyd had had no professional performing career. From her youthful interest in Greek dancing, a British technique based on revived forms of Greek dance, she moved to teaching and then straight into the operation of the Winnipeg company, for which she choreographed, immediately, extensively, and enthusiastically.[56] In a thirteen-year choreographic career, she produced thirty-five works ranging from prairie subjects (*Grain* and *Kilowatt Magic*) to abstract works and even a dance version of *Pride and Prejudice*. By sheer facility and versatility, she thus established herself as a major Canadian choreographer before Canadian choreography was recognized as a serious artistic possibility. Lloyd had come relatively late to ballet training and, except for studies with Margaret Craske, a pupil of Cecchetti's, had had little direct contact with the formative influences in Franca's career. Volkoff, with considerable professional experience, came from an entirely different tradition. He had trained in Moscow, not in St Petersburg, the home of Diaghilev and his dancers, and had danced his way around the world (including a stint in a Shanghai night club and a period with the Adolph Bolm Ballet in Chicago) before settling in Toronto.[57] To Franca, his teaching techniques represented the 'old fashioned Russian training'[58] that was antithetical to her canons of taste. Volkoff, for his part, thought that Franca's standards represented 'the very tidy English-governess school of dance.'[59] In addition to having these differences of taste, experience, and tradition, both Volkoff and Lloyd were a full generation older than Franca. There was little, on the face of it, to suggest a mutually rewarding partnership.

Some attempts at cooperation, however, did take place. Betty Oliphant remembers discussing with Franca ways to make 'both Gweneth and Volkoff feel important parts of this early company.'[60] Franca recalls that she and the board tried to remain on good terms with both of them.[61] According to the minutes of the Ballet Guild's board of directors' meeting for 21 May 1952:

> *Miss Franca had asked Miss Gweneth Lloyd to choreograph a ballet for the National Ballet Guild and Mr. Homburger had followed up this request with a letter. The General Manager then read a letter received from Miss Lloyd thanking the Guild for the invitation, but saying that she found she would be too busy at this time to undertake this work.*[62]

The contentious question of whether or not to invite Lloyd to participate in this way had been vigorously debated. The perfunctory nature of her refusal, as reported in the minutes, suggests that she saw the invitation as too little, too late. From this point on, even though she remained resident in Toronto, Lloyd redoubled her support of the Winnipeg Ballet. The rift between the two companies would eventually reach melodramatic proportions.

Volkoff had a slightly longer, though largely unofficial, association with the company. He agreed to take some of the male classes for the company, prior to its opening performances at Eaton Auditorium in 1951.[63] Subsequently, some of the company's principals, Lois Smith, David Adams, Lawrence Adams, and Galina

Samsova among them, found it useful to take private classes at his studio.[64] In July 1952, after the National's first year of operation, relations were still cordial enough to allow Volkoff and David Adams to form Toronto Theatre Ballet. Volkoff and Adams acted as artistic directors of this summer operation, which included among its dancers Natalia Butko, Angela Leigh, and Colleen Kenney, all charter members of the National. Stewart James, who had served very briefly as the National's company manager, played the same role for Toronto Theatre Ballet. Kay Ambrose, close friend of Franca and a stalwart of the National's production team, did some of the costumes.[65] Whereas Lloyd seems to have severed relations with the company decisively, Volkoff lingered a little while longer on the periphery. His disillusionment and bitterness, however, finally became as public as Lloyd's. After the initial years of agitation for a national company, neither played a role in its development.

Betty Oliphant, Franca, and the first summer school

This shifting pattern of aspiration, rivalry, and suppressed hostility provides the background to the earliest events in Franca's Canadian experience. The experience itself began in November 1950, when, in response to the invitation from the provisional Toronto group, Franca visited the Third Canadian Ballet Festival in Montreal to observe the standards of ballet in Canada. 'I think you need me here,' was her diplomatic comment,[66] and in February 1951, after completing commitments in London, she returned to Toronto, nominally as an employee of the T. Eaton Company but actually to conduct a feasibility study for the proponents of a national ballet for Canada. Gossip among dancers and dance teachers was rife, with Franca seen as the mysterious outsider whose purposes were not entirely clear. At this point, Betty Oliphant made her entrance onto the scene. As Oliphant tells the story, the members of the Canadian Dance Teachers Association were apprehensive that no real change would take place. They feared the much-vaunted national company would simply become an extension of the Volkoff enterprise, which they considered to have a virtual monopoly on dance activity in the city. Volkoff was not a member of the CDTA. When Franca announced her first classes, to be taught in his studio, she received a call from Betty Oliphant, sent by the

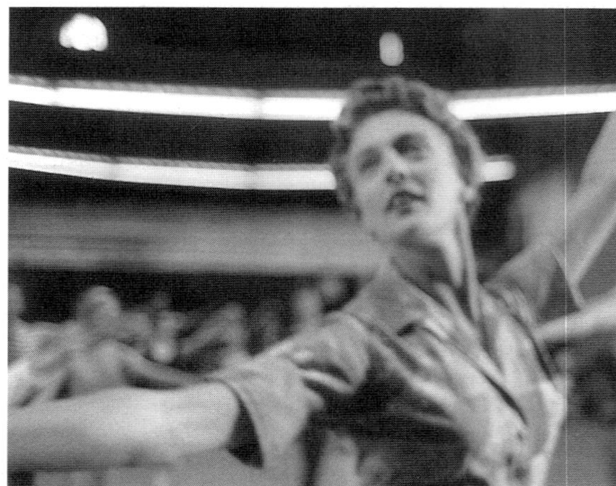

A rare action photo of Betty Oliphant teaching class, demonstrating the Cecchetti style, which she espoused.

CDTA to find out just how open the newcomer was to the full range of talent and experience in the country. 'Why don't they trust me, Miss Oliphant?' Franca asked. 'Well why should they? They don't even know you; they don't have any reason to trust you,' Oliphant responded, and the two women began discussing the new enterprise in earnest.[67]

From this initial conversation sprang an alliance that shaped the development of the National Ballet of Canada. Franca was absolutely clear in her own mind as to the range and scope of the project she had in hand.

> *Ninette de Valois had given advice to the ladies, saying that you should have a national company, that auditions should be held nationally to make sure you get the best possible talent, that your governing body should be national. It was de Valois who really advised them of the set-up; and of course, before I came over I talked to de Valois. I knew all this.*[68]

But she needed as an ally someone sympathetic to her own background and standards *and* someone able to help her navigate the tricky waters of the Canadian dance teaching establishment. Whatever their standards or level of accomplishment, it was from among the students of these teachers that the dancers of the future company must be drawn. Without the teachers' cooperation, the politics of Franca's immediate task would be treacherous. She needed help to overcome the suspicions and hostilities of the teachers who wanted to consider themselves her professional colleagues, yet were unsure of her motives and intimidated by her international qualifications and theatrical experience. Above all, she needed to remain impartial, to avoid identifying her own search for talent with any one studio or teacher.

In Betty Oliphant, a woman of her own generation, Celia Franca found the natural ally that Volkoff and Lloyd could never be. Although they had not met before coming to Canada, the two women had a great deal in common. Both counted Antony Tudor as their first teacher in the Cecchetti syllabus;[69] both had had experience in London's commercial theatre; and both had studied with Marie Rambert. Betty Oliphant recalls their student days:

> *We weren't in the same class, but we were at Marie Rambert's at the same time. Franca wasn't allowed in the professional ballet class because she was in a musical comedy. I did a lot of musical comedy but Rambert didn't know about it, so I was in the professional class; but we were there at the same time.*[70]

Though Oliphant's subsequent career had taken her into teaching rather than performance, she drew her inspiration from essentially the same source as Franca: the

Diaghilev tradition in its British manifestation and as expounded through the teachings of Cecchetti. With such a background, she was certainly not one to be intimidated by Franca; Oliphant understood thoroughly the standards and ideals Franca stood for. But most valuable of all, Oliphant already had a position of some respect among teachers of dance in Canada. As a founding member of the CDTA, she had been animated by a desire to break down hostilities and get dance teachers talking to one another.[71] As emissary from this group to Franca, she came as close as anyone would to representing a group of teachers speaking with a common voice rather than an individual teacher with a vested interest. And that common voice already had a Canadian organizational structure. Through this organization, the impartiality and inclusiveness essential to the founding of the company might actually be realized. If Betty Oliphant and the CDTA had not already existed in 1951, it might have been necessary to invent them.

The crisis which had prompted Oliphant's initial visit to Franca was resolved by having the CDTA take over sponsorship of the classes in question, and thus avoiding the appearance of bias on Franca's part. The classes, advertised by the CDTA, were open to pupils of any teacher, whether a member of the CDTA or not, as long as the students had the requisite amount of training.[72] The opportunity these preliminary classes offered to aspiring dancers to be seen by the artistic director of the future national company needed no emphasis. It was a logical development, then, for the CDTA to co-sponsor Franca's cross-country audition tour, as it did in August 1951.[73] If Franca needed the CDTA to smooth over the rivalries among the local Toronto teachers, how much more did she require the sponsorship of a national organization in dealing with the country's regional sensitivities.

But before the audition tour, a school – or at any rate, a summer school to begin the long-term process of raising the standards of instruction to meet the professional requirements of a national company. Existing standards, in Franca's opinion, were not high, despite the enthusiasm and visionary zeal which had fuelled the national project in the first place.[74] Even though she bruised some feelings with this assessment of the situation,[75] Franca's analysis was crucial to the success of her venture. If money and opportunity alone were enough to give professional ballet a start in Canada, why import someone to do the job? Franca was more than an administrator; she was a teacher of professionals and saw with a teacher's eye that the raw material before her had to be shaped and trained if it was to fulfil anyone's dreams of its future potential and if it was to bear her distinctive stamp. True it was that many fine dancers had left the country to perform; true, also, that they had left for the advanced training that turned promising students into distinctive, professional artists. Teaching would be the key to the company's success and the real justification for Franca's introduction onto the Canadian scene.

Accordingly, she set about organizing the first summer school, to be conducted

In makeshift surroundings, the dancers listen attentively as Oliphant gives corrections (ca. 1953–5). Immediately behind Oliphant, facing the camera, are Myrna Aaron and Grant Strate; facing Olpihant in the front row, left to right, are Sylvia Mason, an unidentified dancer, Howard Meadows (frowning), Judie Colpman, and Jacqueline Ivings; in the back row, far left, is André Dufresne; the three dancers in the upper right corner are Robert Ito and Angela Leigh (rear) and Lois Smith (in front of them); Earl Kraul is silhouetted in the right foreground.

under the sponsorship of the National Ballet Guild but entirely at her personal financial risk.[76] The five-week session, running from 2 July to 4 August 1951,[77] attracted both teachers and advanced students of dance. Through the summer schools, which continued annually until 1965,[78] Franca 'preached the gospel'[79] of high standards and demanding pedagogic practices. She also preached the gospel of the Cecchetti method of teaching basic technique. Although that first summer school at the St Lawrence Hall included both the Cecchetti and the Royal Academy of Dancing methods of instruction, the balance was clearly inclining in favour of Cecchetti, with decisive implications for the development of the company and eventually the National Ballet School.

Franca's emphasis on Cecchetti could be seen as an astute tactical move. She and Oliphant were the only Cecchetti advocates on the scene at the time; by emphasizing this method, Franca ensured that no other teachers, representing other methods, would pose any real threat to her authority. The choice of this method offered a graceful way, if one was needed, of avoiding undue entanglement with either Volkoff or Lloyd.

But the real basis for the choice, one on which Franca and Oliphant agree to this day, was stylistic. As Franca sees it: 'It was important for us to have a system that we believed in as a basic training, which had good scientific reasons behind it about the placement of the body, the use of the arms, and the carriage of the neck.'

The Cecchetti system met those requirements, 'because the Cecchetti system is very pure. And it's very Petipa.'[80] A company that aspired to dance the works of Petipa, the pre-eminent Russian classical choreographer, laid the foundation for that repertoire with this choice of basic schooling.

Oliphant had come to essentially the same conclusions in her own evaluations of teaching methods. For her, Cecchetti was 'probably the best method in the whole world for the use of the head, the use of the arms, the use of *épaulement*, nuances, and subtleties.' One reason, in her view, for the strength of the system is the emphasis it places on basic technique. 'It lays a base which is better than any other method that I've seen, including Vaganova [the technique of the legendary Kirov Ballet and School]. It's death on affectations and mannerisms. It has very, very good lines.'[81] This fundamental agreement on the merits of the Cecchetti system formed the basis of the strong partnership that was to exist between Franca and Oliphant for years to come. It also dictated the stylistic direction in which the new company would develop and, to a large extent, the speed at which that development would take place. The dancers would be taught Cecchetti's pure, unaffected line, however long the process took. They would not be allowed to settle for easier solutions, more theatrical effects, in their pursuit of the ideal. The goal that Franca and Oliphant set was a lofty one; there could be no shortcuts to it. (Like any technique, however, the Cecchetti method was only as good as the teachers espousing it; with the passage of time, the original standards of the Cecchetti syllabus have become eroded, in Oliphant's view,[82] and today the National Ballet School, arguably founded on the Cecchetti method, no longer bases the curriculum on it.)

With the 1951 summer school, Franca and her colleagues took the first, small step towards their goal. Whereas logic might have argued that *all* her efforts should be directed towards education for at least a few years, until she had dancers ready for professional exposure, circumstances dictated otherwise. When George Balanchine was being courted by Lincoln Kirstein to come to America and start a company, he uttered the famous dictum, 'But first a school.'[83] Franca, though fully committed to the same ideal, could acknowledge it in the first instance only by these summer sessions. The reason was purely practical.

> *It didn't take me five minutes to find out that in Canada you had to use the word 'sell,' and I knew damn well I couldn't get anybody to support a school. I had to show why we needed a school. From my own background in England I knew that a school was essential, the type of school that we finally did found, the National Ballet School. But in 1951 there was no way.*[84]

Franca was joined in that first summer session by a number of other teachers, among them Betty Oliphant. Oliphant had scheduled her own summer session that year; on hearing of the National Ballet Guild's plans, she telephoned Franca in panic, frightened that the conflict would reduce her student numbers. When Franca suggested they join forces, Oliphant was happy to agree.[85] The National Ballet of Canada, though not yet officially constituted, had moved out of the planning stages, into the studio.

A youthful Howard Meadows. A stalwart in the company's wardrobe department for many years after his dancing career ended, Meadows died in 1994.

Students came to that first summer session with varying expectations and varying degrees of experience. Judie Colpman arrived, fresh from grade thirteen and from Bettina Byers' Toronto studio, attracted by the luxury of taking class every day of the week for the first time in her life; at first, she had no thought of auditioning for the company.[86] Howard Meadows, a student of Gerald Crevier in Montreal and deeply involved in amateur performances there, attended in the hope that he might be noticed and offered a chance.[87] David Adams already had the promise of a summer performance and a prominent place in the company, if it materialized; he helped to clean up the St Lawrence Hall so that it could be used for class.[88] With him, from Winnipeg, came his wife, Lois Smith, with extensive experience in musical comedy and no clearly formulated ambitions to become a ballerina; she had been taken more or less sight unseen, on the basis of a photograph and the recommendation of her husband.[89] The 1951 summer school functioned as both a training ground for the committed and a means of attracting potential talent to Toronto, thereby heightening interest in the possibility of a national company.

Dr Coppélius mistakenly believes he has brought his mechanical doll to life; Coppélia, however, is bent on causing trouble. Sydney Vousden and Celia Franca, in rehearsal for the performance at Varsity Arena in 1951.

Almost simultaneously with the organization of the summer school, Franca presented a performance, on 14 June of *Coppélia* Act II at the annual Promenade Concerts in Varsity Arena.[90] Ballet performances, usually organized by Boris Volkoff,[91] had been a feature of the Prom Concerts for some years. This performance offered another opportunity for Franca to signal her presence and her intentions in Canada. It met with enough success to be repeated in Montreal on 8 August and again in Toronto on 13 September with the addition of the peasant pas de deux from *Giselle* for Lois Smith and David Adams. None of these could be considered the first performance of the National; they were simply guest spots on a musical program. In the case of the June and August performances, the national audition tour had not yet taken place and no company was as yet formally constituted. Furthermore, these independent performance ventures broke even without any financial support from the Guild; they were crucial precursors to the company's activities, an official preview rather than a formal début.

The national audition tour ignited excitement and controversy in equal measure.

The summer school had turned a profit of one thousand dollars.[92] Under the terms of the start-up loan which the Guild had advanced to her for the school, Franca was obliged to use that profit 'to travel to West Coast and intervening cities for the purpose of auditioning dancers for the Canadian National Ballet Company, if and when formed.'[93] In late August 1951, the tour took place, but not without its share of controversy. The idea of creating a national company using the most talented dancers in the country had seemed a splendid idea in the formative, theoretical stages of discussion; now that a flesh-and-blood artistic director, and a British one at that, was travelling from Toronto to the west coast to have a look at that talent, two contradictory fears arose. One was that the stranger entrusted with this task would overlook the home-grown talent available; the other was that she would find it and steal it away, thus robbing the regions of their principal contact with the art form, which was struggling to establish itself regionally as well as nationally. It was a diplomatic tightrope that Franca walked as adroitly as any human could. But despite tact and diplomacy, reaction was sometimes negative. Halifax, not even a stop on the tour, was 'much annoyed.' The Halifax Ballet should have been approached before the husband-and-wife team of Jury Gotshalks and Irene Apiné was lured away by Franca's offer to join the new company.[94] Winnipeg was irate and complained formally to the Guild, asking the meaning of the word 'National' in the name 'National Ballet Guild of Canada,' and pointing out that the Winnipeg Ballet was already committed to a season of its own.[95] The implication, clearly, was that the National should stick to its own territory and stop stealing dancers from the relatively limited pool of talent and experience available. But what precisely was that territory? National dreams seemed suddenly less potent when confronted with the realities of regional rivalry.

While the Guild tried to mend fences from its base in Toronto, Franca did her best on the road. In Winnipeg, she gave an interview to the *Winnipeg Free Press*.

'*The decision of the* [National Ballet Guild] *board to go ahead with the national compa-*

ny came simultaneously with the decision of the Winnipeg board of directors to continue the Winnipeg Ballet for another year,' Miss Franca explained.

'When I heard this, I didn't approach any Winnipeg dancers afterwards because of an unwritten code of ethics by which the director of one company does not solicit dancers from another company.

'Naturally, unless any Winnipeg dancers came to me of their own free will I wouldn't approach them.' She said she had already signed dancer David Adams and his wife Lois under these circumstances before the Winnipeg Board's decision came out.[96]

After the fact, Franca expressed herself more forthrightly on the subject. 'My whole trip was made in the wake of Arnold Spohr. When our plans were known, the Winnipeg Ballet declared itself professional and sent Spohr ahead of me to see what talent was available.'[97] Spohr, then the Winnipeg Ballet's ballet master, was eventually to direct the company for thirty years, during which time the rivalry between the Winnipeg Ballet and the National would never entirely vanish. Perhaps because of this initial competition, Franca found fewer qualified dancers than she might have hoped for.[98]

The Winnipeg issue was far more complicated than it appears on the surface. From October 1950, the Winnipeg (after 1953, the Royal Winnipeg) Ballet operated under long-distance artistic direction. Gweneth Lloyd did not give up the title of artistic director until June 1955. Throughout this period, however, she remained in Toronto; it was a sign of the distance between them that, when her company performed in Winnipeg in March 1951, it did so, for the first time, without an original Lloyd work on the program.[99] Lloyd and David Yeddeau, in Toronto, had told Franca that 'the Winnipeg Ballet was finished.'[100] In approaching Betty Farrally in Winnipeg regarding studio space for the audition tour, Franca believed that she was dealing with a ballet school, not with another professional performing company. But she reckoned without Lloyd's determination and Winnipeg civic pride. In June 1951, the Winnipeg board announced honoraria for its dancers, thereby reasserting the company's claim to professional status, and in October of the same year it staged a full-blown media event: a command performance before Princess Elizabeth and the Duke of Edinburgh during their Canadian tour.[101] The National was not going to be allowed to claim centre stage unchallenged. If, as Franca had been told, the Winnipeg Ballet was on the verge of collapse early in 1951, her national audition tour goaded a second Canadian company back into being.

Amid such controversy, the whirlwind audition tour rolled on, its methods of selection not always orthodox. Grant Strate, with no ballet training at all, did not audition for the company, but met Franca at a reception in Edmonton.

She came to the studio and she saw a couple of things I had choreographed, after which she looked at me and said, 'Would you join the National Ballet of Canada?' and I said, 'Sure.' And we both wandered away wondering what we'd done. So that was how I joined the National Ballet, an interesting process, something that I think would never happen again and maybe shouldn't even have happened then.[102]

In the right place at the right time, Judie Colpman was among the young hopefuls drawn into the excitement of the company's earliest days.

When Oliphant questioned another choice, Franca explained: 'I wanted someone who looked good stripped to the waist for 'Danse Arabe' in *Nutcracker*.'[103] Earl Kraul, who would become the company's leading male dancer after David Adams' departure, auditioned unsuccessfully. 'I finally did the audition, and at first Celia was not going to take me; but there was supposed to be a boy coming from Vancouver and he had had an accident, and at the last minute she decided to take me.'[104] Judie Colpman, after her participation in the summer school, was invited to audition to fill another unexpected vacancy and was accepted.[105] Natalia Butko didn't go through a formal audition. She had danced extensively with Volkoff's group and appeared in the first Prom Concert performance of *Coppélia* Act II. Perhaps Franca valued her comic and dramatic gifts and saw a place for them in her projected repertoire.[106] David Adams, as an observer of the audition process, still cannot discern the rationale for all of Franca's choices.

Some people were not able to do very much at all, and people who were able were told that they weren't good enough. I didn't see, I don't see to this day, the reason why that group were there. We did, eventually, fit. As a matter of fact we fit like a glove; it was fantastic. But those are the personalities, and in an audition system you don't find out personalities. She was lucky.[107]

Luck surely played its part in the process, but so did Franca's skill and intuition. She was not simply auditioning talent; she was beating the bushes, looking for personalities who were willing to pioneer with her and body types that would be able to take her instruction; if experience and training came with the package, so much the better. Franca had seen enough of the country and its attitudes towards culture to realize just how much depended on her choices. The company she assembled had to make a splash with its very first performance. There wasn't enough experienced, trained talent in the nation to carry the project off on skill alone. She was, in many cases, assessing raw material in order to judge what she might be able to make of it, not what it already was. The cohesiveness of the group of people she finally brought together proved to be one of its strongest initial assets. Natalia Butko assessed the situation astutely: 'We were all equals and we really worked our hearts out.'[108] Given the turbulent climate in that summer of 1951 when the company was formed, this sense of equality and devotion to the cause was the company's strongest suit.

CHAPTER TWO

An Okay Beginning

Franca's challenge: to tailor the repertoire to the dancers' abilities

With that hectic summer of preparatory activity behind her – the preview performances at Varsity Arena and in Montreal, the first summer school, the audition tour – Franca could concentrate all her professional and artistic energies on grooming her dancers for their opening performance as a company. In the disparate group of professionals and aspiring professionals assembled about her, she found malleable material, eager to accept all the direction she had to offer. The principles of taste and style which she applied at this early stage would remain her standards for the duration of her career with the National. Throughout the varying fortunes of the company, its artistic successes and its failures, Franca insisted on the ideals which guided this first performance. Such assumption of authority on her part was no mere display of ego; it was the logical consequence of her uncompromising artistic idealism. Only through firm artistic direction could her artistic vision for the company be realized.

OPPOSITE: Disembarking from the train in Hamilton, David Adams assists his wife and partner, Lois Smith, while George Crum, the company's music director, follows with orchestral scores.

ABOVE: Franca's production of Les Sylphides *was a staple of the early repertoire on tour and at home, from the company's very first performance through its years at the Royal Alexandra Theatre.*

And despite the glowing public rhetoric of the early years, she remained the company's severest critic; she knew all too well the discrepancies between her vision and its realization, just as she recognized the moments of fulfilment.

Franca's fifteen years of professional experience in England had given her an invaluable set of resources for the task at hand. She knew, by memory, much of the standard classical repertoire. Her extensive work with contemporary British choreographers in the process of creation had given her as well a strong sense of the nuances of style appropriate to a given work or period. Like many other professionals, then, she could teach her dancers the steps they had to know; but more than that, she could demand from them the refinements of style and of phrasing that raise a performance out of the realm of the ordinary. She was knowledgeable; she had a discriminating sense of style; and she had the confidence to impose her sense of style on dancers who would have been lost without her guidance.

A studio photo of Judie Colpman illustrates the attention to arms and hands which Franca emphasized in coaching Les Sylphides.

Without hesitation, participants in that first series of performances at Eaton Auditorium give Franca the credit for producing the coherent sense of style that distinguishes a company from a pick-up group. It was no mean feat, given the disparity in background, training, and experience that met her in the rehearsal hall. Franca's response to this challenge showed her mettle immediately. With characteristic practicality, she settled on a choice of works that were choreographically within the range of possibility for her dancers at their present level of experience, the mastery of which would nevertheless begin the painstaking process of discipline and training necessary to achieve her long-term goal – creating a major classical ballet company. Franca recalls the central place which Fokine's *Les Sylphides* occupied in the company's early repertoire: 'If you have a classical ballet company you have to have a well-trained corps de ballet. *Les Sylphides* was the very first thing we did which was the beginning of training a corps and getting a feeling for uniform style.'[1] Judie Colpman remembers rehearsals as a struggle 'to get the turnout, to get the form for a professional company.' But, like many others, she remembers also the sense of shared commitment among the dancers that fuelled the endeavour and made the hours of work worthwhile. For in pursuit of a coherent, authentic style, Franca worked her inexperienced company long and hard. Her attention to detail, especially in the ensemble, was relentless. Colpman also recalls 'particularly in *Les Sylphides*, the hours we used to spend just doing the arms and the hands.'[2] Franca was after a sense of poetically inspired unison that went beyond mere precision. To achieve this end, she drilled her dancers repeatedly, then urged them to contemplate some image, whether of dreams or of moonlight, as she puts it, 'to get their imaginations working, so they would all move in unison without looking like a bunch of soldiers.'[3] Every dancer was expected to be dramatically present – not simply filling up a place in the line, but rather contributing actively to the overall effect. According to Natalia Butko, the company's major objective at this stage was 'to think of the dance as a whole picture, not just as bits and pieces.'[4] Once that picture had been set, Franca maintained it with scrupulous care and attention. The frequent critical notes for the dancers were, by her own admission, 'very tough on them. If I didn't give them a correction after a performance they would feel I was ignoring them.'[5] Such an atmosphere could have been discouraging, but in the young company it bred a 'rivalry in detail' (in Colpman's phrase) in which all the dancers participated, to try to maintain the ensemble playing at the highest possible level.

Behind Franca's emphasis on the detail and coherence of the ensemble lay an innate awareness of musical values. If dance takes its inspiration from music, then choreographic effects can be successful only insofar as they build upon and relate to the music sustaining them. Franca's conception of phrasing in dance, of the linking of movements into a continuous, expressive sequence that 'speaks' to an audience, derived from her sensitivity to phrasing in music. Her criticism of the unmusical dancer is timeless: 'You're thinking in short phrases. You are thinking one step at a time. There is no big phrase-line that you'd see on the score, that lovely beautiful semicircle that goes from this bar to that bar.'[6] The respect for musical values inherent in such criticism is by no means universal in the world of ballet. A yawning chasm separates the dancer for whom music is accompaniment, to be manipulated as may be convenient, from the dancer for whom music is the soul of dance, the muse whose dictates must be obeyed. Franca was the latter kind of dancer. Betty Oliphant describes musicality in a dancer as 'the ability to play with the music, to phrase the music, to know when you can steal this extra moment and make it up,' and recognizes musicality as one of Franca's significant attributes.[7] As a teacher and coach, Franca tried to impart to the young company some of her own sensitivity to musical values. Earl Kraul acknowledges the debt. As his basic technique began to develop, he needed something more to turn him into a dancer. 'And Celia was the one who showed me how to handle technique, how to treat it musically and how to place it.'[8] Franca's determination never to compromise the music placed a stylistic stamp on the emerging company as surely as her attention to the detail of the ensemble had done. She had chosen to stake her reputation, and the reputation of the company, on detailed authenticity of mood and style and on refined musical sensibility rather than on pyrotechnics and dazzling theatrical effects.

The choice was every bit as practical as it was idealistic. With only one or two exceptions, Franca's dancers simply didn't have the technical ability to sustain flamboyant displays and virtuoso tricks. In reporting on the choreography at the Third Canadian Ballet Festival in Montreal for the *Royal Academy of Dancing Gazette* she had written: 'Choreographers must avoid the dangerous tendency to tax dancers beyond their technical ability.'[9] Her conception of professionalism thus involved a

The full company in Les Sylphides. *The dancers wear wet-white, a heavy foundation make-up intended to create a uniformly ethereal appearance. Lilian Jarvis is on the floor, centre. Behind her stand (from left to right) Irene Apiné, Jury Gotshalks, and Colleen Kenney.*

scaling down of aspirations to meet existing abilities on some reasonable middle ground. Franca would, if necessary, make modifications in standard choreography to enable her dancers to realize the spirit of the choreographer's intentions, when the letter might have defeated them. Betty Oliphant admired Franca's skill in this regard.

> *Celia was absolutely brilliant at never giving away the limitations of the dancers. She managed to produce a homogeneous, artistically presented, very well lit company. But always, and this frustrated the dancers very much – 'If you can't do two clean pirouettes, only do one. If you can't lift your leg in the air and balance, then don't lift your leg.' The very, very first performance I ever saw of the company (I wasn't the ballet mistress then), I couldn't believe that out of what I knew were very different styles and, by and large, not very well trained dancers (although some were good), she managed to produce this effect.*[10]

As late as 1956, in her report to the Guild's fifth annual meeting, Franca admitted candidly to the occasional need for this kind of protective camouflage. 'As far as possible, I have tried to insulate the public from any inadequacies by occasionally changing the choreography to fit the dancers' capabilities.'[11] Reflecting on that period, she now says: 'My job was to make dancers who had not had an ideal training look professional. It was a very, very difficult process, because there was an awful lot wrong with their basic technique.'[12] Lois Smith concurs:

> *Franca was a very good teacher, but what she taught us as a whole company was how to dance together, how to be professional about what we were doing, how to really produce, how to move properly. So in that way, we were quite professional looking, even though we didn't have all the technique in the world.*[13]

Theatrical professionalism: that was the value Franca sought to instil and for which the company's charter members still admire her. Those first steps towards its achievement must have looked like a cramped and shrunken version of the grandiose ambitions that had led to the founding of a national company. The dawn of professional activity cast a cold light on the dreams that had preceded it. The dancers who had been proclaimed ready for national exposure were being taken back to the first principles of their art, like neophytes rather than professionals. But Franca recognized the necessity for this humble beginning if the long-term goal of a classical ballet company for Canada was to be placed on a firm footing from the very start.

Opening night: the critical response

On 12 November 1951, after a scant two months of rehearsal as a full company, the Canadian National Ballet (the company's name was changed to the National Ballet of Canada in January 1952)[14] opened a three-night run at Eaton Auditorium in Toronto. The full program consisted of *Les Sylphides*, Franca's own *Dance of Salomé*, the peasant pas de deux from Act I of *Giselle* (for David Adams and Lois Smith), Kay Armstrong's *Etude*, and, as a closing number, the Polovetsian Dances from *Prince Igor*. With the exception of *Etude*, which Franca had admired as one of Vancouver's contributions to the 1950 Ballet Festival in Montreal,[15] the program came entirely out of the storehouse of her own memory. She had choreographed the *Dance of Salomé* for BBC-TV a few years earlier; the rest of the repertoire she had acquired during her years with Ballet Rambert, Sadler's Wells, and the Metropolitan Ballet. As was to be the case throughout the early years, Franca's prodigious memory saved the impoverished company a bundle in choreographic fees.

Her choice of program was judicious as well as practical. It leaned a little heavily on Fokine, but with good cause: *Les Sylphides* exemplified the stylistic virtues Franca had decided to emphasize, and the Polovetsian Dances provided an opportunity to display the men, as well as the vitality of the whole company. If they couldn't be virtuosos, they could at least kindle some sparks of energetic excitement. The excerpt from *Giselle* gave the audience a hint of the romantic repertoire, and of the dance partnership that was to develop between Smith and Adams to sustain the company through its early years; the Franca and Armstrong pieces stood for contemporary and Canadian choreography. The only glaring omission, for the début program of a classical company, was any piece of genuinely classical choreography. There was nothing by Petipa, the pre-eminent classical choreographer, whose work displays the purity of form and technique which ballet attained by the close of the nineteenth century. (Franca added to the repertoire his *Don Quixote* pas de deux, for Jury Gotshalks and Irene Apiné, in less than a month's time.) There was little here that would startle Toronto dance audiences. The Polovetsian Dances and *Les Sylphides* had been staple pieces in the de Basil Ballets Russes touring repertoire. Volkoff had mounted versions of both in Toronto, and in the 1938–9 season had retired from dancing with a final virtuoso performance in the starring role of the Warrior Chief.[16] But the program served its purpose: it introduced the company to Toronto audiences in such a way as to appeal to their own previous knowledge of ballet, assert Franca's arrival on the scene, emphasize the company's strengths, and discreetly mask its weaknesses.

The significance of this conservative beginning lay not in any tumultuous, overnight success, but in its happening at all. For the company's organizers and supporters, the evening represented a culmination of years of hope and aspiration and the beginning, whether they knew it or not, of the real, the herculean efforts to keep the company afloat. For Franca, the performance was simply the first step on the road towards the creation of the kind of company few of her Canadian associates envisioned at the time. For many of those first performers, like Howard Meadows, the euphoria came from the declaration of purpose and sense of professional status which the occasion symbolized. 'We were now part of a professional, full-scale company. How big, how bad, how good, that didn't matter; you had finally stepped over that threshold. You were not an amateur anymore, you were a professional.'[17] But Earl Kraul's memories testify to the realistic response to the performance itself which Franca and her dancers preserved in the face of all the excitement.

> *I mostly remember standing, holding the spear in* Salomé *beside Brian Macdonald, while everyone else was doing the dancing and I was wishing I was doing it. I think that I recall hearing from Celia that it was okay. Not that it was sensational or anything, but we were okay. We pulled it together; it was an okay beginning.*[18]

On the critical front, the opening night demonstrated, not surprisingly, that Toronto had little by way of professional critical experience to evaluate what was being offered. Like its audience, critics of the company would have to be developed. The reviewer for the *Telegram* waxed ecstatic, but his only yardstick for the performance seemed to be the legendary Pavlova, dead for some twenty years. The comparison was too absurd, and too outdated, to be flattering.

> *Enthusiasm of the large audience was inspiring, but not at all surprising. Music was in perfect register with what was happening on the stage. Scenery and costumes were in perfect alignment, too. Dancing of Celia Franca throughout the evening had all the enchantment of Pavlowa's faultless dance technique. Last evening she touched the whole art of ballet as it used to be and can never be again.*[19]

Whether intentionally or not, the nostalgic note of the final sentence lent an air of doomed, if noble, futility to the long-term hopes of the company.

The *Globe and Mail* took things more seriously. It sent its drama critic, Herbert Whittaker, who would become one of the company's most faithful observers and critics, as well as its first official historian. He provided a much fuller, more optimistic account of the proceedings. Although critical of the 'turgid theatricality' of the *Dance of Salomé*, he admired Franca's highly dramatic performance in the ballet and provided a valuable description of some of its choreographic features.

> *After a somewhat cluttered beginning – mock Schéhérazade, not helped by the bulky costuming – the figure of Salomé begins to dominate the action and a genuine tension was achieved. The Dance of the Seven Veils, a pitfall if ever there was one, proved exciting although perhaps it outlasted its excitement a bit.*
>
> *A pas de deux by Salomé and the Young Syrian, danced by David Adams, and another with the Jokanaan, Grant Strate, built to the moment in which Salomé performs her dance for the head of the Prophet. But it was after this that Miss Franca's gift for groupings of fluidity and sustained invention.* [Here the *Globe*'s typesetter cut short Whittaker's intended praise.]
>
> *There is an ingenious passage in which Salomé tries to escape and is blocked by the other dancers, with Herodias* [Natalia Butko] *attempting to aid her daughter. A similarly effective moment came with the death of Salomé behind the soldiers' shields, her hands describing a last tortuous measure.*[20]

With Polovetsian Dances concluding the program, the opening night audience must have gone reeling into the night under the onslaught of so much unabashed exoticism.

Whittaker saved his unstinting praise, however, for the chaster *Etude*:

> *Miss Armstrong's ballet opens with a beautifully sculptured grouping and then proceeds from it through a series of designs which flow rhythmically and interestingly until the first grouping is resumed. The lack of strain and cleanness of this work was worthy of Balanchine.*

At its revival for the company's thirty-fifth anniversary Gala in 1987, the work, in its spare and economical style, bore an uncanny resemblance to Ashton's much later *Monotones*. Whittaker's summary paragraph looked to the future, rather than the nostalgic past as the *Telegram* had done: 'There is great promise here, as well as considerable achievement. There is uniformity of style and attack, and Miss Franca's training has obviously built the foundation for a successful future.' Even if that final sentiment represented pious hope more than confident prediction, Whittaker's assessment of Franca's training of the company reveals that her basic values were visible to an audience from the very first company performance.

Earl Kraul supports (bottom to top) Oldyna Dynowska, Natalia Butko, and Katharine Stewart in one of the sculptured groupings from Kay Armstrong's Etude.

But her strengths, so evident here, implied also some of the weaknesses with which the company would have to deal in years to come. Careful, correct schooling, an unquestioned necessity in the early years, could lead to careful, correct dancing, even when a maturer level of technical accomplishment might have allowed for greater freedom. Franca's limitations as a choreographer ruled out the possibility of her becoming the company's chief source of original works. That elusive creature, the Canadian choreographer, might be welcomed in effusive terms, as Whittaker had welcomed Armstrong, but was to make furtive, isolated appearances at best, overawed, perhaps, by the daunting genius of Balanchine south of the border.

Whittaker's comparison of Armstrong's work to Balanchine, doubtless intended as a compliment, bespoke as early as 1951 the powerful influence of Balanchine in North America: to be good was to be derivative of him; to be outside his frame of reference was dangerous. And Franca stood outside. Her taste as well as her experience allied her with de Valois, Tudor, Ashton, and the British school of choreography, not with Balanchine's experimental neoclassicism. With the rising of Balanchine's star in the United States, critical opinion turned against the British canons of taste that had recommended Franca to these shores. Throughout such criticism, however, she retained the strengths of conviction and self-knowledge. She could create only the kind of ballet company *she* envisioned; and she knew better than anyone the time, the generations of dancers it would take, to reach her goal. As the company developed, an impatient and sometimes ungrateful public came to interpret as inflexibility the dogged determination that Franca exercised in order to create a well-trained, well-disciplined classical company, sufficiently free of stylistic eccentricities to be able to dance convincingly the works of a wide variety of choreographers.

Franca built the administrative team that would shape the company.

While busily whipping her dancers into shape and performing with them, both in Toronto and on tour, Franca also had to turn her attention to the task of assembling an artistic support staff. The company began operations with a healthy representation of the old Volkoff team in its employ. James Pape and Suzanne Mess, two former Volkoff students, designed some of the opening productions. Margaret Clemens, Volkoff's longtime studio pianist and associate, became the first company pianist. Stewart James, after initiating the original negotiations with Franca and managing the first summer school,[21] took on the job of company manager.[22] But James resigned abruptly in March 1952.[23] No reason for the resignation is recorded in the company archives, and the only subsequent reference to James is a mysterious acknowledgment of the Guild's receipt of a letter from a Mr Bolsby regarding Mr James, to which the Guild's solicitors were directed to reply.[24] The record makes no mention of the fact that Stewart James *was* James Bolsby, and no trace of the correspondence exists. To this day, Stewart James, a.k.a. James Bolsby, declines requests to provide the information which would unravel the mystery of his sudden disappearance from the company's management. For whatever reasons, though, by the end of that first season, the last official connections to the Volkoff organization, if such they had been, were severed. Franca quickly began to build the artistic support structure that would see her through her period as artistic director of the company and beyond.

De Valois had advised the founding committee that the new company ought to have a music director,[25] presumably in preference to hiring a succession of visiting conductors as occasion demanded. The fact that Franca and the first board immediately attended to this matter provides some indication of the importance which would be attached to the musical side of the company's activities. By October 1951, Pearl Whitehead, heedful of de Valois' instructions, had introduced George Crum, a young family friend, to Franca. His musical career to this point had been primarily in opera, and for a time he managed to balance commitments to the National Ballet with operatic conducting for the CBC and the precursors of the Canadian Opera Company. Eventually, however, ballet won out. Crum conducted the company's opening performances at Eaton Auditorium, became its first musical director, and guided its musical fortunes until 1984.[26] Throughout that period, he fought for the strengthening and development of the orchestra, which was often far

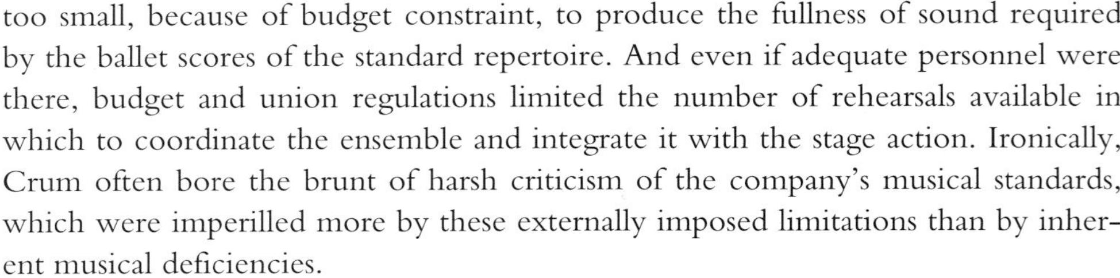

too small, because of budget constraint, to produce the fullness of sound required by the ballet scores of the standard repertoire. And even if adequate personnel were there, budget and union regulations limited the number of rehearsals available in which to coordinate the ensemble and integrate it with the stage action. Ironically, Crum often bore the brunt of harsh criticism of the company's musical standards, which were imperilled more by these externally imposed limitations than by inherent musical deficiencies.

After the musical director, the rehearsal pianist, though rarely seen by the public, provides crucial musical support for the company. Several individuals followed Margaret Clemens in this role until, in 1958,[27] George Crum engaged Mary McDonald, who was to be its principal pianist for the next thirty-one years. McDonald became a close personal friend of Franca's and a staunch supporter of the company and its dancers, a company icon whose level-headed sense of humour and passionate devotion to dance provided stability and support through good times and bad. She locked horns with dancers, from temperamental stars like Rudolf Nureyev to the most junior member of the corps, on questions of musical integrity, she played for their weddings, and she supported them backstage through the terrors and insecurities of performance. On the way, she developed into a rehearsal pianist of international renown who worked with virtually all the greats of the ballet world. But it was the irrepressible McDonald personality that won the love and devotion of those who knew her. The staunch Catholic who prayed the company bus through a harrowing Nova Scotia blizzard to a safe arrival in Amherst,[28] the Irish charmer who unwittingly and unhesitatingly commandeered a police cruiser in Lafayette, Louisiana, to catch up to the shuttle to the theatre which she had missed,[29] is the stuff of legends.

In later years, David Scott and Joanne Nisbet cast a watchful eye over a rehearsal in progress. Dancers Sean Boutilier and Gretchen Newburger can be seen behind Scott.

Two English dancers, who joined the company in 1959, were encouraged by Franca to develop careers as coaches when injuries compelled them to give up dancing with the National.[30] Joanne Nisbet and her husband, David Scott, formed the nucleus of the company's coaching staff through its middle years. Although Scott retired from the position of principal ballet master in 1984, amid critical controversy about the company's artistic standards, Nisbet remains one of its two principal ballet mistresses, one of the company's chief repositories of knowledge of the repertoire.

Among the administrative support staff, too, Franca's loyalty to colleagues from the company's early days was instrumental in building the National Ballet team. David (Kerval) Walker and James Ronaldson made the transition from early performing careers with the company to long-term service in its administration, Walker as assistant to Franca and three subsequent artistic directors, Ronaldson as wardrobe supervisor until 1984. David Haber joined the company as stage director in the spring of 1952. He resigned from that position in 1956[31] to join the William Morris Concert Agency in the United States, where he represented the company on tour. Later, as program director of the National Arts Centre, he remained influential in promoting the company in Canada. Never out of touch with the National, he rejoined the company at Franca's request as her co–artistic director in 1972[32] and finally replaced her briefly, her chosen successor as artistic director, in 1974. The controversy surrounding this succession does little to diminish Franca's overall record for rewarding long-term loyalty and building a strong team. Franca valued dependability and personal loyalty. From the nucleus of her associates and supporters, she created a stability and continuity for the company that would last well beyond the years of her own direct control.

On the senior management side, matters were different. Walter Homburger, who went on to a distinguished career as managing director of the Toronto Symphony and who was already established as an impresario with the International Artists Concert Agency, served as the National's first tour manager and, until 1955, as its general manager.[33] Homburger's was, incredibly, a part-time appointment, but on his departure the position became full time and was filled by a succession of individuals: Carman Guild (1955–64); Anthony B. Lawless (1964–6); John H. Wilson (1966–7); Wallace A. Russell (1967–72); Gerry Eldred (1972–81); and Robert H. Johnston (1981–96).[34] It is significant that during Franca's term as artistic director, the company had six different general managers (including Homburger), whereas the seventh, Robert Johnston, has worked with all her successors but one. This statistical fact reflects Franca's firm belief in the authority of the artistic director to direct the company, and her unwillingness to see that authority eroded. During her time, continuity came not from the administrative but from the artistic side of the organization, where her own contacts and control were strongest. The change to a corporate structure in which the administrative head of the company bore equal responsibilities and authority with the artistic head could not be implemented fully until after her departure.

Betty Oliphant, ballet mistress and friend

Two early associations which Franca established for the National, however, influenced the company's development more decisively than all the others. One was with Betty Oliphant. Aside from her early involvement through the Canadian

Dance Teachers Association and her participation in the company's first summer school, Oliphant's formal association with the company began one full year after its founding, in September 1952, when she joined the staff as ballet mistress.[35] David Adams had served as the company's ballet master in its opening season, during which Franca approached Oliphant to try to interest her in the position of ballet mistress. Oliphant was intensely interested, but there were problems. As a single mother, she depended on regular revenue from her own school to support herself and her young family; and she could hardly abandon two young children to follow the company on tour. But Franca was determined, and suggested a compromise whereby Oliphant became ballet mistress to the company while it was in rehearsal and performing in Toronto, and Shirley Kash, a young and talented pupil of Oliphant's, came on as assistant for the tours. Oliphant's was another ostensibly 'part-time' appointment; she worked for the company from 9:00 until 3:30, then went on to teach at her own school until 9:00 at night, somehow squeezing her children in along the way. The newspapers announced that Miss Oliphant had been 'appointed mistress to Walter Homburger.'[36]

Oliphant devoted her full energies to the company until she took on responsibility for the National Ballet School, and she continued to play a central role in the company even after the school's founding in 1959. After Franca, she exercised the single most decisive influence on the schooling of its dancers, both as ballet mistress and as teacher and mentor of the children who aspired to join the company. Franca had worked to achieve, in her own words, a 'veneer of professionalism'[37] for the company's opening season; Oliphant examined basic technique and began rebuilding it from the ground up. After the exhilaration of the first season's performances, the dancers, understandably, found this approach unpalatable. The rigorously defined demands of the Cecchetti syllabus seemed to confine their movement and hamper their style.[38] Oliphant herself recognizes the challenge she presented to the company.

> *I think the thing about the Cecchetti method, which the company found very, very difficult to accept when I became the ballet mistress, is that it doesn't cater to you in any way. You could almost say of the beginning parts of it, that it doesn't give you a feeling of dance. That isn't fair, because it is a very beautiful syllabus, but it's so hard and so technically uncompromising and so not-catering to everyone's desire to feel good about themselves. It's a very, very difficult method.*[39]

Difficult or not, Franca was so convinced by Oliphant's emphasis on the importance of Cecchetti that she herself underwent the necessary examinations to qualify as an instructor of Cecchetti at the elementary and intermediate levels. (Her own training under Cecchetti's pupil, Idzikowski, had been as a professional performer, not as a teacher of basics.) Betty Oliphant coached her for the exams, which she passed on 1 November 1953. Eventually, they worked out an alternating system, whereby Oliphant concentrated on the minutiae of the dancers' technique and Franca provided some relief with classes that offered an opportunity for broader movement and expression.[40] But some of the dancers still went surreptitiously to Volkoff for classes that would stretch them out. And many found Peggy van Praagh's visit in 1956 to teach the advanced Cecchetti syllabus an invigorating breath of fresh air, not because she was an eminent British ballerina and ballet mistress (who would go on to be the founding artistic director of the Australian Ballet in 1972), but because her fresh approach to the syllabus brought the dancers out of their 'Cecchetti doldrums.'[41]

Oliphant's early involvement gave her a proprietary interest in the company's development which she never lost. Her basic function as trainer of its dancers extended logically and influentially into her role as principal and then artistic director of the National Ballet School. After her transfer to the school in 1959, she maintained a close and careful watch over the company. When Franca abruptly resigned in 1968, it was logical for the board to call on Oliphant to re-join the

As artistic director of the National Ballet School, the training ground for generations of the company's dancers, Betty Oliphant exercised a long and powerful influence on the life of the National.

company officially as its associate artistic director as part of its resolution to the crisis. When Oliphant herself resigned from this position in 1975, amid a flurry of recrimination and publicity, her continuing position as the school's director and principal entitled her to a position ex officio on the company's board of directors, a right which she chose to exercise with active participation in its activities.

Oliphant consequently enjoyed considerable tactical advantage: her position as a director of the company gave her legitimate grounds to criticize the company's development without implying any staff responsibility to answer for its shortcomings. Increasingly, she aligned herself as Franca's opponent rather than her ally. In either role, she was formidable. A woman of infinite charm, iron will, and consummate political skill, she could manoeuvre with the best of the Ottawa bureaucrats or Bay Street lawyers the ballet world came in contact with. Her indisputable authority, however, stemmed from the classroom, from her knowledge of dance basics and her ability to communicate them to students. By the mid-seventies, most of the company's dancers looked to her as the person who had formed their dance technique and given them their start in their chosen profession. Furthermore, her reputation as a dance educator had become international in scope. She had, at Erik Bruhn's invitation, reorganized the school of the Royal Swedish Ballet and had developed close ties with the school of the Bolshoi Ballet. Oliphant's voice counted, both at home and abroad. Her significant influence continued long after her celebrated differences with Franca dissolved the alliance between the two women that had initially introduced her into the company's affairs.

Designer Kay Ambrose had a hand in virtually every aspect of the company's operations.

The second major influence on the company's development, as decisive as Oliphant's but shorter in duration, was that of Kay Ambrose. Deeply loved and deeply hated by various individuals inside and outside the company, the late Kay Ambrose is still remembered with a mixture of veneration and exasperation by those who worked with her. Like Franca and Oliphant, she was English, but unlike them, she was not a professional dancer. As an author and illustrator, she published a number of short works in England on the technical aspects of ballet, including *The Ballet-Lover's Pocket Book* and *The Ballet Lover's Companion*. It was in this connection that she met and became close friends with Franca, who posed for her sketches and helped her with advice on technical matters. The two were collaborating on *Beginners, Please!* (published in North America as *The Ballet Student's Primer*) when Franca moved to Canada to take up her new position. Desperate to meet her publisher's deadlines, Ambrose followed in order to complete the collaboration. She arrived before the opening performance at Eaton Auditorium, saw the impossible array of practical problems confronting her friend, and stayed on to help.[42] For above all, her talents were practical, and she had no hesitation in turn-

Kay Ambrose at work. The sketch she holds is typical of the style she used for her book illustrations.

ing those talents to use, whatever the needs of the occasion might be.

Her readiness to act, coupled with the formidable range of her knowledge and experience, made her a daunting force. She designed costumes and sets; she sewed costumes and quickly discovered the cheapest sources in Toronto for materials and supplies; she did publicity and public relations for the company. On tour, her efforts to advance the company and its interests knew no bounds: in Lethbridge and many other centres, she sketched dancers in the local department store windows as a promotional stunt,[43] while in Victoria she successfully argued before a committee of the legislature for a reduction in the amusement tax as it applied to National Ballet ticket sales.[44] She taught dancers how to apply theatrical make-up[45] and, in the name of promoting the ballet, demonstrated cosmetics in the local Hudson's Bay Company store.[46] Before the days of resident physiotherapists, she treated dancers' injuries with her own nostrums and traditional remedies;[47] a superb cook, she fed countless meals to dancers and company hangers-on. Before coming to

Canada, she had even collaborated with Ram Gopal on a book on Indian dancing and costume and performed briefly with his company on tour in India.[48] Small wonder, then, that charter members of the company spoke of her years later as witch, sorcerer, or shaman,[49] or that some found her quick intelligence and almost compulsive energy intimidating.[50]

Franca relied heavily on that intelligence and dedicated support. In purely practical terms, Ambrose's willingness to turn her hand, for very little pay, to any number of tasks, particularly the designs for early productions, helped to ease the company's perennial insolvency. With characteristic practicality, Franca acknowledges her indebtedness to Ambrose's versatile talents: 'Kay did all that stuff, and whether people liked those sets or not, we had sets; whether they liked the costumes or not, we had costumes; besides which, she knew how to *sew* them.'[51] Furthermore, Ambrose was an accommodating designer, always ready to adjust or find a compromise to solve a practical or financial problem.[52] But many did not like her sets and costumes, nor did they like the increasing power which they saw her gaining in the company and its affairs,[53] as much through her personal relationship with Franca as through her official position.

Kay Ambrose joined the company officially, after almost a year of unofficial association with it, in September 1952, as public relations officer. Jack-of-all-trades would have been a more accurate title; after a further year, 'Artistic Adviser' emerged as the reasonable compromise. 'It is understood,' said the minute recording her appointment as public relations officer, 'that in her position she will assist in the designing of sets and costumes.'[54] Thus she became, in effect, the company's resident designer through its first decade of operation. (This function created union difficulties with IATSE, the International Alliance of Stage and Theatrical Employees, until Ambrose went to New York and qualified for membership in the Alliance.)[55] But she was also the company's moving force, a sympathetic partner on whom Franca could rely for decisive action. Judie Colpman describes Ambrose's tendency to act while others were still debating alternatives: 'If there was a problem with someone making a decision or taking responsibility to do something, Kay would have done it already.'[56] She was clearly a useful ally, but also a headstrong force whose energy could be difficult to live with. And Franca did live with it, both at the company and, for a period when the two women shared an apartment, at home. As the opposition to Ambrose's influence and the criticism of her designs became harsher, Franca found herself trapped between her roles as Ambrose's boss and Ambrose's friend. If she bowed to external pressure, she betrayed a deep personal loyalty; if she defended Ambrose professionally, she appeared to allow personal ties to influence professional judgment. Criticism in the press became intense; as late as 1974, twelve years after Ambrose's departure and three years after her death, an innuendo-laden article in *Chatelaine*[57] pilloried her, and by association, Franca, for her undue influence on the company. Franca always recognized the criticisms to which her friendship with Ambrose left her vulnerable, but she knew as well that she needed Ambrose and that her skills were real. As a reproducer of designs she was without peer, and her original designs for the company's Bavarian-flavoured *Coppélia* are still fondly remembered by many. Moreover, the company, in its early days, simply couldn't afford anyone else.

On the personal level, the demands finally became too intense. Exhausted by the relationship which, paradoxically, gave her strength, Franca could not hold out indefinitely.

> *There wasn't anything she couldn't do. She was so kind to me – I mean* really *kind. But you see I had to be kind to her too, and that was energizing. It was also exhausting, because when people were complaining about her, I had to protect her from all that. I suppose mainly I needed her. Also, I loved her. But she did in the end get too difficult. You see by that time she was having terrible headaches which turned out in the end to be a tumour which killed her. I didn't know what was wrong with her – she didn't know – she was taking aspirins and vitamins and painkillers and smoking and not getting enough sleep because of the headaches, living on nerves, and it really just became too much, in the end, for all of us.*[58]

At the conclusion of the 1961–2 season, Ambrose took a sabbatical from the company, from which she never returned. On her departure, two people had to be hired to fill her shoes.[59] When Kay Ambrose died of cancer in London in 1971, Franca cabled to her surviving relatives: 'Ballet world has lost one of its most talented and best loved artists.'[60] The formal tribute concealed the personal grief which Franca felt at the loss of one of her closest friends.

Grant Strate's long apprenticeship in the art of choreography

The new company was slow to designate a resident choreographer. Franca herself, although she turned her hand to choreography as the need arose, did not aspire to the role. Barring Gweneth Lloyd, whose prolific choreography was more significant as pioneering work than for its inherent artistic value, experienced choreographers simply did not exist in a nation with no professional ballet activity to produce them; and Franca held to the firm belief that a choreographer had to be nurtured with a thorough education in the principles and vocabulary of classical ballet before being turned loose to choreograph. Grant Strate joined the company as a charter member largely on the strength of his promise as a choreographer. While still a student in the University of Alberta's law program, he had come under the influence of Laine Mets, a former pupil of Mary Wigman, the pioneer of modern dance in Germany. With no formal ballet training, Strate had immediately begun to choreograph in the modern idiom. Franca invited him to join the company on the strength of that choreographic potential, not because of his abilities as a dancer. She then promptly required him to dance, principally in character roles like Dr Coppélius, as the necessary prerequisite to undertaking choreography. Strate chafed under the classical discipline Franca imposed.

Besides dancing and choreographing for the company, Grant Strate held a key administrative position as Franca's assistant. Here he consults with her amid the rehearsal clutter of the St Lawrence Hall.

> *She thought I could develop into a choreographer. And then when I joined the company, rather to my surprise, I learned that you really would never get the opportunity to choreograph till you had spent about five years learning the vocabulary. There was a very strong belief in classical ballet, and perhaps there still is, that choreography is something you do at the end of the spectrum, whereas, in fact, creativity doesn't work that way. You must start at earlier stages. So I was somewhat frustrated the first five years.*[61]

Eventually, in 1963, Strate was named the company's first resident choreographer,[62] and he choreographed seventeen works for it before his departure in 1970 to found the dance department at York University.[63] Even in his early years with the company, however, his organizational and administrative skills were put to use immediately. 'I was always, right from the beginning, involved in organizational matters, and eventually became Celia's assistant.'[64] In this capacity, Strate gradually assumed a role of greater and greater importance in the inner counsels of the company. He negotiated directly with choreographers like Balanchine and Cranko for the acquisition of new works and served as Erik Bruhn's assistant throughout the creation of his *Swan Lake* in 1967. He travelled frequently in order to absorb new trends and influences and to scout out talent. Above all, he became the champion of the avant garde, associating himself with young and adventurous company members in choreographic workshops[65] and arguing that the company must look to American rather than European developments if it was to join the mainstream of twentieth-century dance. During a 1963 visit to England, he articulated this position forcefully in a letter home:

> *We must no longer look back to mother England for supplemental dancers and artistic*

inspiration. There is NOTHING here which could possibly set a new trend and we must not be content to follow any more. New York should be our communication line. I am so afraid we will be stranded out of the mainstream of artistic vitality – where England now finds herself. So much talent in N.Y. is unfulfilled but with the potential for fulfilment that, if we must still import talent, we must face Mecca. British ballet can sink into the ocean for all of me. Saccharine romance and pretty dancing still seems to be the standard.[66]

Franca and Joanne Nisbet during an onstage rehearsal break on one of the company's New York trips.

These opinions flew in the face of the tradition Franca herself held dear. Strate was, for many years, her trusted and valuable colleague, but he differed fundamentally from her in his views on the nature of movement and the possibilities of dance.

At that time the classical ballet field tended to think that choreography simply was good arrangement and classical movement that you learn in a classroom. This didn't interest me. What interests me is the manipulation of that movement, or the invention of movement. That's where Celia and I started to part ways.[67]

He could support her loyally, but not from a position of essential agreement on basic principles. Strate was a modernist, an admirer of Balanchine, a seeker after new concepts; Franca was a traditionalist, an admirer of Petipa and Ashton, a custodian of the classics. Inevitably, when he could no longer hope to exercise a decisive influence on the direction the company was taking, when its interests diverged from his own, he drifted away. But through its first nineteen years, he counted as an active force in its development, urging it on to experiments it might not otherwise have attempted.

Franca demanded unswerving loyalty to the cause.

In Oliphant, Ambrose, Crum, Strate, Nisbet, Scott, and many others, Franca brought together with amazing speed a group of extremely strong, highly motivated individuals, all committed to the task of bringing into being the National Ballet of Canada. Their professional roles subjected their personal relationships to severe strains, some so severe that friendships were damaged or broken. Within this remarkable group, Franca's was unquestionably the dominant personality. Her vision of what the company should be took precedence over anyone else's; her own image came to represent the company, visually, to its growing public. She could never have created the company alone, but she alone became inseparable from its identity in the public imagination. Through radical swings in popularity and critical acceptance she remained its symbol and its guiding genius, by turns its whipping-boy and patron saint. The team which she had assembled had no choice but to adjust to the extraordinary force of her personality and dedicated vision. Those who could do so received from Franca the inspiration born of loyalty and labour in the common cause. Those who could not, eventually went their separate ways. This position of pre-eminence exacted its toll from Franca herself in the exhausting demands it placed on her spiritual and physical resources. (She was, for the first years, one of the company's two principal ballerinas as well as its artistic director.) Few individuals could have had the strength to take on such a role, and fewer still could have sustained it for as long as she did. The conflicts and bitternesses which inevitably arose were eloquent testimony to the level of emotional investment which the early company demanded of its creators. For Franca, and for those who threw in their lots with her, the game had to be played for keeps.

With the passage of the years, Franca's striking profile reflected the burden of responsibility involved in running a major arts organization.

CHAPTER THREE

I Won in the First Few Years

Administering on a shoestring: the limits to artistic freedom

If Franca ruled like an autocrat, she ruled over an extraordinarily meagre empire. Rich in aspirations and ambitions, the early company endured financial and material hardships that can, in retrospect, hardly be credited. The rehearsal space at the St Lawrence Hall, destined eventually to become the company's permanent home, could be used only during the summer months; in the winter it served as a hostel for Toronto's street people.[1] The company found makeshift rehearsal locations to fill in the gaps – a restaurant, the Orange Lodge, St Margaret's Church, Eglinton[2] – until, in 1967, a centennial project by the City of Toronto renovated the St Lawrence Hall premises and turned them over for the company's use on a year-round basis.[3] Eventually, the company outgrew even these facilities, ample by the standards of 1967, and spilled out of the Hall into rehearsal and office space in other nearby buildings. With hopes for a full-scale Ballet Opera House crushed, the company nevertheless realized a part of its dream in the summer of 1996, with its move to new production and rehearsal facilities at King's Landing. Named after philanthropist Walter Carsen,

OPPOSITE: The company's early repertoire leaned heavily on works by Franca's earlier contacts, like Andrée Howard. Jocelyn Terelle brought impeccable line and fluidity of movement to her performance in Howard's Death and the Maiden.

ABOVE: Franca reproduced Fokine's Le Carnaval *with great success. Lilian Jarvis and Earl Kraul in a tender moment from the ballet.*

the Carsen Centre amalgamates the company's scattered facilities in one spacious, up-to-date complex the company calls home.

But at the beginning, ambitions were far more modest. It took a full year before Franca could be provided with a telephone,[4] fifteen, apparently, before she got an office for her exclusive use.[5] Production and storage facilities were scattered around the city, and in the resulting confusion the company could, and did, depart on a tour missing crucial drops and set pieces.[6] The dancers, ill paid at best, on one occasion took up a collection among themselves to try to keep the beleaguered company afloat.[7] The adventure of touring took on added suspense when no one knew for sure whether or not the tour would have to be cancelled for lack of funds. It was 1959 before the company could afford even a cursory dress rehearsal prior to setting out on tour,[8] 1963 before it could manage a complete dress and technical rehearsal in Toronto.[9]

Franca with James Ronaldson in Antony Tudor's Lilac Garden. *The psychological subtleties of Tudor's choreography projected well in the small theatres which the company played in its early years.*

With the cumulative deficit mounting annually, Franca poured every penny into the new productions she so desperately needed in order to attract and hold an audience. But even here there was not enough to go around. Mounting new productions and maintaining old ones involved the company in never-ending rounds of robbing Peter to pay Paul, with the inevitable consequences to the onstage picture. 'It is frustrating,' wrote Franca in 1953, 'how every ballet we possess is just not quite right because we have been forced to economise on something. *Lilac Garden* is nearly a perfect production but because we only have two sets of flats instead of three and because they are flats instead of wings it just falls short.'[10] Against this background of enforced penny-pinching, the resourcefulness of an accommodating designer like Kay Ambrose assumes its full value, as does the patience of an Antony Tudor, whose royalty payments from the company, like those for many another choreographer, were frequently in arrears.[11]

Freedom to determine the artistic policy of the company was one thing; the ability to implement that artistic policy effectively, in the face of financial pressures that threatened to terminate the venture at almost every point, was quite another matter. Franca's mandate required a certain basic level of funding in order to make artistic development possible. But in the period before government funding and corporate sponsorship were accepted realities, no such level of funding could be assumed. Franca had to live with the vagaries of inadequate financing from the company's inception, and when the board blew the financial whistle, Franca regarded its actions as interference in artistic matters, her proper sphere within the company. Factions on the board would, in their turn, accuse her of financial irresponsibility.

Celia Franca's twenty-four years as artistic director of the National Ballet of Canada were to be characterized by a 'hands on' approach to artistic management. In her initial advice to the founding committee, de Valois had 'begged them not to tie her hands artistically,'[12] and Franca's first contract, according to the board's minutes, gave her 'the sole and entire artistic direction of the Company.'[13] No copy of that contract survives, but in her 1963 notes for a projected history, Sydney Mulqueen recorded that Franca 'accepted the position of Artistic Director of the proposed National Ballet Company of Canada with the proviso that she would always be given a completely free hand in the artistic direction of the company.'[14] The challenges to Franca's leadership which surfaced during her tenure as artistic director reflected broad questions about the scope of artistic control within an arts organization, and about artistic direction itself, the extent of its authority and the nature of its relationship to non-artistic company activities, particularly financial ones. In her own mind, however, the issue was clear. The direct, personal control she exercised over the company's dancing extended logically into all its other facets. Her responsibility for the artistic product put her in charge of the entire company, with artistic achievement the overriding goal. The board existed in order to serve the same ideals. In an artistic enterprise, what authority could be higher than the artistic director's?

The concept of artistic director as autocrat was not new. Precedents in the world of twentieth-century ballet included those set by the likes of Diaghilev, Rambert, Balanchine, and, above all, de Valois, all of whom provided the 'sole and entire artistic direction' for their companies. But the de Valois model had a fatal structural flaw: it expected the artistic director to exercise a nineteenth-century, autocratic authority, but without the political and economic mechanisms, the direct government financial support, that had made such authority workable. In de Valois' 'begging' of the organizers not to tie Franca's hands, it is just possible to hear the frustrations of an experienced artistic director attempting to come to terms with the paradoxes inherent in this state of affairs, where personal magnetism and tenacity had to fill the gap created by inadequate support.

Much later, Franca herself, in an address to new members of the board of directors, would summarize de Valois' advice as stating that the new artistic director should 'be given complete freedom to set and fulfil artistic policy with no interference from the board.'[15] But changes in society's attitudes towards the arts and in its willingness to provide finances for them were conspiring, even by the mid-point of the century, to invalidate the model of unquestioned authority under which Franca was invited, and chose, to operate. As business responded to the challenge of becoming a partner in artistic enterprise, business principles, inevitably, asked to be heard alongside artistic ones. Franca thus entered into a peculiarly hazardous position in twentieth-century ballet management, asked to organize a company on one model and then required to guide it into the relatively new and unknown territory of corporate cooperation and fiscal responsibility.

Not that she was unfamiliar with the overriding power of the budget. She had, after all, seen through rehearsal *Deidre*, her own choreographic work for the Metropolitan Ballet, only to have it cancelled for lack of funds prior to its London opening by the company's patron, Cecilia Blatch.[16] Nor was she opposed to the idea of working with a board of directors. She herself had made an 'eloquent appeal' that a corporate structure be drafted to strengthen her position, even before a formal commitment to launch the company had been made.[17] She was, furthermore, a shrewd judge of character, with the essential requisite for genuine pioneering work, the ability to adapt old ways to new circumstances. The ways that she knew, through the examples of Rambert and de Valois, represented a method of operation that could not be maintained indefinitely. But before altering them, she would first have to be convinced that they required alteration, and she would never be able to forget the initial, broad-ranging terms of her appointment. Thus, though she was promised sole and entire authority in the running of the company, force of circumstances clipped her wings. As artistic director, however, she never gave up trying to soar.

Franca's intensely practical nature led her quickly to actions designed to make the general public aware of the company's precarious financial position. In 1954, the company undertook an extensive, and financially perilous, tour of Quebec, Ontario, the United States, and western Canada. With debts spiralling, the board, at home in Toronto, gave serious consideration to the possibility of cancelling the tour, while Franca, on the road, took to including in performances a personal appeal from the stage for fifty thousand dollars to help the National through this crisis period. From Montreal, in late January, she wrote: 'Our "appeal-from-the-stage" each night has brought in about $350 so far: not much compared to $50,000, but better than nothing. At least it is worth the trouble of making a little speech!'[18]

Had she known the full effect these little speeches would have, she might have revised her opinion. When the company reached Toronto, Gweneth Lloyd, now completely alienated from the Toronto enterprise and committed more than ever to Winnipeg, got wind of the appeal and took out a pointed advertisement in the Toronto newspapers, on the same page with the National's daily show ads. In it, she reassured the general public that opportunities for professional dance would continue to exist, notably with the Royal Winnipeg Ballet, even if the National were to fold. 'While it is regrettable,' the advertisement concluded, 'that one company finds itself unable to remain solvent despite generous public support, it would be more regrettable that the hard-working young dancers should be misled and disillusioned regarding their opportunities in the future.'[19] The notice was signed 'Gweneth Lloyd, Director, The Royal Winnipeg Ballet.'

Lloyd was throwing down the gauntlet. With this gesture, she brought to a public climax the rivalry and animosity which had long been smouldering and which had flared up sporadically ever since Winnipeg's reaction to Franca's audition tour and recruitment tactics. If Lloyd's words betray the bitterness of frustrated personal hopes, they also bear eloquent testimony to the desperate level of competition for audience support to which she felt her company had been reduced. The advertisement occasioned a flurry of press interest in 'the battle of the ballets,' but Franca's public response was muted. In the eyes of at least one columnist, she emerged from the scuffle smelling a little more sweetly than did Lloyd. 'Miss Franca's retort, ostensibly a "no comment," was as devastating as a long rebuttal. "It isn't in my nature to reply to statements like that," she said.'[20] Nevertheless, the National's board prudently decided that no appeal from the stage would be made when the company played Winnipeg in April, and took steps to reduce the dancers' salaries for a period of three weeks; the decision had already been taken that there would be no appeals on the American portion of the tour.[21]

13x

NOTICE

The well advertised financial straits and predictions of "tragedy for Canadian culture" by one of our ballet companies must be giving considerable alarm to dancers and to those who are interested in the future of this art in Canada.

We feel that this fear should be allayed by a presentation of the true facts regarding the past, present and future of ballet in this country.

We should like to remind the public that:

1. The Royal Winnipeg Ballet, which has toured Canada since 1945 and which was incorporated in 1949, thus making it Canada's first professional ballet, is national in its character, scope and personnel, and for fifteen year has provided an outlet for talented dancers in Canada and will continue to do so. It is soon to show this Canadian talent in Washington, D.C., and in 9 other states of the Union, in addition to a trans-continental tour of Canada.
2. There are ever-increasing opportunities for dancers in theatre and television as these develop in our country.
3. The well-established Canadian Ballet Festival Association gives dancers encouragement and preliminary training in performance and also opportunity to choreographers, musicians and designers from coast to coast to shew their work.
4. There are many opportunities for dancers to gain professional experience in productions such as Theatre Under the Stars, the Canadian National Exhibition, Melody Fair, the Montreal Festivals and small concert groups.

While it is regrettable that one company finds itself unable to remain solvent despite generous public support, it would be more regrettable that the hard-working young dancers should be misled and disillusioned regarding their opportunities in the future.

GWENETH LLOYD,
Director, The Royal Winnipeg Ballet.

Gweneth Lloyd's challenge as it appeared in the Toronto Evening Telegram *of 25 January 1954.*

But as the company tottered from one financial crisis to another, Franca applied herself with optimistic vigour to the immediate challenge of building a repertoire. Through the first ten years of the company's life, repertoire had to be acquired as cheaply as possible; there was no money for new commissions from established international choreographers. Even had there been, the eminent ones would have been unlikely to offer their services, at any price, to a new and untried company without an international reputation. As Franca learned, even the influence of personal friendship had its limitations. 'If I could have got the Ashtons and Tudors,' she was to comment later with some asperity, 'I would have.'[22] This complete lack of a bargaining position was a point frequently lost on the public and the critics, who seemed to think that new works from major choreographers could be had simply for the asking. Few realized that neither love nor money would pry great choreographers loose from the companies that provided their creative context in order to mount a new work on unknown dancers.

In order to establish a new, classically based, company, it made sense to start with the classics of the standard repertoire. Accordingly, Franca undertook what turned out to be a three-stage process in the early acquisition of repertoire, drawing on her own capital before investing tentatively in the volatile and unpredictable market of original choreography. First, she mounted the classics, from her own memory of them; second, she turned to the friends of her past for works from the recent British repertoire; third, she began to commission original Canadian works.

The centrality of the full-length classics

Franca's astonishing memory, her 'little brain-box,' as she calls it,[23] produced a wealth of works for the National in its early years. That retentive memory has never received the full credit it deserves. Today, when the remounting of a single classic involves copious historical research and requires the assistance of an entire community of artists, there has been a tendency to undervalue the precise, efficient mind that stored away countless details of movement and groupings, then brought them out on demand in the recreation for Canadian audiences of *Coppélia*, *Swan Lake*, *Giselle*, and *The Nutcracker*. There were few memories equal to the task, fewer still whose source was as impeccable as Franca's. She had learned the classics, by dancing in them and by watching from the wings, in de Valois' Sadler's Wells Ballet. They had been staged for de Valois by Nicholas Sergeyev, the former director general of the Mariinsky Theatre who fled Russia in 1918, bringing with him an invaluable set of notebooks which recorded the Russian classics.[24] Sergeyev thus became the lifeline for the transmission of the Russian tradition in the West, the authoritative source for the classics throughout the period when, for political reasons, direct contact with Russian ballet and its artists was impossible. Franca never worked with Sergeyev directly, but she danced in his productions while they were still fresh in the Sadler's Wells collective memory.[25] In the art form which depends absolutely on personal transmission of the tradition from generation to generation,

Franca stood in the direct line of that tradition as it was then known in western Europe, and passed it on as she knew it to the artists and audiences of Canada.[26]

A stylized version of Myrtha's headdress, which repeated the moth motif, was used in Kay Ambrose's poster for the 1956–7 season, seen here outside the Royal Alexandra Theatre in Toronto.

Her productions came thick and fast in those early years, often in bits and pieces, as circumstances allowed. *Coppélia* first, and first of all the toy shop scene, 'a very tiny little version of it in Varsity Arena before we had a company.' A complete Act II entered the repertoire during the company's first tour (the Eaton Auditorium stage being too small to house the set) in 1951–2; the two-act version had its première in Calgary, during the company's first western tour (27 October 1952); the third act had to wait until the 1958–9 season, when Franca 'had dancers who I thought could cope with the technical demands of the difficult pas de deux.'[27]

Next, *Giselle*, the second act only, in the company's first season, to be rounded out with the first act in 1952–3. Calgary audiences, once again, saw the première of the company's first complete *Giselle* on the evening of 28 October 1952. With the mounting of *Giselle*, Franca introduced into the repertoire one of its most durable pieces, as well as the role with which she would become most closely identified as a performer in the minds of North American audiences. Although she had made her reputation in England as a dramatic dancer with the cold and forbidding Myrtha, Queen of the Wilis, she would take her official Canadian farewell, deluged with flowers and affectionate good wishes, in 1959 as the fragile Giselle. In this production and the 1956–7 remounting of the complete ballet, Franca, Lois Smith, and David Adams would appear repeatedly, with Smith and Franca alternating the roles of Giselle and Myrtha to Adams' Albrecht.

The Kay Ambrose designs for these productions attracted their share of critical scorn, especially the large, mothlike wings for Myrtha's first entrance.[28] But the designs had the desired effect on one little girl, who went with her family to the Odeon Palace Theatre in Hamilton to see *Giselle* on 6 December 1958.

> *All I remember is Celia Franca. I thought the second act was boring, but I remember the mad scene. She was very dramatic in it. And the costumes. I wanted to wear those costumes. I was enraptured. I actually got to return to the Palace Theatre and dance Giselle myself before they tore it down. I thought that was a lovely completed circle.*[29]

Without Franca to start it, Karen Kain, the child in that Hamilton audience in 1958, could never have completed the circle to become one of the National's authentic, home-grown stars and one of the major figures in Canadian professional dance.

Barnstorming performances of the classics in the movie-theatres and hockey arenas of the nation had their grotesque moments, like the night in Kitchener, Ontario, when local stage-hands forgot to lock the elevating device which had raised an ethereal Giselle from behind her tombstone. Instead of casting himself tragically on top of the grave, Earl Kraul, as a despairing Albrecht in the ballet's final moments, threw himself, quite unexpectedly, into it, his head unfortunately still visible to the audience above the tombstone.[30] But without such performances, the dreams which led to major careers for Canadian dancers like Karen Kain, Veronica Tennant, and Frank Augustyn might never have been born. Franca and her colleagues were dealing in magic, the magic that could build theatrical ambition in a public for whom the theatre itself was almost unknown.

Hard on *Giselle*'s heels in the acquisition of basic repertoire, and once again in instalments, came *The Nutcracker*. 'We are now busy rehearsing Casse Noisette,' wrote Franca to a supporter of the National in November 1951, 'although I haven't as yet dared to mention this to our Directors, as I can't think how we are going to pay for its production.'[31] But pay for it they did, and *Casse-Noisette* Act II entered the repertoire during the company's second Eaton Auditorium engagement in January 1952. Under its English title, the complete *Nutcracker* premièred before Quebec City audiences on 19 November 1955.

Swan Lake completed the company's early sampling of the classics. It might not have found a place in the repertoire at this point, had it not been for the chance which brought Lois Smith into the company along with her husband, David Adams. Smith was, at that time, a dancer with reliable basic training, a long-legged, classically proportioned body, latent powers of dramatic projection, and largely unformed ambitions as far as ballet itself was concerned. Her early experience had been confined almost entirely to musical comedy. In seventeen seasons with the

National, she developed into one of its most reliable ballerinas and its first star. Her partnership with Adams was one of the great drawing cards for the company, both in Toronto and on tour. On the break-up of their marriage, and Adams' departure from the company, she developed a new partnership with Earl Kraul and continued her development, discovering new maturity and expressive powers to her very last season with the company.

In the young Lois Smith, Franca recognized a dancer willing to be trained for *Swan Lake*. 'She was a very willing learner. I could coach her. She wanted to do duets and partnering work.' Franca decided to build this element of her repertoire on the opportunity represented by Smith, the potential classical ballerina. 'I think one has to be an opportunist. If I hadn't had Lois I would have done something else, I expect, at that time.'[32] Fortunately, she did have Lois, and so *Swan Lake* Act II premièred at St Peter's High School auditorium in Peterborough on 17 November 1953, to be followed by the complete *Swan Lake* in Hamilton on 19 January 1955. A program called *Dances from the Classics* had introduced some of the *Swan Lake* divertissements to the stage piecemeal, as the company learned them.[33]

The swan maidens, frightened by the intrusion of Siegfried and his friends, shelter behind Odette (Lois Smith) during rehearsals for the company's first Swan Lake. *Lilian Jarvis (in white headband) and Angela Leigh (extreme right) can be recognized among them.*

One obvious gap waited to be filled. The National had no full-length *Sleeping Beauty*, the crowning achievement of Marius Petipa's career as choreographer at the Imperial Theatre in St Petersburg. It was *Sleeping Beauty* with which Diaghilev had sought to dazzle London in his landmark production of 1921, *Sleeping Beauty* with which de Valois' Sadler's Wells had reopened Covent Garden in 1946, after the war, and *Sleeping Beauty* with which Sadler's Wells and a radiant Margot Fonteyn had conquered New York in 1949. The best the National could muster at this early stage of its development was excerpts, modelled on those of the Ballets Russes, under titles like *Dances from the Sleeping Beauty* and *Princess Aurora*. The company's first full-length production of this touchstone of the classical repertoire would be long in coming, but when it finally arrived, it would herald a significant new phase in the National's development.

The fact that almost all these major premières took place in communities outside Toronto testifies to the importance of touring in the company's early life. Despite frequent criticisms, the company was not an exclusively Toronto phenomenon. The typical pattern for the National's development of a new production was preparation and rehearsal in Toronto, opening night (which was actually the first full dress rehearsal the production would receive) on the first stop on the tour, and performances in Toronto after extensive exposure across the country and in the United States. Toronto audiences were thus denied the prestige of a company première, but the previous exposure didn't necessarily guarantee them the most polished performance possible. The tour's value as road-show try-out before the Toronto opening was negligible. Theatrical conditions on the road in Canada and in many of the American towns the company toured were primitive, more often than not high school auditoriums, gymnasiums, community halls, or arenas without proper lighting facilities and with postage-stamp-size stages. Unlike in England and parts of the United States at the time, and unlike in Canada today, there was no network of established, professionally equipped theatres across the country that could allow a tour to iron out technical difficulties in preparation for a grand opening at the Royal Alexandra Theatre, which became the company's Toronto performance home in January 1953. On tour, every theatre and high school auditorium presented a different challenge in technical improvisation; a new production arrived at the relative splendours of the Royal Alex with many of its technical difficulties intact, waiting to be resolved in the first few performances before the Toronto audience.

Lilian Jarvis as Princess Aurora in an early staging of the Rose Adagio from Sleeping Beauty. *Her suitors (from left to right) are Earl Kraul, Harold da Silva, Lawrence Adams, and Ray Moller.*

Despite these obstacles, the company persevered in its pioneering work of bringing the standard repertoire to audiences in small and often remote centres throughout Canada and the United States. And in doing so, it filled a pressing need. It could not, it is true, claim the first North American production of any of these works. William Christensen, a student of Fokine's and one of three Danish-American brothers who helped to establish dance in the western United States, produced America's first full-length *Coppélia* in San Francisco in 1939, its first complete *Swan Lake* in 1940,[34] and its first full-length *Nutcracker* in 1944.[35] Under the direction of William Christensen, and later of his brother, Lew, the San Francisco Ballet became one of the major ballet companies on the continent. *Coppélia* had been in American Ballet Theatre's repertoire since 1942, *Giselle* since 1940.[36] In 1947, the Ottawa Ballet Company, led by Nesta Toumine, presented a full-length *Nutcracker* featuring the fifteen-year-old Svetlana Beriosova as guest artist. Balanchine's famous and influential complete *Nutcracker* appeared in 1954.[37]

Christensen, however, had never seen a complete *Swan Lake* before producing it, and had had to piece the choreography together at second hand; his complete production was not performed after 1942.[38] Balanchine never mounted the entire *Swan Lake*, his 1951 production being essentially Act II of the original four-act version.[39] So when the National toured its complete *Swan Lake*, based on Franca's recollections of the Sergeyev Sadler's Wells production, in the early 1950s, no other authoritative, professional version of the work was on display anywhere in North America.[40] In bringing *Swan Lake* and other works from the classical repertoire to its far-flung audience, the National not only defined its own identity; it formed its audience, by showing it, often for the first time, what classical ballet could be.

Despite the inevitable compromises forced upon these early productions by lack of funds, the results were good. Knowledgeable critics, at home and in the United States, noticed Franca's care for ensemble style in her mountings of the classics, and commented as well on the considerable promise of the company itself and of some

The corps in the lakeside scene from the company's first Swan Lake. *Barely visible in the foreground are four black cygnets, a feature of traditional stagings of the ballet which Erik Bruhn and other producers dropped from more recent versions.*

of its individual dancers. Franca's strategy of careful schooling and attention to detail paid off with an artistic product that was recognized as modest in its pretensions but of undeniable quality and integrity within those self-imposed limits. Of the company's first full-length production of *Giselle*, Sydney Johnson in the *Montreal Star*, who counted the immortal Markova and Dolin in his personal pantheon of dancers of *Giselle*, wrote that he had 'never seen a *Giselle* in which the drama was expressed with such consistent clarity and with every tiny detail of pantomime so carefully integrated into the whole pattern of the dance.' 'This was not the most exciting *Giselle* I have ever seen,' he went on to say, 'but it may have been the best-balanced production ever danced on Her Majesty's stage.'[41] John Martin, reviewing the new four-act *Swan Lake* when it played the Brooklyn Academy of Music in 1955, expressed his qualified admiration in similar terms.

> *If the* Swan Lake *was perhaps over-ambitious for so inexperienced a company to attempt, nevertheless it was in the famous second act of this work that the best results were obtained. The corps de ballet danced, indeed, better than many a more experienced corps de ballet has danced in this same act. It was precise, unified, and in good style throughout. Furthermore, the very capable young conductor, George Crum, held them strictly to tempo, even in the pas de quatre.*[42]

Martin also concurred with Franca's judgment about Lois Smith as a dancer worth the gamble of a full production of the ballet. He saw in her already the lyric, expressive qualities that were the hallmark of her dancing and waited hopefully for the development of technical skills of speed, agility, and attack that would enable her to command the contrasting aspects of the dual role on which the ballet is built.

> *Her Odette, considerably better than her Odile, has a definite lyric charm and is frequently touching. If the variation was not impeccably achieved, the pas de deux was beautifully danced, and technically it would seem to be only a matter of time and training before we have a swan queen of real distinction.*

Musicality, attention to stylistic detail, and the careful nurturing of individual potential could thus be seen in the company's earliest attempts at the classical repertoire; these qualities became the cornerstone of its early North American reputation.

That early reputation, however, is hard to document today. One of the drawbacks of the pioneering mode was the fact that very little genuinely informed newspaper and magazine coverage was granted the company. Local critics assigned to the company's visit to town were frequently simply writers taken off other beats, with no knowledge of or sympathy for ballet as a performing art. But regional ballet had not yet established itself as a significant force on the continent, and so experienced critics in major centres, with exceptions like Martin, noted above, tended to ignore the company's barnstorming appearances or pass them off with little consideration. Most of the company's early press consists of news stories and public interest items generated by Ambrose, Franca, and the hard-working publicity staff, rather than knowledgeable evaluations of its ambitions and achievements.

Franca supplemented with choreographic borrowings from old friends.

In the second stage of Franca's acquisition of early repertoire, she called upon her British contacts for any existing works they would allow her to have. The international world of professional choreography operated on a far more casual basis in the 1950s than it does today. Friends passed their works on to other friends without formal contracts, and without requiring the direct personal control of the final production that now accompanies the transfer of a work from one company to another. Thus Antony Tudor, far and away Franca's most significant source of twentieth-century repertoire during her first decade of operation, trusted her to mount *Lilac Garden* (in 1953) from her own memory of the work, with just one visit by Franca to Tudor in New York in order to set a few details.[43] *Dark Elegies* entered the repertoire in Kingston on 15 November 1955 in the same fashion. But the company also had significant direct contact with Tudor, who coached *Lilac Garden* when the National visited Jacob's Pillow in the summer of 1953, and set *Gala Performance* on them in person. For the 1954–5 season, he also set *Offenbach in the Underworld*. (Franca did not know the work then, but would, at the time of her retirement in 1975, revive it for the National and for the Joffrey Ballet.) Franca and Joanne Nisbet, the company's principal ballet mistress, travelled to New York together prior to the 1962–3 season to learn *Judgment of Paris* from Tudor so that they could teach it to the company. Tudor then came to Toronto in Franca's absence for final rehearsals of the ballet.[44]

Thus by the 1962–3 season, the National had as the core of its twentieth-century repertoire five Tudor ballets, including the two monuments of his early career, *Lilac Garden* and *Dark Elegies*. The National shared with American Ballet Theatre, which had been Tudor's home since he left England in 1939, the distinction of keeping the Tudor repertoire alive in North America. With *Offenbach in the Underworld*, a version of which Tudor had originally created for the Philadelphia Ballet Guild, the National actually got the jump on Ballet Theatre, by bringing it into the repertoire a full year before ABT and even performing it in New York before Ballet Theatre premièred its own production of the work there.[45] But with the exception of *Offenbach*, the National did not participate in the American phase of Tudor's development. It was the Tudor of Franca's London acquaintance, not the contemporary Tudor of American Ballet Theatre, to whom Canadian audiences were introduced. Given the slump in his own creativity during this period, the Tudor repertoire may have looked slightly passé. But it called to mind an earlier Tudor of variety, complexity, and psychological subtlety, whose example and personality were to affect company members deeply. Grant Strate, who values Tudor for both his strict Cecchetti training and his eclectic openness to other forms of dance, today acknowledges him as the first major influence on his own development as a choreographer.[46] From Franca's point of view, the exposure to Tudor represented a vital part, the 'contemporary classical' part, of her young company's education.[47]

Continuing to draw on her old Ballet Rambert connections, Franca also acquired *The Mermaid* and *Death and the Maiden* from Andrée Howard, and *Winter Night* from Walter Gore, two British choreographers of less substantial reputation than Tudor. The latter ballet, to the Rachmaninoff Piano Concerto in C minor, was a romantic work on the theme of the eternal triangle, with passionate parts for the three principals. It had been a popular, if not a critical, success in London since its first performance in 1950.[48] Howard's 1937 work, *Death and the Maiden*, to the slow movement of the Schubert quartet of the same name, was a brief but intense exploration of the theme of death, remarkable for the concentration of its effects in pure dance terms. Dame Marie Rambert wrote of it that 'everything in it is expressed through sheer movement without the help (or hindrance) of realistic gesture or mime. The deep emotion felt is the result of a moving idea expressed by perfect choreography.'[49]

Negotiations for the acquisition of *The Mermaid* illustrate just how informal such arrangements sometimes were. After several unanswered letters to Howard and some prompting by a common friend in London,[50] Franca finally received the following response to a letter with technical questions about the décor:

> *Well, I think in general the Mermaid costumes and décor should be a bit more glorified than the old production. With the wonderful things in the way of plastics and the like that are made now the Mermaid and undersea corps could look much more* wet! *than in the original production and I'm not at all averse to a bit of sparkle discreetly touching up their headdresses and part of costume. (A bit shiny on one side of their tails and little on the body.) The weeds for the underwater could be mixed with plastic and do have a rock or two if you like!*[51]

A far cry from the rigid control which ensures the faithful reproduction of every detail of the original, as frequently stipulated in current contracts with the company. On the choreographic side, Howard exercised a more watchful eye. Franca, who had danced in the original, travelled to London with Grant Strate to relearn and record the work in descriptive, longhand notes (which survive among her papers in the National Archives of Canada), the method preferred for many years by the company to any of the established systems of notation.[52] Earl Kraul, who was in England studying during that summer of 1959, served there as guinea-pig and model for them[53] and then demonstrated the steps when Franca and Strate later taught the ballet to the company in Canada. Howard herself never worked directly with the company. It was a testimony to the esteem in which Franca was held that this method of acquisition was permitted. As Franca now puts it: 'I had the trust of Antony Tudor, I had the trust of Andrée Howard, so I could bring these things back.'[54]

The same trip to London netted the company another staple of its early repertoire, *Pineapple Poll,* and established a connection with its choreographer, John Cranko, that exercises a decisive influence on the National's character to the present day. Cranko was another of Franca's personal contacts, this time from her Sadler's Wells days.[55] Grant Strate recalls that he was to meet Cranko for the first time at the intermission of a performance of his *Prince of the Pagodas* at Covent Garden in 1959. While Strate, Franca, and Andrée Howard awaited Cranko in the Royal Box, a message was whispered to Howard. Cranko had been arrested. The Canadian contingent had stumbled inadvertently into one of the more sordid encounters between British public morality and the British artistic community.

The newspapers subsequently reported that Cranko had been fined £10 and released after he admitted to 'persistently importuning men for an immoral purpose' on a street in Chelsea. The *Daily Express* took this relatively minor incident

This onstage photograph of Cranko's Pineapple Poll *captures the atmosphere of the Royal Alexandra Theatre, the company's Toronto home until 1964.*

and blew it up into a moralistic vendetta against homosexuals, the 'unpleasant freemasonry' and 'secret brotherhood' which, the newspaper insinuated, controlled London's West End theatre. Cranko, then enjoying enormous popularity as a rising choreographer of serious works and the co-author of *Cranks*, an immensely successful West End review, suffered greatly under the attack. The publicity surrounding the incident contributed in the long term to his disillusionment with England and his departure for Stuttgart,[56] where he gained international recognition for his work until his untimely death in 1973, on a flight home to Stuttgart from his company's appearance in New York.

On that night in 1959 when Cranko was to have met Franca and Strate, the arrest so demoralized and frightened him that he remained locked in his home, refusing to answer his phone. Strate and Franca finally made contact with him, and he agreed to teach them *Pineapple Poll*, as previously arranged, but insisted on doing so in the security of his home, the bachelor flat which had been described in the press as 'almost as weird as the birdcage and chicken-wire scenery of *Cranks*.'[57] 'So,' Strate remembers, 'we spent over a week learning *Pineapple Poll* in his living room.'[58] The friendship which Strate established with Cranko in these unusual circumstances was instrumental in the negotiations for *Romeo and Juliet* which he undertook four years later.

Working in John Cranko's London flat, Grant Strate, seated, takes notes on the choreography of Pineapple Poll, *as demonstrated by Franca and Cranko.*

But two of Franca's major contacts were not to be so easily exploited – Sir Frederick Ashton and Dame Ninette de Valois. Franca's concerted efforts to acquire Ashton's *Symphonic Variations*[59] and *La Fille Mal Gardée*[60] met with polite evasions, every bit as effective as outright refusal. The only Ashton work produced during Franca's tenure as artistic director was *Les Rendezvous*, which Dame Peggy van Praagh mounted for the company during her 1956 visit.[61] *Les Patineurs* was apparently offered, but only in 1963, after it had already been acquired by the Royal Winnipeg Ballet.[62] Franca thought it best not to step on their toes, or to appear to follow their lead. After protracted negotiation, de Valois' *The Rake's Progress* finally entered the repertoire in 1965. De Valois herself never saw the production, despite Franca's invitations to her to participate in its staging.[63] Franca, who was accused by her detractors of turning the National into a mini Royal Ballet, had scant success in gaining the cooperation of Ashton and de

Valois, its two leading lights. By force of circumstance, she relied far more heavily on Cranko and Tudor, both renegades as far as the Royal Ballet was concerned, than she did on the mainstream Royal Ballet tradition.

David Adams, Canadian choreographer and the company's first *premier danseur*

Having restaged the classics and called on old friends from England for twentieth-century works, Franca grasped the thorny problem of developing original Canadian choreography. Box-office of course, constituted a major risk. Everyone, especially the press, and, eventually, the granting agencies, expected a national ballet to produce national works, but few customers were ready to back up this expectation by buying a ticket to a new work by an untried choreographer. In the national and theatrical conditions under which Franca operated, however, two other factors complicated the straight financial problem and gave it delicate political overtones.

The first was the international perspective which Franca applied to her artistic judgments. For her, ballet was an international art form and her responsibility was to maintain its high standards; she strove to recognize a choreographer's talent, not nationality. The rift with Gweneth Lloyd, who had turned out original works at a prodigious rate throughout the thirties and forties, served to up the ante even further. Lloyd had worked in relative isolation, unfettered by fears of comparison with the larger world of ballet; the National, because of its unique combination of high public profile and relative inexperience, was denied that freedom. Having trained her sights on the international stage, Franca could not afford to let a naïve sense of nationalism guide its choreographic development.

The second complicating factor was Franca's firm belief that a classical ballet company should present a modern repertoire consistent with its classical heritage, not antithetical to it. If classical training, to which she was devoting so much of her energy, stood for anything, it mustn't be contradicted every time the company ventured into contemporary work. With a company as new to the classical tradition as this one, she had a point. The pressure to develop contemporary Canadian choreography could not be allowed to sabotage the fundamental purpose for which Franca had committed herself to Canada. She thus had to look for, or develop, a special choreographer, one who would conceive of dance in terms of the vocabulary and traditions of classical ballet, not in reaction to them, and one who might eventually pass the acid test of comparison to international choregraphic standards.

Franca took a principled and reasoned stance on this centrally important issue of contemporary choreography. She paid for her adherence to international artistic standards by appearing to be insufficiently Canadian, and for her loyalty to the classical tradition by seeming to be a hidebound conservative. In the period when chauvinistic fervour and radical artistic experimentation set the dominant tone, she remained her own woman and took the consequences. That her refusal to compro-

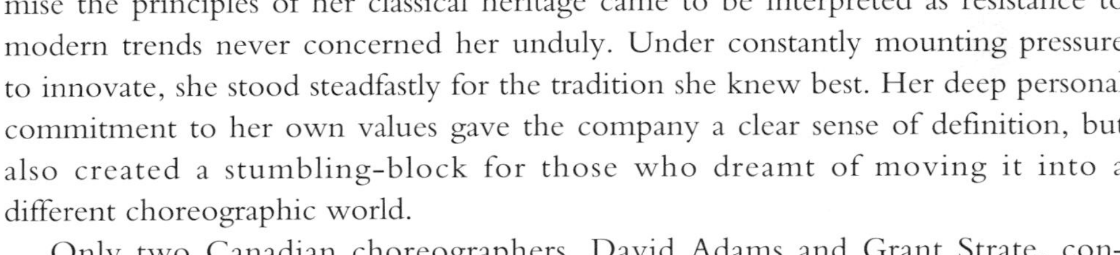

mise the principles of her classical heritage came to be interpreted as resistance to modern trends never concerned her unduly. Under constantly mounting pressure to innovate, she stood steadfastly for the tradition she knew best. Her deep personal commitment to her own values gave the company a clear sense of definition, but also created a stumbling-block for those who dreamt of moving it into a different choreographic world.

Only two Canadian choreographers, David Adams and Grant Strate, contributed with any frequency to the National's early repertoire. Adams had already had some choreographic experience when he joined the company, having created *Ballet Composite* for the Winnipeg Ballet in 1949 and two further works for the same group in 1951.[64] Franca called upon that experience immediately. *Ballet Composite* entered the repertoire in the 1951–2 season, unchanged from the earlier, Winnipeg version of the work. In all, Adams mounted a total of seven ballets for the company before his departure in 1964 – enough to be noticed, but not enough to make a real mark as a choreographer. They ranged from divertissements like *Pas de Six* (to the music of the pas de trois from *Swan Lake*, but otherwise unrelated to it)[65] or *Pas de Deux Romantique* (a gift to his wife, Lois Smith, that capitalized on the remarkable freedom of movement which entered her dancing after her studies with Audrey de Vos in England),[66] to short narrative works like *Barbara Allen*, *Pas de Chance*, and *The Littlest One*. Following Tudor's lead, Adams felt compelled to explore the possibilities of narrative in contemporary ballet. Given the company's emphasis on classical story-ballet, this inclination towards narrative fit in well with the National's emerging character. With *The Littlest One*, Adams ventured into the realm of child psychology. 'The littlest one was the small child in the family, the youngest. She had problems communicating with the rest of the family, and the ballet was done part of it through her eyes and the rest through the eyes of her parents and her sisters and brothers.'[67] In *Barbara Allen* he reworked the sensational American folk narrative of Barbara Allen, object of a fundamentalist preacher's desire, whose love for a mysterious Witch Boy turns her mountain community into a lynch mob. In this ballet, Adams used an original Louis Applebaum score that had been commissioned by the company for *Dark of the Moon* seven years earlier. *Dark of the Moon*, first choreographed in 1953 by another Canadian, Joey Harris, on the same story material, had had to be retitled *Barbara Allen* by 1955, to avoid violation of copyright. An early publicity release describing the piece as 'a dance-drama based on the play by Richardson and Berney' evidently overstepped the bounds.[68] But Harris's version, under either title, was short-lived in the repertoire in any case. Adams thus gave extended life to a score and an idea that might otherwise have faded prematurely.

After a brief performance career with the National, Brian Macdonald went on to become one of Canada's best-known choreographers. Here, Macdonald and Oldyna Dynowska camp it up in a scene from David Adams' Ballet Behind Us*, a satirical look at nineteenth-century ballet conventions. Costumes for the 1952 production were by Suzanne Mess.*

Grant Strate approached the creation of original works as a fully collaborative enterprise. His 1958 Ballad *had a commissioned score by Harry Somers and designs by Mark Negin. Earl Kraul and Angela Leigh in a moment of tense confrontation.*

Even the Kay Ambrose sets for the original, which Adams had admired,[69] were reused, including a backdrop which Franca remembers as being 'quite revolutionary at the time,'[70] with slits in it to allow for entrances and exits.

Despite this exposure as a choreographer, Adams felt finally that he and Strate represented a modern trend within the company which was losing out to Franca's more traditional view of choreography. Adams later remarked: 'Supposing Grant and I had won and said, "Well, we're going to do contemporary works," it would change the whole direction of the company.'[71] His choreographic ambitions frustrated, he maintained his career as the company's premier danseur until his departure, in 1964,[72] to dance with the London Festival Ballet (for whom he also did some choreography) and the Royal Ballet and then to direct the Royal Ballet's Ballet for All.

Grant Strate's inventiveness challenges the traditions.

The other major contender for the role of Canadian choreographer was Grant Strate, whose enforced apprenticeship in the vocabulary and craft of classical dance delayed his choreographic début with the company until 1956, when the National presented his *Jeune Pas de Deux* (in August) and *The Fisherman and His Soul* (in November). After these initial efforts, Strate quickly declared his creative independence by declining, thereafter, to accept Kay Ambrose as his designer, a move that had symbolic as well as practical significance in that it asserted the choreographer's artistic control over the individual choreographic project.[73] He introduced Mark Negin into the company as a designer and, on the single, spectacular occasion of *The House of Atreus*, collaborated with Harold Town, attracted to him because of a scathing public denunciation Town had made of theatrical design at the Stratford Festival.[74] But with the exception of *The House of Atreus*, Strate, by his own admission, had little interest in stage spectacle. As the National, after the transfer to the O'Keefe Centre in 1964, moved more decisively into the spectacular ballets of the classical repertoire, he felt increasingly alienated from its primary goals.[75]

But the more significant mark of his independence could be found not in the area of design, but in the development of his own choreographic principles. More and more, Strate wanted to choreograph in a way that Franca did not admire. After eighteen years in the company, he was quoted as saying: 'Miss Franca and I have almost always been on opposite sides as far as ideas of choreography go. I suppose, though, that's one of the reasons we've worked so well together.'[76] This fundamental difference of opinion, inherent in Strate's early training and interests, declared itself fully after his exposure to contemporary developments in American ballet, most notably the work of George Balanchine. After visits to New York in the early 1960s had introduced him to the work of Paul Taylor, Merce Cunningham, and Anna Sokolow, as well as that of Balanchine himself, Strate dared to articulate an aesthetic in which dance was not subservient to music, in which movement, regardless of its source or provenance, was supreme. Balanchine set the standard. 'He could work with Bach, but he worked with him as an equal partner, if not a superior partner. It was never a kind of obeisance.'[77] Strate's predilection for contemporary scores (he three times commissioned Harry Somers to provide original scores for his work) may well reflect this desire to work with the composer as an equal creative partner. When he was preparing *The House of Atreus*, which had an electronic score by Somers that baffled Strate and the dancers, Strate sometimes set the choreography for a passage before receiving the instalment of music for it from the composer.[78] It is easy to see that such iconoclasm, especially in the area of the relationship between music and dance, would put him at odds with Franca, who must have been perplexed by the creative forces she had unleashed.

A significant portion of Strate's output for the National originated outside the confines of the main company. *Electre*, *Sequel*, and *Time Cycle*, while full company productions, were commissioned by the Stratford Festival, where they received their only performances. *The Arena* and *Cyclus* were created in Belgium in 1966–7, a year Strate spent on sabbatical from the company, teaching and choreographing for the Royal Flemish Ballet.[79] *Cyclus*, with an original score by a Flemish composer, Peter Welffens, had an elaborate design that had worked well on the opera house stage in Antwerp, but caused problems at the O'Keefe Centre and had to be modified beyond recognition on tour. Consequently, a central visual effect of the piece, when large cloth sails flew up, transforming into a cage what had appeared to be a peaceful arena, could never be fully realized. As Strate points out, the ballet made an overt, anti-war, political statement: 'It was not at a time when that kind of political statement was favourably looked on by the National Ballet. I don't know that it ever has been looked on favourably.'[80]

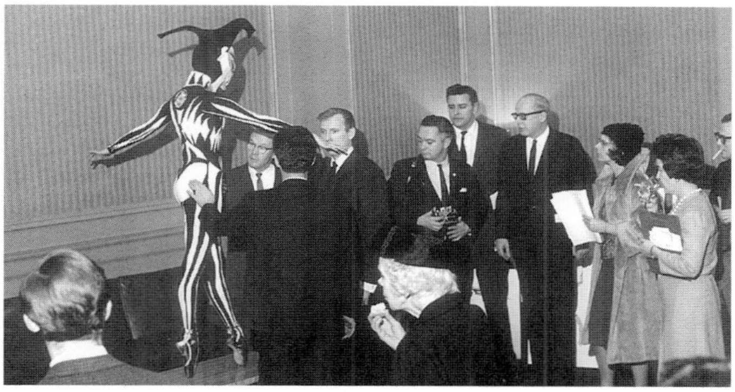

At a special press preview, a dancer, balanced precariously on a coffee table, models one of Harold Town's controversial costumes for The House of Atreus. *Town stands to her right (his face partially obscured by her hand), with ballet and theatre critic Herbert Whittaker (wearing glasses) three to the right of Town.*

The House of Atreus first saw the light of day in New York, at the Juilliard School of Music. Strate went to New York in 1962–3, on a Canada Council Senior Arts Fellowship, and while there was invited to teach at Juilliard by Antony Tudor. The invitation to choreograph a work for the school followed quickly.[81] The young choreographer was suddenly keeping heady company. He wrote home in great excitement: 'On same programme 2 ballets by Tudor – ballets by José Limón, Doris Humphrey, Anna Sokolow. Some competition.'[82] He chose to do a version of the Electra story, 'preliminary to my more epic work for the National Ballet of Canada,'[83] and set it to the String Quartet No. 2 by Alberto Ginastera. The larger-scale work, with the Somers score and Town designs, entered the National's repertoire the following season, to a mixed reception. Allen Hughes, of the *New York Times*, was one of the few critics to have seen the work in both its forms. When the company brought the full-scale *House of Atreus* to the Brooklyn Academy of Music in 1964, he opened his review of it with a reference to the Juilliard version.

> *At that time, the ballet seemed remarkably strong, and it made a telling dramatic impact despite interruptions in the narrative by the multi-movement form of the Ginastera string quartet to which it was set.*
>
> *But the* House of Atreus *shown by the Canadians is not the same thing. The drama, if it is still there, has been concealed completely by Harold Town's rash costumes, masks, headdresses, wigs and whatnot. There is a riot of presumably symbolic drawing on the costumes and much color, all of which adds up to nothing in regard to Electra, Orestes, Clytemnestra, Agamemnon and company.*
>
> *Harry Somers's new score for the ballet has few organic tensions of its own, but its*

> *sound effects might have supported* House of Atreus *in last year's genuinely dramatic version. As things stand now, they seem pointless, especially when they accompany the balletic clichés that have crept into what was terse, expressive dancing.*
>
> *In any case, what appeared once to be a forceful depiction of credible human beings caught in tragic conflicts seems to have been killed by chi-chi.* House of Atreus *deserved a better fate.*[84]

Strate's opinion of the ballet differs from Hughes' because of the position he now sees the work as occupying in his own development as a choreographer.

> *Looking back, I think that of the three elements – the choreography, the design, and the music – the choreography was the most lacking, because it was the beginning of the transition into movement discovery as opposed to movement assimilation.*[85]

Strate's growing interest in teaching and in the discovery of radically different forms of movement led finally to his departure from the company in 1970 to found Canada's first university department of dance at York University. The company's resident choreographer, always something of a maverick on his home turf, had to seek residence elsewhere.

Original Canadian works to round out the repertoire

Aside from Adams and Strate, Franca looked to a succession of isolated contracts to bring Canadian choreography into the company's early repertoire. Kay Armstrong, Joey Harris, Elizabeth Leese, company member Ray Moller, Brian Macdonald (after his departure as a dancer), and Don Gillies were all represented by single works. Franca herself, though she never developed in a concentrated fashion the career in choreography she had begun in England, discovered some of the pitfalls of choreographing in the Canadian cultural climate when she mounted *Le Pommier* for the company's second season. Responding to the need to represent French Canada in the company's offerings, Franca and Ambrose researched French-Canadian folk-songs and arts and crafts, commissioned a score, on George Crum's recommendation, from Hector Gratton, and put together what was intended as a light and amusing ballet on folk themes. It was well received outside Quebec, but met strong opposition in Montreal, where it was seen as the worst kind of tokenism as well as a slight to the true nature of Quebec culture.[86] Paul Roussel, reviewing for *Le Canada*, called into question the validity of its inspiration. He suggested that, suitably revised, it might make an amusing trifle, but could not lay claim to any Québécois cultural authenticity. 'Quelques variations animées, quelques bons solis et le reniement de son inspiration

folklorique, convertiraient *Le Pommier* en un joli divertissement.'[87]

Franca's attempt to include Québécois themes in her choreography misfired badly. Quebec audiences were offended by Le Pommier, *which quickly disappeared from the repertoire.*

Despite such well-intentioned miscalculations, there was enough Canadian content in those early years for Franca to defend herself against her nationalist critics, but clearly nothing that could be looked upon as the careful, concerted development of Canadian choreographic talent. In David Adams' estimation, there was too much 'chopping and changing.' 'We would try something for a short time. Ditch it. All kinds of people were tried, all kinds of people were brought in, and all kinds of things went on, but you don't establish a foundation this way.' But Franca was laying a different kind of foundation. Both Adams and Strate now think that she may have come hoping to create a contemporary company and then radically changed her direction.[88] It is true that Franca had arrived in Canada with a reputation as an emerging avant-garde choreographer. Indeed, her departure from Sadler's Wells had been occasioned, ironically, by a surfeit of *Sleeping Beauties*. 'I went to the first rehearsal to the Royal Opera House and looked at the notice board, and it said they were going to be dancing *Sleeping Beauty* for two months. I thought, "That's it." That's when I left.'[89] But in the new country her firebrand energies burned with a zeal to establish classical ballet, to create the very environment which she, as a dancer, had forsaken. She established those priorities early, in accordance with the terms set out for her at the time of her appointment. In the ongoing debate about the overall direction which the company should take, she never wavered from this determination to create a major classical ballet company for Canada; if that meant that the development of choreographers had to come at a later stage, as Franca herself believed, so be it.

The variety and stimulus of the early programming

For some, including even Franca herself, this first phase of the company's development, before the full-length classics came to dominate the repertoire and the public's expectations, provided its greatest artistic satisfaction. Franca thrived on challenge, the challenge of advancing her artists and their audience, step by step, from the world of the possible to the realm of the ideal. As she acknowledged the challenge, she acknowledged also its elusiveness. 'I didn't win,' she said in summing up her twenty-four-year struggle, and then immediately revised that judgment: 'I won in the first few years.'[90] Only in those first few years, perhaps, did the company remain small enough in size, ambitious enough in temperament, flexible enough in organization, varied enough in repertoire, for Franca's hands-on, authoritative leadership to produce the results she aimed for. As the company itself grew and its dancers gained the experience necessary to present the classics convincingly, it acquired also a complexity of structure and an independence of spirit that inevitably diluted the effect her own personality could have in determining the artistic character of the enterprise.

In its first ten years of operation, the company gained a level of critical and popular acceptance which it found impossible to maintain through its second decade and difficult to regain thereafter. Its early reputation rested on the integrity of purpose which Franca transmitted to every aspect of the organization. By 1961, despite a variable performance standard, the company was riding high. Nathan Cohen, the *Toronto Star*'s acerbic drama critic, had by then developed into a knowledgeable, if cantankerous and eccentric, commentator on the company. His frequent scathing attacks on the company rule out the possibility that the following favourable assessment sprang from an unreasoned bias in the company's favour.

> *It is a company which deserves to be taken with the utmost seriousness, and which is evolving its own character, its own spirit of interpretation, through its dancers, choreographers, composers, designers, and its program balance of full-length classics, important*

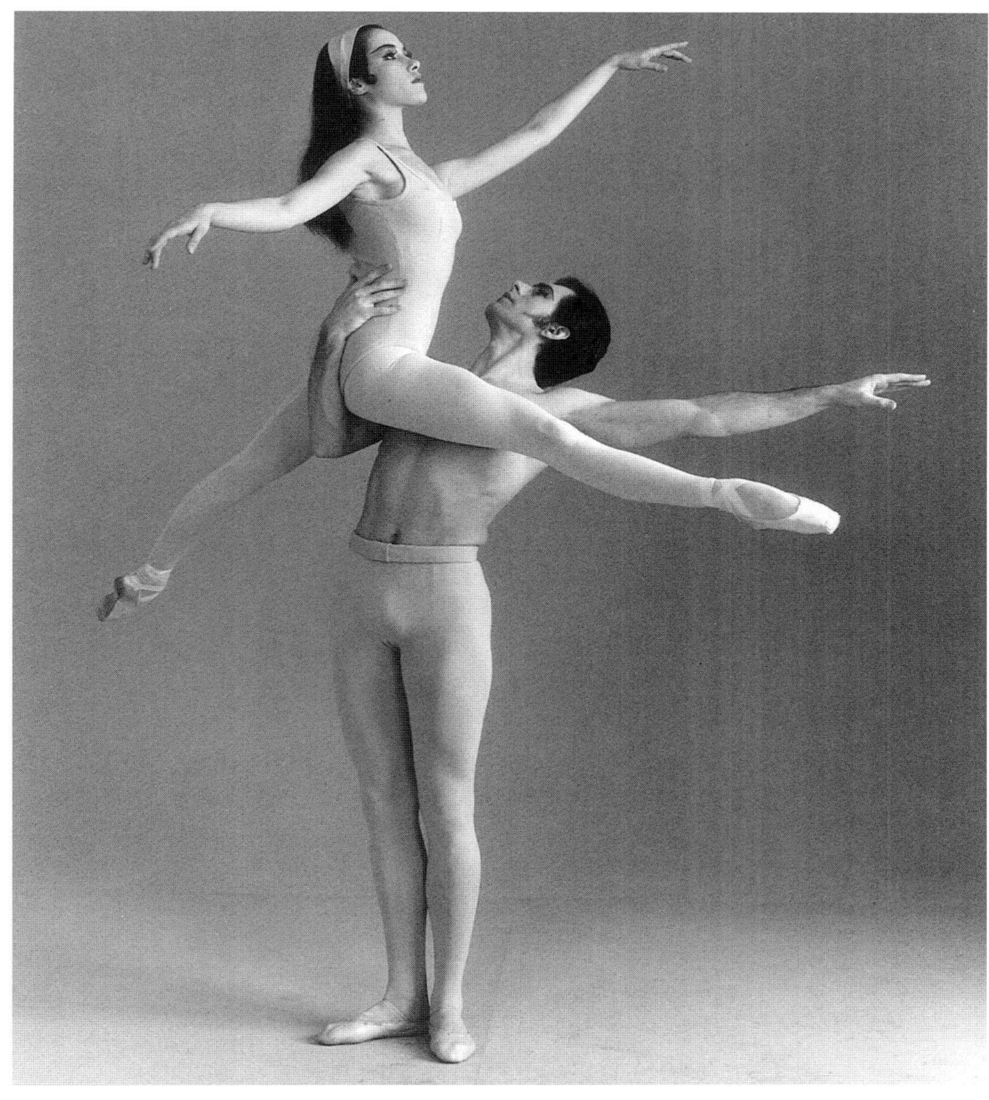

Karen Bowes and Alastair Munro in a serene moment from Grant Strate's Cyclus.

works in the modern repertoire, and original vehicles tailored to the talents and temperaments of the members of the company.

For all these reasons the quality of most of the ballet presentations is greater in sum than their faults, however glaring they may be. There is never an impurity in the essential feeling.[91]

Strong praise from anyone, and especially from Cohen. It speaks of a company building its character slowly and surely, a company whose artistic vision outstripped its technical accomplishments not in a way that exposed its weakness, but that encouraged it to progress to greater achievement.

Even slightly discounted to allow for nostalgic bias, the dancers' recollections testify similarly to the distinctive achievements of the early company. The major Tudor repertoire, though it was carried over into the O'Keefe Centre, had its greatest success at the Royal Alexandra Theatre. Lois Smith remembers:

> *The best time of* Dark Elegies *was in the Royal Alex. O'Keefe's too big. At the O'Keefe you're not close enough to it, you're not part of it. And we did have a very good cast. But all of those works were better at the Royal Alex.* Lilac Garden *was better there too.*[92]

The variety of the repertoire, and particularly the performance opportunities provided by the high proportion of shorter works, made the early company particularly attractive to dancers. Two ballerinas who became international stars after their association with the National pay tribute to the attractiveness of its early repertoire. Galina Samsova joined the company in 1961, just when the Tudor repertoire was giving way to a sprinkling of Balanchine. 'I did a lot of wonderful things, a lot of Balanchine ballets that were there, *Serenade* and *Barocco*, which I really enjoyed very much, Tudor ballets, *Lilac Garden*, *Offenbach in the Underworld*.'[93] Martine van Hamel echoes these sentiments, and draws particular attention to the advantages which a repertoire of short works holds for the dancer beginning her career, hungry for experience and public exposure.

> *The first year I was in the company was absolutely, totally exciting. I did so many things and so many roles that I think I was spoiled forever. When I joined, the repertoire was wonderful. It had a lot of short ballets by Tudor and by Balanchine. You got so much opportunity for versatility.*[94]

Those early years, in retrospect, seem like halcyon days of exploration and development for a group of like-minded individuals sharing a common goal and submitting themselves willingly to dedicated, single-minded leadership. But artistic fulfilment alone could not guarantee financial and political stability, nor could the National rest indefinitely in a niche so similar to the one the Royal Winnipeg already occupied. The National Ballet of the first ten years had not reached artistic equilibrium. The growing pains as it entered the next phase of its development were difficult and protracted.

CHAPTER FOUR

Not without Honour

The demands for a more diverse repertoire

Success could not be bought indefinitely on a shoestring and Franca's personal contacts, and by the company's tenth-anniversary season, the halcyon days were drawing to a close. Franca herself was privately aware of the problems the company faced. Furthermore, she was clear in her own mind as to the source of its difficulties: the constant scramble for funds diverted too much of her own attention from artistic concerns, where it properly belonged; the inevitable inadequacy of the funds procured made a shambles of long-range planning and forced debilitating cutbacks in current activities. The effect on company performances and morale was inevitable and swift. The draft version of her report to the Annual General Meeting of 1961 did not mince matters. 'The general feeling is that our 10th season was a

OPPOSITE: Lois Smith and Jeremy Blanton rehearse the Bedlam scene from The Rake's Progress, *one of the larger-scale ballets with which the company made the transition to the O'Keefe Centre. The inmates of Bedlam, standing behind Smith, are (from left to right) Lawrence Haider, Yves Cousineau, Brian Scott, and Glenn Gilmour.*

ABOVE: The acquisition of Balanchine repertoire began to lessen the company's reliance on the British choreographic tradition. From left to right, Martine van Hamel, Jeremy Blanton, and Veronica Tennant in Serenade.

Pointe shoes are manufactured in England, to individual specifications, and shipped to the company in large quantities. Dancers then modify each pair, pounding and pummelling to get just the right degree of flexibility. Footwear supervisor Carol Beevers, seen here preparing for one of the company's Hurok tours during the 1970s, helps dancers achieve the perfect fit.

ghastly one but nobody wants to admit it publicly. Those of us "in the know" are horribly aware that the future prospects do not look bright – short of miracles.'[1] She then went on, in more positive vein, to enumerate the things the company would be able to do if it had 'a bit to spare right now.' Her budgetary wish-list included adequate rehearsals; technical rehearsals in a theatre, with proper lighting in order to evaluate sets and costumes before putting them onstage; an orchestra rehearsal for each new work, and for each cast in it; a dancing-shoe factory; a physiotherapist on tour; a large enough orchestra to allow choreographers to use full symphonic scores; design budgets that could run to imported materials where necessary; adequate workshop space for scenery and paint frames; an enlarged wardrobe; funds to invite major choreographers to set pieces on the company. 'If the above list sounds greedy and luxurious,' she concluded, 'let me assure you that it barely includes the necessities with which our artists and technicians would be given a fair chance to execute their work competently.' Far from sounding greedy or luxurious, this list, by present-day standards, simply covers the bare minima for a genuinely professional level of performance. Only the shoe factory has not been realized, and even in this area, company staff and services have greatly improved the dancers' lot. Whereas in the company's earliest days Natalia Butko had to prevail on Ruth Carse's brothers, players with the Chicago Black Hawks, to smuggle ballet slippers into Canada for her and her friends in the company,[2] today Carol Beevers, the company's footwear supervisor, coordinates orders from British manufacturers and maintains an extensive stock of shoes fitted to individual dancers' specifications.

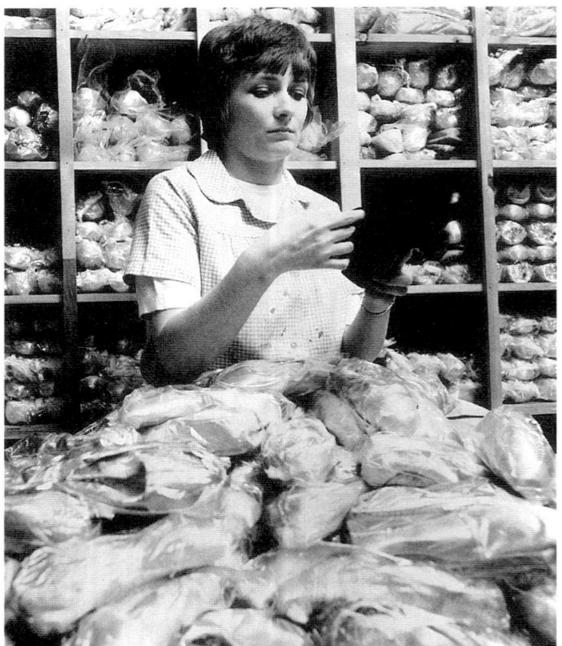

But in the early 1960s, no one would have predicted with confidence the facilities and relative security which the National enjoys today. As the novelty of the company's earliest achievements wore off, stringent criticism of its shortcomings became the dominant public tone, replacing the tolerant optimism of the first decade. The Canada Council, finally created in 1957, six years after the Massey Commission had recommended it, could not supply money to the company fast enough to meet its growing demands, and refused on principle to advance funds to cover its mounting cumulative deficit.[3] Nor could it find a rational basis for allocating funds among the country's three competing, and highly competitive, dance companies.

For by this time another contender for the country's dance loyalties had arrived on the scene – Les Grands Ballets Canadiens. Founded in 1953 by Ludmilla Chiriaeff to provide material for CBC television in Montreal, the group quickly developed a reputation for innovative choreography in the new medium and attracted the interest of no less a figure than George Balanchine. Chiriaeff's pioneering work soon became a significant part of Québécois cultural self-expression. In 1955, Les Ballets Chiriaeff began performing in Montreal theatres, and in 1957 her troupe, rechristened Les Grands Ballets Canadiens, made its début at the Montreal Festival.[4] By the early 1960s, Les Grands Ballets Canadiens had become a strong regional company, competing with the Royal Winnipeg and the National not only for the attentions of the Canada Council, but for the financial support of public and patrons as well. The two smaller companies could claim a clearly defined regional base and regional identity; the National, aspiring to national significance, got backed into the corner of the Toronto establishment. But the Toronto establishment, while generous to a degree, could not support the national enterprise single-handedly.

The National's early fundraising campaigns consistently fell short of their stated goals. This lack of success was enough to prompt the Canada Council, in 1959, to ask E.P. Taylor, one of Canada's richest and most successful businessmen, to provide discreet advice to the company on its fundraising strategies.[5] Every shortfall in fundraising cut with a double edge, forcing reductions in the current production budgets while driving the accumulated deficit still higher.

An inexorable downward spiral had begun. The close scrutiny of the Council placed a greater emphasis than ever before on the company's deficit; efforts to reduce it led to economies in the operating budget that adversely affected the artistic product, just when the public was becoming increasingly demanding; fundraising from the public sector became the only way of closing the gap, yet every shortfall in fundraising widened that gap, reduced the company's credibility, and damaged further the artistic product, thus making the public even less inclined to contribute to its cause; and with every increase in the deficit, the Council increased its scrutiny of the company's operations. There seemed no way out of the dilemma, and Franca, who wanted to concern herself with artistic policy, found herself constrained more and more to concentrate on financial crises.

The effects of the squeeze could most readily be seen in the acquisition of repertoire. The 1961–2 season introduced only two new works. The 1962–3 season looked a little better on paper, with six new works on the official list, but of those, two were Grant Strate's commissions for the Stratford Festival, which were never performed in the company's regular seasons, and two were simply divertissements, the *Corsaire* pas de deux and the pas de six from *Laurencia*. The latter work enjoyed only the briefest of lives in the repertoire; it played eleven times, and never in Toronto.

There could not have been a worse time in the company's development for the stream of new repertoire to dry up. Franca's productions of the full-length classics, all with Ambrose designs, had begun to look shop-worn and to come under heavy critical fire; meanwhile, the repertoire of short works by Tudor, Fokine, and the British had lost much of its original savour; after the 1960–1 season, David Adams choreographed no more; and Grant Strate's work, finally coming onstream during this period, turned out to be too experimental for good box-office. To sell Strate's ballets to a conservative public, the National needed the drawing power of short works with popular appeal by proven choreographers. Franca had played virtually all the cards she held in her own hand during the formative years; she could do little more through her old formula of low-cost personal contacts to replenish the repertoire. Just when the company had to move more aggressively onto the international scene, the deficit decreed a fallow period of consolidation and retrenchment. But by the mercurial measures of box-office and public response, consolidation looked ominously like backsliding; to try to stand still was really to fall behind.

Even in these trying times, Franca's resourcefulness and luck did not forsake her. In the spring of 1961, she asked Strate, then in New York, to call on George Balanchine. Although, according to Strate, she never liked Balanchine's work, she could not neglect the opportunity to acquire an example of it. And the opportunity, briefly, incredibly, was there.

> *Celia had said to me, 'Try to get an appointment with Balanchine and see if he'll let us have a work.' So I set up an appointment. He said, 'Sure, what would you like?' Just at that time, there was an open window. Balanchine was very anxious to give his works for a very short period, including those things he was most fond of. Shortly after that, it all changed.*[6]

Balanchine suggested one of two relatively early works, *Serenade* or *Concerto Barocco*, for the National. Franca, who had seen neither, weighed the merits of each as described to her by Una Kai, the associate ballet mistress of the New York City Ballet, who would mount the work on the company, and chose *Concerto Barocco*. Aside from Miss Kai's very modest fee and expenses, no other financial charges would be involved.[7] The National had acquired its first work by Balanchine, virtually as a gift.

Concerto Barocco is Balanchine's choreographic realization of the contrapuntal intricacies of Bach's Double Violin Concerto in D Minor. A demanding work requiring precision in the execution of steps, a command of syncopated rhythms, and, in its middle movement, a smooth, seamless, legato delivery of line, it challenged the female corps of the company and provided exciting opportunities for soloists like Jocelyn Terelle, Martine van Hamel, and Galina Samsova. It also

Karen Bowes in Concerto Barocco.

brought back to Canada, as one of the company's first guest artists in 1963, Melissa Hayden, by then a star of the New York City Ballet. Franca later complained of Hayden's lack of discipline, which manifested itself not only in last-minute alterations to the Balanchine choreography, but also in her chewing caramels throughout rehearsals. Franca, who strictly forbade gum-chewing among her own dancers, had to hold her tongue out of deference to the visiting celebrity.[8] *Concerto Barocco*, like Balanchine's *Serenade*, has enjoyed a double life in the company's repertoire. After numerous performances in the 1960s, both works dropped out of sight, and then in the 1980s they returned to become staples of the repertoire and essential elements in the company's homage to Balanchine.

Serenade arrived in the 1962–3 season, with the help of direct intervention by Balanchine's staff with the Canada Council. When the National returned to Balanchine to negotiate for *Serenade*, they found Strate's 'open window' closed. Balanchine had come to realize that he could no longer afford the altruistic practice of giving ballets away. In acute embarrassment at having to discuss finances at all, he requested the modest initial fee of one thousand dollars, for which he threw in forty royalty-free performances of the work. (The company's standard contracts with choreographers generally stipulate a fee for acquisition and separate royalties for every performance, usually with a specified date at which performance rights lapse and must be renegotiated.) To help matters along further, Balanchine's general manager, Betty Cage, interceded with the Canada Council on behalf of the cash-strapped National Ballet. She wrote to Carman Guild, her counterpart at the National: 'Mr. Peter Dwyer of the Canada Council telephoned me today and I explained the situation to him. He thought it possible that the Council could help if you apply.'[9] The company did so, and in January 1963 the Canada Council, despite a drastic reduction in its overall operating grant to the National, approved an extraordinary grant of one thousand dollars to cover the costs of acquiring *Serenade*.[10]

For the supplier of the new work thus to have direct conversations with the funding agency was somewhat unusual. For the arm's-length funding agency, which supported Canadian arts organizations without intervening directly in their daily operation, such involvement in the acquisition of a specific work was genuinely remarkable. It had directed its financial support with the clear intention of influencing a specific choice of repertoire and so had crossed over into the area of artistic judgment theoretically reserved for the company, and for its artistic director, alone.

In this instance, given the end result, no one complained. *Serenade*, less challenging technically than *Concerto Barocco*, nevertheless displayed the corps as few other works have done. The impersonality central to Balanchine's conception was warmed, ever so slightly, by the loving, vulnerable characterization which the National's dancers imparted to it. They responded as much to the lush, romantic strains of the Tchaikovsky score (his Serenade in C for string orchestra) as to the abstract demands of Balanchine's choreography. Homespun Balanchine, perhaps, rather than the cool sophistication of a big city approach, but a Balanchine the dancers and their audiences welcomed. Of the many fine performances the work has received, none was more moving than Veronica Tennant's last, as, borne aloft by the men and bathed in offstage light, she was carried slowly into the wings at the ballet's conclusion. In its understated simplicity, it was a farewell to her art as touching as the final Juliets that rounded out her career.

Galina Samsova, in an excerpt from her staging of the Laurencia *pas de six, demonstrates the powerful technique that galvanized the company on her arrival.*

The excursion into Balanchine in the early 1960s was an invigorating departure for the company, a real change from the essentially conservative, predominantly British character which Franca's personal vision had imparted to it. At about the same time, Russian energy and temperament invaded the artistic ranks in the person of Galina Samsova. In the same year in which Rudolf Nureyev's sensational defection started the process of change which redefined ballet in the western world and cast it in a Russian mould, Samsova, a soloist with the Kiev Ballet, entered Canada quietly, and legally, as the wife of a Canadian citizen, Alexander Ursuliak, whom she had met and married in Ukraine. At a time when artistic contact with

Russia was virtually impossible, her arrival generated excitement and artistic ferment within the company. Samsova was an electrifying performer, in full command of the Russian strength and athleticism which Canadian dancers and audiences had only heard about. Moreover, Samsova, who later in her career founded and ran her own company in England, had direct contact with a Russian performance tradition and repertoire which she could transmit in the West. After an initial fallow period in Canada, during which she sold books in a Ukrainian bookshop and took class with Boris Volkoff,[11] Samsova joined the company in 1961, technically at the rank of corps but in fact taking on principal roles from the outset.

Franca drew almost immediately on Samsova's past experience for stagings of two rarities of the Russian repertoire, the pas de six from Chabukiani's *Laurencia* and the pas de deux from Leonid Lavrovsky's *Walpurgis Night.* These two offerings had a limited life-span in the repertoire, but a third, the pas de deux from *Le Corsaire*, established itself firmly with the National just before the work took centre stage internationally as one of Nureyev's bravura show-stoppers. Samsova's version, attributed to Robert Klavin, differed from Nureyev's (based on the Petipa choreography), but it had its première, on tour in Sherman, Texas, two weeks before Nureyev and Fonteyn introduced it at the Royal Ballet.[12]

For the 1963–4 season, Svetlana Beriosova, another one of Franca's contacts from her Metropolitan Ballet days, staged the pas de deux from Petipa's *Don Quixote*, which had been absent from the National's repertoire since its first two seasons, when it served as a vehicle for Jury Gotshalks and Irene Apiné. With the advent of Balanchine, Samsova, and these bravura pieces from the Russian repertoire, the character of the company in the early 1960s began to take on a distinctly Russian flavour.

In December 1962, the Bolshoi Ballet performed in Toronto for the second time in its history. The appearance of any company as prestigious as the Bolshoi was a major artistic event; the appearance of a Soviet company at this period in East-West relations added a political dimension to the visit that escalated the level of excitement immeasurably. The sense of occasion which accompanied the Bolshoi's tour is difficult to re-create today, when artistic exchanges between East and West are relatively commonplace. In 1962, the Bolshoi was exotic, mysterious, and glamorous. It brought with it coaches and teachers of note, like Leonid Lavrovsky and Asaf Messerer, but above all it brought its prima ballerina assoluta, Galina Ulanova, whose international reputation and influence approached the legendary Pavlova's even though her career had been confined for the most part to Russia.

During the Toronto engagement, Lavrovsky, the director of the company, accepted an invitation to teach at the National Ballet School. The senior women's class at that time included Vanessa Harwood, Veronica Tennant, and Martine van Hamel, all on the verge of major professional careers. Betty Oliphant recalls Lavrovsky's arrival:

> *Lavrovsky took one look at the class and said, 'You know, I'm a company director, and I can't teach for nuts. And it never matters because when I give these classes the dancers aren't any good. But now it really matters. Do you mind if I ask Madam Ulanova to come and teach?'*

Ulanova taught at the school the next day. She and Asaf Messerer taught class at the company as well, and the entire Bolshoi company came to watch the National in rehearsal.[13] International recognition for Betty Oliphant as a dance educator and for the National Ballet School as a professional training ground stems from this contact with the Russians. But the Russian connection was crucial for the company as well, in its influence on repertoire and its opening up of the dancers to a new range of influences.

As a result of this contact with Moscow, Eugen Valukin, a young teacher with the Bolshoi, began a series of extended visits to Canada, teaching at the school and mounting several short works for the company. His association with them culminated in his staging of *Bayaderka* Act IV in the 1966–7 season. The company was moving well beyond the familiar territory which Franca had initially staked out for it.

Romeo and Juliet rejuvenates the company.

Franca was skilful at exploiting any and all opportunities that came her way during this period, but such expediency resulted in stop-gap programming at best. Longer-range planning took her company to a much more ambitious level of operation and required proportionally more risk. As so often in the company's history, it required its share of luck, too. In 1960, the O'Keefe Centre had opened in Toronto to immense fanfare and publicity. With twice the seating capacity of the Royal Alexandra Theatre (3,200 seats as opposed to 1,497)[14] and with a much larger and better equipped stage, the O'Keefe could accommodate stage spectacle like the Broadway-bound musical *Camelot*, which inaugurated the new theatre. It could also give spectacular ballet productions the facilities they demanded, but the company decided initially not to move there because the larger capacity of the auditorium would have meant fewer performances and therefore a shorter working year for dancers.[15] It pinned its hopes instead on negotiations with Ed Mirvish, the owner of the Royal Alex, to remodel its stage and dressing-room facilities. In 1963, when these negotiations fell through because of the company's inability to commit to an extended contract with the theatre, the board decided to present the National at the O'Keefe, beginning in April 1964.[16]

The new theatre meant a new kind of dancing and a new standard of production values. The larger stage and auditorium challenged the dancers to extend their powers of dramatic projection and increase their physical stamina. The O'Keefe's improved lighting and cavernous dimensions exposed every limitation of the company's stock of sets and backdrops. The recently acquired Balanchine repertoire alone could not meet the challenge. A large, dramatic gesture was called for.

Franca believed she had one ready. She had prevailed upon Dame Ninette de Valois to mount her production of *The Rake's Progress* for the National. Moreover, she intended to invite Lynn Seymour, the native of Wainwright, Alberta, who had left Canada as a teenager and become a renowned artist and international celebrity with the Royal Ballet, to open the show in Montreal and Toronto.[17] A highly dramatic work, *The Rake's Progress*, to music by Gavin Gordon, had established itself as a classic of the British repertoire since its first performance in 1935. Its sets and costumes by Rex Whistler (eventually adapted for the Canadian production by Lawrence Schafer) were closely modelled on Hogarth's famous series and would show well in the new theatre. The dramatic challenge it represented would help the dancers find their way to the broader style required by the theatre's size and

The full company rehearses The Rake's Progress *in the St Lawrence Hall. Veronica Tennant watches from the barre, while Lois Smith chats with Howard Marcus in the foreground, with Charles Kirby (back to camera) to her left. Stage manager Anthony Clarke, in shirt and tie, leans against the barre at the rear. Mary McDonald, the company pianist of many years, is partially visible at the piano.*

sightlines. The prestige of de Valois' and Seymour's names would divert public attention from the fact that this newest addition to the repertoire was nearly thirty years old. An eminently sensible choice, entirely consistent with Franca's goals for the company and her previous track record, it breathed a pleasing historical appropriateness as well. The move to the new theatre would be sealed by the presence of her early mentor, the woman who had recommended Franca for her job.

But the choice had political pitfalls. Mounting *The Rake's Progress* at this stage in the National's development was bound to raise the spectre of Royal Ballet influence once again. Criticisms that Franca was too bound by British models, that she was not abreast of current developments in choreography, might gain even more strength. Whatever virtues *The Rake's Progress* possessed, no one would claim that it was up to the minute. In fairness, the National's Balanchine repertoire was hardly any more recent. But Balanchine in 1964 represented the dominant contemporary force in North American ballet; de Valois had effectively ceased choreographing in 1950.[18]

Then, in the summer of 1963, with the opening at the new theatre less than a year away, de Valois notified Franca that illness prevented her from mounting the ballet for the National and that it was impossible for her to send a répétiteur to teach it in her place.[19] The company was desperate, and it was also broke. With the stakes high and pressure mounting, Franca gambled and won. The terrifying void created by the withdrawal of *The Rake's Progress* was filled, on amazingly short notice, by a brand-new ballet from an old, old friend. John Cranko's *Romeo and Juliet* found its second home at the National Ballet of Canada.

The credit for acting fast enough to accomplish this coup must be shared. Franca pays tribute to the decisive risk-taking of Carman Guild, the company's general manager, who authorized her to proceed with the project on the basis of a purely speculative budget at a time of dire financial necessity.[20] Franca herself made an impressive leap of faith, backing the work on the strength of others' recommendations rather than personal knowledge, and with scanty information as to its technical requirements. But the lion's share of the credit goes to Grant Strate, who saw the ballet soon after its première in Stuttgart, recognized its significance and its suitability to the National, alerted Franca to the possibility of staging it, and extracted from Cranko the permission to mount it in Canada.

Romeo and Juliet was the first of Cranko's full-length story-ballets, followed shortly by *Onegin* and *The Taming of the Shrew*. These three works gave the genre of story-ballet new life in the twentieth century and brought the Stuttgart Ballet to international attention. The Stuttgart opening of *Romeo and Juliet* in 1962, however, was still an isolated phenomenon, not a major event on the international ballet scene. Strate was present at just the right time to recognize the impending sensation and cash in on it for the National. Despite strong resistance from the Stuttgart management, Strate prevailed on the ties of friendship that had been established when he worked with Cranko learning *Pineapple Poll.* According to Strate, Cranko 'was anxious at that time to do some work somewhere else. It took some talking, but he agreed to do it.'[21] The National became the first, and for many years the only, North American company to carry a full-length Cranko ballet in its repertoire. It was the first company anywhere in the world to acquire *Romeo and Juliet* and the only company, outside Stuttgart, to have the ballet produced by Cranko personally.

It could not have come into the National's repertoire more opportunely. With the brilliance of its costume and set design, the romantic grandeur of the Prokofiev score, already familiar to audiences worldwide as a standard part of the symphonic repertoire, and the vitality and energy of its choreography, it ushered the company not only into a new theatre, but into a new phase in its development. Peter Dwyer, the assistant director of the Canada Council, sensed the significance of the acquisition. Even before opening night, he wrote privately to Guy Glover, whose opinions on ballet were frequently consulted by the Council:

> *It seems to us that a wind of change is blowing through the National Ballet. Grant Strate's recent period of study in New York and Europe on a Canada Council scholarship appears to have had a profound effect on him, and I gather that it was largely at his urging that the National Ballet decided to put on the Cranko ballet which was done originally last year at Stuttgart.*[22]

In *Romeo and Juliet*, Franca and the National got exactly what they needed: a spectacular ballet to meet the opportunities and challenges of the O'Keefe and the other large, new theatres springing up across the country, a popular success, and a significant work with which to win some leverage with the Canada Council. The enormous gamble paid off. The company, by no means out of the woods, had nevertheless turned a decisive corner. The future lay with works of *Romeo and Juliet*'s scope, not with a steady diet of *Lilac Gardens*. *Romeo and Juliet* became one of the company's major box-office attractions and remains in the repertoire to the present day, where it has been joined by the other major Cranko works, *Onegin* and *The Taming of the Shrew*.

On 14 April 1964, the National opened *Romeo and Juliet* in Montreal, playing for the first time in that city's newly constructed Place des Arts. On 21 April it brought the production to the O'Keefe. Thus, in the space of one week, the company made its entrance on two of the country's major new, modern stages. The production itself provided opening night audiences with a dramatic metaphor for this bold, new step. The guests at the Capulet ball, including Romeo and his interloping friends, arrived in shadowy semi-darkness, swathed in voluminous cloaks of pink silk; then, instantaneously, the stage leapt into full, brilliant light and the cloaks were discarded to reveal the dazzling black and gold display of the ballroom scene. The opulence and extroverted swagger of the gesture proclaimed both the new theatres and the company's intent to occupy them with style. Cranko's realization of the drama provided the company with a canvas large enough to support the exotic colour and lavishness of the Jürgen Rose designs. (Kay Ambrose, already on prolonged sabbatical from the company, was not present to experience any unflattering comparisons.) Supported musically by a full-scale orchestra, here was a work that called forth from its dancers precisely the kind of projection needed to communicate to the nether reaches of a large auditorium. And it did so with an abundance of mime and dancing roles for the entire company, from the vivid action in the crowd scenes to the virtuosity of Mercutio and Benvolio and the high drama of Lady Capulet and Tybalt. Franca herself, returning to the stage in the role of Lady Capulet, left an indelible impression on all who saw her with performances that sealed her reputation as one of the great dramatic dancers of the century. Above all, *Romeo and Juliet* was genuinely new. The significance of Cranko's Stuttgart success was just beginning to be felt around the world, and the National had become a part of it. If the glory was borrowed, it was at least newly minted.

Yves Cousineau (as Tybalt) leads Joan Killoran in to the Capulets' ball with a swagger and a flourish of black velvet and cloth of gold. After thirty years of service, the opulent Jürgen Rose costumes were retired in 1995, when Susan Benson designed the new production.

Yet because of the circumstances surrounding its acquisition, the full extent of *Romeo and Juliet*'s significance to the National Ballet is a family affair, little known to observers outside Canada. The first of the company's 'hot' international properties, it was the last to be acquired informally, by verbal arrangement with its creator. As a result of the dispute which subsequently arose regarding the extent of the company's performance rights to it, this ballet, so closely identified with the company, could not be played on tour when the company first set about establishing an international profile. After more than a hundred and fifty complete performances in the National's repertoire,

Romeo and Juliet has never played in New York, London, Paris, or Stuttgart.

This curious state of affairs hinged on a legal ambiguity. Was *Romeo and Juliet* Cranko's to give to another company, or did it belong, as a property, to the Stuttgart Ballet, of which Cranko was technically an employee? In their initial negotiations, Franca and Strate begged this question by going directly to the choreographer, an old friend, and dealing with him, as had been their practice with most of the acquisitions of repertoire in the first fifteen years of the company's existence. But the Stuttgart administration, then headed by Dieter Gräfe, recognized the potential value of the Cranko repertoire. With canny foresight, it saw that the Stuttgart Ballet's international reputation would rest on its exclusive performances of the Cranko full-length ballets, and that its impact on the world stage would be lessened if these works found their way into the repertoires of other companies. Cranko may not have guessed the extent of Stuttgart's international possibilities when he seized the opportunity for immediate international exposure which Strate's request to stage the work for the National represented. As Strate recalls the negotiations, Cranko's agreement did not delight the Stuttgart administration, but they could not prevent the production from being mounted. 'I think Dieter will never forgive me for getting it, because they thought of it as their property. There was a condition on it that we were not to perform it in any major centre outside of Toronto. They were quite angry with me in Stuttgart.'[23] The informal nature of the arrangements, and the speed required to mount the ballet once it had been decided to go ahead, meant that the company's formal agreement with Cranko took the form of a letter from the company to Cranko (not the Stuttgart administration), dated 21 April 1964, *after* the Montreal opening of *Romeo and Juliet*. The letter covered Cranko's fees and royalties, but left the question of performance rights vague. The copy of this document in the National Ballet Archives bears Cranko's signature and that of Carman Guild, for the company. A handwritten addendum to this letter, initialled by Guild but not by Cranko, gives the National the right to perform *Romeo and Juliet* anywhere *except* in 'the New York area and Europe, including the United Kingdom.'[24] The addendum was evidently an attempt to placate Stuttgart's concerns about international exclusivity, while still allowing the National to get some international mileage out of its highly successful acquisition. In the long run, it did more to obscure than to clarify the situation.

In 1965, the National Ballet performed *Romeo and Juliet* during its summer engagement at the outdoor Carter Barron Amphitheatre in Washington, D.C. The company regarded these performances as allowable within the terms of its agreement with Cranko and did not seek his explicit approval.[25] In June 1967, Grant Strate, who was on leave from the company and working in Belgium at the time, arranged to meet Cranko to try to reach a clear, satisfactory agreement about performance rights.

> *I had called ahead and made an appointment to see John in Kiel, about eight hundred kilometres up the coast. I got there to find that John was in Morocco, and Dieter met me and said, 'Oh, so sorry.' I was angry. They had sent John to Morocco so that he wouldn't give me the rights to do it. It was a very bizarre story.*[26]

In August 1967, on the authority of the original agreement, the National again performed *Romeo and Juliet* at the Carter Barron.

The Stuttgart Ballet enjoyed a tumultuous success when it toured North America with its full repertoire of Cranko ballets in 1969. In New York, Strate saw Cranko, for the last time in his life, as it turned out, flushed with his company's triumph. In the euphoria of the moment, Cranko gave Strate his permission for the National to perform *Romeo and Juliet* anywhere it wanted to,[27] but that permission, being verbal, only confused matters further. In 1970, the National Ballet appeared at Expo in Osaka, Japan, in the first high-profile international engagement in its history. On the strength of Strate's report of Cranko's permission, Franca programmed *Romeo and Juliet*. This action finally brought the accumulated grievances of the Stuttgart administration to a head, and Gräfe wrote to forbid the Osaka performances on the ground that Cranko had never given anyone permission to perform *Romeo and Juliet* outside Canada.[28] With the success of the engagement and the future of the company in the balance, Franca cabled frantically to Cranko himself.

> *Have read devastating correspondence regarding Romeo in Japan Stop Tried to reach you by phone Stop Hopeless to try to unravel situation without meeting you but time running out Stop Osaka engagement very important for dancers' morale as it is first opportunity to represent Canada abroad Stop Cannot take different production now as it takes 3 months for shipping effects Stop Cancellation of engagement impossible as could mean end of National Ballet resulting from heavy financial loss and loss of future government subsidies to say nothing of dancers' spirits Stop I implore you as friend and colleague to bestow your blessing.*[29]

Cranko relented, but only partially.

> *Contract invalidated by performance in Washington Stop Under circumstances agree to Osaka performances but not television Stop Condition that ballet dropped from repertoire after Japan Stop Require written confirmation from you.*[30]

The Osaka performances went on as scheduled, and the ballet, except for the hiatus caused by the destruction of its costumes in the fire of 1973, was not dropped from the repertoire. After Cranko's death, once the ballet had lost some of its novelty as an international sensation and money-maker, the two administrations were finally able to come to terms on the question of performance rights. By then, however, *Romeo and Juliet* had established itself firmly as a domestic feature of the National's character. The company's international reputation rested on other repertoire.

Fortunately, such administrative bickering did nothing to diminish the good spirits of the production itself, which bubbled out in the vibrant crowd scenes, filled with individual touches of characterization that gave the company members new-found scope. One of the reasons for its success undoubtedly lay in the happy atmosphere in which Cranko, Jürgen Rose, the designer, and the members of the National worked. A letter which Rose wrote to Franca, in German, the year following their initial collaboration, testifies to the extraordinary sense of camaraderie he experienced in Toronto.

> *Has much changed in your company? – Somehow I'm attached to all the kids. They're a good bunch. You get aggravation everywhere, once in a while, but in your group you get over it quickly, because everyone is so enthusiastic about the work. They all give it their best, and that's a really great feeling!*[31]

Earl Kraul and Celia Franca watch as John Cranko demonstrates a lift with Galina Samsova during rehearsals for Romeo and Juliet.

Earl Kraul learned Romeo from Cranko himself, with Galina Samsova as his Juliet. He remembers the spirit of cooperation that prevailed throughout the rehearsal period. Cranko even modified a few details of the production to suit the characteristics of the National's dancers.

> *Basically the steps are all the same, but some of the sword fights, some of the things in the ballroom scene are a little different. I think it had a lot to do with how he was working with Galina and me at that time, how we reacted towards each other, and how I reacted to Tybalt. After Mercutio had been killed, he said, 'Your best friend is dead. What do you feel like doing?' And it was the reaction between Mercutio, Lawrence Adams at that time, how we reacted to each other.*[32]

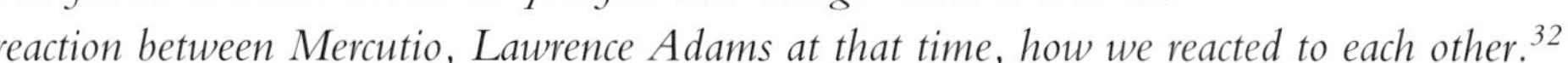

But Cranko could make mistakes, too. At one of the last rehearsals, Samsova, attempting to execute a difficult sequence exactly according to Cranko's instructions, sprained her foot.

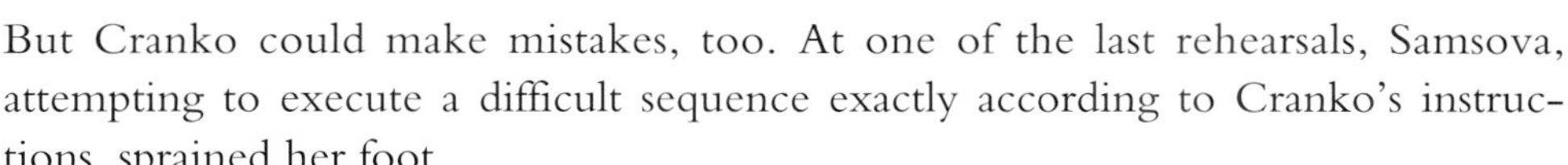

> *And I always said to John it was in a way his fault, because he told me to pirouette in arabesque and the boy catches me at the back. I said, 'That's impossible. It's so difficult.' And he said, 'Well, Marcia does it.' And when Marcia Haydée came, she didn't do it,*

she did plain pirouette, finish in arabesque. So I always told him that, and he said, 'Well it seemed to me that it looked right.'[33]

From its very first performances, audiences loved Cranko's Romeo and Juliet. *Among their favourite pairs of star-crossed lovers were Earl Kraul and Veronica Tennant, seen in the 1965 taping for television (left), and Karen Kain and Frank Augustyn (right).*

With Cranko's personal attention to detail, and with the accumulation of performances over the years, *Romeo and Juliet* has come to 'look right' on the dancers of the National too.

The production of *Romeo and Juliet* represented a watershed for the National's dancers individually as well as for the company as a whole. The expansion which it brought in its wake spelled the end of the close family-feeling that had characterized the company during its earliest years. It also accelerated the inevitable process of turnover among artistic personnel. With the 1961–2 season, David Adams had begun an arrangement whereby he remained with the National as his home company, but guested for as much as six months of the year with London's Festival Ballet (now the English National Ballet). He attributes his decision to leave the National completely to the loss of individuality in the bigger, more highly struc-

tured company called into existence by *Romeo and Juliet*.[34] His departure was influenced as well by the Festival Ballet management's unwillingness to adjust his schedule with them for the spring of 1964, in order to allow him to appear as Romeo with the National.[35] When forced to make a choice, Adams decided to sever his thirteen-year association with the company in favour of a return to England, where he had spent some time early in his career. Guest stars Ray Barra and Marcia Haydée, the Romeo and Juliet of the original Stuttgart production, opened the ballet as planned; but Earl Kraul, not David Adams, became the National's first Romeo and thereby solidified his position as dependable company lead, often eclipsed by the imported superstars but always there to support and partner the dancers who needed him.

This ballet about youthful love was a cruel reminder of the passage of the years and the tyranny of youth in the professional life of the dancer. *Romeo and Juliet* was the first major addition to the repertoire in which Lois Smith, the company's designated prima ballerina, did not dance the leading role. Even though she requested it (the only time she ever asked for a specific role with the company), she was never given the part of Juliet, which went initially to Samsova. Watching from the sidelines during Cranko's rehearsals with the younger ballerina, Smith absorbed the role she would never dance. 'I learned it all, and I did it on the side for my own benefit.'[36] Despite the significant achievements which still lay ahead of her in *La Sylphide*, *The Rake's Progress*, and Erik Bruhn's *Swan Lake*, not dancing Juliet was the signal to her and to the company's first generation of dancers that their time was drawing to a close.

The public did not have long to wait for the new generation to declare itself. Martine van Hamel, who went on to become one of the great stars of American Ballet Theatre, danced one of the gypsies on opening night. And Lois Smith was not the only dancer learning Juliet on the side. Incapacitated by a back injury, the young Veronica Tennant, who would enter the company from the National Ballet School at the rank of principal, watched every rehearsal John Cranko conducted with Galina Samsova.[37] Tennant later interpreted this privilege as a sign that she had been chosen from the beginning for the role of Juliet; Franca acknowledges that she must have had her eye on Tennant even then.[38] Franca was never one to choose repertoire simply as a vehicle for a single dancer; *Romeo and Juliet* was not, in that sense, Tennant's ballet. But as she had done with Lois Smith in *Swan Lake* almost fifteen years earlier, Franca recognized Tennant's unique characteristics and potential for a given role. On 7 January 1965,[39] just one week shy of her nineteenth birthday, Tennant made her début as Juliet, and made the role her own for twenty-four years, until her retirement in 1989. Her blend of classical training and dramatic intensity set a standard that influenced the company's image decisively. Other dancers have also had personal triumphs in this ballet. Franca's Lady Capulet, Tomas Schramek's Mercutio, and Yves Cousineau's Tybalt live on in the memories of those who saw them as ideal examples of the powerful expression of drama through dance. *Romeo and Juliet*, the last-minute substitution, moved the company out of its early stages and onto the path on which its future lay.

Galina Samsova, Martine van Hamel, and the international world of dance

The company could not afford to pause long, even at such a milestone. With the public's appetite whetted by the success of *Romeo and Juliet*, Franca made it her top priority over the next five years to acquire big productions adequate to the new surroundings of the O'Keefe Centre and the new theatres being planned across Canada as national centennial projects: a new *Nutcracker*, with designs by Jürgen Rose, and *La Sylphide*, both in 1964–5; *The Rake's Progress* in 1965–6; *Bayaderka* Act IV and *Swan Lake* in 1966–7; the ill-fated *Cinderella* in 1967–8. An impressive list, with three of these productions, *La Sylphide*, *Nutcracker*, and *Swan Lake*, holding prominent places in the National's repertoire today. (Makarova's Kirov-influenced production of *La Bayadère* Act II has replaced the original Bolshoi-style *Bayaderka* by Valukin.) And of these ballets, only two, *Nutcracker* and *Cinderella*, were mounted by Franca herself. As the National grew from the intimate company of the early years, Franca's control gradually shifted away from the detailed supervision of individual productions into planning and administration, a shift that eventually placed severe strains on her relationship with the company.

But those strains did not manifest themselves immediately. After the relatively fallow period of 1960–3, a golden age was dawning. Finances continued perilous, but onstage the company flourished. A marked improvement in the technical accomplishments of its dancers, particularly of its women, accounted for the change. Galina Samsova's brilliant, extroverted technique and romantic grandeur of style appealed directly to the public. The dancers in the company felt its influence as well. Joanne Nisbet, by then its ballet mistress, could see the difference Samsova's example made in the training of the others:

> *Sometimes we would say to the dancers that a particular dancer was wonderful technically, doing such and such a step, and they'd never quite be able to believe us. But when Galina came, they* saw *it, and that already brought the company up another notch.*[40]

In 1963, while still a member of the National, Samsova created a European sensation dancing a new production of *Cinderella* in Paris. The guest engagement cut into her rehearsals for *Romeo and Juliet*[41] (another monkey-wrench in the works, as far as Franca was concerned), but the attendant international acclaim opened the company's eyes, if only vicariously, to a wider world. Lilian Jarvis, one of the

National's most charming Coppélias since the early days, accompanied her friend Galina to Paris and sent a proud account of the opening back to the troops at home.

> *At the end Galina got a fantastic standing ovation like I've never seen before. The whole stage was filled with flowers. She could hardly walk out for her call – after call – after call. Then people flocked onto the stage. There were literally hundreds of photographers as well. The choreographer – Russian – gave me his flowers, along with numerous hugs and kisses. Thanking me for Galina. You'd think I bore her and made her dance.*[42]

Samsova, now with a distinguished international career to her credit, keeps her Cinderella scrapbooks handy in her London home as a reminder of 'the glamour that doesn't exist any more' in today's theatrical world. Overnight, she was the toast of Paris. She still recalls the post-performance party:

> *By the time I arrived at Régine's, doors were opening, people are screaming, 'Cinderella is coming!' and I had never heard anything like it, being brought up in Soviet Union. And then being in Canada where one was treated as if you were lucky you have a job. It was complete triumph.*[43]

Martine van Hamel added to the lustre of this period by winning the gold medal, counter to her own expectations, in the Junior Women's category at the 1966 International Ballet Competition in Varna. She danced the repertoire she knew from the National – excerpts from *Bayaderka*, *Solitaire*, even Tudor's *Dark Elegies*[44] – but she dazzled the jury with her performance of the pas de deux from *Le Corsaire*, as taught to her by Samsova in the version originally created for Samsova's graduation performance in Russia.[45] In Samsova and van Hamel, whose careers with the company overlapped for the 1963–4 season only, Franca now had distinctive, confident, even flamboyant ballerinas, stronger and more muscular than the restrained and technically less accomplished dancers typical of the early years. Their stage-presence and powers of projection opened the eyes of dancers and audience alike to a new standard of performance.

Van Hamel's success had a special significance. She won at Varna both as a member of the company and as a recent graduate of the National Ballet School. Though she studied at the school for only a few years, her entry into the company signalled the school's emergence as a training ground for company members. Founded in 1959,[46] after years of agitation by Franca and Oliphant, the school was able to graduate female dancers into the company in remarkably short order because Oliphant closed her own studio and absorbed its most serious students into the National Ballet School. Strong male dancers were slower in coming, simply

For a group of invited guests at the St Lawrence Hall, Martine van Hamel and Earl Kraul re-create the excitement of their gold medal performance of the pas de deux from Le Corsaire.

because of the general prejudice of the time against encouraging boys to undertake dance studies. As early as the 1960s, dancers trained by the National Ballet School for performance careers began to enter the ranks. Following hard on van Hamel's heels, Veronica Tennant, Victoria Bertram, Vanessa Harwood, and Nadia Potts graduated into the company, with Karen Kain making the transition a little later. Kain, Potts, Tennant, and Harwood, all products of the school, developed into the ballerinas who defined the company's identity through the sixties and seventies. A few generations later, in the seventies and eighties, the male roster of the company was enriched with graduates of the school like Raymond Smith, Peter Ottmann, Owen Montague, Jeremy Ransom, Rex Harrington, Serge Lavoie, Kevin Pugh, John Alleyne, and Pierre Quinn. In anticipation of the school's opening, Franca had said: 'The day our permanent school opens will be the most important in the Guild's history to date.'[47] She did not overstate the case. The school has shaped the company by giving it the dancers who make it live.

Introducing Erik Bruhn and Rudolf Nureyev

During the expansion of the early 1960s, Franca established two immensely significant contacts, one the result of her own previous experience and perseverance, the other, once again, pure luck. For the 1964–5 season, she had to capitalize on the interest and expectations which *Romeo and Juliet* had aroused. In *The Nutcracker* she had a visually spectacular crowd-pleaser; it has developed into an annual Christmas ritual, delighting generations of dance lovers and their children. It has been danced in midsummer, at Washington's Carter Barron Amphitheatre, where Lois Smith was flown onto the set by a giant construction crane; and, by special request, it formed part of the company's repertoire on its far eastern tour of 1992. It endured until 1995, when it finally bowed to increased demands for spectacle created by shows like *Phantom of the Opera* and *Beauty and the Beast* and was replaced by James Kudelka's production, set in czarist Russia and sumptuously designed by Santo Loquasto. But in 1964, it could not sustain an entire season. For all its popularity,

Nutcracker as it is now danced is probably the least substantial of the surviving Petipa ballets. To follow the success of the previous season's *Romeo and Juliet*, something more was called for.

Franca's choice was inspired. With daring and imagination, she hit upon *La Sylphide*, the first ballet by August Bournonville, the nineteenth-century Danish master, to be included in the National's repertoire. *La Sylphide* would be something old *and* something new. The seemingly effortless, ethereal Bournonville style, which assumed controlled technique and quick precision, would contrast effectively with the company's existing repertoire, but could also build on the careful English training which Franca and Oliphant had given the dancers. A classic of the Danish school of ballet, *La Sylphide* had no connections with the Royal Ballet or Sadler's Wells. Nor had it been staged in North America. In going back to the Danish tradition, Franca was breaking new ground.

Franca had initially approached Niels Bjørn Larsen, ballet master of the Royal Danish Ballet, for permission to mount *La Sylphide* in the 1963–4 season,[48] but hesitations on the part of the Danes delayed plans by a year and led her back to one of her old friends, now the world's greatest exponent of Bournonville style. Erik Bruhn, whom Franca had known as a youngster in his Metropolitan Ballet days, received the invitation to mount *La Sylphide* and thus entered the orbit of the National Ballet, never entirely to leave it until his death in 1986. By chance, he introduced to the company the other blazing talent of the time, Rudolf Nureyev. These two great friends and rivals, who at one time shared an apartment and at others vied for the spotlight on the world's principal stages, revitalized male dance in the latter part of the twentieth century. Through *La Sylphide*, they first encountered the National Ballet; for the next twenty years, they became the two most formative influences on its growth.

La Sylphide: no ordinary première

La Sylphide opened at the O'Keefe Centre on 31 December 1964, with Erik Bruhn dancing the lead role of James, the bewitched young Scot who spurns mortal happiness with his sweetheart for the delusory enchantment of the Sylph. Opposite him on opening night and on the New Year's Day performance on 1 January 1965 was Lynn Seymour in the role of the Sylph. The presence of these two international stars made the opening a major event, but much greater excitement was in store. Rudolf Nureyev, the mere whisper of whose name was by this time enough to attract the press in droves, paid an unscheduled visit to Toronto to see his friend Bruhn and his new production. When Bruhn, suffering under the physical strain of preparing the production and dancing in it, had to withdraw from some of his scheduled appearances, he prevailed on Nureyev, who had never danced the role in his life, to replace him for one performance as James. Nureyev was injured himself, and undertook this remarkable test of skill dancing on two badly twisted, bandaged ankles.[49] The sensational turn of events, like something out of a show-business musical, electrified the press and brought an unprecedented level of publicity and critical attention to the opening run of this charming and delicate nineteenth-century evocation of romanticism. Bruhn returned for a final performance with an added passion that many attributed to rivalry between Bruhn the established star and Nureyev the brash newcomer.[50] But not all the excitement attached to the imported stars. Two of the National's stalwarts gave some of the most memorable performances of their careers in *La Sylphide*.

Earl Kraul had been scheduled to dance James, but not until the company took the work on tour later in January. All the O'Keefe Centre performances were to be by Bruhn. When Bruhn first decided that he was unable to appear as scheduled, Kraul agreed to step in for him, even though he had yet to learn large portions of mime and the scarf dance with the Sylph. Shortly after asking him to help, Bruhn phoned to say that Kraul was off the hook. Nureyev had agreed to dance. Since Kraul was already scheduled to dance the demanding pas de deux from *Le Corsaire* on the program in question, in a repeat of the gala format used on New Year's Eve, he felt considerably relieved. Relief evaporated later the same night when he received a call from Celia Franca, asking him to replace Bruhn as originally suggested, since the company wanted some lead time to publicize the windfall of the upcoming Nureyev performance. For the good of the company, Kraul agreed, but with the stipulation that he get a great deal of help from Bruhn with the sections he had yet to learn. Kraul recalls the events vividly.

An embarrassment of riches. During the opening run of La Sylphide, *Lois Smith and Earl Kraul (left), Lynn Seymour and Rudolf Nureyev (centre), and Seymour and Erik Bruhn (right) all took turns in the central roles.*

> *Erik said he would help, and Lynn Seymour came in. She was marvellous. Erik taught me these sections, but while he was teaching them to me, Rudi was behind me learning them as well. Rudi would say things like, 'Well, no, no, I change that. I do that this*

> *way,' and Erik was saying, 'No you don't change. It's Bournonville. You don't change.' All this was going on while I was trying desperately to get ready.*

After this invigorating day in the studio, Kraul danced *Le Corsaire* removed his body make-up, and got into James' kilt, conscious that he would make his début in the role with minimal preparation, under the watchful eyes of the two greatest male dancers in the world.

La Sylphide opens with a tableau, James dozing in the armchair by the fire, the Sylph kneeling at his side. Kraul and Seymour took their places and waited for the curtain. But before the curtain went up, they heard an announcement over the theatre's public address system that Kraul will never forget: 'that I would be replacing Erik, and that if they wanted to get their money back they could go to the box-office. Lynn, who was already kneeling beside me, put her head up and looked at me, and said, "They didn't say that, did they?."' Kraul took strength from the members of the company who had emerged silently from the wings to wish him luck and launched into his performance. 'After the first scene, I was looking out at the audience, and I knew it was one of those performances where I felt I couldn't put a foot in the wrong place. Through the whole performance, I was five feet off the floor.'[51] Kraul's sense of achievement remained undiminished, even after Nureyev's blaze of glory three days later.

And there were those who thought Nureyev's appearance rode more on its sensation than on the strength of its dancing. In his own account of the evening, Nureyev later stressed the integrity of his performance against the enormous odds of his injuries, not its inherent merits.

> *Very foolishly, I took one of the bandages away, so I let the blood spread even further inside of my ankle. However, I rebandaged again and waited for the second act. I danced. I did all the steps. I didn't change or cut anything. Everything was as was rehearsed. The next day of course my legs were both very enormous, and Erik miraculously suddenly recovered and he danced to glorious acclaim.*[52]

The 'glorious acclaim' of that final performance was not reserved for Bruhn alone. Lois Smith danced her first Sylph that night and remembers it as yet another magic evening in the theatre.

> *It was one of those performances where everything was right. Now there are very few times that this kind of thing really happens. It was like a dream. Everything was working together, it was a wonderful performance, and the audience got up and clapped and cheered at the end, and I thought, 'Great, that's what it's all about, that's wonderful.'*[53]

The Nureyev appearance made all the headlines, and Bruhn's return took whatever space was left, but Kraul and Smith, buoyed up by the excitement of their presence, captured their own places in the hearts of the audience that knew them well.

The company as a whole stood up well under the intense glare of the publicity. Both Ralph Hicklin and Nathan Cohen singled out Lois Smith for special praise. (Cohen found her to be generally more persuasive than Seymour.)[54] Cohen, who would on the following day savage the company's dancing in *Romeo and Juliet*, summed up the closing night of *La Sylphide* with carefully chosen words of praise: 'Altogether it was a moving performance. It reached the heights of grandeur when Mr. Bruhn was the centre of the action, and it never lied or deteriorated into the chic or trivial.'[55]

Offstage as well as on, it was a heady holiday season. The company premièred three new productions (*Nutcracker*, *Sylphide*, and Grant Strate's *Triptych*) within the space of ten days. Celebrating this extraordinary achievement, and the New Year, with them were Erik Bruhn, Lynn Seymour, Rudolf Nureyev, Frank Schaufuss (Martine van Hamel's partner for *Nutcracker*), and his son, Peter, both from the Royal Danish Ballet. For the younger Schaufuss, it was quite a New Year's Eve.

> *I had just started smoking, very young, and Rudolf and Erik were trying to convince me that you shouldn't smoke, you should drink whisky instead. On the New Year's Eve they showed me how to drink whisky, and I was sick for three days afterwards. Ever since I have never smoked, and I haven't really been drinking either.*[56]

(Peter Schaufuss later returned to dance with the National for two separate periods, once as a promising beginner in 1967–9, and again as an established star from 1977 to 1984.) In all this hullabaloo, no one cared very much that the National narrowly missed out on the distinction of mounting North America's first *La Sylphide*. American Ballet Theatre stole the march on them with the première of their production, staged by Harald Lander, in San Antonio, Texas, on 11 November 1964,[57] just a month and a half before the National began its eventful first run of the work.

Erik Bruhn's radical *Swan Lake*

The need for a new *Swan Lake* to replace the worn-out Franca-Ambrose production had been decisively demonstrated by a brief run at the O'Keefe Centre in 1964. In the new theatre, the old warhorse had shown her age; she should no longer be trotted out. By returning to Bruhn with the commission, Franca hoped, as with *La Sylphide*, to gain a fresh, new perspective on an old classic. Bruhn's longstanding desire to give more prominence to the role of Prince Siegfried,[58] as well as his success with *La Sylphide*, augured well for the project. Desmond Heeley's rising reputation at the Stratford Festival made him an obvious choice to provide the opulent designs. Even the Tchaikovsky score would be reconsidered and revised to fit Bruhn's conception of the work. The new *Swan Lake* became the company's major new production for Canada's centennial year and the National's appearances at Expo 67. The world première in Toronto, on 27 March 1967, was one of the most eagerly awaited in the company's history. With this production, Bruhn gave the National an intensely personal statement, a revisionist *Swan Lake* that created controversy from the very beginning.

One of the ways in which Bruhn sought to strengthen the figure of the Prince was by giving him a lyrical and murderously difficult new solo in Act I to establish his brooding, introspective character. Once again, Earl Kraul had the unenviable task of following in Bruhn's footsteps.

> *It was really difficult to do. Erik designed it on himself. He looked positively magnificent doing it, and I didn't have that kind of line. Partnering was my forte. I could jump. I had a lot of strength and energy. But I had to work really hard to get a good line on my body all the time, and I found that type of solo very difficult to pull off.*[59]

According to Rudolf Nureyev, that solo had an interesting genesis. In 1964, Bruhn had been present in Vienna when Nureyev staged a complete *Swan Lake*. Even earlier, however, in 1963, Bruhn had seen the controversial solo for Prince Siegfried which Nureyev choreographed for the Royal Ballet.[60] Bruhn had originally sided with the critical opinion of the time that dismissed this interpolation into the Petipa original, but later, according to Nureyev, changed his mind.

> *Suddenly he got excited, after he'd seen it two or three years. He saw that it worked and it did portray the mood of prince – brooding, melancholy – that essentially prepares for the event of white swans by the lake and makes him unique. So he used the same solo again, with his own modifications.*[61]

In the Act I solo, then, Kraul and the

Sergiu Stefanschi and Vanessa Harwood perform the Black Swan pas de deux from Erik Bruhn's production of Swan Lake.

Siegfrieds who came after him wrestled with choreography born of the formidable combination of Bruhn line and Nureyev virtuosity. Latterly, Jeremy Ransom has come closer than any of them to recapturing the spirit of the original. It was only one of many places where the highly individual nature of Bruhn's choreography made the production resistant to the personalities of dancers other than the original cast.

The Nureyev influence went deep. At the beginning of the project, Bruhn considered, briefly, doing a collaborative production with his friend. Before any contracts were signed, however, he changed his mind. In October 1965, Grant Strate reported to Celia Franca on a meeting he had had with Bruhn about the project in Montreal: 'Bruhn would now rather stage *Swan Lake* alone without Nureyev. He thinks this collaboration could work artistically, but in practice the physical difficulties of getting together are too great.'[62] But if the idea of collaboration came to nothing, the fact of Nureyev's earlier version of the ballet, and Bruhn's familiarity with it, cannot be ignored. According to Nureyev, Bruhn adopted the musical cuts and revisions to the score which he himself had used in Vienna.[63] When Nureyev, in later years, came to dance the Prince, he obtained Bruhn's permission to revert to some of the traditional choreography. In 1977, on tour in Los Angeles, Nureyev was quoted on the subject.

> *We have made some modifications, with Bruhn's permission. I asked to dance the original pas de deux, and he didn't object. And in the last act, I use my own choreography. Erik had modelled his on mine anyway, so I said, 'Why not go whole hog?'*[64]

Going 'whole hog' has meant that many audiences have seen the Bruhn original with a Nureyev face-lift. Over its lifespan, the Bruhn *Swan Lake* has probably sustained more of this kind of modification than any other production still in the National's repertoire.

Two important aspects of the production, however, were Bruhn's and Bruhn's alone. One was the conflation of the original four-act action into two acts of two scenes each. The swift, smooth transition in each act from court to lakeside, without the interruption of a curtain, gave the production dramatic momentum and focused attention on the emotional conflict of the Prince, caught between the forces these two worlds represent. Bruhn had to insist in order to make this radical innovation in the staging of the ballet. The arguments against it were purely practical. Could the elaborate scene-change and the necessary costume-changes be accomplished in the brief space of time allowed by the music that would be used for the transition? The Black Swan had to change back into the Swan Queen's tutu, and virtually all the court ladies had to transform themselves into swans once again. Would the second act, without intermission, prove too gruelling a test of the lead dancers' stamina? Even if these problems could be solved, would the two large acts prove too long for the audience's attention span?[65] Bruhn's insistence, and the technical ingenuity of the production staff, carried the day. Audiences did not notice that the court ladies, one by one, slipped discreetly out of the ballroom scene in order to undo the hooks on the backs of their costumes, careful not to turn their backs on the spectators after their return. Only with this preparation could they manage the quick change necessary for the last lakeside scene. The two-act presentation of *Swan Lake*, which seemed impossible until Bruhn insisted on it, has proved one of the most attractive features of the production, and has been widely imitated by others, among them Rudolf Nureyev in his production for the Ballet of the Paris Opéra.[66]

The other Bruhn trademark which distinguished his production was the transformation of von Rothbart, the evil genius in control of the swans, into a woman. Precedent for the change existed in Myrtha and Carabosse, the other arch-villains of classical ballet, both of them women, but those closely associated with the production believe the change to have been motivated by something deep within Bruhn's own personality, not by any desire for conformity with the rest of the canon. Grant Strate worked with Bruhn as the artistic coordinator of the project and watched the idea of a female von Rothbart grow from its inception. 'That had a lot to do with his own psychology, his own background, his own Danish attitude towards life.'[67] Celia Franca concurs. The entire conception of the character 'was very, very psychological and something deep inside him that I think probably Freud couldn't analyse.'[68] However complicated the origins of the idea, it has never worked successfully in performance. Strate, who worked through the scenario in detail with Bruhn, had great difficulty in making him develop the Black Queen (as von Rothbart was rechristened) as a character and as a choreographic entity beyond his initial idea. At a planning session in Rome, where Bruhn was mounting *La Sylphide*, Strate tried to make Bruhn come to terms with the conception.

> *I spent four days talking to Erik, and we still hadn't gotten to the essential thing. He wanted von Rothbart to be a woman, but he didn't know what that woman should do. And when he choreographed the ballet, he still didn't know. I was trying to force him to materialize that concept. It was the weak point of the ballet, a female doing a male role.*

Franca, the first of the Black Queens, was given the role and then left largely to work it out by herself.[69] The part rode on the strength of her own considerable dramatic presence, rather than on Bruhn's choreography or detailed elaboration of the character.

> *It was only strength of personality that got anything across, just sheer physical and emo-*

> *tional personality. I used to be worn out at the end of it, trying to make it look convincing, but I couldn't get the character in my own mind. I couldn't understand what Erik was getting at.*[70]

After Franca left the role, Bruhn took to tinkering with it in an attempt to make it work. He had Desmond Heeley design a new costume and, when Ann Ditchburn took the part, put her on pointe,[71] but nothing seemed to work.

The Black Queen has baffled many of those who took her on. Lois Smith danced her only once, on the occasion of 'Lois Smith Night,' her farewell appearance with the National on 24 November 1969. 'I didn't have very much rehearsal on it. In that fourth act you were in and out and around, running here and running there, and up and down lines, and it was always, "Where the hell do I go next?"'[72] Probably no dancer, other than Franca, has had more experience in the role than Victoria Bertram, who, during a career spanning more than twenty-five years, has worked her way through the ranks to that of principal character artist, specializing in the character roles that so frequently provide crucial dramatic motivation and continuity in the story-ballets. The Black Queen has presented her with one of the enduring challenges of her career. 'I tried to make it work. I really tried to connect the thing to get a thread of the Black Queen through it. I wanted to make it a little bit more interesting and I wanted to dig down a little bit and see if I could find a whole other side.' Even though Bruhn complimented Bertram warmly on her conception of the role, she herself remains dissatisfied. 'He was quite pleased with that. I don't feel happy about it, but I feel that there's something there and if I keep hammering at it, maybe – .'[73] Bruhn relied too heavily on the force of Franca's own personality in creating the original to give it the choreographic substance it required. A challenge for Franca, the Black Queen remains an enigma to those who came after her, a graphic reminder of the importance of character roles in classical ballet. But despite its shortcomings, Bruhn's *Swan Lake* has endured and even flourished in the repertoire.

The high costs of mounting *Cinderella*

A crueller fate awaited *Cinderella*. The Prokofiev score for this full-length ballet, not nearly as well known or popular as his *Romeo and Juliet*, had inspired major Soviet productions in Moscow and Leningrad (with choreography by Konstantin Sergeyev) and Sir Frederick Ashton's famous version for the Sadler's Wells Theatre Ballet (1948), revived at the Royal Ballet in 1965 with Ashton and Sir Robert Helpmann dancing the roles of the ugly stepsisters. Franca herself undertook the choreography of the National's *Cinderella* with an acute awareness of the company's straitened circumstances. 'I probably wouldn't be choreographing *Cinderella* at all except that it's cheaper if I do it. You can't ask Sir Frederick Ashton when you don't know until the last minute if the money will be available.'[74] Such awareness could not work to her advantage. Now that the National had become a larger organization, her role as artistic director placed her in an invidious position as a creative artist. Administrative responsibility prevented her from allowing artistic ego a free rein. As artistic director, Franca had been able to act as a buffer between the board, with its responsibility for financial prudence, and Cranko or Bruhn, whose primary concern was for the artistic product. As choreographer, she had no one to run similar interference for her. And as artistic director, she did not receive the payment for her choreography that any outsider demanded as a matter of course. The question of performance royalties for *The Nutcracker*, for example, the National's perennial money-maker, was not even raised until after she had left the company.[75] She was the available house choreographer, and her services were more or less taken for granted.

From the outset, financial difficulties bedevilled Franca's *Cinderella*. At a hundred thousand dollars, its budget was uncomfortably high. Then illness prevented Jürgen Rose from meeting some of the design deadlines, and expenses rose by another ten thousand. When Franca requested a further nine thousand, the board's Executive Committee declined her request, unless equivalent savings could be realized elsewhere.[76] The Board had just moved away from its practice of amortizing the cost of a new production over a three-year period; thus all the production costs for *Cinderella* had to be charged within a single, disastrous, financial year.[77] At precisely this time, the Canada Council's scrutiny of the rising cumulative deficit placed the board under intense pressure. Once again, talk of retrenchment filled the air.[78]

Under these clouds of mounting tension, Franca's *Cinderella* opened at the O'Keefe Centre on 15 April 1968. There was some cause for rejoicing. No less a critic than Clive Barnes wrote in the pages of the *New York Times*:

> *Lavishness, spectacle or simple extravagance are not always associated with our neighbor Canada. Yet within the last few years the National Ballet of Canada has, almost unobtrusively, become the most elaborately mounted ballet company in North America. This Cinderella is the most sumptuous looking ballet ever produced in North America.*[79]

Writing in the Toronto *Telegram*, Ralph Hicklin maintained: 'Franca has come much closer to the spirit of the music, and to the unique féerie implicit in the mythic world of Cinderella, than Frederick Ashton or Konstantin Sergeyev, creators of the only other versions I have seen of this ballet.'[80] But there the praise stopped. Barnes' review went on to castigate Franca's choreography:

> *The choreography rarely enchanted or amazed. It had, of course, classroom competence,*

> *but little theatrical magic. I have certain reservations about Frederick Ashton's version for the Royal Ballet, but compared with this Franca version it is outstanding. There are errors of judgement in the Ashton (it was his first full-evening work), but there are also many moments of genius entirely lacking in this Canadian production.*[81]

Veronica Tennant watches as Franca and television producer Norman Campbell argue a point during the taping of Cinderella. *Campbell was instrumental in bringing many of the company's productions to the television screen.*

Significant critical response to this, Franca's first original, full-length work and the first production of *Cinderella* by a North American company, was lukewarm at best. At worst, it amounted to a backlash against the very lavishness and spectacle that had won Barnes' honest admiration. Wendy Michener, writing in the *Globe and Mail*, gave voice to a point of view that would make itself increasingly heard:

> *Just what purpose it serves for the National or the Canadian public at this time I can't see, unless the directors have concluded from the successes of* Swan Lake *and* Romeo and Juliet *that traditional spectacles are all their public really wants from them.*[82]

She, too, went on to lament the absence of choreography sufficiently inspired to justify the spectacle.

Cinderella received only thirteen complete performances (the Act II pas de deux appeared by itself on a few mixed programs) before being retired from the active repertoire. Most of its costumes were destroyed in the fire of 1973.[83] But *Cinderella*'s story does not end in ignominy. The production was taped for television, its choreography appropriately modified by Franca for the demands of a different medium.[84] In this version, it won an Emmy in 1970, in the category of Best Classical Musical Production. The irony of the award, given the production's reception just two years previously, must have cut deep. A new production of *Cinderella*, by Ben Stevenson, the artistic director of the Houston Ballet, entered the repertoire in 1995, long after the memories of Franca's version had faded.

Original choreography failed to excite the public.

Franca's heavy personal involvement in *Cinderella* undercut her overall reputation as artistic director during this crucial period. The contempt for 'traditional spectacles' evident in critical comment like Michener's attached itself, perhaps unfairly, to Franca's artistic policies. She was now thought of as the conservative opponent of radical, new choreography, choreography that would rely less heavily on production values for its effects. While the bulk of her energy in the 1960s had undeniably gone into the development of the spectacular, 'O'Keefe Centred' repertoire, her record was not entirely one-sided. The company produced original works during this period too.

It had its greatest investment, in creative terms, in Grant Strate. His period as apprentice in the vocabulary of classical ballet long since over, he produced the bulk of his output during the sixties. But despite considerable time and energy spent in mounting these works, Strate's ballets failed to find a large public. As his ideas about movement took him further and further away from the methods and assumptions of classical ballet, Strate's work became peripheral to the company's main interests. In 1969 he was in Stockholm, at Erik Bruhn's invitation, working with the Royal Swedish Ballet, of which Bruhn was then the artistic director. In a letter to Franca, Bruhn reported on the work in progress:

> *I saw his ballets today for the first time. Though it is hard to judge from a first orchestra rehearsal I still feel he has not developed choreographically as much as I had hoped. Though my company is not the greatest they have on other occasions responded better, however it all might pull itself more together before the premiere.*[85]

Strate had great difficulty discovering a genuinely distinctive style of movement. Of only one section of his *Triptych*, for example, could Ralph Hicklin say, 'We can think of their dance as Strate movement, not just dance movement.'[86] The demands of the large theatre and its conservative audience were also a problem. Strate took greater pleasure in experiment, working with the radical, younger members of the company to challenge accepted ideas of movement, than in conventional choreography. The smaller-scale surroundings of the Stratford Festival or Ballet Concert, the company's small touring group, provided a more suitable creative environment for him. He did not become the major source of original choreography which the full company needed.

With hopes for Strate's development on the wane, and no other potential resident choreographer in the wings, Franca looked to guest choreographers to supply original repertoire that could succeed at the box-office. The search was scattered and, by and large, unsuccessful. Commissioned works by Zachary Solov, Heinz Poll, Daniel Seillier (then ballet master with the company), and Heino Heiden filled up programs but took the company in no single, distinctive direction. Guest choreographers could not know the company members well enough to choreograph to their particular talents and capabilities. Their work could not spring from a close, continuing relationship with the dancers. Heino Heiden's *La Prima Ballerina*, an elaborate dramatization of events from the life of the nineteenth-century dancer

Marie Taglioni, played like a send-up rather than the serious drama it was intended to be.[87] Its utter failure, in the same season with *Cinderella*, cast a gloomy pall over the company's reputation for encouraging original work. The issuing of another stern warning from the Canada Council about 'the necessity of beginning an effective debt retirement plan'[88] sounded a note as ominous as it was familiar. The decade would apparently close, as it had opened, gloomily.

1968: Franca precipitates a crisis.

The 1960s ended, as far as the National Ballet of Canada was concerned, on 15 November 1968, precisely seven months after the opening of *Cinderella*. On that day, the Guild held its seventeenth Annual General Meeting, the public gathering for its members at the St Lawrence Hall, at which the Guild, its board of directors, and the company's senior staff, with the press routinely in attendance, reported on the year's activities and the ballet's general state of health. The event was usually as carefully choreographed as any of the company's best productions, with nothing left to chance or improvisation. On this occasion, however, Franca astounded the assembled audience by delivering the following carefully worded statement in place of the expected report of the artistic director.

> *I and my policies are currently receiving overwhelming criticism from very many quarters. I am used to criticism, and have weathered much of it, but I have always had enough support to carry on.*
>
> *However, there is reason to believe that the majority of our directors, guild members, staff members, company members, governmental grant-giving bodies and the news media have lost confidence in me. There is no accurate method of assessing the opinions of the general public, but even if there were, and even if those opinions were in my favor, I can't run the company's artistic affairs in an atmosphere of dissension, nor compromise my ideals beyond the point of honesty and self-respect.*
>
> *Of course, I will finish out this season; but in due course our president will receive my official letter of resignation. I am conscious of the wishes of the board for the remainder of this season, and will carry them out. However, as from today I renounce responsibility for any actions I may be pressured to take against my better judgment.*
>
> *Ladies and gentlemen, if I go into details on this occasion, the event will become nauseatingly dramatic and theatrical. I hope you will receive this brief report calmly, so that I may retire gracefully.*[89]

She had her wish. As the audience of the ballet faithful watched in disbelieving silence, Franca made the most dramatic exit of her career, first to her office and then to seclusion at her home.

CHAPTER FIVE

A Voice Crying in the Wilderness

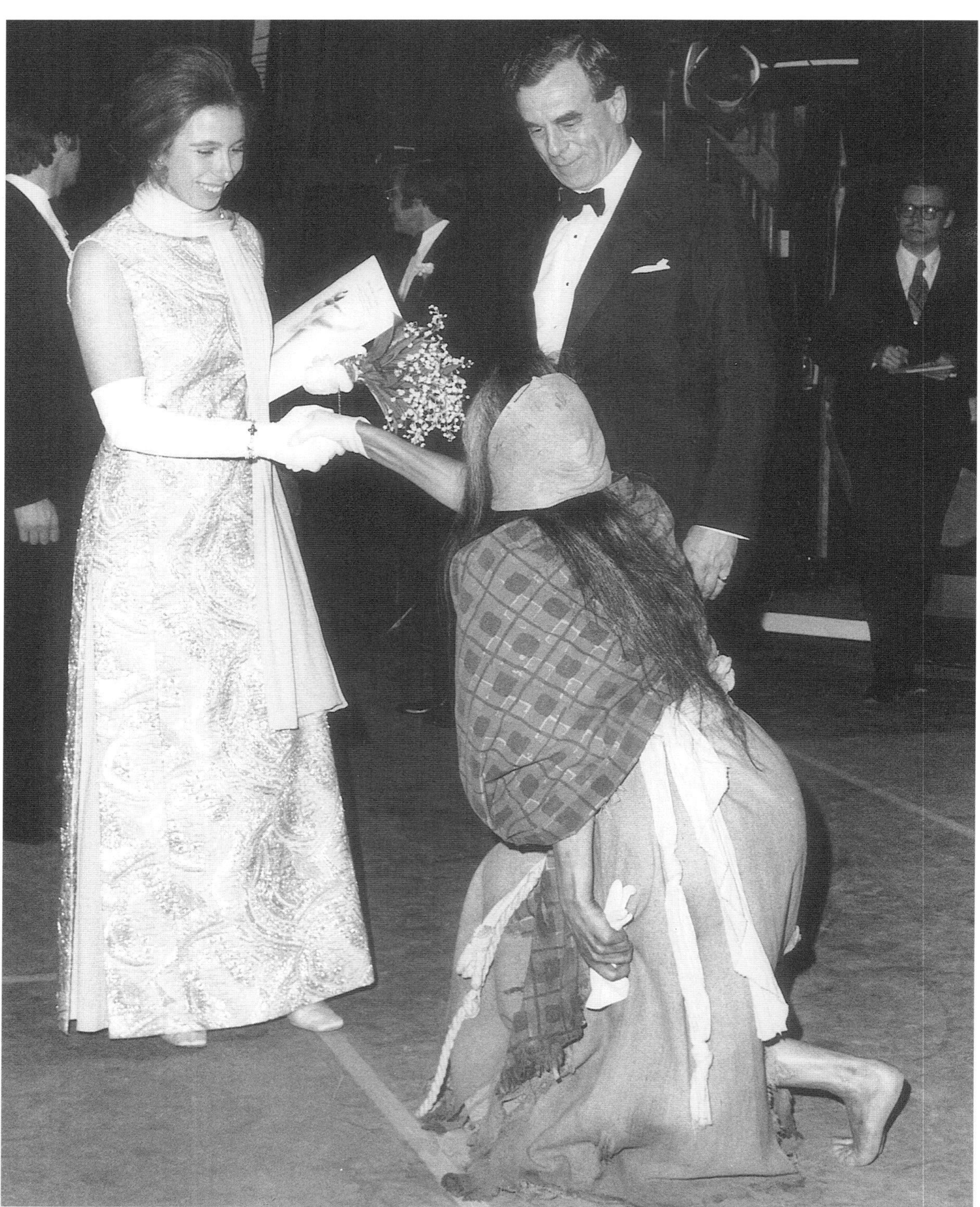

Franca's dramatic statement made the reason for her resignation perfectly clear. She felt that her authority in artistic matters, which was to have been undisputed, had been undermined to the point where she was forced into artistic compromises against her better judgment. With her statement, she intended to shift the blame for those artistic compromises away from herself and place it where it belonged, squarely at the feet of those who controlled the purse-strings. By the 1968–9 season, the National's board of directors had streamlined its structure to eliminate the position of chairman and retain only that of president. John Godfrey was thus chairing the Annual General Meeting, as president of its board of directors, when

Delicate negotiations induced Franca to reconsider her position.

OPPOSITE: Despite internal turmoil, Franca presented the company in its 1972 European début at a gala performance of La Sylphide *in London, attended by HRH the Princess Anne. For the post-performance reception, Franca added a pair of white cotton gloves (from Woolworths) to her costume as Madge, thus satisfying the demands of protocol while protecting the princess's hands from her own heavy makeup. The* Toronto Star*'s dance critic, William Littler, takes notes in the background, with David Haber just visible behind the princess's bouquet.*

ABOVE: Roland Petit's Kraanerg *was included in the European tour to demonstrate the company's range and modernity. Andrew Oxenham and David Gordon support Veronica Tennant in one of the work's small groupings.*

Franca dropped her bombshell. In that position, and completely unaware of Franca's intentions, he spoke to the meeting before she did. He too addressed head-on the issue of fiscal as opposed to artistic responsibility, but from the opposite point of view. 'Although the last thing I, as President, or the Board of Directors, should do is interfere, if the artistic side is not prepared to make recommendations for retrenchment, then in my opinion it is the duty of the General Manager to do so.'[1] The conflict between the board's financial priorities and the director's artistic ones had finally come out into the open. The 1968 crisis played itself out in precisely these dualistic terms, as a conflict between financial responsibility and artistic freedom. Godfrey's statement, however, drew attention to a third factor, the role of the general manager, whose alignment, whether with the board or with the artistic director, thus became a crucial factor in the governance of the company.

Franca's surprise announcement elicited strong reactions from among the dancers, the board, and the company's supporters. For some the National without Franca was unthinkable. From Edmonton, a longtime supporter of the ballet telephoned to say that out west, the National Ballet *was* Celia Franca, and to warn of the serious damage her resignation would cause.[2] Within the company itself, reaction ranged from the extremes of panic and denial to acceptance and planning for the future. Lawrence Adams, David Adams' brother and a member of the recently formed Dancers' Council, was in the vanguard of those for whom the world had not come to an end with Franca's announcement. 'Within the Dancers' Council we took the attitude, "Well, she's gone, so now we just have to get on with the business here."'[3] For Adams, who welcomed the idea of change, Franca's resignation offered a real opportunity to rethink the company along more contemporary, less elaborate (and hence less expensive) lines. The five-member Dancers' Council raised this issue in a cable to John Godfrey:

> *The company has grown to a proportion which imposes on its mobility and versatility, and with no future prospect of a reduction in operational costs. Then a serious reconsideration of the proportions of the company must be made. There has been no precedent set that size and expenditure of a company affect its artistic calibre.*[4]

The same cable spoke of the need to develop a significant body of contemporary repertoire for the company.

The issues had been debated before: financial responsibility, artistic authority, the company's overall character. But this time, the debate was conducted in an atmosphere of tension, consternation, and crisis. The company itself, on tour in the Maritimes when Franca announced her resignation in Toronto, had had no prior warning from her as to her intentions. She flew out a few days later to speak with them in person, but their sense of isolation could not be so easily overcome. With nine of their number absent, performing for the Prologue to the Performing Arts program in the schools, the majority of dancers felt that no genuinely collective opinion could be expressed; the Dancers' Council, though duly elected, thus spoke as a separate entity, not for the entire company.[5] As events played themselves out, the Council found itself more and more isolated from the dancers it sought to represent, identified as an anti-Franca faction rather than a planning group trying to cope with a crisis.[6] Meanwhile, in Toronto, communication between Franca and Godfrey deteriorated even further. The key players in the affair were becoming dangerously isolated from one another.

Staff at the Canada Council kept a careful watching brief on the situation. Lawrence Adams, in Halifax, consulted at least twice with Peter Dwyer, who, along with Jean Roberts of the Council staff, spoke directly with Franca as well.[7] Hamilton Cassels, Jr, who had been chairman of the board before that position was abolished and was the son-in-law of Aileen Woods, conducted diplomatic talks with Franca, Godfrey, Betty Oliphant, and Christopher Knobbs, a dancer who called him from the tour in an attempt to gain a clearer understanding of the situation.[8] Confusion was rife. At all levels, there existed a fundamental difference of opinion as to the best way of handling the resignation. The forces pressing for change saw it as an opportunity to reshape the company completely, under a new artistic director; but a significant faction considered Franca indispensable to the company's well-being and wanted to use the occasion simply as a way of urging on her the values of fiscal restraint and choreographic innovation. The crisis had already registered at the box-office; subscription sales for the Toronto season, which had been initiated only a year earlier, fell off dramatically immediately following Franca's announcement.[9]

After a two-week cooling-off period, during which the Dancers' Council attempted, unsuccessfully, to reach consensus among the dancers and Cassels pursued his diplomatic course with the company's officers, the board met to consider Franca's resignation. It in turn referred the matter to a special three-person committee, made up of Lyman Henderson, James Fleck, and Mrs St Clair Balfour, which was asked to report back to the full board within a month's time.[10] On 20 December 1968, the board met to receive this committee's recommendations. Immediately following the meeting, the company issued a press release stating that the board had refused to accept Franca's resignation and that she had been prevailed upon to remain as artistic director of the company. In the press release announcing this resolution to the crisis, John Godfrey was quoted as saying:

> *The pressures which led to the current difficulties were basically financial, and all have agreed management procedures will be altered so Miss Franca will not have to take sole responsibility for almost every decision in the company.*

> *Better financial disciplines have already been introduced to ensure that Miss Franca has the time she needs to devote to the artistic direction of the company.*[11]

The same meeting that reinstated her invited Betty Oliphant to become the company's associate artistic director and also reaffirmed its confidence in the general manager, Wallace A. Russell. Russell had been doing lighting design for the company since its 1961–2 season and had joined the staff, as production manager, the following year. He remained on the production side, working with both the ballet and the Canadian Opera Company,[12] for some years, before going full time with the ballet. In 1967, following the departure of John H. Wilson from the post of general manager, he made the shift to administration as the company's business administrator. After a year in that position, he became general manager in 1968–9, just before the crisis of Franca's resignation. Though new as general manager, he had a long-standing association with the company and knew its productions and production staff intimately. He also had the confidence of the board. In Oliphant and Russell, Franca was now flanked by two powerful figures, each with considerable influence within the company. This volatile combination of personalities determined the company's internal politics for four tempestuous years.

Though the board invited Franca to take the helm once again, it asked her to steer a different course. The invitation was coupled with the express wish that greater emphasis be laid on contemporary works in the future.[13] Confrontation had, apparently, been negotiated into compromise, but the real issues, financial and artistic, had not been laid to rest.

A gesture as dramatic as Franca's resignation could hardly have been genuine, or so some people thought, particularly when the resolution to the crisis left her in control of the company, nominally at least. But if Franca's resignation was a ploy, it failed in its central purpose, since it returned her to only a conditional leadership, not to the unqualified control she presumably sought. And if her actions looked to some to be contrived or tactical, the evidence nevertheless indicates that there was much heartfelt agony in Franca's decision. Three days after the event, she wrote to Aileen Woods, her friend and supporter from the beginning:

> *I know you must be feeling awful at the turn of events. Please believe me – I thought over my horrible decision very carefully before I made it. I thought particularly of you and the many friends who supported me in building our beloved National Ballet. The truth is, dear, that life with the ballet has become intolerable for me and I feel I cannot continue the struggle. Feeling this way I would let the ballet down if I continued with it. I hope so very much that my successor will be treated with sympathy and understanding for he (or she) will have a monstrous task.*[14]

In the public eye, the Franca of this period was the iron lady, clinging grimly to personal power for her own purposes. Because her dreams of a ballet company dedicated to the full-length classics were becoming critically unfashionable, as well as expensive, the public failed to recognize her unswerving purpose as dedication to the art form itself, as she conceived of it. But Franca's intense personal identification with the art which had been her entire life meant that her fight was for the ballet, and only incidentally for herself as its champion. Public opinion could not recognize such selflessness, especially when it was coupled with such unwavering strength. And public opinion of the time was not inclined to admire this combination of selflessness and strength in an artist, especially a woman. Her resignation could be one of two things only: foolhardy idealism or Machiavellian manipulation. The cynical interpretation of her motives became the easier, though not necessarily the fairer, one to accept. The public eye never saw the vulnerable, discouraged human being revealed in Franca's letter to Woods.

Either as idealistic stand or as tactical manoeuvre, however, Franca's gesture did little to increase her real power base within the company or to resolve the underlying tensions. In withdrawing her resignation, she accepted significant limitations on her authority as artistic director. She who had initially been given 'the sole and entire artistic direction of the company' now had to function within a structure that included an associate artistic director, with strong ideas of her own, and an Artistic Management Council, soon to be renamed the Artistic Management Committee. This committee had been set up in the fall of 1968 to improve liaison between the board and the artistic and management arms of the company.[15] Its membership included Franca, Oliphant, Strate, and, later, George Crum. This emerging company structure contributed to the increasing power of the role of general manager.

In the fall of 1967, the board received from one of its own subcommittees the Townsend Report, which subjected the management side of operations to formal scrutiny. A year later, the board accepted this report's affirmation of the importance of the position of general manager in management's working with the board to exercise budgetary control of the company's affairs.[16] The board evidently hoped that the general manager would function as its instrument for ensuring financial responsibility, with the artistic director virtually removed from the financial sphere and given complete autonomy in the artistic. But as long as finances remained tight, the distinction between financial and artistic authority was illusory at best. Thus the 'better financial disciplines' that the board instituted at the time of Franca's reinstatement came eventually to cramp her style as surely as they were intended to free her to concentrate on artistic matters. Franca herself, though she worked hard to adapt to the new organizational structure, was temperamentally ill suited to function within it. The rival claims of business and artistic principles would have one more day in court.

On the choreographic side, matters moved more swiftly. For a period of three years following this resolution to the administrative crisis, the company's concerted efforts to build the classical side of its repertoire gave way to a pursuit of the avant garde. In part a response to the pressures exerted by critics, board members, Canada Council staff, the Dancers' Council, and individuals like Grant Strate, this emphasis on the contemporary also came about as the result of a unique combination of circumstances and opportunities. The opening of the National Arts Centre in Ottawa made possible a large-scale investment in op-art chic, while, on the home front, the presence of an extraordinary group of young people led the company into a period of radical creative experimentation which prepared the way for some of the important choreography of the seventies. Franca, once a fledgling choreographer herself, was ready to let the members of the next generation test their wings, even if she was not the one who could teach them how to fly.

The *Kraanerg* experience

The opening engagement at the new National Arts Centre in Ottawa, Canada's most lavish and superbly equipped theatre to date, was unquestionably the theatrical plum of 1969. At the National Arts Centre, the National Ballet had influential friends. Hamilton Southam, the director general, had wide-ranging tastes in the arts and the confidence to act upon them; David Haber, formerly the National Ballet's stage manager, was now the Arts Centre's director of programming, and retained strong loyalties to Franca and the company. Between the two of them, they managed to ride out the inevitable controversies attendant upon the decision to offer to the National Ballet the distinction of opening the new house. The National responded to the invitation with the suggestion of a major, commissioned work by Roland Petit, the French choreographer of high fashion who had one foot in Hollywood and the other in the Champs Elysées. Originally planned as a revolutionary ballet about Maiakovsky, then as a modern version of Mary Shelley's *Frankenstein*, the commission eventually became *Kraanerg*, an abstract ballet in two acts. Attempts to interest Petit in working with the internationally acclaimed Quebec artist Jean-Paul Riopelle as his designer came to naught, as did efforts to prevail upon the Royal Opera House, Covent Garden, to release Rudolf Nureyev to star in the production.[17] But even so, *Kraanerg* as it eventually appeared on the stage of the Opera at the National Arts Centre, on 2 June 1969, had international glamour to spare. With a commissioned electronic score by the Greek Iannis Xenakis, stunning op-art designs by the Hungarian-born French artist Victor Vasarely and his son Yvaral, the American composer Lukas Foss as guest conductor, and the French Georges Piletta and expatriate Canadian Lynn Seymour as guest stars, *Kraanerg* represented the last word in contemporary ballet. Petit's and Piletta's names may have been intended to satisfy the need for significant francophone representation on the important occasion of the opening of a national facility. (Les Grands Ballets Canadiens had been strong contenders for the honour at one time.)[18] Seymour's presence provided international stature as well as Canadian content.

The full company in Kraanerg, *in front of Victor Vasarely's eye-catching set. In the foreground (from left to right), Mary Jago, Veronica Tennant, Clinton Rothwell, Timothy Spain, and Karen Bowes do the splits.*

Kraanerg represented a landmark in the company's development. In Haber's view, it proclaimed to the world that the National Ballet, as a Canadian company, was capable of international collaboration on the highest level.[19] The production of *Kraanerg* thus crystallized the debate between the nationalist and the internationalist points of view in the performing arts. To the nationalist, it represented failure because none of its creators was Canadian; to the internationalist, it represented success precisely because its international creators had acknowledged the company's quality by mounting an original work for it. The Arts Centre, which had invested substantial funds in the production, got what it paid for: a glittering event to celebrate the opening of its theatre. The company, in the longer term, got a more mixed return on its investment.

Kraanerg lasted four seasons in the repertoire and played a total of twenty-one performances to generally cool critical response but warm, sometimes heated audience reaction. It served as the occasion for the company's first major experiment in audience research, when its Toronto dress-rehearsal was thrown open to a predominantly young and lower-income audience, whose reactions were surveyed.[20] It unquestionably altered the company's approach to programming and audience-building and probably helped to attract a younger, less conservative element into the theatre. In all these respects, the gamble paid off. Many original creations have shorter lives and less effect on a company than this. And *Kraanerg* did not remain an isolated phenomenon. Balanchine's *The Four Temperaments* entered the repertoire in the same year, to be followed in 1969–70 by Petit's *Le Loup* and Flemming Flindt's *The Lesson* and in 1970–1 by Peter Wright's *The Mirror Walkers*. After *Kraanerg*, continental European and contemporary ballet finally gained a real foothold in the National's repertoire.

Martine van Hamel and Linda Fletcher in Solitaire *(right, above). Van Hamel left the company shortly after the National Arts Centre opening, but returned to Toronto ten years later to perform in* Solitaire *once again, at the National Ballet School's twentieth-anniversary celebration performance (right, below). National Ballet School students (left to right) Sabina Allemann, Kim Lightheart, Susan Dromisky, Joy Bain, and Judy Fielman appeared with van Hamel on this occasion; all but Fielman subsequently joined the company.*

But in other important ways, the National lost the *Kraanerg* gamble. As so frequently happens, the aggressively up-to-date quickly became dated. Despite rumours of European productions, Petit never mounted the work on any other company. It thus failed to gain a place in the international repertoire and died when the National stopped performing it. Even the National was denied the kind of mileage it might have hoped for from the work. *Kraanerg* went along on the company's first European tour in 1972, but, at Petit's request, it did not play Paris. The press at the time reported that he had withheld it because of a planned production in Marseilles. In fact, just three years after its première, Petit was afraid it might look *passé* in the capital of France.[21] Divorced from its occasion, *Kraanerg* soon betrayed the limitations of its occasional origin.

The National opened the Arts Centre, however, with much more than just *Kraanerg*. On opening night, *Kraanerg* was preceded by an eight-minute curtain-raiser, choreographed by Grant Strate in a neo-baroque style, to original music by Louis Applebaum.[22] The company played a full week of performances that included, along with *Kraanerg*, Sir Kenneth MacMillan's *Solitaire* and the company's full-length productions of *Romeo and Juliet* and *Swan Lake*. For David Haber, watching from the rear of the theatre, it was *Swan Lake* danced on the Arts Centre stage that really opened the theatre and put the seal on the company's success.[23] What other Canadian arts organization could have brought such variety, such spectacle, such professionalism, and such artistry to the opening of the nation's showcase theatre? It was a far cry from *Les Sylphides* on the Eaton Auditorium stage.

Experimental workshops for a generation of young rebels

Ironically, Strate's curtain-raiser for the National Arts Centre rang down the curtain on his own career as the National's resident choreographer. It was his last work for the company. But his contribution was not to be measured by his choreographic record alone. Before he left the company, he participated in the development of the choreographic workshops that were to provide an invaluable training ground for the volatile talents of a new generation of choreographers.

> *There was so much I wanted to explore in new territory, and I think this was probably more effective with a certain group of young dancers who came up, like Tim Spain and Ann Ditchburn, David Gordon, David Hatch-Walker, Ross McKim. A number of them were coming through the school with a creative fervour, and I fed into that because I found it very interesting. I helped them as much as I could.*[24]

In April 1969, less than a month before the opening of *Kraanerg*, the company had mounted a week-long season of contemporary ballet at the Edward Johnson Building of the University of Toronto. The program was made up of Strate's Stratford Festival commission, *Electre*, and original works by company members Ann Ditchburn, Charles Kirby, and Ross McKim. Now that the main company was entering more enthusiastically into the acquisition of modern repertoire, the time was right for workshops. With Franca's and Oliphant's blessing, a committee made up of Strate, Karen Bowes, an elegant young dancer whose career with the company was all too brief, and Victoria Bertram[25] set about organizing workshops on a frequent, though not quite annual, basis. The low budgets and the informal surroundings of the smaller theatres they used placed the emphasis on experiment and innovation, without the pressures and risks involved in choreographing for the full company. It was no coincidence that the goals of the workshops bore a close resemblance to the goals defined by the Dancer's Council in its attempt to suggest a restructuring of the company in 1968. Bowes, Bertram, and Spain had been three of that Council's five members.

The 1970 workshop, at the Ryerson Theatre, had two different programs with works by ten company members. It received informal adjudication from four distinguished guests: Monique Michaud of the Canada Council; Peter Brinson, director of the Royal Ballet's Ballet for All; Norman Campbell, the CBC television producer who made a specialty of televising the company; and Selma Jeanne Cohen, the American dance critic and scholar and the editor of *Dance Perspectives*.[26]

During a year's sabbatical spent in London, Ann Ditchburn received encouragement and inspiration from Lynn Seymour. Here, in a London studio, she works on an early version of her ballet Kisses, *with Seymour and Frank Frey, one of Seymour's partners from the Berlin Opera Ballet.*

If Franca had been slow to encourage original choreography from company members up to this point, she now moved a little hastily to incorporate the results of the workshops into the regular repertoire. She acknowledged her eagerness in her own report to the Annual General Meeting of 1971.

> *Encouraged by the highly promising ballets presented by Timothy Spain and Ann Ditchburn for the Workshop, and in my somewhat over-anxious desire to push Canadian choreographers in the hope that we could show their works in Europe next May and June, I programmed Tim's* For Internal Use Only *and Ann's* Brown Earth *on opening night. For several reasons, these ballets were not entirely successful. Nevertheless these young choreographers, while temporarily disillusioned, have regained their spirit, and are at present rehearsing new works for the next workshop performances.*[27]

The process, once begun, could not be hurried. The transition from promising workshop piece to a finished work for the full company required careful judgment and nurturing. But given the extraordinary talents coming from the school into the company at the time, Franca could be forgiven a little haste. Victoria Bertram thinks her willingness to promote these young artists was based on deeply felt personal sympathy. 'They were a very talented, very interesting bunch, and I think she was really taken with their energy and their youth. It probably reminded her of her own youth, because she was terribly rebellious, I believe, and very talented.'[28] Much of the rebellion and talent in the group burned itself out, unfortunately, but not without producing some results. The workshops, over the years, offered young choreographers the congenial environment for experimentation that no longer existed in the large dance organization the National had by now become. They thus provided a starting-point for the work of Ann Ditchburn, James Kudelka, Constantin Patsalas, and David Allan, all of whom choreographed major works for the full company later in their careers. Though the company did not place its highest priority on the development of choreographic talent, it had, through the institution of the workshops, at least allowed Canadian choreography to establish a beachhead.

A new *Giselle* recalled the company to its central emphasis.

By her encouragement of the workshops, Franca bowed to the long-standing pressures to modernize the repertoire; she did not, however, change her fundamental strategy for the company's development. While the winds of fashion blew in a contemporary direction, she maintained her long-term goal of creating a major classical ballet company, a goal which had not yet been reached, despite the company's expansion following *Romeo and Juliet*. The debate at this time regarding the acquisition of a new production of *Giselle* demonstrates just how strongly the winds of fashion did blow.

Since the move to the O'Keefe Centre in 1964, there had been only two renewals of existing classical works, *Swan Lake* and *Nutcracker*. The complete *Giselle*, once a staple in the National's repertoire, had last been danced in Hamilton on 17 January 1964; Toronto had not seen it since 7 March 1963. Franca planned a new production for the 1969–70 season.

Although it is, strictly speaking, the prime example of romantic ballet and thus a precursor of the more formal classical tradition represented by the works of Petipa, *Giselle*, originally choreographed for the Paris Opéra in 1841 by Jean Coralli and Jules Perrot, holds a central place in any classical ballet company's repertoire. Its heroine dominates our conception of ballet itself, gripping audiences with her pathos and ethereal serenity and challenging ballerinas to refine their lyric and dramatic gifts. The National's production of *Giselle*, now in mothballs, had been a cornerstone of the early company's repertoire. For historical, artistic, and sentimental reasons, then, a really first-rate new *Giselle* seemed a self-evident, indeed, a long-overdue, addition to the repertoire. But Franca, speaking on behalf of the Artistic Management Council, had to argue forcefully at the board level in order to secure the necessary commitment of funds. She could have spoken very personally, from her experience as the pre-eminent interpreter of the role in the company's earliest years. Instead, her argument touched on the fundamental objectives of the company, the recent trend towards contemporary work, and the underlying significance of the classics to any ballet company, whatever its specific emphasis.

> *Why present* Giselle *today?*
>
> *So long as it is decided to maintain our original policy and strive towards our aims, we must continue to mount the classics. So long as we are training and producing classical dancers of quality in our school and employing them in our company we must continue to mount the classics. While the world's best classical dancers, actors and musicians enjoy performing contemporary works, none of these artists have the incentive to develop without the challenges the classics present. Many of you must have heard of dancers who switch from 'ballet' to 'modern' because they can 'express' themselves better in modern. This is true – they can – but simply because they lack the talent and ability to meet the technical and artistic challenges the classics present.*
>
> *But, when a company possesses dancers who at the least can come close to meeting those classical challenges, they deserve the opportunity to try. If the opportunities are not present here, they will seek employment elsewhere.*[29]

Franca's presentation pulled no punches. The classics, and here she included the repertoire of both the Classical and the Romantic periods, were and always would be the true test of a dancer's capabilities and hence the pinnacle of a company's achievement. To profess a preference for contemporary work was to evade the ultimate challenge presented by the the classics, and Franca had never been one to baulk at a challenge. The impassioned tone of her presentation, however, indicates that Franca had to argue, and argue strongly, for an acquisition that would have required no justification at all fifteen years earlier. Though Franca's goals had remained the same, the climate in which she worked had changed considerably during those fifteen years. She must have felt like a voice crying in the wilderness.

Despite some grumbling from among the dancers,[30] *Giselle* entered the repertoire on 16 April 1970, with Lynn Seymour and the Stuttgart Ballet's Egon Madsen as guest artists, but otherwise without the fanfare that later came to be associated with a major première. Designed by Desmond Heeley and mounted by Peter Wright, yet another alumnus of the Metropolitan Ballet, it remains one of the most satisfying productions of the standard, full-length works in the National's repertoire. Traditional and tasteful rather than idiosyncratic, it displayed from the outset the company's virtues of impeccable production values and well-schooled execution. Wright's expansion of the first-act peasant pas de deux into a pas de quatre was not universally admired, but on the whole critical response recognized the integrity of the production. During the company's 1975 London engagement, the prominent British critic John Percival, writing in the London *Times*, welcomed it with enthusiasm.

> *To bring Peter Wright's production of* Giselle *to London, where we already have two slightly different editions of it in the Royal Ballet's repertory, might seem risky, but the Canadian National Ballet knew what it was about. For one thing, their version is in some important respects an improvement on ours; for another, the ballet shows several of their principals and soloists to excellent advantage. Another advantage of the Canadian production is the marked superiority of its decor.*[31]

Richard Buckle, not always a friend of the company, said simply, 'The National Ballet of Canada's production of *Giselle*, which they have presented at the Coliseum, is much the most intelligent I have seen.'[32]

Its strength lies in its simplicity. Wright's production does not compete with the dancers for the audience's attention and consequently allows their individual abilities and personalities to shine forth from within the central roles with freshness and vitality. Thirteen years after its première, it proved the ideal ballet for Evelyn Hart's historic début with the National. After winning the gold medal in the Varna International Ballet Competition in 1980, Hart became, in the minds of many, a

Overriding the objections of purists, Peter Wright transformed the peasant pas de deux in Giselle *into a pas de quatre. Here (from left to right) Sergiu Stefanschi, Linda Maybarduk, Mary Jago, and Tomas Schramek hold the final pose. The photo highlights the charming detail of Desmond Heeley's designs.*

ballerina in search of a repertoire. Her special talents cried out for the full-length dramatic ballets that the Royal Winnipeg Ballet could not then command. On 26 February 1983, her first Giselle held the sold-out audience at O'Keefe Centre spellbound and proclaimed Hart's homecoming, not to the company but to the Romantic repertoire she was born to dance. She came on her own terms, as the star of the Royal Winnipeg, not as aspirant to membership in the National. Yet the National's *Giselle* offered her the artistic fulfilment she most needed. In its hospitable setting, and with the strong, tactful partnering of Frank Augustyn, her interpretation of the character, fragile, idealistic, consumed as much by her passion for dance as by her love for Albrecht, glowed with intensity and conviction.

In 1970, however, there was no time to linger over the entry of Wright's *Giselle* into the repertoire. One month after its opening, the company flew to Japan to perform *Swan Lake* and *Romeo and Juliet* at Osaka's Expo 70. Mixed programs of *The Four Temperaments*, *Concerto Barocco*, *The Lesson*, *Le Loup*, *Solitaire*, and Grant Strate's *Phases* reflected the company's excursions into contemporary repertoire. Osaka, however, was but a prelude to even greater things.

The long-awaited European début

Talk of a European tour for the company went back at least as far as 1955.[33] In 1972, the dream was finally to become a reality, and the elaborate preparations for the National's European début had to begin almost immediately upon its return from Japan. Given the origins of the company and Franca's own background, the opening engagement of the tour in London, at the Coliseum, was charged with emotional significance.

But the pragmatic reasons for the venture far outweighed the sentimental. Franca knew that without the experience of performing in the world's major ballet centres, the company would never be more than a good provincial troupe. And without international exposure for the company, she would never be able to entice major international choreographers, unless they were old friends, to work with the National. Her attitude towards European touring was hard-headed rather than sentimental. 'It is not particularly vital that we achieve a resounding success in London and Paris. It is important that our company experiences international competition.'[34] The National had come tantalizingly close to realizing its European dream in 1965, when Ian Hunter, the director general of the Commonwealth Arts Festival in England, expressed strong interest in having the National and the Montreal Symphony appear at the Festival with a repertoire that would include *Romeo and Juliet* and *The House of Atreus*.[35] Collaboration with the Montreal Symphony had contributed greatly to the success of *Romeo and Juliet* at its Montreal opening the previous year. But the federal government gave the nod to the Royal Winnipeg Ballet instead, and when, the following year, the company tried to exploit the politically attractive Montreal connection to participate in a government-sponsored tour of French-speaking European countries, Ottawa chose to send the MSO alone.[36]

By 1969, however, David Haber had returned to Canada following a period of work with the William Morris Concert Agency in the United States. He returned, initially, as producer of theatrical attractions at Expo 67, then served as a consultant to the World Festival for Osaka's Expo 70, and eventually became involved in setting up the Canada Council's Touring Office, in addition to carrying out his duties at the National Arts Centre. Through these international connections and his contacts in the Department of External Affairs, he was well placed to assist the National's strenuous lobbying efforts for government support in travelling to Europe. (He had, indeed, worked to bring about the 1970 Osaka engagement.)[37] In the late fall of 1969, Haber, as government representative for cultural trips abroad, was able to announce to the company that the Department of External Affairs had decided to send the National to Europe in the summer of 1972.[38]

The major challenge in planning for the tour, aside from the logistical problems of transporting a company of fifty-two dancers plus artistic and technical staff, sets, and costumes to seven different European cities, lay in the selection of repertoire. In its European début, the company had to show as a competent exponent of the classical repertoire, yet it had to appear distinctive as well, not simply a country-cousin of the major European classical companies. To that end, the company selected Bruhn's *La Sylphide* and *Swan Lake* as its two full-length programs. Outside Denmark, the complete *La Sylphide* was still something of a novelty, and Bruhn's radical reworking of *Swan Lake* guaranteed the National a degree of critical attention which a more traditionally mounted classic would not have commanded. On the contemporary side, apart from a few performances of *Kraanerg*, the National presented several mixed programs of short works which included Wright's *The Mirror Walkers*, Eliot Feld's *Intermezzo*, and, in a graceful acknowledgement of Antony Tudor's importance to the young company, *Fandango* and *The Judgment of Paris*. *Romeo and Juliet* could not be shown because of the company's agreement with Cranko forbidding its production in major European centres. No original Canadian choreography was presented.

The tour's main purpose was unquestionably to introduce the company to a knowledgeable European audience and to expose it to European critical opinion. But despite a generally hospitable climate, the company was not a hot item on the European circuit; box-office had to be taken into consideration along with artistic goals. A guest star would assure good box-office, but at the risk of obscuring the company itself. Erik Bruhn's name presented itself as the obvious solution. With two of his works as major elements of the tour repertoire, and with his eight-year association with the company as choreographer, coach, and teacher at the school,

Bruhn already had a special status with the National. A guest yet not a guest, by his presence he would build box-office without throwing too large a shadow over the company. Accordingly, Bruhn was engaged to appear as guest artist with the company in *La Sylphide* and perhaps a new pas de deux in London and Paris, the two major stops on the tour.[39]

But Bruhn did not fulfil the engagement. In late December 1971, the undiagnosed chronic pain which he had suffered for some years reached such agonizing proportions that he abruptly announced his retirement from dancing, after a final performance as James in Harald Lander's production of *La Sylphide* with American Ballet Theatre.[40] The National received formal notification in early January 1972 that Bruhn would not appear with them five months hence on the European tour.[41] Bruhn's withdrawal placed Franca in an impossible quandary. Despite her desire to showcase the company itself, despite her long-standing reluctance to rely on guest artists, the company had to turn to guest stars to create some publicity hype for the tour. At Bruhn's suggestion, Niels Kehlet of the Royal Danish Ballet appeared in *La Sylphide* in London and Paris, while Georges Piletta repeated his role in *Kraanerg* in London, Brussels, and Glasgow. Plans for an original pas de deux for Bruhn and Veronica Tennant were scrapped; Stuttgart's Marcia Haydée and Richard Cragun appeared instead at the gala opening in a performance of Cranko's *Legende*. On 17 May 1972, the curtain rose on the National Ballet's all-important London début.

London was home to an influential international ballet press and to a remarkable concentration of ballet professionals whose opinions on matters of dance were authoritative. But for Franca, playing London was like the culmination of a pilgrimage to a holy shrine. In London, all the important people from her past, her mentors and teachers, Rambert, de Valois, and above all Stanislas Idzikowski, would see what she had managed to achieve on her own. The company appeared at the Coliseum, a notch below the Royal Opera House, Covent Garden, whose exclusive portals opened by invitation only, and certainly not to a newcomer like the National, but a distinct notch above Sadler's Wells Theatre, where new touring companies traditionally made their London débuts.[42] (To Ann Ditchburn, the Coliseum was 'a more honest place than Covent Garden for foreign people to play in London.')[43] For company members old enough to remember the Royal Alexandra Theatre, the ornate décor of the Coliseum had a familiar, welcoming air, but to the post-O'Keefe generation, the excitement of the London opening was heightened by the experience of performing in such faded but authentic Edwardian elegance. Those with a sense of history knew that the Coliseum, despite its music hall origins, had presented the greatest dancers of the past, including the Diaghilev Ballets Russes in their triumphant return to London after the First World War.

Stanislas Idzikowski, seated in the Coliseum's auditorium in 1972, had danced Harlequin in *Le Carnaval* on its stage in 1918. A circle, of which many of the young artists on the stage were unaware, had been completed.

Despite his inability to perform, Bruhn did accompany the dancers to lend moral support to their important venture. Veronica Tennant, although deprived of her chance to dance with him, felt his presence in London, as so often in her career. 'Even though he didn't dance with me in London, he was there. Erik was very much there, before the performance, after the performance. Erik has been there, I realize, all my life, from the time I started.'[44] Tentatively but forcefully, the Bruhn influence was asserting itself, preparing the way for his much fuller commitment to the company in years to come.

The London press coverage was positive, but not ecstatic. *Dance and Dancers* gave it three separate articles, and commented favourably on Bruhn's interpolated pas de deux for Effy and James in the first act of *La Sylphide*. Two of its reviewers especially liked his innovative staging of *Swan Lake* in two acts instead of the traditional four.[45] Reporting on the company's visit for the *Dancing Times*, James Monahan commented on both its reception and its characteristics.

The company returned to London's Coliseum in 1987. With portable barres set up on stage, the dancers undertake the daily regimen of company class, looking out past the proscenium arch to the brightly lit auditorium beyond. Principal ballet mistress Magdalena Popa (centre, facing camera) teaches class. Donald Dawson can be identified in the extreme right foreground.

> *Everyone, the critics included, wanted to like them and everyone did like them – but … Not all the critics, of course, put equal stress on that 'but'; nearly all of them, however, made at least as much of what had still to be achieved as of what had been achieved already. London's good-will was tinged with avuncular condescension. Before the event I shared, I must confess, in that attitude. But the company taught me to see it differently.*
>
> *We had been told to expect a company which had no star-ballerina and no choreography, or at least no choreographer, of its own; to expect also to find that it was well-schooled. This description turned out to be dead accurate, and yet misleading; it had not led me to expect that the one plus would so well compensate for the two minuses.*[46]

Though the company could not be said to have taken London by storm, it established its international credentials with this visit. Following the Coliseum engagement, the company made stops in Stuttgart, Paris, Brussels, Glasgow, Lausanne, and Monte Carlo. The Paris press was less enthusiastic than the London, but overall the company's competence in presenting the classical repertoire, its flair for attractive productions and tasteful innovation, its concern for stylistic ensemble, and its reservoir of young, developing talent were seen and duly noted. It had yet to impress the international community, however, as an ensemble of genuinely distinctive style and authority, and, aside from London, Stuttgart, and Paris, the tour had not played cities known as major ballet centres. The National had made its presence felt, but had not yet asserted its own identity.

The Sleeping Beauty forced unprecedented growth.

The effort and accomplishments of the European tour were immediately eclipsed, in that event-filled year of 1972, by the realization of yet another long-standing company dream. Franca knew from the outset that any company claiming to specialize in the classical repertoire had to perform the ultimate test-piece of the canon, the full-length Petipa *Sleeping Beauty*. In the fall of 1972, a scant two months after the company's last performance on the European tour, the complete *Sleeping Beauty* was to enter the repertoire at last. But not just any *Sleeping Beauty*; this lavish production, the largest and most complex undertaking in the company's history, was to be the cornerstone of a major North American tour, culminating in the National's début at the Metropolitan Opera House in New York, under the auspices of the Hurok organization.

Sol Hurok, the foremost artistic and theatrical promoter in the world, had introduced the Royal Ballet to North America and kept its international profile high for many years. He held the key to all the major theatres of the continent; his sponsorship of a theatrical attraction guaranteed access to all the number one houses on the circuit. Moreover, he represented the superstars. Re-enter Rudolf Nureyev, the star on whose drawing power this particular Hurok scheme was predicated. Nureyev was to choreograph the entire production and dance in almost every performance of *Sleeping Beauty* and the other standard repertoire of the National throughout the gruelling, continent-wide tour. This combination of the European début and the Nureyev North American tour gave the National more international exposure in 1972 than ever before, but at the price of a superhuman expenditure of effort from each of its members that stretched the company's organizational structure to the breaking-point.

The National had grown gradually from a troupe of twenty-nine dancers in 1951 to a company that hovered around the forty mark through the late 1950s and early 1960s. The acquisition of *Romeo and Juliet* and the move to the O'Keefe raised that number into the fifties; gradual expansion resulted in an all-time high of fifty-five dancers on the roster for the seasons of 1967–8 and 1968–9. The 1968 financial crisis took its toll on company size, however, reducing the company drastically to its earlier level of forty-one dancers by 1970–1. Reduced numbers limited the choice of repertoire and left the company dangerously understaffed to provide understudies or replacements for injured dancers, a critical problem on tour. In 1971–2, company size jumped from forty-one to fifty-two dancers, to accommodate the needs of the European tour; for *Sleeping Beauty* in 1972–3, the company added thirteen more dancers, for a total of sixty-five. It has stayed above the sixty mark ever since.

These numbers speak of more than mere size. A larger company is a more complex, less informal organization, as David Adams had anticipated at the time of the first major expansion for *Romeo and Juliet*. It can handle a wider range of repertoire, but it also has to cope with a greater range of competing interests among dancers, more of whom are of a calibre to hope for major roles. By the time of the European tour and *Sleeping Beauty*, Lois Smith and Earl Kraul had retired; David Adams was long gone; and Galina Samsova and Martine van Hamel had flashed across the horizon and moved on to major international careers. But the company for the 1970s boasted talent, some of it new and some of it already established, that set a new standard of proficiency and a new character for the ensemble. Five ballerinas vied for attention: Veronica Tennant, Karen Kain, Vanessa Harwood, Mary Jago, and Nadia Potts. Frank Augustyn emerged as the first internationally acclaimed male dancer the National had produced, but the older men – Tomas Schramek, Sergiu Stefanschi, and Hazaros Surmeyan – gave strength and depth to the male roster. *Sleeping Beauty* was a challenge, but it was a challenge the developing company longed for.

Preparations for *Sleeping Beauty* could not wait for the completion of the European tour. Although rehearsals were scheduled for August, after the company's return, with a September opening in Ottawa production of sets and costumes coincided exactly with preparations for the tour and, indeed, with the tour itself. Dieter Penzhorn, at that time the company's production manager, had the job of coordinating the production aspects of this mammoth undertaking. There were, he remembers, 'so many costumes to be done, and there just wasn't the time when the company was here to do it all, so we brought some of the wardrobe staff to England to do a lot of the fittings while we were in London.'[47] Even the National, which by now had had some experience with staging spectacles, had never encountered as opulent an imagination as that of Nicholas Georgiadis, the Greek-born designer of such Covent Garden spectacles as MacMillan's *Romeo and Juliet*, who was to provide the sumptuous visual setting for Nureyev's vision of the work. But once the Hurok contract was signed, there was no looking back, not even when it became apparent that Franca's preliminary budget for the show, an astronomical two hundred and fifty thousand dollars, was inadequate to the commitments that had been made. Franca recalls the frustrations of dealing with Nureyev and Georgiadis, who conceived of the show only as it would appear on the major stages of the continent, without any thought for the exigencies of touring.

Nicholas Georgiadis originally wanted a fleet of coaches in Sleeping Beauty*'s hunting scene. Though he eventually compromised on this point, he still created one of the most lavish, and expensive, stage spectacles in the company's entire repertoire.*

> *By this time we had already signed a contract with Hurok, so there was nothing we could do except try to persuade them to cut down. Poor Jimmy Ronaldson, our wardrobe supervisor, was going crazy in London with Georgiadis, who was picking out the most expensive silks and brocades he could find. Nureyev and Georgiadis were under the impression that they could build the production for the National Arts Centre–size stage. And of course we don't have anything like that anywhere else in Canada.*[48]

The board, which had seen financial crisis in its day, blanched at the cost overruns. Bankruptcy loomed, and the year of the company's greatest achievements to date teetered on the verge of catastrophe.

A major challenge to Franca's authority

Worse was in store. In the midst of all the anticipation, preparation, and confusion caused by the European tour and and the production demands of *Sleeping Beauty*, the administrative tensions that had simmered within the company since 1968 finally came to a rolling boil. The rival interests of artistic and administrative control, which had defined the 1968 crisis, declared themselves decisively in 1972, in a series of events which Lyman Henderson, then president of the board, has come to refer to as the Palace Revolution. Within the board and the staff, the company was split between rival factions, one backing Wally Russell, the National's general manager, the other loyal to Franca and fighting to maintain her position and authority.

On the personal level, the stakes were high and the in-fighting fierce. Franca sees the struggle as a personal attack, an attempt to remove her from the artistic direction of the company. 'The board and Wally Russell were very close, and there were certain members of the board who really wanted to get me out. And so they became in league.'[49] Nor was she alone in this interpretation of events. Lyman Henderson remembers it as a time 'when a dissident section of the board, largely spearheaded by the general manager, decided it was time to get rid of Celia Franca.'[50] Veronica Tennant tells a similar story. In her position as the dancers' representative on the board, she interpreted events as

> *a plot to terminate Miss Franca's directorship. Basically we rallied to stop it because we felt it to be very, very wrong, especially at that particular time. And to be done for reasons that didn't particularly take into account what the dancers might feel. But it didn't seem to originate from within the dancer core of the company; it was more a machination within the board at that time.*[51]

Rumour had it that the dissident group intended to approach Erik Bruhn and offer him the position of artistic director.[52] Just when the company needed to present itself in the best possible light on the international stage, it was rent by internal dissension.

Betty Oliphant, who had been associate artistic director of the company since 1968, had by now achieved a greater independence from Franca than she had had earlier, when she was ballet mistress. She certainly had as fierce a dedication as anyone to the company into which she had poured her energies and whose dancers she groomed at the National Ballet School. Indeed, by 1972 the company was substantially made up of graduates of the school, like Tennant herself, Kain, Potts, and Augustyn, many of whom Oliphant had known and worked with since their childhoods. A more astute political survivor than Franca, she assessed the situation and responded to it, not out of personal loyalty, but out of concern for the future of the company. She recognized that compromise between the opposing forces was no longer a possibility, as it had seemed to be in 1968; however difficult the terms, a choice had finally to be made. And if the choice forced upon the company had to be between an artistic director and a general manager, the issue was clear.

Franca with Dame Ninette de Valois, the woman who had originally recommended her to Canada, at the National Ballet of Canada's London début in 1972.

It reached the point where the board was willing to get rid of Celia and keep Wally

> *Russell. And that's where everybody rallied around to support Celia. Not because we really believed in her that much, but because we certainly did not believe in Wally Russell and we found the whole exercise a really rotten stunt. I organized a meeting, and every single department of the company was represented: the wardrobe, the musical, the artists, every area. And each person presented their point of view, which was that Celia certainly had faults, but there was no way that anybody in the company was prepared to stay if Wally took over and Celia was fired.*[53]

This concerted demonstration of support for Franca forced Russell's hand, and he resigned just two months before the National's departure for London. The company had little warning. He had first tendered his resignation in January 1972, to take effect after the European tour, and then, in March, after the events described by Oliphant, he abruptly walked out.[54] The company was left, on the eve of its first European engagement and in the midst of preparations for *Sleeping Beauty*, without a general manager.

Seen in organizational rather than personal terms, the 1972 crisis simply continued the conflicts that had been deferred, but not resolved, in 1968. At that point, faced with Franca's resignation, the board had tried to assert both the autonomy of the artistic director and the authority of the general manager. But that tenuous balance had not held for long. During the intervening period, the general manager's position, particularly in relation to the board, had strengthened significantly. In the effort to bring sound business principles to bear on an artistic organization, the general manager and the board naturally became allies in a common cause. As Franca puts it, the board 'didn't want the headaches of deficits. They just wanted to be sure that the budget was clean, and the general manager's position became very, very important.'[55] But in the last analysis, however important it may have been to rein in artistic temperament and break it to the bit of financial prudence, artistic vision had to remain in the forefront, driving the entire enterprise. The reassertion, on this occasion, of the centrality of Franca's position within the company amounted to a public declaration that the cart would not be put before the horse. If a working balance could not be achieved between the artistic and the management sides of the company, then the artistic must win out. From a situation she had not precipitated, Franca thus emerged in a much stronger position than the one her 1968 resignation had created for her. But even so, the spectre of artistic versus managerial authority had not been finally laid to rest. Nor would it be, until well after Franca's departure from the company.

Because Russell's successor, Gerry Eldred, could not take over the position in time for the European tour, interim help had to be found. In such circumstances, the fact that the tour could take place as planned testifies to the soundness of

Russell's preliminary arrangements and the competence and efficiency of the company's staff. The interim help came in the person of David Haber, seconded from his duties at the National Arts Centre and the Canada Council Touring Office to guide the company through the administrative details of a tour in whose planning he had already been involved.[56] Haber retained a strong affection for Franca from his days as the company's first stage manager. His reappearance just at the time of Russell's departure rescued Franca from potential disaster; overnight, a serious rival to her authority had been replaced by a staunch ally. Haber's presence provided welcome support for someone who valued personal loyalty as much as Franca did. As events unfolded, he turned out to be more than just an interim replacement.

Succession planning

In all the tumult of the events of 1972, Franca had other important matters to consider. Despite the reassertion of confidence in her leadership following the Palace Revolution, she was ready to lighten her own load. After twenty years of living the National Ballet of Canada night and day, she wanted some relief.

Ever since her arrival in Canada, Franca's personal life had taken a back seat to the concerns of the ballet. Her 1951 marriage to Bert Anderson, whom she had met shortly after coming to Canada, ended in divorce, and in 1960 she married James Morton, the principal clarinet with the National Ballet Orchestra. In the early 1970s, when Morton moved to Ottawa to join the National Arts Centre Orchestra, Franca added the stresses of commuting between Ottawa and Toronto to her already impossible schedule. By 1972, she was ready to think of a successor, and of diminishing her daily involvement with the company so that she could devote more time to herself and her husband.

She discussed possible successors frankly with Betty Oliphant, and, inevitably, Erik Bruhn's name came up in their conversations. But the two women did not see eye to eye on the question of his suitability. His recent retirement from dancing and presence with the company in London served as catalyst for a reconsideration. One night, after the curtain had come down at the Coliseum, Franca and Oliphant returned with Bruhn to Rudolf Nureyev's home for a late-night supper. Their recollections of the evening illustrate the opposing points of view of these two women whose united front on company matters had once been unshakeable. Franca:

> *Betty and I had a dinner with Erik one night after one of our performances at the Coliseum, and I fell asleep after it. It was in Rudi's house; Rudi wasn't there, but Erik was staying in Rudi's house. And I knew immediately then, although Betty and I had discussed Erik, that Erik was not right for the job, not at that time. His health had not*

> *been good, he was very nervous, and I just didn't think that he would be the right person for the company – at that time. But his association with the company and with the school continued, so that when it was the right time he was ready.*[57]

Oliphant:

> *I told her that Erik would be a wonderful director for the company, and she was so scornful. We went out after the show at the Coliseum to Nureyev's place; he wasn't there, and Erik was staying there. We went there about two in the morning, and at six in the morning Erik was still talking in this very neurotic way he has. He used to be very paranoid about people being out to get him. I listened to Erik all that time; she fell asleep. And as we left she said, 'Now you see why he can't be the director of the company.' But anyway, when he was, he was superb.*[58]

Bruhn was not ready for such responsibility at this time. And in 1972, Franca was not in a position to recognize his suitability for the job. The characteristic that she describes as 'nervous,' Oliphant as 'neurotic' and 'paranoid,' constituted a real obstacle for her, when the issue at stake was something as close to her as the National Ballet. Franca had to be able to trust those with whom she worked, and it can be difficult to trust someone who veils his essential character as Bruhn evidently did. Oliphant recognized that inaccessibility herself, but refused to be put off by it. 'He had built his own defences, and you couldn't have reached him in a million years. In fact you might have destroyed him if you'd tried to reach him in the psychological sense.'[59] Franca's reluctance to hand over the company of her creation to someone who could not be reached is hardly surprising. Even though it was an academic argument at this point, it illustrated the significant change that had come into the relationship between Oliphant and Franca. The two women who had so long and so successfully shared a common vision now moved and worked independently.

Franca had another important conversation on the European tour, this one with David Haber while she was in Monte Carlo, the last stop on the tour.[60] At this time, she broached to him the idea of his joining the company permanently as her close associate, someone who could relieve her of significant portions of her professional duties and thus give her the personal freedom she sought. There was no explicit understanding at the time that such a relationship would eventually develop into Haber's taking over the company, but anything might happen. As Haber puts it: 'Celia, consciously and unconsciously, was always keeping options open.'[61] Franca, for her part, recognized in Haber 'an old theatrical friend' who had bailed the company out of a difficult situation after Russell's sudden departure. 'He was always crazy about ballet, and he had worked with me in the early years, and he had a broad theatrical experience that was fantastic.'[62] Haber had proved his worth and won Franca's trust. An old friendship had been re-established and a new alliance formed.

CHAPTER SIX

I Don't Believe in a Flimsy *Sleeping Beauty*

The pros and cons of the Nureyev connection

On the company's return from Europe, the Juggernaut that was *Sleeping Beauty* was already gaining momentum. In choosing to accept the conditions of the association with Nureyev and the Hurok organization, the company had taken a carefully calculated risk. The disadvantages, clearly recognized from the outset, lay in the arbitrary control which Hurok exercised over the venture. Hurok had responsibility for the tour; the company had responsibility for mounting the production; and Nureyev had artistic control over the entire project. The company was left with a huge financial risk and very little ability to control its own destiny.

Hurok had Nureyev under contract and needed a company to show him off in North America in the proper setting of a full-length Petipa classic. The National,

OPPOSITE: The Sleeping Beauty *tested the company, just as the Rose Adagio tested its ballerinas. Veronica Tennant, one of the company's finest Princess Auroras, held aloft triumphantly by her four cavaliers. (David Nixon can be identified on the right.)*

ABOVE: Nureyev demanded both lavish production values and careful attention to stylistic detail. Tennant's arms, shoulders, and feet mirror the line of Nureyev's leg and torso in the final pose of the grand pas de deux from the last act of The Sleeping Beauty.

with its North American reputation for lavish staging and its considerable touring experience, would do. But Nureyev's drawing power at the box-office unquestionably provided the motivating force for the enterprise and consequently gave him what amounted to despotic control. As choreographer and star of the production, slated to appear in virtually every performance, Nureyev had to be kept happy. And the terms of the contract were such that Hurok's financial responsibility applied only to the tour itself; the cost of mounting the production to Nureyev's satisfaction fell to the National alone. Franca summed up the situation succinctly in some private notes she made regarding the 'cons' of accepting the Hurok offer. '1) No Nureyev, no job. 2) No new productions for Nureyev, no job. 3) Nureyev has final artistic say because our contract with Hurok dictates that if Nureyev doesn't dance the N.B. doesn't get paid.'[1]

The advantages lay in the enormously increased number of performance opportunities for the company (except for its leading male dancers, who toured under the shadow of the omnipresent superstar), the entry to the Metropolitan Opera House in New York, which Hurok's connections guaranteed, and the chance for the company to work on a daily basis with an artist of Nureyev's experience and stature. And the National would finally acquire a production of *Sleeping Beauty*, the one major Petipa work missing from its repertoire as a classical company. On balance, these factors were judged to outweigh the real risks and frustrations the collaboration entailed. With their eyes wide open, Franca and the company had decided to take the plunge; now, in late 1972, in the midst of the chaos thus unleashed, it was all the company could do to keep the project going. Reflection and evaluation were luxuries reserved for some later date.

The difficulties which the company experienced in trying to keep the production costs under some semblance of control paled beside the experience of coping with Nureyev's demands in the rehearsal room. Nureyev had already staged a complete *Sleeping Beauty*, with designs by Georgiadis, for La Scala in Milan and thought of the National's production as a 'second reading' of the work.[2] As is frequently the case in such circumstances, the ballet's steps themselves were taught to the company by one of Nureyev's collaborators from the earlier production. The National had closed its European tour in Monte Carlo on 3 July 1972, and, as Franca later reported:

> *In mid-July, 1972, Gilda Majocchi, a ballet mistress from La Scala, Milan, sent by Nureyev, arrived in Toronto to teach our dancers Nureyev's version of the Petipa choreography. She was pleasant and efficient. However, when Nureyev arrived, on August 3rd, he proceeded to change much of what Mme Majocchi had set – and not always necessarily for the better. Further, Nureyev insisted on having the whole company present during his rehearsals, whether they were needed or not, which meant that the other ballets in the*

> *repertoire were insufficiently rehearsed – with the exception of* The Moor's Pavane. *We had difficulty in getting Nureyev's co-operation during our photo calls at Ottawa's National Arts Centre, and the staging and dress rehearsals were nightmarish.*[3]

Not all Nureyev's choreographic changes were whimsical. He had had much larger forces at his disposal at La Scala; for the National (as large as it had ever been at sixty-five dancers), he had to trim numbers and hence modify the choreography. And to cope with the demands of touring (virtually unheard of at La Scala), he had to allow changes in design and construction as well. For all that he seemed intransigent to his Canadian collaborators, Nureyev thought of himself as making concessions.

> *First of all, from this enormous, mammoth production of La Scala, I have to draw out of Georgiadis a production which would be able to tour, that stage-hands could move, and still the story had to be told and the production had to look awesome, because I don't believe in a flimsy* Sleeping Beauty.

Nureyev choreographed *The Sleeping Beauty* in homage to his idealized memories of the Kirov Ballet in Leningrad,[4] the company of his youth and a state-supported organization with hundreds of dancers in its employ. With La Scala and the Kirov as his models, small wonder that he deployed dancers as lavishly as Georgiadis did

His trademark hat firmly in place, Nureyev perches on a chair back and surveys the crowded studio with gimlet eyes. Veronica Tennant concentrates on a pirouette in the foreground, with Karen Kain and Vanessa Harwood visible in the background. Susa Menck, the company choreologist, takes notes.

fabrics and materials. Yet he did nothing simply for the sake of extravagance, everything in obedience to the dictates of his imagination. His imagination, however, functioned on a scale the National had never before encountered.

Even the demands on company rehearsal time, so inefficient from an administrative point of view, had their purpose. Nureyev wanted the whole company immersed in the entire ballet, so that it could give a coherent, convincing account of the work. And he wanted to push all the dancers to go beyond anything they had done before. Mary Jago remembers the gruelling rehearsal period.

> *He made us do run-throughs of* Sleeping Beauty *twice a day. And it's a hard, hard ballet; technically, it's hard, hard, hard. He had all his Auroras running it every single day full out. You never marked anything. He pushed us – he worked us hard – but he also was very giving. He pushed you hard because he knew you were capable of more. His reasons and his intentions were so productive.*[5]

Though Franca, who had other repertoire to think of besides *Sleeping Beauty*, chafed under the difficulties created by Nureyev's all-consuming passion for detail, the dancers thrived on it. For this generation of performers, Nureyev's coaching in *Sleeping Beauty* provided the same zeal for professionalism and authentic classical style that Franca had instilled in another, technically less proficient group twenty years earlier, when she first mounted *Les Sylphides*. For Karen Kain, whose rising career was propelled into the international arena by her association with Nureyev, the fabled tantrums and displays of temper told little of the artist underneath. Before his untimely death, she spoke of the nature of their partnership.

> *He bullied me, but underneath it he always made sure that I knew that he really cared about me. He really believed in me. He was never cruel to me. He did have his tempers sometimes, and I would know when to stay away from him, but he never really took things out on me, and he was very generous. I think that's the key word. Not all artists of his calibre are generous people, but he is a very generous person. I think that's what makes you forgive any of the other little things in his character that are difficult. He was special to me. But he took time with everybody, every member of the corps de ballet, and he made them dance better.*[6]

Not only did they dance better, but, according to Veronica Tennant, the company discovered essential performance values under his teaching and goading.

> *He'd say, 'You must eat up the stage and so audience will go wild.' He gave great lessons in theatricality. I think probably we weren't that theatrical a company before Rudolf, and it was after working with him that you realized that this was very much a reciprocal occasion with the audience. And that it was a communicative art. And that, yes,*

there were ways of getting response, not only in an adulatory sense, but in a sense of the audience being a participatory force in the performance.[7]

Though Nureyev's presence gave the male dancers less opportunity to shine, it nevertheless opened other kinds of experience to them. Frank Augustyn, at the time a young and relatively inexperienced principal dancer, got considerable exposure in the bravura role of the Bluebird and did, on the rare occasions when Nureyev was not dancing, take on the role of the Prince. Tomas Schramek had come to the National from a background in folk-dancing in his native Slovakia. At the time of Nureyev's arrival, he was not yet a principal and did not aspire to the Prince roles that were Nureyev's special domain. He shared the stage with him frequently, however, in supporting male roles like Catalinon in *Don Juan* and Gurn in *La Sylphide*. He remembered a more complex, less directly generous mentor than did the women.

He has helped me quite a bit. I don't mean actually physically, because he is not very generous in teaching and giving you correction – he wouldn't tell you – he would tell somebody else, and then it was up to that person to go to you and say, 'I heard him say that if you do this it will help you.' Hardly ever would he come and say it directly, unless he would do that to his partners.[8]

The *Sleeping Beauty* rehearsal period did far more than simply teach the dancers a new and important piece of repertoire. It opened their eyes to the Russian ballet heritage (albeit interpreted through the westernized experience of the most celebrated defector of the day) and to the imperious demands of a difficult, uncompromising, meticulous, and inspiring imagination. The Nureyev phenomenon unleashed itself unchecked upon the company and moved the dancers to a new level of professionalism, a new conception of their art, and a new set of demands upon their own performances.

The rehearsal hall wasn't big enough for two large egos. Franca, whose real love was working in the studio with the dancers, and who was herself cast as the wicked fairy, Carabosse, the major dramatic character role in the ballet, removed herself to the administrative offices and allowed Nureyev a free rein with the company members. Victoria Bertram, as the second-cast Carabosse, wound up running interference between them.

When we were doing Carabosse together, she'd never show up for any of the rehearsals, because she and Rudolf were not getting on very well. She couldn't stand another master in the studio – one had to give in, and she just would not show up. I had to do all the rehearsals and then write it down and take it upstairs and talk to her about the role because she'd have to do the full rehearsals.[9]

Franca, for her part, was willing to give Nureyev the latitude he required. With the administrative responsibilities involved in the production and the tour, she had not wanted to perform at all.

> *In rehearsal, he was actually quite good to me because he admired me as a performer, ever since 1964, when he saw me do Madge the witch in Erik's production of* La Sylphide. *That was why he insisted that I do the Carabosse role, which I didn't want to do because I knew I was going to have my hands full. There I was with a million things on my mind, trying to remember his choreography for this Carabosse.*

Among her many administrative headaches, she had to deal with Nureyev's cavalier attitude towards union rehearsal regulations, which he had a tendency to ignore if the required break interrupted his creative process.[10] Whether he was aware of causing any difficulties or not, Nureyev appreciated the welcome and the freedom he received. 'Celia Franca greeted me with nice open arms, of course now and then imposing her ideas, remembering Covent Garden version, or Sadler's Wells. But she was tactful and she kept away and didn't get into my soup.'[11] His comment emphasizes the fundamental stylistic difference between the two. *The Sleeping Beauty* had been the Sadler's Wells' (and later the Royal Ballet's) signature piece, the vehicle with which it created a North American sensation and established its international reputation. Like all the de Valois generation, Franca, who had herself danced the Bluebird pas de deux at Sadler's Wells,[12] could lay a special claim to the ballet. But Nureyev, who had by this time had ample experience of the later Royal Ballet versions staged by Ashton and MacMillan and had often partnered its legendary Aurora, Margot Fonteyn, nevertheless considered himself the pipeline to the authentic tradition of the ballet, as preserved at the Kirov, the theatre where *Sleeping Beauty* had had its première. Though the fact received little public recognition, the National's production of this crown jewel of the Royal Ballet's repertoire represented a break from the English tradition, not a perpetuation of it. The production which Franca had long regarded as an absolute necessity for a classical company,[13] and in which she must have had a certain proprietary interest, owed little to the English tradition or to her personal storehouse of knowledge.

On the road with *The Sleeping Beauty*

The Sleeping Beauty opened at Ottawa's National Arts Centre, one of the largest and best equipped stages on the continent, on 1 September 1972. Both Georgiadis and David Hersey, the lighting designer, had worked to the specifications of the NAC, thus assuming conditions that could not be duplicated anywhere else on the tour. Even at the superbly equipped National Arts Centre, the huge, cumbersome set

Because the large flight of steps had to be brought on silently and smoothly, the vision scene caused headaches for the company's long-suffering technical staff, especially on tour. For audiences, however, the entry of Princess Aurora among her court of naiads was one of the highlights of the ballet. Kristine Soleri, as the Lilac Fairy, reveals Veronica Tennant to an adoring Rudolf Nureyev.

pieces, like the grand staircase and the three-dimensional chandelier the size of a small room, created problems onstage and impossibilities for storage in the wings or the flies when not required. The chandelier alone took two stage-hands several hours to assemble and could not be flown out of sight because the spacing of the overhead lines and pipes would not allow free clearance for an object of its depth. (The three-dimensional model was soon replaced with a two-dimensional one that could be flown.) Set pieces designed to take advantage of the maximum NAC stage height snagged on the lines whenever they were moved. Drunk with the technical riches the Arts Centre afforded, Hersey used some three hundred lamps in his lighting plot, many more than the company could travel with.[14] Having survived the chaos of a week's production time at the NAC, the technical crews then had to endure a baptism of fire on the road.

After playing the NAC and the Place des Arts in Montreal, the show went on to Philadelphia, the first of the significantly smaller stages into which Hurok had booked the company on its cross-continent tour. Larry Beevers, who had, after a serious injury, just made the transition from dancer to assistant stage manager, recalls the experience vividly.

> *I remember someone saying to Georgiadis, 'What do we do in these small theatres?' 'Well, that's up to you.' Now we were stuck with a huge set going into smaller theatres. And our intermissions became so long, and our shows became so long. Three and a half hours in those days was nothing for* Sleeping Beauty.[15]

The wear and tear of awkward scene-changes caused damage to the set. Attempts to follow the original lighting plot without the resources of the NAC left parts of the show in semi-darkness. Road crew kept on quitting, unwilling to take the strain of the long hours and the physical demands of assembling and striking the huge set within the unyielding, impossible deadlines of the touring schedule.[16]

Somehow, *Sleeping Beauty* staggered through the autumn portion of the tour, into the O'Keefe Centre and a Toronto opening night as exciting as any in the company's history. Thanks to the resourcefulness of the technical crew, the dedication of the dancers, and the unflagging energy of everyone involved, the curtain rose to reveal not the difficulties and shortcomings of a technically complicated production, but the ornate splendour of Nureyev's vision of *Sleeping Beauty*. It was, as Nureyev had intended, a substantial, even a weighty production, and the dancers, in some cases, had not yet gained the full authority necessary to carry it off. But in Veronica Tennant, the company had an Aurora who could subdue the technical demands of the role to an affecting impersonation of character, and in the Bluebird pas de deux, it rejoiced in the electrifying performances of Karen Kain and Frank Augustyn giving audiences a foretaste of the partnership that was to develop between them. Nureyev may have been the star, but he was far from being the evening's only attraction. This *Sleeping Beauty* was a major achievement in itself as well as a harbinger of things to come. The most extravagant production in the company's history had justified itself as the most vivid realization the National had ever achieved of ballet's central, fairy-tale fantasy.

Following the Toronto run and the television taping in the O'Keefe Centre, *The Sleeping Beauty* was given a brief rest. The dancers embarked on the Christmas round of *Nutcracker*s in Windsor, Ottawa, Toronto, and London (with a few *Swan Lake*s thrown in for good measure), while production regrouped its forces for an assault on *Beauty*'s unsolved problems. After set maintenance and repairs had been effected in the Toronto workshops, the production department, en route to Vancouver for the opening of the 1973 portion of the Hurok tour, took a detour to Regina, where a large enough stage was available for the week of production work essential to the success of the remainder of the tour. At the Hurok organization's expense, the show was set up and properly 'trimmed,' all the pieces positioned so that lighting pipes were masked and wing space would not show from anywhere in the audience. Then proper measurements and markings were made, so that the desired effect could be duplicated in any theatre on the tour. David Hersey returned from England to relight the entire production to the specifications of the touring electrical equipment.[17] With somewhat lighter minds, the company resumed the *Sleeping Beauty* tour; its demands were now merely unmanageable, not completely impossible.

The Hurok itinerary was daunting, exhausting. Carrying as repertoire *Beauty*, *Swan Lake*, and a mixed program of *La Sylphide*, *The Moor's Pavane*, and *Fandango* (with occasional additions of the pas de deux from *The Nutcracker* or *Le Loup*), the National worked its way across the continent for four uninterrupted months, routinely doing a minimum of seven performances in six days with never more than one day off in seven. While *Swan Lake* concluded the run in one city, an advance crew would proceed to the next to begin the set-up for *Sleeping Beauty*. For the dancers, the tour became an endurance test. As Veronica Tennant, who shared the role of Aurora with Nadia Potts and Vanessa Harwood, recalls: 'Absolutely everybody was stretched to their limit. All the ballerinas were on stage all the time. If they were on in Aurora one night, they were doing Fairies the next.' A short break of eight days preceded the final engagement of the tour at the Metropolitan Opera House, but the company was still exhausted when it opened the New York performances.

The Moor's Pavane, *José Limón's dance dramatization of* Othello, *provided a contrast to the classical purity of* The Sleeping Beauty *on the tour. The company learned the work from Limón himself, shortly before his death. From left to right, Nureyev, Winthrop Corey, and Mary Jago in a tense moment from the ballet.*

Nothing in their previous experience had prepared the dancers for the audience response. New York provided the grand climax of the tour for the company and for Nureyev himself, as Veronica Tennant's account of the evening testifies.

> *I was utterly dazed by the whole thing, it was so exciting. And it meant so much to Rudolf too, which was interesting. I think probably the biggest surprise was the roar of the audience. He had already started to tune my ears to an audience response, but nobody roars like a New York audience. That opening night in New York in* Sleeping Beauty *was thrilling.*[18]

Critical response, sensitive to the stature implied by playing the Met, considered Nureyev first, the company second. Clive Barnes, by this time no stranger to the National, summed the matter up in a review article midway through the company's New York stay.

> *The company has style and taste, but little originality. It dances like the Royal Ballet – which is a very good way to dance – but with slightly less conviction. So what is a nice company like this doing at the Metropolitan Opera House when its previous New York engagement was a one-night stand in Brooklyn? The answer can be given in two words: Rudolf Nureyev.*[19]

Barnes, clearly anxious not to accord the National the status of a genuinely front-ranking company, nevertheless struck a generally cordial note in the rest of his reviews. Referring to the La Scala precursor of the National's production, he went on to say: 'This is one of the best productions of *The Sleeping Beauty* around. I thought so when I first saw it – with Fonteyn and Nureyev – at La Scala, and I think so now. But the Canadians dance it better.' The reporter for *Variety*, after the obligatory references to Nureyev, was even more positive. 'But with every acknowledgement of the spectacularity Nureyev brings to this *Beauty*, the ensemble still must and does bear the main responsibility. The evening rests on general merit.'[20] For all that Nureyev garnered the lion's share of the attention, the company itself developed a following among the New York public, with the regulars in the audience returning to watch their favourite dancers and give them the adulation of loyal fans.[21] Nureyev and his *Sleeping Beauty* had triumphed in New York, as anyone could have foreseen and as Hurok so profitably did. The National's thoroughly respectable, if less frenzied, reception by the New York public and press had not been such a foregone conclusion; its significance would endure long after the Nureyev hoopla had died down.

It took years for the company and its public to assess the full impact of the Nureyev experience. The financial accounting was the easiest to perform. At $412,565, *The Sleeping Beauty* had cost almost double its initial projected budget and broken all former records for production costs.[22] Attempts to secure corporate sponsorship for the production having proved largely unsuccessful, the company once again faced a staggering deficit and bleak short-term financial prospects. As a long-term financial investment, however, the production proved to be a sound one. Its immense and continuing popularity soon helped to recover those enormous costs, and by the time of its 1975 submission to the Canada Council, the company's management could point to the *Beauty* experience as evidence of its ability to emerge if not triumphant, then at least unscathed from the brink of financial catastrophe.[23] One other statistical assessment was easy, and revealing. The

Hurok connection had increased the National's number of annual performances from one hundred and seven in 1971–2 (to the end of the European tour in July) to one hundred and ninety-eight, a record that has yet to be exceeded. The company estimated that its dancers would reach an audience of four hundred thousand people, compared with one hundred and ninety-three thousand the year before.[24] Never before had the company been so large, danced so continuously, or brought the pleasures of a full-scale production of the classical repertoire to so many.

Herein lay one of the principal intangible values of the experience. In associating itself with Nureyev in such a marathon of travel and performance, the National had, like Pavlova in her day, become one of the major popularizers of ballet on the North American continent. From this perspective, it mattered less that the company had been seen in New York than that smaller centres like Champaign, Iowa City, and Seattle had had the riches of Nureyev's production spread before them. (The tyranny of Hurok economics eliminated all but the major Canadian cities from this first tour.) And in this enterprise, the company members had been full partners with Nureyev; they had the satisfaction of equal participation in an artistic venture that might well inspire individuals and thus perpetuate the art form through successive generations.

But the full appreciation of Nureyev's significance to the company and its development could come only from another professional, and only, perhaps, with the perspective of the passage of time. Nureyev, one of the great performers of his or any generation, paid the dancers of the National a compliment by demanding of them no less than he demanded of himself. Franca recognizes the value of his unyielding concern for accurate Petipa style. 'In order to present his ballet – his Petipa as he had got it into his head and into his muscles and into his bones from his background – he was a stickler for academic accuracy with the dancers.' His insistence that each position be carefully defined and clearly marked resulted at times in a certain staccato academicism, at the expense of lyrical style. As Franca recalls it, the dream vision scene of the second act could have been more mysterious. 'My memory goes back to Fonteyn, and she was very ethereal. Our ballerinas were not ethereal in that particular scene.' But for Franca the resultant purity of style far outweighed any such disadvantages. 'It was really because of his insistence on that kind of accuracy that Karen and Frank won the silver medal in Moscow in 1973.' And she acknowledges that Nureyev's uncompromising stylistic example inspired the company members as much as his demands challenged them.

> *He was a stickler with himself. He prided himself on that solo at the end, in the wedding scene of* Sleeping Beauty. *He prided himself on the* tours en l'air *finished in absolute clean fifth position; he'd grit his teeth, and there was no way he wasn't going to finish that whole solo, spinning away and getting as dizzy as hell and then standing up in a*

clean fifth position, saying, 'I did it.' Well that was a very good example for the dancers.[25]

Both example and precept worked forcefully on virtually every dancer. In the final analysis of the Nureyev experience, one factor outweighed all the others: the company danced differently, and danced better, as a result of its association with Nureyev.

Like *Romeo and Juliet* in 1964, *The Sleeping Beauty* in 1972 propelled the company as a whole onto a different level of activity, from which there could be no retreat. As Dieter Penzhorn, of the company's production department, puts it: 'If you have a circle, you can't make a bubble in it on one side – the whole circle will expand. And that's what *Beauty* did to the company.'[26] Expanded production facilities and skills broadened the company's horizons and raised its public's expectations; the larger company of dancers had to be supplied with appropriate material. The energies and resources that had been required to sustain *Sleeping Beauty* thus became the norm and called into being a more elaborate repertoire and an even higher standard of production values. And like *Romeo and Juliet* before it, *The Sleeping Beauty* put the seal on Franca's vision of the National as a large-scale classical company, at a time when debate about the appropriate direction for it to take had once again opened up genuine alternatives in the minds of some of its critics. *Beauty* stood as a spectacular vindication of Franca's long-standing goals, a gorgeous roadblock in the way of anyone who sought to streamline and modernize at the expense of the standard repertoire.

The National's Bluebirds, Kain and Augustyn, at the Moscow ballet competition

An important by-product of the *Sleeping Beauty* experience, with intrinsic, long-lasting significance for the life of the company, was the success of Karen Kain and Frank Augustyn at the Second International Ballet Competition in Moscow in the summer of 1973. The invitation to send competitors to the event was in itself a signal honour to the two women without whom there would have been no competitors to send. Betty Oliphant had strengthened the Bolshoi connections she had established in 1962 with a visit in 1969, during which, as she recalls, she 'was given the run of the school for six weeks,'[27] a clear acknowledgment of her international reputation as a teacher of professional dancers. Franca's international eminence was recognized with an invitation to sit on the competition's jury, which included the likes of the British critic Arnold Haskell, the famed Kirov ballerina Irina Kolpakova, and the American choreographer Jerome Robbins. The participation of Kain and Augustyn in Moscow thus paid tribute to the two formative influences in their careers: the National Ballet School and the National Ballet Company.

The competition itself was a harrowing experience. The dancers had just completed the marathon *Sleeping Beauty* tour. The Bluebird pas de deux, at least, was well rehearsed, but little time remained to rest or to prepare any other repertoire. The difficulties of understanding the intricacies of competition protocol and dealing with a foreign language and culture hit the Canadians hard. As a result, they used their strongest piece, the Bluebird pas de deux, for the first elimination round, unaware that in that round it would not be marked, and that it could not then be repeated later in the competition. The raked stage and wooden, rather than linoleum, floor were unfamiliar to them. Not knowing exactly when they would be called on to dance, they warmed up countless times, in a constant state of nervous tension, and found themselves rehearsing at one in the morning, the only time they could get the stage.[28] Against these odds, and competing against older and more experienced artists at a time before the competition was sectioned into junior and senior categories, Kain won the silver medal; as a pair, Kain and Augustyn, nominated by Kolpakova,[29] won a special prize for the best pas de deux in the competition. Kain attributes part of their success with the Russians to the Nureyev experience of the year preceding.

In New York, in 1973, the spotlight picks out Karen Kain and Frank Augustyn in the finale of the Bluebird pas de deux. Their partnership made them popular favourites at home and abroad for years to come.

> *They loved the way we did Bluebird because of the schooling, and that was from him so much. It was our schooling too, but the* port de bras *and the style were directly from him. They didn't know that, but they were very impressed by what we were doing.*[30]

Whatever finish Nureyev had put on the dancers, it was the school and the company that had produced them. Their Moscow victory finally awoke the Canadian public to the extraordinary achievement of these two institutions.

It was not the first time that company members had placed well in international competition. At Varna, Martine van Hamel had won a gold medal in 1966, Nadia Potts and Clinton Rothwell a prize for the best pas de deux (from *Le Loup*) in 1970.[31] But the enormous prestige of the Bolshoi, where the competition was held, contributed to a higher public awareness of Kain and Augustyn's success. It was as much a personal as an official triumph. Kain, who did win one of the top three medals, remembers the reception the Bolshoi audience gave on the final night to Augustyn, who did not. 'Some of the people who won gold medals got booed and hissed by the audience, and when Frank got up they wouldn't let him go, because they liked him so much.'[32] And this competition received prominent coverage in Canada from the outset. John Fraser, then writing regular dance criticism for the *Globe and Mail*, gave the venture the attention it deserved with regular feature stories covering the dancers' progress through the competition.

Coppélia and Erik Bruhn's return to performing

Even the trials and successes of *The Sleeping Beauty* could not entirely distract Franca from her intention to lighten her own load and step back somewhat from the active artistic leadership of the company. Her conversation with David Haber in Monte Carlo at the end of the European tour had led to further negotiations and resulted finally in the announcement, on 30 November 1972, of his appointment as co–artistic director of the company.[33] There was no indication at the time that this appointment would one day translate itself into the artistic directorship, a point which gave rise to enormous controversy when that translation eventually took place. Franca, indeed, remained open to any possibilities, and as late as the following July put out highly tentative feelers to John Neumeier, the American-born, German-based choreographer whose work with the Royal Winnipeg Ballet was attracting favourable attention and whose *Don Juan* was about to enter the National's repertoire.[34] Nureyev, meanwhile, strengthened his already close ties to the company through his annual return visits for the Hurok-sponsored tours that continued until 1977. Nor was Erik Bruhn ever very far away. His appointment as resident producer of the company, beginning with the 1974–5 season, formalized his long-standing association with the National and guaranteed his presence in Toronto for three months of the year.[35] The aura of three such plausible candidates hovering about the company at this crucial time provided ample material for gossip and speculation.

In the meantime, however, the public's hungry maw had to be fed with new ballets, and Franca and Haber applied themselves to the never-ending task of building repertoire with two additions that had an appropriately valedictory air about them. *Les Sylphides* and *Coppélia*, Franca's very first choices for the company's repertoire, would see out her final years with the National. Both were to be Bruhn productions, but the recurring illness which had caused his retirement from dancing plagued him during the rehearsal period for *Les Sylphides* and resulted in Franca's stepping into the breach.[36] Fittingly enough, the new *Les Sylphides* became a Bruhn-Franca co-production.

Coppélia, the staple of the National's early repertoire, had played in every season from the opening one to 1962–3, the last before the move to the O'Keefe Centre. There then followed a hiatus of nearly twelve years before it rejoined the repertoire, although there had been talk of a new production at least as early as 1972.[37] Rehearsals for *Coppélia* were delayed by Bruhn's surgery, in December 1973 and January 1974, which finally treated the perforated ulcer from which he had suffered, his ailment undiagnosed, for eleven years.[38] But rather than turn to someone else to keep to their original timetable, Franca and Haber accommodated their plans to Bruhn's revised schedule,[39] with the result that *Coppélia* premièred on 8 February 1975, seven months after Franca had stepped down as artistic director of the company.

At the suggestion of Robert A. Laidlaw, longtime benefactor of the National, the company dedicated this new *Coppélia* to its founding triumvirate, Sydney Mulqueen, Pearl Whitehead, and Aileen Woods.[40] The dedication highlighted the striking contrast between the company's tentative beginnings in 1951 and its confident professionalism in 1975. Three casts alternated in the roles of the young lovers: Veronica Tennant and Tomas Schramek, Mary Jago and Hazaros Surmeyan, and Vanessa Harwood and the Australian-born Gary Norman. Among the dancers portraying Dr Coppélius was none other than Erik Bruhn himself. Maurice Strike's evocative designs transformed the O'Keefe stage into a cheerful idealization of a European village, then a sinister, claustrophobic realization of Coppélius' workshop. Nostalgia and remembrance for days gone by complemented the youthful self-assurance of the new generation of dancers that now made up the National.

Leaving the handsome princes of his danseur noble *days far behind, Erik Bruhn moved into the character roles which allowed him to display a different side of his dramatic personality. In the toyshop scene, the crazed Dr Coppélius believes he is removing the soul of the sleeping Franz in order to animate his life-size doll, Coppélia.*

As he had done with *Swan Lake*, Bruhn compressed the staging of *Coppélia* in the interests of dramatic continuity, so that the traditional three acts became two. His first act, in two closely linked scenes, tells the entire E.T.A. Hoffmann story of the toymaker who thinks he has brought his doll to life, while his second becomes simply the wedding celebration for Franz and Swanilda, with divertissements.

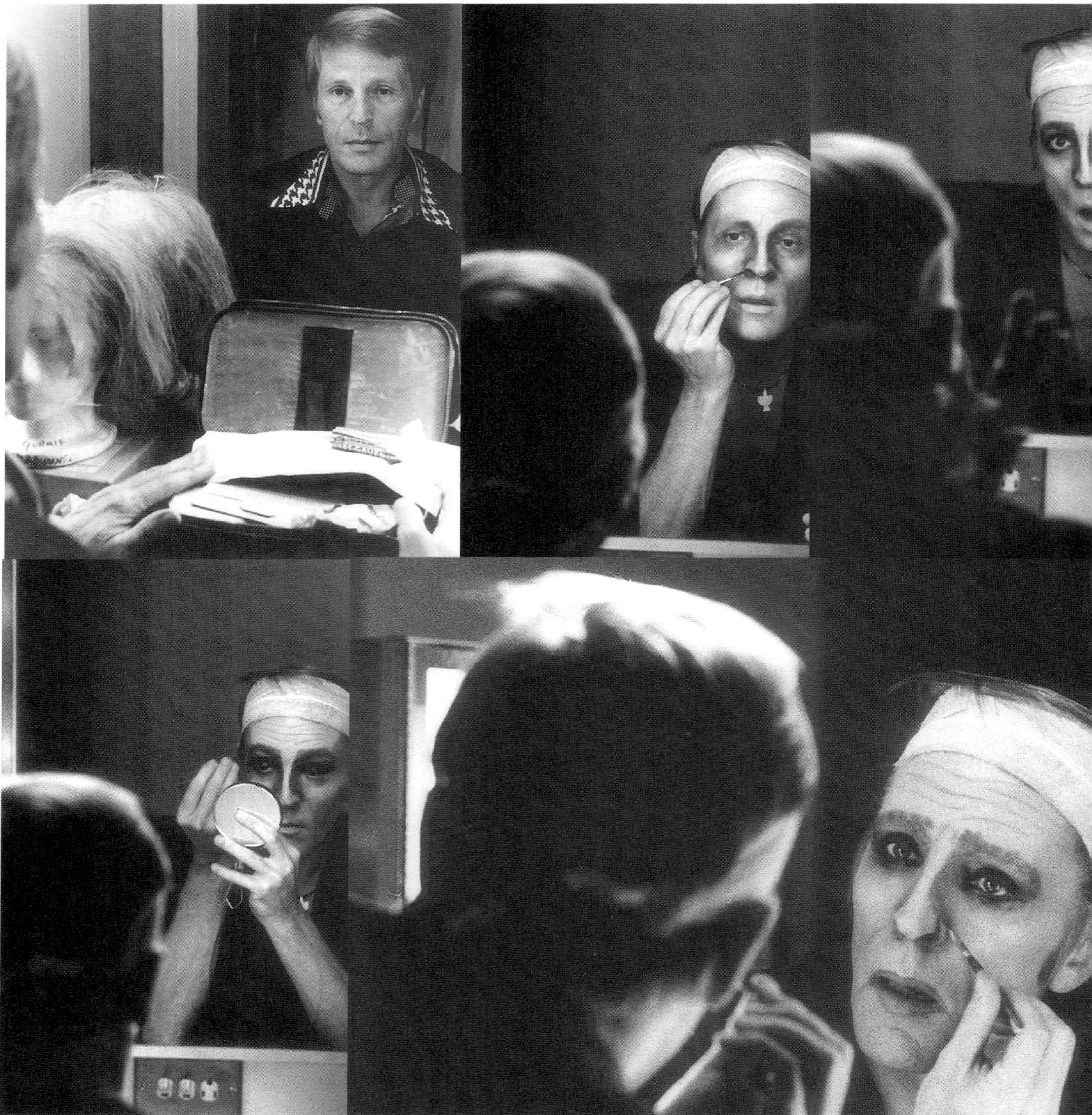

This structure places great emphasis, in the first act, on the grotesque pathos of Dr Coppélius as a species of diabolical Pygmalion to Coppélia's Galatea, only to have the role descend to its more traditional level of buffoonery and compromise in the second act. Bruhn's *Coppélia* makes of Franz and Swanilda a pair of callous, middle-class opportunists, of Dr Coppélius a crazed visionary. As characters, they inhabit separate worlds, which cannot be bridged as easily as the concluding festivities suggest. In the unthinking victory of vigorous youth over thoughtful age, one can see mirrored some of the frustrations Bruhn must have felt at having to surrender the *danseur noble* roles of his youth to younger, less finished artists. With the role of Dr Coppélius, Bruhn created one of the major vehicles of his mature career as a character artist. The macabre events of the second scene, in which Dr Coppélius believes he is stealing Franz's soul in order to infuse life into Coppélia, speak poignantly of the desire to preserve and manipulate youthful energy, the energy for which the mature dancer must envy his younger, less experienced colleagues.

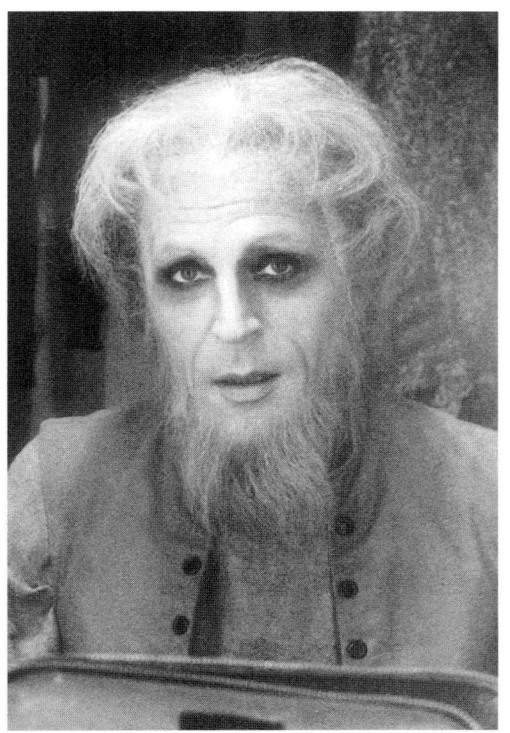

The mirror tells the tale as the skilful application of make-up reveals the anguish of Dr Coppélius, hidden beneath Erik Bruhn's handsome, impenetrable features.

Bruhn's *Coppélia* thus provided a highly charged setting for a joint appearance by Bruhn and Nureyev. In April 1975, on the company's second European tour, the two friends and rivals whose careers had so influenced the National danced together on the stage of the Coliseum, one as the decrepit toymaker and the other as the vigorous young man. Bruhn spent a week in London prior to the performance, teaching his younger friend the ballet.[41] Exactly ten years earlier, the two had competed on equal terms in the New Year's performances of *La Sylphide* at the O'Keefe Centre. At the Coliseum in 1975, the plot of *Coppélia* told a different story, in which the great age-gap between Dr Coppélius and Franz acknowledged the ten-year difference in age between Bruhn and Nureyev. In the physically demanding world of ballet, that age difference favoured Nureyev for just a little while longer. In purely dramatic terms however, Bruhn, by yielding the field to his junior, had laid claim to a new territory in which his gifts were unrivalled.

Bruhn had retired from the stage for good, he thought, in 1971. But as he recuperated and adjusted to his changed life, he was prevailed upon by the National to attempt the character role of Madge, the witch, in his own production of *La Sylphide*.[42] A greater departure from the prince roles he had reluctantly forsaken could not be imagined. His first character role, and an exercise in cross-dressing at that, made the transition easier for Bruhn, if not for his adoring public.[43] Bruhn the character artist made his début on the stage of the Metropolitan Opera House on 9 August 1974, dancing with the National Ballet of Canada. Rudolf Nureyev appeared onstage with Bruhn for the first time ever on that August night,[44] dancing the role of James, which he had taken on such short notice during *La Sylphide*'s opening run. With the National, Bruhn would appear frequently thereafter as Madge and as Dr Coppélius, his personal identity concealed behind the make-up, wigs, and costumes which, paradoxically, gave his dramatic personality a freedom it had never before enjoyed.

Celebrity by association: the Baryshnikov defection

August 1974 brought the company another major triumph and another intimation of the relentless progress of time in the short professional lives of dancers. Just five days after the New York *La Sylphide*, at its opening performance at Ontario Place, the company played host to yet another Soviet defector, the new arrival who would edge Nureyev out of his position as ballet's international superstar, Mikhail Baryshnikov. The vehicle, once again, was *La Sylphide*, and Bruhn was in the audience. The cloak and dagger conspiracy of Baryshnikov's defection in Toronto had occupied the better part of a month and had involved some of the company's dancers in elaborate efforts to elude the press.[45] His television appearance with the National (in excerpts from *La Sylphide*) and his New York début with American Ballet Theatre (dancing in *Giselle* opposite Natalia Makarova)[46] served to whet the Canadian audience's appetite further. On 14 August 1974, with public interest whipped into a frenzy by rumours of romance and the political intrigue of the event, and despite a public transit strike that paralysed Toronto traffic, the Forum, Ontario Place's outdoor amphitheatre, began filling in the early afternoon for the evening performance. The scheduled afternoon rehearsal of *La Sylphide*, without Baryshnikov himself, took place before the attentive, patient crowd. By late afternoon, with every inch of seating space taken, the hillside surrounding the forum began swarming with the overflow, anxious for at least a glimpse of Baryshnikov and for a sense of participation in the event. By performance time on that hot August night, an estimated ten thousand people were on hand to greet the new sensation.

He did not disappoint them, even though it was Baryshnikov's first attempt not only at the role, but at any Bournonville choreography, which offers few opportunities for the kind of athletic display many were expecting from a Russian star. His performance as James, a haunting amalgam of grace and passion, conferred artistic grandeur on an evening that might otherwise have been merely a celebrity event. Admission to the Forum was, as usual, free with the price of general admission to the park. The egalitarian atmosphere of this tradition of popular entertainment contributed to the ecstatic, cheering welcome Baryshnikov received.

With David Haber looking on, Sergiu Stefanschi, acting as interpreter, points out some of the features of Ontario Place to Mikhail Baryshnikov, prior to Baryshnikov's appearance with the company at the Forum following his defection in 1974.

The short reign of David Haber

Celia Franca had announced her decision to resign the artistic directorship of the company in early January 1974.[47] She intended, however, to maintain a close working relationship with the company and asked the board to ratify her choice of David Haber as her successor, effective 1 July 1974. She thus planned an orderly transfer of power to the deputy whom she had selected and trained over the past fourteen months. Had things worked as planned, comparisons might have been drawn yet again between Franca and de Valois, who had handed over the running of the Royal Ballet to her chosen successor, Sir Frederick Ashton, in 1963, without the benefit of selection committees or advertised vacancies.[48] But although the board initially acquiesced in Franca's choice, it was clear from the very beginning that there was significant opposition within the board both to the choice and to the procedures which had put it in place. Haber himself acknowledged openly this opposition to his appointment in his report, as artistic director, to the Annual General Meeting of 9 September 1974. 'I am of course aware that some members of the Board were against my appointment. I sincerely hope the continuing development of the company will allay their fears.'[49] His hopes were ill founded.

As Franca remembers events, it was she who made the first approach to Haber and asked him whether he felt ready, after his work with the company, to take over the artistic directorship. After a few days' reflection, he decided he was, and the two put their plan to Ian H. McLeod, then the president of the board of directors, who agreed to it without bringing it before the full board.[50] This procedure in itself lay at the root of many of the troubles to come. Board members felt they had been slighted in the process, among them Betty Oliphant, who was, of course, much more than just a board member.[51] There were also fears that Haber, whose experience was in management rather than in the studio, might encroach uncomfortably upon the sphere of the general manager at the time, Gerry Eldred.[52] Haber could not escape criticism on the grounds that he had never been a dancer or a choreographer, even though there were illustrious precedents in the history of ballet companies for the non-dancing ballet administrator. (In fact, Haber had studied dance and had even appeared on the Quebec night-club circuit in his youth.)[53] Haber never claimed to be anything he wasn't. He went into the job hoping to show that his own blend of skills and experience could bring advantages to the company different from those which a dancer might offer. Haber's appointment, then, was contentious on two separate grounds: it violated the sense of procedure of at least some of the board members, and it plunged the company into debate about appropriate qualifications for the position. But had there not been fundamental discontent with the choice itself, these debates of principle would never have surfaced.

For those still hoping for a radical change of artistic direction for the company, Haber's appointment merely continued the old régime, and it thwarted their desire for change. As Haber himself puts it: 'Celia wanted a certain amount of freedom, but she didn't want to let go.' To the degree that Haber's appointment was seen as merely Franca's strategy for not letting go, it never had a chance. His close personal identification with her and with her ideals and goals for the company branded him as her creature and stood in the way of any independent assessment of his achievements.

For the brief period during which he held it, Haber was uncomfortable with the title 'Artistic Director.' He hoped the position would evolve into that of 'Director General,' or *Intendant*, on the model of continental European opera houses, with artistic, musical, technical, and managerial staff reporting to him on an equal footing. On such a model, his experience in management would be an asset, and his lack of experience as a dancer no impediment to his effective functioning. Given the inherent tension between the artistic director and the general manager in the company structure as it then existed, his scheme might even have solved some of its long-standing problems of power sharing as well. But his essentially conservative approach did not allow these ideas a chance to emerge. 'I moved too slowly, and I didn't create waves at the beginning, and say, "Ah, here's a new presence."'[54] Haber had very little time to establish any kind of presence at all.

He did manage, however, to initiate a number of projects that bore fruit after his departure. The major one of these was *Mad Shadows*, Ann Ditchburn's most ambitious work. Ironically, given the never-ending pressures on the company to mount Canadian work, Haber had to fight hard to persuade the board to take a risk on this thoroughly Canadian project, based on Marie-Claire Blais' *La Belle Bête*, with an original score by André Gagnon and designs by Jack King. Originally conceived as a joint choreographic venture between Ditchburn and James Kudelka, then a rising young choreographer in the company's ranks, *Mad Shadows* became Ditchburn's exclusive property when the proposed collaboration proved too difficult to carry out. *Mad Shadows* played twenty-two performances over four seasons, but reached a much wider audience through a very successful telecast and enjoyed the distinction, as well, of playing the Royal Opera House, Covent Garden, and the Metropolitan Opera in New York during its life-span. Ditchburn herself now describes *Mad Shadows* as a naïve work, at least in the international context, but sees its naïveté as appropriate to its subject matter and theme. David Haber still considers it a good theatrical piece and an important opportunity for Ditchburn, even though, as things turned out, it proved to be her last work for the company. Attending the première, not as artistic director but as Ditchburn's guest, Haber commented, with a mixture of bitterness and satisfaction, 'It was worth the fight, wasn't it?'[55]

Even though the proposed choreographic collaboration with Ann Ditchburn on Mad Shadows *failed to materialize, the young James Kudelka danced in the work as Ditchburn created it. He is seen here opposite Cynthia Lucas.*

Another of Haber's acquisitions, *Whispers of Darkness* by Norbert Vesak, the Canadian choreographer who had created the Royal Winnipeg Ballet's highly successful *The Ecstasy of Rita Joe*, gave less cause for satisfaction. By Haber's own admission, the ballet did not work out,[56] and it closed after only ten performances. Haber helped to sow the seeds of interest, at the board level, in the acquisition of Sir Frederick Ashton's *La Fille Mal Gardée*[57] and tried to bring John Neumeier back to choreograph an original work for the company,[58] but the project which was undoubtedly closest to his heart reached only partial fruition, as a production stored in the company's videotape files but never fully mounted or performed in public. *Le Coq d'Or*, the ballet that would not be, remains the phantom monument to Haber's aspirations for the repertoire.

First produced in 1914, in Diaghilev's heyday, Fokine's *Le Coq d'Or* (a spectacular opera-ballet to a score by Rimsky-Korsakov) had been revived by de Basil in the thirties and had thereafter fallen out of sight, along with most of the Fokine repertoire. The opportunity to acquire the ballet arose through Franca's old contact, from her Metropolitan Ballet days, Nicholas Beriosoff. 'Papa' Beriosoff, as he was universally known in the ballet world by the seventies, was the self-appointed champion of the out-of-favour Fokine repertoire. He offered to mount *Coq d'Or* for the National and suggested furthermore that the company could buy sets and costumes (by André Delfau, after the originals by Gontcharova) at a cut-rate price from the Ballet de Wallonie in Charlevoi, which had revived the work in 1966.[59] Haber, backed by Franca, saw Beriosoff's offer as an opportunity to perform an important act of historical preservation. Restoring this gem of the Fokine era would not only add a novel piece of exotica to the repertoire, but also demonstrate the historical line of descent from Petipa through Fokine to the present day.[60] Beriosoff, then sixty- nine, would not live forever. The time was ripe to take advantage of his offer, and his memory, in order to preserve *Coq d'Or* and thus transmit it to future generations.

Haber pursued this acquisition vigorously, not only for its potential box-office value but for the general direction it represented for the company. There was talk of Fokine's *Schéhérazade* and *Petrushka* as well, both of which Beriosoff offered to produce.[61] But Haber encountered serious difficulty, within the board and within the company, in defending what he describes as 'one of those wonderful, wonderful antique pieces' against the doubts of those who had not seen, or even heard of, the work.[62] Since he was a non-dancer, his own judgment carried less weight in such matters than it might have, and Franca, having resigned the artistic directorship, could not defend the choice too actively without appearing to call into question Haber's own ability to do so. As internal opposition to the production grew, Beriosoff entered negotiations with London's Festival Ballet to mount *Coq d'Or* for them in 1976.[63] If the company was to capitalize on the originality of the plan, it would have to act fast. Beriosoff was engaged to come and teach the work, even though funds for the production itself, in the post-*Beauty* era of economic restraint, had not been fully committed.

But before the issue could be resolved, other events complicated matters even further. In March 1975, midway through Haber's first year as artistic director, Betty Oliphant announced her resignation as associate artistic director of the company, the position she had held since the 1968 crisis. She explained the reasons for her resignation in a full statement to the press.

> *Although I think that David Haber has many good qualities, I do not believe they are all the ones needed to be an effective artistic director. I was informed last year that he was to succeed Celia only a few hours before the press was, and although I had strong reservations, I also felt there was some hope. He did have some artistic background to draw on and with proper consultation and a reasonable acceptance of his own limitations, I thought he might make it. So I kept quiet.*
>
> *Since Celia's resignation, however, it has become increasingly clear that her time*

> *with the company has become more and more limited and that this situation will likely increase in the future. Since David's appointment, I have had to demand two meetings with the artistic staff to present important problems. Since the last of those, there has been virtually no communication between us on the future plans of the company.*
>
> *At a recent board meeting, the problems surfaced because I brought them up. I hated doing this since I feel artistic decisions should be made by the artistic staff, but the situation had reached, in my opinion, a crucial point.*
>
> *I am terribly concerned about the choice of repertoire that is being proposed right now. I am worried about how the dancers are being used – and not used – and I feel particularly terrible about the fact that I have to train kids who will be joining a company that has weak leadership and appears to be drifting toward real trouble artistically.*
>
> *Since the artistic staff have made it abundantly clear over the past season that they did not want to discuss anything with me, I have decided to resign. When you stop being useful, you clear out.*[64]

The enormous respect which Oliphant enjoyed in the international ballet community made this announcement far more than a mere intimation of discord. It was a motion of non-confidence in Franca's chosen successor and a challenge to the board to do something about his artistic policies. Oliphant's comments about lack of communication probably referred to the fact that the Artistic Management Committee had ceased to function and had resisted Haber's efforts to revive it.[65] The complaint about repertoire, deliberately non-specific, could have referred to any number of initiatives, including the ill-fated *Whispers of Darkness*, which had closed in February, but the proposed move to Fokine must have been one of them.

Oliphant's highly public gesture and the board's general discontent with Haber coalesced to bring matters to a head over the issue of *Coq d'Or*. Lyman Henderson, still an active member of the board at the time, recalls the pursuit of *Coq d'Or* as one of many aspects of Haber's direction to come under heavy criticism.

> *The board became extremely critical about his choice of resurrecting* Le Coq d'Or*, which he could do economically because he knew where the costumes were. It didn't strike the imagination of the board. It was just one of the heaps of criticism.*[66]

The board instituted a review of senior artistic and management staff. It also declined, for financial reasons, to authorize funds for the full production of *Coq d'Or*. In May 1975, Haber wrote to Beriosoff, explaining that the board had authorized only that the company learn and videotape the work for future reference.[67] It was a compromise, and clearly an unsatisfactory one, between the company's prior commitments to Beriosoff and the board's desire to cancel the production. In October 1975, after efforts to secure corporate sponsorship for *Coq d'Or* had failed, the production, which had been fully cast, rehearsed, and videotaped, was finally shelved.[68] But before that, on 3 June, the board asked Haber to leave.[69]

The company announced Haber's resignation on 7 June, to take effect 31 July, 1975. The press release, though not detailed, was extraordinarily candid.

> *Mr. Haber said that his decision is the result of irreconcilable differences with the Board of Directors of the Ballet. These differences revolve around the choice of repertoire, cuts in productions and the procedure followed by a committee of the Board of Directors in their assessment of senior artistic and management staff.*[70]

In the final analysis, Oliphant's public statement was less significant than the decision of the board to remove an artistic director in whom it no longer had full confidence. The authority to do so had always existed, but had never previously been exercised. Challenges to Franca's authority had resulted in the board's reaffirming its confidence in her and in her artistic policies, as it had done in 1972. In removing Haber, the board asserted its ultimate responsibility for the overall fate of the company. In effect, it resolved the tension between artistic authority and board and management authority that had existed from the very beginning of Franca's appointment. Such resolution was possible only after her departure, and made inevitable by her attempt to establish her own successor. Perhaps any individual, or at any rate any non-dancer, she had tried to place in the position would have suffered Haber's fate. Implicitly at least, the removal of David Haber came out of a desire to allow a genuinely new broom the chance to sweep clean. Lyman Henderson recognizes this possibility. 'There may have been a feeling in the board that it really was time for a change in artistic direction and that pure succession might not achieve that. That certainly must have been in the minds of some, although it was not publicly expressed.'[71] This direct board intervention and assertion of board interest in overall artistic policies stood as precedent in the even more controversial case of Alexander Grant just a few years later.

David Haber served as artistic director of the company for just thirteen months, far too short a period to allow for any meaningful critical evaluation of his contribution or, indeed, for his direction to have assumed a distinctive character. However, in losing him the National lost his considerable range of international theatrical contacts, which might have brought about a higher international touring profile for the company in the seventies and eighties. And his attempt to resurrect the Fokine repertoire demands one further historical footnote. The London Festival Ballet did stage *Le Coq d'Or*, under Beriosoff's direction, in 1976. Although the production failed to set the world on fire, it earned the company a small place in the history books for its contribution to the preservation of an important piece of repertoire. In later years, the Joffrey Ballet enjoyed great success with its historical reconstructions of *Petrushka* and Nijinsky's *Rite of Spring*. Les Grands Ballets Canadiens, seizing the opportunity which the National passed up, became the repository for important historical reconstructions of the Diaghilev repertoire, including Massine's *The Three-Cornered Hat* and Balanchine's early work *La Chatte*. As ballet companies became collaborators with dance scholars in the archival task of preserving significant repertoire, the pendulum swung, and the attempts to preserve little-known repertoire found critical respect as well as popular acceptance. When the National vetoed *Le Coq d'Or*, it effectively gave up the chance to be in the vanguard of these efforts at authentic historical reconstruction.

The press release announcing Haber's resignation also stated that a search for his successor was being instituted immediately, 'not only in Canada but throughout the rest of the world.'[72] But such an extensive search took time, and in the interim, the company required leadership. Given Franca's intense personal disappointment at the forced resignation of David Haber,[73] her willingness to act as artistic director through this difficult period testified to her deep loyalty to the institution which owed its existence to her and was now in the process of outgrowing her. She resumed the office from Haber's departure on 31 July until 30 September 1975. On 18 September, she wrote to McLeod, resigning thereafter from any position with the National Ballet. 'As you may remember, I had originally asked for a year's leave of absence with the idea of returning to work with David Haber. However, it would not be fair to the incoming artistic director, should he or she be saddled with my presence.'[74] In attempting to secure the successor of her choice as artistic director, Franca had gambled and lost. As a result, she had to forfeit the chance for a continuing direct relationship with the National. The demands of her personal life required that she live in Ottawa, at some remove from the activities of the company. Once she had no formal position within the National's structure, her ability to influence the direction of the company she had watched over for twenty-four years was abruptly cut off. At fifty-three, with her creative energy intact and her company just one year shy of its silver anniversary, she found herself sidelined. At an age when many mature dancers were just beginning the transition to administration (Alexander Grant was fifty-one, Erik Bruhn fifty-five, when they took over the direction of the company), Franca's career with the National was over. Partly because she was the company's founder, with a strong reputation for hands-on management, partly because she had taken on the role of artistic director at such a remarkably early age, partly because there was no other dance company in Canada that could absorb the force of her personality and give scope to her talents and energy, Franca had no choice but to enter retirement, interrupted by involvement in dance education, both in Canada and in the People's Republic of China, and by a period of membership on the Canada Council, and punctuated by occasional diplomatic statements in the press. After a career which had repeatedly landed her in the headlines and at the centre of controversy, Celia Franca withdrew from public life with dignity and restraint. It took years before the press and public at large recognized the extraordinary nature of her contribution and loyalty to dance in Canada, or the full magnitude of her achievement.

Striking as it was, this portrait of Franca and David Haber as co–artistic directors did nothing to counter his opponents' claims that Haber's subsequent appointment as artistic director was simply a blind to allow Franca to continue directing the company.

CHAPTER SEVEN

A Ballet Company Is Not a School

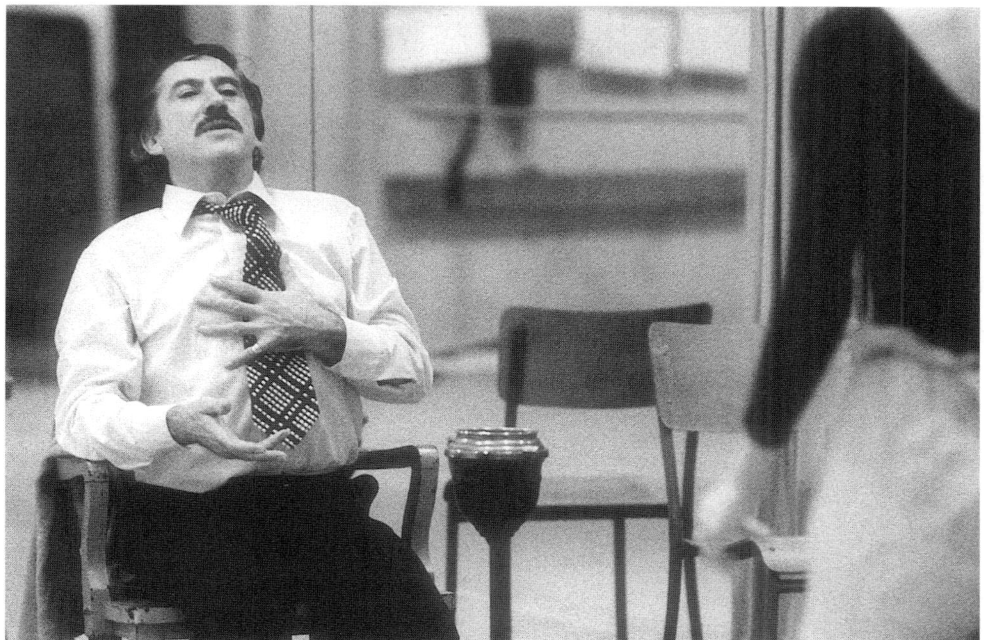

Speculation and uncertainty at a time of change

The search for a new artistic director for the company was influenced by the inevitable attraction of two superstars. Erik Bruhn and Rudolf Nureyev had been close friends almost from the moment of Nureyev's defection to the West; they had also been professional rivals, the two greatest male dancers of their time, vying for public attention and lucrative engagements. Bruhn's genius was an inspiration and a source of plunder, from which Nureyev sought to learn and appropriate anything that he could use to fulfil his own artistic ambitions. Nureyev's youth and inexhaustible passion to perform reminded Bruhn of the limits which age and health imposed on his own career. Nor was he indifferent to the fact that Nureyev, the younger, less experienced artist, commanded astronomical fees, far in excess of his own earning capacity. 'I am sure you know what Margot

OPPOSITE: Overcoming the scepticism of dancers and critics alike, Peter Schaufuss, seen here with Karen Kain in the exuberant finale, produced a landmark Napoli *for the company. It was a landmark in Alexander Grant's association with the National as well. Victoria Bertram stands between Kain and Schaufuss with children from the National Ballet School looking on.*

ABOVE: Alexander Grant's extroverted personality made him one of the most beloved character dancers of his day. His professional reputation, spanning generations, made him a strong candidate for the artistic direction of the National, even if his star burned less brightly than Bruhn's or Nureyev's.

and Rudi make, so what I am mentioning here for myself, is not only reasonable, but far below what I even get in Denmark,' Bruhn wrote to Franca in 1964, during negotiations for his *La Sylphide*.[1] Nureyev and Bruhn had frequently been compared in their onstage roles; with Franca's departure from the National, public speculation had them competing once again, this time for the offstage role of artistic director of the company. Both had established strong ties with the National, Bruhn as resident producer and as choreographer of four of its major productions, Nureyev as presiding genius of *The Sleeping Beauty* and as annual guest artist for the Hurok tours. The only other high-profile contender for the position, John Neumeier, effectively took himself out of the running when he told David Haber privately that the National could not match the ideal conditions for creation which the opera houses of Frankfurt and Hamburg offered him.[2]

At the height of their remarkable careers, Erik Bruhn and Rudolf Nureyev each possessed an arrogant beauty to match a fabulous technique. For almost twenty years, their personalities inspired the dancers and influenced the life of the company.

Both Nureyev and Bruhn were approached informally and sounded out about the artistic directorship. Betty Oliphant and Gerry Eldred, the company's general manager, discussed the selection of a new artistic director with Bruhn directly and asked him to speak with Nureyev 'regarding any thoughts he may have for a new director for the company.'[3] Nureyev, who by this time felt a real rapport with the company,[4] had to fend off the dancers' pointed questions. According to Veronica Tennant, Nureyev was genuinely concerned about the fate of the company. 'It mattered to him. I remember the dancers saying, "Would you consider being our director?" But he just giggled. I was never quite sure what that meant. Rudolf would giggle a lot when he just didn't want to say anything.'[5] Nureyev later acknowledged that talk of his directing the company was always 'in the air. But it was never offered.' In any case, 'It really didn't attract me to be in one place,'[6] and the company needed a resident artistic director, not a glorified visitor.

Bruhn, who was already spending three months a year with the company and had received landed immigrant status in Canada by late 1974,[7] could not be lured into a fuller commitment to the National. His period as the artistic director of the Royal Swedish Ballet from 1967 to 1972 was one of self-doubt, overwork, and public criticism. It had done nothing to attract him to artistic administration. More important, just eight months before Franca's retirement, he had made a comeback to the full performing career he thought he had forsaken forever, savouring the sweetness of a triumphant return to the stage with American Ballet Theatre in the kitchen scene from *Miss Julie* at ABT's thirty-fifth anniversary gala.[8] Bruhn had to come to terms with his own performing career before he could commit himself wholeheartedly to directing the development of other dancers.

As the issue of its artistic leadership came to a head, the company experienced another of the ructions brought about by press coverage and nationalist sentiments that materially altered its reputation and sense of self. In the summer of 1975, the company made its annual summer appearance at the Metropolitan Opera House with Rudolf Nureyev as guest artist. On 27 July 1975, the *New York Times* published a lengthy and prominently displayed guest column by the *Globe and Mail*'s dance critic, John Fraser. 'Nureyev, Leave Canadian Ballet Alone,' trumpeted the headline; the article itself was hardly less incendiary. In it, Fraser mounted a concerted attack on the Nureyev presence and its effect, over the years, on the growth and development of the company. His brief analysis of the company itself was even-handed.

> *It has often enough been observed that the Canadian company is as old as the Royal Ballet and the New York City Ballet, but has never come close to achieving the same stature. While that's true enough, it's a fairly specious argument. Toronto is not New York or London, and Canadian artistic and economic resources are correspondingly limited. The National started in a void, and a considerable part of its mandate has been to educate Canadians in a tradition that never before existed. The building-up of the company was a slow process, hampered initially as much by public indifference as by an overly cautious and unexciting repertoire. This began to change when the school started providing dancers who could live up to demanding works which, in turn, aroused audiences and grant-giving institutions.*
>
> *Things were moving ahead nicely, albeit slowly, when Nureyev arrived on the scene. The company was expanding while remaining true to the classical traditions under founder Celia Franca. Erik Bruhn had been enticed to help, and he fleshed out the repertoire with distinctive productions of the old war-horses that flattered the dancers rather than showed off their weaknesses. There was no distinctive new choreography, though. There never has been, and this, predictably, has always put the National on the defensive. With the mighty Russian, the company saw a chance of leaping to prominence through someone else's greatness – an old trap that many companies have fallen into.*

The ensuing evaluation of Nureyev's direct influence tried to retain a similar sense of balance, but it stressed the debits of his extravagance and temperament far more than it did the credits of his encouragement to the company, and it frankly criticized the level of his recent performances.

> *If only his own technique and artistry remained at a consistently high level, perhaps his behaviour might be acceptable even inside Canada. But, of course, they haven't. Nureyev's stage presence is always awesome, but his dancing certainly isn't consistently so anymore.*

The tone of the concluding paragraph, more in sorrow than in anger, did little to moderate the harshness of the previous comments.

> *In the end, Nureyev remains what he always has been since he left Russia – a stranger in strange lands. He is doomed to adoration and lack of appreciation, enthusiasm and resentment, to using and being used. Once again, in Canada this time, he will not find it surprising to hear that he must pack up and move somewhere else.*[9]

The international prominence of the publication and the timing of the article, in the middle of the National's New York season and in the middle of the search for an artistic director, added immeasurably to its impact. If there *was* a serious courtship under way between the company and its guest star, Fraser's final words lent it no public encouragement. Nureyev was always sensitive to commentary in the press; the climate for negotiation suddenly became decidedly frosty.

Fraser's article provoked vigorous debate, including a condescending response from Clive Barnes which called attention to Fraser's relative inexperience as a dance critic and to the fact that Fraser, immediately after writing the piece in question, had forsaken dance criticism for drama at the *Globe and Mail*.[10] All ten of the company's principal dancers, the men included, sent a letter to the *Times*, dissociating themselves unequivocally from the sentiments expressed in Fraser's article. The president of the board, Ian H. McLeod, wrote to rebut Fraser's arguments, saying that the company, through its association with Nureyev, had achieved its two primary objectives, of increasing the number of performance opportunities for its dancers and of gaining access to the Metropolitan.

> *The National does not share Mr. Fraser's eagerness to end an association which has been so helpful for our young company in its developing stage. Instead, we look forward to a continuing association with Mr. Nureyev as opportunities arise in the future.*[11]

No amount of rebuttal, however, could undo the effect of the article's publication.

By characterizing the National's continued appearances at the Metropolitan as a species of colonial exploitation, Fraser had both insulted the company's foreign guest star and undercut its own achievement. Though his intention had been to urge the company on to a vigorous pursuit of its own identity, his words encouraged introspection and self-doubt. No one had claimed that the company on its own had taken New York by storm; now its more modest achievement there had been called into question, and by a fellow Canadian in a major American newspaper at that. Whether the laundry was dirty or clean remained open to dispute, but it had certainly been hung out for all the neighbours to see.

The emphasis on Nureyev himself, both in Fraser's article and in the heated response it provoked, unfortunately clouded a real and important issue. The Hurok organization, not Nureyev personally, had exploited the company in the colonial manner Fraser described. Nureyev had treated the company members as fellow artists; Hurok saw them as back-up for his big star. Having contracted for *Sleeping Beauty* as the initial vehicle for Nureyev, Hurok did not scruple to specify other selections of repertoire for the company, always with an eye to box-office and to

When Hurok toured The Sleeping Beauty, *one of his organization's staff members, Simon Semenoff, occasionally walked on in the mime role of Catalabutte, here being humiliated by Celia Franca's vengeful Carabosse. Mary Jago is visible as one of the captured fairies, right of centre.*

displaying Nureyev to advantage. *The Moor's Pavane*, which Hurok bought from its choreographer, José Limón, as a birthday present for Nureyev,[12] was a welcome addition, but his strong pressure to add Roland Petit's *Carmen* to the repertoire met with resistance and even prompted a Canada Council staff member to ask, 'Who's running the National Ballet, anyway?'[13] Such interference in artistic policy was old hat for Hurok. American Ballet Theatre had suffered a similar fate at his hands during its association with him in the forties;[14] in 1965 the Royal Ballet had capitulated to his demand that Fonteyn and Nureyev dance the Covent Garden opening performance of MacMillan's *Romeo and Juliet*, rather than Lynn Seymour and Christopher Gable, on whom the roles had been created, in order to build better box-office for the Royal's upcoming North American Hurok tour.[15]

The National's management also had to fight Hurok in order to get decent exposure on the tours for its own male principals. The Hurok organization, not the National, handled tour publicity. It promoted Nureyev heavily and gave short shrift to the infrequent non-Nureyev performances (usually the less popular matinees).[16] The predictable results – sold-out houses for Nureyev and poor attendance for the company on its own – contributed further to the public perception of the company as mere stage-dressing for the star. But even this state of affairs was part of the National's calculated risk in signing on with Hurok. Impressing the promoter was as important a part of the game as building an audience, and took just as long. Not until 1977, and then because of circumstances beyond his control, did Hurok risk presenting the National in New York without Nureyev. Fraser, by couching his argument as a personal criticism of Nureyev, glossed over these complex issues of the economics and politics of promotion in the arts and shifted attention away from Hurok's pivotal role in the game. Furthermore, by publicly writing off one of the candidates with the inside track, he helped to throw the competition for the position of artistic director of the company wide open. With both Bruhn and Nureyev ruling themselves out, the committee now had to search in earnest. Their choice fell on Alexander Grant.

Alexander Grant, the dark-horse candidate

A New Zealander by birth, Alexander Grant had joined the Sadler's Wells Ballet at Covent Garden in 1946. He remained at Covent Garden, with Sadler's Wells and then the Royal Ballet, for thirty years, rising to the rank of principal and establishing himself not as a romantic lead, but in the subtle and demanding role of the character artist. Alexander Grant was the consummate actor-dancer, whose dramatic presence on stage projected the depth, humanity, pathos, and, at times, melodrama of the choreographer's vision. Short and stocky, with penetrating eyes and expressive features, he had the knack of appearing larger than life onstage without detracting from the main action. He was malevolent as Carabosse in *The Sleeping*

Beauty, pathetic and vulnerable as Alain in *La Fille Mal Gardée*, a rustic contemplative as Bottom in *The Dream*, and, a few months before his departure from Covent Garden, a haunting Yslaev, the neglected husband, in *A Month in the Country*. An internationally respected artist, Grant was a mainstay of the Royal Ballet. He would not suffer the disparaging criticisms of lack of stage experience that had plagued David Haber in his attempt to direct the company.

During his thirty-year association with Sadler's Wells and then the Royal Ballet, Grant worked closely with Sir Frederick Ashton in the creation of many of his most famous ballets, developing a special affinity for Ashton's style and for his method of operation as a choreographer. Grant particularly admired the independence which Ashton encouraged his dancers to exhibit as creative artists. Ashton invited them to improvise, then selected what was best from what he had seen and fashioned his own creation out of their contributions. As Grant, frequently Ashton's guinea-pig in this process, put it: 'You felt you could do anything in front of him and he would not let you be put in a bad light.' Grant's professional collaboration with Ashton turned into a close personal friendship as well. In his will, Ashton left to Grant the performing rights to his enduringly popular ballet *La Fille Mal Gardée*.[17]

The other great influence in Grant's Covent Garden background was Dame Ninette de Valois. Like Franca, Grant held her in high esteem, but his perception of de Valois and her administrative style differed from Franca's. He had seen de Valois relinquish the strict control of her Sadler's Wells days and grow with the company into a director and coach who encouraged her dancers to exert their own artistic independence as their capabilities increased.[18] Grant represented the Royal Ballet tradition proper, as it had developed through the first thirty years of its existence, rather than the Sadler's Wells experience of its genesis, which was all that Franca had known directly. He also had some experience as an administrator himself, having directed the Royal Ballet's small educational ensemble, Ballet for All, from 1972 until his departure for Canada.[19] He had worked with Franca in 1946, when, in her *Khadra*, she had been the first choreographer to create a role on the young dancer,[20] but their paths had not crossed since then.

Grant's Royal Ballet background, with its emphasis on the classics as the basis for all the company's activities, his personal connections with Ashton, and his independence from Franca herself made him an attractive candidate for the job. Though a stranger to the National, he was nevertheless well acquainted with its founding traditions, someone who could bring a fresh, independent approach to questions of repertoire and casting without radically altering the course which the company, under Franca, had charted for itself. As Grant later put it: 'I had come from a company that had also looked after the classics, as well as doing its own works. This formula I was endeavouring to accomplish for the National Ballet.'[21]

Not everyone welcomed his appointment. Lauretta Thistle, commenting in the *Ottawa Citizen*, said, 'Dear God, they've done it again. By "done it again" I mean they've gone to the Royal Ballet, and thereby refused to cut the umbilical cord which has tied the National to the Royal all these years.'[22] The spectre of the Royal Ballet haunted Grant in his efforts to lead the company as surely, and almost as unjustly, as it had Franca.

He was haunted as well by the elusive but formidable spirit of Erik Bruhn. Grant himself recognized from the beginning that Bruhn was the obvious choice for the job, and said as much to Bruhn privately when he visited the company to consider its offer.[23] When Grant accepted the position of artistic director, Bruhn resigned his own as resident producer, not in protest, but in order to give the new artistic director complete freedom. As early as the transition period, however, Bruhn felt slighted by what he saw as Grant's lack of attention. In June 1976, he wrote privately to Gerry Eldred, the company's general manager:

> *Perhaps I expected Alex to contact me about various things since he expressed he needed my support when we talked, but I also suppose that he has found the people he needs to work with by now and since I am not exactly in search of a job I consider my relation with the National has come to an end. It has been a good and happy ten years for me and I think it's time to make a change for all concerned.*[24]

Having evaded the responsibilities of the artistic directorship, Bruhn nevertheless expected a role in the affairs of the company. It required infinite tact and diplomacy to negotiate successfully such a minefield of unspoken assumptions and delicate feelings. Tact and diplomacy were not Grant's strong suits, but he did his best. He invited Bruhn back, to teach, to dance, and to add the pas de trois to his production of *Swan Lake*,[25] a variation which Bruhn had omitted when he originally staged the ballet because the company of 1967 lacked second soloists strong enough to cope with its technical demands. Grant used this expanded version of Bruhn's production to open the company's Covent Garden engagement in 1979. Even so, the two men remained on distant terms. For a period of about six months, from July 1976 to January 1977, Bruhn went so far as to have his name removed from the credits for *Swan Lake* and *La Sylphide*.[26]

Reworking the repertoire: Ashton and others

The search committee decided on Grant for the position of artistic director in the fall of 1975,[27] with the appointment to take effect 1 July 1976. Grant thus had the better part of a year to work on the repertoire for his first season, which inevitably combined the advance planning of previous administrations with his own initiatives. The 1976–7 season, Grant's first as artistic director, also marked the company's twenty-fifth anniversary. The new repertoire planned for the season did justice to the special occasion.

After years of avoiding the company's advances, Jerome Robbins finally agreed to its acquisition of his *Afternoon of a Faun*.[28] It premièred during Grant's first season, as did Ditchburn's *Mad Shadows* (already in the planning stages prior to Grant's appointment) and Hans van Manen's *Four Schumann Pieces*, continuing the Dutch connection that had been initiated with *Monument for a Dead Boy* in 1975–6. To encourage the company's own burgeoning choreographic talent, Grant took James Kudelka's *A Party* and Constantin Patsalas' *Black Angels* into the 1976–7 repertoire directly from the company's April 1976 workshop, which he saw prior to his official arrival.[29] The centrepieces of Grant's first season, however, were a previously planned revival of *Romeo and Juliet*, whose costumes had been destroyed in the fire of 1973 and which had not been performed since 22 April 1972, and new productions of Sir Frederick Ashton's *Monotones II* and *La Fille Mal Gardée*, acquired by Grant after his appointment.

It was an exciting, well-balanced season, that accurately foreshadowed Grant's influence on the company. Throughout his seven years with the National, he functioned as the custodian of the existing standard repertoire and the developer of short new works by company choreographers and outsiders, but also as the source of the Ashton repertoire that had so long eluded the company. Ashton's active career as a choreographer had enjoyed a late flowering with his production of *A Month in the Country* in 1976, in which Grant created his last Ashton role.[30] Ashton's reputation rested on his story-ballets, lyrical narratives which revealed the humour, pathos, and irony of human interactions. His achievements in this form had made him the only twentieth-century choreographer whose name could be mentioned in the same breath with Balanchine, who still dominated the North American imagination with his vision of plotless, abstract ballet. Grant's personal friendship with Ashton gave him ready access to his works; he was well equipped to challenge the Balanchine monopoly on public taste and test the extent of Canada's appetite for the Ashton style.

In his first three years with the company, Grant mounted five Ashton ballets – *Fille*, *Monotones*, *The Dream*, *Les Patineurs*, and *The Two Pigeons*. *Monotones*, a miniature to a score by Erik Satie, showed Ashton in his purely abstract vein. *Fille* and *The Dream*, after inconspicuous starts, established themselves as staples of the National's repertoire, ballets whose popularity serves to reveal the careful design and deft manipulation of narrative structure that become apparent on repeated viewing. With their economical exploitation of musical and dramatic values (Ashton story-ballets are generally short, concentrated works), they have proved particularly well suited to the talents of generations of the National's dancers. Key elements of Ashton style – an emphasis on fast footwork, inherent musicality, an abundance of effective character roles – challenged the company's abilities and forced it to develop in new directions. The role of Titania, especially when she was partnered by the Royal Ballet's Anthony Dowell, was instrumental in bringing Veronica Tennant's dancing into its maturity. *Fille* and *The Dream* in themselves justified the Ashton emphasis that Grant brought to the National.

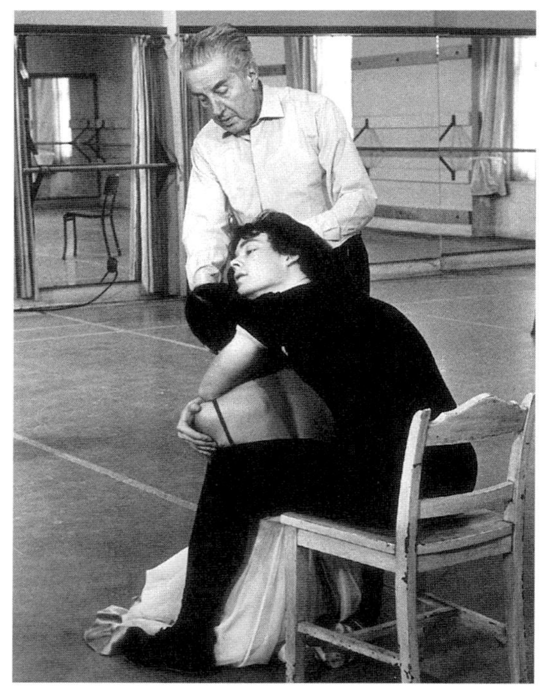

The exploration of young love was one of Sir Frederick Ashton's recurrent themes. Though The Two Pigeons *failed to win popular approval, its duets for the artist and the young girl are among Ashton's finest achievements in this vein. Here, Ashton works on a point of detail with Karyn Tessmer and Raymond Smith, who gave memorable performances in the roles.*

The other Ashton imports, however, failed to win over Canadian popular and critical tastes. The acquisition of Ashton's 1937 *Les Patineurs* was a mistake. It had already been reproduced all over the world – in Canada by the Royal Winnipeg Ballet in 1966, and by the National Ballet School for its 1978 school performance. (Grant himself gave the school permission to use the company's sets and costumes before the first company performance of the work.)[31] On the full company it looked dated, rather than quaint. *The Two Pigeons* was scarcely better received, even though it was a much more novel choice, never before produced in North America and regarded by connoisseurs as one of Ashton's 'sleepers,' a ballet that requires a second chance to reach its audience.[32] The lukewarm reception these two ballets received, coupled with Ashton's well-known aversion to trans-Atlantic travel, put an end to the promising connection Grant was establishing between the National and his friend and former mentor. The company enjoyed the enormous benefit of working directly with Ashton himself during the staging of *The Two Pigeons*, but missed out on a cherished dream – the opportunity to have him choreograph an original work on its dancers.

By the late seventies, Grant had developed a balanced artistic roster, with experienced principal dancers and character artists complemented by an energetic young generation of talent recruited largely from the National Ballet School. Karen Kain, Veronica Tennant, Mary Jago, Vanessa Harwood, Nadia Potts, Frank Augustyn, Tomas Schramek, and Peter Schaufuss were coming into their own as principals;

Charles Kirby, the company's most experienced character artist, was supported by the likes of Hazaros Surmeyan, Jacques Gorrissen, Constantin Patsalas, Victoria Bertram, and Lorna Geddes, all making the transition to character roles; younger dancers like Gizella Witkowsky, Karyn Tessmer, Peter Ottmann, and Linda Maybarduk, along with new recruits such as David Allan, Kimberly Glasco, and Kevin Pugh gave the company a variety and potential it had never known before. With such strength and depth, the National could have done justice to Ashton's *A Month in the Country*, perhaps even attempted his idiosyncratic, quintessentially British masterpiece, *Enigma Variations*. Both were ballets with which Grant had been closely associated. Had he been able, over time, to pry either of them loose from their creator and from the Royal Ballet, Ashton's significance to the National would have stood on an entirely different plane. As it was, the Ashton connection lay unexploited for almost twenty years, until the 1994–5 season, when the National, by then a substantially different company as far as its artistic personnel was concerned, acquired *A Month in the Country* as a tribute to Karen Kain in the twenty-fifth year of her professional career.

Without a really significant core of Ashton works to define his direction, the rest of Grant's acquisitions, though interesting in themselves, failed to focus the company. Neither MacMillan's *Elite Syncopations* (a last-minute substitute for *Song of the Earth*, which had been promised and then withdrawn),[33] nor Lander's *Etudes*, nor Béjart's *Song of a Wayfarer* established a clear direction for the company's future development. Both *Etudes* and *Elite Syncopations*, however, found lasting popularity in the repertoire, where they provided a valuable measuring stick of the company's technical competence judged against that of other major companies that carried these works. In the 'Calliope Rag' variation of *Elite Syncopations*, Cynthia Lucas' witty, tongue-in-cheek performances as the bored vamp set standards for this little cameo role that have never been surpassed.

Only one of the new works, Glen Tetley's *Sphinx*, set the stage for a significant future collaboration between an outside choreographer and the company. Ironically, its arrival in Grant's final year with the National was almost completely overshadowed by the controversy surrounding his departure. The nurturing of the Tetley connection became one of Erik Bruhn's achievements, and few remembered that Grant had been the one to establish it.

Grant's encouragement of Canadian choreographers

Within the company, focus was equally hard to achieve. The company had two aspiring young choreographers, James Kudelka and Constantin Patsalas, with a third, Ann Ditchburn, just beginning to shift her interests to other endeavours. Grant tried to find a way to develop their talents and give them the opportunity to create within the strictures of low budgets and limited audience tolerance for new and experimental repertoire. Kudelka, a brilliant and temperamental prodigy at the National Ballet School, had joined the company at the age of sixteen and was soon choreographing for company workshops; the Greek-born, German-trained Patsalas was a close friend and protégé of Erik Bruhn's with a flair for character roles and ambitions to choreograph works on a grand scale. Both came to prominence under Grant, Kudelka with *A Party*, *Washington Square*, *Playhouse*, and *Hedda*, Patsalas with *Black Angels*, *The Rite of Spring*, *Angali*, *Nataraja*, and *Canciones*. Not since Grant Strate's most productive period had the National given such emphasis to original choreography. The challenge was to find a distinctive, coherent direction for the company in the midst of such choreographic variety.

New works continued to do poorly at the box-office, relative to the standard repertoire, but Grant persevered with the policy of introducing short new ballets on the same program with popular favourites like *The Dream* or *Elite Syncopations*.[34] He thus exposed audiences to original choreography along with the familiar while increasing the number of performance opportunities, an important part of his strategy for making the dancers feel as comfortable onstage as in the rehearsal hall.

But despite this level of activity, the National throughout this period had trouble retaining and nurturing its own choreographers. After *Mad Shadows*, Ann Ditchburn, as part of a small group of the company's younger dancers, experimented with a touring program called Ballet Revue, performing short works from the standard and contemporary repertoire integrated into a highly personal format. Ballet Revue's phenomenal popularity sealed its fate. In a cross-country tour of twenty-one performances, it sold out 108 per cent. As future plans became more elaborate, the implicit competition with company activities forced the dancers and Grant to make hard choices. Tomas Schramek, one of the members of Ballet Revue, recounts the experience: 'We wanted to do it again but met some resistance in the company, for obvious reasons. We were too successful.' Originally active only during the dancers' vacation period, when Ballet Revue's performance schedule began to conflict with the main company's rehearsal and touring, it folded, with vague hopes for the future that never materialized.[35] The disappointment of Ballet Revue's short life-span, coupled with changes in Ditchburn's personal life and the possibility of a movie career, led her to resign from the company, an action which she accompanied with statements to the press regarding her disagreements with Grant's artistic policies.[36] These statements she later came to regret. 'I was a pawn. I thought that I was doing something right for the company. I talked badly about Alex in the press and I'll never forgive myself for that.' Ditchburn left the company after the 1978–9 season, halfway through Grant's term as artistic director. After his departure, she attempted to return, but without success,[37] and subsequently left the dance world to experiment with writing and film. Her resignation and the press coverage accompanying it contributed to a growing perception that the company under Grant was not doing enough to develop its own choreographers.

James Kudelka came to prominence just in time to fill the gap created by Ditchburn's going. Although, in his later international career, Kudelka has worked in many different forms, his major works for the National during this period had a narrative component and a literary source appropriate to the company's traditions and emphasis on story-ballet. *Washington Square*, based on the Henry James novel, and *Hedda*, based on Ibsen's play, united an interest in psychological portraiture with a clearly recognizable narrative line. In both instances, Kudelka used as his designer Jack King, who had remained the designer for *Mad Shadows* after Kudelka's withdrawal from the project. King modelled his designs for *Hedda* on the sombre work of the Norwegian painter Edvard Munch and used back projections derived from his tortured images to enhance the feeling of psychological oppression in the ballet. Both ballets had commissioned scores by Canadian composers, *Washington Square*'s by Michael Conway Baker (its original, workshop version had been set to selections of chamber music by Brahms) and *Hedda*'s, a combination of orchestral score and sound collage, by Norma Beecroft. With their emphasis on psychological observation, both works also provided striking roles for the company's dramatic ballerinas. Veronica Tennant's Catherine Sloper and Gizella Witkowsky's Hedda were serious, substantial creations, challenging to the dancers and audience alike. Despite the difficulties of finding his way beyond gesture and mime to tell his stories in pure dance terms,[38] Kudelka had clearly established himself as one of the most promising choreographers ever to come through the company when he, too, resigned. He left after the 1980–1 season, a year and a half before the première of *Hedda*, to join Les Grands Ballets Canadiens. Despite the considerable choreographic opportunities he had enjoyed with the company, he later spoke

First workshopped in 1977, then revised for the mainstage in 1979, James Kudelka's Washington Square *received a major revival in 1996, the first time that a work created for the company has had the benefit of this kind of retrospective consideration. This photograph, from the original workshop production, features Stephen Jefferies and Cynthia Lucas.*

of the frustrations with Alexander Grant's artistic policies that led to his departure. Kudelka's passion was for creation, not reproduction.

> *Grant's whole career happened because people created roles for him. He should have brought choreographers in to set works on Mary Jago – or me, for that matter – instead of the Ashton repertoire. It's important to work with live people and not a notator from England with the score of* The Dream*! It's more important to be a creator than an interpreter.*[39]

Sir Frederick Ashton came to put the finishing touches on the company's première of The Two Pigeons *in 1979. Here, he watches Alexander Grant rehearsing James Kudelka and Colleen Cool. In the background, George Crum looks over Mary McDonald's shoulder.*

As a creator, Kudelka had had to share the choreographic limelight with Ditchburn and with Constantin Patsalas, with whom he also shared the title of company choreographer.[40] Les Grands offered him the chance to dance a repertoire which he admired and gave him a clear field to choreograph his own works on a regular basis. His subsequent choreographic career with them and with companies in the United States all but eclipsed his beginnings with the National; his complaints at the time of his departure hung in the air, an implicit reproach to Grant and to the company for its failure to meet his expectations. The reproach was mitigated nine years later, in the spring of 1990, when Kudelka accepted the company's invitation to choreograph an original work. The success of Pastorale, an enigmatic ballet set to Beethoven's Symphony No. 6 and depicting an eighteenth-century aristocratic ramble in the countryside, began healing the rift. In September 1992, he was appointed artist in residence with the National, a post which enabled him to resume a close and productive relationship with the company that had given him his start, and which, as things turned out, prefigured much, much more.

By 1981, Grant was left with only one of the three young choreographers he had inherited at the time of his arrival. Constantin Patsalas' *Angali*, *Nataraja*, *The Rite of Spring*, and *Canciones* made striking additions to the repertoire during his administration. The full flowering of Patsalas' brief and turbulent career, however, came later, under Erik Bruhn.

Grant's only other experiment with original Canadian choreography occurred in the 1980–1 season, with Brian Macdonald's *Newcomers*. After two seasons as a dancer with the National in its very first years, Macdonald had gone on to become Canada's best-known choreographer. He had worked extensively with both the Royal Winnipeg Ballet and Les Grands Ballets Canadiens, had preceded Erik Bruhn as artistic director of the Royal Swedish Ballet, and had directed the Harkness Ballet and the Batsheva company in Israel.[41] With works like *Les Whoops-de-Doo* and *Rose Latulippe*, Macdonald had developed a domestic idiom in dance that modified classical ballet with popular elements. He showed early the willingness to draw on the full spectrum of dance traditions, from classical ballet to show-dancing, that later characterized his enormously successful Stratford Festival productions of Gilbert and Sullivan and Broadway musicals and established over time a reputation for working with Canadian music and Canadian themes. But for his past criticism of Franca, Oliphant, and Ambrose, he might have seemed a logical successor to Franca as artistic director of the company. Macdonald had contributed nothing to the National's repertoire since *Post Script* in 1956–7. Grant's commission of a Macdonald work was as much a political gesture of reconciliation as an artistic decision.

Newcomers had a distinctive business dimension as well, as a work sponsored by Imperial Oil in conjunction with its television series of the same name, to celebrate its one-hundredth anniversary in 1980. The National thus gained a new, original work for its repertoire, virtually gratis, but had to accept quite specific conditions from Imperial Oil regarding its commitment to give the new work a significant number of performances.[42] This was raising corporate sponsorship to the level of direct patronage.

The terms of the commission included the specific requirement that the ballet deal with Canadian themes. The end result was well meaning, sincere, and uninspiring. The score, in four separate sections by four different Canadian composers, contributed to a lack of continuity and coherence in the ballet, which depicted the waves of immigration from various points of origin that had settled the nation and transformed the country. The full ballet premièred in Toronto on 19 November 1980, although its first movement, 'Fantasmes,' was performed on tour in St John's, Newfoundland, on 17 October. Despite spirited and energetic performances by Mary Jago and Clinton Rothwell, the ballet, after its contracted number of performances, dropped out of sight. There were no further collaborations with Macdonald. As a self-conscious experiment in nationalism, *Newcomers* fractured the performance image of the company. Somewhere between the anglicized vocabulary of Ashton and the naïve fervour of commissioned nationalism, the company had to assert an identity of its own.

The National's North American reputation and the recruitment of Peter Schaufuss

International touring highlighted this issue of the company's self-definition from a different perspective. In New York, which the National continued to visit annually until 1979, critical and public response began to take note of the company itself as distinct from its superstar guest artist Nureyev. In 1977, Walter Terry, writing in the *Saturday Review*, summed up the company's slow, steady progress towards establishing its own profile in the cutthroat New York dance scene.

> *In recent years, the National had Rudolf Nureyev as guest artist to assure its box office solvency, and Nureyev did an unforgettable job in leading the National into the big time. This year the company made it comfortably on its own with its own excellent stars (Karen Kain and Frank Augustyn among them), a fine supporting group of soloists and corps, and the two young guests Fernando Bujones and Peter Schaufuss, who may well become superstars within a year or two.*[43]

Earlier in the article, Terry had placed the National on an equal footing with the Stuttgart Ballet, saying that 'each of them maintained the high level of performance the ABT had established' during the season they shared at the Met.

Schaufuss' presence, by a combination of lucky chance and conscious choice, opened the way for his future association with the company. Along with his mother, the character artist Mona Vangsaae, the young Schaufuss had been a member of the National briefly in the late sixties, shortly after his graduation from the school of the Royal Danish Ballet. By

When he brought Peter Schaufuss into the company, Alexander Grant caught a rising star. As both a virtuoso dancer and a controversial company director, Schaufuss went on to positions in London, Berlin, and his native Copenhagen.

1977, he had appeared with the London Festival Ballet and was a rising star with the New York City Ballet under Balanchine. The combination of his training and experience, his inborn muscular virtuosity, and his inherent star quality identified him early, as Terry had seen, as a major contender for public recognition. That recognition came, however, in the international arena, and not during the years of his association with the National.

Alexander Grant invited Schaufuss to appear with the National at the Metropolitan Opera after Nureyev, who had been scheduled as usual, withdrew to mount *Romeo and Juliet* for the London Festival and after the New York City Ballet's Peter Martins, who had been secured as his replacement, was denied permission by Balanchine to appear with the company in *Swan Lake*.[44] Schaufuss, who was ready to broaden his horizons, realized that the National's invitation was incompatible with his own position under Balanchine, given Balanchine's stand on Martins' participation in the season.

> *I knew by accepting that engagement that I had to leave New York City Ballet, and I took that risk, accepted the engagement, and danced with the Canadians in New York. Then, after the summer season, they invited me to join the company, and I took up the offer.*[45]

The arrangement which he eventually worked out gave him prominent status within the National but also allowed him to accept the numerous other engagements he was offered worldwide. He became a full company member, but functioned as a resident guest artist, regularly, though not exclusively, associated with the National. Schaufuss later combined his superstardom as a performer with a major career in dance administration in England, Germany, and his native Denmark. As artistic director of the London Festival Ballet (rechristened the English National Ballet), he welcomed Alexander Grant back to a performing career after his stint with the National, brought Lynn Seymour out of retirement, and cajoled Sir Frederick Ashton into reconstructing his *Romeo and Juliet*, which had long been considered irretrievably lost.

Rite of passage: Covent Garden, 1979

During Grant's administration, the National's emerging identity received a chastening, if not ignominious, set-back in London, the other dance capital of the world after New York. The National's associations with British ballet had long made London the foreign centre that mattered most. A London triumph would be particularly sweet. Although no one ever said so out loud, a London triumph would also affix a seal of approval on the company and legitimize its efforts. If there was anything genuinely colonial about the National, its audiences, and its Canadian press, it was this unspoken veneration of the opinion of the mother country. New York had simply been a tough nut to crack; London was the parent whose approval was necessary to the child's sense of self-esteem. To reach real maturity, the National had to come to the bitter realization that its sense of self could not depend on the approval of mother-London. The Covent Garden engagement of 1979 became the company's arduous and painful rite of passage.

Franca's low-key attitude towards the company's first London appearance in 1972 had reflected in part her own independence of spirit and the middle level of the company's entry into the London theatrical circuit. The National had appeared at London's Coliseum Theatre in 1972 and again in 1975. The Coliseum implied high standards, but not the highest, which were associated uniquely with the prestige and social status of the Royal Opera House, Covent Garden. The company had always aimed for Covent Garden, home of the Royal Ballet, and had been advised by Peter Brinson, the British dance journalist and pioneer of Ballet for All, as early as 1973 to hold out for it for its next London engagement.[46] Alexander Grant's long-standing connections with the Royal Opera House had undoubtedly helped him secure his appointment to the National. In 1978, those connections paid off with an invitation from the Royal Opera House to appear for one week during the summer of 1979.[47] The preparation time for such a major engagement was short, and, as Grant knew, a week offered scant opportunity to show the full range of the company's repertoire and artists.[48] Even so, the offer was far too good to refuse.

The opening, on 6 August 1979, was a gala occasion, starring the company's own Karen Kain and Frank Augustyn in *Swan Lake*, with Princess Margaret in attendance, a house liberally sprinkled with enthusiastic Canadian fans and the happy assurance of an entirely sold-out run. But the night, despite a gorgeously bedecked theatre and all the social trappings of a major début, received lukewarm reviews; as the week progressed, the criticisms became harsher and eventually painted a picture of complete disaster. Galina Samsova, by 1979 a resident of London and a seasoned performer on its ballet stages, recalls that the company itself danced well. The problem, in her judgment, lay with the choice of repertoire. 'It had nothing to do with their dancing. It was just – "Don't bring us what we know better."'[49]

As much as the week-long run would allow, Grant chose repertoire which would present the National as a classically based company of international stature, with both depth and versatility. In order to demonstrate its classical base, he scheduled Bruhn's 1967 *Swan Lake*, newly refurbished for the occasion and with the first-act pas de trois inserted in order to show off the capabilities of some of the younger dancers, along with the 1966 Valukin production of *Bayaderka*, which he had revived for the 1977 season.[50] *Mad Shadows* and Gerald Arpino's *Kettentanz*

completed the mixed program (along with *Bayaderka*). The company's spanking-new *La Fille Mal Gardée* rounded out the week's offerings. There was very little security in these choices. Except for *Kettentanz* (which had been shown in London during the company's 1975 visit), each work represented a real gamble. *Mad Shadows* was a gamble of the right kind. However inclined towards condescension the London audience might be, it was vital to show some of the company's original choreography on an occasion of such importance. And *Fille* was probably worth the risk as well. Though the ballet clearly belonged to the Royal, there might have been a cheeky kind of novelty in showing what it looked like, mounted on a different company. But *Swan Lake* and *Bayaderka* were less carefully calculated risks. Bruhn's *Swan Lake*, no longer a novelty, had been seen in London during the company's first visit in 1972. *Bayaderka* was bound to look upstart on the Royal Opera House stage. Nureyev's production for the Royal Ballet, based on the Kirov rather than the Bolshoi tradition, had come to be regarded as definitive by its fervent British admirers. For its first engagement on the foremost ballet stage in Europe, the National had brought coals to Newcastle. The critics were happy to point out that the coals were hardly up to Newcastle's demanding standards.

Even Peter Schaufuss' pyrotechnics and Mary Jago's purity of line could not save Bayaderka *from the wrath of the British critics. The Valukin production was especially offensive to the British, who thought the Royal Ballet's execution of the work set a standard that was unassailable.*

Response to the company's classical repertoire ranged from indifference to outright scorn. *Bayaderka* suffered the most. Alexander Bland, writing in the *Observer*, led the charge.

> *To bring 'La Bayadère' to Covent Garden is an act of recklessness, given the standard of the Royal Ballet production and the fanatical devotion of some of the audience to the ballet. To go to the Bolshoi for a version of a work which is the supreme expression of the Kirov style seems even more foolhardy.*
>
> *'Bayaderka,' as the Canadians call it, was apparently mounted for them by a Moscow choreographer in 1966 and restaged by him only two years ago. The result is a travesty, with Minkus's simple, sweet tunes and Petipa's celestially pure, romantic choreography souped up into a kind of circus display.*[51]

Mary Clarke, commenting on the same ballet in the *Guardian*, was close behind.

> *Sadder than the production, however, was the way the company danced it. It is, in this Kingdom of the Shades scene from the complete ballet, the supreme test of a corps de ballet. And the Canadians gave it a staccato style totally at odds with the flow of movement this masterpiece from St Petersburg demands.*[52]

The opening night *Swan Lake* fared no better as a production, although the critics, restraining themselves slightly at the beginning of the engagement, were inclined to be somewhat kinder to the dancers themselves. Clement Crisp, of the *Financial Times*, wrote:

> *The style of the ensemble is neat, well-mannered, but the staging is one of those wilful exercises which perverts the accepted text of* Swan Lake *in order to reassert Siegfried as the focal point of the ballet. Given the dubious merits of the staging, the National Ballet do well, with sound ensemble playing and promising soloists.*[53]

Mary Clarke was still willing to give the dancers the benefit of the doubt. 'The company, which must not be judged too harshly on this showing, are well drilled but have little opportunity to be more competent.'[54] The expatriate Canadian dancer and critic Fernau Hall deplored the Bruhn staging outright in his review for the *Daily Telegraph*. 'As it turned out, the decision to present *Swan Lake* was unwise, for the defects of the production and the dancing stood out all too clearly. One of the most disturbing features of the Canadian production was Erik Bruhn's choreography.'[55]

Mad Shadows met with blank incomprehension, tempered by disdain. In Alexander Bland's opinion:

> *It took us deep into silent-film territory, with fornication, drink, a blind boy, a murdering moppet and a retarded nine-year-old who takes to the bottle, all hamming it up in the French-Canadian outback.*
>
> *At moments gleams of genuine talent shone out in the choreography and the performances were admirable. But, with its undistinguished score and celluloid antics, the ballet trembled all the way on the brink of farce.*[56]

Mary Clarke was nonplussed: 'About Ann Ditchburn's *Mad Shadows* I am at a loss to know what to say. I'd put it on my very short list of ballets never to be endured again but I was told very firmly by a critic I respect that I was wrong.'[57] Clement Crisp was not: 'The cast work their emotional fingers to the bone; there is a score that should accompany a soap-opera, many set changes and copious use of gauzes. Oh.'[58]

There were a few bright spots. Mary Jago received some of the best notices of

Peter Schaufuss, with artists of the ballet, as Alain in La Fille Mal Gardée. *The dancers' ribbons create the effect of turning wheels, while Alain mimes the horse pulling the carriage.*

her career, and in the demanding classical test-piece of Nikiya in *Bayaderka* at that. Peter Schaufuss was much admired, but at the expense of the rest of the company; 'Danish Artist Saves Canadian Ballet,' said the headline of one of Fernau Hall's reviews, thereby using Schaufuss' achievement as a stick to beat the company with.[59] Despite a succession of onstage accidents with sets and props,[60] which the company borrowed from the Royal Ballet to save shipping expenses, and with its own costumes (the cockerel's splendid tail actually fell off during performance),[61] *La Fille Mal Gardée* fared relatively well, though even here praise came mixed with condescension. As Nicholas Dromgoole, in the *Sunday Telegraph*, put it: 'Their *La Fille Mal Gardée* was another matter, because this ballet is good enough to carry any average company home to success, but it showed up the rest of the repertory on view rather too sharply.'[62]

Summing up the entire season at a later date for the monthly *Dance and Dancers*,[63] John Percival gave a far more balanced and sympathetic account of the company than did his colleagues in the daily press. He was alone in suggesting that the company should have brought more original choreography, one piece by each of Kudelka, Patsalas, and Ditchburn.

If a work by each of them had been given, making clear (as the Stuttgart Ballet did last year) that they are newcomers to choreography, I believe the London audience would have watched them sympathetically and would have been more enthusiastic about the season as a whole.

He himself responded critically but with great sympathy to *Mad Shadows.*

The first and most obvious thing to say about it is that the work is seriously flawed. But it was unfair that so many comments left it at that, without going on to the equally important facts that it was a courageous and ambitious endeavour by a young choreographer and that some aspects of it succeeded in an imaginative and individual way.

He then devoted a full column to an extended discussion of the piece's characteristics, successes, and failures. But even Percival, though he tempered his overall comments, had to admit disappointment with the company's Covent Garden showing. Commenting on Mary Jago's development since the company's 1975 London appearance, he said:

Unfortunately her progress draws attention by contrast to the absence of development in other leading dancers: good before, good now, but not progressing as they need to do for fulfilment. Could it be that the paucity of specially created work is a factor in this, stultifying talent and potential?

And Percival's comments, appearing in a monthly magazine for specialists, received far less circulation than did the harsh criticisms of the dailies, which had been quoted at length in Canadian press reports on the engagement. There was no softening the blow: Covent Garden had been a disaster.

The chastening effects of the experience could be seen in a number of ways. Silently, *Bayaderka* disappeared from the repertoire, never to be danced again until *La Bayadère: Act II* (the Kingdom of the Shades scene from the full-length work), in Natalia Makarova's Kirov-inspired staging, entered the repertoire in 1983–4. More publicly, the pages of the *Globe and Mail* became the forum for a debate about the responsibility for company technique and schooling. Grant had defended himself against some of the London criticisms about schooling by saying: 'It is not our job to teach technique. I must take the very best that is available.' Betty Oliphant's response became the subject of a news story in the *Globe.* 'It is easy not to take responsibility for this, but a company, if it is not responsible for teaching technique, is definitely responsible for maintaining it.'[64] The frustrated hopes of the Covent Garden début thus became the focal point for public criticism of Grant's administration of the company and for the tension between Grant and Oliphant, which increased alarmingly over the next two years.

But criticism of the company's level of execution and technical competence paled in significance beside the fundamental questioning of its taste and artistic judgment. London critics had treated the National as provincial in the worst sense of the word, a company so far removed from the centre that it neither recognized nor shared the standards of taste that prevailed in the sophisticated world. For both the company and its home audience, the shock of this dismissal was hardest to bear but proved most salutary in the long run. It took some time for the company and its supporters to recover from the bludgeoning they had received, but when they did, they could look upon themselves and their mission with washed eyes.

In brutal fashion, the London critics had put paid to the secret hope that the National might one day conquer London just as decisively as the Sadler's Wells had conquered New York in 1949. The myth of the plucky little company, emerging from local obscurity to international acclaim, would no longer serve. Relinquishing that myth freed the company to pursue its own artistic course, indifferent to the approval or criticism of the Old Guard. There can be little doubt that the National deserved some of the harsh criticism it received; there can be equally little doubt that it had to learn to dance for itself and for its own audience, without undue regard for external approval, before it could develop a character of its own. Likewise the Canadian public, waiting eagerly for reports of praise and approbation, had to learn to look with its own eyes and make its own judgments. It had long since changed its allegiance from the imported to the domestic artistic product. London, 1979, taught it to forego the dubious luxury of imported critical opinion and to undertake the task of self-education that would allow it to evaluate the domestic product with confidence. Covent Garden forced the company and its audience into the mature, if rueful, realization that our centre was not elsewhere; our centre was here.

The complex series of events leading to the dismissal of Alexander Grant

Troubled as Grant's career at the National became, it nonetheless brought a flowering of young talent into the company, comparable to the influx of women from the National Ballet School in the early sixties. Kimberly Glasco, Kim Lightheart, Sabina Allemann, and Amalia Schelhorn all entered the company during this period. All had distinguished careers with the company, Glasco's longer than any of the others'. Even more remarkable, however, was the deluge of male talent that descended on the National at this time. Grant had brought Stephen Jefferies from the Royal Ballet for his first season. (He later brought Anthony Dowell, the Royal's undisputed star, for extended visits which inspired and educated the National's own principals, both male and female.) Jefferies' experience and vigour proved a welcome addition to a company which, like many, had decidedly more strength and depth among its women than its men. But when Jefferies left after only one season, to

A galaxy of the company's stars (from left to right, David Nixon, Nadia Potts, Raymond Smith, Veronica Tennant, Peter Schaufuss, Karen Kain, Kevin Pugh, Mary Jago, David Roxander and Vanessa Harwood) in the final act of Napoli. *With strength like this in the company, and a reluctance on Grant's part to deny his dancers the roles they requested, his casting policies eventually became a source of concern.*

return to London and the Royal Ballet, his place was quickly filled, not by another visitor, but by a succession of strong, distinctive male dancers drawn entirely from the National Ballet School. Kevin Pugh, David Nixon, William Stolar, Paul Chalmer, Jeremy Ransom, Serge Lavoie, Anthony Randazzo, and Owen Montague were all taken into the company by Grant. Ransom and Lavoie became principals, and mainstays of the company. Pugh, Nixon, and Montague made substantial impacts on the National before leaving, Nixon and Montague for careers in Europe, Pugh, following debilitating injuries and a courageous attempt to resume his career, for other pursuits. Stolar, Randazzo, and Chalmer, after briefer associations with the National, made important dance careers with American Ballet Theatre, the San Francisco Ballet, and the English National Ballet. From the junior ranks of the National, the future stared Grant in the face and asked to be acknowledged.

As both the repertoire and the influx of new dancers indicated, Grant had charge of the company during a volatile and difficult period of transition. Years of stability and careful, incremental growth had suddenly given way to all the tensions, competition, and instability of an explosion of talent. That this explosion occurred during a period of economic recession, which, inevitably, cut into box-office receipts for all the performing arts,[65] didn't make the task of managing the company any easier. Grant came under increasing fire, from within the company and from without. One of the criticisms, which he still found illogical long after his depar-

ture, was that he gave too many dancers too many opportunities to dance,[66] in effect, that he refused to make the difficult choices among individual dancers that were necessary to a sound, carefully considered casting policy. In his defence, it must be said that if ever any artistic director suffered from an embarrassment of riches, it was Alexander Grant. Five senior ballerinas and two internationally experienced premiers danseurs constituted a sizeable block to the burgeoning talent in the lower ranks of the company. Casting was a major diplomatic, as well as artistic, challenge. The departures of Chalmer, Glasco (who returned after two seasons with American Ballet Theatre), and Stolar during this period hinted at some of the frustrations the younger generation felt. But Grant was not the man to tell experienced company members that their services would be in less demand, or not required at all, in order to give younger dancers their chance. That purge came later, at other hands.

Grant's contract had been renewed in the spring of 1979,[67] just prior to the company's Covent Garden appearance. In the period immediately following, the many pressures under which he had been operating came to a head. The press once again became the forum for a discussion of the state of the company and Grant's record as artistic director. Two of the credentials which had certainly helped him win the post, his access to the Ashton repertoire and his associations with Covent Garden, had lost their original lustre in the public eye. When company morale, always a volatile commodity, reached dangerously low levels, several of the dancers themselves entered the fray.

By the early eighties, Karen Kain and Frank Augustyn were two of the National's undisputed stars and had the informal role of leadership within the company which that status and their seniority conferred. Kain, who had been expressing her concerns privately to Grant himself and to various members of the board of directors, finally decided to speak out publicly on the issues which troubled her. Frank Augustyn acknowledged the same responsibility. As he later expressed their dilemma: 'Whether we wanted it or not, we had a certain responsibility towards the National Ballet Company and so it was better to speak out. It was a necessary evil.'[68] Their speaking out took the form of criticisms in the press of Grant's administrative policies. In an interview in the *Globe and Mail* in May 1982, they commented specifically that Grant assigned too many alternate casts to works, and that he had not brought enough new, original ballets into the repertoire to stimulate the company creatively.[69] Public criticism from artists of this calibre could not be ignored.

But public criticism alone did not dislodge Grant from his position with the company. Opposition to his reappointment and concern about his artistic policies were expressed to the board privately, independent of the dancers' initiative. Betty Oliphant had written to the president of the board of directors at the time of the expiration of Grant's first contract, to say that, in her opinion, he ought not to be renewed. She saw him as the cause of the doldrums into which the company had fallen and, when his contract was renewed, wrote again to predict that only a radical slump in box-office would bring the board round to her opinion. Erik Bruhn, who continued to perform as guest artist with the company, also became concerned about its condition. Aware of the weight Bruhn's opinion would carry with the board, Oliphant undertook to mobilize his concern.

> *I got a reputation, which I always feel was rather unfair, for being a stirrer up of trouble. But nobody else would fight for saving the company. I walked into Erik's dressing room one day when he was performing the witch in* La Sylphide, *and he said, 'Betty, what are we going to do?' I said, 'Well Erik, it's not really what* we're *going to do, because I have done all I can. But if you would also speak to people on the board –.' He said, 'I'll speak to anyone. You just arrange it.' And that was a big step for Erik. So I arranged for him to meet with the chairman of the board.*[70]

The cumulative power of such opposition proved impossible to resist. In late June 1982, the board terminated Grant's appointment.[71]

In speaking out about the company's problems, Karen Kain had not anticipated such drastic action and had, indeed, been unaware that the board was about to move. Coming, as it did, hard on the heels of her press statements of late May, the board's announcement looked like a direct response to her complaints, rather than the independent action it was. Kain, while she stood by the comments she had made, regretted the timing of events and the lack of full communication between board and dancers which made this interpretation of her actions possible. 'I hurt Alexander's feelings terribly. It was not a very pleasant thing, and it was only because I wasn't informed. I reached a breaking-point and I said what I felt. I wasn't happy about the way that was handled.'[72] The crisis over Grant's direction thus brought to light an important side issue, that of the dancers' right to express themselves, and to be heard, on matters of general company management. Dancers had had formal representation on the board since 1970,[73] but Kain's and Augustyn's actions really heralded the new era of self-awareness and independence. As Kain describes the issue:

> *We are not always as articulate as we would like to be because we are not used to using words. But we have very good instincts, and we know when things aren't right, and we know when the ship doesn't have a captain. It's part of our training to be quiet, to do what we are told. It's part of the discipline that you don't argue, you don't fight back. I think all of those things are changing. I think that we demand more of the people in front of the rehearsal room than we used to.*[74]

Like the Covent Garden experience, the painful self-examination of the Grant crisis formed part of the company's necessary maturation process. For the dancers, rising on pointe had never been a problem; as individuals and as an organization, they now faced the greater challenge and responsibilities of standing on their own feet.

But analysis of the larger issues cannot gloss over the personal pain of the dismissal. Alexander Grant was in Jackson, Mississippi, serving on the jury of the International Ballet Competition there, when André Galipeault, the president of the board, flew down to see him. His response, as quoted in the *Toronto Star* at the time, came as something of a surprise. 'I said I didn't want to resign. I wouldn't do it. It was the responsibility of the board to ask me if they felt I must, but I wouldn't offer it to them. I think you could say I'm more than a little hurt.'[75] Rather than bow out quietly, Grant forced the board's hand. He commented on its decision publicly and furthermore chose to work out his year's notice of termination to the bitter end, in the full glare of the attendant publicity.[76] From July 1982 to June 1983, Grant worked without the confidence of the board that employed him.

Peter Schaufuss' *Napoli* restored the company's self-confidence.

It would be an exaggeration to say of Grant's career with the National that nothing in his artistic directorship became him like the leaving it. It is ironically true, however, that his final eighteen months in the job saw a distinct upswing in the company's fortunes, and that public opinion once again looked more favourably upon him. In November 1981, just as the storm clouds began to gather, the National opened Peter Schaufuss' landmark production of Bournonville's *Napoli*. Grant had suggested the project to Schaufuss, who was still a member of the company at this time, during the National's appearance at the Chicago Festival in 1979. He thereby beat out the Australian National Ballet, which was also negotiating with Schaufuss for his first *Napoli*. Schaufuss recalls the allegiance he felt to the National. 'I really wanted to do it here, because I was a member of the company at that time and I felt that that was what I should accept, and then not do it in Australia.'[77]

Napoli, the most popular of the Bournonville ballets in the Royal Danish Ballet's repertoire, was largely unknown outside its native Denmark. Received opinion held that the complete work, with its heavy emphasis on mime, Roman Catholicism, and the supernatural, would be unplayable outside the tradition that had nurtured it. The third-act divertissements enjoyed great popularity around the world, but the complete work remained a piece of relatively arcane ballet lore to all except the Danes and their followers. Schaufuss had not mounted *Napoli* before. He had, however, danced in a production of the complete work which Poul Gnatt, of the Royal Danish Ballet, staged for the Scottish Ballet in 1978,[78] and had received critical acclaim for his own production of Bournonville's *La Sylphide* for the Festival Ballet in 1979. The plan was daring and its scope was huge. Grant and

Schaufuss proposed to give North America its first full-length production of a certified, if obscure, Danish masterpiece. If they succeeded, the National would gain new stature for its imaginative, independent approach to programming: no longer a provincial imitator of others; no longer a clone of the Royal Ballet; no longer a passenger on Nureyev's coattails.

But getting the production onstage took perseverance and determination. The obvious risks involved made many people nervous, from board members apprehensive about the production's cost (approximately $450,000),[79] to Canada Council officials sceptical about the 'creative deficit' into which it forced the company,[80] to dancers less than enthusiastic about the ballet itself,[81] to members of the press doubtful that the first and second acts could be successfully staged outside Denmark.[82] Difficulties in scheduling adequate rehearsal time led to a postponement of the production from the spring to the fall of 1981.[83] Preparations were filled with equal portions of apprehension and excitement.

Napoli tells the story of a young Neapolitan fisherman's love for the beautiful Teresina, who is courted by old and inappropriate rival suitors. During a storm at sea, Teresina is washed away, and Gennaro, her youthful lover, survives only to be blamed by the townspeople for her loss. Aided by a medallion of the Madonna, Gennaro ventures forth to rescue his beloved from the Blue Grotto of Capri and the supernatural clutches of Golfo, the King of the Sea, who has transformed her into a naiad. As a concession to twentieth-century scepticism, Schaufuss played the entire Blue Grotto sequence as a tortured dream of Gennaro's. (No one pointed out that twentieth-century scepticism accepts without a murmur the supernatural transformations from woman to swan to evil seductress on which *Swan Lake* is built.) In deference, however, to the eternal appeal of stage spectacle, he retained the breakaway costumes which transform Teresina twice, in full view of the audience, from human to naiad and back to human form once again. Reunited, the lovers return to Naples, clear Gennaro of the false accusation of his rivals that he is in league with the devil, and preside over the famous pas de six and tarantella which end the ballet. In a formula well known to classical story-ballet, two acts of complicated narrative are concluded with an act of pure celebration and dance.

Opening night, on 10 November 1981, proved that superlative dancing and strong production values could redeem even a contrived and creaky plot like *Napoli*'s. The O'Keefe Centre stage overflowed with vibrant colour and youthful, energetic dance. The company looked rejuvenated, free and graceful, riding high on the spectacular production itself. The first-act mime sequences, for which Schaufuss had invited Denmark's Niels Bjørn Larsen as guest, communicated clearly and comically to the audience; the revised Blue Grotto scene of the second act continued to trouble some critics, but held audience attention with Teresina's breakaway costumes and a clever substitution trick for the male lead that enabled

Gennaro to disappear at stage left and re-enter at stage right just a split-second later; the procession and tarantella of the last act, in which the full company and scores of children from the National Ballet School crowded the stage, pulsated with unquenchable energy and radiated pure joy. The presence of the schoolchildren testified, as well, to the School's important role in turning out dancers able to do justice to the technical demands of Bournonville's elegant, buoyant choreography. If anything proved the wisdom of mounting the full work, it was the last act which, presented in context as the celebration of the peasant love-story that had gone before, created its proper effect as conclusion to the drama, not a mere string of unmotivated divertissements. The company's special way with Bournonville style, which Schaufuss describes as slightly bigger and more powerful than the Danish,[84] showed off to great advantage. They had, after all, been dancing Bournonville since *La Sylphide* in 1964. It was as unqualified a success as was possible in the international dance world of the eighties. And it was a truly international event. Instead of going, cap in hand, to another world centre for inspection and approval, the National brought the international critical establishment to Toronto for the occasion. Special pre-performance talks on aspects of Bournonville style prepared the audience for what it was about to see. *Napoli* was a major acquisition for the company, and a major accomplishment for both Schaufuss and Grant.

Erik Bruhn as Peppo and Alexander Grant as Giacomo confront each other in the first act of Napoli *in a bravura display of comic character dancing.*

Although the ballet was not an instant success, box-office built satisfactorily over the forty-one performances which the ballet received to the end of the 1990–1 season. When Erik Bruhn took over the company, he chose not to capitalize on the production's potential. He did not authorize the construction of a touring set, and so the full production was seen only in Toronto, Ottawa, and Montreal. Act III alone was performed more widely on tour, but Act III alone could not give a full impression of the nature of the production and its achievement. The Schaufuss production has, however, been mounted on the English National Ballet and on the company of the Teatro San Carlo, in Naples, the scene of the ballet's action.[85] Though the impact of *Napoli* was insufficient to rescue Grant's own career with the company, it did much to wipe out memories of Covent Garden. With a distinctive achievement like this to its credit, the company no longer needed to look back.

But look back it did, in an especially appropriate way, just two days after *Napoli*'s opening. On 12 November 1981, the company celebrated its thirtieth anniversary with a dazzling special performance of *Napoli*. Schaufuss and Veronica Tennant danced the leads, with Niels Bjørn Larsen, Alexander Grant, and Erik Bruhn in the principal character roles. Vanessa Harwood, Mary Jago, Karen Kain, and Nadia Potts appeared in the pas de six and tarantella, perhaps the first time since *Sleeping Beauty* that all five of the company's senior ballerinas had danced together in the same performance. Yves Cousineau, the redoubtable Tybalt of many a *Romeo and Juliet*, came out of retirement, as did Lois Smith, to take minor parts. And swanning about in the widow's weeds and black veil of one of the walk-on parts was none other than Celia Franca. Grant still looks back on the accomplishment of that evening with pride.[86] It was a real celebration of the company's stature as well as a merciful hiatus in his personal tribulations.

Ashton's The Dream, *an enduring legacy for the company, with Karen Kain as Titania, and Luc Amyôt (before the injury that curtailed his performing career) as Oberon.*

Alexander Grant's final exit

The repertoire of Grant's final season with the company was mixed but respectable. Nicholas Beriosoff, who was to have staged *Le Coq d'Or* for the company in 1975, produced *Don Quixote* on a shoestring, the production itself purchased from the London Festival Ballet. It met with only partial success, mainly because the sets and costumes proved, on arrival, to be garish and in disrepair. But Grant did thereby give the company its first full-length *Don Quixote*, a ballet which, redesigned by Desmond Heeley in 1985, figured prominently in Erik Bruhn's repertoire planning. Grant's revival of John Neumeier's 1974 production of *Don Juan* was distinguished by guest performances by the Royal Ballet's Anthony Dowell, appearing for the first time, anywhere in the world, in the role of the Don. His elegantly restrained interpretation of the central role challenged the memory of Nureyev's more flamboyant approach to it, while his generous presence served as example and inspiration to the company's dancers. His discreet partnering highlighted Mary Jago's Lady in White, which had always been one of her most effective roles in the repertoire. The revival of Tudor's *Offenbach in the Underworld* (Grant had revived *Dark Elegies* just two seasons earlier) proved to have more sentimental than intrinsic value. But Glen Tetley's *Sphinx* held spectators spellbound and revealed a dark and mysteriously sensual side of the dancers that had seldom been seen before. Frank Augustyn and Karen Kain, whose partnership in the standard classical roles was waning, enjoyed an enormous success as Oedipus and the Sphinx, dramatizing a relationship in which romantic attachment is replaced by sexual tension and the struggle for power. Had Grant stayed one more year, he would have been able to leave to the glorious strains of *Onegin*, a ballet which he programmed but did not see through production.[87] Its première on 14 June 1984, as the National's contribution to the Toronto International Festival, added the second Cranko story-ballet to the National's repertoire, a dramatic vehicle for many of the company's ballerinas, and a perennial audience favourite. But even without the high point of *Onegin* to soften his departure, the coda of Grant's last months with the National reverted to a major key.

The bitterness and recrimination of the parting of the ways between Grant and the company had the unfortunate effect of obscuring his real achievements with the National. In repertoire and the hiring of dancers, he made choices for the company from which it still benefits today. And perhaps his failure rate in such areas was no worse than the average. But his managerial style, the antithesis of Franca's firm, direct control, was too liberal and accommodating for an organization in a state of transition. Company members complained of lack of direction; Grant, in his own defence, saw himself as trying to introduce them to the freedom and responsibility of the full professional. The responsibilities that accompanied such freedom could be frightening.

Under coaches like Franca and Nureyev, the dancers of the National had been drilled in the minutiae of performance. Lois Smith recalled, of the mad scene in Franca's *Giselle*, that every move, every reaction was carefully choreographed.[88] Very little was left to chance or the spontaneity of the moment. Such rigorous attention to detail gave the company the uniformity of style which had gained it its early distinction, but it also prompted the criticisms of hesitancy and lack of individuality that had later been applied to it. To achieve full creative expression, the dancers had to learn to take individual risks. For Grant, the difference was that between a company and a school. 'A ballet company,' says Grant now, 'is not a school. A ballet company are professional artists who have been trained in a school. And you don't run a ballet company like a school.' What the dancers experienced as lack of direction, Grant thought of as adult, professional treatment. In Grant's view:

> *Dancers never stop learning to polish their technique and develop their artistry. You give an artist a certain degree of independence. You don't tell an artist to raise an eyebrow here or an eyelash there unless that artist is raising that eyebrow in the wrong way. But he might raise it in a wonderful way that surprises even the person who is doing the coaching, and that's all to the good.*

Grant had seen de Valois grow with her company from a strict teacher to a more liberal coach, willing to give her artists creative independence. As he recalls: 'In the beginning, when she first had the company, she had to tell them, because it's a school in the beginning. De Valois, being the great woman that she was, grew, and as she grew, and the company grew, this whole attitude changed.'[89] Undirected laissez-faire or room to grow? Grant's attitude of benign detachment came out of a combination of his own past experience and a genuine desire to move the company on to the next stage of its development. But the company was not ready to hear this message of increased artistic independence, or at any rate not willing to accept it from Alexander Grant. Erik Bruhn, his successor, was to deliver a strikingly similar message to the company, but with markedly greater success.

CHAPTER EIGHT

Outspoken in Our Work and in Our Dancing

Bruhn takes the plunge.

As early as 1952, Erik Bruhn had turned down a half-joking invitation from Celia Franca to join the National Ballet of Canada;[1] since 1964, he had circled on its periphery, almost always involved, never at its centre. With the announcement of Grant's departure, the stage was set, but for whose entrance? Bruhn had played the reluctant débutante for so long that his name was no longer the first to become the subject of speculation. One newspaper report of Grant's dismissal mentioned Veronica Tennant, Brian Macdonald, and Peter Schaufuss as possible successors,[2] but not Erik Bruhn. He was finally chosen only after a rigorous public search, carried out at his own insistence. Despite his disclaimers to the contrary, Bruhn had considerable skills as a politician. In an early display of those skills, he used his genuine reluctance to emerge too quickly as the company's artistic director in order to assure himself of an enthusiastic welcome to

OPPOSITE: Mary Jago took on the role of Giselle late in her career and danced it only eighteen times. Nevertheless, when she retired from dancing in 1984, she chose Giselle *for her official farewell. A curtain call at the O'Keefe Centre.*

ABOVE: As part of his strategy for change, Erik Bruhn challenged the company's younger dancers with creative opportunities. Corps members Barbara Smith and Owen Montague, seen here in 1983 in rehearsal for Constantin Patsalas' L'Ile Inconnue, *rose to Bruhn's challenge.*

the post. He needed such enthusiasm to support him through the difficult reorganization of artists and staff that constituted his first responsibility.

By discreetly intimating to a number of key people that he might, finally, be interested in the position, Bruhn encouraged the groundswell of support that made it his. As in 1975, so in 1982 he was an obvious adviser to the search committee and to all those concerned about the National's future. The man who had so steadfastly resisted the company's previous blandishments became, in private, remarkably amenable to suggestion. Robert Johnston, who had replaced Gerry Eldred as the company's general manager in 1979, remembers his approach to Bruhn in the matter.

Bruhn's long-standing ties with the company and the school went back to his staging of La Sylphide. *After one of its first performances in 1965, he chatted backstage with the school's artistic director, Betty Oliphant, and principal dancer Earl Kraul.*

> *I had arranged with Erik to have a drink with him. One of the things I wanted to find out was whether there was the remotest chance that he'd be interested in this job. As we walked down to San Lorenzo's to have our glass of wine, he said, 'You know, if you really can't find anybody else, I might be willing to take it on.' Well, we knew the search was over the minute he said that. He literally volunteered, which, given how he felt in '75, was quite a transition.*[3]

Lyman Henderson chaired the board's search committee for a new artistic director.[4]

Following up a tip from Betty Oliphant, he too consulted Bruhn, again with an eye to interesting him in the position.

> *I asked his advice, and then I said, as we were coming to the close of the conversation, 'Would you be interested yourself?' And he said something to this effect: 'I swore I would never take on the artistic direction of any company again, but I love the National Ballet so much that maybe I might change my mind.' We certainly went through the whole search process, but the target was obvious pretty early on.*[5]

Valerie Wilder had, by 1982, left a career as a dancer with the National and become a dancers' agent. Among her clients was Erik Bruhn. She too was surprised by Bruhn's easy acquiescence to the idea of directing the company.

> *He was in town in the early summer of '82 when, in the course of our conversation, one of my topics was: 'As you know, the National Ballet has started a search. It has been speculated that you will certainly be asked to do it. How do you want to respond to this?' Much to my surprise he said, 'Well, you know, I am getting sick and tired of travelling around. I think I might like to do it, but I don't really know if we will be able to reach an agreement. You can negotiate it for me.' And off he went.*[6]

Betty Oliphant sums up the informal part of the search procedure most succinctly: 'Well, we all asked him to consult, and then he said, "How about me?"'[7]

Bruhn's strategy in the matter was carefully thought out, as he indicated in an interview in *Dance and Dancers* shortly after his appointment.

> *When the time came to decide for a new director, I was willing to be an advisor to the search committee, to help and recommend. I said 'if you come to a point where you feel that there is no-one right for the moment, I wouldn't mind helping you out for a short time, 2 or 3 years.' That gave a seed to all the committee and board people here. So I said 'you have to go through all the Canadians and even all the foreigners who are interested. That will give me the chance to rethink whether or why I want to come back and help you out as a temporary director.'*[8]

It also protected him from any subsequent accusations of having stolen a march on other qualified candidates and unquestionably heightened the anticipation surrounding the final announcement. Thus indirectly did Bruhn sidle into the job that had long awaited him.

Bruhn's interest was kept strictly confidential, but even so the search, though rigorously conducted, took on a certain pro forma air. David Adams, having returned to Canada from England, was among those interviewed for the position.

'Although I made application, I had a sneaking suspicion that they had already chosen the person, and of course they had.'[9]

The fact that Bruhn already held Canadian landed immigrant status smoothed the way for his appointment in one significant respect. During the search process, the committee received a delegation from the Department of Employment and Immigration which stressed the importance of appointing a Canadian (broadly defined to include naturalized citizens and landed immigrants) to the job. With the target of the search already clearly in mind, Henderson was able to say, 'If we depart from that, I'll let you know.' Public opinion, as well as government regulations, made the nationalist issue a particularly sensitive one. Despite strong pressures to make citizenship status one of the deciding criteria for the position, the search committee was looking for the best possible candidate anywhere in the world. In a profession as international in its orientation and methods of operation as ballet, the chances of finding the citizenship and artistic criteria embodied in a single individual were slim indeed. As a landed immigrant, Bruhn passed the citizenship test on a technicality. And, from Henderson's point of view, 'that was purely a fortuitous circumstance.'[10] The committee took seriously its responsibility to find the best possible artistic director for the company, regardless of nationality.

Bruhn's appointment brought an interesting perspective to bear on the ongoing debate about nationalism and the arts. As the following three years proved, he was undoubtedly the right choice for the position, the individual capable of restoring to the company its sense of self-confidence, and hence of its own identity, and the one to push it into a more active relationship with other parts of the Canadian dance scene. Had he not been appointed, it is impossible to predict with any certainty where the National would stand in its own country or in the world today. Had his appointment been blocked on nationalist grounds, it is unlikely that the company, reeling as it still was from the bad publicity surrounding its handling of Alexander Grant's dismissal, would have survived the experience with any sense of its primary mission intact. Nor is it likely, given Bruhn's general hesitancy to assume administrative responsibility after his unpleasant experiences of government intervention in Sweden, that he would have been willing to let his name stand through that kind of highly politicized examination and debate. Bruhn's landed immigrant status and his insistence on a full-scale search for qualified Canadians constituted the necessary preconditions for his appointment. Yet his citizenship status was the least of his qualifications for the job.

His long-standing association with the company gave him the insight he needed to function sympathetically and effectively as its artistic director. His international experience allowed him to consider its problems objectively. And his international reputation helped immeasurably to restore the dancers' own sense of self-confidence and to win the Canadian public's respect. Through a stroke of pure luck,

Bruhn's appointment satisfied the political considerations inherent in the choice of an artistic director for a national cultural institution. But it also pointed up the fact that in this instance, the political considerations contributed nothing materially to the choice itself; had they been applied in such a way as to block it, they could have done real harm.

One other factor did, however, complicate Bruhn's appointment. Knowing his own limitations and his distaste for certain aspects of the administrative responsibilities he must face, Bruhn made his interest in the job contingent upon the appointment of two colleagues who would work with him to form a three-person administrative team. As Bruhn's negotiator, Valerie Wilder had the responsibility of winning the board over to this new concept of artistic administration. It was a hard sell, as she recalls the negotiations. 'It wasn't an easy concept to sell. The board wanted one star. They didn't really see the value of a team and couldn't see why that would be necessary.' As negotiations proceeded, Bruhn agreed to begin his term with only one of the two colleagues in place, the other to be added after his first year in the job. At about the same time, he specified that he wanted Valerie Wilder to become the first member of the team.

> *I think it was a little bit later in the process that he backed down from the three and named me as the first team member. When I first began negotiating, I was negotiating in a kind of loose, theoretical sense, and in fact there came a time when I couldn't continue. As soon as I became that person, and finances became involved, it really did become impossible, and I had to back off a little bit.*[11]

The new generation of male dancers struts its stuff in Erik Bruhn's Here We Come *(1983). From left to right, Anthony Randazzo, Serge Lavoie, Pierre Quinn, and Owen Montague. All were graduates of the National Ballet School, and all went on to distinguished careers with the National or with other companies.*

Thus Valerie Wilder, who herself had extensive experience with the National Ballet as well as an established working relationship with Bruhn, became Bruhn's artistic administrator.

She was joined after one year by Lynn Wallis, in the position of artistic coordinator. Wallis, whose background was with the Royal Ballet School in England, had initially had contact with the National during Alexander Grant's administration, when she mounted *Les Patineurs* and *Monotones* for the National Ballet School, and *The Two Pigeons* for the company. During one of her visits to the School, she had seen Bruhn's *Here We Come*, which he created as a special tribute to the School's extraordinary male students for its 1978 graduation program. She later invited him to mount it for the Royal Ballet School. It was, as she recalls, 'his first time back with the Royal Ballet establishment after he had left as a dancer.' In 1984, she accepted his invitation to work as guest ballet mistress with the National for three months. After that trial period, she became the third member of the administrative team.[12]

The concept of genuine teamwork was new in artistic administration and absolutely central to Bruhn's approach. He used it, not only as a way to lighten his own load, particularly of the duties to which he was ill suited, but also to bring the artistic side of the company back to a sense of real collaboration and cooperation. The early company had often been characterized as a kind of family. Under Bruhn, 'team' replaced 'family' as the metaphor for community. The difference was significant. The authority of the artistic director, as team leader, was less obtrusive, though no less real, than it had been as family head. More important, the responsibility for the success of the joint venture devolved in a more direct way onto each member of the team. Bruhn stressed administrative teamwork that went beyond a simple division of duties, teamwork in which each member could do parts of the other's job, in which real opportunity existed to contribute to artistic policy-making.[13] That sense of opportunity and responsibility worked its way through to all levels of the company, drawing individuals together in the common artistic enterprise. As Bruhn noted in a private memorandum in Copenhagen, following the European tour of 1985: 'A strong team of a ballet staff must be based on mutual respect and artistic understanding before a fruitful collaboration can be expected to take place.'[14] It was Bruhn's response to the problem that had defeated Alexander Grant. Neither family nor school, a company, in Bruhn's terms, should be a team.

But when Bruhn finally decided to take the company on, his only assurance was of the challenges involved, not the success he would enjoy. Those challenges were, if anything, greater in 1983 than they had been in 1975. What accounted for his change of heart? Veronica Tennant supplies part of the answer in highly personal terms.

> *I believe that it took Erik many, many years to get over the fact that he was no longer a dancer. I think he suffered deeply and greatly from stopping dancing. It was the kind of suffering that was almost physical for him. I think that by the time '83 came along, he had resolved this within himself. He was a great artist, and so to cut off that part of his self-expression would take him longer than it would take somebody else. By the time '83 came along he was ready and resolved within himself. He had matured enough now to want to be challenged again, and he called us his ultimate challenge.*[15]

Another part of the answer lay with the nature of the company itself, and of Bruhn's relationship with it, as he pointed out in the *Dance and Dancers* interview.

> *I did 5 months of good thinking, and came to the conclusion that although I would not accept to be director of any other company in the world (I've refused Denmark twice, and La Scala, and the Paris Opera even, and at one time I was a candidate for ABT after Lucia Chase) I liked this company. The possibility was there, the organization as such, not just the dancers whom I knew very well, but the office people, the musicians, the wardrobe.*[16]

But something else had changed in the years since Bruhn had last sidestepped the artistic directorship. Two very large and influential personalities had receded from the company's view. In 1975, he would inevitably have had to work in the shadows of Celia Franca and Rudolf Nureyev. By 1982, Bruhn could take over without appearing to supplant Franca, whose retirement to Ottawa and participation in other dance activities had removed her from direct involvement in the company's life. And with the Nureyev connection far less prominent than it had been in the years immediately following *Sleeping Beauty*, he could avoid even the appearance of a rekindling of those old rivalries. The timing was right and the coast was clear.

Because he so successfully mobilized his team, Bruhn's three years at the head of the company instituted a surprising number of different initiatives. Radical re-evaluation of the repertoire and the artistic complement of the company; an aggressive approach towards development and marketing; daring experiments with choreographers from at home and abroad; continued, direct contact with the dancers in the studio; effective long-range planning; a passion for youth and for developing international contacts – Bruhn and his colleagues touched on all of these areas in their planning for the development of the company. No single event characterized the tactical astuteness and artistic daring of Bruhn's approach more dramatically than his choice of programming for his first gala on 18 February 1984. A manifesto in the guise of a fundraiser, it served notice on the National's established audience that a new era was about to dawn.

A fearless commitment to new choreography

The gala made its obligatory bow towards superstardom with Mikhail Baryshnikov, partnering Elaine Kudo in Twyla Tharp's *Sinatra Suite*, but his presence was merely a hook to lure the patrons. The real program, light years away from standard gala fare, was carefully constructed to announce to the world the shape of the National Ballet's future, as Erik Bruhn conceived it. It opened with a full company master class, conducted by Bruhn himself. The class presented the entire company to its public, not as stars and supporting dancers, but as equal participants in the rigorous demands of the preparation for dance. It demonstrated both the discipline of the art form and the concept of teamwork with which Bruhn intended to approach it. And it revealed Bruhn in relation to his dancers: personal, ironic, challenging, goading them on to new discoveries about their technique and about themselves, daring them to risk failure in pursuit of impossible ideals. Only Baryshnikov, the company outsider, resisted Bruhn's onstage, impromptu invitation to come on from the wings and join the class for a warm-up. Even though it was a staged event, the master class gave the public an authentic glimpse of Bruhn where he most loved to be – in the studio coaching dancers, watching, perhaps, to see if there were any who could challenge his own past accomplishments. It showed them, too, the extraordinary respect and admiration which his dancers accorded him. Here, at the heart of the company's enterprise, the relationship between dancers and artistic director was healthy, edgy, and stimulating.

The bulk of the program consisted of modern works, all of them new to National Ballet audiences, only one of them danced by company members. It was the standard gala formula of guest artists coming in to do their star turns, but with a twist. The star turns, instead of being warhorses from the traditional repertoire, were radical examples of contemporary choreography; the guests, not the usual string of international celebrities, were for the most part Canadian artists from outside the National Ballet. The landed immigrant had landed with his eyes wide open to the Canadian cultural scene.

Mary Jago and Veronica Tennant joined Tomm Ruud, of the San Francisco Ballet, in a performance of his *Mobile (1969)*, which later entered the company's repertoire for six performances on the 1984–5 tour of eastern Canada. The company's resident choreographer, Constantin Patsalas, created a new pas de deux, *S'Agapo*, for the Royal Winnipeg Ballet's Evelyn Hart and John Alleyne, then with the Stuttgart Ballet. Hart, under Grant's administration, had established a friendly guest-artist relationship with the National that Bruhn would foster and encourage. Alleyne, a graduate of the National Ballet School, would leave Stuttgart to join the National at the beginning of the 1984–5 season. James Kudelka and members of Les Grands Ballets Canadiens performed the first movement of Kudelka's *In Paradisum*. Bruhn's invitation to them could be seen as a gesture of reconciliation towards Kudelka, an indication that, in the company's view at least, past differences should be forgotten.

The program's centrepieces, however, were performances by three of Toronto's modern dance groups. Danny Grossman performed his *Curious Schools of Theatrical Dancing: Part I – 1977*; Toronto Dance Theatre brought the 'Miserere' section from David Earle's *Exit, Nightfall*; and, to an onslaught of rock and electronic music unlike anything the National's audiences had ever experienced, the Desrosiers Dance Theatre initiated the gala patrons into the mysteries of Robert Desrosiers' *L'Hôtel perdu*. Grossman's *Endangered Species* had entered the company's repertoire just three days earlier; all three choreographers had been invited to create original works for the company in the very near future. With the exception of

Like a primal scream in a polite drawing room, Danny Grossman's Endangered Species *assailed any preconceptions the National may have had about decorous programming. Barbara Smith (top), Yolande Auger (left), and Mark Raab (right).*

Baryshnikov's appearance, every item on the program had a specific purpose closely related to Bruhn's plans for the National. The three major Canadian ballet companies had been included. Canadian modern dance had given the evening its central emphasis. Bruhn had converted the gala into a political gesture, a declaration of his own forthcoming agenda more potent than a thousand press releases. No more debates in the public press; the company would henceforth speak through its performances, with a voice that had not been heard before.

The gala concluded with a performance by the full company, led by Kain and Augustyn, of the last act of *The Sleeping Beauty*. As a gesture, it was intended to acknowledge Bruhn's awareness of the significance to the company of the classical heritage, and of the need to preserve that element of the repertoire. As a part of this gala, however, it looked curiously old-fashioned and over-dressed. Was the gesture actually ironic, a silent demonstration that the classical repertoire could not remain central to the kind of company Erik Bruhn had in mind? Such iconoclasm was not outside the scope of Bruhn's personality, for whom change was the essence of progress. Or was it merely an afterthought, a dutiful acknowledgment of first principles that showed where Bruhn's real interests lay? Whether deliberately or not, its presence foreshadowed future developments. Bruhn would maintain the classics in the National's repertoire, but he would add very little to their number and, at a time when many of the existing productions needed overhaul or replacement, would direct his energies elsewhere. The freshness and vitality of Bruhn's vision came with a cost.

Part of that cost was borne quite directly by stalwarts who had carried the company through its earlier years. One of Bruhn's first responsibilities was to conduct the housecleaning that was necessary for the company to move forward in the directions he planned for it. In order to establish his own authority, he had to dismantle and reorganize at least some of the structure that remained from Franca's days. As Franca had had to distance herself from Volkoff and Lloyd, so Bruhn had to establish his autonomy and surround himself with individuals who would share his goals. The process was swift and direct. Within a year of his arrival, George Crum, the music director, and David Scott, the principal ballet master, announced their retirements; by the end of his three-year contract, Mary Jago had retired from dancing, and Nadia Potts and Vanessa Harwood had left the company. Transition was hard. Bruhn's judgment that the time for retirement had come didn't necessarily coincide with that of his dancers and staff. Bruhn himself shied away from the confrontations implied in restructuring; that duty often fell to Valerie Wilder. In a later newspaper interview, she recounted the painful process. 'Helping Erik effect some of those draconian changes was tough. Usually it was left to me to tell them they could no longer dance a favourite role. Or that it was time to consider retirement. It wasn't easy.'[17]

In some cases, however, the necessary changes were accomplished amicably, as with Mary Jago, who came to the decision to retire independently and received from Bruhn the help and encouragement she needed to enter the next phase of her career as a ballet mistress with the company.[18] None of the departures was easy. Those who left had made major contributions to the company over a long span of years. They became casualties in the necessary process of change, sacrifices to the youthful resurgence of the company.

Bruhn and his team also brought about a significant change in company organization: the shift to aggressive marketing and development, and the emergence of a large arm of the company devoted exclusively to these activities. Responding to the temper of the times, the company had already started moving in this direction prior to Bruhn's arrival. But in the six months of activity before he officially took over, he and Valerie Wilder played a part in the board's decision to change, for the second time in the company's history, from single-ticket to subscription sales for the Toronto season. (The first experiment in subscription sales, begun in 1967, had ended in 1971 when the massive commitment to touring for Hurok made a Toronto subscription season difficult.)[19] Effective subscription marketing implied detailed long-range planning, since subscribers wanted to know repertoire and principal casting before they would lay out their money. It also implied a more commercial focus than the company had had before,[20] and the independence of marketing as a separate activity of the company. Wendy Reid, hired to put the subscription campaign in place, eventually became the director of Marketing and Development, a greatly expanded division of the company that worked hand in hand with its artistic and administrative sectors in planning for the company's future growth.[21] In this position, Reid became one of the senior officers of the company and went on, after a successful career with the National, to become director general of Les Grands Ballets Canadiens.

Although Bruhn personally disliked the public relations chores that went with aggressive fundraising, he could be extremely good at them,[22] and the team that he assembled recognized the necessity of sophisticated marketing and development practices to the survival and growth of the company. Bruhn's concept of teamwork thus extended horizontally, to the company's financial and administrative divisions, as well as vertically, down through the artistic ranks of its operations. Without sacrificing his personal authority, Bruhn had surrendered the absolute control of the old-fashioned artistic director and entered the new age of corporate cooperation.

The emphasis on marketing and development put a new bureaucratic structure in place that made the company less personal than it had been and was even seen by some as representing a divergence from its primary artistic purposes. Did the company exist to dance, or to fundraise and market its product? But the new age of development and marketing brought with it two undeniable advantages. Subscription sales, whose phenomenal success came as a surprise even to their most enthusiastic proponents, brought working capital into the company's coffers twelve to eighteen months before the beginning of the season,[23] thus alleviating the cash-flow problems that had kept the company teetering on the verge of bankruptcy through much of its life. Instead of waiting for box-office to finance expenditures after the fact, the company could now pay for many of the costs of the season out of its advance revenues, without having to go into debt. The very first campaign pre-sold 45 per cent of the seats at the O'Keefe Centre and brought working capital in excess of $900,000 in to the company. Subscription sales began at 13,000 subscribers, almost double the initial goal, and rose quickly to 20,000;[24] by the early nineties they had levelled off to about 17,500, providing a solid basis of financial and audience support for the company. The second advantage could be seen in the new attitude towards budget shortfall which professional, highly organized fundraising made possible. As long as fundraising had remained a volunteer, ancillary activity, shortfalls in the annual campaign had had to be absorbed directly, by a corresponding cut in production budgets, usually at very short notice. With the advent of professional fundraising, development became an independent revenue-generating aspect of company activities, with its own goals, its own mechanisms for assessing the likelihood of a shortfall, and its own responsi-

Though his career was plagued by injuries, virtuoso dancer Kevin Pugh (seen here in the pas de deux from Don Quixote*) was one of the company's major attractions during the Bruhn years. He was frequently paired with Yoko Ichino (in costume for* Oiseaux Exotiques*), who was recruited by Bruhn from American Ballet Theatre and later left the National to dance in Europe.*

bilities for compensating for one. However much some might lament the intrusion of big-business principles in the arts, those principles brought with them a level of financial security which made possible the long-range artistic planning that had long been a goal of the artistic administration.

Bruhn and his team took full advantage of these new possibilities with a careful and specific plan for the company's development and re-emergence on the world stage. The company would build up a significant body of new repertoire, unique to it, over a period of four or five years, and would then concentrate on touring that repertoire internationally for a year or two.[25] As a result of Bruhn's international prestige and the inherent attraction of the planned repertoire, that touring would be done more on the National's own terms than ever before. After the European tour of 1985, whose planning had been largely in place before he took over the company, Bruhn announced this part of his strategy in an internal memo.

> *In particular, we must begin planning NOW for our appearances in the most important venues abroad – London, Paris, Copenhagen, Hamburg, Spoleto – all of which have expressed a great interest in having us. So prepared, we will be able to negotiate more directly with my contacts in Europe and design tours that present us to our best advantage.*[26]

Revision of the repertoire and then touring: this logical ordering of priorities revealed a strategist of the first order.

Bruhn took a three-pronged approach to the building of repertoire, reaching out to Canadian modern dance choreographers, encouraging choreographers from within the company itself, and developing long-term relationships with two internationally established choreographers. The process of reaching out had been clearly established at the 1984 gala. Grossman, Desrosiers, and Earle introduced the National's dancers to dance forms and approaches towards movement that few of them had encountered before. In mounting *Endangered Species*, Grossman brought his entire company into the rehearsal studio and assigned the dancers from the National opposite numbers within his own company, who taught their own roles to their 'buddies' in the National. Thus a real bond between the two companies was formed. His decision to mount *Hot House: Thriving on a Riff* primarily on younger members of the company, many of them having a role created for them for the first time in their lives, won him a great deal of commitment and created excitement at the junior levels of the company. Desrosiers, who had danced with the National for one season in 1971–2 before leaving to explore less classical, more theatrical types of performance, introduced the dancers to exotic and primitive effects and handed the production department some of the most difficult challenges of their experience. The resources of the National gave his visual imagination unprecedented scope; *Blue Snake* turned out to be a phantasmagoria of vaguely tropical sights and sounds, mixed with European iconography and touches of eastern mysticism. Desrosiers later went on to use some of the National's dancers in his own productions. The company had rarely experienced such freedom of association, either imaginatively or professionally.[27]

In opening the company up to more recent trends in modern dance, Bruhn, almost overnight, broke down long-standing barriers and fostered a sense of community in the Canadian dance scene, where, previously, uneasy rivalries and tension had been the order of the day. It was a political gesture as much as an artistic choice. The success or failure of individual works was of secondary importance to the links which this type of programming forged with other dance organizations and with a different kind of audience. Of all these works, *Blue Snake* enjoyed the greatest success in the repertoire, with thirty-two full performances and eight of excerpts on a mixed program at Ontario Place. *Hot House* achieved a respectable twenty-two, seven of them at the Metropolitan Opera House in New York, but did not remain in the repertoire beyond its second season. David Earle's *Realm*, with six performances, and Grossman's *Endangered Species*, with five, did not survive beyond their initial runs. But statistics like these told little of the real significance of this aspect of Bruhn's programming, which established him in the public mind as a friend of the avant garde and a supporter of young Canadian talent. The introduction of such experimental programming, especially so soon after his appointment as artistic director, was one of the shrewdest moves he could have made.

Pursuing the elusive company choreographer: David Allan, John Alleyne, and Constantin Patsalas

While Bruhn was thus reaching out to Canadian modern dance choreographers, he also took care to encourage young choreographic talent within the company. David Allan, one of the National's second soloists, had first tried his hand at choreography during the 1983 workshop. Veronica Tennant saw his ballet and liked it enough to invite Allan to create a pas de deux for her upcoming engagement at Ontario Place. *Khachaturian Pas de Deux* impressed Bruhn so much that he took it into the company's repertoire for an engagement by a small group of its dancers in Hamilton, Bermuda, in January 1984. There followed a series of small commissions from outside the company, mostly occasional pieces, which Allan undertook with company support. Bruhn then used his influence to assist Allan and a group of eight company dancers in arranging a tour of Italy which featured 'Le Stelle e Solisti Balletto Canadese' in a program made up primarily of Allan's choreography. After the success of that tour, Bruhn took five more of Allan's short pieces into the National's repertoire for the 1985–6 season. The next logical step, a large-scale commission for the O'Keefe stage, was initiated by Bruhn, but completed only after his death. *Masada*, a daring and controversial piece set to Rachmaninoff's

Symphonic Dances, took as its subject matter the ritual suicides of the Jewish zealots at Masada under Roman siege. It represented a real departure for Allan, as for the

A tableau from Masada, *featuring Gregory Osborne (centre), who died of AIDS-related causes in 1993. With Veronica Tennant, centre, Kim Lightheart on the floor at left, Cynthia Lucas on her haunches (foreground), Owen Montague to Osborne's left, and Raymond Smith standing, right.*

company, and was put together in some haste, partly because it was moved forward by several months from its original time slot, partly because the pressures of other repertoire limited the available rehearsal time, partly because Allan's own conception of the piece expanded after schedules had already been set.[28] *Masada* provoked a few outraged reactions among its audience, some of whom walked out on the performance, unable to accept its graphic depiction of suicide. But it also elicited dramatic and emotional performances from the dancers, especially Veronica Tennant (always a strong supporter of Allan's work), Kim Lightheart, and Gregory Osborne. Although flawed in places, *Masada* was a striking first work for large-scale resources that promised much for the future.

But the company's perennial inability to nurture its own choreographers over the long haul struck again. After *Masada*, with no hard feelings on either side, Allan left the company to look for choreographic opportunities in his native United States. He wanted to gain a range of experience that could not be provided in the shelter of the company, but he also sensed an obstacle in the company's structure. 'The way the company is structured, I don't think there's room for a resident choreographer.'[29] Allan's departure, and subsequent success as a choreographer in

American regional ballet, repeated a familiar pattern. As with James Kudelka, the company had nurtured a promising choreographic talent only to see it move to greener pastures.

John Alleyne, the other budding choreographer of the eighties, received less encouragement from Bruhn. Almost immediately after graduating from the National Ballet School, Alleyne had accepted a contract to dance with the Stuttgart Ballet, under Marcia Haydée, and had worked there with the influential forces in contemporary European ballet, choreographers like John Neumeier, Maurice Béjart, William Forsythe, and Jiří Kylián. There too, he undertook his first attempts at choreography, producing ballets for the company workshop which were subsequently taken into the repertoire and which resulted in his being offered a choreographer's contract by Haydée. By the time this offer came, Alleyne was already feeling the strong gravitational pull back to Toronto, where Bruhn, his former mentor and teacher at the National Ballet School, had just taken charge of the company. Unsure of the extent of his commitment to choreography, Alleyne returned to Toronto, where, ironically, Bruhn's indifference to this facet of his talents served to crystallize Alleyne's choreographic ambitions. Bruhn saw Alleyne primarily as the dancer of extraordinary power and presence that he was to become and showed little interest in promoting him as a choreographer. But neither did he attempt to hold him back. When Alleyne received commissions from Stuttgart, and later from Ballet B.C., Bruhn readily gave him leave to fulfil them.[30] Alleyne's début as a choreographer with the National, however, did not take place until after Bruhn's death.

There may well have been another reason Bruhn did not develop Alleyne as a choreographer, aside from the urgency of encouraging his dancing career while he was in his prime. The company already had a resident choreographer, Constantin Patsalas, a close personal friend, whom Bruhn supported actively in what proved to be the final period of his career. With David Allan beginning to show considerable promise, Bruhn had to avoid placing himself in the awkward position of having too many in-house choreographers to keep busy, the problem Alexander Grant had had to face in the days of Ditchburn, Kudelka, and Patsalas. Bruhn had first met Patsalas in Europe in 1971 and had suggested that the expatriate Greek, who was looking for a safe haven in troubled political times, audition for the National during its upcoming European tour.[31] Patsalas joined the company for its 1972–3 season and soon after his arrival demonstrated his interest in choreography at the company's workshops. Franca, Haber, and Grant all encouraged his work, which began appearing in the company's repertoire in the 1974–5 season. Meanwhile, his close personal relationship with Bruhn grew, and Bruhn also took an active interest in his development as a choreographer.[32] In 1980–1, Alexander Grant, who introduced a total of five Patsalas works into the National's repertoire, named him com-

Patsalas' L'Ile Inconnue *was filled with lyrical pas de deux and ensembles like this one, in which Gizella Witkowsky's arms seem to go on forever. She is supported by David Nixon (left) and Owen Montague (right), with Rex Harrington kneeling in front of her.*

pany choreographer, along with James Kudelka, and in 1982, after Kudelka's departure, Grant made him resident choreographer,[33] the first individual to hold that title since Grant Strate.

Patsalas' regular exposure as a choreographer during Alexander Grant's administration paved the way for even greater prominence during the early year's of Bruhn's. In the 1983–4 season the company premiered two large-scale Patsalas works, *L'Ile Inconnue*, to Berlioz' orchestral song cycle 'Les Nuits d'Été,' and *Oiseaux Exotiques*, to an original score by Harry Freedman. In the following season, it presented his *Piano Concerto*, a reworking of the ballet set to Alberto Ginastera's Piano Concerto No. 1, with which he had taken first prize at the Boston Ballet choreographic competition in 1979. The work was subsequently retitled *Concerto for the Elements* and would later still become the focus for Patsalas' acrimonious and protracted feud with the company. Appearing in two consecutive seasons, these three works established Patsalas as a vivid and popular choreographic presence. They were markedly different in character – *L'Ile Inconnue* with its sustained lyricism; *Oiseaux Exotiques* in a sexy and flirtatious vein, bordering on nightclub and cabaret dancing; *Piano Concerto* powered by an aggressive tension. Yet they defined a recognizable, coherent Patsalas style which emphasized a sinuous, long line and showed great skill in the handling of pas de deux, less confidence in manipulating larger numbers of dancers. Most important, they sprang out of a long-standing, close working relationship between choreographer and company. Patsalas had taken the measure of the National's dancers, particularly its younger generation, and had choreographed out of that knowledge. The ideal of the resident choreographer seemed finally to be fulfilling itself in a series of works, unique to the company, dependent on the company's character for their own sense of style.

The creative exertions of these two years seemed to drain Patsalas, as well they might. His *Sinfonia*, originally commissioned by the McGill Chamber Orchestra, entered the repertoire in 1985–6 for three performances at Ontario Place; the following year, *Lost in Twilight*, especially created for the company's joint appearances with the Royal Winnipeg Ballet and Les Grands Ballets Canadiens at Expo 86 in Vancouver, became Patsalas' last work for the National. He had planned a sabbatical year, for travel and gathering new ideas for forthcoming projects. A cruel and arbitrary personal fate decreed otherwise.

A strategic alliance with Glen Tetley

However much attention Bruhn paid to his company's own choreographers, he knew that the international touring and refurbished image he planned for the company would not rest on such domestic achievements. He needed choreographers of international stature to build the repertoire that would gain access to the great opera houses of the world. He himself was not that choreographer. True, he had mounted *Here We Come*, his fantasy on Morton Gould march tunes, originally created for the National Ballet School, as a kind of calling-card in his first season, but that was a slight work. There had also been talk, going back as far as 1968,[34] of an original work by Bruhn for the company. He even had a subject in mind, as he wrote to Franco Zeffirelli, probably in 1983, attempting to interest him in some form of collaboration. 'For about 15 years I have had this crazy idea of doing a full length ballet based on the true story of the Dead Queen Donna Inez de Castro.'[35] But these plans came to naught. Bruhn had a facility for choreography, but not a real genius for it. His procrastination may have sprung from an awareness of this limitation. As artistic director, he knew that the development of the repertoire could not wait on his uncertain inspiration. He needed a ready source of repertoire from a name that had international prestige. Bruhn had two such sources in mind.

In one of the press stories announcing his appointment, Bruhn had been quoted as saying, 'For my first year, I want to bring Jiří Kylián in to look at the company and do a work for us.'[36] Kylián, the Czech-born director of the Netherlands Dance Theatre, had already earned an impressive reputation for his distinctive mix of folk-dance, modern dance, and ballet vocabularies and for the strong musicality of his work. But, though he was cooperative, he could not so easily be wooed away from the Netherlands for the long-term commitment implied by an original creation for the company. Kylián's *Transfigured Night* entered the repertoire in the 1985–6 season, but Kylián did not visit the company in person until two years later, when he was present for the rehearsals of *Forgotten Land*.[37] The light-hearted *Dream Dances* in 1989 and the deeply moving *Soldiers' Mass* in 1995 rounded out the National's sampling of Kylián's choreography. None of these was created specifically for the company. Kylián provided valuable additions to the repertoire, but not the original work, exclusive to the company, that was essential to Bruhn's plan.

In Glen Tetley, Bruhn found the creative collaborator he needed. Alexander Grant had introduced Tetley to the company, hoping initially to persuade him to create an original work for the National, but then revising his request to ask for an existing work, *Sphinx*. Tetley's curiosity about the company had been piqued when he saw Karen Kain and Peter Ottmann dance at the Spoleto Festival; he knew, as well, that Martine van Hamel, on whom he had originally created *Sphinx* for American Ballet Theatre, was a product of the School and the company. When Grant scaled down his request, Tetley agreed. He found the experience of working with the company fruitful and rewarding.

> *Grant said, 'We would like to have* Sphinx,*' and that was a very concrete thing, so I agreed to come and do* Sphinx, *with Karen Kain, Frank Augustyn, Kevin Pugh, all wonderful dancers. And I had three casts, Gizella Witkowsky with David Nixon and Peter Ottmann; and Owen Montague and Sabina Allemann with Raymond Smith. They worked beautifully on it. It was a very exciting rehearsal period, and I was impressed with the way the company was set up, by the atmosphere in the studios, also the technical part of the company and the excellent way in which they constructed the set. It worked for me and it worked for the company too.*

The company had won Tetley's trust and respect, not only by the way in which they worked with him, but also by the high standards with which they maintained *Sphinx* in the repertoire during his subsequent absence. When Bruhn took over the company, he could prevail upon this strong rapport between company and choreographer, as well as on his long-standing friendship with Tetley, which went back to their days together at American Ballet Theatre.

> *Erik and I were friends for many years, going back into the late fifties and sixties when Erik was a premier danseur with American Ballet Theatre. I admired Erik as one of the greatest dancers I'd ever seen, and Erik gave me a lot of confidence in my development as a dancer.*

Bruhn wanted nothing less than an original Tetley work for the company, and now Tetley was happy to agree. *Alice*, a sixty-five-minute ballet set to David del Tredici's 'Child Alice, Part I: In Memory of a Summer Day,' explored the relationships that bound together Lewis Carroll, the people in his life, and the characters in his work. It premièred on 19 February 1986.[38]

In *Alice*, Tetley was able to use his previous experience of the company to match his choreographic ideas unerringly to the talents and personalities of individuals. The ballet gave particular scope to the younger generation of dancers, especially Kimberly Glasco, returned to the company from American Ballet Theatre during Bruhn's first year, and Rex Harrington, in their respective roles of Child Alice and Lewis Carroll. But the mature Karen Kain played a key role as well, growing from a passionate, adult Alice Hargreaves into Alice alone in old age. Both

Kimberly Glasco and Rex Harrington in Tetley's Alice. *Harrington, who later developed a worldwide partnership with Evelyn Hart, was launched as a matinée idol with the role of Lewis Carroll.*

generations of dancers within the company were thus represented, and in a fashion that took creative advantage of their generational differences. Furthermore, Tetley's personal fusion of modern dance vocabulary and techniques, particularly those of Martha Graham and Hanya Holm,[39] with classical dance synchronized perfectly with Bruhn's desire to bring the National into the twentieth century, to modify its classical schooling with movement ideas based on other traditions. The result was a work tailored to the company's personality, yet different from anything it had done before.

Tetley gave the company the precise blend of qualities it most needed in a choreographer: the international clout of a big name and the sensitivity of a resident choreographer to the dancers' individual characteristics. *Alice* opened the door of the Metropolitan Opera to the company once again, and finally on its own terms, as a company in its own right, with distinctive repertoire to offer. Since the death of Sol Hurok and the collapse of his organization, the Metropolitan itself had booked visiting attractions into the house. Jane Hermann, at that time its director of programming, saw *Alice* in Toronto and, when a last- minute cancellation created a vacancy in her upcoming summer schedule, invited the company to bring it to New York that July.[40] In what turned out to be Bruhn's final season with the company, his strategy for its development was already bearing fruit.

For Bruhn, repertoire planning held the key to the company's development.

The classical and standard sides of the repertoire interested Bruhn less than these excursions into new territory. Of the three purely classical works to enter the repertoire during his administration, two were associated in one way or another with his predecessor. Alexander Grant had arranged with Natalia Makarova that she would stage *La Bayadère: Act II – Kingdom of the Shades*,[41] to replace Valukin's *Bayaderka*, which had fared so badly at the hands of the British critics in 1979. Makarova's production, based on her recollections of the Kirov version and mounted originally for American Ballet Theatre, premièred during Bruhn's first season. Bruhn also revamped the Beriosoff *Don Quixote*, which Grant had acquired for the company, by commissioning new décor and costumes from Desmond Heeley to replace the disastrous ones purchased from the London Festival Ballet. Heeley's vivid colours and fanciful designs shored up the National's initial investment in *Don Quixote* and gave the company a durable, popular favourite for the repertoire.

On his own initiative, Bruhn invited his old friend Terry Westmoreland to produce the third act of Marius Petipa's *Raymonda* for the company during its 1984–5 season. Bruhn had, in 1975, danced in Rudolf Nureyev's staging of the complete ballet for American Ballet Theatre,[42] but the standard practice outside Russia was usually to mount only the final act. By 1984, it was virtually the only one of the standard works in the classical canon which the company had yet to perform.

In selecting *Raymonda* Act III Bruhn made a significant addition to the company's classical foundation, but that was not the primary motive behind his choice. *Raymonda* Act III exposed the company to a teacher and coach who held a special place in Bruhn's heart. Westmoreland had been a member of Bruhn's artistic team at the Royal Swedish Ballet, where he had been appointed ballet master and principal teacher by Bruhn in 1968.[43] Bruhn took the concept of the artistic team over from his Swedish experience to his Canadian task, and had hoped to take over at least one of the team members as well. Though he was unsuccessful in his attempt to lure Westmoreland to the company on a permanent basis, as associate director,[44] Bruhn engaged him as guest ballet master for his first two seasons at the head of the National. It was exposure to Westmoreland, more than *Raymonda* itself, that Bruhn wanted to provide for the company. The classical repertoire as such was not the absolute ideal for Bruhn that it had been for Franca. He used it not as an end in itself, but as part of his consistent strategy to extend the range of the company by bringing it into contact with as diverse a spectrum of influences as he could attract. In this case, the personal contact was of more value than the addition to the repertoire. Westmoreland's *Raymonda*, visually heavy and unappealing, disappeared in 1987, after thirty-one performances.

Still trying to challenge his dancers with divergent influences, Bruhn also reintroduced the company to the work of Balanchine. As a memorial shortly after his death, Bruhn mounted 'A Tribute to George Balanchine,' an evening devoted entirely to Balanchine's work, for which he revived *Serenade* and *The Four Temperaments* and added to the repertoire *Symphony in C*. The company had never before presented an exclusively Balanchine evening. Indeed, the company had never been particularly identified with the Balanchine legacy. The tribute was a generous piece of programming, because Bruhn's personal relationship with Balanchine during his brief associations with the New York City Ballet had been a troubled one. Bruhn had felt that Balanchine had misunderstood him, attributing to him the temperamental tactics of a star, when all Bruhn wanted was the chance to learn firsthand from the master.[45] The tribute to Balanchine proved to be a huge

In November 1989, the Royal Winnipeg Ballet and the National Ballet of Canada collaborated in a performance of George Balanchine's Symphony in C. *The four ballerinas are, from left to right, Gizella Witkowsky and Karen Kain of the National, and Caroline Gruber and Elizabeth Olds of the Royal Winnipeg.*

success and opened the way for further acquisitions of Balanchine's repertoire as it became more readily available in the years following his death. The company responded to the challenge and grew into the repertoire over the ensuing years, thus confirming the foresight of Bruhn's vision for it.

Only one of Bruhn's acquisitions for the repertoire, *The Merry Widow*, appeared to be selected primarily for audience appeal and box-office durability. Even this choice, however, played its part in Bruhn's larger plans for the development of the company and testified to his diplomatic skills. *The Merry Widow* was the property of the Australian National Ballet, which, developing it from an idea of Sir Robert Helpmann's, had used it as a vehicle for guest appearances by Dame Margot Fonteyn.[46] According to Bruhn's correspondence, its three original creators, choreographer Ronald Hynd, designer Desmond Heeley, and orchestral arranger John Lanchbery, conceived the idea of mounting the production in Canada. Bruhn reported the idea in a letter to Helpmann, written in 1985.

> *Recently Ronald Hynd, Desmond Heeley and Jack Lanchbery, at Jack's suggestion, approached me with the idea of doing a similar production for the National Ballet. Needless to say, I was thrilled and thought it would be just right for the company to pre-*

> *sent in November, 1986. While Ronnie, Desmond, and Jack are all ready and willing, the Australian Ballet seems to have certain rights and they are unwilling to release the work until after 1988.*[47]

The copy of this letter in the National Ballet's archives, dated 1 October 1985, bears a handwritten emendation that reads: 'has finally agreed to give us the rights.' What persuaded the Australian Ballet to change its mind, along with mutually agreeable financial terms, was Bruhn's visit to Australia, in the fall of 1985, to stage and appear in *La Sylphide* for them. Bruhn saw his visit there in the nature of a diplomatic mission, from which he hoped to reap the rewards of increased cooperation and mobility. As he wrote to the company's artistic director, Maina Gielgud, concerning *La Sylphide*: 'I feel strongly that this could be a beginning of an exchange on various artistic levels for the future offering perhaps first an exchange for young dancers visiting and joining the forces between our companies for certain periods of time.'[48] Bruhn had himself experienced frustration, early in his career, when he attempted to gain leave from the Royal Danish Ballet to appear elsewhere,[49] and had since then championed mobility and cooperation in the ballet world. Even the acquisition of this undisputed blockbuster, then, formed part of his overall campaign to break down barriers and open the world of ballet to its own potential as an international creative community.

His visionary leadership enabled the dancers to take new risks.

But Bruhn the strategist, the diplomat, the long-range planner must finally yield to Bruhn the teacher and coach, working with his dancers. In the studio, his public demeanour at least partially forgotten, the mysteries and contradictions of his sometimes difficult personality worked a wonderful alchemy on those dancers who had the initiative to accept his oblique style of guidance. Bruhn's determination to set the dancers on their own feet, to make them take charge of their own art, never wavered, no matter how frightening the process might be. Veronica Tennant describes this part of his purpose.

> *It took Erik Bruhn to help us make that transition – his stature and magnitude and depth as an artist and his great leadership quality. He was the one that was able to take this child and shake it out of the nest, and say, 'The time has come to fly. And if you don't fly, if you fall and stumble, it's because you haven't got what it takes. You haven't dared and you have no wings. But the time has come.'*[50]

The 'housecleaning' which Bruhn had instituted formed part of this process of establishing a company that could proceed on its own initiative. Karen Kain, one of the survivors of the housecleaning, reflects on the confidence of knowing that one's place in the company was earned, not simply left over by default. 'That put everybody on edge. But we all knew it was the best thing for the company, when we saw the results and we knew that those he had there in the end were the people he really considered worthy of the positions. And he let us know that.'[51] With his team-members in place, and with a clear statement of his confidence in them, Bruhn proceeded to give them challenges of an order they had rarely experienced before.

Bruhn's lined face already showed signs of illness and fatigue in this photograph of him in conversation with Glen Tetley, whose choreography formed a key element in Bruhn's long-term planning for the company.

Bruhn did not 'produce' his dancers, in the sense of giving them detailed instructions for every movement and gesture. Instead he worked indirectly, almost mysteriously, challenging them to find their own ways to the secret knowledge he had discovered. Only by self-discovery would they make that knowledge their own. For Veronica Tennant, it was coaching as inspirational example, rather than command. When Bruhn demonstrated a movement in the studio, 'it was always a demonstration which gave you a glimpse into the possibilities of what could be done, without ever telling you exactly how to do it.' According to Tennant, his coaching, though difficult for some to accept, annihilated the complacency that can grow out of routine.

> *He in no way told you what to do. He only made suggestions and those suggestions could change daily. Many dancers found that very difficult with Erik, because he would give you different ideas and different suggestions every single day. He would come up to you just before a performance and change something, if only to unsettle you, if only to take away any kind of automatic response that you might have ingrained in yourself, just to shake you, to force you to be spontaneous.*[52]

John Alleyne recalls a similarly oblique process.

> *I remember him giving me roles, and he'd say, 'I'm giving this to you, John, because I think you can do something with it.' And that is as much as he would say, and that meant that the way it was done was wrong and you had better find new ways to do it.*

And then he would come up a couple of months later, out of the blue, before a performance, and he would say, 'You did it, John. Thank you.' And just that was enough.[53]

Alexander Grant had defined the same needs in the company as the criterion necessary for its emergence as a fully professional, artistically mature organization. He had lacked the ruthless determination, however, to prune its membership and force a streamlined version of the team into this process of self-discovery. Bruhn liberated the company, but not by the simple removal of constraint. The freedom he fostered did not grant licence to perform exactly as one wished. Karen Kain comments on the powerful, though largely unspoken, control which his very presence exerted.

Somebody called him 'laser eyes.' He didn't miss anything from anybody. He didn't miss you if you were in the back row and you thought nobody could see you. He would see everything you were doing, and he let you know. He knew how to guide people without over-producing them, without having to mould them to his way. He knew how to guide them and pull things out of them. He made you feel like an adult, but he also made you know that there was absolutely nothing you could get away with that he wouldn't notice. And I think that being made to feel like an adult was an extremely liberating thing for most of us. Because he really did allow you to think for yourself. He didn't tell you what you were supposed to do.[54]

Bruhn's secret touch stemmed from his ability to maintain the necessary control without resorting to the authoritarian structures that had been ingrained in ballet organizations for centuries. Frank Augustyn felt the invigorating force of being 'treated as a human being, as an individual, as an adult. He had tremendous respect for dancers, being a dancer himself.'[55] Having faced the challenge of developing their art for themselves under Bruhn's formidable 'laser eyes,' many dancers found a new sense of their own individuality and a revaluation of their activity as central to the purpose of the company. According to John Alleyne, this rejuvenated sense of initiative permeated other aspects of the organization as well.

He had every single person in the corps de ballet feeling like an extremely important member of the company. Every facet counted. He was aware of the needs of the crews, the orchestra, and he didn't have to do much. I guess it's because what he was aiming for was right, so we all could stand behind him.[56]

Some degree of idealization has crept into comments like these. Bruhn the human individual has become conflated with his vision for the company. Those who venerate him most may be the ones who discovered most about themselves under his direction. But the potency of his ideals cannot be overstated. The greatest of his many gifts to the company was this courage of conviction. Believing they were standing behind him, the dancers learned to stand on their own. The draft notes for one of Bruhn's reports as artistic director state these ideals in his own words.

> *There is more to ballet than straight lines and correct steps! I would appeal to each of you to maintain that breadth of vision; to stay close to that inspiration, that 'something' that people talk about without analyzing. It is my dream to talk less and less, and rather just show results. I am confident that our struggles are worth their work. If we were an overnight success, we would be an overnight gone. Let us go from there. Let us be outspoken in our work and in our dancing. Let us take the risks that are ultimately responsible for great art.*[57]

When Bruhn finally took the helm of the company, he took it as a visionary leader with his sights set on the open waters of the future, not the confining channels of the past.

Bruhn's 'temporary' assumption of the artistic directorship should have extended beyond his initial three-year stint. Towards the end of that period, he signed a contract for one further year with the company,[58] a contract he did not live to fulfil. On the evening of 1 March 1986, he officiated at Nadia Potts' farewell performance as Lise in *La Fille Mal Gardée*. It was a bittersweet occasion, with Bruhn doing his best to put a diplomatic gloss on the reluctant retirement of one of the company's best-loved ballerinas. It was also the last time the company as a whole saw him alive.[59]

Bruhn had always been a heavy smoker and, like many dancers, had turned a blind eye to the risks which the habit presented to his health and to his performance as a professional. His great preoccupation with his health had been focused on the stomach problems which devastated his performance career. It came as a shocking surprise, therefore, when the tests which he underwent shortly after the Potts farewell indicated lung cancer. Surprise turned to grief and consternation when, on 1 April Bruhn died of the disease[60] without ever leaving the hospital he had entered for tests less than a month before, and without returning to the company to put his affairs in order or bid a last farewell. Only one or two of his most independent dancers broke into the inner circle to visit him in the hospital before his death. For the company as a whole, and even for his close associates, there was virtually no warning.[61] Within the space of a month, the company had to adjust to the loss of the leader who had set the National on a new and daring path. Personal grief mingled with professional shock at the prospect of a future without him.

Even as he battled for his life, Bruhn showed the sense of leadership that had inspired his career with the company. From his deathbed, he wrote the company a letter which dancers and staff read through their tears on company bulletin boards, in offices, hallways, and the dancers' lounge. It was dated 19 March 1986.[62]

Dear Company,

From all of my irregular but honest 'spies,' I have heard some wonderful reports on our *'Don Quixote' in Hamilton and London. For most of you who knew me when we began working on 'Don Quixote' nearly three years ago, it was worth it all – from a production point of view and musical point of view – but it was all of your potential and talent that inspired me and overthrew the many doubts I had over the years. We have now a treasure that we can share together for many years to come.*

My illness as it comes now is at the most unfortunate time, but then illnesses always are. However, I have come to realize in the last year that my nearly three years with you as a director have become the most fulfilling and rewarding experience in my entire professional life. Coming from a former first class egomaniac, this is not a small thing to admit!

I do hope that you will continue to support all that the last three years have stood for, and 'you' means all of my staff. Indeed, there is no one left in the organization that I can complain of, only praise.

Let's go on from here, spirits up; with confidence, belief, and mutual respect for each other – not only go on, but go on inspiring each other. This way, you will really help me through this difficult time of mine, knowing that the outcome will be something we can share forever.

Much love to you all
as always,
Erik

CHAPTER NINE

He Who Pays the Piper: Of Finances and Friends

The search for government subsidy

Erik Bruhn's creative accomplishment with a mature company rested on the artistic groundwork which had been established during its formative years. But this artistic legacy provided only one part of the support essential to the company's growth and success. Without organizational support, the artists could accomplish little. From the very beginning, the three women who willed the company into being, Sydney Mulqueen, Pearl Whitehead, and Aileen Woods, knew that a strong board structure was essential to raise funds, lobby for support, and give credibility to the venture. Looking to their friends, and their husbands' associates, they recruited board members, largely businessmen and lawyers, from among Toronto's upper middle class. The presidents of the board have reflected these origins, predominantly, though not exclusively, WASP (Eddie Goodman and Arthur Gelber, two early and influential presidents, were Jews), almost all of them male (Judith Loeb Cohen, president from 1987–90, the only woman to date). A prior

OPPOSITE: As production values have risen, so have production costs. The Volunteer Committee's Build-a-Ballet Fund has for many years underwritten at least one production annually. Glen Tetley's Sphinx, *with its sculptural set by Rouben Ter-Arutunian and costumes by Willa Kim, was one of them. Gizella Witkowsky (seen here as the Sphinx, with David Nixon as Oedipus) chose the ballet for her farewell performance in May 1996.*

ABOVE: The National has had many friends, but none truer than Sydney Mulqueen (left), Pearl Whitehead (centre), and Aileen Woods (right), who fought tenaciously to make the dream a reality.

knowledge of ballet was not a prerequisite; it could be learned. Absolute, if contradictory, essentials, judging by the records of the early presidents, were the willingness to exercise real control over the company's spending (which often put them in conflict with the artistic director) and the ability to defend the company's right to exist, and to cost money, against all comers. Watchdogs on the inside, attack dogs on the outside, board presidents and the boards they headed led a Janus-like existence, looking both ways to keep the company in line and the public onside.

By a process of trial and error, the National's friends discovered the organizational structures and strategic approaches necessary to support the company. Somewhere between the extremes of full state subsidy and complete abandonment to the economics of the marketplace lay the formula for financing professional artistic enterprise in Canada. The National's volunteer organizers committed themselves, vigorously and tenaciously, to discovering that formula and arguing its acceptance before the appropriate government officials, as well as the general public. In the process, they established a working model for the governance of a state-assisted artistic organization in Canadian society that assigned specific, well-defined roles to public subsidy, private philanthropy, and box-office revenues. The National was not alone in charting this territory; in the early fifties, the Canadian Opera Company, the Stratford Festival, and the Toronto and Montreal Symphonies had exactly the same task before them. In the sixties and seventies, as professional artistic activity burgeoned across the nation, many newer, smaller organizations learned from their experiences and made their own contributions to the enterprise. But the National stood in the vanguard of this development and provided significant impetus towards the creation of the various infrastructures that today support the professional performing arts in Canada.

According to an argument that was as self-evident to its supporters as it was mysterious to its detractors, the existence of a professional company necessarily implied a level of financial support adequate to its needs; absence of financial support did not constitute grounds for curtailing or abandoning the enterprise. The National's board and host of volunteer supporters accepted this argument enthusiastically. Deficits did not mean failure. Given the existence of a company, they set about to rearrange social and political priorities in accordance with its needs. Had they accepted the logic of the balance-sheet or the dictates of the bottom line, they would have admitted defeat a hundred times or more. Fortunately for the existence of the National, they operated according to a different logic, dictated by their passion for dance.

The Massey Commission, the Royal Commission on National Development in the Arts, Letters, and Sciences, which submitted its final report on 1 June 1951, foresaw the development of professional cultural organizations in postwar Canada and, with its recommendations regarding the establishment of the Canada Council, paved the way for an 'arm's-length' mechanism for federal funding of the arts.[1] On 4 November 1949, the Canadian Ballet Festival Association, represented by Kay Ransom, its secretary, and Joseph A. Whitmore, its chairman, had submitted a brief to the Massey Commission, arguing for the importance, in Canadian culture, of the development of ballet in general and of the annual Ballet Festivals in particular. Financial support for the Festivals, the Association argued, would enable it to pursue its long-term goal, 'to organize and create a National Ballet Company with suitable headquarters in some particular city.'[2] This order of proceeding, establishing federal financial support first and then applying it to the creation of a company, had a certain logic to recommend it.

The company's earliest organizers, like Sydney Mulqueen, were certainly aware of the Canadian Ballet Festival Association, its aims, and the contents of its brief. (The copy of the brief in the archives of Dance Collection Danse bears the handwritten name of 'S. Mulqueen' on the title page.) They may have thought, by going ahead with their first season in 1951 without federal financial support, that they were anticipating only slightly the logical order of the Association's brief and the Massey Commission's recommendations. If so, they reckoned without the stately pace at which the government implemented the commission's suggestions. The six-year delay in the creation of the Canada Council subverted this logical order of funding first, dancing later. When the Council finally convened in 1957, it considered as one of its first items of business a desperate plea from the thriving but insolvent National Ballet Guild of Canada.

Under this umbrella organization, the company conducted business for its first twenty-one years. The National Ballet Guild of Canada was the nominal employer of all company personnel and the sponsor of both the company and the regional branches of the Guild which supported the company's activities at a local level. (From 1955 until 1964, matters were further confused by the fact that the Guild employed as the company's general manager one Carman Guild who, mercifully, pronounced his surname to rhyme with 'child.') As long as the branches remained active, the distinction between Guild and company retained real significance. With the gradual decline of the branches, however, this distinction became a polite fiction. In time, the Guild came to serve solely as the governing board of the company, and in 1972, it moved to change the name of the National Ballet Guild to the National Ballet Company,[3] thus recognizing formally the actual state of affairs.

The company's first season very nearly broke even. Its first audited statement reported a deficit of $24.18 on overall expenses of $91,450.91.[4] With expanding activities and the fluctuations of the box-office, however, the company's ability to balance its books quickly faded, and significant deficits became the order of the day. Despite frequent claims to the contrary, the company did not thereby abandon fiscal responsibility completely. A balanced budget remained an ideal, however elusive, and at the twenty-ninth annual meeting in 1980, the treasurer was able to report that the company found itself in a surplus position for the first time in its history,[5] with its cumulative deficit eliminated and some cash in hand. The fact of deficit financing indicated, rather, the high cost of starting professional theatrical activity without government support in a country with little by way of prior tradition, and of maintaining it in a country whose demographics dictated extensive touring to small and medium-sized centres as a way of life.

Supporters knew from the beginning that some form of continuing subsidy would be necessary to the company's survival. As an art form, ballet had a history of significant patronage, either from governments or from wealthy individuals. Lucia Chase's careful but generous support of American Ballet Theatre provided a striking example of private philanthropy close to home. After a 1954 reconnaissance trip to New York, to speak on behalf of the Guild with the owner of the Shubert chain of theatres there, Dr Alan Skinner reported back to the board. His account illustrates both the high cost of producing ballet, even in a thriving market like New York, and the frightening demands it could place on personal generosity.

> *Mr. Shubert referred to the experience of Ballet Theatre in New York in the past and told me that on the first occasion when Miss Chase rented one of his New York theatres she was losing money at the rate of $12,000 a week although playing to fairly good houses. After two weeks he told me that he went to see Miss Chase and pleaded with her to close as he felt it was unfair to keep asking her to contribute $12,000 a week of her own money to keep the company going.*[6]

Organized fund-raising started in a small but glamorous way. An early board of the Guild raffled off a mink coat, modelled here by a visiting Margot Fonteyn while Celia Franca and board member Tom Whitley look on.

The National had no Lucia Chase, who combined her role as philanthropist with those of dancer and director of the company, but it did enjoy the friendship of remarkably generous individuals who, in the days of less structured fundraising, could be counted on, on short notice, to bail the company out of an impossible financial situation. Among them was R.A. (Bobby) Laidlaw, remembered by many of the dancers as the 'angel' back home in Toronto who got them out of scrapes when the money ran out on tour. A.G.S. Griffin, president of the board from 1954 to 1957, recalls the memorable occasion when Laidlaw, with no prior softening up whatever, covered the cost of hotels and transportation for the entire company from Edmonton to Calgary to Toronto. Without his instant response to Griffin's desperate appeal, the company would have been stranded in Edmonton, its tour a shambles. Other friends responded to the company's pressing needs by digging into their own pockets repeatedly and by providing annually their personal guarantees for the sizeable bank loans without which the company could not operate.[7] Without such personal generosity, the fledgling company would have folded many times over.

Early boards did not assume, however, that private philanthropy alone could or should make up the shortfall between box-office income and company expenditures. Accepting the European rather than the American model for financing the arts, they argued that government had a direct role to play in creating and sustaining national cultural institutions. The Guild's 1961 submission to the Canada Council, for example, presented comparative figures of government support for ballet in Sweden, England, and Denmark as part of its argument for an increased grant.[8] The luxuries of complete state support in countries like France, Germany, or Russia were irrelevant. The National was pressing for a distinctively Canadian model that posited a partnership made up of government, private philanthropy, and the company as income-producer, as the formula to provide realistic financial support for professional dance on a large scale. Before 1957, while the will-o'-the-wisp of the Canada Council danced before their eyes, the company's boards had no choice but to press their case by direct appeal to the highest authorities. Neither the provincial nor the federal government had any structure in place to hear applications for financial support for cultural activities.

Throughout its formative years, the Guild was fortunate to have the enthusiastic participation of Mabel Hees, whose husband, George, had in 1950 been elected as a Conservative member of Parliament, the start of his long and vigorous career in federal politics. In 1954, she shrewdly advised immediate attempts to secure government funding, given the political climate of the time.

> *Both the federal and provincial governments have large majorities with ministers who have held office long enough to be reasonably confident to try new things. These conditions may not last forever as new ministers and new governments are inclined to try to practice stringent economies and are nervous of untried ideas. Economic problems, too, are arising that may make it more difficult to obtain government assistance for the arts.*[9]

Some approaches had already been made. In 1952, Sydney Mulqueen had written directly to the prime minister, Louis St Laurent, to request an annual grant of fifty thousand dollars to cover the costs of national touring,[10] but to no avail. A 1953 approach to the premier of Ontario, Leslie Frost, did no better.[11] In 1956, in light of an extraordinary grant made by the House of Commons to the National Gallery,

Mrs Hees was asked to prepare a brief on behalf of the National Ballet. The prime minister responded regretfully, saying that financial support for the ballet would have to await the formation of the Canada Council.[12] Provincially, the problem was the same: there was no government agency with the specific mandate to consider requests for funding the arts. Prior to the creation of the Ontario Arts Council in 1963, the Guild did receive a ten-thousand-dollar grant from the Province of Ontario, but administered through the Miscellaneous Grants Branch of the Department of Education.[13] The Guild made the case for government support as directly and persistently as possible, but in the absence of the appropriate agencies to consider its case, these aggressive efforts met with only limited success.

The Canada Council had to weigh the merits of three competing ballet companies.

The Guild would eventually obtain significant support from the Province of Ontario and from the City of Toronto, but without doubt the most important factor in breaking the log-jam and establishing the principle that government had a role in supporting the arts was the creation of the Canada Council in 1957. This event was delayed for six years after the Massey Commission report by the indifference of the Liberal government in power, under Louis St Laurent, to matters cultural, and by the appointment of Massey as Governor-General, which complicated procedurally the discussion of recommendations he himself had made to the government. When, in 1956, death duties from the estates of Izaak Walton Killam and Sir James Dunn, two Maritimes magnates, produced an unexpected windfall of a hundred million dollars, the government seized upon the opportunity to create a fifty-million-dollar endowment, the interest of which would finance the operations of the Canada Council. In April 1957, six years after Massey's recommendation, the Canada Council held its first meeting.[14]

The National Ballet Guild struck swiftly, with a brief requesting short-term assistance and long-term aid in the amount of $230,000.[15] The Council, however, was not prepared to begin disbursing funds quite so quickly. It had, first of all, to set its own priorities for awarding grants, and had spent part of its first meeting hearing from Dean Rusk of the Rockefeller Foundation, who noted that 'organizations would say they were certain to collapse unless they were assisted, but "this imposed no claim upon a Foundation, and that a Foundation should not regard such misfortunes as operating principles."'[16] Rusk's hard-headed advice presumably strengthened Council's resolve not to be unduly swayed by the perilous straits in which the company found itself. A.W. Trueman, the first director of the Canada Council, explained its position to the Guild.

> *Your letter to me of April 29 was placed before the first meeting of the Canada Council that same day.*

> *The opinion of the Council is that at present, before income has become available, before the Council has had any opportunity to discuss and establish the principles which will govern its grant-giving programme and before the Council has made any investigation whatever of the general needs which no doubt exist in Canada in the area of the arts, it is impossible for the Council to take action in reference to the situation which your letter discloses.*[17]

These words offered cold comfort to an organization which had kept its head above water for six years in the hope of federal financial assistance and now faced the bleak prospect of bankruptcy just as that assistance hove into view. A.G.S. Griffin, the president of the Guild, responded with a set of figures summarizing the company's financial picture since its inception. The positive construction he placed on the deficit illustrated neatly the Guild's attitude towards the necessity of government support for the arts.

> *It has required an expenditure of $1,536,000 to bring the Company to its present stage of development. Net earnings at the box office have amounted to $1,012,000. The difference of $524,000 has been covered to the extent of $412,000 by contributions from the public leaving a net deficit after six seasons of $112,000. You find this deficit hard to accept. We find it hard to believe, upon reviewing the Company's history, that so much could have been produced for so little.*[18]

In the eyes of the Guild, the crippling cumulative deficit simply represented the federal government's share, at the rate of less than nineteen thousand dollars a year, of the expenses of the past six years of operation. The National's aggressive tactics paid off, but not without causing a degree of ill feeling about the unreasonable demands coming from the nation's wealthiest city. Larry Mackenzie, a member of the Massey Commission and a charter member of the Council, complained to Brooke Claxton, its first chairman. 'Larry was also annoyed at being "bludgeoned" by an imperious lady into giving a hundred thousand dollars for the Toronto Ballet. She conducted both a lobby before the meeting and a performance during it. Claxton agreed.'[19] Council staff, however, recommended aid to the company, and on 27 August 1957, following the second meeting of Council, the National received notification of a grant of a hundred thousand dollars, less than it had requested, but the largest grant made to any single organization.[20] The principle of significant government funding had been established; prophetically, however, the amount, though generous, was inadequate to the need.

Thus began a pattern that would determine relations between Council and the company over the next decade. With the spectre of the cumulative deficit constantly hovering near, Council's evaluation of the company's plans inevitably considered fiscal responsibility at least as much as it did creativity and artistic accomplishment. Whenever potshots at Ontario or Toronto seemed to be in order, the fact of the deficit gave ammunition to the Council itself, whose makeup stressed political and regional considerations more than it did knowledge of the arts.[21] In the end, however, Council members took advice about the actual levels of funding from their professional staff. That staff, headed by Trueman and Peter Dwyer, treated the company's applications with respect and sympathy, tempered always by an awareness of the limits of Council's policies and likely generosity. Timothy Porteous, who was director of the Council at a slightly later period, describes the delicate balance between Council members and Council staff that prevailed from the first.

Funding issues aside, it was no easy matter to mount productions in cramped and unsuitable facilities. In the early days, set painters had to work on the floor of a hangar at the Toronto Island airport (left), while seamstresses laboured in crowded quarters above the old market building near the St Lawrence Hall (right).

> *You have to understand that the recommendations were being prepared for the Council to approve, so the people who were preparing those recommendations were being careful to prepare them in such a way that the Council would approve them. And they would know what the Council's views were, what the Council would think was reasonable.*[22]

The fate of the company's applications hung in the balance between the knowledgeability of the professional staff and the political sensitivities of the Council itself.

With respect to ballet, the Council immediately found itself confronted with two distinct species of problems. One, ironically, was a problem of quantity. By 1957, contrary to all theoretical wisdom and thanks to hard work and rivalry at the local levels, Canada had not one, but three professional dance companies, the National, the Royal Winnipeg, and Les Grands Ballets Canadiens, each one laying legitimate claim to federal funding. The other was a problem of quality. All three companies were still emerging as professional ensembles; consequently, it was difficult to know how severely to judge their efforts, even assuming that anything approaching an objective standard of judgment could be hoped for in the factional atmosphere in which they operated. These two types of problem coalesced to bedevil the Council in its early approach to funding dance.

Population and economics dictated that three ballet companies were two too many for the country to sustain. In 1960, A.W. Trueman enunciated the dilemma before Council clearly, but without any suggestions as to a solution.

> *Your officers have previously warned the Council that the problems entailed by the maintenance of three ballet companies in a country with a population of 18 million would become rapidly aggravated. It would now appear that some radical decision must be taken since we cannot support the companies at the level they require; nor do we see in the circumstances how we can abandon any of these companies since each has a unique quality.*[23]

A country with a greater tolerance for the arts would have rejoiced at such evidence of artistic activity. In Canada, it became a bureaucratic problem. In every round of applications, the three companies necessarily competed for funds from a single allocation. That sense of competition inevitably affected their relationships with one another, which were fragile to begin with. Because of their locations, that competition played into the country's regional rivalries as well. By one method of reckoning, the Council's first grants to the three companies for their 1957–8 seasons translated into subsidies of '36 cents for each person attending the National Ballet, $3.45 for each person attending the Royal Winnipeg Ballet and $4.35 for each person attending Les Grands Ballets Canadiens.'[24] Though such discrepancies would be substantially reduced as soon as Winnipeg and Les Grands undertook more extensive touring, they seemed to indicate at the very least that the National's share of the pie had not been over-large. In comparative terms, however, the $20,000 given to the Royal Winnipeg and the $10,000 for Les Grands looked small indeed, next to the National's $100,000, as critics of any 'Toronto-centric' action were quick to point out. Knowing that it would be impossible to please everyone, Council quickly discovered that it was hard-pressed to satisfy anyone in the game of funding ballet.

The critical climate in Canada at the turn of the decade only exacerbated the problem. By the early sixties, partly because of its perennial financial difficulties, the National had hit a plateau. The novelty of its existence had worn off and was no longer enough to ensure a critical welcome for the company; the serious problems in its repertoire and its level of performance began to attract increasingly pointed comment from the reviewers. Such comment, damaging under any circumstances, was potentially disastrous given the new competitiveness for scarce federal funding. As the unofficial gauge by which the company's eligibility for funding was measured, critical comment began to wield enormous power. The Council had trouble enough justifying large grants to a Toronto-based company that called itself National and ran up enormous deficits. If that company's artistic achievement was called into question into the bargain, the game might well be over.

As the stranglehold exerted by these forces tightened, the Council took refuge in the only expedient available to it: a survey of ballet in Canada by external authorities. On the basis of the survey results, Council would set priorities for future funding of the three major dance companies. On 26 September 1961, the Council issued a press release announcing its intention.

> *The existing companies must look to the Council for substantial help. Therefore, the funds available to the Council, scarcely adequate for a single company of any size, must be distributed among three. We are hoping that impartial, widely experienced experts may be able to point the way out of a dilemma which so far has seemed insoluble.*[25]

Neither Lincoln Kirstein (left) nor George Balanchine (right) was an admirer of British ballet. Their exacting standards and discriminating tastes found little to praise in the struggling National Ballet of Canada.

The difficulty, of course, was to find the impartial experts. De Valois was mentioned, but given her role in the founding of the National and her close identification with the ideals of British ballet, there was reluctance to approach her.[26] In the international arena, the other alternative was George Balanchine, who, on 22 November 1961, was announced as the survey committee's first member.[27] To balance Balanchine's Russian-American point of view, the Council obtained the services of Richard Buckle, the British critic and ballet historian. Before the committee could begin its work, however, Balanchine bowed out and sent his close associate, Lincoln Kirstein, the co-founder of the New York City Ballet.

Peter Dwyer had previously consulted informally with Kirstein, who had expressed himself forcefully on the lamentable state of Canadian ballet, the superiority of Russian over British training, and the inability of women to administer a ballet company. Indeed, Kirstein had even suggested to Dwyer that his own service on such a committee might damage the value of the report, given his well-known views on the subject of the National Ballet.[28] Under the pressure of circumstances, however, such hesitations were swept aside. The 1962 Kirstein-Buckle ballet survey was on.

The perils of expert opinion

The two worked completely independently, seeing performances by all three companies, inspecting their schools, and interviewing their most prominent supporters. They then submitted separate reports and returned to their respective homes, their tasks completed. Council was left with the tricky problem of reconciling two quite distinct and at times divergent expert opinions. Kirstein ranked Les Grands at the top of his list, with the Royal Winnipeg a distant second and the National an even more distant third. Buckle liked the Royal Winnipeg the best of all, but failed to state a clear preference between Les Grands and the National.[29] On the basis of the reports, then, the Council would have had difficulty in assigning an undisputed ranking to the three companies. Both assessors also suggested schemes for cooperation or pooling of resources among the three companies, for the presentation of a joint season of the highest possible quality. But the mere thought of amalgamation was anathema to the three companies themselves and, because it forced the choice of a single location, an affront to regional interests. This suggestion, admirable in theory, simply could not be put into practice. The survey failed to resolve the difficult problems it was intended to address.

Worse than that, having raised expectations across the country, it proceeded to insult the very institutions which stood to learn from its comments. No one would have been surprised at negative judgments from the assessors. At this stage of the companies' development, national standards would inevitably suffer by international comparisons. But Council staff must have been taken aback by the casual imperiousness of Kirstein's tone. He dismissed the National in short order.

> *Its insistence on the so-called classics (the canonical four act 19th century opera-house ballets with ballerina stellar roles) have drawn a certain public which in its innocence assumes it is competing with international ballet standards. Its execution is undistinguished; its visual and musical taste alarming. Its direction is so muscularly strong that nothing short of revolution can much change the present situation. Its best dancer* [Samsova] *is Russian-born and trained. The best teacher at its school is a Canadian-Ukrainian, Russian-trained* [Alex Ursuliak, then Samsova's husband]. *The artistic direction suffers as much from complacency as from ignorance, but it is doubtful if it can be much altered by the mere palliative of temporary guests.*

The school got even shorter shrift.

> *The Toronto school has an elaborate paper-plan and provides a far stronger general secondary liberal education than training in theatre-dance. A slackness pervades its classrooms. There is an excellent male teacher of character dance* [Ursuliak]. *Masculine strength is needed to get the best out of girls in classic ballet classes.*[30]

In 1974, Kirstein, on a return visit to Toronto in pursuit of Erik Bruhn as a teacher for the American School of Ballet, referred obliquely to these latter comments and revised them drastically.

> *I don't want to be too rude in print, but the school I saw 10 years ago wasn't much to write home about. But now, my God, it is the equal in essence and potential of the Kirov school in Leningrad and the Royal Ballet School (in England). I'm envious of you.*[31]

Buckle admired the school, though he criticized Betty Oliphant's sense of discipline. His most disdainful comments he reserved for the designs of Kay Ambrose. Though he gave a much fuller account of his observations, he too found the company wanting. 'A means must be found to give Franca a more creative artistic policy, to improve her company's schooling and to stop the flow of money into channels of dubious value.'[32] So potentially damaging was the tone of the reports that the Council, acting on legal advice,[33] decided not to release them publicly in their full form. Edited versions were supplied to the individual companies, but the full reports remained confidential documents.

Since this selective release of information ran counter to its previously advertised intentions, the Council now found itself in an even more delicate position with respect to the nation's three ballet companies than it had before commissioning the survey. As a publicly acknowledged basis for formulating policy, the survey's value was negligible. As a goad to inspire the three companies to raise their standards, it was potentially useful, but largely unusable in its complete form. If the comments contained in the survey materially affected the Council's future funding decisions, the companies would quite legitimately ask to see the full text of such influential documents. But any member of Council or its staff who had read the incendiary report (and the survey had been circulated internally) could scarcely ignore the tenor of its comments when drawing up funding advice or reaching a decision. Impossible to ignore, the Kirstein-Buckle report would, on the whole, be best forgotten.

Spurred on by negative criticism and audience demand, the company adopted ever more sophisticated production standards. The elaborate detail of Kay Ambrose's designs for Gala Performance *(1953) contrasts dramatically with the sleek stylization of Jürgen Rose's for* Romeo and Juliet *(1964), to highlight this development.*

The 1962–3 season saw a dramatic change in funding levels for the three companies. The staff memo accompanying the Kirstein-Buckle survey when presented to Council said, in part:

> *If we have seized correctly on the essential points of what has been said about the three companies, it would appear that Les Grands Ballets Canadiens should command the Council's particular attention; that continued support is justified to the Royal Winnipeg Ballet, and that (while we should not abandon the National Ballet) it has been weighed in the balance and found in a number of respects wanting.*

In response to the companies' annual application for operating grants, it went on to suggest levels of funding based explicitly on this interpretation of the sensitive survey.

> *Your officers' general view is that greater recognition should be immediately given to Les*

> *Grands Ballets Canadiens and that a grant of approximately $50,000 would be justified. This would be an increase of nearly 50% over last year. That the Royal Winnipeg Ballet should be given less than Les Grands Ballets Canadiens and that therefore its grant should be not more than $45,000. Both these grants to be subject to the officers' scrutiny of financial statements and budgets.*
>
> *We cannot recommend that the amount of money allotted to ballet be increased beyond $170,000 since it already receives a high percentage of the funds available for arts organizations. This means therefore that the grant to the National Ballet would be $75,000, a reduction of 25% over last year.*[34]

It followed this recommendation with a careful financial analysis that suggested that such a grant would just enable the National to get by. Without abandoning the National (it still received more than either of the other two companies), this recommendation clearly attempted to reorder the Council's priorities with respect to the country's three ballet companies. At its August meeting, in response to a desperate argument from the Guild that the reduction in Council support had come upon them without adequate warning, the Council approved an additional grant of $12,000, but without any commitment to increased levels of support in the future. The final allocations for 1963 were as follows: Les Grands Ballets Canadiens, $40,000 (+ $1,500 for staging two ballets by Balanchine); the Royal Winnipeg Ballet, $45,000; the National Ballet of Canada, $87,000 (+ $1,000 for staging Balanchine's *Serenade*).[35] The National's operating grant from Council (exclusive of the special grant for *Serenade*) had dropped in a single year from $100,000 to $87,000, an absolute decrease of 13 per cent in direct support.

More significantly, perhaps, Council's response to the Kirstein-Buckle report established a proportional division of funds among the three ballet companies that was to prevail for the next twenty-five years. In 1958, the National had received a whopping 77% of the funds allotted to the three companies by the Council. That proportion had declined slowly to a still substantial 59% by 1962. During the same period, Les Grands had received at most 17% of the pot, and in 1958 as little as 8%. In varying proportions, the Royal Winnipeg scooped up the rest.[36] The final allocation for 1963 gave the National 50% of the funds shared by the three companies, raised Les Grands' share significantly to 24% of the total, and gave 26% to the Royal Winnipeg. With minor variations, this pattern has continued over the years, with half the funds available to the three companies assigned to the National and the remainder divided more or less equally between the other two. The Kirstein-Buckle report enabled the Canada Council to redress the inequity between the two smaller companies, at the expense of the larger.

The letter notifying the Guild of the initial grant of seventy-five thousand dollars made explicit reference to the Kirstein-Buckle survey and promised to forward a condensed version of it as soon as possible.[37] When Peter Dwyer, as a representative of the Canada Council staff, attended a board meeting of the National Ballet Guild on 11 September 1962, he was asked if the complete reports would be available to the company and indicated that the Council was not in a position to release them.[38] Thereafter, the issue of release was dropped, as the Guild faced the more pressing task of finding alternate sources of funding. The much-heralded ballet survey sank into the oblivion of confidentiality.

If the entire exercise proved anything, it proved that Canadian standards of professional dance were not yet up to international ones, that external assessors could do little to solve the problems of Canadian regional rivalries, and that ballet itself had no powerful advocates at the federal level. No one suggested, as a solution, that the proportion of the Council's budget allocated to dance should be increased. In allowing the Royal Winnipeg and Les Grands a bigger share of the pie, it also forced a cutback on the National from which it would take years to recover. The deficit was in no sense caused by the 1962–3 cutback, but the discrepancy between the Guild's expectations and the grant it finally received pushed the company to the brink of disaster. Given the overall climate of the times and the severe criticisms of the survey, the Guild could count itself lucky to have survived at all. The Council's reduction of its grant was an unambiguous reprimand; the decision not to cut it off completely reflected a grudging faith in its long-term potential. The overall message was clear: the company would have to improve and the Guild would have to trim its sails or else find other sources of funding to help it meet its objectives.

Deficits had to be dealt with in order to get on with the job at hand.

Underlying the annual negotiations about levels of funding to the Guild was the policy issue of whether or not the Canada Council had any responsibility to assist arts organizations in the task of deficit reduction. The Council made its own position clear from the outset. Its business was to assist in the ongoing operations of the company; deficit reduction was someone else's problem. Brooke Claxton, the council's first chairman, expressed this principle as one of leverage rather than bail-out.

> *If the Council is to make the best possible use of the money appropriated to it for the national interest, it must do so in a way which exercises 'leverage,' that is, results in an organization raising increased funds and in adding to its activities with the Council's money rather than using it to keep in existence. This general point of view is expressed throughout the first Annual Report.*[39]

From the Guild's point of view, it was difficult to 'add to its activities' when the harsh realities of deficit financing occupied much of the staff's energy and imagination in keeping creditors at bay. The sixties, a period of remarkable growth for the company, were also a period of unmanageable deficits, which threatened with alarming regularity to close the entire company down. The problem was not unique to the ballet among arts organizations.

Thanks to the initiative of Frank McEachren, then president of the board of the Toronto Symphony, and to the financial commitment of the Province of Ontario Council for the Arts, the Canada Council did, in 1970, change its stand on deficit reduction. Lyman Henderson, the chairman of the ballet's board of directors at the time, remembers the negotiations that laid the groundwork for an approach to Ottawa.

> *It was really spearheaded by Frank McEachren. Because he was the senior aide-de-camp to the Lieutenant-Governor, he had a pretty close 'in' to the Ontario government. He went to John Robarts and said, 'You are in danger of losing your five major performing arts companies, the Canadian Opera Company, the National Ballet, the Shaw Festival, the Toronto Symphony, and the Stratford Festival. How would your government like to go down in history as having allowed these five majors to collapse?' I can remember sitting down with Frank in those days, and with representatives of the other ones, and Frank carried the ball. That was a major turning-point. It started at the provincial level.*[40]

With a substantial grant in hand from the provincial government, earmarked explicitly for deficit reduction, Henderson then tackled the Canada Council on behalf of the ballet. In May 1970, he wrote to the Council:

> *There is a limit to the amount of volunteer and staff time and effort. For the past few years we have been devoting entirely too much of this precious asset to our major weakness, our financial deficit; and too little to our major strength, our artistic product. Now we feel that having fed the wolf at the door at least half a meal, we must change our emphasis. We are looking to you for the other half of the wolf's meal.*[41]

The Council responded with a grant specifically aimed at deficit reduction, to be spread over a period of five years.[42] At the 1975 annual meeting, the company was able to announce that in this, the last year of the Council's deficit reduction program, the cumulative deficit had been 'dramatically reduced,' that fundraising over the previous three years had increased by 90 per cent, and that, in 1974, the National Ballet reported 'the largest profit ever generated by any performing arts organization in Canada.'[43] With the wolf appeased, the company's efforts to promote its major strength had begun to pay off.

Despite the inevitable tensions of the financial tug-of-war, the National maintained excellent overall relations with the Canada Council, as it did with the Ontario Arts Council. Professional staff at both councils, as they developed experience in the field of arts administration, were happy to put their knowledge at the company's disposal. Together, Council and company refined the application and reporting procedures so that applications could effectively be considered on artistic merit rather than financial grounds alone, and so that the company could render its financial accounts to the Council efficiently and meaningfully. The genuine partnership which developed between the Canada Council and the company, quite unlike the relationship of suppliant to patron, can be illustrated by the degree of assistance and advice which officers like Jean Roberts and Monique Michaud willingly offered to the company. During the presidency of Lyman Henderson, the board began sending copies of its minutes to the Council on a regular basis. Michaud responded to the first set of these with real gratitude and with a careful statement of her desire not to intrude.

Lyman Henderson, whose involvement with the board goes back to 1963, chaired the search committees which appointed Erik Bruhn, Reid Anderson, and James Kudelka.

> *I would not hazard comments any more than I would speak if I attended a meeting myself, unless asked a specific question. However I believe that the board members of the National Ballet as well as its artistic and managerial staff all know that the Council is very 'approachable.'*[44]

That 'approachability' had, of course, to be kept in check so as not to constitute undue interference. The opinions of the staff members of a grant-giving organization, however guardedly expressed, carry a special significance for the recipients of the grant. Lyman Henderson recognizes the potential power inherent in the Council's holding of the purse-strings.

> *I even said to Monique Michaud, 'If you were a shareholder you would demand a position on the board. You can call it arm's length, but in fact you are very much calling some of the shots.' I found Monique to be tremendously helpful; she played a very definitive role in 1972, when we had the Palace Revolution with Celia Franca. She spoke to the board in no uncertain terms and said, 'You've got a wonderful woman here, you're doing a silly thing.'*[45]

The company's management, however, does not see Council's involvement as an unwarranted intrusion in the company's day-to-day affairs.[46] In the curious relationship, half partnership and half patronage, which the Council and the company have developed, some compromises are inevitable.

Since the expansionist seventies, during which support for the company from all levels of government increased significantly, the company has had to decrease its reliance on government funding. For three years during the 1980s, the Canada Council straight-lined its basic operating grant to the company, providing the same level of funding year over year, unadjusted even for inflation. The same straight-lining applied to the Royal Winnipeg and Les Grands Ballets Canadiens.[47] In 1989, the Canada Council again allowed increases in its annual operating grant, which remains the largest single grant the company receives. The general downward trend of the eighties and nineties, however, is unmistakable. Grants from all sources, taken as a percentage of the company's overall revenue, have declined from 41% in 1986–7 to 34% in 1991–2. The Ontario government's 1995 cut in direct funding to the company of 25% of its grant (approximately $425,000) disastrously accelerated the trend, which forces the company to make up the difference in box-office and, in an increasingly competitive market, fundraising from the private sector.[48] The board and the company are no strangers to fundraising.

The branches of the Guild provided grass-roots support.

From the outset, the Guild attempted to give the company a national scope, and provide a national base for fundraising, by creating centres of interest and volunteer activity across the country. The branches of the Guild were, in theory, autonomous, regional, volunteer organizations. Working in close cooperation with the Guild and the company, they had a local mandate to encourage interest in the ballet, and in the National Ballet of Canada in particular. With the hard-working support of Franca and the entire company staff, the Guild actively promoted the formation of these branches wherever local interest seemed to warrant it or their own contacts could dragoon a local organizer into manufacturing such interest. Authority for the branches' activities descended to them from the central organization of the Guild; their support flowed back to sustain the Guild in various tangible and intangible ways. Although the Guild never succeeded in its aim of having a fully national structure, it did, in its heyday, have active branches in Toronto, Hamilton, Oakville, St Catharines, Kitchener-Waterloo, London, Windsor, Belleville, Montreal, Sherbrooke, Quebec City, and even Buffalo, N.Y. In their prime, they created grass-roots support for the company in their communities, but the concept of the branches was too fragile to survive over time. As volunteers became exhausted and local constituencies began to question the direct benefits to themselves of the branch activities, the branches themselves gradually dwindled and died. But before they did so, they presented the company in their home communities, often under primitive conditions where goodwill and improvisation had to substitute for genuinely professional organization.

The touring company's actual presence in any given community was necessarily brief. The branches of the Guild conducted year-round activities to develop and maintain interest in the dance during the company's absences. They also, inevitably, raised money, both to finance their own operations (if they became a financial drain on central resources, their entire purpose was defeated) and to contribute to the running of the company. With this kind of community investment in the company, its appearance in the branch city became an event of genuine local pride, as well as the occasion for the resources of the local organization to come into full play. In cities where there was a branch of the Guild, it became the sponsor of the company's appearance there, doing advance publicity, selling tickets, handling arrangements with the local theatre, and, in the earliest days, providing lodging and hospitality for company members. To inspire this level of hard work, there had to be a strong relationship and mutual goodwill between the Guild in Toronto and the outlying branch. The Guild looked for real support from its branches, in the form of tickets sold and financial contributions made to the operation of the company. The branches in turn looked for direct contact with the company on its tours and a significant voice in the larger affairs of the company.

The system had its weaknesses. Inexperience in the details of theatrical management could make branch members uncertain impresarios when they presented the company locally. A harried Franca sent back this description of one such engagement.

> *The muddle here is fantastic. The newspaper ads are frightful. None of Walter's* [Homburger's] *stuff has been used. He was asked to send 2,000 window cards – not a sign of them. The box office opened this morning – no one knew how the sale was going except that they thought we had $15,000 worth – quite right except that they forgot to deduct the tax. The volunteers left their committee office with the telephone ringing just so that they could go to the Mayor's office with the dancers & sign the beastly book.*[49]

Franca, accustomed to an established theatrical circuit with professional management in her native England, was driven to distraction by such inefficiency. But success could breed its own problems. As the company's touring schedule increased, its appearances in any given locality became less frequent. If the National came to town only once every two years, or less often, even the most successful branch could feel left out and lose motivation during the fallow periods. As branches improved as presenters of the company, many of their members became disillusioned with the eternal round of selling tickets and fundraising, especially when all the funds went straight to the financially hard-pressed national headquarters. With increased experience, even the most responsible branch members wanted, understandably, to try more interesting work (often related to dance education),[50] to control at least some of the money they had raised and use it for purposes of obvious local benefit. On the other hand, as active branches requested direct company support for their local activities, these could become a drain on central company resources and personnel. In the extreme instance, where did Franca's primary responsibility lie – in coaching the dancers in Toronto, or in hitting the road with yet another lecture demonstration for one of the Ontario branches? Branch activities were supposed to support the company, after all, not the other way around.

But for all these built-in problems, the branch organization of the Guild had undeniable strengths. Within Ontario, and to a limited extent in Quebec, branches of the Guild prospered through the fifties and sixties in their efforts to encourage an interest in ballet. London, Ontario, showed the way in December 1951, with the formation of the first branch outside Toronto.[51] This branch could call on some impressive workers. During its 1953 membership renewal campaign, no less a theatrical personality than Hume Cronyn, London's native son, took to the telephones to cajole renewals out of recalcitrant members.[52]

Signing the visitors' book remained a diplomatic obligation in the early days of touring. In Quebec City in 1959, years after the incident that had so annoyed her, Franca, with Lois Smith and local dignitaries looking on, was happy to oblige.

The fruits of such labour were realized when the company enjoyed a successful tour engagement with one of the branches. At their best, the branches turned the company's visit into a major community event, making the performances themselves a glamorous social occasion, duly chronicled in the local press, then providing hospitality and friendship for the dancers billeted in their homes. This level of personal involvement was integral to the company's first successes. At a time when the artistic product would not bear comparison with the world's best, the presence of dancers in homes throughout the community engendered a level of goodwill and acceptance no critical praise could buy.

A firsthand account (written in 1964) of the company's earliest appearance in Belleville, in 1956, vividly portrays the kind of community feeling that sustained it in its barnstorming days.

> *Unskilled in the arts of Theatrical Impresario-ism, Joan and Bob Tanner and their small brave committee plunged into the fray with enthusiasm untempered by experience. Since they knew nothing, they did everything; ignorant of the support available from headquarters in Toronto, they organized and wrote their own publicity, signed an agreement with*

the High School Board (at the rate of $35.00 for the night as a non-profit organization), and were all set to produce their own posters, when they found much to their surprise, that official ones beautifully designed by Kay Ambrose, the like of which Belleville had never seen before, were available from Head Office. There were gasps of amazement from passers-by when these appeared in every shop window in Belleville, Trenton, Marmora, Madoc, Picton, Tweed, Brighton, etc.

With no local theatre box office to fall back on, they printed their own tickets and arranged to sell them at Ed Thomas' Cigar Store (operated by his son, Don) which was the traditional outlet for hockey, wrestling and raffle tickets, as well as hunting and fishing licenses. Don Thomas, whose slow smile and imperturbability had hitherto been known mainly among Belleville's sporting set, bravely took on the position of Business Manager, a post he has held with distinction ever since: he still invariably refers to the different seat prices as 'reds,' 'blues' and 'greys.'

Another staunch supporter at this time was Jules Abramsky, Treasurer of the Theatre Guild, who handled all the financial side of the visit and subsequently filled the same office when the local branch of the National Ballet Guild was formed. Dynamic yet shrewd, and with an underlying kindliness which endeared him to all his colleagues, he firmly controlled the purse strings and was largely responsible for the financial success of the Belleville operations. The third male member of the committee was Bob Tanner, who handled publicity and later became Corresponding Secretary of the Branch. A man of charm and wit, he provided a calm pivot for the often hectic operations of the group. These three men, so different in character, outlook and background, worked together in harmony and mutual respect and became the backbone of the National Ballet in Belleville. Their adherence to the cause did much to counteract the suspicion initially displayed by Belleville's male population.

A short time before the visit, a stern letter was received from the Kingston local of the Musicians' Union demanding the hiring of several extra musicians. The facts that there were no suitable players in Belleville, and that to accommodate even the unaugmented orchestra, it was necessary to remove several front rows of seats in the auditorium, appeared to be of little importance. However, after a telephone call to Carman Guild, the letter was ignored and nothing further was heard from Kingston, to the great relief of the committee, who were expecting a picket line to form any moment.

One of the conditions imposed by the School was that nothing could be done by the Company until after 3:30 p.m. when classes stopped, so that only four and a half hours remained before the auditorium doors were opened. All sets, costumes, properties and lighting equipment had to be carried up to the second floor, and about eight high school boys were hired (at an exorbitant $2.00 per hour) to help with this task. Amongst the organized confusion, the dancers found themselves corners in the classroom–dressing rooms to limber up, while the orchestra took over another classroom for practice.

Miraculously enough, by 8 p.m. all was ready; and the audience, in spite of

> *reserved tickets, had arrived early and was lined up outside the doors. They were all shown to their seats by teenage daughters of Belleville families, dressed in their formal gowns, adding a touch of colour and also encouraging an interest in ballet among the young people of the town. By 8:30 p.m. every seat in the house was occupied, and an expectant throng awaited the entry of the Conductor, George Crum.*[53]

This appearance, under the auspices of the Belleville Theatre Guild, led to the formation, in Belleville, of one of the National Ballet Guild's most active branches. For years thereafter, the Belleville branch sustained a level of interest in the ballet completely out of proportion to the city's population. From its base in Belleville, the Quinte Dance Centre outlived the Belleville branch to provide dance instruction and performance opportunities in the eastern Ontario region.

The Christian Culture series of Father Stanley Murphy sponsored the National's first appearance in Windsor. Soon after, an energetic branch of the Guild, initially chaired by Maggie Reid, promoted the company from early disaster (a stage floor specially waxed for the occasion, which made a secure footing for the dancers impossible) through to its inauguration of the Cleary Auditorium, a theatre capable of housing the full *Swan Lake* in Desmond Heeley's production. The Windsor branch and the National itself contributed materially to the final stages of planning for this important regional facility.[54]

The branches' lasting achievements can be measured by the local institutions and activities they sustained, but their value came also from the individual personalities from outside Toronto whom they brought into the orbit of the National Ballet, personalities like Maggie Reid, whose personal support and friendship, unflagging through crises, Franca found invaluable, or Alan Skinner of London, whose influence ranged from informed contributions to policy discussions to arranging for the distribution of free vitamin supplements to the company's dancers.[55] With all their inefficiencies of small-scale, decentralized operation, the branches of the Guild had political and human significance for the company out of all proportion to their actual size and activity.

They also made large-scale, lasting contributions to the National, significant by any standards. The Montreal branch was crucial to the company's attempts to gain a foothold in Quebec. In the long run, the delicacy of French-English relations combined with the vicissitudes common to all branch politics to defeat this effort. Les Grands Ballets Canadiens inevitably commanded greater loyalty in Montreal than did the National.[56] But before activities on the company's behalf ceased, the Montreal branch, initially under the leadership of André Marcil, had successfully applied to the Canada Council for separate funding to enable the Montreal Symphony to perform with the company at the Montreal opening of *Romeo and*

Juliet;[57] it had sponsored numerous fundraising events, the most ambitious, perhaps, being 'Gaieté à la Bourse,' a benefit ball for the National held in the newly com-

Antony Tudor's Fandango, *the first production sponsored entirely by volunteer fund-raising efforts, with (from left to right) Vanessa Harwood, Linda Maybarduk, Karen Kain, Colleen Cool, and Nadia Potts.*

pleted Montreal Stock Exchange building; and it had for some years operated Paper Things, a successful small business, the proceeds of which went to the National Ballet Guild.

Paper Things, a brainchild of the Toronto branch,[58] eventually became a mainstay of the fundraising operations of the Guild, providing branch members with the challenges of entrepreneurial activity as a welcome relief from the constant round of organized social events. At its 1964 opening in the Colonnade, the Toronto Paper Things raised $3,800 for the ballet, then went on to generate a profit of $4,000 in its first three months of business.[59] At the height of their success, there were two Paper Things in Toronto, one in Windsor, and one in Montreal. Only one Toronto outlet survives today, moved from the Colonnade to nearby Yorkville, but its activities help to underwrite significant company activity. In 1972, proceeds from Paper Things sponsored the production of Antony Tudor's

Fandango[60] and thereby established a tradition which continues today in the Volunteer Committee's Build-a-Ballet Fund, which has sponsored more than twenty major productions in the repertoire.

The branches also provided scholarships to dancers from the company and, later, students at the National Ballet School. The Windsor branch supported the early studies of the young Glenn Gilmour,[61] who went on to become a principal with the company, to dance for a year with Ballet Rambert in London, and eventually to become a teacher at the National Ballet School. Earl Kraul travelled to England to study with Stanislas Idzikowski in 1959 with money raised by the Guild's London branch to support its native son.[62] Scholarship support became a hot item among the various branches. It had the appeal attached to things educational and the added advantage of local interest when the student who benefited came from the branch's own community. With the emergence of the National Ballet School in 1959, such endeavours became even more attractive. Out of all the best motives in the world, the branches' growing preoccupation with dance education began to compete with their role as promoters of the company itself.

The Windsor Branch's investment in dancer education paid off. After a performing career with the company, their scholarship winner, Glenn Gilmour, went on to become a teacher at the National Ballet School.

Other factors contributed to their eventual demise as well. Women, acting as volunteers, had traditionally provided the backbone of support and labour for branch activities. As social values changed, and as more and more women who might have worked as volunteers entered the work force instead, many of the branches lost the source of labour and organization on which they had depended. At roughly the same time, the initial high ideals of the company as a national touring organization changed; the growing company forsook barnstorming in small communities and travelled less frequently, and then to the new, better-equipped theatres of major centres. The Canada Council Touring Office emerged to sponsor such touring on a level the branches could never have supported. The company itself, as it grew, took some of the functions originally assigned to the branches over into its own professional organization, especially those relating to publicity and fundraising. In the long term, centralization proved too powerful a force to resist. The branches had been used to promote interest in the company and to provide, on an amateur level, services which should have been available through a professional support system of theatrical circuits, impresarios, and company ancillary services. The branches certainly succeeded in promoting interest in the company; but as support services became professionalized and absorbed into the company structure, they found themselves without a function. One by one, they wound up operations within their communities. The last to close had been the first to open. The London branch sent formal notification of its dissolution to the Annual General Meeting of 1987,[63] thereby closing a significant chapter in the history of community involvement in professional arts activity in the country.

The Toronto branch did not close, but rather metamorphosed itself, in 1978,[64] into the present Volunteer Committee, whose special project is the Build-a-Ballet Fund. This group, in essence volunteer fundraisers in the accepted tradition, now makes such a major contribution to the company's budget ($475,000 in 1988–9, $315,000 in each of 1989–90 and 1990–1, and $215,000 in 1991–2)[65] that it has achieved a degree of political and economic clout within the organization quite foreign to the old-school concept of volunteers as compliant workhorses. The Volunteer Committee exercises the right to choose which production it wishes to sponsor and has, on one occasion, withheld its funds pending a fuller explanation of the company's proposals. This incident led eventually to a better understanding between the company and its Volunteer Committee. Instead of assuming the Committee's support for a specific project, the company now approaches it with as full a proposal and as carefully worded an appeal as it would use for a major corporation.[66] As it has in other large arts organizations, volunteerism at the National, while maintaining its amateur status, has taken on all the trappings of big business.

The professional management structure needed for arts administration

As the company developed, its management became big business too. Though some members of the earliest company lamented the passing of the more intimate, hectic, and often less organized days of yore, the streamlining and effective organization of management were essential to the realization of Bruhn's ambitious plans and the company's survival after his sudden death. Over the years, the board and the company's professional management team arrived at a cooperative model for administration uniquely adapted to the company's needs. One of the keys to the company's financial survival was the emergence of fundraising as a central part of the company's own professional activity.

The company's early efforts at fundraising, conducted almost entirely by volunteers from the board, proved inadequate to stave off the crippling deficits which overtook the company. At the Branch Liaison Meeting of the fateful 1968 Annual General Meeting of the board, when Franca announced her resignation, the company's general manager reported that volunteer fundraising over the preceding ten years had lagged behind the rate of inflation for the same period. While the level of government support was at least holding its own, fundraising was on the decline.[67] The board's emphasis, through the sixties, on securing adequate levels of government support, had distracted it from the attention that needed to be paid to fundraising. By 1970, however, after the reallocation exercise prompted by the Kirstein-Buckle report and the temporary relief of the federal-provincial deficit reduction program, the message was clear: the company would have to find major sources of revenue in the private sector if it was to survive.

In the carnage following the 1972 'Palace Revolution,' both the chairman of the campaign committee and the director of development resigned. The huge burden of the post–*Sleeping Beauty* deficit left no room for manoeuvring. For three years, board members spearheaded the fundraising drive for corporate donations and corporate sponsorships of individual performances, with enough success to keep the company afloat through a period of enormous financial risk and unprecedented artistic activity. In 1976, the company entered the world of professional fundraising in earnest with the appointment of William Poole as development director. By 1979, the Fundraising Committee, comfortably ahead of its previous year's record, was able to accept an increase in its campaign objective of approximately $50,000, bringing its goal for the year to $789,000.[68] By 1982, Robert Johnston, the company's general manager, gave credit to the Fundraising Committee, to Poole, and to his successor Mary Carr for bringing in the largest amount of money raised in any one year by a performing arts organization in Canada.[69] Subsequently, under the direction of Wendy Reid, Paul Mack, and, most recently, Wendy McDowall, private sector fundraising has come to account for roughly 20 per cent of the company's total sources of revenue, $3,543,000 in 1989–90, $2,945,000 in 1990–1, and $4,209,000 in 1991–2.[70] Within that envelope, corporate donations, largely a creation of the worldwide ballet boom of the seventies, have levelled off, while donations from foundations and individuals have risen sharply, in part because of sizeable donations from single individuals, like Walter Carsen's sponsorship of *The Taming of the Shrew* in 1991–2, or cooperative efforts like the joint sponsorship of the company's 1995–6 remounting of *The Nutcracker* by BPI Financial Corporation, Sandra and Jim Pitblado, and Lawrence and Ann Heisey. This new trend signals the effort to tap the resources of private philanthropy on the American model, which has traditionally relied on private wealth to a much larger extent than on direct government subsidy.

As Development assumed a higher profile and met with greater success within the organization, Publicity went through a similar change. With the appointment in 1973 of Mary Jolliffe, the promotion of the company took on new dimensions. If anyone in Canadian theatre was aware of the performing arts as commodity, a product that could and should be exploited to its full potential and sold, Mary Jolliffe, with her experience at the Stratford Festival, Expo 67, and the National Arts Centre,[71] was that person. In 1976, Jolliffe warned the company against what she called the 'nose in the trough' syndrome, a comfortable reliance on government funding that could lull an arts organization into a false sense of security and into neglecting the tough job of selling its product to a paying public in an increasingly competitive marketplace.[72]

Under the guidance of Jolliffe and her successors, Marcia McClung, Roz Gray, Gregory Patterson, and Julia Drake, the company's Publicity Department has developed a distinctive public image for the National and used it to promote the company aggressively, in Toronto and on tour. Magazine articles, cover photographs, television spots, and other forms of press coverage do not occur spontaneously. They are the result of careful strategy, diplomatic cajoling, and quantities of hard work. The extent to which the National is today considered newsworthy and receives coverage in the press is a direct result of the labours of an energetic Publicity Department, working from a position of central influence within the organization.

Today, international guest stars are a recognized tool for promoting the company at home and on tour. But when Marcia Haydée and Richard Cragun appeared in John Cranko's Legende *at the company's European début in 1972, some critics saw their presence as indicative of a lack of confidence in the company's own talent.*

Initially considered strictly as an adjunct to the artistic side of the operations, Publicity was reorganized around the time of Alexander Grant's arrival at the company, so that it reported to the general manager rather than the artistic director.[73] This change recognized the necessary links between Publicity and all the administrative operations of the company. It also helped to pave the way for the shift from the absolute authority of an old-style artistic director like Franca to the cooperative model of management ultimately championed by Bruhn.

One of the key elements in the consultative style was the approach of Robert Johnston, the company's general manager since 1979. Johnston's previous experience, as deputy minister of culture and recreation for the Province of Ontario,[74] gave him invaluable background and contacts when negotiating grants with the provincial government or trying to interpret its policies. But the secret of his success as an arts administrator lay in his attitude towards the exercise of his position's power within the company's corporate structure, in which both the general manager and the artistic director report directly to the board. This parallel structure might easily have led to conflict of the kind that caused major upheaval within the company in 1972. Johnston would regard such conflict as an indication of failure.

> *I start with the premise that my number one job here is to support the artistic management. So I think if I was to get into a situation where there was some kind of Mexican stand-off between me and the artistic director and we had to go to the board to have it resolved, I would figure I wasn't doing my job. And that has never happened, and I hope it will never happen. On the other hand, I think it is a useful kind of checks-and-balances arrangement in terms of things like budgeting, for example, and financial management, and things of that kind. I think it's also useful, maybe, to the artistic management in some areas to be able to say, 'That's primarily somebody else's responsibility, not ours.'*

In November 1995, the company collected thousands of letters from supporters protesting the Ontario government's cut in funding to the arts. When Karen Kain and Rex Harrington, accompanied by toy soldiers from The Nutcracker, *attempted to deliver them to the Ontario Legislature, they were refused entry. Premier Mike Harris subsequently apologized for the snub.*

With Johnston's arrival, division of responsibility and the assumption that such division best serves the interests of the National had thus become the fundamentals of its management style. From the artistic point of view, the partial surrender of authority may represent a compromise; from the business point of view, the sharing of authority may seem inefficient. But the National Ballet of Canada is no stranger to compromise. In Johnston's words, 'It may not be every master of commerce's idea of a perfect organizational structure, but in this case it seems to work.'[75]

An organizational structure that worked was precisely what the National needed most in 1986. Erik Bruhn had motivated the company by the sheer force of his personality, but he had run it by the determined delegation of authority and sharing of responsibility. There was no comparable personality standing in the wings, ready to take over on short notice. For the company to survive his loss, it had to run, for a time at least, on the efficiency of its organization and sound practical sense.

CHAPTER TEN

Discovering the Centre

Power struggle in the aftermath of Bruhn's death

Bruhn's death overtook the National with immense speed; the shock-waves it created rippled through the company at a much slower rate. While maintaining without interruption an active performance schedule, the community of artists and staff had to come to terms with the abrupt removal of the man who had touched virtually all of them in deeply personal ways. Valerie Wilder and Lynn Wallis, as Bruhn's closest associates, had to step into the breach. By Wilder's assessment, they took over a grieving company.[1] For reasons of public image and company well-being, the board and administration sought to characterize the period following Bruhn's death as years of consolidation and stability. In

OPPOSITE: Reid Anderson's guest appearances in Onegin *opposite Karen Kain presaged his own arrival as artistic director and the central importance of the Cranko repertoire for the company of the nineties.*

ABOVE: John Alleyne's Have Steps Will Travel *in the 1988–9 season featured striking costumes by Kim Nielsen, at that time a member of the company's production and technical staff. From left to right, Nina Goldman, Raymond Smith, Sally-Anne Hickin, and Barbara Smith.*

fact, they were years of transition and adjustment to a world without Bruhn, during which the company clung to the vestiges of his legacy while attempting, yet again, to redefine its destiny. Wilder and Wallis, thrust without warning into the daunting role of guiding the company through this emotionally difficult time, had the advantage of Bruhn's approval and of their close firsthand knowledge of his plans. But to the extent that their authority derived from their association with him, they worked at a disadvantage: they were not Erik Bruhn and could only suffer by comparison with the dead hero. Whatever their own merits, the world saw them primarily as caretakers. The brevity of their tenure as co–artistic directors was inevitable. What was remarkable was the positive contribution they were able to make to the company's development in such a short time, and the healthy state in which they passed it on to Reid Anderson. Grief could easily have torn the company apart. In the event, it played itself out during the Wallis-Wilder years, enabling Anderson to refocus the dancers' energies, unimpeded, on the challenges of artistic growth in the difficult economic climate of the nineties.

From his hospital bed, Bruhn tried to use the time remaining to him to put the company's affairs in order. Just one day before his farewell letter to the company, he wrote personally to Edmund C. Bovey, the president of the board, declaring his confidence that Wilder and Wallis would guide the company in the directions he had charted for it. His intentions with respect to Wilder and Wallis were clear enough: they were to provide leadership for the company in fulfilling the plans already set by Bruhn and his team. His hopes for Constantin Patsalas, his protégé and friend, were open to interpretation. The statement of his wishes in this respect became the centre of a troubling management controversy.

Valerie Wilder (left), Lynn Wallis (centre), and Constantin Patsalas (right), the three associates to whom Bruhn entrusted the running of the company immediately after his death.

As my first two years were marked by a certain amount of upheaval, including major staff changes, I feel that anything other than maintenance of the current direction would be damaging to the company at this point.

Should I be unable to continue in my position as Artistic Director at all, it would be my wish that Constantin Patsalas join Valerie and Lynn as Artistic Advisor. Having worked closely with me for many years, Constantin is also familiar with my goals for the company and is dedicated to the National Ballet. It is not my desire, nor his, that he become Artistic Director, but as Advisor he would fill a gap left by my absence.[2]

The exact nature of Patsalas' role in this triumvirate quickly became a matter of acrimonious dispute. By specifying that an artistic adviser was *not* an artistic director, Bruhn implied a gradation of authority, but he offered no further guidance on this important subject. It was left to the board and the triumvirate of Wilder, Wallis, and Patsalas to try to work out the practical consequences of the scheme.

At a special meeting held on 7 April 1986, the board confirmed Bruhn's deathbed wishes for the artistic direction of the company, at least for an initial period, and put in abeyance the issue of establishing a search committee to look for a successor.[3] It named Wilder and Wallis as associate artistic directors of the company, and Patsalas, according to Bruhn's wishes, as artistic adviser. Almost as soon as it had been instituted, however, the arrangement began to unravel. As associate artistic directors (later renamed co–artistic directors), Wilder and Wallis saw themselves as the source of leadership for the National, with Patsalas providing an added creative spark. As Valerie Wilder describes the situation, Patsalas saw things differently.

Constantin's interpretation of the role of artistic adviser was, in everything except title, artistic director. He saw the team continuing really as it had. He felt that Erik had put him in that position as the artistic influence in the team, the artistic sensibility, and that we would continue helping make his artistic vision happen in the way we had with Erik. Our understanding of it was quite the reverse, that we should run the company with his assistance.[4]

It was a fundamental difference of opinion that could not be reconciled in compromise. Both parties stood their ground. Wilder and Wallis, with considerable administrative experience in their favour and with at least as great a claim on Bruhn's personal approval as Patsalas, quickly established the dominant position. In the autumn of 1986, Patsalas, denied the role he felt was his, filed suit for constructive dismissal against the National and against Wilder and Wallis as its associate artistic directors. At virtually the same time, he sought an injunction to prevent the company from performing his *Concerto for the Elements*, scheduled for the 1986 November season.[5]

With respect to the injunction, Mr Justice W. Gibson Gray of the Ontario Supreme Court found in favour of the company,[6] thus establishing the company's right, in law, to maintain and perform works to which it had title, without the direct presence and cooperation of the choreographer. He thereby confirmed the way in which ballet companies traditionally work, with ballet masters and mistresses taking responsibility for the faithful reproduction of a work once the choreographer has set it on the company.[7] The decision allowed the November 1986 performances of *Concerto for the Elements* to go ahead as scheduled, but did nothing to resolve the overall problem of the status of Patsalas' works in the National's repertoire. Even with a legal judgment in its favour, the company would not persist in programming his works against the choreographer's express wishes. The National had lost its resident choreographer of four years and effectively, if not legally, been cut off from the repertoire which he had created for the company over a much longer span of time. And the suit for constructive dismissal dragged on, poisoning the atmosphere as far as any resolution to the repertoire problem was concerned.

From left to right, Rex Harrington, Ronda Nychka, and John Alleyne in Constantin Patsalas' Concerto for the Elements. *Its sleek design and angular movements were reminiscent of his earlier* Angali *and* Nataraja.

Constantin Patsalas left the National Ballet in the autumn of 1986. In October 1987, he presented an evening of his works at the Premiere Dance Theatre in Toronto, using independent dance artists, students from the National Ballet School, and a handful of dancers from the National Ballet. Thereafter, he went to Denmark to create a work for the Royal Danish Ballet.[8] On 19 May 1989, Patsalas died in a Toronto hospital of AIDS-related causes.[9] Before his death, the company reached an out-of-court settlement with him in the matter of his outstanding lawsuit, but despite behind-the-scenes efforts, it could not wrest from him his blessing to perform his works again in the future, as it had done so successfully in the past. Once she learned of his illness, after the board had decided to search for a new artistic director for the company, Valerie Wilder tried to resolve this issue.

> *When we heard how ill he was, my main concern was a wish for him to somehow, through some intermediary, come to terms with his feeling on his repertoire and whether we could do it. So I spoke to several of his close friends and pleaded for someone to try to get through to him; obviously it couldn't be me. I was very hopeful that before he died we would get some sort of indication from him that, yes, all is forgiven, the National Ballet can continue to do his work, especially in light of the fact that Lynn and I were not even going to be there any more, presumably his main antagonists. But that never occurred.*[10]

Constantin Patsalas died embittered, his personal grievances against the company unresolved, and without the full command of his faculties that might have allowed him to respond differently to Wilder's unofficial overtures. As a consequence, the work of one of the company's resident choreographers, made for its own artists from within its own creative community, disappeared. Once again, as had been the case with Grant Strate, Ann Ditchburn, the young James Kudelka, and David Allan, the company was frustrated in its attempts to build an enduring body of repertoire by developing and supporting its own choreographers. There was no memorial tribute. When Veronica Tennant, at her farewell performance in November 1989, danced the lullaby from Patsalas' *Canciones* with Kevin Pugh, she pronounced a personal benediction on her friend and colleague. It was the last performance of a Patsalas work by dancers of the National Ballet. The company itself remained, officially, silent.

Patsalas' illness materially affects one's judgment on the litigious nature of his concluding relationship with the company. In the final stages of AIDS, he suffered from dementia, which drove him to endless litigation and uncontrollable spending.[11] His grievances against the company unquestionably sprang from real conflicts about the nature of his role within it. The extent and bitterness of his pursuit of those grievances, however, may have been exaggerated by the psychiatric disorders over which he had no control and which must have crept upon him gradually, clouding his vision only slightly at first, then controlling more and more of his behaviour. At this point the company's history mingles inextricably with private affliction. In *L'Ile Inconnue*, the National had embodied for Patsalas his vision of romantic yearning for an unknown destiny. In his own life, that yearning spent itself in a bitter separation from the company that had been his home, a separation that effectively thwarted the possibility of keeping his memory alive through the performance of his work.

In the fall of 1986, the full significance of Patsalas' actions and departure could not be known. Clearly, however, his absence created a gap in the company's artistic administration. Bruhn had sensed the need to bring onto the team someone with artistic vision and creative daring to complement the experience and administrative skills provided by Wallis and Wilder. In Patsalas' absence, the board looked to another individual whose association with the company Bruhn had fostered. Glen Tetley, albeit hesitantly, stood ready to join the team.

After the success of *Alice*, Bruhn had suggested to Tetley some more permanent relationship with the company as a choreographer, but Tetley had shied away from any commitment that would tie him down. In the trying period after Bruhn's death and Patsalas' departure, the board turned to him for help of an even more binding nature. As Tetley recounts the events, he was sounded out about the possibility of taking on the artistic directorship. 'The title that was offered me was not artistic associate, it was artistic director, to take over where Erik left off. I felt I just could not do it. I just could not take on the responsibility, because I know what that responsibility is.' Having directed other major companies, including the Netherlands Dance Theatre and the Stuttgart Ballet, Tetley had firsthand experience of the trials of being an artistic director. Tetley felt a strong bond with the National, however, and was willing to accept the position of artistic associate, in which he would be relieved of administrative responsibility but would involve himself intimately in discussions of 'the artistic future and policies of the company, the repertoire, the dancers, the decisions on dancers' futures.'[12] Thus began a two-year period (1987–9) during which, working closely with Wilder and Wallis, he exercised a fundamental influence on the company's activities. Ironically, he thus came to fulfil precisely the role that had been envisaged for Patsalas.

The company's rift with Patsalas occurred in September 1986; Tetley's appointment was announced on 27 January 1987, to take effect on 1 March of that year.[13] Had Patsalas been displaced in order to make way for a bigger name? As Wilder now recalls the sequence of events, Tetley's availability was not the cause of Patsalas' departure. 'I don't think the Tetley role had evolved far enough at that stage, so I don't think he felt edged out by Tetley.'[14] Wilder acknowledges readily, however, that Patsalas' penchant for large-scale works (he had already created *Rite of Spring* and *L'Ile Inconnue* and had at one point worked on a scenario for a fifty-minute ballet to a score by Olivier Messiaen)[15] conflicted with plans already in place for major new works by Tetley and the acquisition of MacMillan's *Song of the Earth*. From budget considerations alone, the company could sustain only a limited number of such initiatives. Patsalas had gambled to become the company's main creative force and lost. Fortunately for the company, Tetley was available to step into the breach.

Tetley brought to the company a distinctive sense of movement that blended the principles of classical ballet with the techniques of modern dance. A student of Margaret Craske (one of Cecchetti's pupils) and of Antony Tudor but also of the modern dance exponents Martha Graham and Hanya Holm,[16] Tetley forced company members to confront the second half of the twentieth century from the vantage point of their strong classical training.

Glen Tetley's influence on company style

> *I love the classical training because it's logical. You always can go back to the beginning plié, relevé, tendu, fondu exercises because they are what give you your strength and freedom at the same time. And there is no reason they can't be used in all of the other rediscoveries of the contemporary technique. If you know where your centre is, why can't you know where your off-centre is, and use that also, consciously?*

In *La Ronde*, *Tagore*, and *Oracle*, his original creations for the company following the success of *Alice*, Tetley placed his imprint on its style of movement. 'I think that's what makes a successful company, that when you think of the company in your mind's eye you see the movement quality of the company. The movement quality of the company should be as distinctive as that of one dancer to another.'[17] In addition to these works created expressly for the National, Tetley mounted significant works from his own earlier repertoire on the company. *Voluntaries* and *Daphnis and Chloe*, added in the late eighties, and *Rite of Spring*, acquired in 1992 when illness postponed the creation of *Oracle* to 1994, demonstrated just what capable exponents of Tetley's style the National's dancers had become. Under his guidance, they discovered a new centre from which their dance could flow. With their sleek, streamlined movement animated by a controlled sensuality, the dancers' stage personalities flowered under the stimulus of Tetley's rigorous demands. No single role dramatized the revolution more graphically than that of the Prostitute in *La Ronde*, whose lonely, self-absorbed preening opened and closed the ballet on an acrid note of spent desire. The role became so closely identified with Ronda Nychka, on whom it was created, that no substitute seemed possible. Yet when Nychka left the company, Tetley grafted it onto the talents of Jennifer

Ronda Nychka as the Prostitute in La Ronde.

Fournier so successfully that it seemed to have belonged to her from the beginning. In the transfer of the role, Tetley's influence could be seen, moulding the company to the new look he had defined for it.

Valerie Wilder and Lynn Wallis maintained the direction that Bruhn had established.

In committing themselves to Tetley, Wallis and Wilder also committed themselves to the emphasis on contemporary repertoire which Bruhn had initiated. During their leadership of the company, only one quasi-classical work, the slight *Diana and Acteon* pas de deux, entered the repertoire. The existing productions of the classics were rotated through the performance schedule, but the real excitement came from the presence of major contemporary choreographers like Jiří Kylián, William Forsythe, and David Parsons, and from the opportunities which Wallis and Wilder gave to company members David Allan and John Alleyne to develop their choreographic ambitions. As part of their strategic planning, Wallis and Wilder used the subscription program to ensure that audiences would be exposed to new and experimental works along with the more standard crowd-pleasers. According to Wilder: 'We forced it, in that there has never been a series that is all classical. You cannot buy a subscription to the National Ballet and not be exposed to at least one new work. That was a principle, and I think it served what we wanted it to serve.'[18]

In addition, they successfully negotiated the entry into the repertoire of major works by Sir Kenneth MacMillan. The company had been trying to obtain his *Song of the Earth* since 1977;[19] in the 1987–8 season it finally arrived, accompanied by *Concerto* and followed, two years later, by *Gloria*. These acquisitions, no longer genuinely contemporary, nevertheless rounded out the company's sampling of works by this major figure of twentieth-century dance. The National's audiences, which had hitherto known only *Elite Syncopations* and, if their memories were long enough, *Solitaire*, now saw a much more representative range of his art. But these new MacMillan works, historically significant though they were, did not make a forceful impression. Only John Alleyne's stunning performances as the Messenger of Death sustained the level of passion, commitment, and concentration that had given *Song of the Earth* such a shattering impact at its Stuttgart première in 1965. These additions of MacMillan repertoire did, however, signal another subtle rite of passage for the company. Wilder and Wallis were able to add these works without attracting the charge of imitating the Royal Ballet that had dogged Franca and Grant before them. The historical exercise could be assessed for what it was, an attempt to strengthen the representation of a major world choreographer in the company's repertoire, without dragging in the red herring of colonial domination.

Wallis and Wilder also revived the idea of the touring group, geared to play smaller centres with less fully equipped stages and provided with a repertoire made up partially of works from the main company, partially of works created specifically for its needs. As Ballet Concert, such a unit had existed in the late sixties and early seventies. The new Concert Group, as it came to be known, served the needs of a particular audience and enabled the company to experiment with new choreography on a smaller scale than that required for the stages of the O'Keefe Centre or the Place des Arts. It also highlighted members of the corps. Alleyne's *Trapdance*, created for the Concert Group in the spring of 1988, revealed the dramatic talents of Nina Goldman, Sally-Ann Hickin, and Barbara Smith and led to his using them for roles in *Have Steps Will Travel* the following season at the O'Keefe Centre. Reid Anderson continued to use the Concert Group as a development ground for new choreography by a variety of choreographers from inside and outside the company. In May 1994, Christopher House's *Cafe Dances*, Jean Grand-Maître's *Frames of Mind*, John Alleyne's *Split House Geometric*, and Serge Bennathan's *The Strangeness of a Kiss*, all works originally commissioned for the Concert Group, rounded out the O'Keefe Centre mixed program in which Glen Tetley's *Oracle* received its world première.

With Tetley's assistance, and relying on the structures Bruhn had put in place, Wilder and Wallis thus urged the company forward, taking as their point of departure the plans Bruhn had developed, but giving them their own emphasis as well. Because Bruhn had encouraged real participation in his administrative team, it was impossible to tell precisely where his influence left off and their independent planning began. After several years in the job, however, it was evident that they directed the company not according to a mandate Bruhn had established, but by virtue of their own clear vision for its future. That vision included a distinctive contemporary repertoire for the company. It also called for the construction of a Ballet Opera House in Toronto and a new scale of operations appropriate to such a permanent home. Wilder and Wallis, working closely with the board, the production department, the Canadian Opera Company, and the Ballet Opera House Foundation, guided the company through years of effort which took the project to the stage of architect selection and identification of a site, before the economic recession and change in Ontario's government put the Ballet Opera House on indefinite hold. The announcement, in June 1994,[20] that the company would move its rehearsal, wardrobe, and administrative facilities out of existing space in and around the St Lawrence Hall to King's Landing on Queen's Quay West confirmed the abandonment of the Ballet Opera House plan, which had sought to provide all such facilities in the same building with a major new performance space. One of Wallis and Wilder's strongest initiatives, and one of Bruhn's long-standing dreams, evaporated with the demise of the project.

With a different project, however, they fulfilled one of Bruhn's explicit wishes for the company. Bruhn had been a professional free spirit, fighting against the rigid codes of loyalty and obligation that made a dancer's movement from one company to another a difficult and emotionally trying experience. Having escaped the sheltered protection of the Royal Danish Ballet, he knew that variety of experience contributed immeasurably to the development of an individual dancer. Even as director of a company, Bruhn maintained a generosity of spirit in such matters at the expense of administrative inconvenience. Less than a year before his death, he wrote to the ballerina Sonia Arova, to whom he had been engaged during the early years of his own vagabond career, now teaching and directing a company of her own in Birmingham, Alabama.

> *You express frustration over not being able to 'hold onto' your best pupils and my only advice on this is 'don't!' It is unreasonable to expect them to stay. Even in a company like my own, this is my experience. The need for growth and change is a constant and when a dancer leaves you cannot take it personally. You can only take pride in what you have given them and where they go when they leave.*[21]

Recognizing the mature artistry of Kain and Augustyn, Glen Tetley reunited them as the Actress and the Count in La Ronde, *long after their youthful partnership had ended.*

Bruhn's active attempts to encourage the interchange of dancers among companies led him to provide in his will for the establishment of an annual prize, to be awarded to the winners (one female and one male) of a competition among the four companies with which Bruhn himself had felt most closely associated: American Ballet Theatre, the National, the Royal Ballet, and the Royal Danish Ballet.[22] In the spring of 1988, Wilder and Wallis presided over the first Erik Bruhn Competition in Toronto, sponsored by the National Ballet of Canada.

The terms of the competition left it open to a good deal of sceptical criticism. Since participation was by invitation rather than open, and since the judges were to be the artistic directors of the four companies sending competitors, its status as a major international competition immediately came into question. Furthermore, the ambience of the first competition, determined as much by fundraising considerations as by a disinterested concern for the international standards of dance, struck some observers as antithetical to the competition's presumed purpose.

'Competition' was, as it turned out, a misnomer, Bruhn's central idea being both more radical and more useful than the institution of yet another international contest run along established lines. As subsequent versions of the competition have shown, the real value of the Erik Bruhn Prize lies in the international showcase it provides for promising young dancers and in the opportunity it creates for cooperation among the four companies named in the will. Behind-the-scenes activity at the very first competition demonstrated that point clearly as, for two days, artistic staff from three different companies worked with the National's artistic and technical divisions at the O'Keefe Centre to coordinate the single performance of the event. The company has taken advantage of these contacts to foster the dancer exchanges so dear to Bruhn's heart. In 1990, one year after competing for the first Erik Bruhn Prize, Silja Wendrup-Schandorff and Henning Albrechtsen spent a brief period working with the National. Alexander Ritter, not a competitor, worked with their home company, the Royal Danish, in exchange. The spirit of cooperation extended beyond the terms of the competition itself when, in 1989, David McAllister of the Australian Ballet and Jeremy Ransom traded places. The real memorial to Bruhn became not the sculpture which the winners of the competition received, but the influence on their careers, and the careers of other young dancers, which the spirit of free exchange made possible.

Wallis and Wilder worked to realize this last element of Bruhn's aspirations for the company knowing that their time as its directors was drawing to a close. With less acrimony and better diplomacy on all sides than had characterized such transitions in the past, the board had, in December 1987, extended their contracts for two more years and announced that, 'in response to Wilder's and Wallis' expressed wish that they not continue as Co-Artistic Directors beyond the two year period,' it would institute search procedures for a new artistic director for the company to take over at the end of their contracts in 1989.[23]

The search committee, chaired once again by Lyman Henderson, discussed matters with Glen Tetley, who remained unwilling to allow his own name to stand for the position of artistic director. Tetley, a strong supporter of Wilder and Wallis, was not happy with the board's decision to institute search procedures at this point. He saw no need to change the current arrangements.[24] With no obvious in-house candidate to turn to, the committee considered a wide range of international candidates and settled eventually on the name of Reid Anderson, no stranger to the company, yet in significant ways an outsider to its traditions.

Reid Anderson's appointment strengthened the Cranko connection.

As a dancer, Anderson had been a long-standing member of John Cranko's Stuttgart Ballet, and was, by the time of the search in 1988, making a reputation for himself as an interpreter and coach of his mentor's repertoire. Anderson's first direct contact with the company had come in 1984, when he staged Cranko's *Onegin* for the National. Coming just at the difficult moment of transition from Grant's régime to Bruhn's, *Onegin* was the National's contribution to the Toronto International Festival, which required new works for the Festival that would then remain unperformed for a decent interval in Toronto in order to preserve the Festival's exclusive aura. *Onegin*, the second of the full-length story-ballets with which Cranko catapulted the Stuttgart Ballet to international prominence, was to become a staple of the National's repertoire after its initial Festival run. Another lavish spectacle in the romantic tradition, it provided a dramatic challenge, in the central role of Tatiana, for the company's mature ballerinas, among them Kain and Tennant, who had cut their teeth on the challenges of Cranko's Juliet twenty years earlier. Anderson himself danced two performances of the title role opposite Marcia Haydée,[25] Cranko's original Juliet and Tatiana, during the opening run. In subsequent years, he returned to partner Natalia Makarova in the work and to supervise some of its later performances.

With his experience and reputation almost exclusively European, Anderson's roots were in Canada. Not, however, in the National Ballet of Canada. Anderson traced his lineage from the western branch of Canadian ballet. Almost forty years after their territorial rivalries, the pioneering work of Gweneth Lloyd and Celia Franca came together in the appointment of Reid Anderson to direct the National Ballet. A native of New Westminster, B.C., Anderson received his training in dance from Dolores Kirkwood, a teacher for whom he still expresses great admiration. At an early age, he encountered both Gweneth Lloyd and Betty Farrally as adjudicators on the western festival circuit. 'It was actually Betty Farrally who told my father to start me into ballet lessons,' says Anderson now. With his love of performing channelled into ballet, he worked his way through the Royal Academy of Dancing sequence of examinations and, as a young teenager, attended the first of four summer sessions at the Banff School of Fine Arts. There, in Betty Farrally's classes, he got his first taste of the discipline and regimen of a professional ballet company, and encountered other pillars of the Royal Winnipeg Ballet tradition, like Arnold Spohr, Brian Macdonald, and Eva von Gencsy. Anderson's closest approach to the National came when he auditioned, unsuccessfully, for admission to the National Ballet School. The refusal left no hard feelings. 'Thinking back on myself at that time, I probably wasn't good enough to get into the school,' he admits. Much later, at seventeen, he went to England for a year of study at the Royal Ballet School. Following a short stint in the Royal Opera Ballet, he joined the Stuttgart Ballet on 4 February 1969. There he fell under the spell of John Cranko, who was to become the dominant artistic influence of his life.

Anderson joined the Stuttgart company on the eve of its enormously successful New York début and stayed with it after Cranko's sudden death in 1973 to work under his successors, Glen Tetley and then Marcia Haydée. Among the choreographers active in Stuttgart during this period were Tetley, Jiří Kylián (a classmate of Anderson's at the Royal Ballet School), William Forsythe, and John Alleyne. Anderson thus absorbed the Stuttgart tradition of encouraging original choreography at the same time that he experienced the power of Cranko's personality and the intimate, family atmosphere which he created in his company. Cranko's example affected Anderson and his approach to his profession. An eye for detail, a sense of discipline and decorum, positive support for every artist, and pride in the artistic enterprise – these were some of the qualities which Anderson admired in his mentor, and which he tried to bring to the task of directing a ballet company, first, Ballet B.C., during his brief association with it, and then the National.

Anderson thus came to the National as a hybrid: while he never considered himself a purely classical dancer, he had a deep-rooted respect for the classics; an exponent of Cranko's works, which had a firm place in the National's repertoire, he was also familiar with choreographers like Kylián and Forsythe, who were just beginning to enter the company's range of vision; a product of western Canadian ballet rather than the National, he nevertheless shared in some of its traditions by virtue of his association with Cranko. And through his earlier visits to the company, he already knew its dancers and was known to them. This combination of qualities made Anderson the right choice for the time. As an outsider yet not a complete foreigner, he could help the company set its eyes firmly on the future without disregarding its past.[26]

It was a measure of Anderson's political astuteness that he invited Valerie Wilder to remain with the company as his associate director, and a testimony to diplomatic skills on both sides that her transition to the position was accomplished smoothly and efficiently. The team approach to administration, which Bruhn had pioneered with his own appointment, had become too deeply entrenched for Anderson to claim the autocratic control of an old-style artistic director along with his assumption of the title. Anderson chose to place himself at the head of a functioning team rather than dismantle it and start anew. Thus he was able to build on the organization and momentum of the past in steering the company's future course.

The transition was not painless. Anticipating the debilitating effects of the recession, Anderson and company management made changes to both the artistic roster and the administrative staff in the early years of his appointment. Kim Lightheart and Kevin Pugh left the company; Owen Montague took a year's leave of absence to dance with the Netherlands Dance Theatre, from which he did not return. Administrative staff was reduced. Touring was curtailed. Balanchine's *Divertimento No. 15*, announced for the 'Glory of Mozart' festival in 1991, had to be postponed to 1993. But by taking difficult decisions early, Anderson and his team avoided greater pain later on. By the forty-first Annual General Meeting in 1992, the company had ended its fiscal year in the black, yet Anderson could point to a successful tour of the Far East and the addition of major new repertoire, assisted by generous private donations and the continuing work of the Volunteer Committee, as signs of artistic health.[27] And balancing the loss of some of the well-loved principal dancers were the additions of exciting new talent like Margaret Illmann, Yseult Lendvai, and Chan Hon Goh. At the 1992 Annual General Meeting, which celebrated the reduction of the deficit, the board also announced that Anderson's contract had been renewed for a further four years.[28] It was a testimony to Anderson's staying power in difficult economic times, but more than that, it acknowledged decisive artistic leadership which took the company further into Cranko territory, as was to be expected, but which also returned the company to its classical origins with significant additions to repertoire and a demanding eye for detail.

The return of James Kudelka

Anderson concentrated a great deal of company energy on the development of new, original choreography. His first investment was in the appointment of John Alleyne as resident choreographer, a position he took on in 1990 only to surrender it in 1992 when he became artistic director of Ballet B.C., the company Anderson himself had left in order to take over the National. Since joining the National under Bruhn's aegis in 1984, Alleyne had pursued a dual career as dancer and choreographer. Although Bruhn had seen him primarily as a dancer, Wallis and Wilder had encouraged his interest in choreography with commissions for the Concert Group (*Trapdance*) and the main company (*Have Steps Will Travel*). They had also taken one of his outside commissions (*Blue-Eyed Trek*, for the National Ballet School) into the repertoire for the company's German tour of 1989. With his appointment as resident choreographer, Alleyne retired from dancing in order to devote himself completely to choreography. In 1991–2, the company premièred his *Interrogating Slam* and performed his *Split House Geometric*, a revision of a work created two years earlier for the Concert Group. In naming Alleyne resident choreographer, Anderson sought once again to place the creation of original works at the heart

Martine Lamy and Robert Tewsley in Pastorale*, the work which sealed James Kudelka's return to the company that had given him his start.*

of the dancers' experience. Alleyne's departure, while a sign of personal success, interrupted yet again the continuity of choreographic collaboration that had eluded the company so often in the past.

Anderson moved quickly to compensate for Alleyne's loss by appointing James Kudelka as artist in residence. The title, deliberately more general than that of resident choreographer, was chosen by Kudelka himself, who was careful not to claim more than he could initially deliver.

> *I felt that the definition of a resident choreographer at the National Ballet was an incorrect one. I find that with a company like the National Ballet of Canada, to be a choreographer who works with a core group of about twelve dancers on esoteric work on a yearly basis is not a resident choreographer.*

Having thus kept expectations in check, he began producing at a rate that exceeded all expectations. *Pastorale*, which he had made for the company in 1990, was followed in quick succession by *Musings* (1992), *The Miraculous Mandarin* (1993), *The Actress* and *Spring Awakening* (1994), and, his first venture into a full-length ballet, the company's spectacular new *Nutcracker* (1995). Two recurring thematic interests could be traced in this body of work: the deep, sometimes tortured, never insignificant, relationship between the worlds of children and of adults (*The Miraculous Mandarin, Spring Awakening,* and *The Nutcracker*); and the enigmatic solitude of the individual in society — admired, adored, but never fully integrated (*Pastorale, Musings, The Actress*). In this latter group, Karen Kain emerged as the muse who inspired Kudelka's art. Of this late-blooming creative relationship, Kudelka says, 'If you'd told me a year before, that it was going to start up, I would have said nonsense.' The collaboration has resulted in haunting tributes to a great ballerina and substantial works for the company's repertoire.

A fabulous dancing horse, being commanded here by Jeremy Ransom, was only one of the many theatrical wonders James Kudelka and his designer, Santo Loquasto, provided for audiences in the company's new Nutcracker, *which premièred in 1995.*

Kudelka turned his residency into an apprenticeship that brought him into contact with a wide variety of the company's operations.

> *I wanted to be able to perform, to be able to teach, to coach. I haven't done all of those things, but I took the company out on concert groups and really did a strange kind of apprenticeship for about a four-year period.*[29]

In all these ways, he fostered the direct rapport with the dancers that is essential to the realization of the company's mission to create original works and thus resumed the role which he had abandoned so abruptly in 1981.

Anderson charted an aggressive course for the nineties.

Anderson also fostered the addition of works to the National's repertoire by noted outside choreographers, including Balanchine (*Divertimento No. 15*), Glen Tetley (*Rite of Spring*), and John Neumeier (with the original creation *Now and Then*, his first collaboration with the company since *Don Juan* in 1974). Given his Stuttgart background, however, it was natural that Anderson placed a heavy emphasis on Cranko in his programming and repertoire. *Concerto for Flute and Harp*, set to Mozart's music, proved to be a pleasing exercise in Cranko classicism for ten men and two women. *Onegin* and *Romeo and Juliet* made regular appearances. But none of this was very surprising. It was a different Cranko ballet that the public anticipated, waiting to see if Anderson held it up his sleeve. Anderson indulged in a little bit of tantalization. At a gala occasion early in his appointment, like Erik Bruhn before him, he signalled to the world his most significant intention with respect to the Cranko repertoire while at the same time honouring one of the company's undisputed stars.

Susan Benson, who had designed Shrew *in 1992, also designed Reid Anderson's new production of* Romeo and Juliet *in 1995. Intricate Renaissance detailing, as seen here in the costumes for the ballroom scene, replaced the dramatic contrasts of Jürgen Rose's earlier designs.*

Veronica Tennant had built a major career and impressive artistic reputation almost entirely within the National Ballet of Canada. One of the company's best-loved ballerinas, she was also a figure of national prominence in the Canadian cultural scene, an eloquent spokesperson for the importance of cultural values in the life of the nation. As such, she enjoyed a popularity and influence that went far beyond the confines of the dance world. In 1988, she caught scores of admirers completely off guard by announcing her retirement from the ballet stage. Her scheduled performances in Cranko's *Romeo and Juliet* in the spring season of 1988 would be her last. She was then just forty-one years old, and in full command of her expressive and technical powers as a dancer. Her final Juliet, on 12 February 1989, was covered on nationally televised news broadcasts. Tickets to see her one last time in the role that had brought her stardom over a twenty-five-year career were impossible to come by. Those fans lucky enough to be in the theatre poured

Veronica Tennant's performance, at her retirement gala, of the Act I pas de deux from The Taming of the Shrew *whetted the audience's taste for the complete Cranko work. When it entered the repertoire after Tennant's retirement, Serge Lavoie and Karen Kain, seen here on the way to the wedding, were amoung the dancers who revelled in the comic opportunities of the ballet's lead roles.*

their love unstintingly across the footlights at the end of the performance with a profusion of flowers and a seemingly endless ovation. On the eve of the company's change in leadership, one of its biggest stars bowed out in a blaze of glory.

The official Tennant farewell, however, took place the following fall, just after Anderson had assumed his new position. It was a gala retrospective on 21 November 1989, with Tennant re-creating some of her finest classical roles as well as excerpts of the original choreography which had been associated with her throughout her career. The new artistic director's curtain speech was gallant and unobtrusive. The evening belonged to Tennant, and to her alone. But Anderson's influence was palpable in the evening's greatest coup, the surprise appearance by Richard Cragun, star of the Stuttgart Ballet, to partner Tennant in a Cranko role she had never before performed. Her spitfire performance that evening as Katherina in the Act I pas de deux from *The Taming of the Shrew* convinced the audience that she had retired too early; it also displayed, even in the absence of any official announcement, Anderson's trump card. He would bring the complete ballet, the only one of the Cranko full-length story-ballets still missing from the National, to the repertoire of his new company.

It took two and a half more years, and the extraordinary generosity of a single donor, Walter Carsen, who underwrote all the costs of the new production, but in February 1992, *Shrew* arrived on the stage of the O'Keefe Centre. It was the blockbuster ballet of Anderson's first term as artistic director, the first new full-length production for the National since *The Merry Widow* in 1986. Just as Alexander Grant's connections had brought access to some of the Ashton repertoire, Reid Anderson's connections completed for the company the Cranko trilogy and confirmed the special significance of Cranko's work in defining the character of the National for the nineties. Under Anderson's leadership, the popular appeal of the Cranko repertoire was to be one of the central supports of the company.

This emphasis, though hardly surprising, represented a highly significant choice for the National. In a period of increasingly constrained resources, Anderson chose to spend those resources not on a badly needed new production of *Swan Lake* or *Giselle*, the standards of the classical repertoire, but on *The Taming of the Shrew*, an entertaining comedy but hardly a work of central significance to a classically based company. In an ideal world, he could have done both. In the consumer-driven world of financial austerity, his choice, completely defensible, confirmed a trend that dated back at least as far as Erik Bruhn: while the standard works of the classical repertoire languished in productions from the sixties and the seventies, new production money was being devoted consistently to new choreography or to lightweight crowd-pleasers like *The Merry Widow*, *The Taming of the Shrew*, and Ben Stevenson's *Cinderella*. The company's classical emphasis was still there, but was it a high priority?

The answer was, after Cranko, yes. Anderson continued the company's longstanding practice of rotating the standard classics – *Swan Lake*, *The Sleeping Beauty*, *Coppélia*, *Giselle*, *Don Quixote* – through the performance schedule as ballast for the modern repertoire of Cranko, Ashton, and Balanchine and contemporary works by Tetley, Kylián, Forsythe, Alleyne, and Kudelka. To a cynic, this decision might represent nothing more than sound business sense; the standard classics were essential to the success of the subscription campaign. But careful observers saw something more: as each of the classics appeared on its appointed round, performance standards were improving. By direct supervision and by careful choice of coaches, Anderson kept a demanding eye on details, scrutinizing the corps, introducing new dancers into prominent roles, and fine-tuning the productions that were in danger of being taken for granted. If Anderson chose not to replace the old productions with new ones, he proved his ability to rejuvenate them by presenting carefully rehearsed, intelligent, and respectful readings of the old favourites.

Furthermore, he demonstrated his commitment to the Petipa heritage by the introduction into the repertoire in 1991 of *Paquita*, in Makarova's production. This single act of divertissements, all that is now produced of Petipa's two-act original, is a test-piece of technique and classical style that exposes mercilessly a company's classical character and abilities. Anderson saw it through its initial, tentative year of entry into the repertoire and brought it back the following year in a much-improved reading that revealed a stylistically cohesive and mature ensemble. Anderson's approach to the classical repertoire, while not a return to Celia Franca's single-minded vision of its centrality to the company's identity, nevertheless shifted the balance back to a recognition of its importance and thus modified the concerted emphasis on the contemporary that had characterized the company from Erik Bruhn's time onward.

Anderson's artistic directorship also spanned another significant era of change for

Trained at the Vaganova Academy in St Petersburg, principal ballet mistress Magdalena Popa has coached the dancers of the National since her defection from Romania in 1982. This photograph was taken in Paris, with her classmate from the Academy, Natalia Makarova.

the company, as measured by its artistic roster. A ballet company's makeup is constantly changing, as dancers mature or move on and as the individual eye of different artistic directors or choreographers identifies and singles out a young new dancer in the company for prominence and recognition. Anderson's period with the company was no different in this respect. His encouragement of its young women was particularly notable, especially in that he brought forward young dancers like Margaret Illmann, Jennifer Fournier, Yseult Lendvai, and Chan Hon

Goh while simultaneously advancing the careers of more established ballerinas like Kimberly Glasco and Martine Lamy. Most significantly, however, with the departure of Tennant, the mature Karen Kain claimed the role of the company's undisputed senior artist, in a class by herself where once she was the first among equals. No longer simply the star who guaranteed box-office, she matured into something far more interesting, the committed artist who seized every opportunity to increase her scope, unconcerned with the dire necessities of advancing a career. Her collaborations with Glen Tetley (in *Alice*) and James Kudelka (in *Musings*, *The Miraculous Mandarin*, and *The Actress*) revealed the depth of her commitment to her art by her willingness to sacrifice star quality to the uncompromising demands of the choreographer's vision. Her twenty-fifth anniversary season, in 1994–5, honoured the mature artist with a relinquishing of the past and a brave step into the future. Her sentimental farewell to the role of the Swan Queen in *Swan Lake* was balanced by the dramatic challenge of Natalia Petrovna in Ashton's *A Month in the Country*, in the first performances of the work by any company other than the Royal Ballet. But even Kain could not avoid the inevitable. With the announcement of a projected seven-city Canadian farewell tour under the auspices of Garth Drabinsky's Livent Inc., Kain signalled her intention to retire from dancing at the end of the 1996–7 season.[30] With this change in her own status, she confirmed the more subtle change that had gradually overtaken the company under Anderson. The National, in its most recent years, has ceased trading on the star quality of its best and brightest dancers and become instead a coherent ensemble, proud of its individual dancers but prouder still of the overall look and standard of the entire company.

On the male side of the house, this change in character was occasioned as much by necessity as by conscious choice. The remarkable contingent of men brought into the company from the National Ballet School during the eighties by Grant and Bruhn had matured and begun to disperse. During his first term as artistic director, Anderson had to say goodbye to more recent recruits from the school like Alexander Ritter and Stephen Legate, on whom the company had placed great hopes, and to Owen Montague, arguably one of the most distinctive male dancers the company ever had. All went on to dance elsewhere. All had helped to account for the strengthening of the male side of the company that had made possible the new choreographic directions of the eighties and nineties. Rex Harrington, Serge Lavoie, and Raymond Smith remained to provide reliable support among the ranks of the male principals, with Jeremy Ransom and Pierre Quinn moving into new prominence. To provide new blood in the junior male ranks, Anderson began to recruit from diverse sources around the world, but without the heavy reliance on National Ballet School graduates that had characterized the company before his arrival. Subtly but decisively, the look of the company began to change.

Some of Reid Anderson's international recruits in James Kudelka's sparkling new Nutcracker. *From left to right, Aleksandar Antonijevic, born and trained in the former Yugoslavia, Greta Hodgkinson, born in the United States and trained at the National Ballet School, and Robert Tewsley, born in England and trained at the Royal Ballet School.*

Male dancers are always at more of a premium in the dance world than female; international competition for strong male dancers is always intense, and no company is immune to raiding. Anderson arrived just at the sunset of a golden age in male dancers within the company that could never have been expected to extend indefinitely. The extraordinary burgeoning of male talent from the National Ballet School in the late seventies and early eighties, directly influenced by Betty Oliphant and Erik Bruhn, produced a generation of men who energized the company and then became fair game in the international world of dance. Where once the company had Frank Augustyn as its male claim to fame, it suddenly had the likes of Montague, Ransom, Harrington, Lavoie, Paul Chalmer, John Alleyne, Kevin Pugh, and Anthony Randazzo. Bruhn was able to play on their loyalty towards their former teacher to keep them in the company together, but he himself realized that their departure was inevitable, a sign, as he had written to Arova, of their own success rather than his failure to keep them at home. In less bountiful times, Anderson had to do all he could to attract and keep a strong male contingent, and did so with the international recruitment of soloists like Aleksandar Antonijevic, Robert Conn, Johann Persson, Robert Tewsley, and Vladimir Malakhov. Of these, only Persson had received his training at the National Ballet School. Anderson opted for the long and arduous task of maintaining a strong overall ensemble instead of relying on a star strategy, a reflection of the hard realities of supply and demand as well as a conscious strategy for the long-term artistic development of the company.

On both the male and the female sides of the house, however, a significant trend emerged. The new dancers of the National, as recruited by Anderson, came from all over the world, trained in many different schools. The dominant influence of the National Ballet School, and, indirectly, of Betty Oliphant, for so many years its defining force, has been significantly diminished. Anderson thereby changed the look of the company and severed, gently but decisively, the last of the direct ties to the company's origins. The westerner from Stuttgart asserted his independence.

A highly significant development of Anderson's first term as artistic director took place not on the stage of the O'Keefe Centre, but in the secondary schools, the community halls, and the senior citizens' homes of the province. Here, an innovative new community and educational outreach program, developed by Assis Carreiro, at the time the National's manager of educational services, assembled dancers, choreographers, musicians, and scenic artists for week-long residencies in secondary schools, during which they assisted students in developing and producing their own dance creations in their schools and for their local communities. 'Creating Dances in the Schools' began with a project in Toronto-area schools and was repeated in Markham; its more ambitious sibling, 'Stepping Out,' moved into the Niagara region and then Ottawa. While the National acted as catalyst for the project, it used artists from outside the company in addition to its own dancers or, in the case of the Ottawa stint, professional dancers from that city's companies, to carry out the work. Students had the satisfaction of seeing their completed work performed on the O'Keefe stage at one of the company's regular school matinees, but the real value of the program rested in the collaboration between professionals and students that enabled them to make the choreographic art part of their living experience.

The program was an extension of earlier and more traditional outreach efforts like Prologue to the Performing Arts (which took small-scale demonstrations of dance and theatrical craft into the schools), the Shell student matinees, pre-performance lectures and chats, and the various open-houses and backstage tours which have long formed a part of the National's activities. The distinctive feature of the new program, however, was its strong community base and its attempt to preach not to the converted, but to those who had never heard the good news. By moving the participating artists into the local community, by using, as much as possible, the artistic resources available within that community itself, and by offering the program explicitly to students who had had no previous experience of dance, the

National came to future audiences on their terms, and made genuine efforts to relate the creative principles of its art to the lives of its community. Audience-building might be a happy by-product of the process, but the immediate result was the exchange of ideas that took place, eradicating the distinction between performer and spectator and replacing it with the common purpose of artistic collaboration.

In 'Stepping Out,' the National found one practical solution to the problem confronting all the so-called museum arts in justifying their substantial claims on the public purse. The keepers of the purse, understandably enough, want to see some evidence of the arts' adapting to the needs of the society they serve. By his support for this program, Anderson demonstrated the National's ability to move with the times without sacrificing its essential identity.

Coming into its inheritance: the National's place on the world stage

This ability to adapt to the political and social requirements of the times and to synthesize the existing elements of the National's tradition into a coherent course for future development proved to be Anderson's greatest strengths as artistic director of a dance organization during radically changing times. The politician had to be as strong as the artist in his temperament in order to maintain this delicate balance. But even the adroit politician eventually got tired. In the fall of 1995, the recently elected Progressive Conservative government in Ontario cut the province's support of the Ontario Arts Council by 10 per cent; the Council in turn cut its direct support to several large arts organizations, including the National Ballet, by 25 per cent.[31] In the National's case, this percentage decrease translated into a reduction of almost $425,000[32] to its budget, an overwhelmingly disheartening move coming, as it did, on top of the various freezes and gradual cuts in funding which had characterized the late eighties and nineties. Anderson had a right to be discouraged; he also had other opportunities opening to him.

On 9 November 1995, Anderson was announced as that year's recipient of the John Cranko Prize, awarded annually by the John Cranko Society of Stuttgart in recognition of excellence in interpreting or staging Cranko's legacy. In Anderson's case, the award acknowledged his success in producing Cranko's works around the world.[33] At the company's O'Keefe Centre performance the following day, Karen Kain, in a curtain speech on behalf of the entire company, shocked the capacity audience by announcing that Anderson was resigning the artistic directorship of the company, effective the following year. Visibly moved, the company members dedicated that night's performance to Anderson.

Trying to maintain and improve artistic standards in the face of constantly diminishing resources had finally become too much. Anderson had been lured away to become the artistic director at Stuttgart, the company he had long called home. In the press release announcing his departure, he took aim at the debilitating effects of government underfunding.

> *My seven years at the National Ballet of Canada have been the most satisfying artistically, and personally, in my career. The continued lack of appreciation by government for art and artists and their contribution to quality of life and the economy is particularly frustrating. So is the failure of government arts agencies to give special recognition, and support, to flagship arts organizations of international stature which provide leadership through proven excellence. The recent cuts from the Ontario Arts Council have greatly discouraged me, and I feel it is time for someone else to take on the challenge of running this extraordinary company.*[34]

At the press conference announcing his appointment, Karen Kain congratulates James Kudelka, the new artistic director of the National Ballet of Canada.

When it least expected to, the National had to look for a new leader.

A search committee was quickly constituted, once again under the leadership of Lyman Henderson. Working amid press speculation that included names like Veronica Tennant, Frank Augustyn, Karen Kain, and even the Royal Ballet's Anthony Dowell,[35] the committee produced a surprising, yet obvious, candidate – James Kudelka. For the first time in its history, the National would be led by an internationally known, practising choreographer, a product of the National Ballet School and of the company itself. The prodigal son, so recently returned, was suddenly shouldering all the responsibilities of the family head.

But in the years since 1981, when he left the company as a dancer, the prodigal son had hardly wasted his patrimony; he had, instead, increased his worth, first by gaining additional experience as both a choreographer and a dancer in the congenial environment of Les Grands Ballets Canadiens, then by working internationally as a choreographer with the Joffrey Ballet in New York, the San Francisco Ballet, and American Ballet Theatre. And although he stood by his earlier criticisms that the company had relied too heavily on reproduced, rather than original, works for its repertoire, he had returned to the National in 1992 as an experienced artist, no longer an angry young man. The company to which he returned had changed as well.

> *That was the period we were going through then and I'm not angry about any of that any more. But it was true. Erik really grabbed hold of that. I wasn't here, but you could*

> *tell, he opened it right up. And yet Erik didn't do it all. Reid had a lot to do with it too, and Valerie and Lynn. I used to hear about Reid talking to the company and saying, 'You know, you just don't know how to act with a choreographer. You have to do what the choreographer says. That's what this is all about.' And that was news to a lot of people.*

Experience with a smaller, more innovative company away from home, international exposure, then a period of practical apprenticeship in the National — it all sounded more like a carefully-rehearsed plan than a spontaneous act of rebellion. On the eve of assuming his duties, Kudelka half-jokingly acknowledged as much.

> *Here I am. This is probably a little bit earlier in my career than I thought that this kind of thing might happen and yet I always knew in my master plan, in my master plan as a younger man, that this was something that I would do one day. I suddenly realized that this was the time.*[36]

He takes on the direction of the company with optimistic idealism, but with a clear-headed awareness of the challenges facing him; with a continuing commitment to his own original choreography, but, his appetite whetted by *Nutcracker*, an eye to restaging the full-length classics of the canon as well; with the creative artist's fervour, but the administrator's awareness of practical considerations. And he enters into an administrative structure that is significantly changed as well. On 1 May 1996, the company announced that Robert Johnston, its general manager since 1979, would retire the following December. Valerie Wilder would become the executive director and co–chief executive officer of the company on 1 June,[37] a partner to Kudelka as the artistic director. It was the team approach to artistic direction as pioneered by Erik Bruhn, but with a much smaller line-up. Whereas Bruhn had worked with Johnston, Wilder, and Wallis, Kudelka and Wilder together constituted the entire team leading the company into the new century.

That company inhabits a national and international dance world that is markedly different from the one Celia Franca knew in 1951. Franca came from one of the acknowledged dance capitals of the world to a region where dance was barely known. Today, the company exists as one of numerous Canadian dance enterprises, all vying for the public's attention and patronage. Internationally, the very concept of a dominant centre has been challenged. New York remains the city where one can probably see more dance than anywhere else in the world, but with Balanchine's death in 1983 the dominance of the New York City Ballet, suddenly forced to redefine its own creative direction, has ended. In England, the retirement of de Valois, the death of Ashton, and the aggressive competition provided by the English National Ballet combined to shake the Royal from its previously undisputed position of leadership. With the end of the cold war and the more frequent visits to the West of both the Kirov and the Bolshoi, the Russian companies have lost their legendary status and come to be seen instead as dance companies with undeniable strengths, but with weaknesses as well, notably in their presentation and encouragement of new developments in choreography. Both the Bolshoi and the Kirov have undergone serious crises of leadership, undreamt of in the autocratic days of the communist regime. In the international world of ballet, there is no longer a uniform, unassailable standard, determined by the ballet of capitals of the world.

As a result, the 'descendant' companies, usually founded by experienced dancers from the old established ones, usually removed from the major centres, have come into their own. Ballet is where you find it; the tradition lives where it is practised, and that may as easily be in our own backyard as in a distant capital. Miami, Seattle,

Sir Frederick Ashton's Symphonic Variations, *once the exclusive property of Britain's Royal Ballet, can now be seen in other major companies. In 1996, it entered the National's repertoire, with (from left to right) Yseult Lendvai, Robert Tewsley, Martine Lamy, and Chan Hon Goh.*

Birmingham, Vancouver, Winnipeg, Toronto, or Montreal may now show us something rich and rare that London, New York, or Leningrad has not seen, and may never see. A vigorous sense of independence, as providing the freedom for renewed creativity, is emerging. Along with it has come an acknowledgment of the legitimacy of the descendant companies as custodians of the central traditions of ballet, not pale imitations of a superior original. With the old ballet capitals shaken from their former positions of undisputed authority, judgment of the descendant companies solely in relation to their forebears gives way to the objective assessment of their achievements within their proper context.

In the case of the National Ballet of Canada, that assessment reveals a company not of international stars, but of disciplined, highly individual artists, competent to interpret a variety of different styles. It reveals a company which now, after nearly fifty years of professional activity, has the depth of generations. Some senior artists and coaches have been working with the National for twenty-five or even thirty years. Their experience imparts to the company's performances the authority of tradition, the experience of continuous performance central to the art of ballet. Finally, objective assessment reveals a company which has matured to the point where it can forsake the elusive dream of conquering the world and recognize the dignity and worth of establishing its roots at home. The National Ballet of Canada has not displaced the legendary ballet companies of the world; it has, instead, claimed its own inheritance, and has established ballet as a flourishing, indigenous art form where once it was an exotic rarity. Founded on the dreams of imitating an art form that had been developed and had its major exponents elsewhere, the National succeeded in creating not only a company, but a context. The centre is no longer elsewhere. For the National, and for its audiences, the centre is here.

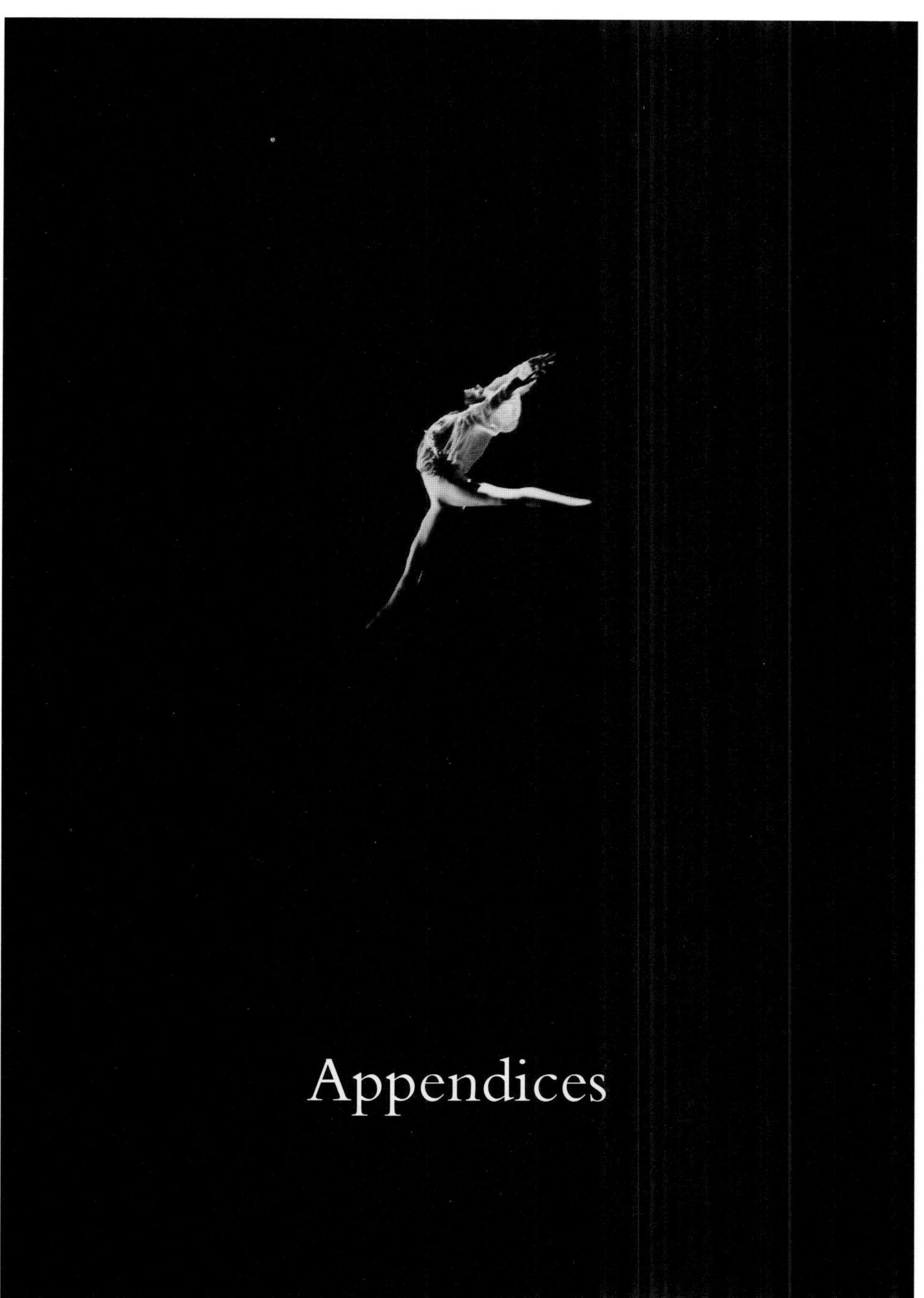

Appendices

Statistics don't have to lie. Performance statistics for an arts organization like the National Ballet of Canada provide important, useful information – interesting to the casual reader who wants to check a fact or confirm a personal recollection, essential to the student of dance who needs to verify the details of performance or back up an analysis of the company's activities. Who made up the company? What did it dance? How often? Where, and when? These facts form the essential basis of our knowledge of the company, however casual or sophisticated our approach. The following appendices present these facts for the company's first forty years, with a minimum of comment or interpretation.

Glance through the itinerary (Appendices A and B) to see the rigours of the early tours of one-night stands, and how these have been mitigated as the company's growing size and changing repertoire led to more concentrated tours of larger centres. Study the theatres in which the company has performed and judge for yourself the changes in the company's scope and aspirations that took it from venues like the drill hall at Camp Petawawa and the innumerable high school auditoriums of the early days to the National Arts Centre, the Metropolitan Opera, and London's Coliseum. Or spend some time with the company's programs over the years and assess the shifts in emphases in its repertoire, and the extent to which repeats of the full-length works have replaced mixed programs of shorter pieces. How strong has the company's support of experimental choreography actually been? Appendix C provides the basis for an answer with a listing of its choreographic workshops. The dancers' roster (Appendix D) records the dancers who have performed with the National in its first forty years, and the years of their association with the company. Finally, the list of board members (Appendix E) acknowledges the more than four hundred volunteers who have contributed to the company's organization and operations during this period. Together, these appendices allow the reader to piece together the basic facts of the company's existence at any point during the period 1951 to 1991.

The statistical research for this book was originally focused on the company's first forty years, and research assistance for the project was awarded accordingly. Hence the appendices record the essential facts relating to the company's first forty seasons, to the end of the 1990–1 season. The statistics were compiled by Lynn Neufeld, with the assistance of the company's archivist at the time, Assis Carreiro, using the invaluable resources of the National Ballet of Canada's archives. The company's current archivist, Sharon Vanderlinde, has also provided assistance in completing and verifying these appendices.

Appendix A

National Ballet of Canada Itinerary 1951–52 to 1990–91

The performance records are for the full company (Appendix A) and for Ballet Concert, Ballet in Action, and the Concert Group (Appendix B), but do not include performances by Prologue to the Performing Arts. Seasons run from 1 July to 30 June of the following calendar year, with the exception of the 1972 full company season, when the European tour ran over into the first days of July 1973. Each season in Appendix A is preceded by a brief statistical summary for the year, indicating total number of performances, number of performances outside Toronto, and additions to the repertoire for the season, with choreographer indicated in parentheses following the title of the work. The summary for Appendix B follows the same pattern, but aggregates all Concert Group activities from 1967 to 1991 in a single summary. The summaries of repertoire do not include works which were brought into the company on special occasions (like gala performances) or by guest artists for limited runs. Such works, which do not form part of the company's official repertoire, are indicated with a dagger (†) immediately following the title when they appear in the detailed itinerary listings. In Appendix B, works which were performed by the Concert Group only, and were never taken into the main company's repertoire, are preceded by a double dagger (‡). Each entry in the itineraries indicates the date, place, and theatre, followed by the repertoire performed on that occasion. The dates of repeat performances of the same program in the same location are indicated in italic type immediately following the initial entry, with minor modifications to the programming, if any, recorded for the date to which they apply. The titles of some ballets have been shortened to conserve space.

Wherever possible, performances have been verified by at least two independent sources, either the original program, the company's production sheet (filed by the stage manager at the conclusion of each performance), or a contemporary newspaper clipping, either advertising the specific performance or reviewing it after the fact. This double-checking was particularly important in establishing the performance record for the company's early years, for which archival resources are incomplete. For more recent years, the company's own record of its performances is complete and reliable. Despite our best efforts to achieve completeness and accuracy, some errors or omissions may yet exist, and for these the author accepts full responsibility. I would be extremely grateful to hear from any readers who may have company memorabilia which could provide corrections or additions to this record.

Abbreviations

Aud	Auditorium
pdd	pas de deux
pdtr	pas de trois
S.S.	Secondary School
*	matinée performance
**	student matinée performance (program frequently shortened)
†	a work not part of the regular repertoire (see explanation, above)
‡	a work performed by the Concert Group only, and not taken into the main company repertoire
•	a work initially performed in workshop and subsequently taken into the repertoire of either the main company or the concert group
§	workshop choreographer not a member of the company

SEASON: 1951-2; **PERFORMANCES:** 23 (12 outside Toronto); **PREMIERES:** Ballet Behind Us (Adams); Ballet Composite (Adams); Casse-Noisette - Act II (Franca after Ivanov); Coppélia - Act II (Franca after Saint-Léon); The Dance of Salomé (Franca); Don Quixote pas de deux (Petipa); Etude (Armstrong); Giselle - Act II (Franca after Coralli/Perrot); Giselle - Peasant pas de deux (Franca after Coralli/Perrot); L'Après-midi d'un Faune (Franca); Les Sylphides (Franca after Fokine); The Polovetsian Dances from Prince Igor (Franca after Fokine).

NOVEMBER, 1951:

12 TORONTO, ON - Eaton Aud: Les Sylphides; Dance of Salomé; Giselle - Act I pdd; Etude; Polovetsian Dances - *repeated, November 13, 14*

DECEMBER, 1951:

10 TORONTO, ON - Forest Hill Collegiate Aud: Les Sylphides; Giselle - Act I pdd; Etude; Don Quixote pdd; Coppélia - Act II

JANUARY, 1952:

14 GUELPH, ON - Guelph Collegiate Aud: Les Sylphides; Giselle - Act I pdd; Etude; Don Quixote pdd; Coppélia - Act II

15 KITCHENER, ON - K-W Collegiate Aud: Les Sylphides; Giselle - Act I pdd; Etude; Don Quixote pdd; Coppélia - Act II

28 TORONTO, ON - Eaton Aud: Giselle - Act II; Ballet Composite; Casse-Noisette - Act II - *repeated, January 29, 30*

31 MONTREAL, QC - His Majesty's Theatre: Les Sylphides; Dance of Salomé; Casse-Noisette - Act II

FEBRUARY, 1952:

1 MONTREAL, QC - His Majesty's Theatre: Ballet Composite; Coppélia - Act II; Etude; Don Quixote pdd; Polovetsian Dances

2* Les Sylphides; Coppélia - Act II; Casse-Noisette - Act II

2 Giselle - Act II; Dance of Salomé; Giselle - Act I pdd; Polovetsian Dances

7 LONDON, ON - Grand Theatre: Les Sylphides; Dance of Salomé; Casse-Noisette - Act II

8 Les Sylphides; Coppélia - Act II; Etude; Don Quixote pdd; Polovetsian Dances

9 Giselle - Act II; Coppélia - Act II; Giselle - Act I pdd; Polovetsian Dances

10 HAMILTON, ON - Savoy Theatre: Program unknown

26 TORONTO, ON - Maple Leaf Gardens: (Tor. Police Assoc. 33rd Ann. Concert) Don Quixote pdd; Polovetsian Dances

APRIL, 1952:

2 ST CATHARINES, ON - Palace Theatre: Coppélia - Act II; Les Sylphides; Casse-Noisette - Act II

21 TORONTO, ON - Eaton Aud: Etude; L'Après-midi d'un Faune; Ballet Behind Us; Casse-Noisette - Act II - *repeated, April 22, 23*

24 HAMILTON, ON - Savoy Theatre: Les Sylphides; Coppélia - Act II; Casse-Noisette - Act II

SEASON: 1952-3; **PERFORMANCES:** 63 (55 outside Toronto); **PREMIERES:** Coppélia (Franca after Saint-Léon); Giselle (Franca after Coralli/Perrot); Le Pommier (Franca); Lilac Garden (Tudor).

OCTOBER, 1952:

27 CALGARY, AB - Grand Theatre: Coppélia; Polovetsian Dances

28* Les Sylphides; L'Après-midi d'un Faune; Etude; Casse-Noisette - Act II

28 Giselle; Ballet Behind Us

29* RED DEER, AB - Red Deer Memorial Centre: Etude; L'Après-midi d'un Faune; Coppélia; Casse-Noisette - Act II

29 Les Sylphides; Ballet Behind Us; Casse-Noisette - Act II

30 EDMONTON, AB - Victoria School Aud: Les Sylphides; Le Pommier; Casse-Noisette - Act II

31 Giselle; Ballet Behind Us

NOVEMBER, 1952:

1* EDMONTON, AB - Victoria School Aud: Les Sylphides; Coppélia - Act II; Polovetsian Dances

1 Etude; L'Après-midi d'un Faune; Coppélia

3 VANCOUVER, BC - International Cinema: Les Sylphides; Le Pommier; Casse-Noisette - Act II

4 Giselle; Ballet Behind Us

5 Etude; L'Après-midi d'un Faune; Coppélia

6 VICTORIA, BC - Royal Theatre: Coppélia; Polovetsian Dances

7 Les Sylphides; Ballet Behind Us; Casse-Noisette - Act II

10 NELSON, BC - Civic Theatre: Les Sylphides; Coppélia - Act II; Casse-Noisette - Act II

13 LETHBRIDGE, AB - Capitol Theatre: Coppélia; Polovetsian Dances

14 Les Sylphides; Ballet Behind Us; Casse-Noisette - Act II

17 SASKATOON, SK - Capitol Theatre: Les Sylphides; Le Pommier; Casse-Noisette - Act II

19 REGINA, SK - Darke Hall: Etude; L'Après-midi d'un Faune; Ballet Behind Us; Casse-Noisette - Act II

21 WINNIPEG, MB - Playhouse Theatre: Coppélia; Casse-Noisette - Act II

22 Giselle; Le Pommier

24 FORT WILLIAM, ON - Voc. School Aud (Selkirk): Les Sylphides; Coppélia - Act II; Casse-Noisette - Act II

JANUARY, 1953:

19 TORONTO, ON - Royal Alexandra Theatre: Les Sylphides; Coppélia

20 Giselle; Ballet Behind Us

21* Casse-Noisette - Act II; Etude; L'Après-midi d'un Faune; Polovetsian Dances

21 Coppélia; Le Pommier

22 Les Sylphides; Lilac Garden; Polovetsian Dances

23 Etude; L'Après-midi d'un Faune; Lilac Garden; Casse-Noisette - Act II

24* Ballet Composite; Coppélia

24 Giselle; Le Pommier

26 LONDON, ON - Grand Theatre: Les Sylphides; Coppélia

27 Giselle; Ballet Behind Us

28 Casse-Noisette - Act II; Etude; L'Après-midi d'un Faune; Le Pommier

29 Les Sylphides; Lilac Garden; Polovetsian Dances

30 Etude; L'Après-midi d'un Faune; Lilac Garden; Casse-Noisette - Act II

31* Ballet Composite; Coppélia

31 Giselle; Le Pommier

FEBRUARY, 1953:

3 BRANTFORD, ON - Capitol Theatre: Coppélia; Casse-Noisette - Act II

4 HAMILTON, ON - Palace Theatre: Giselle; Le Pommier

9 MONTREAL, QC - Her Majesty's Theatre: Les Sylphides; Coppélia

10 Giselle; Ballet Behind Us

11* Casse-Noisette - Act II; Etude; L'Après-midi d'un Faune; Polovetsian Dances

11 Coppélia; Le Pommier

12 Les Sylphides; Lilac Garden; Polovetsian Dances

13 Etude; L'Après-midi d'un Faune; Lilac Garden; Casse-Noisette - Act II

14* Ballet Composite; Coppélia

14 Giselle; Le Pommier

16 FREDERICTON, NB - Devon School Aud: Les Sylphides; Coppélia; Casse-Noisette - Act II

17 SAINT JOHN, NB - Saint John High School Aud: Casse-Noisette - Act II; Coppélia - Act I, Mazurka, Czardas; Giselle - Act I pdd; Coppélia - Act II

18 Les Sylphides; Etude; L'Après-midi d'un Faune; Casse-Noisette - Act II

20 SYDNEY, NS - St Andrew's Hall: Les Sylphides; Coppélia; Casse-Noisette - Act II

21 Giselle - Act I - dances; Etude; Coppélia - Act I, Mazurka, Czardas; Casse-Noisette - Act II

23 HALIFAX, NS - Capitol Theatre: Coppélia; Polovetsian Dances

24 Giselle; Casse-Noisette - Act II

25* Coppélia; Casse-Noisette - Act II

25 Les Sylphides; Ballet Behind Us; Le Pommier

26 SACKVILLE, NB - Charles Fawcett Memorial Hall: Les Sylphides; Coppélia - Act II; Casse-Noisette - Act II

MARCH, 1953:

2 QUEBEC CITY, QC - Palais Montcalm: Coppélia; Casse-Noisette - Act II

4 OTTAWA, ON - Capitol Theatre: Giselle; Casse-Noisette - Act II

10 ST CATHARINES, ON - Palace Theatre: Giselle - Act I pdd; Etude; L'Après-midi d'un Faune; Le Pommier; Polovetsian Dances

11 KITCHENER, ON - K-W Collegiate Aud: Coppélia; Polovetsian Dances

12 Giselle; Casse-Noisette - Act II

13 OAKVILLE, ON - Oakville-Trafalgar H.S.: Les Sylphides; Coppélia; Casse-Noisette - Act II

SEASON: 1953-4; **PERFORMANCES:** 103 (88 outside Toronto); **PREMIERES:** Dances from the Classics (Franca after Petipa/Ivanov); Dark of the Moon [listed as Barbara Allen after 2 February 1955] (Harris); Gala Performance (Tudor); Swan Lake - Act II (Franca after Petipa/Ivanov).

AUGUST, 1953:

4 LEE, MA - Jacob's Pillow: Giselle - Act I pdd; Don Quixote pdd; Lilac Garden; Coppélia - Act II - *repeated, August 5*

6* L'Après-midi d'un Faune; Don Quixote pdd; Lilac Garden; Casse-Noisette - Act II

6 Giselle - Act I pdd; Don Quixote pdd; Lilac Garden; Coppélia - Act II

7* L'Après-midi d'un Faune; Don Quixote pdd; Lilac Garden; Casse-Noisette - Act II

7 Giselle - Act I pdd; Don Quixote pdd; Lilac Garden; Coppélia - Act II

8* L'Après-midi d'un Faune; Don Quixote pdd; Lilac Garden; Casse-Noisette - Act II
8 Giselle - Act I pdd; Don Quixote pdd; Lilac Garden; Coppélia - Act II

NOVEMBER, 1953:

16 PETERBOROUGH, ON - St Peter's High School Aud: Les Sylphides; Don Quixote pdd; L'Après-midi d'un Faune; Giselle - Act I pdd; Coppélia - Act II
17 Swan Lake - Act II; Lilac Garden; Casse-Noisette - Act II
18 OTTAWA, ON - Capitol Theatre: Coppélia - Act II; Lilac Garden; Gala Performance
20 QUEBEC CITY, QC - Palais Montcalm: Swan Lake - Act II; Casse-Noisette - Act II; Gala Performance
23 FREDERICTON, NB - High School Aud: Swan Lake - Act II; Don Quixote pdd; L'Après-midi d'un Faune; Giselle - Act I pdd; Coppélia - Act II
24** Coppélia - Act II; Les Sylphides; Casse-Noisette - Act II
24 Les Sylphides; Dances from the Classics; Casse-Noisette - Act II
25 SAINT JOHN, NB - Capitol Theatre: Giselle; Casse-Noisette - Act II
26* Les Sylphides; Dances from the Classics; Polovetsian Dances
26 Swan Lake - Act II; Coppélia
30 HALIFAX, NS - Capitol Theatre: Les Sylphides; Gala Performance; Polovetsian Dances

DECEMBER, 1953:

1 HALIFAX, NS - Capitol Theatre: Swan Lake - Act II; Dark of the Moon; Gala Performance
2* Les Sylphides; Coppélia
2 Giselle; Casse-Noisette - Act II
3 SACKVILLE, NB - Charles Fawcett Mem. Hall: Swan Lake - Act II; Dances from the Classics; Coppélia
4 Les Sylphides; Don Quixote pdd; L'Après-midi d'un Faune; Giselle - Act I pdd; Casse-Noisette - Act II

JANUARY, 1954:

19 MONTREAL, QC - Her Majesty's Theatre: Casse-Noisette - Act II; Lilac Garden; Gala Performance
20* Program unknown
20 Swan Lake - Act II; Dark of the Moon; Polovetsian Dances
21 Giselle; Gala Performance
22 Dances from the Classics; Don Quixote pdd; Lilac Garden; Casse-Noisette - Act II
23* Swan Lake - Act II; Polovetsian Dances; Dances from the Classics
23 Swan Lake - Act II; Gala Performance; Dark of the Moon
25 TORONTO, ON - Royal Alexandra Theatre: Casse-Noisette - Act II; Lilac Garden; Gala Performance
26 Coppélia; Dark of the Moon
27* Les Sylphides; Coppélia
27 Giselle; Gala Performance
28 Swan Lake - Act II; Dark of the Moon; Polovetsian Dances
29 Giselle; Polovetsian Dances
30* Swan Lake - Act II pdtr; Don Quixote pdd; Casse-Noisette - Act II
30 Swan Lake - Act II; Lilac Garden; Gala Performance

FEBRUARY, 1954:

1 LONDON, ON - Grand Theatre: Casse-Noisette - Act II; Lilac Garden; Gala Performance
2 Coppélia; Dark of the Moon
3* Les Sylphides; Coppélia
3 Giselle; Gala Performance
4 Swan Lake - Act II; Dark of the Moon; Polovetsian Dances
5 Giselle; Polovetsian Dances
6* Swan Lake - Act II pdtr; Don Quixote pdd; Casse-Noisette - Act II
6 Swan Lake - Act II; Dark of the Moon; Gala Performance
8 BRANTFORD, ON - Capitol Theatre: Les Sylphides; Gala Performance; Polovetsian Dances
9 ST CATHARINES, ON - Palace Theatre: Swan Lake - Act II; Don Quixote pdd; Dances from the Classics; Gala Performance
10 HAMILTON, ON - Palace Theatre: Swan Lake - Act II; Lilac Garden; Casse-Noisette - Act II
11 Les Sylphides; Dark of the Moon; Gala Performance
12 BUFFALO, NY - Erlanger Theatre: Giselle; Gala Performance
13* Les Sylphides; Coppélia
13 Swan Lake - Act II; Lilac Garden; Dances from the Classics; Casse-Noisette - Act II
14 DETROIT, MI - Cass Theatre: Les Sylphides; Coppélia
15 Casse-Noisette - Act II; Lilac Garden; Don Quixote pdd; Polovetsian Dances
16 Giselle; Gala Performance
17 L'Après-midi d'un Faune; Giselle - Act I pdd; Dark of the Moon; Casse-Noisette - Act II
18 Swan Lake - Act II; Dark of the Moon; Swan Lake pdtr; Polovetsian Dances
19 Swan Lake - Act II; Lilac Garden; Dances from the Classics; Gala Performance
20* Les Sylphides; Coppélia
20 Giselle; Casse-Noisette - Act II
22 MILWAUKEE, WI - Davidson Theatre: Swan Lake - Act II; Coppélia
23 Les Sylphides; Lilac Garden; Casse-Noisette - Act II
25 MINNEAPOLIS, MN - Lyceum Theatre: Giselle; Gala Performance
26 Program unknown
27* Les Sylphides; Coppélia
27 Program unknown

MARCH, 1954:

4 SEATTLE, WA - Metropolitan Theatre: Giselle; Gala Performance
5 Casse-Noisette - Act II; Dances from the Classics; Giselle - Act I pdd; Polovetsian Dances
6* Les Sylphides; Coppélia
6 Swan Lake - Act II; Dark of the Moon; Casse-Noisette - Act II
8 VANCOUVER, BC - International Cinema: Swan Lake - Act II; Dark of the Moon; Gala Performance
9 Giselle; Polovetsian Dances
10* Les Sylphides; Coppélia
10 Swan Lake - Act II; Lilac Garden; Casse-Noisette - Act II
11 Coppélia; Dark of the Moon
12 Les Sylphides; Lilac Garden; Gala Performance
13* Casse-Noisette - Act II; Dances from the Classics; Polovetsian Dances
13 Giselle; Dances from the Classics
15 VICTORIA, BC - Royal Theatre: Giselle; Casse-Noisette - Act II
16 Swan Lake - Act II; Dark of the Moon; Gala Performance
17 Dances from the Classics; Don Quixote pdd; Lilac Garden; Gala Performance
22 NELSON, BC - Civic Theatre: Swan Lake - Act II; Giselle - Act I pdd; Don Quixote pdd; Casse-Noisette - Act II
23 Les Sylphides; Dances from the Classics; Coppélia - Act II
25 LETHBRIDGE, AB - Capitol Theatre: Swan Lake - Act II; Don Quixote pdd; Giselle pdd; Casse-Noisette - Act II
26 Les Sylphides; Dances from the Classics; Coppélia - Act II
29 CALGARY, AB - Grand Theatre: Swan Lake - Act II; Giselle - Act I pdd; Don Quixote pdd; Gala Performance
30 Les Sylphides; Dark of the Moon; Casse-Noisette - Act II
31 Swan Lake - Act II; Dances from the Classics; Gala Performance

APRIL, 1954:

1 EDMONTON, AB - Victoria School Aud: Swan Lake - Act II; Gala Performance; Swan Lake pdtr; Polovetsian Dances

2 Casse-Noisette - Act II; Dark of the Moon; Don Quixote pdd; Dances from the Classics
3* Coppélia; Casse-Noisette - Act II
3 Giselle; Gala Performance
5 WINNIPEG, MB - Playhouse Theatre: Les Sylphides; Dark of the Moon; Casse-Noisette - Act II
6 Swan Lake - Act II; Don Quixote pdd; Dances from the Classics; Gala Performance
19 TORONTO, ON - Royal Alexandra Theatre: Swan Lake - Act II; Dark of the Moon; Gala Performance
20 Les Sylphides; Dances from the Classics; Don Quixote pdd; Gala Performance
21* Swan Lake - Act II; Dances from the Classics; Casse-Noisette - Act II
21 Swan Lake - Act II; Lilac Garden; Don Quixote pdd; Gala Performance
22 Giselle; Casse-Noisette - Act II
23 Dances from the Classics; Giselle - Act I pdd; Dark of the Moon; Polovetsian Dances
24* Coppélia; Giselle - Act I pdd; Polovetsian Dances

SEASON: 1954-5; **PERFORMANCES:** 66 (50 outside Toronto); **PREMIERES:** Offenbach in the Underworld (Tudor); dances from The Sleeping Princess (Petipa, add. choreography by Franca); The Lady from the Sea (Leese); Swan Lake (Petipa/Ivanov, produced by Franca).

JANUARY, 1955:
17 ST CATHARINES, ON - Palace Theatre: Les Sylphides; Lilac Garden; Offenbach in the Underworld
18 HAMILTON, ON - Palace Theatre: Casse-Noisette - Act II; Barbara Allen; Offenbach in the Underworld
19 Swan Lake
20 BRANTFORD, ON - Capitol Theatre: Swan Lake - Act II; Lilac Garden; Offenbach in the Underworld
21 KITCHENER, ON - Memorial Aud: Swan Lake
24 LONDON, ON - Grand Theatre: Coppélia; Offenbach in the Underworld
25 Swan Lake
26* Casse-Noisette - Act II; Les Sylphides; Offenbach in the Underworld
26 Les Sylphides; Barbara Allen; Gala Performance
27 Swan Lake
28 Casse-Noisette - Act II; Lilac Garden; Offenbach in the Underworld
29* Swan Lake - *repeated, January 29*
31 TORONTO, ON - Royal Alexandra Theatre: Swan Lake

FEBRUARY, 1955:
1 TORONTO, ON - Royal Alexandra Theatre: Coppélia; Offenbach in the Underworld
2* Les Sylphides; Coppélia
2 Les Sylphides; Barbara Allen; Gala Performance
3 Gala Performance; Lilac Garden; Offenbach in the Underworld
4 Swan Lake - *repeated, February 5**
5 Casse-Noisette - Act II; Barbara Allen; Offenbach in the Underworld
7 Giselle; Gala Performance
8 Swan Lake - *repeated, February 9**
9 Casse-Noisette - Act II; Lilac Garden; Offenbach in the Underworld
10 Les Sylphides; Barbara Allen; Gala Performance
11 Coppélia; Offenbach in the Underworld
12* Giselle; Offenbach in the Underworld
12 Swan Lake
14 CHICAGO, IL - Great Northern Theatre: Swan Lake
15 Casse Noisette - Act II; Lilac Garden; Offenbach in the Underworld
16* Coppélia; Gala Performance
16 Giselle; Gala Performance
17 Swan Lake
18 Les Sylphides; Barbara Allen; Offenbach in the Underworld
19* Swan Lake - *repeated, February 19*
21 DETROIT, MI - Shubert Theatre: Swan Lake
22* Coppélia; Offenbach in the Underworld
22 Casse-Noisette - Act II; Barbara Allen; Offenbach in the Underworld
23 Les Sylphides; Lilac Garden; Offenbach in the Underworld
24 Giselle; Gala Performance
25 Swan Lake - *repeated, February 26**
26 Swan Lake - Act II; Lilac Garden; Offenbach in the Underworld
28 MONTREAL, QC - Her Majesty's Theatre: Swan Lake

MARCH, 1955:
1 MONTREAL, QC - Her Majesty's Theatre: Gala Performance; Lilac Garden; Offenbach in the Underworld
2* Casse-Noisette - Act II; Les Sylphides; Offenbach in the Underworld
2 Giselle; Offenbach in the Underworld
3 Coppélia; Gala Performance
4 Les Sylphides; Barbara Allen; Casse-Noisette - Act II
5* Swan Lake - *repeated, March 5*
7 OTTAWA, ON - Capitol Theatre: Swan Lake - Act II; Barbara Allen; Offenbach in the Underworld
8 KINGSTON, ON - Kingston Comm. Mem. Centre: Casse-Noisette - Act II; Les Sylphides; Offenbach in the Underworld
25 BROOKLYN, NY - Brooklyn Academy of Music: Swan Lake
26 Barbara Allen; Lilac Garden; Offenbach in the Underworld

JUNE, 1955:
9 WASHINGTON, DC - Carter Barron Amphitheatre: Gala Performance; Lilac Garden; Offenbach in the Underworld; Sleeping Princess pdtr
10 Coppélia; L'Après-midi d'un Faune; Casse-Noisette
12 Giselle; Sleeping Beauty - Bluebird pdd; Offenbach in the Underworld
13 Les Sylphides; Giselle - Peasant pdd; Lady from the Sea; Offenbach in the Underworld
14 Swan Lake
15 Lady from the Sea; Sleeping Beauty - Bluebird pdd; Barbara Allen; Offenbach in the Underworld
16 Gala Performance; Barbara Allen; Coppélia
17 Swan Lake
18 Les Sylphides; Sleeping Princess pdtr; Lilac Garden; Offenbach in the Underworld

SEASON: 1955-6; **PERFORMANCES:** 73 (56 outside Toronto); **PREMIERES:** Dark Elegies (Tudor); The Nutcracker/ Casse-Noisette (Franca after Ivanov).

NOVEMBER, 1955:
14 BELLEVILLE, ON - Belleville Collegiate Inst.: Les Sylphides; Lilac Garden; Offenbach in the Underworld
15 KINGSTON, ON - Kingston Comm. Mem. Centre: Swan Lake - Act II; Dances from the Classics; Dark Elegies
17 OTTAWA, ON - Capitol Theatre: Swan Lake
19* QUEBEC CITY, QC - Capitol Theatre: Nutcracker
19 Swan Lake - Act II; Dark Elegies; Offenbach in the Underworld
21 MONTREAL, QC - Her Majesty's Theatre: Nutcracker
22 Gala Performance; Dark Elegies; Offenbach in the Underworld
23* Sleeping Princess pdtr; L'Après-midi d'un Faune; Dark Elegies; Gala Performance
23 Les Sylphides; Lady from the Sea; Offenbach in the Underworld
24 Swan Lake
25 Coppélia; Lady from the Sea
26* Nutcracker
26 Swan Lake

28 BRANTFORD, ON - Capitol Theatre: Nutcracker - Snow Scene; Lady from the Sea; Offenbach in the Underworld
29 HAMILTON, ON - Palace Theatre: Nutcracker
30 Dark Elegies; Offenbach in the Underworld; Lady from the Sea

DECEMBER, 1955:
1 KITCHENER, ON - Memorial Aud: Nutcracker
2 ST CATHARINES, ON - Palace Theatre: Swan Lake - Act II; Lady from the Sea; Offenbach in the Underworld

JANUARY, 1956:
1* TORONTO, ON - Shea's Theatre: Nutcracker - Acts I, II, & III
16 TORONTO, ON - Royal Alexandra Theatre: Nutcracker
17 Gala Performance; Dark Elegies; Offenbach in the Underworld
18* Nutcracker - Snow Scene; Lady from the Sea; Offenbach in the Underworld
18 Nutcracker
19 Les Sylphides; Coppélia
20 Dark Elegies; Lady from the Sea; Offenbach in the Underworld
21* Swan Lake
21 Nutcracker
23 Coppélia; Lady from the Sea
24 Sleeping Princess pdtr; L'Après-midi d'un Faune; Pas de Deux; Lilac Garden; Offenbach in the Underworld
25* Nutcracker
25 Swan Lake
26 Les Sylphides; Offenbach in the Underworld; Dark Elegies
27 Gala Performance; Lilac Garden; Offenbach in the Underworld
28* Nutcracker
28 Swan Lake
30 LONDON, ON - Grand Theatre: Nutcracker
31 Les Sylphides; Dark Elegies; Offenbach in the Underworld

FEBRUARY, 1956
1* LONDON, ON - Grand Theatre: Nutcracker - Snow Scene; Lady from the Sea; Gala Performance
1 Coppélia; Dark Elegies
2 Swan Lake
3 Lady from the Sea; Lilac Garden; Offenbach in the Underworld
4* Nutcracker
4 Swan Lake
10 ROCHESTER, NY - Eastman Theatre: Nutcracker
11 BUFFALO, NY - Erlanger Theatre: Swan Lake
12* Nutcracker
12 Les Sylphides; Lilac Garden; Offenbach in the Underworld
13* Coppélia; Offenbach in the Underworld
13 Swan Lake - Act II; Lady from the Sea; Gala Performance
14 Sleeping Princess pdtr; L'Après-midi d'un Faune; Dark Elegies; Gala Performance
15* Les Sylphides; Lady from the Sea; Offenbach in the Underworld
15 Nutcracker
17 BROOKLYN, NY - Brooklyn Academy of Music: Les Sylphides; Dark Elegies; Offenbach in the Underworld
18* Nutcracker
18 Swan Lake - Act II; Coppélia
20 NEWARK, NJ - Mosque Theatre: Swan Lake - Act II; Lady from the Sea; Offenbach in the Underworld
21 PHILADELPHIA, PA - Academy of Music: Les Sylphides; Dark Elegies; Offenbach in the Underworld
22 Coppélia; Lilac Garden; Gala Performance
24 BALTIMORE, MD - Lyric Theatre: Swan Lake
25* Nutcracker
25 Gala Performance; Dark Elegies; Offenbach in the Underworld
27 HUNTINGTON, WV - Keith-Albee Theatre: Coppélia; Offenbach in the Underworld
28 KNOXVILLE, TN - University of Tennessee Aud: Les Sylphides; Coppélia
29 GREENSBORO, NC - Aycock Aud: Les Sylphides; Lady from the Sea; Offenbach in the Underworld

MARCH, 1956:
1 COLUMBIA, SC - Columbia Township Aud: Coppélia; Offenbach in the Underworld
2 SAVANNAH, GA - Municipal Aud: Nutcracker - Act IV; Gala Performance; Offenbach in the Underworld
3 DAYTONA, FL - Peabody Aud: Nutcracker - Act IV; Gala Performance; Offenbach in the Underworld
5 MONTGOMERY, AL - Sidney Lanier Aud: Nutcracker - Act IV; Gala Performance; Offenbach in the Underworld
6 BIRMINGHAM, AL - Municipal Aud: Gala Performance; Dark Elegies; Offenbach in the Underworld
7 NASHVILLE, TN - Ryman Aud: Les Sylphides; Dark Elegies; Offenbach in the Underworld
8 Nutcracker
10* ATLANTA, GA - Tower Theatre: Nutcracker
10 Gala Performance; Dark Elegies; Offenbach in the Underworld

---

SEASON: 1956-7; **PERFORMANCES:** 130 (105 outside Toronto); **PREMIERES:** The Fisherman and His Soul (Strate); Giselle - new production (Coralli/Perrot, produced by Franca); Jeune Pas de Deux (Strate); La Llamada (Moller); Les Rendez-vous (Ashton); Pas de Chance (Adams); Post Script (Macdonald).

AUGUST, 1956:
2 WASHINGTON, DC - Carter Barron Amphitheatre: Les Sylphides; Jeune Pas de Deux; Dark Elegies; Offenbach in the Underworld
3 Swan Lake
4 Nutcracker
5 Coppélia; Pas de Trois; Gala Performance
6 Swan Lake
7 Nutcracker
8 Les Sylphides; Jeune Pas de Deux; Lilac Garden; Offenbach in the Underworld
9 Nutcracker
10 Coppélia; Pas de Trois; Offenbach in the Underworld
11 Swan Lake
12 Nutcracker
13 Coppélia; Pas de Trois; Offenbach in the Underworld
14 Swan Lake
15 Nutcracker

NOVEMBER, 1956:
5 HAMILTON, ON - Odeon Palace Theatre: Les Rendez-vous; Fisherman and His Soul; Post Script
6* Nutcracker - Act IV; La Llamada; Post Script
6 Jeune Pas de Deux; L'Après-midi d'un Faune; Pas de Chance; Giselle
7 ST CATHARINES, ON - Palace Theatre: Les Rendez-vous; Jeune Pas de Deux; L'Après-midi d'un Faune; Pas de Chance; Nutcracker - Act III
8 Nutcracker - Act IV; La Llamada; Post Script
9 KITCHENER, ON - Kitchener Memorial Aud: Giselle; Gala Performance
10 BELLEVILLE, ON - Belleville Collegiate Inst.: Nutcracker - Act IV; Les Rendez-vous; Post Script
13 OTTAWA, ON - Capitol Theatre: Les Rendez-vous; Fisherman and His Soul; Offenbach in the Underworld
14 La Llamada; Giselle

15 SHERBROOKE, QC - Theatre Granada: Les Sylphides; Jeune Pas de Deux; L'Après-midi d'un Faune; Pas de Chance; Post Script
17* QUEBEC CITY, QC - Capitol Theatre: Nutcracker - Act III; Coppélia
17 Swan Lake
19 MONTREAL, QC - Her Majesty's Theatre: La Llamada; Giselle
20 Les Rendez-vous; Dark Elegies; Post Script
21* Nutcracker
21 Les Rendez-vous; Fisherman and His Soul; Offenbach in the Underworld
22 Giselle; Offenbach in the Underworld
23 Les Sylphides; Lilac Garden; Gala Performance
24* Nutcracker
24 Coppélia; Post Script
26 Swan Lake
27 Jeune Pas de Deux; L'Après-midi d'un Faune; Pas de Chance; Fisherman and His Soul; La Llamada
28* Swan Lake
28 Fisherman and His Soul; Coppélia
29 Nutcracker
30 Giselle; Post Script

DECEMBER, 1956:

1* MONTREAL, QC - Her Majesty's Theatre: Les Sylphides; Jeune Pas De Deux; L'Après-midi d'un Faune; Pas de Chance; Nutcracker - Act IV
1 Les Rendez-vous; Lilac Garden; Offenbach in the Underworld

JANUARY, 1957:

7 TORONTO, ON - Royal Alexandra Theatre: Les Rendez-vous; Dark Elegies; Post Script
8 Les Sylphides; Fisherman and His Soul; Offenbach in the Underworld
9* Nutcracker
9 La Llamada; Giselle
10 Les Sylphides; Lilac Garden; Pas de Chance; Post Script
11 Les Rendez-vous; Fisherman and His Soul; Gala Performance
12* Nutcracker
12 Giselle; Post Script
14 Swan Lake
15 Nutcracker
16* Swan Lake
16 Jeune Pas de Deux; L'Après-midi d'un Faune; Pas de Chance; Fisherman and His Soul; Post Script
17 Les Rendez-vous; Dark Elegies; Offenbach in the Underworld
18 Les Rendez-vous; La Llamada; Offenbach in the Underworld
19* Jeune Pas de Deux; L'Après-midi d'un Faune; Pas de Chance; Giselle
19 La Llamada; Fisherman and His Soul; Post Script
21 Jeune Pas de Deux; L'Après-midi d'un Faune; Pas de Chance; Lilac Garden; Offenbach in the Underworld
22 Les Rendez-vous; Offenbach in the Underworld; Post Script
23* Nutcracker - *repeated, January 23*
24* Les Rendez-vous; Nutcracker - Act III; Post Script - *repeated, January 24 (Fisherman and His Soul substituted for Nutcracker - Act III)*
25 La Llamada; Dark Elegies; Offenbach in the Underworld
26* Coppélia; Post Script
26 Swan Lake
28 LONDON, ON - Grand Theatre: Les Rendez-vous; Fisherman and His Soul; Post Script
29 La Llamada; Giselle
30* Les Rendez-vous; Jeune Pas de Deux; L'Après-midi d'un Faune; Pas de Chance; Post Script
30 Les Rendez-vous; La Llamada; Offenbach in the Underworld
31 Swan Lake

FEBRUARY, 1957:

1 LONDON, ON - Grand Theatre: Jeune Pas de Deux; L'Après-midi d'un Faune; Pas de Chance; Giselle
2* Swan Lake
2 Les Sylphides; Fisherman and His Soul; Post Script
3 WINDSOR, ON - Capitol Theatre: Nutcracker
6 SIOUX FALLS, SD - Sioux Falls Coliseum: Les Rendez-vous; Fisherman and His Soul; Offenbach in the Underworld
7 ALBERT LEA, MN - Albert Lea High School Aud: Les Sylphides; Jeune Pas de Deux; L'Après-midi d'un Faune; Pas de Chance; Post Script
8 MINNEAPOLIS, MN - Northrop Memorial Aud: Les Rendez-vous; Fisherman and His Soul; Offenbach in the Underworld
9* Coppélia; Nutcracker - Act IV
9 Les Sylphides; Jeune Pas de Deux; L'Après-midi d'un Faune; Pas de Chance; Post Script
12 EAST LANSING, MI - University Aud: Les Sylphides; Fisherman and His Soul; Offenbach in the Underworld
13 Nutcracker - Act IV; Les Rendez-vous; Post Script
15 LAWRENCE, KS - Hich Aud: Nutcracker - Act IV; Coppélia
16 KANSAS CITY, MO - Civic Music Hall: Swan Lake
17 OKLAHOMA CITY, OK - Civic Aud: Les Rendez-vous; Fisherman and His Soul; Offenbach in the Underworld
19 WACO, TX - Baylor Univ., Waco Hall: Swan Lake - Act II; Fisherman and His Soul; Offenbach in the Underworld
20 FORT WORTH, TX - Will Rogers Memorial Aud: Les Sylphides; Nutcracker - Act IV; Post Script
21 AUSTIN, TX - U. of Texas, Gregory Gym.: Les Rendez-vous; Nutcracker - Act IV; Offenbach in the Underworld
22 DALLAS, TX - State Fair Aud: Les Rendez-vous; Fisherman and His Soul; Offenbach in the Underworld
23 Swan Lake
25 BATON ROUGE, LA - Southern U. Aud-Gymnasium: Les Sylphides; Jeune Pas de Deux; L'Après-midi d'un Faune; Pas de Chance; Offenbach in the Underworld
26 GALVESTON, TX - City Aud: Les Rendez-vous; Fisherman and His Soul; Offenbach in the Underworld
27 SHREVEPORT, LA - Municipal Aud: Les Rendez-vous; Jeune Pas de Deux; L'Après-midi d'un Faune; Pas de Chance; Offenbach in the Underworld
28 OXFORD, MS - U. of Miss., Fulton Chapel: Les Rendez-vous; Jeune Pas de Deux; L'Après-midi d'un Faune; Pas de Chance; Offenbach in the Underworld

MARCH, 1957:

1 COLUMBUS, MS - Whitfold Hall: Les Rendez-vous; Nutcracker - Act IV; Post Script
4 TAMPA, FL - Municipal Aud: Les Rendez-vous; Nutcracker - Act IV; Post Script
5 TALLAHASSEE, FL - Westcott Aud: Les Rendez-vous; Fisherman and His Soul; Offenbach in the Underworld
6 Les Sylphides; Nutcracker - Act IV; Post Script
7 ORLANDO, FL - Municipal Aud: Les Rendez-vous; Fisherman and His Soul; Post Script
8 MIAMI, FL - Dade County Aud: Les Rendez-vous; Fisherman and His Soul; Offenbach in the Underworld
9* Coppélia; Post Script
9 Swan Lake
10 FORT LAUDERDALE, FL - War Memorial Aud: Les Rendez-vous; Nutcracker - Act IV; Post Script
12 ATLANTA, GA - City Aud: Swan Lake
13 SAVANNAH, GA - Civic Aud: Coppélia; Post Script
14 MACON, GA - Porter Family Memorial Aud: Les Rendez-vous; Les Sylphides; Post Script

19 PITTSBURGH, PA - Mount Lebanon Aud: Coppélia; Offenbach in the Underworld
20 ANN ARBOR, MI - A.W.S. Butterfield Theatre: Les Rendez-vous; Offenbach in the Underworld; Post Script
21 INDIANAPOLIS, IN - Murat Theatre: Giselle; Post Script
22 LAFAYETTE, IN - Purdue Hall of Music: Les Rendez-vous; Fisherman and His Soul; Offenbach in the Underworld
23 Coppélia; Post Script
24 LOUISVILLE, KY - Memorial Aud: Swan Lake
25 CORNING, NY - Corning Glass Center: Les Sylphides; Jeune Pas de Deux; L'Après-midi d'un Faune; Pas de Chance; Post Script
27 BINGHAMTON, NY - Capitol Theatre: Nutcracker - Act IV; Les Sylphides; Offenbach in the Underworld
29 BURLINGTON, VT - Memorial Aud: Nutcracker - Act IV; Les Sylphides; Offenbach in the Underworld
30* BROOKLYN, NY - Brooklyn Academy of Music: Les Rendez-vous; Fisherman and His Soul; Post Script
30 Nutcracker - Act IV pdd; L'Après-midi d'un Faune; Pas de Chance; Giselle

APRIL, 1957:
1 NEWARK, NJ - Mosque Theatre: Les Rendez-vous; Fisherman and His Soul; Offenbach in the Underworld
29 BARRIE, ON - Barrie Arena: Les Sylphides; Offenbach in the Underworld; Post Script
30 HUNTSVILLE, ON - Memorial Arena: Les Sylphides; Offenbach in the Underworld; Post Script

MAY, 1957:
1 SUDBURY, ON - Sudbury Community Arena: Les Sylphides; Offenbach in the Underworld; Post Script
2 SAULT STE MARIE, ON - Sault Memorial Gardens: Les Sylphides; Offenbach in the Underworld; Post Script
4 HAILEYBURY, ON - Armouries: Les Sylphides; Offenbach in the Underworld; Post Script
6 NORANDA, QC - Noranda Recreation Centre: Les Sylphides; Offenbach in the Underworld; Post Script
7 TIMMINS, ON - McIntyre Arena: Les Sylphides; Offenbach in the Underworld; Post Script
8 KAPUSKASING, ON - Community Club: Les Sylphides; Offenbach in the Underworld; Post Script
10 CAMP PETAWAWA, ON - Drill Hall #1: Les Sylphides; Offenbach in the Underworld; Post Script
11 KINGSTON, ON - Kingston Community Centre: Les Sylphides; Offenbach in the Underworld; Post Script
13 PETERBOROUGH, ON - Peterborough Mem. Centre: Les Sylphides; Offenbach in the Underworld; Post Script

---

SEASON: 1957-8; **PERFORMANCES:** 189 (155 outside Toronto); **PREMIERES:** Dances from The Sleeping Beauty (after Petipa); La Farruca (Moller); Le Carnaval (Franca after Fokine); The Willow (Strate); Winter Night (after Gore).

NOVEMBER, 1957:
4 HAMILTON, ON - Odeon Palace Theatre: Le Carnaval; Winter Night; Offenbach in the Underworld
5* Swan Lake - Act II; Pas de Chance; Willow; La Farruca; Le Carnaval
5 Swan Lake
6 ST CATHARINES, ON - Palace Theatre: Swan Lake - Act II; Winter Night; Le Carnaval
7 Dances from The Sleeping Beauty; La Farruca; Willow; Pas de Chance; Offenbach in the Underworld
8 KITCHENER, ON - Kitchener Memorial Aud: Les Rendez-vous; Winter Night; Offenbach in the Underworld
9* BELLEVILLE, ON - Belleville Collegiate Aud: Swan Lake - Act II; Pas de Chance; Willow; La Farruca; Dances from The Sleeping Beauty
9 Le Carnaval; Winter Night; Offenbach in the Underworld
12 OTTAWA, ON - Capitol Theatre: Swan Lake
13* Pas de Chance; Willow; La Farruca; Nutcracker - Acts II & IV
13 Nutcracker - Act III; Winter Night; Le Carnaval
14 SHERBROOKE, QC - Theatre Granada: Nutcracker - Act III; La Farruca; Willow; Offenbach in the Underworld pdd; Pas de Chance; Dances from The Sleeping Beauty
16* QUEBEC CITY, QC - Capitol Theatre: Dances from The Sleeping Beauty; Winter Night; Le Carnaval - *repeated, November 16*
18 MONTREAL, QC - Her Majesty's Theatre: Swan Lake
19 Nutcracker
20** Coppélia
20 Le Carnaval; Winter Night; Dances from The Sleeping Beauty
21 Giselle; Offenbach in the Underworld
22 Swan Lake
23* Coppélia; Offenbach in the Underworld
23 Swan Lake
25 Nutcracker
26 Giselle; Le Carnaval
27* Dances from The Sleeping Beauty; Winter Night; Offenbach in the Underworld
27 Coppélia; Le Carnaval
28 Swan Lake
29 Pas de Chance; Willow; La Farruca; Giselle
30* Nutcracker
30 Le Carnaval; Winter Night; Offenbach in the Underworld

JANUARY, 1958:
6 TORONTO, ON - Royal Alexandra Theatre: Swan Lake
7 Les Sylphides; Winter Night; Offenbach in the Underworld
8* Nutcracker
8 Giselle; Offenbach in the Underworld
9 Les Sylphides; Winter Night; Offenbach in the Underworld
10 Nutcracker
11* Swan Lake
11 Les Rendez-vous; Winter Night; Le Carnaval
13 Le Carnaval; Lilac Garden; Offenbach in the Underworld
14 Nutcracker - Act IV; Les Sylphides; Offenbach in the Underworld
15* Les Sylphides; Coppélia
15 Le Carnaval; Winter Night; Gala Performance
16 Swan Lake
17 Nutcracker
18* Giselle; Gala Performance
18 Les Rendez-vous; Fisherman and His Soul; Offenbach in the Underworld
20 Swan Lake
21** Les Sylphides; Coppélia - Act II
21 Nutcracker
22* Dances from The Sleeping Beauty; Nutcracker - dances from; Willow; Pas de Chance; Offenbach in the Underworld
22 Swan Lake - Act II; Lilac Garden; Le Carnaval
23 Nutcracker
24 Swan Lake
25* Les Sylphides; Nutcracker - Act III; Le Carnaval
25 Giselle; Le Carnaval
27 Nutcracker
28** Swan Lake - Act II; Offenbach in the Underworld

28 Swan Lake
29* Nutcracker
29 Les Rendez-vous; Winter Night; Le Carnaval
30 Le Carnaval; Fisherman and His Soul; Offenbach in the Underworld
31 Pas de Chance; Nutcracker - dances from; Willow; Giselle

FEBRUARY, 1958:

1* TORONTO, ON - Royal Alexandra Theatre: Nutcracker
1 Swan Lake
3 LONDON, ON - Grand Theatre: Swan Lake
4 Nutcracker
5* Dances from The Sleeping Beauty; Coppélia
5 Pas de Chance; Nutcracker - Buffon; Willow; Giselle
6 Swan Lake
7 Le Carnaval; Dances from The Sleeping Beauty; Offenbach in the Underworld
8* Nutcracker
8 Le Carnaval; Winter Night; Offenbach in the Underworld
9* WINDSOR, ON - Capital Theatre: Swan Lake - Act II; Pas de Chance; Willow; La Farruca; Le Carnaval
9 Dances from The Sleeping Beauty; Winter Night; Offenbach in the Underworld
10 ANN ARBOR, MI - A.W.S. Butterfield Theatre: Dances from The Sleeping Beauty; Winter Night; Le Carnaval
11 WARREN, OH - Packard Music Hall: Dances from The Sleeping Beauty; Winter Night; Offenbach in the Underworld
12 BINGHAMTON, NY - Capitol Theatre: Swan Lake - Act II; Nutcracker - dances from; Offenbach in the Underworld pdd; Pas de Chance; Le Carnaval
13 HARTFORD, CT - Bushnell Hall: Swan Lake - Act II; Winter Night; Le Carnaval
14 COLLEGE PARK, MD - Cole Activities Centre: Swan Lake - Act II; Nutcracker - dances from; Pas de Chance; Offenbach in the Underworld
16 PITTSBURGH, PA - Syria Mosque: Giselle; Le Carnaval
19 RALEIGH, NC - Memorial Aud: Le Carnaval; Winter Night; Offenbach in the Underworld
20 SAVANNAH, GA - City Aud: Swan Lake
21 AUGUSTA, GA - Bell Memorial Aud: Le Carnaval; Winter Night; Offenbach in the Underworld
22* ATLANTA, GA - Tower Theatre: Swan Lake - Act II; Nutcracker - dances from; Pas de Chance; Dances from The Sleeping Beauty
22 Le Carnaval; Winter Night; Offenbach in the Underworld
24 EAST LANSING, MI - Michigan State U. Aud: Swan Lake
25 Le Carnaval; Winter Night; Offenbach in the Underworld
26 LAFAYETTE, IN - Elliott Hall of Music: Swan Lake
27 Le Carnaval; Winter Night; Offenbach in the Underworld
28 INDIANAPOLIS, IN - Murat Theatre: Le Carnaval; Winter Night; Offenbach in the Underworld

MARCH, 1958:

1* LOUISVILLE, KY - Memorial Aud: Le Carnaval; Winter Night; Offenbach in the Underworld
1 Swan Lake
2 MILWAUKEE, WI - Oriental Theatre: Swan Lake - Act II; Nutcracker - dances from; Swan Lake - Act III Czardas; Offenbach in the Underworld pdd; Pas de Chance; Dances from The Sleeping Beauty
3 BLOOMINGTON, IN - Indiana University Aud: Le Carnaval; Winter Night; Offenbach in the Underworld
4 ST LOUIS, MO - Kiel Opera House: Swan Lake - Act II; Winter Night; Le Carnaval
5 DAVENPORT, IA - Orpheum Theatre: Le Carnaval; Winter Night; Offenbach in the Underworld
6 DES MOINES, IA - K.R.N.T. Theatre: Le Carnaval; Winter Night; Offenbach in the Underworld
7 KANSAS CITY, MO - Music Hall: Giselle; Dances from The Sleeping Beauty
8* Le Carnaval; Winter Night; Nutcracker - Act IV
8 Swan Lake
9 OKLAHOMA CITY, OK - Municipal Aud: Le Carnaval; Winter Night; Offenbach in the Underworld
10 FORT WORTH, TX - Will Rogers Aud: Dances from The Sleeping Beauty; Nutcracker - dances from; Pas de Deux; Pas de Chance; Le Carnaval
11* RUSTON, LA - Howard Aud: Dances from The Sleeping Beauty; Nutcracker - dances from; Pas de Chance; Le Carnaval
11 Swan Lake - Act II; Winter Night; Offenbach in the Underworld
12 COLLEGE STATION, TX - G. Rollie White Coliseum: Le Carnaval; Winter Night; Offenbach in the Underworld
13 HARLINGEN, TX - Municipal Aud: Le Carnaval; Winter Night; Offenbach in the Underworld
14 CORPUS CHRISTI, TX - Delmar Aud: Le Carnaval; Winter Night; Offenbach in the Underworld
15 LAREDO, TX - Martin High School Aud: Le Carnaval; Winter Night; Offenbach in the Underworld
17 SAN ANGELO, TX - Municipal Aud: Dances from The Sleeping Beauty; Winter Night; Offenbach in the Underworld
18 Swan Lake - Act II; Nutcracker - dances from; Pas de Chance; Le Carnaval
19 MIDLAND, TX - High School Aud: Le Carnaval; Winter Night; Offenbach in the Underworld
20 EL PASO, TX - Liberty Hall: Swan Lake - Act II; Winter Night; Offenbach in the Underworld
22 DENVER, CO - Denver Aud: Swan Lake
24 LOGAN, UT - Utah State Coll. Field House: Swan Lake - Act II; Nutcracker - dances from; Pas de Chance; Offenbach in the Underworld
25 SALT LAKE CITY, UT - Capitol Theatre: Swan Lake - *repeated, March 26**
26 Le Carnaval; Winter Night; Offenbach in the Underworld
28 TUCSON, AZ - University of Arizona Aud: Le Carnaval; Winter Night; Offenbach in the Underworld
29* PHOENIX, AZ - West Phoenix High School Aud: Swan Lake - Act II; Nutcracker - dances from; Dances from The Sleeping Beauty
29 Le Carnaval; Winter Night; Offenbach in the Underworld
31 LOS ANGELES, CA - Philharmonic Aud: Swan Lake

APRIL, 1958:

1 SAN BERNARDINO, CA - California Theatre: Swan Lake - Act II; Le Carnaval; Offenbach in the Underworld
2 LONG BEACH, CA - Wilson Hight School Aud: Le Carnaval; Winter Night; Offenbach in the Underworld
3 PASADENA, CA - City of Pasadena Aud: Le Carnaval; Winter Night; Offenbach in the Underworld
4 SAN DIEGO, CA - Russ Aud: Swan Lake - Act II; Le Carnaval; Offenbach in the Underworld
5* LOS ANGELES, CA - Philharmonic Aud: Swan Lake
5 Le Carnaval; Winter Night; Offenbach in the Underworld

7 BAKERSFIELD, CA - Harvey Aud: Le Carnaval; Winter Night; Offenbach in the Underworld
8 SANTA CRUZ, CA - Civic Aud: Swan Lake - Act II; Nutcracker - dances from; Pas de Chance; Offenbach in the Underworld
9 RICHMOND, CA - Memorial Aud: Swan Lake - Act II; Nutcracker - dances from; Pas de Chance; Offenbach in the Underworld
10 SAN JOSE, CA - Civic Aud: Swan Lake - Act II; Le Carnaval; Offenbach in the Underworld
11 SAN FRANCISCO, CA - War Memorial Opera House: Le Carnaval; Winter Night; Offenbach in the Underworld
12 Swan Lake
13 VISALIA, CA - Montgomery Aud: Swan Lake - Act II; Nutcracker - dances from; Offenbach in the Underworld
14 FRESNO, CA - Roosevelt High School Aud: Le Carnaval; Winter Night; Offenbach in the Underworld
15 SACRAMENTO, CA - Sacramento Memorial Aud: Le Carnaval; La Farruca; Nutcracker - dances from; Sleeping Princess - Aurora pdd; Offenbach in the Underworld
17 EUGENE, OR - U. of Oregon-MacArthur Court: Le Carnaval; La Farruca; Nutcracker - dances from; Pas de Chance; Offenbach in the Underworld
18 CORVALLIS, OR - Gill Coliseum: Swan Lake - Act II; Nutcracker - dances from; Pas de Chance; Offenbach in the Underworld
19 SEATTLE, WA - Moore Theatre: Dances from The Sleeping Beauty; Winter Night; Offenbach in the Underworld
21 WALLA WALLA, WA - Walla Walla High School Gym.: Swan Lake - Act II; Offenbach in the Underworld
22 Le Carnaval; La Farruca; Nutcracker - dances from; Pas de Chance; Offenbach in the Underworld
25 VICTORIA, BC - Royal Theatre: Swan Lake
26* Dances from The Sleeping Beauty; Le Carnaval; Offenbach in the Underworld
26 Le Carnaval; Winter Night; Offenbach in the Underworld
28 VANCOUVER, BC - Orpheum Theatre: Le Carnaval; Winter Night; Offenbach in the Underworld
30* PENTICTON, BC - High School Aud: Dances from The Sleeping Beauty; La Farruca; Nutcracker - dances from; Pas de Chance; Le Carnaval
30 Swan Lake - Act II; Winter Night; Offenbach in the Underworld

MAY, 1958:
1 TRAIL, BC - Cominco Arena: Swan Lake - Act II; Winter Night; Offenbach in the Underworld
3* LETHBRIDGE, AB - Capitol Theatre: Dances from The Sleeping Beauty; La Farruca; Nutcracker - dances from; Pas de Chance; Le Carnaval
3 Swan Lake - Act II; Winter Night; Offenbach in the Underworld
5 CALGARY, AB - Jubilee Aud: Swan Lake
6 Le Carnaval; Winter Night; Offenbach in the Underworld
7 EDMONTON, AB - Jubilee Aud: Swan Lake
8 Le Carnaval; Winter Night; Offenbach in the Underworld
10* SASKATOON, SK - Capitol Theatre: Le Carnaval; La Farruca; Nutcracker - dances from; Pas de Chance; Dances from The Sleeping Beauty
10 Swan Lake - Act II; Winter Night; Offenbach in the Underworld
12* REGINA, SK - Capitol Theatre: Le Carnaval; La Farruca; Nutcracker - dances from; Pas de Chance; Dances from The Sleeping Beauty
12 Swan Lake - Act II; Winter Night; Offenbach in the Underworld
14 WINNIPEG, MB - Winnipeg Playhouse Theatre: Le Carnaval; Winter Night; Offenbach in the Underworld
15 Swan Lake
17* FORT WILLIAM, ON - Fort William Gardens: Le Carnaval; La Farruca; Nutcracker - dances from; Pas de Chance; Dances from The Sleeping Beauty
17 Swan Lake - Act II; Winter Night; Offenbach in the Underworld
19 SAULT STE MARIE, ON - Sault Memorial Gardens: Swan Lake - Act II; Winter Night; Le Carnaval
20 SUDBURY, ON - Sudbury Arena: Swan Lake - Act II; Winter Night; Le Carnaval
31 MEXICO CITY, MEXICO - Palacio de Bellas Artes: Swan Lake

JUNE, 1958:
1 MEXICO CITY, MEXICO - Palacio de Bellas Artes: Les Rendez-vous; L'Après-midi d'un Faune; Dark Elegies; Offenbach in the Underworld - *repeated, June 2 (without Faune), 3*
4 La Farruca; Pas de Chance; Sleeping Princess - Aurora pdd; Giselle
5 Swan Lake
7* Les Sylphides; Winter Night; Gala Performance
7 Swan Lake
8* Les Sylphides; Winter Night; Gala Performance - *repeated, June 8*
9 Les Sylphides; La Farruca; L'Après-midi d'un Faune; Pas de Chance; Offenbach in the Underworld
10 Les Sylphides; Winter Night; Gala Performance
11 Nutcracker - *repeated, June 12*
13 Nutcracker - Act III; Coppélia
14* Les Sylphides; Fisherman and His Soul; Le Carnaval
15* Le Carnaval; Fisherman and His Soul; Offenbach in the Underworld
15 Le Carnaval; Giselle
16 Les Rendez-vous; Coppélia
17 Le Carnaval; Giselle
18 Les Rendez-vous; Lilac Garden; Sleeping Princess - Aurora pdd; Offenbach in the Underworld
19 MEXICO CITY, MEXICO - Auditorio Nacional: Swan Lake - *repeated, June 20*
21* Les Rendez-vous; Nutcracker - Acts III & IV
21 Giselle; Offenbach in the Underworld

SEASON: 1958-9; **PERFORMANCES:** 150 (117 outside Toronto); **PREMIERES:** Ballad (Strate); Coppélia - new production (Franca after Saint-Léon).

OCTOBER, 1958:
27 PETERBOROUGH, ON - Peterborough Memorial Centre: Swan Lake - Act II; Lilac Garden; Les Rendez-vous
28 BELLEVILLE, ON - Belleville High School Aud: Les Rendez-vous; Les Sylphides; Nutcracker - Act IV
29 OTTAWA, ON - Capitol Theatre: Les Sylphides; Ballad; Les Rendez-vous
30* Coppélia - *repeated, October 30*

NOVEMBER, 1958:
1* SHERBROOKE, QC - Granada Theatre: Les Rendez-vous; Lilac Garden; Nutcracker - Act IV
1 Les Rendez-vous; Lilac Garden; Nutcracker - Act IV
3 BURLINGTON, VT - Memorial Aud: Swan Lake - Act II; Lilac Garden; Les Rendez-vous
4** Coppélia - *repeated, November 4*
7 FREDERICTON, NB - Lady Beaverbrook Rink: Swan Lake - Act II; Ballad; Offenbach in the Underworld

8★ SAINT JOHN, NB - High School Aud: Les Sylphides; Ballad; Les Rendez-vous
8 Swan Lake - Act II; Lilac Garden; Offenbach in the Underworld
10★ HALIFAX, NS - Capitol Theatre: Coppélia
10 Les Rendez-vous; Ballad; Offenbach in the Underworld
12★ MONCTON, NB - Moncton High School Aud: Nutcracker - Act IV; Les Sylphides; Offenbach in the Underworld - *repeated, November 12*
13 EDMUNDSTON, NB - Cormier High School Aud: Nutcracker - Act IV; Les Sylphides; Offenbach in the Underworld
15★ QUEBEC CITY, QC - Capitol Theatre: Coppélia
15 Les Sylphides; Ballad; Offenbach in the Underworld
17 TROIS-RIVIERES, QC - Capitol Theatre: Les Sylphides; Lilac Garden; Nutcracker - Act IV
19 MONTREAL, QC - Her Majesty's Theatre: Coppélia
20 Les Rendez-vous; Giselle
21 Les Rendez-vous; Ballad; Offenbach in the Underworld
22★ Nutcracker
22 Swan Lake - *repeated, November 23*★★
24 Nutcracker
25 Les Rendez-vous; Ballad; Offenbach in the Underworld
26★ Coppélia
26 Les Sylphides; Ballad; Gala Performance - *repeated, November 27 (Lilac Garden substituted for Ballad)*
28 Giselle; Offenbach in the Underworld
29★ Coppélia - *repeated, November 29*

DECEMBER, 1958:

1 ST CATHARINES, ON - Palace Theatre: Les Sylphides; Ballad; Les Rendez-vous
2 Swan Lake - Act II; Lilac Garden; Nutcracker - Act IV
3 KITCHENER, ON - Kitchener Memorial Aud: Les Sylphides; Ballad; Les Rendez-vous
4 HAMILTON, ON - Odeon Palace Theatre: Coppélia
5★ Nutcracker - Acts III & IV
5 Les Sylphides; Ballad; Les Rendez-vous
6★ Coppélia
6 Giselle; Gala Performance

JANUARY, 1959:

2 BALTIMORE, MD - Lyric Theatre: Giselle; Offenbach in the Underworld
4★ Coppélia
5 LYNCHBURG, VA - H.C. Glass High School Aud: Giselle; Offenbach in the Underworld
6 NORFOLK, VA - Center Theatre: Les Sylphides; Winter Night; Offenbach in the Underworld
7 RALEIGH, NC - Memorial Aud: Les Sylphides; Ballad; Coppélia - Act III
8 DURHAM, NC - Duke University, Page Aud: Les Sylphides; Winter Night; Offenbach in the Underworld
9 ASHEVILLE, NC - City Aud: Les Sylphides; Ballad; Offenbach in the Underworld
10 ATLANTA, GA - Municipal Aud: Coppélia
12 THOMASVILLE, GA - Municipal Aud: Les Sylphides; Ballad; Offenbach in the Underworld
13 PENSACOLA, FL - Municipal Aud: Coppélia - Act III; Winter Night; Offenbach in the Underworld
14 BIRMINGHAM, AL - Municipal Aud: Coppélia
15 TALLAHASSEE, FL - Westcott Aud: Coppélia
16 MIAMI, FL - Dade County Aud: Giselle; Offenbach in the Underworld
17 Coppélia
18 JACKSONVILLE, FL - National Guard Armory: Giselle; Offenbach in the Underworld
19 DAYTONA BEACH, FL - Peabody Aud: Coppélia
22 PHILADELPHIA, PA - Academy of Music: Les Sylphides; Winter Night; Offenbach in the Underworld
23 HARTFORD, CT - Bushnell Aud: Coppélia
24 ROCHESTER, NY - Eastman Theatre: Ballad; Coppélia - Act III; Winter Night
25 WINDSOR, ON - Capitol Theatre: Les Sylphides; Ballad; Les Rendez-vous
26 LONDON, ON - Grand Theatre: Giselle; Offenbach in the Underworld
27 Swan Lake - *repeated, January 28*★
28 Coppélia - *repeated, January 29*★★
29 Les Sylphides; Ballad; Offenbach in the Underworld
30 Le Carnaval; Winter Night; Gala Performance
31★ Le Carnaval; Ballad; Coppélia - Act III
31 Coppélia

FEBRUARY, 1959:

2 TORONTO, ON - Royal Alexandra Theatre: Coppélia
3 Le Carnaval; Winter Night; Gala Performance
4★★ Nutcracker - Acts III & IV
4 Coppélia - *repeated, February 5*
6 Swan Lake - *repeated, February 7*★
7 Les Rendez-vous; Winter Night; Offenbach in the Underworld - *repeated, February 9 (Gala Performance substituted for Offenbach)*
10 Les Sylphides; Ballad; Offenbach in the Underworld
11★ Les Rendez-vous; Ballad; Gala Performance
11 Le Carnaval; Winter Night; Offenbach in the Underworld - *repeated, February 12 (Lilac Garden substituted for Winter Night)*
13 Giselle; Gala Performance
14★ Coppélia - *repeated, February 14*
16 Nutcracker - *repeated, February 17*
18★ Les Rendez-vous; Lilac Garden; Offenbach in the Underworld - *repeated, February 18*
19★ Winter Night; Gala Performance
19 Les Sylphides; Dark Elegies; Gala Performance - *repeated, February 20 (Les Rendez-vous substituted for Gala Performance)*
21★ Nutcracker - *repeated, February 21*
23 Giselle; Coppélia - Act III
24 Les Sylphides; Fisherman and His Soul; Coppélia - Act III - *repeated, February 25*★
25 Les Sylphides; Ballad; Gala Performance
26 Swan Lake - *repeated, February 27*
28★ Coppélia - Act III; Ballad; Offenbach in the Underworld
28 Les Rendez-vous; Giselle

MARCH, 1959:

2 MOUNT PLEASANT, MI - Warringer Aud: Les Rendez-vous; Winter Night; Offenbach in the Underworld
3 COLUMBUS, OH - Mershon Aud: Les Rendez-vous; Winter Night; Offenbach in the Underworld
4 DAYTON, OH - National Cash Register Aud: Coppélia
5 LOUISVILLE, KY - Memorial Aud: Giselle; Coppélia - Act III
7 FORT WAYNE, IN - Scottish Rite Aud: Giselle; Offenbach in the Underworld
9 MADISON, WI - Wisconsin Union Theatre: Coppélia
10 Les Sylphides; Ballad; Offenbach in the Underworld
11 MINNEAPOLIS, MN - Northrop Aud: Giselle; Offenbach in the Underworld
12 Coppélia
13 MILWAUKEE, WI - Pabst Theatre: Ballad; Coppélia - Act III; Winter Night
14 CEDAR RAPIDS, IA - Coe College Aud: Les Sylphides; Winter Night; Offenbach in the Underworld
16 BURLINGTON, IA - Memorial Aud: Les Rendez-vous; Winter Night; Offenbach in the Underworld
17 ST LOUIS, MO - Kiel Opera House: Coppélia

18 COLUMBIA, MO - Jesse Aud: Giselle; Offenbach in the Underworld
19 TOPEKA, KS - Municipal Aud: Les Rendez-vous; Ballad; Offenbach in the Underworld
20 KANSAS CITY, MO - Music Hall: Coppélia
21** Coppélia - Act II
21 Les Rendez-vous; Ballad; Offenbach in the Underworld
23 LUBBOCK, TX - Lubbock Aud: Les Sylphides; Ballad; Offenbach in the Underworld
24 DALLAS, TX - State Fair Music Hall: Giselle; Offenbach in the Underworld
25 AUSTIN, TX - Gregory Gymnasium: Les Sylphides; Ballad; Coppélia - Act III
26 HOUSTON, TX - Music Hall: Coppélia
27 SAN ANTONIO, TX - Municipal Aud: Giselle; Offenbach in the Underworld
28 BEAUMONT, TX - City Aud: Coppélia - Act III; Ballad; Offenbach in the Underworld
30 NEW ORLEANS, LA - Municipal Aud: Coppélia
31 SHREVEPORT, LA - Municipal Aud: Coppélia

APRIL, 1959:
20 GUELPH, ON - Guelph Memorial Gardens: Les Sylphides; Nutcracker - Act IV; Offenbach in the Underworld
21 BRANTFORD, ON - Capitol Theatre: Les Rendez-vous; Ballad; Nutcracker - Act IV
22 CHATHAM, ON - Kinsmen Aud: Les Sylphides; Ballad; Nutcracker - Act IV
23 OWEN SOUND, ON - Owen Sound C.V.I. Aud: Les Rendez-vous; Ballad; Nutcracker - Act IV
24 BARRIE, ON - Barrie Arena: Les Rendez-vous; Ballad; Nutcracker - Act IV
25* COBOURG, ON - Cobourg Opera House: Les Sylphides; Nutcracker - Act IV; Les Rendez-vous
25 Les Rendez-vous; Ballad; Offenbach in the Underworld
27 CORNWALL, ON - Cornwall Community Arena: Les Rendez-vous; Ballad; Offenbach in the Underworld
28 MONTREAL, QC - Comédie Canadienne: Les Sylphides; Ballad; Offenbach in the Underworld
29* RENFREW, ON - Recreation Centre: Les Sylphides; Nutcracker - Act IV; Les Rendez-vous
29 Les Rendez-vous; Ballad; Offenbach in the Underworld
30 PEMBROKE, ON - Pembroke Memorial Centre: Les Rendez-vous; Ballad; Offenbach in the Underworld

MAY, 1959:
1 NORTH BAY, ON - Memorial Gardens: Les Rendez-vous; Ballad; Nutcracker - Act IV
2 SAULT STE MARIE, ON - Sault Memorial Gardens: Les Rendez-vous; Ballad; Nutcracker - Act IV
4 NORANDA, QC - Recreation Centre: Les Rendez-vous; Ballad; Nutcracker - Act IV
5 TIMMINS, ON - McIntyre Arena: Les Rendez-vous; Ballad; Nutcracker - Act IV
6* KAPUSKASING, ON - Kapuskasing Community Club: Les Sylphides; Nutcracker - Act IV; Les Rendez-vous
6 Les Rendez-vous; Ballad; Nutcracker - Act IV
8 BRACEBRIDGE, ON - Memorial Community Centre: Les Rendez-vous; Ballad; Nutcracker - Act IV

SEASON: 1959-60; **PERFORMANCES:** 110 (78 outside Toronto); **PREMIERES:** Death and the Maiden (Howard); The Littlest One (Adams); The Mermaid (Howard, in collaboration with Susan Salaman); Pas de Deux Romantique (Adams); Pas de Six (Adams); Pineapple Poll (Cranko).

NOVEMBER, 1959:
2 HAMILTON, ON - Odeon Palace Theatre: Nutcracker
3** Coppélia - Acts I & II
3 Le Carnaval; Mermaid; Pineapple Poll
4** Coppélia - Acts II & III
4 Les Rendez-vous; Death and the Maiden; Sleeping Princess - Aurora pdd; Littlest One; Pineapple Poll
5 KITCHENER, ON - Kitchener Memorial Aud: Littlest One ; Sleeping Princess - Aurora pdd; Death and The Maiden ; Mermaid; Winter Night
6 ST CATHARINES, ON - Palace Theatre: Mermaid; Pas de Six; Littlest One; Sleeping Princess - Aurora pdd; Pineapple Poll
7* Coppélia
7 Le Carnaval; Nutcracker - Act III pdd; Death and the Maiden; Offenbach in the Underworld
9 BELLEVILLE, ON - Belleville Collegiate Aud: Swan Lake - Act II; Pas de Six; Death and the Maiden; Sleeping Princess - Aurora pdd; Le Carnaval
11 MONTREAL, QC - Her Majesty's Theatre: Swan Lake
12 Les Rendez-vous; Mermaid; Offenbach in the Underworld
13 Coppélia
14* Les Rendez-vous; Mermaid; Le Carnaval
14 Pas de Six; Death and the Maiden; Littlest One; Ballad; Gala Performance
15** Swan Lake
17 Pas de Six; Death and the Maiden; Sleeping Princess - Aurora pdd; Dark Elegies; Pineapple Poll
18* Le Carnaval; Winter Night; Pineapple Poll
18 Coppélia
19 Swan Lake
20 Les Sylphides; Ballad; Gala Performance
21* Les Sylphides; Pas de Six; Death and the Maiden; Sleeping Princess - Aurora pdd; Offenbach in the Underworld
21 Mermaid; Dark Elegies; Pineapple Poll
22** Le Carnaval; Nutcracker - Acts II & IV
24 QUEBEC CITY, QC - Capitol Theatre: Swan Lake
25* Les Rendez-vous; Death and the Maiden; Pas de Six; Coppélia - Act III
25 Le Carnaval; Mermaid; Pineapple Poll
26 TROIS RIVIERES, QC - Capitol Theatre: Swan Lake - Act II; Littlest One; Sleeping Princess - Aurora pdd; Death and the Maiden; Le Carnaval
27 OTTAWA, ON - Capitol Theatre: Les Rendez-vous; Mermaid; Pineapple Poll
28* Le Carnaval; Littlest One; Gala Performance
28 Swan Lake - Act II; Dark Elegies; Pineapple Poll

JANUARY, 1960:
6 DANVILLE, VA - George Washington H.S. Aud: Nutcracker - Act IV; Death and the Maiden; Sleeping Princess - Aurora pdd; Pas de Six; Offenbach in the Underworld
7 GREENSBORO, NC - Aycock Aud: Nutcracker - Act IV; Ballad; Pineapple Poll
8 SAVANNAH, GA - City Aud: Les Rendez-vous; Death and the Maiden; Pas de Six; Sleeping Princess - Aurora pdd; Pineapple Poll
9 COLUMBIA, SC - Columbia Township Aud: Nutcracker - Act IV; Death and the Maiden; Pas de Six; Sleeping Princess - Aurora pdd; Pineapple Poll
11 CLEMSON, SC - Clemson College Field House: Les Rendez-vous; Ballad; Offenbach in the Underworld

12 ATLANTA, GA - Municipal Aud: Les Rendez-vous; Death and the Maiden; Pas de Six; Sleeping Princess - Aurora pdd; Pineapple Poll
13 BIRMINGHAM, AL - Municipal Aud: Les Rendez-vous; Death and the Maiden; Pas de Six; Sleeping Princess - Aurora pdd; Pineapple Poll
14 KNOXVILLE, TN - Alumni Memorial Aud: Pas de Six; Death and the Maiden; Sleeping Princess - Aurora pdd; Ballad; Nutcracker - Act IV
16 JOHNSTOWN, PA - Cochran Jr. High School Aud: Les Rendez-vous; Death and the Maiden; Pas de Six; Sleeping Princess - Aurora pdd; Offenbach in the Underworld
17* CLEVELAND, OH - Music Hall - Public Aud: Nutcracker - Act IV; Death and the Maiden; Pas de Six; Sleeping Princess - Aurora pdd; Offenbach in the Underworld
25 LONDON, ON - Grand Theatre: Les Rendez-vous; Mermaid; Pineapple Poll
26 Swan Lake
27** Swan Lake - excerpts Acts I & III, complete Acts II & IV
27 Pas de Six; Death and the Maiden; Sleeping Princess - Aurora pdd; Mermaid; Pineapple Poll
28 Coppélia
29 Les Sylphides; Pas de Six; Death and the Maiden; Nutcracker - Act III pdd; Pineapple Poll
30* Coppélia
30 Les Sylphides; Ballad; Gala Performance

FEBRUARY, 1960:

1 TORONTO, ON - Royal Alexandra Theatre: Les Rendez-vous; Pas de Deux Romantique; Lilac Garden; Pineapple Poll
2 Les Rendez-vous; Mermaid; Offenbach in the Underworld
3** Pas de Deux Romantique; Pineapple Poll
3 Les Sylphides; Ballad; Pineapple Poll
4 Pas de Chance; Death and the Maiden; Sleeping Princess - Aurora pdd; Ballad; Gala Performance
5 Coppélia
6* Swan Lake
6 Les Sylphides; Mermaid; Pineapple Poll - *repeated, February 8 (Ballad substituted for Mermaid)*
9 Pas de Six; Death and the Maiden; Sleeping Princess - Aurora pdd; Fisherman and His Soul; Offenbach in the Underworld
10** Swan Lake - excerpts Acts I, II, III, complete Act IV
10 Pas de Chance; Death and the Maiden; Pas de Deux Romantique; Mermaid; Pineapple Poll
11 Les Rendez-vous; Lilac Garden; Pineapple Poll
12 Le Carnaval; Fisherman and His Soul; Coppélia - Act III
13* Coppélia
13 Swan Lake
15 Le Carnaval; Winter Night; Coppélia - Act III
16 Swan Lake
17** Coppélia - excerpts Acts I & III, complete Act II
17 Nutcracker - Act IV; Mermaid; Pineapple Poll
18 Nutcracker - Act IV; Ballad; Offenbach in the Underworld
19 Mermaid; Winter Night; Le Carnaval
20* Nutcracker - *repeated, February 20*
22 Swan Lake
23 Coppélia
24* Le Carnaval; Winter Night; Nutcracker - Act IV
24 Pas de Six; Pas de Deux Romantique; Pas de Chance; Dark Elegies; Pineapple Poll
25 Les Rendez-vous; Fisherman and His Soul; Offenbach in the Underworld
26 Les Sylphides; Dark Elegies; Coppélia - Act III
27* Les Rendez-vous; Coppélia - Acts II & III
27 Pas de Six; Pas de Deux Romantique; Death and the Maiden; Mermaid; Pineapple Poll

MARCH, 1960:

1* RED BANK, NJ - Carlton Theatre: Nutcracker - Act IV
2 HARTFORD, CT - Bushnell Aud: Swan Lake
3 RED BANK, NJ - Carlton Theatre: Les Rendez-vous; Pas de Six; Death and the Maiden; Coppélia - Act III pdd; Offenbach in the Underworld
4 BALTIMORE, MD - Lyric Theatre: Pas de Six; Death and the Maiden; Pas de Deux Romantique; Fisherman and His Soul; Pineapple Poll
5 MT LEBANON, PA - Mt Lebanon High School Aud: Swan Lake - Act II; Pas de Chance; Death and the Maiden; Pas de Six; Pineapple Poll
8 MADISON, WI - Orpheum Theatre: Nutcracker - Act IV; Pas de Chance; Sleeping Princess - Aurora pdd; Pas de Six; Offenbach in the Underworld
9 STEVENS POINT, WI - Pacelli High School Aud: Nutcracker - Act IV; Pas de Chance; Sleeping Princess - Aurora pdd; Pas de Six; Offenbach in the Underworld
10 GREEN BAY, WI - Variety Theatre: Nutcracker - Act IV; Pas de Chance; Sleeping Princess - Aurora pdd; Pas de Six; Offenbach in the Underworld
13 WAUWATOSA, WI - Wauwatosa High School Aud: Swan Lake - Act II; Death and the Maiden; Pas de Chance; Pas de Deux Romantique; Offenbach in the Underworld
15 SAGINAW, MI - Temple Theatre: Nutcracker - Act IV; Pas de Six; Sleeping Princess - Aurora pdd; Pas de Chance; Offenbach in the Underworld
16* FLINT, MI - Capitol Theatre: Les Rendez-vous; Nutcracker - Act IV
16 Swan Lake
17 LAFAYETTE, IN - Elliott Hall of Music: Nutcracker - Act IV; Death and the Maiden; Pas de Chance; Pas de Deux Romantique; Pineapple Poll
18 Swan Lake - Act II; Pas de Six; Death and the Maiden; Sleeping Princess - Aurora pdd; Offenbach in the Underworld
19 LOUISVILLE, KY - Memorial Aud: Nutcracker - Act IV; Pas de Chance; Death and the Maiden; Sleeping Princess - Aurora pdd; Pineapple Poll
21 NEW ORLEANS, LA - Municipal Aud: Swan Lake
22 GRAMBLING, LA - College Aud: Swan Lake - Act II; Pas de Chance; Death and the Maiden; Pas de Six; Offenbach in the Underworld
23* RUSTON, LA - Howard Aud: Swan Lake - Act II; Pas de Chance; Pas de deux Romantique; Pas de Six; Les Rendez-vous
23 Swan Lake - Act II; Fisherman and His Soul; Les Rendez-vous
24 HOUSTON, TX - Music Hall: Nutcracker - Act IV; Fisherman and His Soul; Pineapple Poll
25 FORT WORTH, TX - Will Rogers Aud: Les Rendez-vous; Death and the Maiden; Pas de Six; Sleeping Princess - Aurora pdd; Offenbach in the Underworld
26 TULSA, OK - Municipal Theatre: Nutcracker - Act IV; Fisherman and His Soul; Offenbach in the Underworld
27* WICHITA, KS - East High School Aud: Les Rendez-vous; Death and the Maiden; Pas de Six; Pas de Deux Romantique; Nutcracker - Act IV
28 LINCOLN, NE - Pershing Memorial Aud: Les Rendez-vous; Pas de Six; Death and the Maiden; Pas de Deux Romantique; Offenbach in the Underworld

29 OMAHA, NE - Omaha Civic Aud: Swan Lake - Act II; Pas de Chance; Death and the Maiden; Pas de Deux Romantique; Pineapple Poll
30 CEDAR FALLS, IA - Teachers College Aud: Les Rendez-vous; Pas de Six; Death and the Maiden; Sleeping Princess - Aurora pdd; Offenbach in the Underworld
31 LAWRENCE, KS - Hoch Aud: Les Rendez-vous; Death and the Maiden; Pas de Six; Pas de Deux Romantique; Offenbach in the Underworld

APRIL, 1960:
1 KANSAS CITY, MO - Music Hall: Swan Lake
2 TOPEKA, KS - Municipal Aud: Les Rendez-vous; Death and the Maiden; Pas de Six; Pas de Deux Romantique; Offenbach in the Underworld

---

SEASON: 1960-1; **PERFORMANCES:** 170 (129 outside Toronto); **PREMIERES:** Antic Spring (Strate); Barbara Allen (Adams); Princess Aurora (Petipa, add. choreography by Franca); The Remarkable Rocket (Gillies).

AUGUST, 1960:
23 WASHINGTON, DC - Carter Barron Amphitheatre: Les Sylphides; Ballad; Pas de Deux Romantique; Les Rendez-vous
24 Coppélia
25 Swan Lake
26 Les Sylphides; Ballad; Sleeping Princess - Aurora pdd; Les Rendez-vous
27 Swan Lake
28 Coppélia
29 Les Sylphides; Ballad; Pas de Deux Romantique; Les Rendez-vous

OCTOBER, 1960:
24 HAMILTON, ON - Odeon Palace Theatre: Princess Aurora; L'Après-midi d'un Faune; Pas de Deux Romantique; Antic Spring
25** Pineapple Poll
25 Swan Lake
26 Remarkable Rocket; Barbara Allen; Princess Aurora
27 ST CATHARINES, ON - Palace Theatre: Remarkable Rocket; Pas de Deux Romantique; L'Après-midi d'un Faune; Princess Aurora
28 Coppélia
29* Les Rendez-vous; Swan Lake - Act II; Pineapple Poll
29 Les Sylphides; Barbara Allen; Antic Spring

NOVEMBER, 1960:
1 KITCHENER, ON - Kitchener Memorial Aud: Coppélia
2 BELLEVILLE, ON - Belleville Collegiate Aud: Les Sylphides; Princess Aurora - excerpts; Pas de Deux Romantique; L'Après-midi d'un Faune; Antic Spring
3 OTTAWA, ON - Capitol Theatre: Antic Spring; L'Après-midi d'un Faune; Pas de Chance; Pas de Deux Romantique; Pineapple Poll
4 Princess Aurora; Barbara Allen; Remarkable Rocket
5* Pineapple Poll
5 Swan Lake
7 QUEBEC CITY, QC - Capitol Theatre: Princess Aurora; Barbara Allen; Remarkable Rocket
8* Coppélia
8 Giselle; Antic Spring
9 SHERBROOKE, QC - Theatre Granada: Coppélia - Act III; Princess Aurora - excerpts; Pas de Deux Romantique; L'Après-midi d'un Faune; Antic Spring
11* BROCKVILLE, ON - Civic Aud: Swan Lake - Act II; Antic Spring; Les Rendez-vous
11 Swan Lake - Act II; Antic Spring; Les Rendez-vous
12 PETERBOROUGH, ON - Memorial Centre: Princess Aurora; Barbara Allen; Antic Spring
15 MONTREAL, QC - Her Majesty's Theatre: Remarkable Rocket; Lilac Garden; Princess Aurora
16 Giselle; Antic Spring
17 Les Sylphides; Winter Night; Pineapple Poll
18 Les Rendez-vous; Pas de Deux Romantique; Pas de Chance; L'Après-midi d'un Faune; Princess Aurora
19* Coppélia - *repeated, November 19*
20** Nutcracker - Acts III & IV
21 Pas de Chance; Pas de Deux Romantique; L'Après-midi d'un Faune; Lilac Garden; Remarkable Rocket
23 Swan Lake
24 Les Rendez-vous; Pas de Chance; L'Après-midi d'un Faune; Sleeping Beauty - Bluebird pdd; Pineapple Poll
25 Les Sylphides; Lilac Garden; Antic Spring
26* Nutcracker
26 Swan Lake
27** Pineapple Poll

DECEMBER, 1960:
26* VICTORIA, BC - Royal Theatre: Les Sylphides; Coppélia - Act II; Princess Aurora
26 Princess Aurora; Ballad; Pineapple Poll
27 Coppélia
29 VANCOUVER, BC - Queen Elizabeth Theatre: Princess Aurora; Ballad; Pineapple Poll
30 Les Sylphides; Lilac Garden; Pineapple Poll
31* Coppélia - *repeated, December 31*

JANUARY, 1961:
3 CALGARY, AB - Jubilee Aud: Princess Aurora; Ballad; Pineapple Poll
4* Coppélia - *repeated, January 4*
5 EDMONTON, AB - Jubilee Aud: Princess Aurora; Ballad; Pineapple Poll
6 Les Sylphides; Lilac Garden; Pineapple Poll
7* Coppélia - *repeated, January 7*
9 SASKATOON, SK - Capitol Theatre: Les Sylphides; Coppélia - Act II; Princess Aurora
11 WINNIPEG, MB - Playhouse Theatre: Les Sylphides; Coppélia - Act II; Princess Aurora
12 GRAND FORKS, ND - Central High School Aud: Les Sylphides; Coppélia - Act II; Princess Aurora
14 RAPID CITY, SD - High School Aud: Les Sylphides; Coppélia - Act II; Princess Aurora
16 VERMILLION, SD - Stagle Aud: Les Sylphides; Coppélia - Act II; Princess Aurora
17 WORTHINGTON, MN - High School Aud: Les Sylphides; Coppélia - Act II; Princess Aurora
18 AUSTIN, MN - Senior High School Aud: Les Sylphides; Coppélia - Act II; Princess Aurora
19 DES MOINES, IA - K.R.N.T.: Les Sylphides; Coppélia - Act II; Princess Aurora
20 MILWAUKEE, WI - Oriental Theatre: Les Sylphides; Coppélia - Act II; Princess Aurora
21 SHEBOYGEN, WI - North High School Aud: Les Sylphides; Coppélia - Act II; Princess Aurora
22* APPLETON, WI - Senior High School Aud: Les Sylphides; Coppélia - Act II; Princess Aurora
23 WINDSOR, ON - Cleary Aud: Swan Lake
24 Les Sylphides; Ballad; Pineapple Poll
25** Coppélia - Act II - *repeated (complete), January 25*
26 Giselle; Antic Spring
27 Remarkable Rocket; Winter Night; Pineapple Poll
28* Princess Aurora; Death and the Maiden; Pas de Six; Nutcracker - Act IV
28 Swan Lake
30 TORONTO, ON - Royal Alexandra Theatre: Giselle; Antic Spring

31 Les Sylphides; Winter Night; Remarkable Rocket

FEBRUARY, 1961:

1** TORONTO, ON - Royal Alexandra Theatre: Coppélia - Act II
1 Coppélia
2 Princess Aurora; Antic Spring; Offenbach in the Underworld
3 Giselle; Remarkable Rocket
4* Swan Lake
4 Princess Aurora; L'Après-midi d'un Faune; Death and the Maiden; Pineapple Poll
6 Coppélia
7 Les Rendez-vous; Remarkable Rocket; Offenbach in the Underworld
8** Swan Lake - Act II
8 Les Sylphides; Barbara Allen; Pineapple Poll
9 Princess Aurora; L'Après-midi d'un Faune; Pineapple Poll
10 Antic Spring; Lilac Garden; Offenbach in the Underworld
11* Nutcracker - *repeated, February 11*
13 Princess Aurora; Pas de Chance; Death and the Maiden; Remarkable Rocket
14 Antic Spring; Lilac Garden; Pineapple Poll
15** Nutcracker - Acts III & IV
15 Giselle; Antic Spring
16 Swan Lake
17 Les Sylphides; Dark Elegies; Pineapple Poll
18* Coppélia - *repeated, February 18*
20 Swan Lake
21 Remarkable Rocket; Barbara Allen; Antic Spring
22* Les Rendez-vous; Pas de Six; Pas de Deux Romantique; Nutcracker - Act IV pdd; Pineapple Poll - *repeated, February 22*
23 Le Carnaval; Barbara Allen; Princess Aurora - *repeated, February 24 (Winter Night substituted for Barbara Allen)*
25* Swan Lake - *repeated, February 25*
27 Nutcracker
28 Les Sylphides; Ballad; Offenbach in the Underworld

MARCH, 1961:

1** TORONTO, ON - Royal Alexandra Theatre: Les Rendez-vous; Ballad
1 Les Sylphides; Dark Elegies; Offenbach in the Underworld
2* Sleeping Princess - dances from; L'Après-midi d'un Faune; Pas de Six; Nutcracker - Act IV
2 Pas de Six; L'Après-midi d'un Faune; Giselle
3 Nutcracker
4* Les Rendez-vous; Pas de Six; Pas de Deux Romantique; Pas de Chance; Pineapple Poll
4 Remarkable Rocket; Barbara Allen; Princess Aurora
6 LONDON, ON - Grand Theatre: Giselle; Offenbach in the Underworld
7 Swan Lake
8* Les Sylphides; Antic Spring - *repeated, March 8 (with Princess Aurora added)*
9 Les Rendez-vous; Winter Night; Antic Spring
10 Pas de Six; Pas de Deux Romantique; Pas de Chance; Barbara Allen; Offenbach in the Underworld
11* Nutcracker - *repeated, March 11*
13* Les Rendez-vous; Nutcracker - Act IV
13 Les Sylphides; Pas de Chance; Death and the Maiden; Pas de Deux Romantique; Princess Aurora
14 Les Rendez-vous; Lilac Garden; Princess Aurora
15 Nutcracker
16 Giselle; Antic Spring
17 Nutcracker
18* Swan Lake - *repeated, March 18*

APRIL, 1961:

3 ROCHESTER, NY - Eastman Theatre: Coppélia
4 SYRACUSE, NY - Lincoln Aud: Coppélia
5** BUFFALO, NY - Kleinhans Music Hall: Coppélia - Act II - *repeated (complete), April 5*
7 HARTFORD, CT - Bushnell Aud: Coppélia
8 BALTIMORE, MD - Lyric Theatre: Coppélia
9 STATE COLLEGE, PA - Schwab Aud: Coppélia
10 HUNTINGTON, WV - Keith-Albee Theatre: Coppélia
11 CHARLESTON, WV - Municipal Aud: Coppélia
12 LYNCHBURG, VA - E.C. Glass High School Aud: Coppélia
13 DURHAM, NC - Page Aud: Coppélia
14 ROCK HILL, SC - Winthrop Aud: Coppélia
15 KNOXVILLE, TN - Alumni Memorial Aud: Coppélia
17 FLORENCE, AL - Coffee High School Aud: Coppélia
18 COLUMBUS, GA - Royal Theatre: Coppélia
19 TALLAHASSEE, FL - Westcott Aud, Fla. State U.: Coppélia
20 Swan Lake
22 LAFAYETTE, LA - Lafayette Municipal Aud: Swan Lake
23* Coppélia
24 BATON ROUGE, LA - Southern University Aud: Coppélia
25 HOUSTON, TX - Music Hall: Swan Lake
26 CORPUS CHRISTI, TX - Del Mar Theatre: Coppélia
27 SAN ANTONIO, TX - Municipal Aud: Swan Lake
28 HOUSTON, TX - Music Hall: Coppélia
29 DALLAS, TX - State Fair Music Hall: Coppélia

MAY, 1961:

1 BIG SPRING, TX - Municipal Aud: Coppélia
2 PAMPA, TX - Jr High School Aud: Coppélia
3 FORT HAYS, KS - Sheridan Coliseum, State Coll.: Coppélia
4 SALINA, KS - Fine Arts Theatre: Coppélia
5 KANSAS CITY, MO - Music Hall: Coppélia
7 CHICAGO, IL - Opera House: Coppélia
8 GRAND RAPIDS, MI - Civic Aud: Coppélia
9 EAST LANSING, MI - University Aud: Coppélia
10 LEXINGTON, KY - Memorial Aud: Coppélia
11 LOUISVILLE, KY - Memorial Aud: Coppélia
12 CINCINNATI, OH - Music Hall: Coppélia
14 CLEVELAND, OH - Music Hall: Coppélia
15 PITTSBURGH, PA - Syria Mosque: Swan Lake

SEASON: 1961-2; **PERFORMANCES:** 104 (71 outside Toronto); **PREMIERES:** Concerto Barocco (Balanchine, staged by Una Kai); One in Five (Powell).

NOVEMBER, 1961:

20 BROCKVILLE, ON - Civic Aud: Swan Lake
21 OTTAWA, ON - Capitol Theatre: Giselle; Concerto Barocco
22 Les Sylphides; One in Five; Lilac Garden; Antic Spring
23 MONTREAL, QC - Her Majesty's Theatre: Swan Lake
24 Les Sylphides; One in Five; Dances from The Sleeping Princess pdtr; Giselle - Act I pdd; Dances from The Sleeping Princess - Bluebird pdd; Pineapple Poll
25* Swan Lake - *repeated, November 25*
26** One in Five; Princess Aurora
26 One in Five; Dances from The Sleeping Princess pdtr, Bluebird pdd; Concerto Barocco; Lilac Garden; Antic Spring
27 QUEBEC CITY, QC - Capitol Theatre: Les Sylphides; One in Five; Concerto Barocco; Pineapple Poll

28 SHERBROOKE, QC - Granada Theatre: Sleeping Princess pdtr; Giselle - Act I pdd; Dances from The Sleeping Princess; Swan Lake - Act III pdd; Concerto Barocco; Lilac Garden; One in Five
30** HAMILTON, ON - Odeon Palace Theatre: One in Five; Princess Aurora
30 Giselle; Concerto Barocco

DECEMBER, 1961:

1 KITCHENER, ON - Memorial Aud: Giselle; Concerto Barocco
2 BELLEVILLE, ON - Belleville Collegiate Aud: Concerto Barocco; Princess Aurora; Giselle - Act I pdd; Dances from The Sleeping Princess pdtr; One in Five

JANUARY, 1962:

22 WINDSOR, ON - Cleary Aud: Giselle; One in Five
23 Concerto Barocco; Les Sylphides; Pineapple Poll
24** Pineapple Poll
24 Princess Aurora; Ballad; Offenbach in the Underworld
25 Giselle; Offenbach in the Underworld
26 Les Rendez-vous; One in Five; Dances from The Sleeping Princess pdtr; Swan Lake - Act III pdd; Pineapple Poll
27* Swan Lake - *repeated, January 27*
29 TORONTO, ON - Royal Alexandra Theatre: Princess Aurora; One in Five; Pineapple Poll
30 Les Sylphides; Concerto Barocco; Giselle - Act I pdd; Pineapple Poll
31** Nutcracker
31 Les Sylphides; Concerto Barocco; One in Five; Offenbach in the Underworld

FEBRUARY, 1962:

1 TORONTO, ON - Royal Alexandra Theatre: Giselle; Offenbach in the Underworld - *repeated, February 2 (Antic Spring substituted for Offenbach)*
3* Coppélia - *repeated, February 3*
5 Giselle; One in Five
6 Coppélia
7* Swan Lake - Acts II, III, IV - *repeated (complete), February 7*
8 Les Sylphides; Ballad; Antic Spring
9 One in Five; Dances from The Sleeping Princess pdtr; Ballad; Princess Aurora
10* Swan Lake - *repeated, February 10, 12*
13 Les Rendez-vous; Concerto Barocco; Pas de Chance; Pineapple Poll
14* Coppélia
14 Les Rendez-vous; Dances from The Sleeping Princess pdtr; Lilac Garden; Offenbach in the Underworld
15 One in Five; L'Après-midi d'un Faune; Lilac Garden; Pineapple Poll
16 Nutcracker - *repeated, February 17*, 17*
19 Les Sylphides; Ballad; Princess Aurora
20 Dances from The Sleeping Princess pdtr; Giselle - Act I pdd; L'Après-midi d'un Faune; Pas de Chance; Concerto Barocco; Lilac Garden; Antic Spring
21* One in Five; Giselle - Act I pdd; Pineapple Poll
21 Concerto Barocco; Giselle - Act I pdd; L'Après-midi d'un Faune; One in Five; Pas de Chance; Offenbach in the Underworld - *repeated, February 22* (without Pas de Chance)*
22 Coppélia
23 Concerto Barocco; Dances from The Sleeping Princess - Bluebird pdd; Les Rendez-vous; Nutcracker - Act IV pdd; L'Après-midi d'un Faune; Antic Spring
24* Giselle; One in Five
24 Swan Lake

MARCH, 1962:

12 LONDON, ON - Grand Theatre: Les Sylphides; One in Five; Concerto Barocco; Princess Aurora
13 Coppélia
14* Les Sylphides; One in Five; Pineapple Poll
14 Giselle; Pineapple Poll
15 Les Sylphides; Lilac Garden; Offenbach in the Underworld
16 Concerto Barocco; Dances from The Sleeping Princess - Bluebird pdd; Lilac Garden; Offenbach in the Underworld
17* Coppélia
17 Concerto Barocco; Princess Aurora; Antic Spring
19 NEWTON, MA - High School Aud: One in Five; Lilac Garden; Princess Aurora
21 NEW KENSINGTON, PA - New Kensington H.S. Aud: Les Sylphides; Concerto Barocco; Giselle - Act I pdd; L'Après-midi d'un Faune; Antic Spring
22 PHILADELPHIA, PA - Academy of Music: One in Five; Concerto Barocco; Princess Aurora; Giselle - Act I pdd; Antic Spring
23a* RED BANK, NJ - Carlton Theatre: One in Five; Giselle - Act I Peasant pdd; L'Après-midi d'un Faune; Antic Spring - *repeated, March 23b*, 23c* (without Giselle pdd) (three matinees on one day)*
24* BALTIMORE, MD - Lyric Theatre: Princess Aurora; One in Five; Antic Spring - *repeated, March 24 (Giselle - Act I pdd; Sleeping Princess pdtr; L'Après-midi d'un Faune substituted for One in Five)*
26 WILMINGTON, NC - Brogden Hall: Swan Lake - Act II; One in Five; Princess Aurora
27 CLEMSON, SC - Clemson College Field House: One in Five; Lilac Garden; Concerto Barocco; Antic Spring
30 MIAMI, FL - Dade County Aud: Swan Lake - Act II; Nutcracker - Act IV pdd; Swan Lake - Act I pdtr; Princess Aurora
31 Swan Lake - Act II; One in Five; Sleeping Princess pdtr; Swan Lake - Act I pdtr; L'Après-midi d'un Faune; Concerto Barocco

APRIL, 1962:

2 ALBANY, GA - Albany Theatre: Les Sylphides; Giselle - Act I pdd; L'Après-midi d'un Faune; Princess Aurora
3 ATLANTA, GA - Municipal Aud: One in Five; L'Après-midi d'un Faune; Lilac Garden; Princess Aurora
4 TALLAHASSEE, FL - Westcott Aud: Les Sylphides; One in Five; Giselle - Act I pdd; L'Après-midi d'un Faune; Antic Spring
5 PANAMA CITY, FL - Municipal Aud: Les Sylphides; One in Five; Sleeping Princess pdtr; Giselle - Act I pdd; Antic Spring
6 COLUMBUS, MS - Whitfield Aud: Swan Lake - Act II; Giselle - Act I pdd; L'Après-midi d'un Faune; Princess Aurora
7 MEMPHIS, TN - Ellis Aud: Les Sylphides; One in Five; Lilac Garden; Antic Spring
9 GRAMBLING, LA - College Aud: Les Sylphides; One in Five; Princess Aurora
10* RUSTON, LA - Howard Aud: Les Sylphides; One in Five; Princess Aurora - *repeated, April 10*
11 FORT WORTH, TX - Will Rogers Memorial Aud: One in Five; Giselle - Act I pdd; Sleeping Princess pdtr; Swan Lake - Act II; Antic Spring
12 SAN ANTONIO, TX - Municipal Aud: One in Five; Giselle - Act I pdd; Sleeping Princess pdtr; Les Sylphides; Antic Spring
13 HOUSTON, TX - Music Hall: Les Sylphides; One in Five; Princess Aurora
14 Concerto Barocco; Giselle - Act I pdd; Pas de Chance; L'Après-midi d'un Faune; Sleeping Princess pdtr; Lilac Garden; Antic Spring
16 WACO, TX - Waco Hall: One in Five; Princess Aurora; Antic Spring
17 TYLER, TX - Municipal Aud: Swan Lake - Act II; One in Five; Pas de Chance; Swan Lake - Act I pdtr; Antic Spring

18 AUSTIN, TX - Municipal Aud: One in Five; L'Après-midi d'un Faune; Concerto Barocco; Princess Aurora
19 WICHITA FALLS, TX - Municipal Aud: Swan Lake - Act II; One in Five; Princess Aurora
21 LAWTON, OK - McMahan Aud: Les Sylphides; One in Five; Concerto Barocco; Antic Spring
23 OMAHA, NE - Omaha Civic Aud Music Hall: Les Sylphides; Princess Aurora; Antic Spring
24 ALBERT LEA, MN - High School Aud: One in Five; Giselle - Act I pdd; Sleeping Princess pdtr; Concerto Barocco; Lilac Garden; Antic Spring
25 MINNEAPOLIS, MN - Northrop Aud: One in Five; Concerto Barocco; Princess Aurora; Antic Spring
27 KANSAS CITY, MO - Music Hall: Swan Lake - Act II; One in Five; Princess Aurora
30 EMPORIA, KS - Civic Aud: Les Sylphides; One in Five; Princess Aurora

MAY, 1962:

1 COLUMBIA, MO - Jesse Hall: Swan Lake - Act II; One in Five; Giselle - Act I Peasant pdd; L'Après-midi d'un Faune; Antic Spring
2 ST LOUIS, MO - Kiel Opera House: One in Five; L'Après-midi d'un Faune; Lilac Garden; Princess Aurora
3 CINCINNATI, OH - Music Hall: One in Five; L'Après-midi d'un Faune; Princess Aurora; Antic Spring
4 LEXINGTON, KY - Memorial Coliseum Aud: One in Five; Swan Lake - Act I pdtr; L'Après-midi d'un Faune; Nutcracker - Act IV pdd; Swan Lake - Act II; Antic Spring
5 PITTSBURGH, PA - Syria Mosque: Swan Lake - Act II; Sleeping Princess pdtr; L'Après-midi d'un Faune; Nutcracker - Act IV pdd; Princess Aurora

---

SEASON: 1962-3; **PERFORMANCES:** 115 (85 outside Toronto); **PREMIERES:** Judgment of Paris (Tudor); Laurencia Pas de Six (Chabukiane, staged by Samsova); Le Corsaire pas de deux (Klavin, staged by Samsova); Sequel (Strate); Serenade (Balanchine, staged by Kai); Time Cycle (Strate).

JULY, 1962:

13 STRATFORD, ON - Festival Theatre: Sequel; Time Cycle - *repeated, July 15*

OCTOBER, 1962:

15 MIDLAND, TX - Municipal Aud: Swan Lake - Act II; Concerto Barocco; Offenbach in the Underworld
16 BIG SPRING, TX - City Aud: Swan Lake - Act II; Concerto Barocco; Offenbach in the Underworld
17 DENTON, TX - North Texas State U. Aud: One in Five; Giselle - Act I pdd; Judgment of Paris; Lilac Garden; Serenade
18 NACHITOCHES, LA - Fine Arts Aud: One in Five; Giselle - Act I pdd; Judgment of Paris; Lilac Garden; Serenade
19 SHERMAN, TX - Sherman High School Aud: One in Five; L'Après-midi d'un Faune; Le Corsaire pdd; Lilac Garden; Offenbach in the Underworld
20 OKLAHOMA CITY, OK - Municipal Aud: Serenade; Swan Lake - Act II; Offenbach in the Underworld
23 CORPUS CHRISTI, TX - Del Mar Aud: Serenade; Swan Lake - Act II; Offenbach in the Underworld
24 NACOGDOCHES, TX - Fine Arts Aud: One in Five; Judgment of Paris; Le Corsaire pdd; L'Après-midi d'un Faune; Laurencia Pas de Six; Les Rendez-vous
25 KERRVILLE, TX - Municipal Aud: One in Five; Judgment of Paris; Les Rendez-vous; Offenbach in the Underworld
26 KINGSVILLE, TX - Jones Aud: Swan Lake - Act II; Concerto Barocco; Offenbach in the Underworld
27 HOUSTON, TX - Music Hall: Serenade; Laurencia Pas de Six; Judgment of Paris; Offenbach in the Underworld
30* GRINNEL, IA - Roberts Theatre: Concerto Barocco; Judgment of Paris; One in Five; L'Après-midi d'un Faune; Les Rendez-vous
30 Serenade; Lilac Garden; Offenbach in the Underworld
31 DES MOINES, IA - K.R.N.T.: Concerto Barocco; Judgment of Paris; One in Five; L'Après-midi d'un Faune; Giselle - Act I pdd; Les Rendez-vous

NOVEMBER, 1962:

1 WAVERLY, IA - Chapel-Aud: One in Five; Giselle - Act I pdd; L'Après-midi d'un Faune; Le Corsaire pdd; Judgment of Paris; Offenbach in the Underworld
2 KANSAS CITY, MO - Music Hall: Serenade; Giselle - Act I pdd; Le Corsaire pdd; Judgment of Paris; Laurencia Pas de Six; Les Rendez-vous
3 AMES, IA - I.S.U. Armory: One in Five; Giselle - Act I pdd; Le Corsaire pdd; Concerto Barocco; Offenbach in the Underworld
5 DAYTON, OH - National Cash Register Aud: One in Five; Concerto Barocco; Giselle - Act I pdd; L'Après-midi d'un Faune; Le Corsaire pdd; Les Rendez-vous
6 LEXINGTON, KY - Memorial Coliseum: Serenade; Swan Lake - Act III, dances from; Swan Lake - Act III Black Swan pdd; Judgment of Paris; Offenbach in the Underworld
7 LOUISVILLE, KY - Memorial Aud: Serenade; Giselle - Act I pdd; Judgment of Paris; Laurencia Pas de Six; Lilac Garden; Les Rendez-vous
8 COLUMBUS, OH - Mershon Aud: Serenade; Laurencia Pas de Six; Giselle - Act I pdd; L'Après-midi d'un Faune; Le Corsaire pdd; Judgment of Paris; One in Five
9 ANN ARBOR, MI - Hill Aud: One in Five; Concerto Barocco; Lilac Garden; Judgment of Paris; Les Rendez-vous
10 PITTSBURGH, PA - Syria Mosque: Swan Lake

DECEMBER, 1962:

31 HARTFORD, CT - Bushnell Memorial Aud: One in Five; Judgment of Paris; Les Rendez-vous; Offenbach in the Underworld

JANUARY, 1963:

2 CHARLOTTE, NC - Ovens Municipal Aud: One in Five; Concerto Barocco; Giselle - Act I pdd; Laurencia Pas de Six; Judgment of Paris; Les Rendez-vous
3 ASHEVILLE, NC - Municipal Aud: Les Sylphides; Giselle - Act I pdd; L'Après-midi d'un Faune; Offenbach in the Underworld
4 KNOXVILLE, TN - Knoxville Civic Aud: Les Sylphides; Winter Night; Les Rendez-vous
5 CHATTANOOGA, TN - Municipal Aud: Les Sylphides; Winter Night; Les Rendez-vous
7 COLUMBUS, GA - Jordan Aud: Serenade; Giselle - Act I pdd; Pas de Deux Romantique; Pas de Chance; Les Rendez-vous
8 FLORENCE, AL - Coffee Aud: One in Five; Death and the Maiden; Pas de Chance; Winter Night; Les Rendez-vous

9 ATLANTA, GA - Municipal Aud: Serenade; Giselle - Act I pdd; Le Corsaire pdd; Pas de Deux Romantique; Judgment of Paris; Offenbach in the Underworld
10 BIRMINGHAM, AL - Temple Theatre: Serenade; One in Five; Pas de Deux Romantique; Le Corsaire pdd; Judgment of Paris; Concerto Barocco
11 MEMPHIS, TN - Music Hall: Serenade; Pas de Chance; Death and the Maiden; Le Corsaire pdd; Judgment of Paris; Les Rendez-vous
12 NEW ORLEANS, LA - Municipal Aud: Serenade; Winter Night; Offenbach in the Underworld
13 LAFAYETTE, LA - Municipal Aud: One in Five; Pas de Chance; Death and the Maiden; Lilac Garden; Offenbach in the Underworld
14 SHREVEPORT, LA - Municipal Aud: Les Sylphides; Laurencia Pas de Six; L'Après-midi d'un Faune; Swan Lake - Act III pdd; Judgment of Paris; Concerto Barocco
15 JACKSON, MS - Municipal Aud: One in Five; L'Après-midi d'un Faune; Pas de Deux Romantique; Lilac Garden; Le Corsaire pdd; Judgment of Paris; Concerto Barocco
18 MIAMI, FL - Miami Beach Aud: Swan Lake
19 ST PETERSBURG, FL - St Petersburg H.S. Aud: Concerto Barocco; Death and the Maiden; Judgment of Paris; Pas de Chance; Giselle - Act I pdd; Les Rendez-vous
20 MIAMI, FL - Municipal Aud: One in Five; Concerto Barocco; L'Après-midi d'un Faune; Pas de Deux Romantique; Judgment of Paris; Offenbach in the Underworld
21 ORLANDO, FL - Municipal Aud: One in Five; Death and the Maiden; Judgment of Paris; Le Corsaire pdd; Pas de Chance; Laurencia Pas de Six; Les Rendez-vous
22 JACKSONVILLE, FL - Municipal Aud: Les Sylphides; Winter Night; One in Five; Judgment of Paris
23 COLUMBIA, SC - Township Aud: Les Sylphides; One in Five; Death and the Maiden; Laurencia Pas de Six; Les Rendez-vous
24 CHARLESTON, SC - Memminger Theatre: Concerto Barocco; Pas de Chance; Lilac Garden; Offenbach in the Underworld
25 WINSTON-SALEM, NC - Reynolds Memorial Theatre: Serenade; Le Corsaire pdd; L'Après-midi d'un Faune; Pas de Chance; Death and the Maiden; Les Rendez-vous
26 RADFORD, VA - Radford College Aud: One in Five; Judgment of Paris; Les Sylphides; Les Rendez-vous
28 RED BANK, NJ - Carlton Theatre: Concerto Barocco; Judgment of Paris; Pas de Chance; Giselle - Act I pdd; Death and the Maiden; Le Corsaire pdd; Les Rendez-vous
30 UTICA, NY - Stanley Theatre: Les Sylphides; Winter Night; Offenbach in the Underworld
31 ROCHESTER, NY - Eastman Theatre: One in Five; Judgment of Paris; Laurencia Pas de Six; Pas de Chance; L'Après-midi d'un Faune; Le Corsaire pdd; Les Rendez-vous

FEBRUARY, 1963:

1 SYRACUSE, NY - Lincoln Aud: Serenade; One in Five; Death and the Maiden; Giselle - Act I pdd; Offenbach in the Underworld
2 BUFFALO, NY - Kleinhans Music Hall: One in Five; Judgment of Paris; Death and the Maiden; Pas de Chance; Giselle - Act I pdd; L'Après-midi d'un Faune; Le Corsaire pdd; Les Rendez-vous
4 WINDSOR, ON - Cleary Aud: Serenade; Winter Night; Offenbach in the Underworld
5 One in Five; Judgment of Paris; Le Corsaire pdd; L'Après-midi d'un Faune; Laurencia Pas de Six; Pineapple Poll
6** Coppélia - *repeated, February 6*
7 Pas de Chance; Judgment of Paris; Giselle
8 Concerto Barocco; Death and the Maiden; Les Sylphides; Nutcracker - Act IV
9* Les Sylphides; One in Five; Nutcracker - Act IV
9 Swan Lake
13 TORONTO, ON - Royal Alexandra Theatre: Serenade; One in Five; Judgment of Paris; Winter Night
14* Swan Lake - Act II; Nutcracker - Act IV
14 Serenade; Winter Night; Offenbach in the Underworld
15 One in Five; Judgment of Paris; L'Après-midi d'un Faune; Pas de Chance; Le Corsaire pdd; Pineapple Poll
16* Swan Lake - *repeated, February 16, 18*
19* Swan Lake - Act II; Nutcracker - Act IV
19 Les Sylphides; One in Five; Death and the Maiden; L'Après-midi d'un Faune; Don Quixote pdd*; Judgment of Paris
20 Concerto Barocco; Le Corsaire pdd; Death and the Maiden; Les Rendez-vous; Nutcracker - Act IV - *repeated, February 21*
22 One in Five; Pas de Chance; Giselle - *repeated, February 23*, 23*
25 Serenade; Lilac Garden; Pineapple Poll - *repeated, February 26*
27** Coppélia - *repeated, February 27*
28 Les Rendez-vous; Le Corsaire pdd; Lilac Garden; Pineapple Poll

MARCH, 1963:

1 TORONTO, ON - Royal Alexandra Theatre: Les Rendez-vous; Le Corsaire pdd; Lilac Garden; Pineapple Poll
2* Coppélia - *repeated, March 2*
4 Swan Lake
5 Les Sylphides; Pas de Chance; Le Corsaire pdd; Judgment of Paris; Nutcracker - Act IV
6* One in Five; Le Corsaire pdd; Giselle - Act I pdd; Les Rendez-vous
6 Les Sylphides; Winter Night; Offenbach in the Underworld
7 One in Five; Concerto Barocco; Giselle
8 Serenade; Giselle - Act I pdd; L'Après-midi d'un Faune; Le Corsaire pdd; Nutcracker - Act IV
9* Les Sylphides; Coppélia - Act II; Nutcracker - Act IV
9 Swan Lake
11 HAMILTON, ON - Odeon Palace Theatre: Serenade; One in Five; Le Corsaire pdd; Judgment of Paris; Les Rendez-vous
12** Pas de Chance; Giselle - Act I pdd; Nutcracker - Act IV pdd; Offenbach in the Underworld
12 Swan Lake
13 ST CATHARINES, ON - Palace Theatre: Serenade; One in Five; Judgment of Paris; Nutcracker - Act IV
14 PORT HURON, MI - Henry McMorran Memorial Aud: Les Sylphides; Winter Night; Offenbach in the Underworld
15 Serenade; Pas de Chance; Giselle - Act I pdd; Le Corsaire pdd; Nutcracker - Act IV
16 Swan Lake - Act II; Concerto Barocco; Le Corsaire pdd; Judgment of Paris; Les Rendez-vous
18 LONDON, ON - Grand Theatre: Serenade; Pas de Chance; Le Corsaire pdd; Judgment of Paris; Les Rendez-vous
19 Swan Lake
20* Serenade; Winter Night; Les Rendez-vous

20 Concerto Barocco; Winter Night; Pineapple Poll
21 Swan Lake
22 Pas de Chance; Le Corsaire pdd; Les Sylphides; Pineapple Poll
23* One in Five; Giselle
23 Les Sylphides; One in Five; Death and the Maiden; Judgment of Paris; Nutcracker - Act IV
25 OTTAWA, ON - Capitol Theatre: Serenade; Pas de Chance; Le Corsaire pdd; Judgment of Paris; Nutcracker - Act IV
26 Swan Lake - Act II; Winter Night; Death and the Maiden; Concerto Barocco
27 BROCKVILLE, ON - Civic Theatre: One in Five; L'Après-midi d'un Faune; Le Corsaire pdd; Les Sylphides; Nutcracker - Act IV
28 QUEBEC CITY, QC - Capitol Theatre: Serenade; Pas de Chance; Le Corsaire pdd; Judgment of Paris; Winter Night
29 MONTREAL, QC - Her Majesty's Theatre: Serenade; Pas de Chance; Le Corsaire pdd; Judgment of Paris; Winter Night
30* One in Five; Giselle - Act I pdd; L'Après-midi d'un Faune; Les Sylphides; Les Rendez-vous
30 Les Sylphides; One in Five; Concerto Barocco; Nutcracker - Act IV
31* Swan Lake - Act II; One in Five; Nutcracker - Act IV
31 Serenade; Pas de Chance; Giselle - Act I pdd; Le Corsaire pdd; Winter Night

---

SEASON: 1963-4; **PERFORMANCES:** 75 (60 outside Toronto); **PREMIERES:** Allégresse (Solov); Don Quixote pas de deux (Petipa, staged by Beriosova); Don Quixote pas de deux (Valukin); House of Atreus (Strate); Romeo and Juliet (Cranko); Walpurgis Night pas de deux (Lavrovsky, staged by Samsova).

OCTOBER, 1963:

15 CONCORD, NH - Capitol Theatre: One in Five; Le Corsaire pdd; Judgment of Paris; Lilac Garden; Les Rendez-vous
16 BOSTON, MA - Donnelly Memorial Theatre: One in Five; Giselle
17 PORTLAND, ME - State Theatre: One in Five; Allégresse pdd; Concerto Barocco; Don Quixote pdd; Judgment of Paris; Les Rendez-vous
18 PROVIDENCE, RI - Veterans Memorial Aud: Allégresse; One in Five; Judgment of Paris; Offenbach in the Underworld
19 BINGHAMTON, NY - Capitol Theatre: Allégresse; One in Five; Judgment of Paris; Offenbach in the Underworld
21 FLINT, MI - I.M.A. Aud: Le Corsaire pdd; Les Rendez-vous pdtr; Don Quixote pdd; Serenade; Offenbach in the Underworld
22 PITTSBURGH, PA - Syria Mosque: Serenade; Giselle - Act I pdd; Don Quixote pdd; Le Corsaire pdd; Offenbach in the Underworld
24 ST LOUIS, MO - Kiel Opera House: Giselle; Offenbach in the Underworld
25 CARTHAGE, IL - Carthage College Aud: One in Five; Judgment of Paris; Lilac Garden; Les Rendez-vous pdtr; Don Quixote pdd; Giselle - Act I pdd; Concerto Barocco
26 MILWAUKEE, WI - Pabst Theatre: Serenade; One in Five; Le Corsaire pdd; Judgment of Paris; Les Rendez-vous
28 SALINA, KA - Fine Arts Theatre: One in Five; Giselle
29 SIOUX CITY, IA - Orpheum Theatre: One in Five; Don Quixote pdd; Judgment of Paris; Concerto Barocco; Offenbach in the Underworld
30 RAPID CITY, SD - High School Aud: One in Five; Judgment of Paris; Lilac Garden; Giselle - Act I pdd; Le Corsaire pdd; Les Rendez-vous
31 SIOUX FALLS, SD - Sioux Falls Aud: Allégresse; Don Quixote pdd; Le Corsaire pdd; Concerto Barocco; Judgment of Paris; One in Five

NOVEMBER, 1963:

2 ST PAUL, MN - St Paul Aud Theatre: Serenade; Lilac Garden; Don Quixote pdd; Le Corsaire pdd; Les Rendez-vous
3 ROCHESTER, MN - Mayo Civic Aud: Serenade; Lilac Garden; Giselle - Act I pdd; Don Quixote pdd; Les Rendez-vous
4 ROCKFORD, IL - Coronado Theatre: Serenade; Don Quixote pdd; Judgment of Paris; Offenbach in the Underworld
5 MADISON, WI - Orpheum Theatre: Les Rendez-vous; Lilac Garden; Giselle - Act I pdd; Offenbach in the Underworld
6 ISHPEMING, MI - High School Aud: One in Five; Don Quixote pdd; Judgment of Paris; Concerto Barocco; Le Corsaire pdd; Les Rendez-vous
7 FOND DU LAC, WI - Fond du Lac Theatre: Allégresse; One in Five; Don Quixote pdd; Offenbach in the Underworld
8 DULUTH, MN - Denfeld Aud: Serenade; Offenbach in the Underworld; Les Rendez-vous
9 APPLETON, WI - Appleton High School Aud: One in Five; Concerto Barocco; Giselle - Act I pdd; Don Quixote pdd; Offenbach in the Underworld
11 EVANSVILLE, IN - Coliseum Theatre: Serenade; One in Five; Giselle - Act I pdd; Offenbach in the Underworld

JANUARY, 1964:

13 OTTAWA, ON - Capitol Theatre: Serenade; House of Atreus; Allégresse
14 One in Five; Pas de Deux Romantique; Giselle
15 QUEBEC CITY, QC - Capitol Theatre: One in Five; Don Quixote pdd; Walpurgis Night pdd; Swan Lake - Act I pdtr; Serenade; Allégresse
17 HAMILTON, ON - Palace Theatre: Allégresse; Giselle
18* Swan Lake - Act I pdtr; Swan Lake - dances from; Swan Lake - Act II
18 Les Sylphides; House of Atreus; Serenade
20 WINDSOR, ON - Cleary Aud: Concerto Barocco; Walpurgis Night pdd; Judgment of Paris; House of Atreus; Allégresse - *repeated, January 21*
22** Swan Lake - Act III, dances from; Swan Lake - Act IV
22 Swan Lake
23 Serenade; Lilac Garden; Don Quixote pdd; Les Rendez-vous - *repeated, January 24*
25* One in Five; Le Corsaire pdd; Swan Lake - Act II; Allégresse
25 Allégresse; House of Atreus; Offenbach in the Underworld
27 ST CATHARINES, ON - Palace Theatre: Les Sylphides; Don Quixote pdd; Giselle - Act I pdd; Concerto Barocco; Allégresse
28 KITCHENER, ON - Lyric Theatre: One in Five; Giselle - Act I pdd; Le Corsaire pdd; Concerto Barocco; Lilac Garden; Les Rendez-vous
29 BELLEVILLE, ON - High School Aud: Les Rendez-vous; Swan Lake - Act I pdtr; Swan Lake - Act II pdd; Le Corsaire pdd; Judgment of Paris; Allégresse
30 BROCKVILLE, ON - Civic Aud: Allégresse; House of Atreus; Pineapple Poll

FEBRUARY, 1964:

1 BROOKLYN, NY - Brooklyn Academy of Music: Les Rendez-vous; Le Corsaire pdd; Judgment of Paris; House of Atreus; Concerto Barocco

2* STRATFORD, CT - Stratford Theatre: One in Five; Giselle - Act I pdd; Don Quixote pdd; Swan Lake - Act II; Les Rendez-vous
2 Allégresse; House of Atreus; Offenbach in the Underworld
3 HARTFORD, CT - Bushnell Memorial Theatre: Serenade; House of Atreus; Allégresse
4 ALBANY, NY - Palace Theatre: Serenade; One in Five; Le Corsaire pdd; Offenbach in the Underworld
6 PHILADELPHIA, PA - Academy of Music: Serenade; Offenbach in the Underworld; Allégresse
7 CARLISLE, PA - Carlisle High School Aud: One in Five; Giselle - Act I pdd; Don Quixote pdd; Concerto Barocco; Walpurgis Night pdd; Offenbach in the Underworld
8 BALTIMORE, MD - Lyric Theatre: Swan Lake - Act II; One in Five; Walpurgis Night pdd; Offenbach in the Underworld
9* One in Five; Don Quixote pdd; Swan Lake - Act I pdtr; Les Rendez-vous; Le Corsaire pdd; Allégresse
12 COLLEGE PARK, MD - Gymnasium: Serenade; Don Quixote pdd; Walpurgis Night pdd; Offenbach in the Underworld
13 HAMPTON, VA - Ogden Hall: Swan Lake - Act II; Don Quixote pdd; Allégresse; Les Rendez-vous
14 WILLIAMSBURG, VA - Phi Beta Kappa Aud: Swan Lake - Act II; Giselle - Act I pdd; Le Corsaire pdd; Offenbach in the Underworld
15 NORFOLK, VA - Center Theatre: Swan Lake - Act II; One in Five; Concerto Barocco; Allégresse
14 MONTREAL, QC - Place des Arts: Romeo & Juliet

APRIL, 1964:
15 MONTREAL, QC - Place des Arts: Serenade; House of Atreus; Princess Aurora pdd; Les Rendez-vous
16 Concerto Barocco; Princess Aurora pdd; Swan Lake pdtr; Allégresse; House of Atreus
17 Swan Lake
18* Swan Lake - Act II; One in Five; Swan Lake - Act III pdd; Concerto Barocco; Les Rendez-vous
18 Romeo & Juliet
21 TORONTO, ON - O'Keefe Centre: Romeo & Juliet
22 Les Sylphides; House of Atreus; Offenbach in the Underworld
23 Romeo & Juliet - *repeated, April 24*
25* Swan Lake - Act II; One in Five; Swan Lake - Black Swan pdd; Offenbach in the Underworld
25 Swan Lake
26** One in Five; Allégresse pdd; Giselle - Act I pdd; Concerto Barocco; Offenbach in the Underworld
27 Swan Lake
28 Serenade; House of Atreus; Allégresse
29* Les Rendez-vous; Le Corsaire pdd; Pineapple Poll
29 Serenade; Swan Lake - Black Swan pdd; Allégresse pdd; Le Corsaire pdd; Pineapple Poll
30 Les Rendez-vous; Walpurgis Night pdd; Concerto Barocco; Lilac Garden; Allégresse

MAY, 1964:
1 TORONTO, ON - O'Keefe Centre: Romeo & Juliet
2* Concerto Barocco; Les Sylphides; Pineapple Poll
2 Romeo & Juliet

SEASON: 1964-5; **PERFORMANCES:** 100 (81 outside Toronto); **PREMIERES:** Clair de Lune (Valukin); Electre (Strate); La Sylphide (Bruhn after Bournonville); The Nutcracker - new production (Franca after Petipa); Pas de Deux (Strate); Pas de Deux (Cranko); Triptych (Strate).

AUGUST, 1964:
9 STRATFORD, ON - Festival Theatre: Electre

DECEMBER, 1964:
26* TORONTO, ON - O'Keefe Centre: Nutcracker - *repeated, December 26, 27*, 28, 29*, 30, 31**
31 Walpurgis Night pdd; Clair de Lune; Le Corsaire pdd; Pas de Deux (Cranko); La Sylphide

JANUARY, 1965:
1* TORONTO, ON - O'Keefe Centre: Nutcracker
1 Serenade; La Sylphide
2 Pas de Deux (Strate); Clair de Lune; Le Corsaire pdd; Pas de Deux (Cranko); La Sylphide
4 Triptych; House of Atreus; Offenbach in the Underworld
5 Les Rendez-vous; La Sylphide - *repeated, January 6 (Serenade substituted for Les Rendez-vous)*
7 Romeo & Juliet - *repeated, January 8*, 8, 9*, 9*
11 LONDON, ON - Grand Theatre: Serenade; La Sylphide
12 Nutcracker - *repeated, January 13**
13 One in Five; Claire de Lune; Le Corsaire pdd; Triptych; Les Rendez-vous
14 La Sylphide; Offenbach in the Underworld
15 Concerto Barocco; Pas de Deux (Strate); Walpurgis Night pdd; House of Atreus; Les Rendez-vous
16* Nutcracker - *repeated, January 16*
18 WINDSOR, ON - Cleary Aud: Serenade; La Sylphide
19 Nutcracker - *repeated, January 20**, 20, 21***
21 One in Five; Clair de Lune; Nutcracker - Act II pdd; House of Atreus; Concerto Barocco
22 Pas de Deux (Strate); Clair de Lune; Nutcracker - Act II pdd; La Sylphide
23* Nutcracker
23 Les Rendez-vous; Pas de Deux (Cranko); Triptych; La Sylphide - Act II
26 MONTREAL, QC - Place des Arts: Triptych; La Sylphide
27 Romeo & Juliet
28 Nutcracker
29 Serenade; Clair de Lune; Pas de Deux (Cranko); Le Corsaire pdd; House of Atreus
30* One in Five; Clair de Lune; Triptych; Les Rendez-vous
30 Romeo & Juliet
31* Nutcracker - *repeated, January 31*

FEBRUARY, 1965:
2* SHERBROOKE, QC - U. of Sherbrooke Aud: Nutcracker
2 La Sylphide; Triptych
3 OTTAWA, ON - Capitol Theatre: Triptych; La Sylphide
4 Nutcracker
5 QUEBEC CITY, QC - Capitol Theatre: Triptych; La Sylphide
6 BELLEVILLE, ON - Belleville High School Aud: Triptych; Pas de Deux (Strate); Clair de Lune; Pas de Deux (Cranko); Le Corsaire pdd; Nutcracker - Act II
8 HAMILTON, ON - Palace Theatre: Triptych; La Sylphide
9* Nutcracker - *repeated, February 9*
10 BRANTFORD, ON - Capitol Theatre: Serenade; Pas de Deux (Strate); Clair de Lune; Le Corsaire pdd; Pas de Deux (Cranko); Nutcracker - Act II
11 KITCHENER, ON - Lyric Theatre: Serenade; Nutcracker - Act II; Triptych
12 ST CATHARINES, ON - Palace Theatre: Triptych; Pas de Deux (Strate); Clair de Lune; Pas de Deux (Cranko); Le Corsaire pdd; Nutcracker - Act II
13* STRATFORD, ON - Avon Theatre: Serenade; Nutcracker - Act II; Les Rendez-vous
13 Triptych; One in Five; Clair de Lune; Offenbach in the Underworld

17 SYRACUSE, NY - Loew's Theatre: Nutcracker
19 HARTFORD, CT - Bushnell Theatre: Nutcracker - *repeated, February 20**
20 One in Five; Concerto Barocco; Pas de Deux (Strate); Clair de Lune; Pas de Deux (Cranko); Le Corsaire pdd; Triptych
23 NASHVILLE, TN - Kean Hall: Serenade; Nutcracker - Act II; Pas de Deux (Cranko); Les Rendez-vous
24 MEMPHIS, TN - Aud Memphis: Triptych; Clair de Lune; Pas de Deux (Strate); Pas de Deux (Cranko); Offenbach in the Underworld
25 JACKSON, MS - Municipal Aud: Les Rendez-vous; Triptych; Offenbach in the Underworld
26 BATON ROUGE, LA - Southern University Aud-Gym.: Triptych; One in Five; Clair de Lune; Nutcracker - Act II
27 TYLER, TX - Tyler High School Aud: Triptych; Nutcracker - Act II; Offenbach in the Underworld

MARCH, 1965:
1 EL PASO, TX - Liberty Hall: Nutcracker
3 LAS VEGAS, NV - Las Vegas High School Aud: Serenade; One in Five; Nutcracker - Act II pdd; Offenbach in the Underworld
4 SANTA MONICA, CA - Santa Monica Civic Aud: Nutcracker
5 PASADENA, CA - Civic Aud: Serenade; One in Five; Clair de Lune; Offenbach in the Underworld
6* Nutcracker
6 Triptych; Pas de Deux (Strate); Clair de Lune; Le Corsair pdd; Judgment of Paris; Les Rendez-vous
7* SAN DIEGO, CA - San Diego Civic Theatre: Nutcracker
7 Serenade; Clair de Lune; Judgment of Paris; Offenbach in the Underworld
9 FRESNO, CA - Memorial Aud: Nutcracker
10 SANTA CRUZ, CA - Civic Aud: Triptych; One in Five; Judgment of Paris; Nutcracker - Act II
11 SAN JOSE, CA - Civic Aud: Triptych; One in Five; Clair de Lune; Le Corsair pdd; Les Rendez-vous
12 OAKLAND, CA - Oakland Aud Theatre: Nutcracker
13 SAN FRANCISCO, CA - War Memorial Opera House: Serenade; Les Rendez-vous; Offenbach in the Underworld
15 SACRAMENTO, CA - Memorial Aud: Serenade; Nutcracker - Act II; Offenbach in the Underworld
17 OGDEN, UT - Ogden High School Aud: One in Five; Judgment of Paris; Triptych; Les Rendez-vous
19 DENVER, CO - Denver Aud Theatre: Nutcracker
20 Serenade; One in Five; Clair de Lune; Offenbach in the Underworld
22 HAYS, KS - Sheridan Coliseum: Triptych; One in Five; Concerto Barocco; Les Rendez-vous
23 LAWTON, OK - McMahon Aud: Triptych; Clair de Lune; Pas de Deux (Strate); Walpurgis Night pdd; Offenbach in the Underworld
25 JOPLIN, MO - Memorial Aud: Nutcracker
26 KANSAS CITY, MO - Music Hall: Nutcracker
27 AMES, IA - I.S.U. Armory: Serenade; Clair de Lune; Judgment of Paris; Triptych
28* ST PAUL, MN - St Paul Aud: Triptych; One in Five; Clair de Lune; Nutcracker - Act II
30 MINNEAPOLIS, MN - Northrop Aud: Nutcracker
31 ROCHESTER, MN - Mayo Civic Theatre: Triptych; One in Five; Nutcracker - Act II

APRIL, 1965:
1 WATERLOO, IA - Paramount Theatre: Nutcracker
3 ANN ARBOR, MI - Hill Aud: Serenade; Nutcracker - Act II, dances from; Offenbach in the Underworld
5 INDIANAPOLIS, IN - Clowes Memorial Hall: Les Rendez-vous; Offenbach in the Underworld; Triptych
6 LOUISVILLE, KY - Memorial Aud: Nutcracker
7 CHARLESTON, WV - Municipal Aud: Nutcracker
8 HUNTINGTON, WV - Keith-Albee Theatre: Nutcracker
10 FLUSHING, NY - Charles S. Colden Aud: Serenade; Nutcracker - Act II; Triptych

---

SEASON: 1965-6; **PERFORMANCES:** 89 (63 outside Toronto); **PREMIERES:** Adagio Cantabile (Poll); Lilac Garden - revival (Tudor); Pulcinella (Strate); The Rake's Progress (de Valois, staged by Worth); Rivalité (Seillier); Solitaire (MacMillan, staged by Worth).

AUGUST, 1965:
2 WASHINGTON, DC - Carter Barron Amphitheatre: Romeo & Juliet
3 Nutcracker
4 Triptych; Solitaire
5 La Sylphide; Solitaire
6 Romeo & Juliet
7 Nutcracker
8 Romeo & Juliet
9 One in Five; Clair de Lune; Solitaire; Triptych
10 La Sylphide; Triptych
11 Nutcracker
12 Romeo & Juliet
13 Nutcracker
14 La Sylphide; Offenbach in the Underworld
15 Nutcracker

SEPTEMBER, 1965:
2 TORONTO, ON - O'Keefe Centre: Romeo & Juliet

NOVEMBER, 1965:
6 MONTREAL, QC - Place des Arts: Rivalité; Adagio Cantabile; Rake's Progress; Nutcracker - Act II
7* Nutcracker, Acts I & II - *repeated, November 7*
9 Serenade; Rake's Progress; Solitaire
10 La Sylphide; Pulcinella
11 Serenade; Solitaire; Pulcinella
12 Solitaire; Rake's Progress; Triptych
13* Romeo & Juliet - *repeated, November 13*
14* Concerto Barocco; Rivalité; Pulcinella; Solitaire
14 La Sylphide; Pulcinella
16 OTTAWA, ON - Capitol Theatre: Adagio Cantabile; Rivalité; Rake's Progress; Solitaire
17 Triptych; Pulcinella; Nutcracker - Act II
19* QUEBEC CITY, QC - Capitol Theatre: Solitaire; Clair de Lune; Adagio Cantabile; Nutcracker - Act II
19 Adagio Cantabile; Rivalité; Rake's Progress; Solitaire
20 SHERBROOKE, QC - U. of Sherbrooke Aud: Solitaire; Concerto Barocco; Rake's Progress; Clair de Lune
21 One in Five; Pulcinella; Triptych
22 BELLEVILLE, ON - High School Aud: Solitaire; Rake's Progress; Triptych
23 PETERBOROUGH, ON - Memorial Centre: One in Five; Clair de Lune; Rivalité; Adagio Cantabile; Solitaire
24 OSHAWA, ON - Regent Theatre: One in Five; Clair de Lune; Solitaire; Nutcracker - Act II
26 BARRIE, ON - Central Collegiate Aud: Triptych; One in Five; Clair de Lune; Solitaire
27* STRATFORD, ON - Avon Theatre: Concerto Barocco; Rivalité; One in Five; Adagio Cantabile; Solitaire
27 Solitaire; Rake's Progress; Triptych

29★ HAMILTON, ON - Odeon Palace: Nutcracker
29 Rake's Progress; Adagio Cantabile; Rivalité; Solitaire
30★ Nutcracker
30 Solitaire; One in Five; Clair de Lune; Pulcinella

DECEMBER, 1965:

1 KITCHENER, ON - Lyric Theatre: One in Five; Adagio Cantabile; Solitaire; Rivalité; Concerto Barocco
2 BRANTFORD, ON - Capitol Theatre: Adagio Cantabile; Rivalité; Rake's Progress; Solitaire
3 ST CATHARINES, ON - Palace Theatre: Triptych; Rake's Progress; Adagio Cantabile; Rivalité
4★ One in Five; Adagio Cantabile; Rivalité; Nutcracker - Act II
4 Solitaire; Pulcinella; Concerto Barocco
26★ TORONTO, ON - O'Keefe Centre: Nutcracker - *repeated, December 27★, 27, 28★, 29★, 30★, 31a★, 31b★ (two matinees on one day)*

JANUARY, 1966:

1★ TORONTO, ON - O'Keefe Centre: Nutcracker - *repeated, January 1*
17 LONDON, ON - Grand Theatre: Solitaire; La Sylphide
18 Adagio Cantabile; Rivalité; Rake's Progress; Triptych
19★ Nutcracker - *repeated, January 19, 20*
21 La Sylphide; One in Five; Clair de Lune; Solitaire; Pulcinella
22 One in Five; Adagio Cantabile; Rake's Progress; Solitaire
24 WINDSOR, ON - Cleary Aud: Rivalité; Adagio Cantabile; Rake's Progress; Solitaire
25 Serenade; Pulcinella; Triptych
26★★ La Sylphide - *repeated, January 26 (with Solitaire added), 27★★*
27 Nutcracker - *repeated, January 28*
29★ Triptych; Pulcinella; Solitaire
29 Rake's Progress; One in Five; Clair de Lune; Pulcinella

APRIL, 1966:

12 TORONTO, ON - O'Keefe Centre: Concerto Barocco; Rake's Progress; Solitaire
13 Romeo & Juliet
14★ La Sylphide
14 Romeo & Juliet
15 Serenade; Rivalité; Adagio Cantabile; Pulcinella
16★ One in Five; Adagio Cantabile; La Sylphide
16 Solitaire; Rake's Progress; Triptych
17★ Pulcinella; Offenbach in the Underworld
18 Triptych; One in Five; Clair de Lune; Pulcinella
19 Solitaire; Lilac Garden; Offenbach in the Underworld - *repeated, April 20 (Serenade substituted for Solitaire)*
21 La Sylphide; Solitaire
22 Concerto Barocco; Rivalité; Adagio Cantabile; Lilac Garden; Rake's Progress
23★ Romeo & Juliet - *repeated, April 23*

SEASON: 1966-7; **PERFORMANCES:** 98 (66 outside Toronto); **PREMIERES:** Bayaderka - Act IV (Petipa, produced by Valukin); Mélodie (Valukin); Swan Lake - new production (Bruhn after Petipa)

NOVEMBER, 1966:

1★ HAMILTON, ON - Palace Theatre: Solitaire; Bayaderka - Act IV - *repeated, November 1 (with Adagio Cantabile and Mélodie added)*
2★ Solitaire; Offenbach in the Underworld - *repeated, November 2 (Serenade and Lilac Garden substituted for Solitaire)*
3 BRANTFORD, ON - Capitol Theatre: Bayaderka - Act IV; Lilac Garden; Offenbach in the Underworld
4 WELLAND, ON - Welland Centennial S.S. Aud: Nutcracker
5★ ST CATHARINES, ON - Palace Theatre: Bayaderka - Act IV; Mélodie; Solitaire
5 Bayaderka - Act IV; Lilac Garden; Offenbach in the Underworld
7 KINGSTON, ON - Grand Theatre: Bayaderka - Act IV; Lilac Garden; Solitaire
8 BROCKVILLE, ON - Civic Aud: Solitaire; Lilac Garden; Nutcracker - Act II
9 PETERBOROUGH, ON - Memorial Centre: Bayaderka - Act IV; Lilac Garden; Offenbach in the Underworld
10 KITCHENER, ON - Lyric Theatre: Bayaderka - Act IV; Lilac Garden; Mélodie; Giselle - Act I Peasant pdd; Nutcracker - Act II pdd
11 PORT CREDIT, ON - Port Credit S.S. Aud: Solitaire; One in Five; Clair de Lune; Nutcracker - Act II
12 GUELPH, ON - Ross Hall: One in Five; Mélodie; Adagio Cantabile; Lilac Garden; Solitaire
14 OTTAWA, ON - Capitol Theatre: Serenade; Lilac Garden; Offenbach in the Underworld
15 Bayaderka - Act IV; Mélodie; Giselle - Act I Peasant pdd; Solitaire
16 NORTH BAY, ON - Capitol Theatre: Solitaire; Lilac Garden; Offenbach in the Underworld
17 BARRIE, ON - Central Collegiate Aud: Bayaderka - Act IV; Mélodie; Giselle - Act I Peasant pdd; Offenbach in the Underworld
18 CHATHAM, ON - Kinsmen Aud: One in Five; Giselle - Act I Peasant pdd; Adagio Cantabile; Lilac Garden; Solitaire
19 PORT HURON, MI - Henry McMorran Memorial Aud: Solitaire; Bayaderka - Act IV; Offenbach in the Underworld
20★ Nutcracker

DECEMBER, 1966:

26★ TORONTO, ON - O'Keefe Centre: Nutcracker - *repeated, December 26, 27a★, 27b★ (two matinees on one day), 28a★, 28b★ (two matinees on one day), 29a★, 29b★ (two matinees on one day), 30a★, 30b★ (two matinees on one day), 31★*

JANUARY, 1967:

4 VANCOUVER, BC - Queen Elizabeth Theatre: Nutcracker - *repeated, January 5★, 6★, 6, 7★, 7, 8a★, 8b★ (two matinees on one day)*
19 MONTREAL, QC - Place des Arts: Bayaderka - Act IV; Lilac Garden; Solitaire - *repeated, January 20 (La Sylphide substituted for Lilac Garden and Solitaire)*
21★ Nutcracker - *repeated, January 21, 22★*
24 WINDSOR, ON - Cleary Aud: Bayaderka - Act IV; Mélodie; Giselle - Act I Peasant pdd; Solitaire
25★★ Bayaderka - Act IV; Solitaire
25 Bayaderka - Act IV; Lilac Garden; Offenbach in the Underworld
26★★ Bayaderka - Act IV; Solitaire
26 One in Five; Rake's Progress; Offenbach in the Underworld
27 One in Five; Clair de Lune; Adagio Cantabile; Lilac Garden; Solitaire
28★ Nutcracker - *repeated, January 28*
30 HALIFAX, NS - Capitol Theatre: Serenade; Lilac Garden; Solitaire
31 La Sylphide; Nutcracker - Act II

FEBRUARY, 1967:

3 ST JOHN'S, NF - Holy Heart of Mary Aud: Serenade; One in Five; Solitaire
4★ One in Five; Bayaderka - Act IV; Nutcracker - Act II
4 La Sylphide; Nutcracker - Act II
6 SAINT JOHN, NB - Saint John High School Aud: Serenade; Giselle - Act I Peasant pdd; Clair de Lune; Solitaire
7 Bayaderka - Act IV; One in Five; Mélodie; Nutcracker - Act II pdd; Solitaire
9★ CHARLOTTETOWN, PE - Confederation Centre: Nutcracker - *repeated, February 9*

10 SACKVILLE, NB - Mount Allison U. Aud: Solitaire; Lilac Garden; Nutcracker - Act II
11★ FREDERICTON, NB - Playhouse Theatre: Serenade; One in Five; Solitaire
11 One in Five; Adagio Cantabile; Bayaderka - Act IV; Nutcracker - Act II
13 RIMOUSKI, QC - Centre Civique: One in Five; Adagio Cantabile; Nutcracker - Act II; Solitaire
14 QUEBEC CITY, QC - Capitol Theatre: Bayaderka - Act IV; Lilac Garden; Nutcracker - Act II
15 CHICOUTIMI, QC - Aud du Séminaire: Solitaire; One in Five; Mélodie; Nutcracker - Act II
17 SHERBROOKE, QC - U. of Sherbrooke Aud: Nutcracker
18 SOREL, QC - Sorel Theatre: Solitaire; Lilac Garden; Nutcracker - Act II

MARCH, 1967:

27 TORONTO, ON - O'Keefe Centre: Swan Lake - *repeated, March 28, 29, 30, 31*

APRIL, 1967:

1★ TORONTO, ON - O'Keefe Centre: Swan Lake - *repeated, April 1*
3 Bayaderka - Act IV; Lilac Garden; Solitaire - *repeated, April 4, 5 (La Sylphide substituted for Lilac Garden and Solitaire)*
6 One in Five; Mélodie; La Sylphide - *repeated, April 7 (Solitaire substituted for One in Five and Mélodie), 8★ (without Mélodie)*
8 Bayaderka - Act IV; Rake's Progress; Offenbach in the Underworld - *repeated, April 10 (Serenade substituted for Bayaderka)*
11 Serenade; La Sylphide
12 Romeo & Juliet - *repeated, April 13, 14, 15★, 15*
18 LONDON, ON - Grand Theatre: Bayaderka - Act IV; Lilac Garden; Solitaire
19 La Sylphide; Serenade - *repeated, April 20★★ (without Serenade)*
20 Bayaderka - Act IV; Rake's Progress; Solitaire
21 Swan Lake - *repeated, April 22★, 22*

SEASON: 1967-8; **PERFORMANCES:** 142 (107 outside Toronto); **PREMIERES:** Cinderella (Franca); EH! (Franca); La Prima Ballerina (Heiden); Rondo Giocoso (Poll); Studies in White (Strate).

AUGUST, 1967:

7 WASHINGTON, DC - Carter Barron Amphitheatre: Romeo & Juliet
8 Swan Lake
9 Bayaderka - Act IV; Lilac Garden; Solitaire
10 Romeo & Juliet
11 Bayaderka - Act IV; Lilac Garden; Solitaire
12 Swan Lake
13 Romeo & Juliet

OCTOBER, 1967:

24 MONTREAL, QC - Place des Arts: Romeo & Juliet - *repeated, October 25*
26 Bayaderka - Act IV; La Prima Ballerina
27 Swan Lake - *repeated, October 28★, 28*
30 OTTAWA, ON - Capitol Theatre: La Sylphide; Le Corsaire pdd; Swan Lake - Neapolitan Dance; Swan Lake - Waltz
31 La Prima Ballerina; Swan Lake - Black Swan pdd; Don Quixote pdd; Swan Lake - Czardas

NOVEMBER, 1967:

1 BROCKVILLE, ON - Civic Aud: Bayaderka - Act IV; Swan Lake - Waltz, Black Swan pdd; Don Quixote pdd; Swan Lake - Czardas, Clowns' Dance, Neapolitan Dance; EH!
2 KINGSTON, ON - Grand Theatre: La Prima Ballerina; Don Quixote pdd; Le Corsaire pdd; Swan Lake - Waltz, Clowns' Dance, Black Swan pdd
3 BELLEVILLE, ON - Centennial Secondary School: One in Five; Le Corsaire pdd; EH!; Don Quixote pdd; Solitaire
4 Bayaderka - Act IV; Nutcracker pdd; Swan Lake - Black Swan pdd; Rondo Giocoso; Lilac Garden
6 PETERBOROUGH, ON - Peterborough Mem. Comm. Centre: Swan Lake - Waltz, Black Swan pdd; Studies in White; Death and the Maiden; Rondo Giocoso; Don Quixote pdd; EH!
7 KITCHENER, ON - Lyric Theatre: Swan Lake - Waltz, Black Swan pdd; Studies in White; Death and the Maiden; Rondo Giocoso; Nutcracker pdd; EH!
8 BARRIE, ON - Central Collegiate Aud: Swan Lake - Clowns' Dance, Black Swan pdd, Waltz; Nutcracker pdd; Lilac Garden; Le Corsaire pdd; Death and the Maiden; EH!
9★ BRANTFORD, ON - Capitol Theatre: One in Five; Nutcracker pdd; Rondo Giocoso; Don Quixote pdd; EH!
9 One in Five; Studies in White; Death and the Maiden; Swan Lake - Clowns' Dance, Czardas, Neapolitan Dance; Nutcracker pdd; Swan Lake - Waltz; EH!
10 PORT CREDIT, ON - Port Credit S.S. Aud: Bayaderka - Act IV; Lilac Garden; Don Quixote pdd; Nutcracker pdd; EH!
11 GUELPH, ON - Ross Hall: Bayaderka - Act IV; Swan Lake - Clowns' Dance, Waltz, Neapolitan Dance, Black Swan pdd, Czardas; Nutcracker pdd; EH!
14★★ HAMILTON, ON - Odeon Palace: Swan Lake - Act I - *repeated, November 14 (complete)*
15★ La Prima Ballerina - *repeated, November 15 (with EH! added)*
16 ST CATHARINES, ON - Palace Theatre: Studies in White; Death and the Maiden; La Sylphide pdd; Swan Lake - Czardas, Clowns' Dance; Don Quixote pdd; Nutcracker pdd; Le Corsaire pdd; Swan Lake - Waltz; EH!
17 WELLAND, ON - Centennial Aud: Swan Lake
20 MINNEAPOLIS, MN - Cyrus Northrop Aud: Swan Lake
21 Solitaire; La Sylphide
24 FORT WILLIAM, ON - Fort William Gardens: Solitaire; Lilac Garden; Bayaderka - Act IV
27 REGINA, SK - Sheldon Williams Coll. Aud: Solitaire; Nutcracker - Act II; EH!
28 Bayaderka - Act IV; Lilac Garden; Don Quixote pdd; EH!
29 SASKATOON, SK - Capitol Theatre: La Sylphide; Solitaire

DECEMBER, 1967:

1 EDMONTON, AB - Jubilee Aud: Solitaire; La Sylphide
2★ Nutcracker - *repeated, December 2*
4 CALGARY, AB - Jubilee Aud: Solitaire; La Sylphide
5 Nutcracker
22a★ TORONTO, ON - O'Keefe Centre: Nutcracker - *repeated, December 22b★ (two matinees on one day), 23a★, 23b★ (two matinees on one day), 25★, 26★, 26, 27a★, 27b★ (two matinees on one day), 28, 29a★, 29b★ (two matinees on one day), 30a★, 30b★ (two matinees on one day)*

JANUARY, 1968:

2 VANCOUVER, BC - Queen Elizabeth Theatre: Romeo & Juliet - *repeated, January 3*
4 Nutcracker - *repeated, January 5★, 5, 6★, 6*
7 Romeo & Juliet
11★ SEATTLE, WA - Seattle Opera House: Nutcracker - *repeated, January 11, 12, 13★, 13, 14★, 14*
18 EAST LANSING, MI - University Aud: Swan Lake
19 Nutcracker

20 CLEVELAND, OH - Music Hall: Nutcracker
21 PORT HURON, MI - Henry McMorran Memorial Aud: Swan Lake
23 WINDSOR, ON - Cleary Aud: Swan Lake - *repeated, January 24★, 24, 25★, 25*
26 Concerto Barocco; Nutcracker pdd; La Prima Ballerina
27★ Nutcracker pdd; Don Quixote pdd; Le Corsaire pdd; La Prima Ballerina - *repeated, January 27*
30 LONDON, ON - Grand Theatre: Swan Lake - *repeated, January 31★, 31*

FEBRUARY, 1968:
1 LONDON, ON - Grand Theatre: Swan Lake
2 Concerto Barocco; Don Quixote pdd; La Prima Ballerina
3★ La Prima Ballerina; Le Corsaire pdd; Nutcracker pdd - *repeated, February 3 (Bayaderka - Act IV substituted for Corsaire and Nutcracker pdd)*
6 MEXICO CITY, MEXICO - Teatro de Belles Artes: Romeo & Juliet - *repeated, February 8*
9 La Sylphide; Solitaire - *repeated, February 10★*
10 Swan Lake
11 Romeo & Juliet
12 Swan Lake
13 One in Five; Le Corsaire pdd; Concerto Barocco; Don Quixote pdd; Nutcracker - Act II - *repeated, February 15*
16 La Sylphide; Solitaire
17★ One in Five; Le Corsaire pdd; Concerto Barocco; Don Quixote pdd; Nutcracker - Act II
17 Swan Lake
18 La Sylphide; Solitaire
19 Romeo & Juliet
20 Swan Lake
21 JALAPA, MEXICO - Teatro del Estado: La Sylphide; Solitaire
22 One in Five; Le Corsaire pdd; Concerto Barocco; Don Quixote pdd; Nutcracker - Act II
25 GUADALAJARA, MEXICO - Teatro Degollado: La Sylphide; Solitaire
26★ Nutcracker - Act II
26 One in Five; Le Corsaire pdd; Concerto Barocco; Nutcracker - Act II

MARCH, 1968:
1 FREEPORT, TX - Brazosport Senior High Aud: Solitaire; Concerto Barocco; Swan Lake - Black Swan pdd; Nutcracker - Act II
2 HOUSTON, TX - Jones Hall: Swan Lake
3★ DALLAS TX - State Fair Music Hall: Swan Lake
4 NEW ORLEANS, LA - Municipal Aud: La Sylphide; Solitaire
7 EMPORIA, KS - Civic Aud: Solitaire; Don Quixote pdd; Swan Lake - Black Swan pdd; Nutcracker - Act II
8 KANSAS CITY, MO - Music Hall: Swan Lake
9 ST LOUIS, MO - Kiel Opera House: Nutcracker
11 TERRE HAUTE, IN - Tilson's Music Hall: Concerto Barocco; Swan Lake - Black Swan pdd; Don Quixote pdd; Le Corsaire pdd; Solitaire
12 PEORIA, IL - Shrine Mosque: Concerto Barocco; Nutcracker pdd; Don Quixote pdd; Swan Lake - Black Swan pdd; Solitaire
13 BURLINGTON, IA - Memorial Aud: Nutcracker

APRIL, 1968:
15 TORONTO, ON - O'Keefe Centre: Cinderella - *repeated, April 16, 17, 18, 19, 20★, 20*
22 Swan Lake - *repeated, April 23, 24, 25, 26, 27★, 27*
29 Concerto Barocco; Don Quixote pdd; La Prima Ballerina
30 Bayaderka - Act IV; La Prima Ballerina

MAY, 1968:
1 TORONTO, ON - O'Keefe Centre: Concerto Barocco; Le Corsaire pdd; La Prima Ballerina
2 Bayaderka - Act IV; Lilac Garden; Don Quixote pdd; Solitaire
3 Romeo & Juliet - *repeated, May 4★, 4*

SEASON: 1968-9; **PERFORMANCES:** 110 (85 outside Toronto); **PREMIERES:** Curtain-Raiser for NAC opening (Strate); Cyclus (Strate); Flower Festival in Genzano pas de deux (Bournonville); The Four Temperaments (Balanchine); Kraanerg (Petit); Phases (Strate).

OCTOBER, 1968:
29 HAMILTON, ON - Palace Theatre: Serenade; Cyclus; Solitaire
30★ Nutcracker - *repeated, October 30*
31 BRANTFORD, ON - Capitol Theatre: Nutcracker - Act II; Cyclus; Solitaire

NOVEMBER, 1968:
1★ WELLAND, ON - Centennial Aud: Nutcracker - Act II; Solitaire
1 Serenade; Cyclus; Solitaire
2 ST CATHARINES, ON - Palace Theatre: Serenade; Cyclus; Solitaire
4 BELLEVILLE, ON - Collegiate Aud: Serenade; Cyclus; Solitaire
5 Studies in White; Phases; Concerto Barocco; Flower Festival in Genzano pdd; Nutcracker - Act II
6★ KINGSTON, ON - Grand Theatre: One in Five; Flower Festival in Genzano pdd; Nutcracker - Act II
6 Serenade; Cyclus; Nutcracker - Act II
8 BROCKVILLE, ON - Civic Aud: Serenade; Cyclus; Solitaire
9★ OTTAWA, ON - Capitol Theatre: Solitaire; Nutcracker - Act II
9 Solitaire; Cyclus; Flower Festival in Genzano pdd; Nutcracker pdd; Swan Lake - Black Swan pdd
11 SHERBROOKE, QC - U. of Sherbrooke Aud: Swan Lake
12 QUEBEC CITY, QC - Capitol Theatre: Serenade; Cyclus; Solitaire
13 Swan Lake
15 FREDERICTON, NB - Fredericton Playhouse: Concerto Barocco; Flower Festival in Genzano pdd; Cyclus; Swan Lake - Black Swan pdd; EH!
16 SACKVILLE, NB - Convocation Hall: One in Five; Flower Festival in Genzano pdd; Cyclus; Serenade
18 HALIFAX, NS - Capitol Theatre: Swan Lake
19 One in Five; Solitaire pdd; Cyclus; Bayaderka - Act IV
20 ANTIGONISH, NS - St Francis Xavier U. Aud: One in Five; Studies in White; Concerto Barocco; Phases; EH!
21★ CHARLOTTETOWN, PE - Playhouse Theatre: One in Five; Phases; Solitaire; EH!
21 Serenade; Cyclus; Solitaire
22 SAINT JOHN, NB - Saint John High School: Studies in White; Phases; Cyclus; Swan Lake - Black Swan pdd; Concerto Barocco
25 FALL RIVER, MA - Durfee Theatre: Nutcracker
26 HARTFORD, CT - Bushnell Aud: Swan Lake - *repeated, November 27*
30★ PITTSBURGH, PA - Syria Mosque: Nutcracker
30 Swan Lake

DECEMBER, 1968:
1 BALTIMORE, MD - Lyric Theatre: Swan Lake
2 HAMPTON, VA - Ogden Hall: One in Five; Flower Festival in Genzano pdd; Cyclus; Phases; Concerto Barocco
3 WEST CHESTER, PA - Philips Memorial Aud: One in Five; Nutcracker pdd; Concerto Barocco; Flower Festival in Genzano pdd; Solitaire

5 CHAMPAIGN, IL - University Assembly Hall: Serenade; Cyclus; Solitaire
7★ ALTON, IL - Hatheway Hall: Serenade; One in Five; Phases; Flower Festival in Genzano pdd; EH!
7 Bayaderka - Act IV; Cyclus; Solitaire
26★ TORONTO, ON - O'Keefe Centre: Nutcracker - *repeated, December 26, 27a★, 27b★ (two matinees on one day), 28a★, 28b★ (two matinees on one day), 29★, 30a★, 30b★ (two matinees on one day), 31★*

JANUARY, 1969:

4★ SEATTLE, WA - Seattle Opera House: Swan Lake - *repeated, January 4, 5, 6*
7 Nutcracker - *repeated, January 8, 9, 10*
11 VANCOUVER, BC - Queen Elizabeth Theatre: Swan Lake - *repeated, January 13★, 14, 15*
16★ Nutcracker - *repeated, January 17★, 18★, 18*
28 CALGARY, AB - Jubilee Aud: Swan Lake
29 Nutcracker
30 EDMONTON, AB - Jubilee Aud: Swan Lake
31 Nutcracker

FEBRUARY, 1969:

4★ SASKATOON, SK - Saskatoon Centennial Aud: Swan Lake
5 Nutcracker
6 WINNIPEG, MB - Manitoba Centennial Centre: Swan Lake
7★ Nutcracker - *repeated, February 7*
18 WINDSOR, ON - Cleary Aud: Studies in White; Cinderella - Act II pdd; Cyclus; Solitaire
19★★ Nutcracker - Act II; Cinderella - Act II pdd
19 Nutcracker
20★★ Nutcracker - Act II; Cinderella - Act II pdd
20 Nutcracker
21 Serenade; Cyclus; Solitaire
22★ Swan Lake - *repeated, February 22*
25 LONDON, ON - Grand Theatre: Nutcracker
26★ Nutcracker - Act II; Cinderella - Act II pdd
26 Nutcracker
27★ Solitaire pdd; Nutcracker - Act II
27 Serenade; Cyclus; Solitaire
28 Swan Lake

MARCH, 1969:

1★ LONDON, ON - Grand Theatre: Swan Lake - *repeated, March 1*
18a★ TORONTO, ON - O'Keefe Centre: Cinderella - *repeated, March 18b★ (two matinees on one day), 19a★, 19b★ (two matinees on one day)*
21a★ Romeo & Juliet - *repeated, March 21b★ (two matinees on one day), 22★, 22*
24 Four Temperaments; Nutcracker pdd; Phases; Tchaikowsky Pas de Deux†; Cyclus
25 Serenade; Cyclus; Four Temperaments
26 Concerto Barocco; Four Temperaments; Tchaikowsky Pas de Deux†; Serenade
27 Serenade; La Sylphide - *repeated, March 28 (Solitaire substituted for Serenade)*
29★ Swan Lake - *repeated, March 29*
30★ MONTREAL, QC - Place des Arts: Cinderella - *repeated, March 30*

JUNE, 1969:

2 OTTAWA, ON - National Arts Centre: Curtain-Raiser; Kraanerg
3 Romeo & Juliet
4 Solitaire; Kraanerg
5 Romeo & Juliet
7★ Swan Lake - *repeated, June 7*

SEASON: 1969-70; **PERFORMANCES:** 94 (58 outside Toronto); **PREMIERES:** Giselle - new production (produced by Wright after Coralli/Perrot/Petipa); Le Loup (Petit); The Lesson (Flindt after Ionesco).

SEPTEMBER, 1969:

29 MILWAUKEE, WI - Uihlein Hall: Les Rendez-vous; Four Temperaments; Solitaire
30 Swan Lake

OCTOBER, 1969:

1 MILWAUKEE, WI - Uihlein Hall: Les Rendez-vous; Four Temperaments; Solitaire
2 Swan Lake
3 Nutcracker - *repeated, October 4★, 4*
6 OSHKOSH, WI - Civic Aud: Swan Lake
7 WAVERLEY, IA - Neumann Aud: Solitaire; Four Temperaments; Nutcracker - Act II
8 ROCKFORD, IL - Coronado Theatre: Les Rendez-vous; Four Temperaments; Solitaire
9 TERRE HAUTE, IN - Tilson Music Hall: Les Rendez-vous; Four Temperaments; Nutcracker - Act II
10 KOKOMO, IN - Havens Hall: Les Rendez-vous; Bayaderka - Act IV; Solitaire
11 CLEVELAND, OH - Music Hall: Nutcracker
13 MT CLEMENS, MI - Mt Clemens H.S. Aud: Les Rendez-vous; Four Temperaments; Solitaire
14 KALAMAZOO, MI - Central H.S. Aud: Les Rendez-vous; Bayaderka - Act IV; Nutcracker - Act II
15 BATTLE CREEK, MI - W.K. Kellogg Aud: Les Rendez-vous; Bayaderka - Act IV; Solitaire
16 SAGINAW, MI - City Aud: Swan Lake
17 ANN ARBOR, MI - Hill Aud: Solitaire; Four Temperaments; Nutcracker - Act II
19 PITTSBURGH, PA - Syria Mosque: Swan Lake
20 TOLEDO, OH - Toledo Museum of Art: Les Rendez-vous; Four Temperaments; Solitaire
21 CHARLESTON, WV - Municipal Aud: Les Rendez-vous; Bayaderka - Act IV; Solitaire
22 REIDSVILLE, NC - High School Aud: Les Rendez-vous; Four Temperaments; Solitaire
23 CHARLESTON, SC - Municipal Aud: Les Rendez-vous; Bayaderka - Act IV; Solitaire
24 ASHEVILLE, NC - City Aud: Les Rendez-vous; Four Temperaments; Nutcracker - Act II
25 RICHMOND, VA - Virginia Museum Theatre: Bayaderka - Act IV; Solitaire; Les Rendez-vous
27 RALEIGH, NC - Reynolds Coliseum: Les Rendez-vous; Four Temperaments; Solitaire
28 Bayderka - Act IV; Four Temperaments; Nutcracker - Act II
29 Les Rendez-vous; Four Temperaments; Solitaire
31 HERSHEY, PA - Community Theatre: Swan Lake

NOVEMBER, 1969:

1 STORRS, CT - Jorgensen Aud: Solitaire; Four Temperaments; Nutcracker - Act II
2 MONTCLAIR, NJ - Montclair H.S. Aud: Solitaire; Nutcracker - Act II; Les Rendez-vous
3 RED BANK, NJ - Carlton Theatre: Les Rendez-vous; Nutcracker - Act II; Solitaire
18 TORONTO, ON - O'Keefe Centre: Kraanerg - *repeated, November 19, 20, 21, 22★, 22*
24 Swan Lake - *repeated, November 25*
26 La Sylphide; Lesson
27 Bayaderka - Act IV; Le Loup; Four Temperaments
28 Lesson; Bayaderka - Act IV; Le Loup
29★ La Sylphide; Le Loup
29 Lesson; Four Temperaments; Le Loup

DECEMBER, 1969:

18★ OTTAWA, ON - National Arts Centre: Nutcracker - *repeated, December 18, 19, 20★, 20*

26a★ TORONTO, ON - O'Keefe Centre: Nutcracker - *repeated, December 26b★, 27★, 27, 28★, 29★, 30★, 31★*

JANUARY, 1970:

2a★ TORONTO, ON - O'Keefe Centre: Nutcracker - *repeated, January 2b★ (two matinees on one day), 3★, 3*

FEBRUARY, 1970:

16 HAMILTON, ON - Palace Theatre: Swan Lake

17 WINDSOR, ON - Cleary Aud: Lesson; Bayaderka - Act IV; Les Rendez-vous

18 La Sylphide; Solitaire

19★ La Sylphide

19 Lesson; Solitaire; Four Temperaments

20 Bayaderka - Act IV; Le Loup; Les Rendez-vous

21★ Les Rendez-vous; Le Loup; Solitaire

21 Swan Lake

24 LONDON, ON - Grand Theatre: Bayderka - Act IV; Four Temperaments; Les Rendez-vous

25★ La Sylphide

25 Lesson; Solitaire; Le Loup - *repeated, February 26 (Les Rendez-vous substituted for Solitaire)*

27★ La Sylphide

27 Lesson; Four Temperaments; Les Rendez-vous - *repeated, February 28★ (Bayaderka - Act IV substituted for Lesson)*

28 Swan Lake

APRIL, 1970:

16 TORONTO, ON - O'Keefe Centre: Giselle - *repeated, April 17, 18★, 18, 19★*

21 Swan Lake

22 Lesson; Concerto Barocco; Phases; Solitaire

23 Swan Lake

24 Lesson; Concerto Barocco; Phases; Solitaire

25★ Swan Lake - *repeated, April 25*

MAY, 1970:

24 OSAKA, JAPAN - Festival Hall - Expo: Romeo & Juliet - *repeated, May 25, 26*

28 Four Temperaments; Le Loup; Solitaire - *repeated, May 29*

SEASON: 1970-1; **PERFORMANCES:** 92 (60 outside Toronto); **PREMIERES:** Brown Earth (Ditchburn); For Internal Use As Well (also titled For Internal Use Only) (Spain); The Mirror Walkers (Wright); Pas de Deux (Spain); Sagar (Spain).

OCTOBER, 1970:

29 OTTAWA, ON - National Arts Centre: Giselle - *repeated, October 30*

31★ Lesson; Le Loup; Mirror Walkers - *repeated, October 31*

NOVEMBER, 1970:

5 OTTAWA, ON - National Arts Centre: Giselle

6 Swan Lake - *repeated, November 7★, 7*

DECEMBER, 1970:

16★ OTTAWA, ON - National Arts Centre: Nutcracker - *repeated, December 16, 17★, 17, 18, 19★, 19*

26★ TORONTO, ON - O'Keefe Centre: Nutcracker - *repeated, December 26, 27★, 28★, 29★, 29, 30★, 31★*

JANUARY, 1971:

2★ TORONTO, ON - O'Keefe Centre: Nutcracker - *repeated, January 2, 3★*

14 TUCSON, AZ - Univ. of Arizona Aud: Les Rendez-vous; Le Loup; Serenade

15 Solitaire; Nutcracker - Act II; Four Temperaments

16 TEMPE, AZ - Gammage Aud: Swan Lake - *repeated, January 16★*

18 LAS VEGAS, NV - Las Vegas High School Aud: Solitaire; Four Temperaments; Les Rendez-vous

19 SAN BERNARDINO, CA - Cal. Theatre of Performing Arts: Solitaire; Le Loup; Les Rendez-vous

20 SAN DIEGO, CA - Civic Theatre: Solitaire; Le Loup; Nutcracker - Act II

21 Kraanerg

22 LOS ANGELES, CA - Royce Hall, U.C.L.A.: Kraanerg

23★ Solitaire; Le Loup; Les Rendez-vous

23 Serenade; Le Loup; Four Temperaments

24★ Swan Lake - *repeated, January 24*

25 FRESNO, CA - Convention Centre Theatre: Serenade; Le Loup; Solitaire

27 BERKELEY, CA - Zellerbach Aud: Kraanerg - *repeated, January 28*

29 Solitaire; Le Loup; Four Temperaments

30★ Serenade; Nutcracker - Act II; Les Rendez-vous

30 Solitaire; Le Loup; Les Rendez-vous

31★ Swan Lake - *repeated, January 31*

FEBRUARY, 1971:

1 SACRAMENTO, CA - Memorial Aud: Serenade; Les Rendez-vous; Solitaire

3 VANCOUVER, BC - Queen Elizabeth Theatre: Kraanerg

4 Solitaire; Le Loup; Nutcracker - Act II

5 PORTLAND, OR - Civic Aud: Swan Lake

6★ Serenade; Les Rendez-vous; Nutcracker - Act II

6 Swan Lake

7★ SEATTLE, WA - Seattle Opera House: Serenade; Les Rendez-vous; Nutcracker - Act II

7 Swan Lake

15 HAMILTON, ON - Palace Theatre: Giselle

16 Nutcracker

17 WINDSOR, ON - Cleary Aud: Giselle

18★ Nutcracker - *repeated, February 18*

19 Four Temperaments; Pas de Deux (Spain); Sagar; Mirror Walkers

20★ Giselle - *repeated, February 20*

23 LONDON, ON - Grand Theatre: Giselle

24★ Nutcracker - *repeated, February 24, 25★*

25 Four Temperaments; Pas de Deux (Spain); Sagar; Mirror Walkers - *repeated, February 26*

27★ Giselle - *repeated, February 27*

APRIL, 1971:

21★★ TORONTO, ON - O'Keefe Centre: Brown Earth; For Internal Use As Well; Pas de Deux Idyllic†; Journey Tree; Sagar; Mirror Walkers - *repeated, April 21 (without Journey Tree)*

22 Kraanerg

23 Romeo & Juliet - *repeated, April 24★*

24 Brown Earth; For Internal Use As Well; Pas de Deux Idyllic†; Sagar; Mirror Walkers

28 Romeo & Juliet

29 Kraanerg

30 Giselle

MAY, 1971:

1★ TORONTO, ON - O'Keefe Centre: Giselle - *repeated, May 1, 2★*

4 Brown Earth; For Internal Use As Well; Pas de Deux Idyllic†; Sagar; Mirror Walkers - *repeated, May 5 (Le Corsaire pdd substituted for Sagar)*

6 Swan Lake - *repeated, May 7, 8★, 8*

JUNE, 1971:

16 TORONTO, ON - Ontario Place: One in Five; Giselle - Peasant pdd (from pas de quatre); Swan Lake - Princesses' dance; Le Corsaire pdd; Nutcracker - Chinese dance; Swan Lake - Czardas; EH!; Brown Earth - *repeated, June 23, 30*

SEASON: 1971-2; **PERFORMANCES:** 107 (69 outside Toronto); **PREMIERES:** Evocation (staged by Seillier); Fandango (Tudor); Intermezzo (Feld); Session (Iscove).

JULY, 1971:

21 TORONTO, ON - Ontario Place: One in Five; Giselle - Peasant pdd (from pas de quatre); Swan Lake - Princesses' dance, Black Swan pdd; Nutcracker - Chinese dance; Swan Lake - Czardas; EH!; Brown Earth - *repeated, July 28*

AUGUST, 1971:
4 TORONTO, ON - Ontario Place:One in Five; Giselle - Peasant pdd (from pas de quatre); Swan Lake - Princesses' dance, Black Swan pdd; Nutcracker - Chinese dance; Swan Lake - Czardas; EH!; Brown Earth - *repeated, August 11 (Swan Lake - Black Swan Solo and Corsaire - Female solo substituted for Black Swan pdd), 18*
SEPTEMBER, 1971:
8 TORONTO, ON - Ontario Place: One in Five; Giselle - Peasant pdd (from pas de quatre); Swan Lake - Princesses' dance; Le Corsaire pdd; Nutcracker -Chinese dance; Swan Lake - Czardas; EH!; Brown Earth - *repeated, September 15 (Nutcracker - Act II pdd substituted for Corsaire pdd), 22 (Nutcracker - Act II pdd substituted for Corsaire pdd)*
DECEMBER, 1971:
15* OTTAWA, ON - National Arts Centre: Nutcracker - *repeated, December 15, 16*, 16, 17, 18*, 18*
26* TORONTO, ON - O'Keefe Centre: Nutcracker - *repeated, December 26, 27*, 28*, 29*, 29, 30*, 31**
JANUARY, 1972:
1* TORONTO, ON - O'Keefe Centre: Nutcracker - *repeated, January 1, 2**
14 HAMILTON, ON - Palace Theatre: La Sylphide; Judgment of Paris; Fandango
15 Swan Lake
16 WINDSOR, ON - Cleary Aud: La Sylphide; Judgment of Paris; Session
17* La Sylphide
17 Evocation; Session; Fandango; Mirror Walkers
18 La Sylphide; Intermezzo
19* Swan Lake - *repeated, January 19*
22 LONDON, ON - Grand Theatre: La Sylphide; Judgment of Paris; Fandango
23* La Sylphide
23 Evocation; Judgment of Paris; Fandango; Session
24* La Sylphide
24 Evocation; Judgment of Paris; Session; Intermezzo
25 Swan Lake - *repeated, January 26*, 26*
MARCH, 1972:
24 MONTREAL, QC - Place des Arts: La Sylphide; Intermezzo - *repeated, March 25* (Evocation substituted for Intermezzo)*
25 Swan Lake - *repeated, March 26**
APRIL, 1972:
5* OTTAWA, ON - National Arts Centre: Fandango; Session; Kraanerg - *repeated, April 5*
6 La Sylphide; Intermezzo - *repeated, April 7 (Evocation substituted for Intermezzo)*
8* Swan Lake - *repeated, April 8*
19 TORONTO, ON - O'Keefe Centre: Romeo & Juliet - *repeated, April 20, 21, 22*, 22*
23* La Sylphide; Fandango; Session
26 Swan Lake - *repeated, April 27, 28, 29*, 29, 30**
MAY, 1972:
2** TORONTO, ON - O'Keefe Centre: Swan Lake - *repeated, May 3***
3 Evocation; Fandango; Judgment of Paris; Intermezzo
4 Mirror Walkers; La Sylphide - *repeated, May 5 (Intermezzo substituted for Mirror Walkers)*
6* Mirror Walkers; Fandango; Session; Evocation
6 Mirror Walkers; La Sylphide
17 LONDON, ENGLAND - Coliseum: Mixed Program (Gala); Mirror Walkers; Legende†; La Sylphide
18 La Sylphide; Intermezzo - *repeated, May 19 (Mirror Walkers substituted for Intermezzo), 20**
20 Fandango; Judgment of Paris; Kraanerg - *repeated, May 22*
23 Swan Lake - *repeated, May 24, 25*
26 Evocation; Fandango; Session; Intermezzo - *repeated, May 27*, 27*
30 STUTTGART, GERMANY - Staatstheater: La Sylphide; Intermezzo
JUNE, 1972:
5 PARIS, FRANCE - Théâtre des Champs-Elysées: Mirror Walkers; La Sylphide - *repeated, June 6, 7*
8 Evocation; Session; Fandango; Intermezzo - *repeated, June 9, 10*
11 Swan Lake - *repeated, June 13*
15 BRUSSELS, BELGIUM - Théâtre Royal de la Monnaie: La Sylphide; Intermezzo - *repeated, June 16 (Evocation substituted for Intermezzo)*
17 Fandango; Session; Kraanerg
20 GLASGOW, SCOTLAND - King's Theatre: La Sylphide; Evocation
21 Swan Lake
22* La Sylphide; Evocation
22 La Sylphide; Fandango; Judgment of Paris
23 Fandango; Judgment of Paris; Kraanerg
24* Swan Lake - *repeated, June 24*
27 LAUSANNE, SWITZERLAND - Théâtre de Beaulieu: Evocation; Judgment of Paris; Session; Intermezzo
28 Swan Lake
JULY, 1972:
1 MONTE CARLO - Casino de Monte Carlo: Swan Lake - *repeated, July 2*
3 Evocation; Judgment of Paris; Session; Intermezzo

SEASON: 1972-3; **PERFORMANCES:** 198 (165 outside Toronto); **PREMIERES:** The Moor's Pavane (Limón); The Sleeping Beauty (Nureyev after Petipa).

SEPTEMBER, 1972:
1 OTTAWA, ON - National Arts Centre: Sleeping Beauty - *repeated, September 2*, 2, 3*, 3*
5 MONTREAL, QC - Place des Arts: Swan Lake - *repeated, September 6, 7*
8 Sleeping Beauty - *repeated, September 9, 10*, 10*
13 PHILADELPHIA, PA - Academy of Music: Sleeping Beauty - *repeated, September 14*
15 La Sylphide; Nutcracker pdd; Fandango; Le Corsaire pdd
16* Swan Lake - *repeated, September 16, 17*
19 BOSTON, MA - Music Hall Theatre: La Sylphide; Nutcracker pdd; Fandango; Le Corsaire pdd
20 Swan Lake - *repeated, September 21, 22*
23 HARTFORD, CT - Bushnell Memorial Hall: Nutcracker pdd; Fandango; Le Corsaire pdd; La Sylphide
24* Swan Lake - *repeated, September 24*
26 ROCHESTER, NY - Eastman Theatre: Swan Lake - *repeated, September 27*
28 CLEVELAND, OH - Music Hall: Swan Lake
29 La Sylphide; Nutcracker pdd; Fandango; Le Corsaire pdd
30 COLUMBUS, OH - Veterans Memorial Aud: La Sylphide; Nutcracker pdd; Fandango; Le Corsaire pdd
OCTOBER, 1972:
1* COLUMBUS, OH - Veterans Memorial Aud: Swan Lake - *repeated, October 1*
3 BIRMINGHAM, AL - Municipal Aud: La Sylphide; Nutcracker pdd; Fandango; Le Corsaire pdd
4 Swan Lake
5 ATLANTA, GA - Maddox Civic Aud: Swan Lake - *repeated, October 6*
7* La Sylphide; Nutcracker pdd; Fandango; Le Corsaire pdd - *repeated, October 7*
8 CHARLOTTEVILLE, VA - University Hall Aud: Swan Lake
10 BALTIMORE, MD - Morris A. Mechanic Theatre: La Sylphide; Nutcracker pdd; Fandango; Le Corsaire pdd - *repeated, October 11 (Moor's Pavane substituted for Nutcracker pdd and Corsaire pdd)*
12 Swan Lake - *repeated, October 13, 14*, 14*

17 TORONTO, ON - O'Keefe Centre: Sleeping Beauty - *repeated, October 18, 19, 20, 21★, 21*
25 La Sylphide; Fandango; Moor's Pavane - *repeated, October 26, 27*
28★ Swan Lake - *repeated, October 28, 29★, 29*
31★★ Sleeping Beauty

NOVEMBER, 1972:
1 TORONTO, ON - O'Keefe Centre: Sleeping Beauty - *repeated, November 2, 3, 4★, 4, 5★*

DECEMBER, 1972:
6 WINDSOR, ON - Cleary Aud: Swan Lake - *repeated, December 7★★ (Act II only), 7*
8 Nutcracker - *repeated, December 9★, 9*
13★ OTTAWA, ON - National Arts Centre: Nutcracker - *repeated, December 13, 14★, 14, 15, 16★, 16*
21 TORONTO, ON - O'Keefe Centre: Nutcracker - *repeated, December 22★, 22, 23★, 23, 26★, 26, 27★, 28★, 28, 29, 30★, 30*

JANUARY, 1973:
3★★ LONDON, ON - Grand Theatre: Nutcracker - *repeated, January 3, 4★★, 4*
5 Swan Lake - *repeated, January 6★, 6*
29 VANCOUVER, BC - Queen Elizabeth Theatre: Sleeping Beauty - *repeated, January 30, 31*

FEBRUARY, 1973:
1 VANCOUVER, BC - Queen Elizabeth Theatre: La Sylphide; Fandango; Moor's Pavane
2 Swan Lake - *repeated, February 3★, 3*
5 SEATTLE, WA - Seattle Opera House: Sleeping Beauty - *repeated, February 6*
7 La Sylphide; Fandango; Moor's Pavane
8 PORTLAND, OR - Portland Civic Aud: Swan Lake - *repeated, February 9*
10★ La Sylphide; Nutcracker pdd; Fandango; Sleeping Beauty - Act III pdd - *repeated, February 10 (Moor's Pavane substituted for Sleeping Beauty pdd and Nutcracker pdd)*
12 SAN FRANCISCO, CA - San Francisco Opera House: Sleeping Beauty - *repeated, February 13*
15 CUPERTINO, CA - Flint Center: La Sylphide; Fandango; Moor's Pavane
16 Swan Lake
17 SAN FRANCISCO, CA - San Francisco Opera House: Sleeping Beauty - *repeated, February 18★, 18*
19 La Sylphide; Fandango; Moor's Pavane - *repeated, February 20*
22 BERKELEY, CA - Berkeley Community Theatre: Swan Lake
23 SACRAMENTO, CA - Sacramento Memorial Aud: Swan Lake
24 SAN FRANCISCO, CA - San Francisco Opera House: Swan Lake - *repeated, February 25★, 25*
27 LOS ANGELES, CA - Shrine Aud: Sleeping Beauty - *repeated, February 28*

MARCH, 1973:
1 LOS ANGELES, CA - Shrine Aud: Sleeping Beauty - *repeated, March 2*
3★ Swan Lake - *repeated, March 3, 4★*
6 HOUSTON, TX - Jesse H. Jones Hall: Sleeping Beauty - *repeated, March 7, 8*
9 La Sylphide; Fandango; Moor's Pavane
10★ Swan Lake - *repeated, March 10, 11★*
12 NEW ORLEANS, LA - Municipal Aud: Swan Lake
13 La Sylphide; Fandango; Moor's Pavane
15 MEMPHIS, TN - North Hall: Swan Lake
16 La Sylphide; Fandango; Moor's Pavane
17 ST LOUIS, MO - Kiel Opera House: Swan Lake - *repeated, March 18★, 18*
20 KANSAS CITY, MO - Capri Theatre: La Sylphide; Fandango; Moor's Pavane
21 Swan Lake
22 IOWA CITY, IA - Hancher Aud: Sleeping Beauty - *repeated, March 23*
24 La Sylphide; Fandango; Moor's Pavane
25★ Swan Lake - *repeated, March 25*
27 CHAMPAIGN, IL - Assembly Hall, U. of Illinois: Sleeping Beauty
28 La Sylphide; Le Loup pdd; Fandango; Moor's Pavane
29 BLOOMINGTON, IN - Indiana Univ. Aud: Sleeping Beauty
30 Swan Lake
31 INDIANAPOLIS, IN - Clowes Memorial Hall: Swan Lake

APRIL, 1973:
1 INDIANAPOLIS, IN - Clowes Memorial Hall: Swan Lake
3 GARY, IN - West Side High School Aud: Swan Lake
4 La Sylphide; Le Loup pdd; Fandango; Moor's Pavane
5 CHICAGO, IL - Opera House: Sleeping Beauty - *repeated, April 6*
7 Swan Lake - *repeated, April 8★, 8*
10 GRAND RAPIDS, MI - Civic Aud: La Sylphide; Le Loup pdd; Fandango; Moor's Pavane
11 Swan Lake
12 EAST LANSING, MI - University Aud: Swan Lake
13 La Sylphide; Le Loup pdd; Fandango; Moor's Pavane
14 DETROIT, MI - Masonic Aud: Swan Lake - *repeated, April 15★*
15 La Sylphide; Fandango; Moor's Pavane
24 NEW YORK, NY - Metropolitan Opera House: Sleeping Beauty - *repeated, April 25, 26, 27, 28★, 28, 29★, 29*

MAY, 1973:
1 NEW YORK, NY - Metropolitan Opera House: La Sylphide; Fandango; Moor's Pavane - *repeated, May 2*
3 Swan Lake - *repeated, May 4, 5★, 5, 6★, 6*
8 Sleeping Beauty - *repeated, May 9, 10, 11, 12★, 12, 13★, 13*

SEASON: 1973-4; **PERFORMANCES:** 144 (102 outside Toronto); **PREMIERES:** Don Juan (Neumeier); Flower Festival in Genzano pas de deux - new production (Bournonville, arranged by Bruhn); Les Sylphides - new production (Fokine, produced by Franca and Bruhn).

JULY, 1973:
31 TORONTO, ON - Ontario Place: Swan Lake

AUGUST, 1973:
2 TORONTO, ON - Ontario Place: Swan Lake - *repeated, August 7, 9, 13, 15, 17*

SEPTEMBER, 1973:
26 WINDSOR, ON - Cleary Aud: Les Sylphides; Le Loup; Solitaire - *repeated, September 27★★ (without Solitaire), 27*
28 Giselle - *repeated, September 29★, 29*

OCTOBER, 1973:
1 HAMILTON, ON - Hamilton Place: Les Sylphides; Le Loup; Solitaire
2 Giselle - *repeated, October 3*
4 LONDON, ON - Grand Theatre: Les Sylphides; Le Loup; Solitaire - *repeated, October 5*
6★ Giselle - *repeated, October 6*
15 EDMONTON, AB - Jubilee Aud: Giselle - *repeated, October 16*
17 CALGARY, AB - Jubilee Aud: Swan Lake - *repeated, 18, 19★★, 19*
23 WINNIPEG, MB - Man. Centennial Concert Hall: Swan Lake - *repeated, October 24, 25*
27 Giselle - *repeated, October 28★, 28*
30 REGINA, SK - Sask. Centre of the Arts: Swan Lake - *repeated, October 31★★ (Act II only), 31*

NOVEMBER, 1973:
1 REGINA, SK - Sask. Centre of the Arts: Giselle
5 SASKATOON, SK - Saskatoon Centennial Aud: Giselle
6 Swan Lake - *repeated, November 7★★, 7*

DECEMBER, 1973:
12★ OTTAWA, ON - National Arts Centre: Nutcracker - *repeated, December 12, 13★, 13, 14, 15★, 15, 16★*

19★★ TORONTO, ON - O'Keefe Centre: Nutcracker - *repeated, December 20★★, 21, 22★, 22, 23★, 23, 26★, 26, 27★, 28★, 28, 29★, 29*

FEBRUARY, 1974:

13 TORONTO, ON - O'Keefe Centre: Les Sylphides; Don Juan; Solitaire - *repeated, February 14, 15, 16★ (Moor's Pavane substituted for Solitaire)*

16 Les Sylphides; Le Loup; Moor's Pavane - *repeated, February 17★, 17*

20 Sleeping Beauty - *repeated, February 21, 22, 23★, 23, 24★, 24*

26 Giselle - *repeated, February 27★★, 27, 28*

MARCH, 1974:

1 TORONTO, ON - O'Keefe Centre: Giselle - *repeated, March 2★, 2*

7 OTTAWA, ON - National Arts Centre: Les Sylphides; Don Juan; Solitaire - *repeated, March 8★★ (Le Loup substituted for Don Juan)*

8 Les Sylphides; Don Juan; Moor's Pavane

9★ Giselle - *repeated, March 9, 10*

12 BOSTON, MA - Boston Music Hall: Les Sylphides; Flower Festival in Genzano pdd; Le Loup; Moor's Pavane - *repeated, March 13, 14*

15 Giselle - *repeated, March 16★, 16*

19 CHICAGO, IL - Chicago Opera House: Sleeping Beauty - *repeated, March 20, 21*

22 Giselle - *repeated, March 23★, 23, 24★*

26 SAN FRANCISCO, CA - San Francisco Opera House: Les Sylphides; Flower Festival in Genzano pdd; Don Juan

27 CUPERTINO, CA - Flint Center: Giselle

28 SAN FRANCISCO, CA - San Francisco Opera House: Les Sylphides; Flower Festival in Genzano pdd; Don Juan - *repeated, March 30★ (Le Loup substituted for Flower Festival), 30 (Le Loup substituted for Flower Festival)*

31★ Giselle - *repeated, March 31*

APRIL, 1974:

2 LOS ANGELES, CA - Shrine Aud: Les Sylphides; Flower Festival in Genzano pdd; Don Juan - *repeated, April 3*

4 Giselle

6★ Sleeping Beauty - *repeated, April 6, 7★, 7*

9 MILWAUKEE, WI - Uihlein Hall: Les Sylphides; Flower Festival in Genzano pdd; Don Juan

10 Giselle

11 Les Sylphides; Flower Festival in Genzano pdd; Don Juan

12 DETROIT, MI - Masonic Temple: Giselle

13 ★Les Sylphides; Don Juan - *repeated, April 13*

16 HARTFORD, CT - Bushnell Memorial Theatre: Giselle

17 Les Sylphides; Don Juan - *repeated, April 18*

19 PROVIDENCE, RI - Veteran's Memorial Aud: Les Sylphides; Don Juan

20★ Giselle - *repeated, April 20*

23 NEW YORK, NY - Metropolitan Opera House: Sleeping Beauty - *repeated, April 24, 25*

26 Les Sylphides; Flower Festival in Genzano pdd; Don Juan - *repeated, April 27★, 27, 28★ (Le Loup substituted for Flower Festival), 28, 30*

MAY, 1974:

1 Giselle - *repeated, May 2, 3*

4★ Sleeping Beauty - *repeated, May 4*

5★ Les Sylphides; Flower Festival in Genzano pdd; Don Juan - *repeated, May 5*

SEASON: 1974-5; **PERFORMANCES:** 119 (73 outside Toronto); **PREMIERES:** Coppélia - new production (Bruhn); Inventions (Patsalas); Kettentanz (Arpino, staged by Barnard); Whispers of Darkness (Vesak).

JULY, 1974:

23 NEW YORK, NY - Metropolitan Opera House: Sleeping Beauty - *repeated, July 24, 25, 26, 27★, 27, 28★, 28*

30 Giselle - *repeated, July 31*

AUGUST, 1974:

1 NEW YORK, NY - Metropolitan Opera House: Giselle

2 Swan Lake - *repeated, August 3★, 3, 4★, 4, 6, 7*

8 La Sylphide; Le Loup; Moor's Pavane - *repeated, August 9, 10★, 10*

14 TORONTO, ON - Ontario Place: La Sylphide - *repeated, August 15, 16, 17*

19 Swan Lake - *repeated, August 21, 23, 26, 28, 30*

OCTOBER, 1974:

3 QUEBEC CITY, QC - Le Grand Théâtre de Québec: Giselle

4 Les Sylphides; Inventions; Kettentanz

5 Kettentanz; Whispers of Darkness; Le Loup

8 SHERBROOKE, QC - Le Centre Culturel, U. de Sherbrooke: Giselle

9 Les Sylphides; Le Loup; Kettentanz

11 FREDERICTON, NB - The Playhouse: Giselle

12 SACKVILLE, NB - Marjorie Young Bell Convocation Hall: Les Sylphides; Inventions; Kettentanz

16 ST JOHN'S, NF - Newfoundland Arts & Cultural Centre: Giselle - *repeated, October 17★★, 17*

18★★ Les Sylphides; Inventions; Kettentanz

18 Kettentanz; Whispers of Darkness; Le Loup

22 CHARLOTTETOWN, PE - Confederation Centre: Giselle

23 Les Sylphides; Le Loup; Kettentanz

24 ANTIGONISH, NS - Aud, St Francis Xavier University: Les Sylphides; Inventions; Kettentanz

25 HALIFAX, NS - Rebecca Cohn Aud: Les Sylphides; Inventions; Kettentanz - *repeated, October 26★ (Whispers of Darkness substituted for Inventions), 26 (Whispers of Darkness substituted for Inventions)*

31★★ LONDON, ON - Grand Theatre: Les Sylphides; Kettentanz

31 Kettentanz; Whispers of Darkness; Inventions

NOVEMBER, 1974:

1★★ LONDON, ON - Grand Theatre: Les Sylphides; Kettentanz

1 Kettentanz; Whispers of Darkness; Inventions

2 Giselle

4 WINDSOR, ON - Cleary Aud: Kettentanz; Whispers of Darkness; Inventions

5★★ Les Sylphides; Kettentanz

5 Kettentanz; Whispers of Darkness; Inventions

6 La Sylphide; Kettentanz

7 HAMILTON, ON - Hamilton Place: La Sylphide; Kettentanz - *repeated, November 8★★ (without Kettentanz), 8*

DECEMBER, 1974:

18★★ TORONTO, ON - O'Keefe Centre: Nutcracker - *repeated, December 19★★, 19, 20, 21★, 21, 22★, 23★, 23, 26★, 26, 27, 28★, 28*

FEBRUARY, 1975:

8 TORONTO, ON - O'Keefe Centre: Coppélia - *repeated, February 9★, 9*

12 Kettentanz; Whispers of Darkness; Inventions - *repeated, February 13*

14★★ Coppélia - *repeated, February 14, 15★, 15, 16★*

19 Don Juan; Kettentanz - *repeated, February 20, 21*

22★ Giselle - *repeated, February 22, 23★, 23*

26 Sleeping Beauty - *repeated, February 27, 28*

MARCH, 1975:

1★ TORONTO, ON - O'Keefe Centre: Sleeping Beauty - *repeated, March 1*

7 OTTAWA, ON - National Arts Centre: Sleeping Beauty - *repeated, March 8★, 8, 9★*

APRIL, 1975:
2 LONDON, ENGLAND - Coliseum: Don Juan; Flower Festival in Genzano pdd; Kettentanz
3 Giselle - *repeated, April 4*
5* Don Juan; Kettentanz - *repeated, April 5*
7 Coppélia - *repeated, April 8*
9 Giselle - *repeated, April 10*
11 Coppélia - *repeated, April 12*, 12*
15 THE HAGUE, NETHERLANDS - Nederlands Congresgebouw: Coppélia
17 EINDHOVEN, NETHERLANDS - Stadsschouwburg: Giselle
18 AMSTERDAM, NETHERLANDS - Stadsschouwburg: Giselle
19 Don Juan; Kettentanz
20 Giselle

SEASON: 1975-6; **PERFORMANCES:** 127 (77 outside Toronto); **PREMIERES:** Kisses (Ditchburn); Monument for a Dead Boy (van Dantzig); Offenbach in the Underworld - revival (Tudor, restaged by Franca).

JULY, 1975:
22 NEW YORK, NY - Metropolitan Opera House: Sleeping Beauty - *repeated, July 23*
24 Coppélia - *repeated, July 25*
26* Sleeping Beauty - *repeated, July 26*
27* Coppélia - *repeated, July 29*
30 Swan Lake - *repeated, July 31*
AUGUST, 1975:
1 NEW YORK, NY - Metropolitan Opera House: Swan Lake
2* Coppélia - *repeated, August 2*
3* Swan Lake - *repeated, August 3*
5 La Sylphide; Don Juan - *repeated, August 6*
7 Sleeping Beauty - *repeated, August 8*
9* La Sylphide; Don Juan - *repeated, August 9*
10* Sleeping Beauty - *repeated, August 10*
19 TORONTO, ON - Ontario Place: Les Sylphides; Offenbach in the Underworld - *repeated, August 20, 21*, 21, 22, 23*, 23*
SEPTEMBER, 1975:
26 MONTREAL, QC - Place des Arts: Swan Lake - *repeated, September 27*
28* Kettentanz; La Sylphide - *repeated, September 28*
OCTOBER, 1975:
2 VANCOUVER, BC - Queen Elizabeth Theatre: Coppélia - *repeated, October 3**, 3*
4 Don Juan; Offenbach in the Underworld
6 EDMONTON, AB - Jubilee Aud: La Sylphide; Kettentanz - *repeated, October 7 (Offenbach in the Underworld substituted for Kettentanz)*
10 BANFF, AB - Eric Harvie Theatre: Kettentanz; Kisses; Offenbach in the Underworld
11 CALGARY, AB - Jubilee Aud: La Sylphide; Kettentanz
12 La Sylphide; Offenbach in the Underworld
14 REGINA, SK - Sask. Centre of the Arts: Coppélia - *repeated, October 15**, 15*
17 SASKATOON, SK - Saskatoon Centennial Aud: Coppélia - *repeated, October 18*, 18*
20 WINNIPEG, MB - Manitoba Centennial Concert Hall: Don Juan; Kisses; Offenbach in the Underworld - *repeated, October 21 (Kettentanz substituted for Offenbach)*
22 Coppélia - *repeated, October 23, 24**, 24*
30 HAMILTON, ON - Hamilton Place: Don Juan; Kisses; Offenbach in the Underworld
31** Les Sylphides; Offenbach in the Underworld - *repeated, October 31 (with Kisses added)*
NOVEMBER, 1975:
1 HAMILTON, ON - Hamilton Place: Don Juan; Kisses; Kettentanz
3 WINDSOR, ON - Cleary Aud: Don Juan; Kisses; Offenbach in the Underworld - *repeated, November 4** (without Don Juan), 4*
5 Les Sylphides; Kisses; Kettentanz
6 LONDON, ON - Grand Theatre: Les Sylphides; Kisses; Offenbach in the Underworld
7** Kisses; Offenbach in the Underworld
7 Les Sylphides; Kisses; Kettentanz
8 Don Juan; Kisses; Offenbach in the Underworld
DECEMBER, 1975:
2** OTTAWA, ON - National Arts Centre: Coppélia - *repeated, December 3, 4*, 4, 5, 6*, 6*
10 HAMILTON, ON - Hamilton Place: Nutcracker - *repeated, December 11**, 11, 12*
23* TORONTO, ON - O'Keefe Centre: Nutcracker - *repeated, December 23, 24*, 26, 27*, 27, 29*, 29, 30, 31*, 31*
JANUARY, 1976:
2 TORONTO, ON - O'Keefe Centre: Nutcracker - *repeated, January 3*, 3*
FEBRUARY, 1976:
7 TORONTO, ON - O'Keefe Centre: Kettentanz; Monument for a Dead Boy; Offenbach in the Underworld
8* Don Juan; Kisses; Offenbach in the Underworld - *repeated, February 8*
11 Swan Lake - *repeated, February 12, 13, 14*, 14, 15*
18 Coppélia - *repeated, February 19**, 19, 20, 21*, 21, 22*, 22*
25 La Sylphide; Monument for a Dead Boy
26 Kettentanz; La Sylphide
27 La Sylphide; Monument for a Dead Boy
28* Kettentanz; La Sylphide
28 La Sylphide; Monument for a Dead Boy
29* La Sylphide; Offenbach in the Underworld
29 Kettentanz; La Sylphide
MARCH, 1976:
3 TORONTO, ON - O'Keefe Centre: Sleeping Beauty - *repeated, March 4, 5, 6*, 6*
10 OTTAWA, ON - National Arts Centre: Swan Lake - *repeated, March 11**, 11*
12 Kettentanz; Kisses; Offenbach in the Underworld
13* Swan Lake
13 Kettentanz; Monument for a Dead Boy; Offenbach in the Underworld

---

SEASON: 1976-7; **PERFORMANCES:** 123 (63 outside Toronto); **PREMIERES:** Afternoon of a Faun (Robbins); Black Angels (Patsalas); Four Schumann Pieces (van Manen); La Fille Mal Gardée (Ashton); Mad Shadows (Ditchburn); Monotones II (Ashton); A Party (Kudelka); Romeo and Juliet - revival (Cranko).

JULY, 1976:
11 MONTREAL, QC - Place des Arts: Romeo & Juliet - *repeated, July 13, 14*
20 NEW YORK, NY - Metropolitan Opera House: Sleeping Beauty - *repeated, July 21*
22 La Sylphide; Four Schumann Pieces
23 Four Schumann Pieces; La Sylphide - Act II; Sleeping Beauty - Act III
24* Sleeping Beauty - *repeated, July 24, 25*, 27*
28 Swan Lake - *repeated, July 29*
30 Giselle
31* Swan Lake - *repeated, July 31*
AUGUST, 1976:
1* NEW YORK, NY - Metropolitan Opera House: Giselle - *repeated, August 1, 3*
4 La Sylphide; Monument for a Dead Boy; Four Schumann Pieces
5 Giselle - *repeated, August 6*

7* La Sylphide; Monument for a Dead Boy; Four Schumann Pieces - *repeated, August 7*
8* Sleeping Beauty - *repeated, 8*
16 TORONTO, ON - Ontario Place: Swan Lake - *repeated, August 17, 18**
18 Kettentanz; Le Corsaire pdd; Offenbach in the Underworld - *repeated, August 19, 20, 21**
21 Swan Lake

SEPTEMBER, 1976:
22* ST JOHN'S, NF - Arts & Culture Centre: Coppélia - *repeated, September 22, 23*
24** Four Schumann Pieces; Offenbach in the Underworld
24 Four Schumann Pieces; Sleeping Beauty - Grand pdd; Black Angels; Offenbach in the Underworld
25 Kettentanz; Le Corsaire pdd; Kisses; Offenbach in the Underworld
29 HALIFAX, NS - Rebecca Cohn Aud: Four Schumann Pieces; Sleeping Beauty - Grand pdd; Black Angels; Offenbach in the Underworld
30** Kettentanz; Offenbach in the Underworld - *repeated, September 30 (with Le Corsaire pdd, Kisses added)*

OCTOBER, 1976:
1 HALIFAX, NS - Rebecca Cohn Aud: Four Schumann Pieces; Sleeping Beauty - Bluebird pdd; A Party; Kettentanz
2 Four Schumann Pieces; Monument for a Dead Boy; Le Corsaire pdd; Offenbach in the Underworld
5 CHARLOTTETOWN, PE - Confederation Centre: Coppélia - *repeated, October 6** (Act I only)*
6 Four Schumann Pieces; Sleeping Beauty - Grand pdd; Black Angels; Offenbach in the Underworld
8 FREDERICTON, NB - Playhouse Theatre: Coppélia
9* Kettentanz; Le Corsaire pdd; Kisses; Offenbach in the Underworld - *repeated, October 9 (with Monument for a Dead Boy added)*
12 SHERBROOKE, QC - Cultural Centre, U. of Sherbrooke: Coppélia
13 Four Schumann Pieces; Sleeping Beauty - Bluebird pdd; A Party; Offenbach in the Underworld

NOVEMBER, 1976:
12 TORONTO, ON - O'Keefe Centre: Romeo & Juliet - *repeated, November 13*, 13, 14*, 14*
17 La Fille Mal Gardée - *repeated, November 18**, 18, 19, 20*, 20*

DECEMBER, 1976:
8 HAMILTON, ON - Hamilton Place: Coppélia - *repeated, December 9*, 9, 10*
12 WINDSOR, ON - Cleary Aud: Coppélia - *repeated, December 13, 14** (Act I only), 14*
16 LONDON, ON - Grand Theatre: Coppélia - *repeated, December 17, 18*, 18*
23* TORONTO, ON - O'Keefe Centre: Nutcracker - *repeated, December 23, 24, 27*, 27, 28, 29*, 29, 30, 31*, 31*

FEBRUARY, 1977:
10 TORONTO, ON - O'Keefe Centre: Romeo & Juliet - *repeated, February 11, 12*, 12, 13*
16 A Party; Monotones II; Mad Shadows; Four Schumann Pieces
17 Four Schumann Pieces; Afternoon of a Faun; Black Angels; Mad Shadows
18 La Fille Mal Gardée - *repeated, February 19*, 19, 20*
23 Giselle - *repeated, February 24*, 24, 25, 26*, 26*
27 Kettentanz; Afternoon of a Faun; Monotones II; Four Schumann Pieces

MARCH, 1977:
2 TORONTO, ON - O'Keefe Centre: Swan Lake - *repeated, March 3, 4*
5* Kettentanz; A Party; Monotones II; Mad Shadows
5 Kettentanz; Afternoon of a Faun; Black Angels; Mad Shadows
6 Swan Lake
9 Sleeping Beauty - *repeated, March 10, 11, 12*, 12*
15 OTTAWA, ON - National Arts Centre: Romeo & Juliet - *repeated, March 16, 17*
18 La Fille Mal Gardée - *repeated, March 19, 20**

JUNE, 1977:
5 TORONTO, ON - Leah Posluns Theatre: Bayaderka - Act IV

SEASON: 1977-8; **PERFORMANCES:** 162 (102 outside Toronto); **PREMIERES:** Bayaderka - Act IV - revival (Petipa, produced by Valukin); Collective Symphony (van Manen/van Schayk/van Dantzig); The Dream (Ashton).

JULY, 1977:
12 NEW YORK, NY - Metropolitan Opera House: La Fille Mal Gardée - *repeated, July 13*
14 Kettentanz; Flower Festival in Genzano pdd; Monotones II; Le Corsaire pdd; Mad Shadows
15 La Fille Mal Gardée - *repeated, July 16* (with Le Corsaire pdd added)*
16 Kettentanz; Mad Shadows; Collective Symphony
19 Swan Lake
20 Giselle
21 Swan Lake - *repeated, July 22*
23* Giselle - *repeated, July 23*

AUGUST, 1977:
17 TORONTO, ON - Ontario Place: Kettentanz; Sleeping Beauty - Act III - *repeated, August 18*, 18, 20*, 21**
23 WINNIPEG, MB - Manitoba Theatre Centre: Monotones II (participation in 5th annual Dance in Canada Conference)
29 LOS ANGELES, CA - New Greek Theatre: Giselle - *repeated, August 30, 31*

SEPTEMBER, 1977:
1 LOS ANGELES, CA - New Greek Theatre: Giselle
2 Bayaderka - Act IV; Offenbach in the Underworld; Four Schumann Pieces - *repeated, September 3, 4*
6 Swan Lake - *repeated, September 7, 8, 9, 10*
13 CHICAGO, IL - Arie Crown Theatre: Sleeping Beauty - *repeated, September 14, 15*
16 Bayaderka - Act IV; Offenbach in the Underworld; Four Schumann Pieces
17 La Fille Mal Gardée - *repeated, September 18*, 18*
21 MONTREAL, QC - Place des Arts: Sleeping Beauty - *repeated, September 22, 23, 24*, 24*
25* Bayaderka - Act IV; Mad Shadows; Four Schumann Pieces - *repeated, September 25*
27 QUEBEC CITY, QC - Le Grand Théâtre de Quebec: Sleeping Beauty - *repeated, September 28, 29*

OCTOBER, 1977:
2 WINDSOR, ON - Cleary Aud: Swan Lake - *repeated, October 3, 4*
5* Bayaderka - Act IV; Kettentanz - *repeated, October 5 (with Four Schumann Pieces added)*
6 HAMILTON, ON - Hamilton Place: Swan Lake - *repeated, October 7*, 7*
8 Bayaderka - Act IV; Four Schumann Pieces; Kettentanz
12 WINNIPEG, MB - Manitoba Centennial Concert Hall: Romeo & Juliet - *repeated, October 13, 13*, 14*
16 REGINA, SK - Sask. Centre of the Arts: La Fille Mal Gardée - *repeated, October 17, 18, 18** (Act I only)*
20 SASKATOON, SK - Saskatoon Centennial Aud: La Fille Mal Gardée - *repeated, October 21*, 21*
25 VANCOUVER, BC - Queen Elizabeth Theatre: Romeo & Juliet - *repeated, October 26*, 26, 27*
28 La Fille Mal Gardée - *repeated, October 29*, 29*
31 EDMONTON, AB - Jubilee Aud: Coppélia

NOVEMBER, 1977:
1** EDMONTON, AB - Jubilee Aud: Coppélia - Act I - *repeated, November 1 (complete)*
4 BANFF, AB - Eric Harvey Theatre: Coppélia
5 CALGARY, AB - Jubilee Aud: Coppélia - *repeated, November 6*
7** Bayaderka - Act IV; Collective Symphony - *repeated, November 7 (with Afternoon of a Faun, Monotones II added)*
17* TORONTO, ON - O'Keefe Centre: Coppélia - *repeated, November 17, 18, 19*, 19*
20 Bayaderka - Act IV; Collective Symphony; Mad Shadows - *repeated, November 23, 24*
25 Afternoon of a Faun; Monotones II; La Sylphide - *repeated, November 26*, 26*
DECEMBER, 1977:
13** OTTAWA, ON - National Arts Centre: Nutcracker - *repeated, December 14, 15**, 15, 16, 17*, 17*
20 TORONTO, ON - O'Keefe Centre: Nutcracker - *repeated, December 21*, 21, 22, 23*, 23, 24*, 27, 28*, 28, 29, 30*, 30, 31**
FEBRUARY, 1978:
8 TORONTO, ON - O'Keefe Centre: Sleeping Beauty - *repeated, February 9, 10, 11*, 11*
15 Four Schumann Pieces; Afternoon of a Faun; Don Quixote pdd†; Tchaikowsky Pas de Deux†; Dream
16 La Fille Mal Gardée - *repeated, February 17, 18*, 18, 19*
21 Swan Lake - *repeated, February 22, 23, 24, 25*, 25, 26*
MARCH. 1978:
1 TORONTO, ON - O'Keefe Centre: Dream; Don Juan - *repeated, March 2, 3*
4* A Party; Dream; Collective Symphony - *repeated, March 4, 5*
8 Romeo & Juliet - *repeated, March 9**, 9, 10, 11*, 11*
16 HAMILTON, ON - Hamilton Place: Sleeping Beauty - *repeated, March 17**, 17*
20 OTTAWA, ON - National Arts Centre: Bayaderka - Act IV; Collective Symphony; Dream
21 Dream; Afternoon of a Faun; Monotones II; Mad Shadows
22 Bayaderka - Act IV; Collective Symphony; Dream
MAY, 1978:
17 FRANKFURT, GERMANY - Jahrhunderthalle: Sleeping Beauty
18 Bayaderka - Act IV; Dream; Kettentanz
20 LUDWIGSHAFEN, GERMANY - Neuer Pfalzbau: Romeo & Juliet
22 Sleeping Beauty
24 LEVERKUSEN, GERMANY - Forum: Romeo & Juliet
25 Sleeping Beauty
27 STUTTGART, GERMANY - Württembergisches Staatstheater: Sleeping Beauty
28 MUHLHEIM, GERMANY - Staatshalle Muhlheim: Bayaderka - Act IV; Dream; Kettentanz
JUNE, 1978:
1 UTRECHT, NETHERLANDS - Staddschouwburg: Bayaderka - Act IV; Dream; Kettentanz
2 DEN HAAG, NETHERLANDS - N.V. Nederlands Congresgebouw: Bayaderka - Act IV; Kettentanz; Mad Shadows
3 Sleeping Beauty
4 AMSTERDAM, NETHERLANDS - Carré Theatre: La Fille Mal Gardée

---

SEASON: 1978-9; **PERFORMANCES:** 123 (63 outside Toronto); **PREMIERES:** Elite Syncopations (MacMillan); Les Patineurs (Ashton); The Rite of Spring (Patsalas); The Two Pigeons (Ashton); Washington Square (Kudelka).

JULY, 1978:
17 TORONTO, ON - Ontario Place: Bayaderka - Act IV; Sleeping Beauty - Act III - *repeated, July 19*
26 NEW YORK, NY - State Theatre: Swan Lake - *repeated, July 27*
28 A Party; La Fille Mal Gardée - *repeated, July 29*, 29,*
30* Bayaderka - Act IV; Dream; Collective Symphony - *repeated, July 30, 31*
AUGUST, 1978:
4 TORONTO, ON - Ontario Place: Bayaderka - Act IV; Sleeping Beauty - Act III - *repeated, August 6*, 6, 8*
16 LEWISTON, NY - Artpark: Sleeping Beauty - *repeated, August 17*, 17*
18 La Fille Mal Gardée - *repeated, August 19*
20* Dream; Don Juan - *repeated, August 20*
SEPTEMBER, 1978:
20** ST JOHN'S, NF - Arts & Culture Centre: La Fille Mal Gardée - *repeated, September 20, 21*
22* Afternoon of a Faun; Monotones II; Dream - *repeated, September 22 (with Rite of Spring added)*
23 Bayaderka - Act IV; Collective Symphony; Sleeping Beauty - Act III
27 SACKVILLE, NB - Convocation Hall, Mt Allison: Collective Symphony; Monotones II; La Fille Mal Gardée - Act I, Scene 2 pdd; Sleeping Beauty - Act III
28 HALIFAX, NS - Rebecca Cohn Aud: Bayaderka - Act IV; Monotones II; Don Quixote pdd; Rite of Spring
29** Bayaderka - Act IV; Sleeping Beauty - Act III
29 Bayaderka - Act IV; Monotones II; Don Quixote pdd; Collective Symphony
30 Bayaderka - Act IV; Rite of Spring; Sleeping Beauty - Act III
OCTOBER, 1978:
3 CHARLOTTETOWN, PE - Confederation Centre: La Fille Mal Gardée - *repeated, October 4**, 4*
6 FREDERICTON, NB - Playhouse Theatre: Dream; Afternoon of a Faun; Monotones II; Rite of Spring
7* La Fille Mal Gardée - *repeated, October 7*
9 QUEBEC CITY, QC - Le Grand Théâtre de Québec: La Fille Mal Gardée - *repeated, October 10*
12 MONTREAL, QC - Place des Arts: La Fille Mal Gardée - *repeated, October 13, 14*
15* Dream; Afternoon of a Faun; Monotones II; Collective Symphony - *repeated, October 15*
17 BROCKVILLE, ON - Civic Aud: Bayaderka - Act IV; Monotones II; Don Quixote pdd; Rite of Spring
18 KINGSTON, ON - Grand Theatre: Bayaderka - Act IV; Monotones II; Don Quixote pdd; Rite of Spring
20 WINDSOR, ON - Cleary Aud: Dream; Monotones II; Don Quixote pdd; Sleeping Beauty - Act III - *repeated, October 21*
22* La Fille Mal Gardée - *repeated, October 22, 23**
NOVEMBER, 1978:
8 TORONTO, ON - O'Keefe Centre: Giselle - *repeated, November 9**, 9*
10 Les Patineurs; Mad Shadows; Elite Syncopations - *repeated, November 11*, 11, 12**
15 Bayaderka - Act IV; Afternoon of a Faun; Don Quixote pdd; Elite Syncopations - *repeated, November 16 (Monotones II substituted for Afternoon of a Faun)*
17 Giselle - *repeated, November 18*, 18*
DECEMBER, 1978:
6 HAMILTON, ON - Hamilton Place: Nutcracker - *repeated, December 7*, 7, 8, 9*, 9*
19 TORONTO, ON - O'Keefe Centre: Nutcracker - *repeated, December 20, 21*, 21, 22, 23*, 23, 24*, 27, 28*, 28, 29, 30*, 30*

FEBRUARY, 1979:
8 TORONTO, ON - O'Keefe Centre: Romeo & Juliet - *repeated, February 9, 10★, 10, 11★*
14 Les Sylphides; Taming of the Shrew pdd†; Don Quixote pdd; Le Corsaire pdd†; Legende†; Elite Syncopations
16 Les Sylphides; Washington Square; Kettentanz - *repeated, February 17★, 17, 18★, 18*
22 Swan Lake - *repeated, February 23*
24 Les Patineurs; Rite of Spring; Le Loup - *repeated, February 25★, 25*
28 Two Pigeons; Elite Syncopations
MARCH, 1979:
1 TORONTO, ON - O'Keefe Centre: Two Pigeons; Elite Syncopations - *repeated, March 2, 3★, 3, 4★*
7 La Fille Mal Gardée - *repeated, March 8★★, 8, 9, 10★, 10*
14 OTTAWA, ON - National Arts Centre: Swan Lake - *repeated, March 15★★, 15*
16 Les Sylphides; Washington Square; Elite Syncopations
17★ Swan Lake
17 Les Sylphides; Washington Square; Elite Syncopations
JUNE, 1979:
26 CHICAGO, IL - Civic Opera House: Coppélia pdd; Swan Lake (contributions to Third International Ballet Festival)
27 Sleeping Beauty - Bluebird pdd; Swan Lake (contributions to Third International Ballet Festival)
28 Le Loup pdd; Monotones II (contributions to Third International Ballet Festival)
29 Swan Lake (contribution to Third International Ballet Festival)
30 Flower Festival in Genzano pdd; Romeo & Juliet pdd; Swan Lake (contributions to Third International Ballet Festival)

SEASON: 1979-80; **PERFORMANCES:** 159 (95 outside Toronto); **PREMIERES:** Etudes (Lander); Le Spectre de la Rose (Fokine staged by Beriosoff); Serenade - revival (Balanchine); Song of a Wayfarer (Béjart); Swan Lake - revival (Bruhn after Petipa).

JULY, 1979:
3 NEW YORK, NY - State Theatre: Sleeping Beauty
Sleeping Beauty - *repeated, July 5, 6, 7★, 7, 8★*
10 Monotones II; Coppélia - *repeated, July 11, 12*
13 Giselle; Elite Syncopations - *repeated, July 14★ (Le Loup substituted for Elite), 14 (Le Loup substituted for Elite), 15★*
AUGUST, 1979:
6 LONDON, ENGLAND - Royal Opera, Covent Garden: Swan Lake
7 Bayaderka - Act IV; Mad Shadows; Kettentanz
8 La Fille Mal Gardée - *repeated, August 9★, 9*
10 Swan Lake - *repeated, August 11★*
11 Kettentanz; Mad Shadows; Swan Lake - Act II
19★ TORONTO, ON - Ontario Place: Les Patineurs; Elite Syncopations - *repeated, August 19*
21 LEWISTON, NY - Artpark: Giselle - *repeated, August 22★,* 22
23 Les Sylphides; Washington Square; Elite Syncopations - *repeated, August 24*
25 Coppélia - *repeated, August 26★, 26*
SEPTEMBER, 1979:
6 MONTREAL, QC - Place des Arts: Swan Lake - *repeated, September 7, 8*
9 Les Sylphides; Washington Square; Elite Syncopations
18 WINNIPEG, MB - Manitoba Centennial Concert Hall: Swan Lake - *repeated, September 19★★, 19*
20 Dream; Collective Symphony; Elite Syncopations - *repeated, September 21*
25 VANCOUVER, BC - Queen Elizabeth Theatre: Swan Lake - *repeated, September 26★★, 26*
27 Dream; Collective Symphony; Elite Syncopations - *repeated, September 28*
29★ Les Sylphides; Washington Square; Elite Syncopations - *repeated, September 29*
30 Swan Lake
OCTOBER, 1979:
2 PRINCE GEORGE, BC - Vanier Hall: Les Sylphides; Collective Symphony; Elite Syncopations - *repeated, October 3★ (without Collective), 3*
5 EDMONTON, AB - Jubilee Aud: Swan Lake - *repeated, October 6★, 6*
8 CALGARY, AB - Jubilee Aud: Swan Lake - *repeated, October 9★★, 9*
12 SASKATOON, SK - Saskatoon Centennial Aud: Dream; Collective Symphony; Elite Syncopations
13 Swan Lake
15 REGINA, SK - Saskatchewan Centre for the Arts: Les Sylphides; Washington Square; Elite Syncopations - *repeated, October 16★★ (without Washington Square), 16*
17 Swan Lake
NOVEMBER, 1979:
7 TORONTO, ON - O'Keefe Centre: Sleeping Beauty - *repeated, November 8, 9, 10★, 10, 11*
14 Four Schumann Pieces; Dream; Collective Symphony - *repeated, November 15*
16 Four Schumann Pieces; Dream; Rite of Spring - *repeated, November 17★, 17*
18★ Four Schumann Pieces; Dream; Collective Symphony
21 Coppélia - *repeated, November 22★★, 22, 23, 24★, 24*
DECEMBER, 1979:
13★★ OTTAWA, ON - National Arts Centre: Nutcracker - *repeated, December 13, 14, 15★, 15*
18 TORONTO, ON - O'Keefe Centre: Nutcracker - *repeated, December 19, 20★, 20, 21, 22★, 22, 23★, 26, 27★, 27, 28, 29★, 29*
FEBRUARY, 1980:
6 TORONTO, ON - O'Keefe Centre: Giselle - *repeated, February 7*
8 Flower Festival in Genzano pdd; Harlequinade Solo†; Don Juan pdd; Angali; Birds†; Dying Swan; Le Corsaire pdd; Giselle
9★ Giselle - *repeated, February 9, 10★*
13 Serenade; Le Spectre de la Rose; Monotones II; Washington Square - *repeated, February 14 (Song of a Wayfarer substituted for Spectre), 15, 16★, 16 (Song of a Wayfarer substituted for Spectre), 17★*
20 Romeo & Juliet - *repeated, February 21, 22, 23★, 23, 24★*
27 Two Pigeons; Etudes - *repeated, February 28★★ (without Etudes), 28, 29*
MARCH, 1980:
1★ TORONTO, ON - O'Keefe Centre: Two Pigeons; Etudes - *repeated, March 1, 2★*
5 Swan Lake - *repeated, March 6, 7, 8★, 8*
11 LONDON, ON - Grand Theatre: Giselle - *repeated, March 12, 13★★, 13*
14 Serenade; Le Spectre de la Rose; Washington Square
15★ Giselle
15 Serenade; Le Spectre de la Rose; Washington Square
18 HAMILTON, ON - Hamilton Place: Giselle - *repeated, March 19, 20*
21 Serenade; Le Spectre de la Rose; Washington Square - *repeated, March 22*
25★★ OTTAWA, ON - National Arts Centre: Giselle - *repeated, March 25, 26*
28 Two Pigeons; Etudes - *repeated, March 29★, 29*
APRIL, 1980:
27 GUANAJUATA, MEXICO - Teatro Juarez: Giselle - *repeated, April 28*
30 MEXICO CITY, MEXICO - Teatro de la Ciudad: Giselle - *repeated, April 1*

JUNE, 1980:
23 WASHINGTON, DC - Carter Barron Amphitheatre: Giselle
24 Serenade; Rite of Spring; Elite Syncopations
25 Giselle
26 Serenade; Rite of Spring; Elite Syncopations
27 Giselle
28 Serenade; Rite of Spring; Elite Syncopations

SEASON: 1980-1; **PERFORMANCES:** 153 (76 outside Toronto); **PREMIERES:** Angali (Patsalas); Dark Elegies - revival (Tudor); The Dying Swan (Fokine, staged by Beriosoff); Newcomers (Macdonald); Playhouse (Kudelka).

JULY, 1980:
2 NERVI, ITALY - Teatro Maria Taglioni: La Fille Mal Gardée - *repeated, July 3, 4*
5 NERVI, ITALY - Teatro Maria Taglioni: Serenade; Song of a Wayfarer; Le Corsaire pdd; Elite Syncopations

AUGUST, 1980:
13 TORONTO, ON - Ontario Place: Serenade; Le Corsaire pdd; Elite Syncopations - *repeated, August 14★, 14, 15 (Rite of Spring substituted for Elite), 16★, 16 (Rite of Spring sub-stituted for Elite), 17★, 17 (Personal Essay† added, Rite of Spring substituted for Elite)*
19 LEWISTON, NY - Artpark: Romeo & Juliet - *repeated, August 20★, 20*
21 Serenade; Rite of Spring; Elite Syncopations - *repeated, August 22*
23 Swan Lake - *repeated, August 24★, 24*

SEPTEMBER, 1980:
25 MONTREAL, QC - Place des Arts: Two Pigeons; Etudes - *repeated, September 26*
27★ Giselle
27 Two Pigeons; Etudes
28 Giselle
30 SAINT JOHN, NB - Saint John High School Aud: Serenade; Angali; Dying Swan; Song of a Wayfarer; Elite Syncopations

OCTOBER, 1980:
1★★ SAINT JOHN, NB - Saint John High School Aud: Serenade; Elite Syncopations - *repeated, October 1 (with Angali, Dying Swan, Song of a Wayfarer added)*
3 SACKVILLE, NB - Convocation Hall: Les Patineurs; Angali; Dying Swan; Song of a Wayfarer; Elite Syncopations
6 CHARLOTTETOWN, PE - Confederation Centre: Swan Lake - *repeated, October 7★★ (Act I, Scene 2 and Act II, Scene I only), 7*
9 HALIFAX, NS - Rebecca Cohn Aud: Serenade; Angali; Dying Swan; Song of a Wayfarer; Elite Syncopations - *repeated, October 10★★ (without Angali, Dying Swan, Song of a Wayfarer)*
10 Les Patineurs; Swan Lake - Act II, Scene I; Elite Syncopations - *repeated, October 11*
15★★ ST JOHN'S, NF - Arts & Culture Centre: Swan Lake - Act I, Scene II; Act II, Scene I - *repeated, October 15 (complete), 16 (complete)*
17★★ Newcomers - (part I only); Elite Syncopations
17 Serenade; Angali; Dying Swan; Song of a Wayfarer; Elite Syncopations
18 Les Patineurs; Playhouse; Elite Syncopations

NOVEMBER, 1980:
12 TORONTO, ON - O'Keefe Centre: Playhouse; La Sylphide - *repeated, November 13★, 13, 14, 15★, 15, 16★*
19 Les Patineurs; Newcomers; Mad Shadows - *repeated, November 20★, 20, 21, 22★, 22, 23★*
26 La Fille Mal Gardée - *repeated, November 27★★, 27, 28, 29★, 29, 30*

DECEMBER, 1980:
16 HAMILTON, ON - Hamilton Place: Nutcracker - *repeated, December 17★★, 17, 18, 19, 20★, 20*
23 TORONTO, ON - O'Keefe Centre: Nutcracker - *repeated, December 24★, 26, 27★, 27, 28★, 28, 30★, 30, 31★, 31*

JANUARY, 1981:
2★ TORONTO, ON - O'Keefe Centre: Nutcracker - *repeated, January 2, 3★, 3*

FEBRUARY, 1981:
11 TORONTO, ON - O'Keefe Centre: Swan Lake - *repeated, February 12★, 12, 13, 14★, 14, 15★*
18 Dream; Dark Elegies; Etudes - *repeated, February 19★ (without Dark Elegies), 19, 20, 21★, 21, 22*
25 Romeo & Juliet - *repeated, February 26★, 26, 27, 28★, 28*

MARCH, 1981:
1★ TORONTO, ON - O'Keefe Centre: Romeo & Juliet
4 Kettentanz; Le Spectre de la Rose; Song of a Wayfarer; Newcomers - *repeated, March 5*
6 Plus One†; Spring Dances†; All Night Wonder†; Reflections†; Belong†; Le Corsaire pdd; Diary†; La Sylphide
7★ Kettentanz; Le Spectre de la Rose; Song of a Wayfarer; Newcomers - *repeated, March 7, 8★*
11 Sleeping Beauty - *repeated, March 12★, 12, 13, 14★, 14*
17 OTTAWA, ON - National Arts Centre: Sleeping Beauty
18★ Kettentanz; Sleeping Beauty - Act III
18 Sleeping Beauty - *repeated, March 19*
20 Kettentanz; Le Spectre de la Rose; Song of a Wayfarer; Newcomers - *repeated, March 21*
24 Sleeping Beauty - *repeated, March 25*
27 WINDSOR, ON - Cleary Aud: Swan Lake - *repeated, March 28★, 28*
29★ Kettentanz; Poèmes Intimes†; Angali; Song of a Wayfarer; Etudes - *repeated, March 29 (without Poèmes Intimes†)*
31 HAMILTON, ON - Hamilton Place: Sleeping Beauty

APRIL, 1981:
1★ HAMILTON, ON - Hamilton Place: Sleeping Beauty - *repeated, April 1, 2★, 2*

MAY, 1981:
3 LUXEMBOURG, BELGIUM - Théâtre Municipal Luxembourg: Swan Lake - *repeated, May 4*
6 STUTTGART, GERMANY - Württembergisches Staatstheater: Swan Lake
7 Kettentanz; Etudes; Elite Syncopations
9 LUDWIGSHAFEN, GERMANY - Theater im Pfalzbau: Swan Lake
10 Etudes; Monotones II; Song of a Wayfarer; Elite Syncopations
12 LEVERKUSEN, GERMANY - Forum: Swan Lake - *repeated, May 13*
15 BERLIN, W. GERMANY - Internationales Congress Centrum Berlin: Swan Lake - *repeated, May 16*
19 FRANKFURT, GERMANY - Jahrhunderthalle: Swan Lake - *repeated, May 20*
22 DUSSELDORF, GERMANY - Opernhaus Düsseldorf: Kettentanz; Etudes; Elite Syncopations - *repeated, May 23*
28 OTTAWA, ON - National Arts Centre: Romeo & Juliet - Ballroom Scene (contribution to CAPDO Gala) - *repeated, May 29, 30*

SEASON: 1981-2; **PERFORMANCES:** 168 (83 outside Toronto); **PREMIERES:** Los Siete Puñales/The Seven Daggers (Susana); Napoli (Schaufuss after Bournonville); Nataraja (Patsalas); Portrait of Love and Death (Nebrada); Three Easy Tangos (de Layress).

AUGUST, 1981:
19★ TORONTO, ON - Ontario Place: Swan Lake - *repeated, August 19, 20, 21★, 21, 22★, 22*
25 LEWISTON, NY - Artpark: La Fille Mal Gardée - *repeated, August 26★, 26*
27 Newcomers; Angali; Dying Swan; Song of a Wayfarer; Etudes - *repeated, August 28*

29 Sleeping Beauty - *repeated, August 30★, 30*

SEPTEMBER, 1981:

1 LEWISTON, NY - Artpark: Sleeping Beauty - *repeated, August 2★, 2, 3*

10 MONTREAL, QC - Place des Arts: Sleeping Beauty - *repeated, September 11*

12★ Kettentanz; Le Spectre de la Rose; Angali; Song of a Wayfarer; Newcomers - *repeated, September 12*

13 Sleeping Beauty

16 THUNDER BAY, ON - Fort William Gardens: Kettentanz; Sleeping Beauty - Act II excerpts; Le Corsaire pdd; Sleeping Beauty - Act III

16 VICTORIA, BC - University Centre: Les Sylphides pdd; Angali; Dying Swan; Monotones II; Song of a Wayfarer; Le Corsaire pdd; Sleeping Beauty - Act III Grand pdd; Kettentanz - selections

17★★ THUNDER BAY, ON - Fort William Gardens: Kettentanz; Sleeping Beauty - Act III

17 VICTORIA, BC - University Centre: Les Sylphides; Angali; Dying Swan; Monotones II; Song of a Wayfarer; Le Corsaire pdd; Sleeping Beauty - Act III Grand pdd; Kettentanz - selections

20 EDMONTON, AB - Jubilee Aud: Newcomers; Angali; Dying Swan; Song of a Wayfarer; Etudes

21 Sleeping Beauty

23 VANCOUVER, BC - Queen Elizabeth Theatre: Newcomers; Angali; Dying Swan; Song of a Wayfarer; Etudes

24★★ Kettentanz; Sleeping Beauty - Act III

24 Newcomers; Angali; Dying Swan; Song of a Wayfarer; Etudes

25 Sleeping Beauty - *repeated, September 26, 27★, 27*

30 CALGARY, AB - Jubilee Aud: Sleeping Beauty

OCTOBER, 1981:

1 CALGARY, AB - Jubilee Aud: Newcomers; Angali; Dying Swan; Song of a Wayfarer; Etudes

4 SASKATOON, SK - Saskatoon Centennial Aud: Sleeping Beauty - *repeated, October 5*

7 REGINA, SK - Sask. Centre of the Arts: Sleeping Beauty - *repeated, October 8★★ (Act III only), 8*

12 WINNIPEG, MB - Man. Centennial Concert Hall: Sleeping Beauty

13★★ Kettentanz; Sleeping Beauty - Act III

13 Sleeping Beauty

14 Newcomers; Angali; Dying Swan; Song of a Wayfarer; Etudes

NOVEMBER, 1981:

10 TORONTO, ON - O'Keefe Centre: Napoli - *repeated, November 11, 12, 13, 14★, 14, 15★*

18 Giselle - *repeated, November 19★, 19, 20, 21★, 21, 22★*

25 Les Sylphides; Los Siete Puñales; Elite Syncopations - *repeated, November 26★, 26, 27, 28★, 28, 29*

DECEMBER, 1981:

15 HAMILTON, ON - Hamilton Place: Nutcracker - *repeated, December 16★, 16, 17, 18, 19★, 19*

22 TORONTO, ON - O'Keefe Centre: Nutcracker - *repeated, December 23★, 23, 24★, 26, 27★, 27, 29★, 29, 30, 31★*

JANUARY, 1982:

2★ TORONTO, ON - O'Keefe Centre: Nutcracker - *repeated, January 2, 3★, 3*

27 HAMILTON, ON - Hamilton Place: La Fille Mal Gardée - *repeated, January 28★★, 28, 29*

30★ Four Schumann Pieces; Etudes; Elite Syncopations - *repeated, January 30*

FEBRUARY, 1982:

3 KITCHENER, ON - The Centre in the Square: La Fille Mal Gardée - *repeated, February 4★, 4, 5*

10 TORONTO, ON - O'Keefe Centre: La Fille Mal Gardée - *repeated, February 11★★, 11, 12, 13★, 13, 14★*

17 Four Schumann Pieces; Nataraja; Etudes - *repeated, February 18★, 18, 19, 20★, 20, 21★*

24 Swan Lake - *repeated, February 25★, 25, 26, 27★, 27, 28★*

MARCH, 1982:

23 WEST PALM BEACH, FL - West Palm Beach Aud: Sleeping Beauty - Bluebird pdd; Sylvia pdd†; Dream pdd; Le Corsaire pdd; Don Juan pdd; Top Hat†; Don Quixote pdd; Sleeping Beauty pdd†; Elite Syncopations

24 Monotones II; Giselle pdd; Dying Swan; Don Quixote pdd; La Sylphide

25 La Fille Mal Gardée - *repeated, March 26*

27★ Four Schumann Pieces; Angali; Swan Lake - Act II pdd; Song of a Wayfarer; Tchaikowsky Pas de Deux†; Etudes - *repeated, March 27*

28★ Monotones II; Le Corsaire pdd; Dying Swan; Flower Festival in Genzano pdd; Don Quixote pdd; La Sylphide

30 HOUSTON, TX - Jesse H. Jones Hall: La Fille Mal Gardée

31 Swan Lake

APRIL, 1982:

1 HOUSTON, TX - Jesse H. Jones Hall: Swan Lake

2 FORT WORTH, TX - Tarrant County Convention Centre: La Sylphide; Don Quixote pdd; Dying Swan; Elite Syncopations - *repeated, April 3 (Etudes substituted for Elite), 4★ (Four Schumann Pieces substituted for Elite)*

MAY, 1982:

5 TORONTO, ON - O'Keefe Centre: Napoli - *repeated, May 6★, 6, 7, 8★, 8, 9★*

12 Four Last Songs - (First Song)†; Monotones II; Dream pdd; Portrait of Love and Death; Kermesse in Bruges pdd†; Three Easy Tangos - (excerpts from 'Late Afternoon'); Adagio†; Le Corsaire pdd; Manon pdd†; Etudes

13★ La Sylphide; Washington Square - *repeated, May 13, 14, 15★, 15, 16★*

19 Romeo & Juliet - *repeated, May 20★, 20, 21, 22★, 22, 23★*

26 LONDON, ON - Grand Theatre: La Fille Mal Gardée - *repeated, May 27★★, 27, 28*

29★ Four Schumann Pieces; Monotones II; Song of a Wayfarer; Etudes - *repeated, May 29*

JUNE, 1982:

1 OTTAWA, ON - National Arts Centre: Napoli - *repeated, June 2, 3★, 3*

4 Four Schumann Pieces; Nataraja; Los Siete Puñales - *repeated, June 5*

SEASON: 1982-3; **PERFORMANCES:** 135 (55 outside Toronto); **PREMIERES:** Canciones (Patsalas); Don Juan - revival (Neumeier); Don Quixote (Beriosoff after Petipa and Gorsky); Hedda (Kudelka); Offenbach in the Underworld - revival (Tudor); Quartet (Peters); Sphinx (Tetley).

AUGUST, 1982:

18 TORONTO, ON - Ontario Place: La Sylphide - *repeated, August 20*

24 LEWISTON, NY - Artpark: Giselle - *repeated, August 25★, 25*

26 Les Sylphides; Los Siete Puñales; Four Schumann Pieces - *repeated, August 27*

28 La Sylphide; Washington Square - *repeated, August 29★, 29*

SEPTEMBER, 1982:

16 MONTREAL, QC - Place des Arts: Napoli - *repeated, September 17, 18, 19*

21 FREDERICTON, NB - Playhouse Theatre: Giselle - *repeated, September 22*

24 CHARLOTTETOWN, PE - Confederation Centre: Giselle - *repeated, September 25*

27 SACKVILLE, NB - Convocation Hall: Kettentanz; Rite of Spring; Don Quixote - Act III

29★★ HALIFAX, NS - Rebecca Cohn Aud: Giselle - Act I - *repeated, September 29 (complete), 30 (complete)*

OCTOBER, 1982:
1★★ HALIFAX, NS - Rebecca Cohn Aud: Newcomers
1 Les Sylphides; Rite of Spring; Newcomers
2 Kettentanz; Los Siete Puñales; Don Quixote - Act III
6★★ ST JOHN'S, NF - Arts & Culture Centre: Giselle - *repeated, October 6, 7, 8★★, 8*
9 Les Sylphides; Los Siete Puñales; Newcomers
10★ Kettentanz; Three Easy Tangos; Le Corsaire pdd; Portrait of Love and Death; Don Quixote - Act III - *repeated, October 10*
17 HAMILTON, ON - Hamilton Place: Rite of Spring - *repeated, October 18*
NOVEMBER, 1982:
10 TORONTO, ON - O'Keefe Centre: Don Quixote - *repeated, November 11★, 11, 12, 13★, 13, 14★*
17 Kettentanz; Three Easy Tangos; Portrait of Love and Death; Le Corsaire pdd; Rite of Spring
18★ Rite of Spring; Los Siete Puñales; Elite Syncopations - *repeated, November 18*
19 Newcomers; Three Easy Tangos; Portrait of Love and Death; Le Corsaire pdd; Rite of Spring
20★ Newcomers; Le Spectre de la Rose; Song of a Wayfarer; Los Siete Puñales - *repeated, November 20*
21★ Kettentanz; Angali; Portrait of Love and Death; Le Corsaire pdd; Rite of Spring
24 Sleeping Beauty - *repeated, November 25★, 25, 26, 27★, 27, 28★*
DECEMBER, 1982:
14 OTTAWA, ON - National Arts Centre: Nutcracker - *repeated, December 15★, 15, 16, 17, 18★, 18*
21★ TORONTO, ON - O'Keefe Centre: Nutcracker - *repeated, December 21, 22, 23★, 23, 24★, 27★, 27, 28, 29★, 29, 30, 31★*
JANUARY, 1983:
2★ TORONTO, ON - O'Keefe Centre: Nutcracker - *repeated, January 2*
25 KITCHENER, ON - Centre in the Square: Kettentanz; Monotones II; Dying Swan; Song of a Wayfarer; Le Corsaire pdd; Napoli - dances from
26 Kettentanz; Angali; Don Juan pdd; Portrait of Love and Death; Don Quixote pdd; Napoli pas de six
28 WINDSOR, ON - Cleary Aud: Les Sylphides - excerpts; Le Corsaire pdd; Three Easy Tangos - excerpts from 'Late Afternoon'; Portrait of Love and Death; Don Quixote pdd; Napoli - dances from - *repeated, January 29★ (Romeo & Juliet pdd substituted for Three Easy Tangos excerpt)*
29 Canciones; Le Corsaire pdd; Three Easy Tangos - excerpts from 'Late Afternoon'; Don Juan pdd; Sleeping Beauty pdd; Napoli - dances from
30★ Canciones; Le Corsaire pdd; Monotones II; Romeo & Juliet pdd; Dying Swan; Portrait of Love and Death; Napoli - dances from
FEBRUARY, 1983:
3★ HAMILTON, ON - Hamilton Place: Kettentanz; Angali; Song of a Wayfarer; Le Corsaire pdd; Napoli - dances from - *repeated, February 3 (Monotones II substituted for Angali)*
4 Kettentanz; Canciones; Le Corsaire pdd; Nelligan†; Napoli - dances from
5 Kettentanz; Don Juan pdd; Le Corsaire pdd; Angali; Don Quixote pdd; Nelligan†; Napoli - dances from
9 TORONTO, ON - O'Keefe Centre: Coppélia - *repeated, February 10★★, 10, 11, 12★, 12, 13★*
16 Giselle - *repeated, February 17★, 17*
18 Dream; Hedda; Offenbach in the Underworld - *repeated, February 19★, 19, 20★*
23 Canciones; Quartet; Hedda; Offenbach in the Underworld - *repeated, February 24★ (Dream substituted for Canciones and Quartet), 24*
25 Giselle - *repeated, February 26★, 26, 27★*
APRIL, 1983:
19 OTTAWA, ON - National Arts Centre: Don Quixote - *repeated, April 20, 21*
22 Dream; Hedda; Offenbach in the Underworld - *repeated, April 23*
MAY, 1983:
4 TORONTO, ON - O'Keefe Centre: Swan Lake - *repeated, May 5★, 5, 6, 7★, 7, 8★*
11 Collective Symphony; Sphinx; Don Juan - *repeated, May 12★, 12, 13 (Nataraja substituted for Collective), 14★ (Nataraja substituted for Collective), 14, 15★ (Nataraja substituted for Collective)*
18 Napoli - *repeated, May 19★, 19, 20, 21★, 21, 22★*

SEASON: 1983-4; **PERFORMANCES:** 147 (59 outside Toronto); **PREMIERES:** Components (McFall); Endangered Species (Grossman); Here We Come (Bruhn); Khatchaturian Pas de Deux (Allan); L'Ile Inconnue (Patsalas); La Bayadère - Act II Kingdom of the Shades (Petipa staged by Makarova); Mobile (Ruud); Oiseaux Exotiques (Patsalas); Onegin (Cranko reproduced and staged by Anderson); Sylvia pdd (staged by Lland after Balanchine and Eglevsky).

AUGUST, 1983:
2 TORONTO, ON - Ontario Place: Offenbach in the Underworld; Sleeping Beauty - Act III Grand pdd; Napoli - Act III, dances from
3★ Napoli - Act III, dances from; Offenbach in the Underworld - *repeated, August 3, 10★, 10*
16 LEWISTON, NY - Artpark: Don Quixote - *repeated, August 17, 18★, 18*
19 Coppélia - *repeated, August 20, 21★, 21*
SEPTEMBER, 1983:
6 QUEBEC CITY, QC - Le Grand Théâtre de Québec: Don Quixote - *repeated, September 7*
8 MONTREAL, QC - Place des Arts: Don Quixote - *repeated, September 9, 10*
14 WINNIPEG, MB - Manitoba Centennial Concert Hall: Don Quixote - *repeated, September 15*
17 REGINA, SK - Sask. Centre of the Arts: Don Quixote - *repeated, September 18*
20 SASKATOON, SK - Saskatoon Centennial Aud: Don Quixote - *repeated, September 21*
23 CALGARY, AB - Jubilee Aud: Don Quixote - *repeated, September 24★, 24*
25 EDMONTON, AB - Jubilee Aud: Don Quixote - *repeated, September 26*
28 LETHBRIDGE, AB - Performing Arts Centre: Canciones; Romeo & Juliet pdd; Angali; Don Quixote pdd; Napoli - dances from
30 VICTORIA, BC - Royal Theatre: Les Sylphides; Canciones; Offenbach in the Underworld
OCTOBER, 1983:
1★ VICTORIA, BC - Royal Theatre: Les Sylphides; Canciones; Offenbach in the Underworld - *repeated, October 1*
4 VANCOUVER, BC - Queen Elizabeth Theatre: Don Quixote - *repeated, October 5*
6 Les Sylphides; Canciones; Offenbach in the Underworld
7 Don Quixote - *repeated, October 8a*
8b FORT MCMURRAY, AB - Keyano Theatre: Canciones; Romeo & Juliet pdd; Angali; Don Quixote pdd; Napoli - dances from
NOVEMBER, 1983:
9 TORONTO, ON - O'Keefe Centre: Romeo & Juliet - *repeated, November 10★★, 10, 11, 12★, 12, 13★*
16 Here We Come; Sylvia pdd; L'Ile Inconnue; Elite Syncopations - *repeated, November 17★, 17, 18, 19★, 19, 20★*
23 Don Quixote - *repeated, November 24★, 24, 25, 26★, 26, 27★*

DECEMBER, 1983:
13 KITCHENER, ON - The Centre in the Square: Nutcracker - *repeated, December 14, 15★, 15, 16, 17★, 17*
20★ TORONTO, ON - O'Keefe Centre: Nutcracker - *repeated, December 20, 21, 22★, 22, 23★, 23, 26, 27★, 27, 28, 29★, 29, 30★, 30*

JANUARY, 1984:
9 HAMILTON, BERMUDA - City Hall Theatre: Napoli - dances from; Coppélia - Wedding pdd; Don Juan pdd; Khatchaturian Pas de Deux; Elite Syncopations - *repeated, January 10*
11 Song of a Wayfarer; Sylvia pdd; Romeo & Juliet pdd; Sleeping Beauty - Act III pdd; Napoli - dances from - *repeated, January 12*

FEBRUARY, 1984:
8 TORONTO, ON - O'Keefe Centre: La Fille Mal Gardée - *repeated, February 9★, 9, 10, 11★, 11, 12★*
15 Serenade; Endangered Species; Components; Etudes - *repeated, February 16★, 16, 17*
18 Master Class†; Curious Schools of Theatrical Dancing: Part I - 1977†; Mobile; In Paradisum - First Movement from†; S'Agapo†; L'Hôtel perdu†; Exit, Nightfall - Miserere from†; Sinatra Suite†; Sleeping Beauty - Act III
19★ Serenade; Endangered Species; Components; Etudes
22 Swan Lake - *repeated, February 23★, 23, 24, 25★, 25, 26★*
29 OTTAWA, ON - National Arts Centre: Romeo & Juliet

MARCH, 1984:
1 OTTAWA, ON - National Arts Centre: Romeo & Juliet - *repeated, March 2, 3★, 3*
7 SAULT STE MARIE, ON - White Pines Aud: Napoli - dances from; Coppélia - Wedding pdd; Don Juan pdd; Khatchaturian Pas de Deux; Elite Syncopations
19 WEST PALM BEACH, FL - West Palm Beach Aud: Don Quixote - *repeated, March 20, 21★, 21*
22 Giselle
23 Here We Come; Sylvia pdd; L'Ile Inconnue; Elite Syncopations - *repeated, March 24★*
24 Giselle

APRIL, 1984:
25 TORONTO, ON - O'Keefe Centre: Giselle - *repeated, April 26★, 26, 27, 28★, 28, 29★*

MAY, 1984:
2 TORONTO, ON - O'Keefe Centre: La Bayadère - Act II; Sphinx; Oiseaux Exotiques - *repeated, May 3★, 3, 4, 5★, 5, 6★*
9 Sleeping Beauty - *repeated, May 10★, 10, 11, 12★, 12, 13★*
14 Onegin - *repeated, May 15, 16★, 16, 17★, 17*

SEASON: 1984-5; **PERFORMANCES:** 145 (78 outside Toronto); **PREMIERES:** Blue Snake (Desrosiers); Concerto for the Elements: Piano Concerto (Patsalas); The Four Temperaments - revival (Balanchine, staged by Dunleavy); Raymonda - Act III (Westmoreland after Petipa); Realm (Earle); Symphony in C (Balanchine, staged by Dunleavy).

AUGUST, 1984:
2 TORONTO, ON - Ontario Place: Here We Come; Sylvia pdd; Oiseaux Exotiques - *repeated, August 3★, 3, 10★, 10, 11★, 11*

SEPTEMBER, 1984:
5 MONTREAL, QC - Place des Arts: Here We Come; Sylvia pdd; L'Ile Inconnue; Elite Syncopations
6 Coppélia - *repeated, September 7, 8*
11 FREDERICTON, NB - Playhouse Theatre: Coppélia - *repeated, September 12★★, 12*
14 CHARLOTTETOWN, PE - Confederation Centre: Coppélia - *repeated, September 15*
17 SACKVILLE, NB - Convocation Hall: Canciones; Mobile; Swan Lake - Black Swan pdd; Oiseaux Exotiques
19 HALIFAX, NS - Rebecca Cohn Aud: Here We Come; Sylvia pdd; L'Ile Inconnue; Elite Syncopations - *repeated, September 20, 21★★ (without L'Ile Inconnue)*
21 Canciones; Mobile; Le Corsaire pdd; Oiseaux Exotiques - *repeated, September 22 (Black Swan pdd substituted for Corsaire)*
24 CORNER BROOK, NF - Arts & Culture Centre: Canciones; Mobile; Le Corsaire pdd; Elite Syncopations
26★ ST JOHN'S, NF - Arts & Culture Centre: Coppélia - *repeated, September 26, 27, 28★★, 28*
29 Here We Come; Sylvia pdd; L'Ile Inconnue; Elite Syncopations
30★ Canciones; Mobile; Swan Lake - Black Swan pdd; Oiseaux Exotiques - *repeated, September 30*

OCTOBER, 1984:
12 OTTAWA, ON - National Arts Centre: Here We Come; Sylvia pdd; L'Ile Inconnue; Elite Syncopations - *repeated, October 13*
31 HAMILTON, ON - Hamilton Place: Coppélia

NOVEMBER, 1984:
1 HAMILTON, ON - Hamilton Place: Coppélia - *repeated, November 2*
7 TORONTO, ON - O'Keefe Centre: Coppélia - *repeated, November 8★★ (Act I only), 8, 9, 10★, 10, 11★*
14 Serenade; Four Temperaments; Symphony in C - *repeated, November 15★★ (Symphony in C only), 15, 16, 17★, 17, 18★*
22 Components; La Sylphide - *repeated, November 23, 24★, 24, 25★*

DECEMBER, 1984:
11 OTTAWA, ON - National Arts Centre: Nutcracker - *repeated, December 12, 13★, 13, 14, 15★, 15*
18 HAMILTON, ON - Hamilton Place: Nutcracker - *repeated, December 19, 20★★, 20, 21, 22★, 22*
26 TORONTO, ON - O'Keefe Centre: Nutcracker - *repeated, December 27★, 27, 28, 29★, 29, 30★, 30*

JANUARY, 1985:
2 TORONTO, ON - O'Keefe Centre: Nutcracker - *repeated, January 3★, 3, 4, 5★, 5, 6★, 6*

FEBRUARY, 1985:
20 TORONTO, ON - O'Keefe Centre: Napoli - *repeated, February 21★★ (Act III only), 21, 22, 23★, 23, 24★*
27 Les Sylphides; Canciones; Blue Snake - *repeated, February 28*

MARCH, 1985:
1 TORONTO, ON - O'Keefe Centre: Les Sylphides; Canciones; Blue Snake - *repeated, March 2★, 2, 3★*
5 KITCHENER, ON - Centre in the Square: Don Quixote
7 WINDSOR, ON - Cleary Aud: Don Quixote - *repeated, March 8, 9★, 9*
13 OTTAWA, ON - National Arts Centre: Onegin - *repeated, March 14, 15, 16★, 16*

APRIL, 1985:
24 TORONTO, ON - O'Keefe Centre: Romeo & Juliet - *repeated, April 25, 26, 27★, 27, 28★*

MAY, 1985:
1 TORONTO, ON - O'Keefe Centre: Piano Concerto; Realm; Raymonda - Act III - *repeated, May 2, 3, 4★, 4, 5★*
13 LUXEMBOURG, BELGIUM - Nouveau Théâtre Municipal Luxembourg: Don Quixote - *repeated, May 14*
17 BERLIN, W. GERMANY - Internationales Congress Centrum Berlin: Don Quixote
18 L'Ile Inconnue; Sphinx; Elite Syncopations
20 LUDWIGSHAFEN, GERMANY - Theater am Pfalzbau: Don Quixote
21 L'Ile Inconnue; Sphinx; Elite Syncopations

22 Don Quixote
23 LEVERKUSEN, GERMANY - Forum: Don Quixote
25 WIESBADEN, GERMANY - Hessisches Staatstheater Wiesbaden: Don Quixote
26 Canciones; Coppélia pdd; Components; Raymonda - Act III
28 ZURICH, SWITZERLAND - Opernhaus Zürich: Don Quixote - *repeated, April 29*

JUNE, 1985:
2 STUTTGART, GERMANY - Württembergisches Staatstheater: Don Quixote
3 Canciones; Components; Raymonda - Act III
6 MUNICH, GERMANY - Bayerische Staatsoper: Don Quixote
7 Canciones; Components; Raymonda - Act III
12 MILAN, ITALY - Teatro Lirico: Don Quixote - *repeated, June 13, 14*
15 Canciones; Components; Elite Syncopations - *repeated, June 16*
17 Don Quixote - *repeated, June 18*
21 AMSTERDAM, NETHERLANDS - Theatre Carré: Don Quixote
22 L'Ile Inconnue; Components; Raymonda - Act III

SEASON: 1985-6; **PERFORMANCES:** 122 (48 outside Toronto); **PREMIERES:** Alice (Tetley); Capriccio (Allan); Don Quixote - new production (Beriosoff after Petipa and Gorsky); Etc! (Allan); Hot House: Thriving on a Riff (Grossman); On Occasion (Allan); Pastel (Allan); Reminiscence (Amyôt); Sinfonia (Patsalas); Transfigured Night (Kylian); Villanella (Allan).

AUGUST, 1985:
7* TORONTO, ON - Ontario Place: Raymonda - Act III; Pastel; Capriccio; Blue Snake - excerpts - *repeated, August 7 (Sinfonia substituted for Capriccio), 8, 9* (Sinfonia substituted for Capriccio), 9, 10*, 10 (Sinfonia substituted for Capriccio)*
27 LEWISTON, NY - Artpark: Onegin - *repeated, August 28*
29* Components; Canciones; Raymonda - Act III - *repeated, August 29, 30*
31 Onegin

SEPTEMBER, 1985:
1* LEWISTON, NY - Artpark: Onegin - *repeated, September 1*
10 OTTAWA, ON - National Arts Centre: Components; Canciones; Blue Snake - *repeated, September 11*
17 SAULT STE. MARIE, ON - White Pines Collegiate Aud: On Occasion; Coppélia - Wedding pdd; Canciones; Reminiscence; Le Corsaire pdd; Etc!
21 VICTORIA, BC - Royal Theatre: On Occasion; Reminiscence; Coppélia - Wedding pdd; Villanella; Le Corsaire pdd; Raymonda - Act III - *repeated, September 22*, 22*
25 VANCOUVER, BC - Queen Elizabeth Theatre: Onegin - *repeated, September 26, 27, 28*
29* Components; Coppélia - Wedding pdd; Villanella; Sleeping Beauty - Act III pdd; Raymonda - Act III

OCTOBER, 1985:
2 CALGARY, AB - Jubilee Aud: Onegin - *repeated, October 3, 4*
6 LETHBRIDGE, AB - University Theatre: On Occasion; Coppélia - Wedding pdd; Raymonda - Act III; Reminiscence; Le Corsaire pdd; Etc!
7 EDMONTON, AB - Jubilee Aud: Onegin - *repeated, October 8, 9*
11 FORT MCMURRAY, AB - Keyano Theatre: On Occasion; Coppélia - Wedding pdd; Raymonda - Act III; Reminiscence; Le Corsaire pdd; Etc!

NOVEMBER, 1985:
6 TORONTO, ON - O'Keefe Centre: Don Quixote - *repeated, November 7** (Acts I & III only), 7, 8, 9*, 9, 10**
13 L'Ile Inconnue; Sphinx; Elite Syncopations - *repeated, November 14** (without Sphinx), 14, 15, 16*, 16, 17*
19 Onegin - *repeated, November 20, 21, 22, 23*, 23, 24*, 24*

DECEMBER, 1985:
17 HAMILTON, ON - Hamilton Place: Nutcracker - *repeated, December 18, 19*, 19, 20, 21*, 21*
24* TORONTO, ON - O'Keefe Centre: Nutcracker - *repeated, December 26*, 26, 27, 28*, 28, 29*, 29, 31**

JANUARY, 1986:
2* TORONTO, ON - O'Keefe Centre: Nutcracker - *repeated, January 2, 3, 4*, 4, 5*, 5*
8 BELLEVILLE, ON - Centennial S.S. Aud: On Occasion; Coppélia - Wedding pdd; Canciones; Reminiscence; Swan Lake - Black Swan pdd; Etc!
17 THUNDER BAY, ON - Thunder Bay Community Aud: On Occasion - excerpts; Coppélia - Wedding pdd; Canciones - excerpts; Reminiscence - excerpts; Swan Lake - Black Swan pdd; Etc!

FEBRUARY, 1986:
19 TORONTO, ON - O'Keefe Centre: La Bayadère - Act II; Alice - *repeated, February 20, 21, 22*, 22, 23**
26 La Fille Mal Gardée - *repeated, February 27**, 27, 28*

MARCH, 1986:
1* TORONTO, ON - O'Keefe Centre: La Fille Mal Gardée - *repeated, March 1, 2**
6 HAMILTON, ON - Hamilton Place: Don Quixote - *repeated, March 7, 8*
12 LONDON, ON - Grand Theatre: Don Quixote - *repeated, March 13, 14, 15*, 15*
25 OTTAWA, ON - National Arts Centre: La Fille Mal Gardée - *repeated, March 26**, 26, 27*

APRIL, 1986:
30 TORONTO, ON - O'Keefe Centre: Hot House: Thriving on a Riff; Transfigured Night; Dream

MAY, 1986:
1** TORONTO, ON - O'Keefe Centre: Hot House: Thriving on a Riff; Dream
1 Hot House: Thriving on a Riff; Transfigured Night; Dream - *repeated, May 2, 3*, 3, 4*
7 Swan Lake - *repeated, May 8, 9, 10*, 10, 11*, 11*
21 A Tribute to Erik Bruhn; Realm - excerpt; Piano Concerto - excerpt; Blue Snake - excerpt; Components - excerpt; Oiseaux Exotiques - excerpts; Villanella - excerpt; Alice - excerpt; Hot House: Thriving on a Riff - excerpt; L'Ile Inconnue - excerpt; Dying Swan*; La Sylphide - excerpt

JUNE, 1986:
1* TORONTO, ON - Joey & Toby Tanenbaum Opera Centre: A Tribute to John Goss; Boy's Ballet Demonstration (NBSch)†; Angali; Kinderen Variations (NBSch)†; Bits and Pieces† (NBC Workshop Repertory); Nutcracker - Act II pdd; Dream pdd; Recital† (NBC Workshop Repertory); Oiseaux Exotiques - excerpts; La Fille Mal Gardée pdd

---

SEASON: 1986-7; **PERFORMANCES:** 159 (70 outside Toronto); **PREMIERES:** Inner Drop (Dawson); Lost in Twilight (Patsalas); Masada (Allan); The Merry Widow (Hynd, scenario by Helpmann); Overture: A Dance for a Celebration (curtain-raiser for 35th Anniversary Celebration) (Desrosiers); Tuwat (Jörgen).

JULY, 1986:
22 NEW YORK, NY - Metropolitan Opera House: Hot House: Thriving on a Riff; Angali; Alice - *repeated, July 23, 24, 25, 26*, 26 (with Villanella added), 27* (with Villanella added)*

30★ TORONTO, ON - Ontario Place: Swan Lake - Act I, Scene 2; Elite Syncopations
30 Swan Lake - Act I, Scene 2; Khatchaturian Pas de Deux; Hot House: Thriving on a Riff - *repeated, July 31*

AUGUST, 1986:
1★ TORONTO, ON - Ontario Place: Swan Lake - Act I, Scene 2; Khatchaturian Pas de Deux; Hot House: Thriving on a Riff
1 Swan Lake - Act I, Scene 2; Elite Syncopations - *repeated, August 2★*
2 Swan Lake - Act I, Scene 2; Khatchaturian Pas de Deux; Hot House: Thriving on a Riff
14 VANCOUVER, BC - Queen Elizabeth Theatre: (with RWB and Les Grands Ballets Canadiens); Collisions (Les Grands)†; Lost in Twilight; Steps (RWB)† - *repeated, August 15, 16, 16★*
22 VIENNA, VA - Wolftrap Park: (with Les Grands Ballets Canadiens and RWB); Lost in Twilight; Collisions (Les Grands)†; Steps (RWB)† - *repeated, August 23, 24*

SEPTEMBER, 1986:
12 ORILLIA, ON - Orillia Opera House: On Occasion; Angali; Canciones; Don Quixote pdd; Inner Drop; Etc!
13 OSHAWA, ON - Eastdale Aud: On Occasion; Angali; Canciones; Don Quixote pdd; Inner Drop; Etc!
23 FREDERICTON, NB - Playhouse Theatre: Don Quixote - *repeated, September 24★ (Acts I and III only), 24*
26 CHARLOTTETOWN, PE - Confederation Centre: Don Quixote - *repeated, September 27*
29 SACKVILLE, NB - Convocation Hall: Swan Lake - Act I, Scene 2; Transfigured Night; Khatchaturian Pas de Deux; Hot House: Thriving on a Riff

OCTOBER, 1986:
1 HALIFAX, NS - Rebecca Cohn Aud: Swan Lake - Act I, Scene 2; Transfigured Night; Khatchaturian Pas de Deux; Hot House: Thriving on a Riff - *repeated, October 2★ (without Transfigured Night, Etc! substituted for Hot House), 2*
3 On Occasion; Les Sylphides pdd; Angali; Reminiscence; Don Quixote - Act III - *repeated, October 4*
6 CORNER BROOK, NF - Arts & Culture Centre: On Occasion; Angali; Transfigured Night; Don Quixote pdd; Reminiscence; Etc!
8★★ ST JOHN'S, NF - Arts & Culture Centre: Don Quixote - Acts I & III - *repeated, October 8 (complete), 9 (complete), 10★★ (Acts I & II), 10*
11 Swan Lake - Act I, Scene 2; Transfigured Night; Angali; Hot House: Thriving on a Riff
12 GANDER, NF - Arts & Culture Centre: On Occasion; Don Quixote pdd; Transfigured Night; Angali; Reminiscence; Etc!

NOVEMBER, 1986:
7 TORONTO, ON - O'Keefe Centre: Merry Widow - *repeated, November 8, 9★, 11, 12, 13★★, 13, 14, 15★, 15, 16★*
19 Concerto for the Elements: Piano Concerto; Song of a Wayfarer; Etudes
20 Giselle - *repeated, November 21*
22★ Concerto for the Elements: Piano Concerto; Song of a Wayfarer; Etudes - *repeated, November 22, 23★*
25 Giselle - *repeated, November 26★★, 26*
27 Concerto for the Elements: Piano Concerto; Song of a Wayfarer; Etudes - *repeated, November 28*
29★ Giselle - *repeated, November 29, 30★*

DECEMBER, 1986:
17 TORONTO, ON - O'Keefe Centre: Nutcracker - *repeated, December 18, 19, 20★, 20, 21★, 21, 23★, 23, 24★, 27★, 27, 28★, 28, 29, 30★, 30, 31★*

JANUARY, 1987:
2★ TORONTO, ON - O'Keefe Centre: Nutcracker - *repeated, January 2*
12 HAMILTON, BERMUDA - City Hall Theatre: On Occasion; Les Sylphides pdd; Transfigured Night; Inner Drop; Swan Lake - Black Swan pdd; Etc!
13 Canciones; Coppélia pdd; Reminiscence; Monotones II; Don Quixote pdd; Tuwat
14 On Occasion; Les Sylphides pdd; Transfigured Night; Inner Drop; Swan Lake - Black Swan pdd; Etc!
15 Canciones; Coppélia pdd; Reminiscence; Monotones II; Don Quixote pdd; Tuwat

FEBRUARY, 1987:
11 TORONTO, ON - O'Keefe Centre: Coppélia - *repeated, February 12★★, 12, 13, 14★, 14, 15★, 15*
18 Serenade; Four Temperaments; Symphony in C - *repeated, February 19★★ (without Serenade), 19, 20, 21★, 21, 22★*
25 (35th Anniversary Celebration) Overture; Etude; Offenbach in the Underworld pdd; Barbara Allen - excerpt; Pas de Deux (Spain); Mad Shadows - excerpt; Washington Square - excerpt; Polovetsian Dances - excerpt; Impromptu†; Don Quixote pdd; Song of a Wayfarer
26 Here We Come; Monotones II; Transfigured Night; Raymonda - Act III - *repeated, February 27, 28★, 28*

MARCH, 1987:
1 TORONTO, ON - O'Keefe Centre: Here We Come; Monotones II; Transfigured Night; Raymonda - Act III
13 MINNEAPOLIS, MN - Northrop Memorial Aud: Serenade; Alice
14★ Coppélia - *repeated, March 14*
16 CHICAGO, IL - Auditorium Theatre: Serenade; Swan Lake - White Swan pdd†; Alice - *repeated, March 17*
21★ MIAMI, FL - Dade County Aud: Coppélia - *repeated, March 21*
22★ Serenade; Alice - *repeated, March 22*
24★ CLEARWATER, FL - Ruth Eckerd Hall: Coppélia - *repeated, March 24, 25★*
25 Serenade; Alice
27★ WEST PALM BEACH, FL - West Palm Beach Aud: Coppélia - *repeated, March 27*
28★ Serenade; Alice - *repeated, March 28*
31 WASHINGTON, DC - Kennedy Centre: Serenade; Alice

APRIL, 1987:
1 WASHINGTON, DC - Kennedy Centre: Merry Widow
2 Serenade; Alice - *repeated, April 3*
4★ Merry Widow - *repeated, April 4, 5★*
22 TORONTO, ON - O'Keefe Centre: Sleeping Beauty - *repeated, April 23, 24, 25★, 25, 26★, 28, 29*
2★ Les Sylphides; Masada; Blue Snake

MAY, 1987:
2 TORONTO, ON - O'Keefe Centre: Les Sylphides; Masada; Blue Snake - *repeated, May 3★, 5, 6★★ (without Masada), 6, 7, 8*
21 MONTREAL, QC - Place des Arts: Merry Widow - *repeated, May 22, 23*
27 OTTAWA, ON - National Arts Centre: Merry Widow - *repeated, May 28, 29, 30*

SEASON: 1987-8; **PERFORMANCES:** 156 (65 outside Toronto); **PREMIERES:** Concerto (MacMillan, staged by Wallis); Concerto Barocco - revival (Balanchine, staged by Simon); Death of a Lady's Man (Allan); Forgotten Land (Kylián); La Ronde (Tetley); Song of the Earth (MacMillan); Voluntaries (Tetley).

JUNE, 1987:
30 LONDON, ENGLAND - Coliseum: Serenade; Alice

JULY, 1987:
1 LONDON, ENGLAND - Coliseum: Serenade; Alice - *repeated, July 2, 3, 4★, 4*
29 LEWISTON, NY - Artpark: Merry Widow - *repeated, July 30, 31*

AUGUST, 1987:

1 LEWISTON, NY - Artpark: Merry Widow - *repeated, August 2★*

6★ TORONTO, ON - Ontario Place: Les Sylphides; Sleeping Beauty - Act III - *repeated, August 6, 7, 8★, 8*

SEPTEMBER, 1987:

12 TAMPA, FL - Tampa Bay Performing Arts Centre: Elite Syncopations - *repeated, September 13★*

17 THUNDER BAY, ON - Thunder Bay Community Aud: Merry Widow - *repeated, September 18*

21 WINNIPEG, MB - Manitoba Centennial Concert Hall: Merry Widow - *repeated, September 22, 23★, 23*

25 REGINA, SK - Sask. Centre of the Arts: Merry Widow - *repeated, September 26*

28 SASKATOON, SK - Saskatoon Centennial Aud: Merry Widow - *repeated, September 29*

OCTOBER, 1987:

1 CALGARY, AB - Jubilee Aud: Merry Widow - *repeated, October 2, 3*

5 EDMONTON, AB - Jubilee Aud: Merry Widow - *repeated, October 6, 7*

10 VANCOUVER, BC - Queen Elizabeth Theatre: Merry Widow - *repeated, October 11, 12, 13, 14*

NOVEMBER, 1987:

6 TORONTO, ON - O'Keefe Centre: Concerto Barocco; La Ronde; Concerto - *repeated, November 7★, 7, 8*

11 La Fille Mal Gardée - *repeated, November 12★★, 12, 13, 14★, 14, 15★*

18 Swan Lake - *repeated, November 19★★, 19, 20, 21★, 21, 22★*

24 Concerto Barocco; La Ronde; Concerto - *repeated, November 25, 26*

27 Swan Lake - *repeated, 28★, 28, 29★*

DECEMBER, 1987:

8 OTTAWA, ON - National Arts Centre: Nutcracker - *repeated, December 9, 10, 11, 12★, 12, 13*

15 TORONTO, ON - O'Keefe Centre: Nutcracker - *repeated, December 16, 17, 18, 19★, 19, 20★, 20, 22★, 22, 23★, 23, 26★, 26, 27★, 27, 29★, 29, 30*

JANUARY, 1988:

2★ TORONTO, ON - O'Keefe Centre: Nutcracker - *repeated, January 2, 3★*

24 CALGARY, AB - Jubilee Aud: Olympic Arts Festival with Les Grands Ballets Canadiens; Symphony in C (with Les Grands); Le Sacre du Printemps† (Les Grands); La Ronde - *repeated, January 25, 26*

FEBRUARY, 1988:

10 TORONTO, ON - O'Keefe Centre: La Bayadère - Act II; Forgotten Land; Elite Syncopations - *repeated, February 11, 12, 13★, 13, 14*

17 Don Quixote - *repeated, February 18★★, 18, 19, 20★, 20, 21★, 21*

24 Components; Reminiscence; Dream

25★★ Dream

25 Components; Reminiscence; Dream - *repeated, February 26, 27★, 27, 28★*

MARCH, 1988:

24 OTTAWA, ON - National Arts Centre: Four Temperaments; Alice - *repeated, March 25, 26*

APRIL, 1988:

28 TORONTO, ON - O'Keefe Centre: Four Temperaments; Voluntaries; Song of the Earth - *repeated, April 29, 30★, 30*

MAY, 1988:

1 TORONTO, ON - O'Keefe Centre: Four Temperaments; Voluntaries; Song of the Earth

4 Onegin - *repeated, May 5★★, 5, 6, 7★, 7, 8★*

10 Four Temperaments; Voluntaries; Song of the Earth - *repeated, May 11, 12*

13 Onegin

14 First Erik Bruhn Competition; Swan Lake - Act II Black Swan pdd (National Ballet of Canada); Don Quixote - Act III Grand pdd† (Royal Ballet - England); La Sylphide - Act II pdd† (Royal Danish Ballet); Sleeping Beauty - Act III pdd† (American Ballet Theatre); Four Seasons - Summer† (Royal Ballet - England); Four Seasons - Autumn† (Royal Ballet - England); Romeo & Juliet - Act I pdd† (American Ballet Theatre); Blue Snake - Balloon Head Solo (National Ballet of Canada); Rite of Spring (Tetley)† - Dance of the Chosen One (National Ballet of Canada); Leaves Are Fading† (Royal Danish Ballet); Swan Lake - White Swan pdd† - Special Appearance by Natalia Makarova; Voluntaries

15 Onegin

26 SAN DIEGO, CA - Civic Aud: Onegin - *repeated, May 27*

28★ Four Temperaments; Alice - *repeated, May 28*

30 PASADENA, CA - Pasadena Civic Aud: Onegin - *repeated, May 31*

JUNE, 1988:

1 PASADENA, CA - Pasadena Civic Aud: Onegin - *repeated, June 2*

4 Four Temperaments; Alice - *repeated, June 5★, 5*

7 COSTA MESA, CA - Orange County Perf. Arts Centre: Four Temperaments; Alice - *repeated, June 8, 9*

10 Onegin - *repeated, June 11, 11★, 12★*

SEASON: 1988-9; **PERFORMANCES:** 151 (54 outside Toronto); **PREMIERES:** Blue-Eyed Trek (Alleyne); Daphnis and Chloe (Tetley); Diana and Acteon Pas de Deux (Vaganova, staged by Bujones); Have Steps Will Travel (Alleyne); Steptext (Forsythe); Tagore (Tetley); Trapdance (Alleyne).

JULY, 1988:

18 NEW YORK, NY - Metropolitan Opera House: La Ronde; Blue Snake

19 Onegin - *repeated, July 20★, 20*

21 La Ronde; Blue Snake - *repeated, July 22*

23★ Onegin - *repeated, July 23*

AUGUST, 1988:

11★ TORONTO, ON - Ontario Place: La Bayadère - Act II; Concerto - *repeated, August 11, 12, 13★, 13, 14★, 14*

SEPTEMBER, 1988:

11 SAINT JOHN, NB - Saint John High School Aud: Concerto Barocco; Concerto pdd; Trapdance; Sleeping Beauty - Act III pdd; Death of a Lady's Man; Etc!

13 FREDERICTON, NB - Playhouse Theatre: Serenade; Trapdance; Sleeping Beauty - Act III pdd - *repeated, September 14*

16 CHARLOTTETOWN, PE - Confederation Centre: Serenade; Trapdance; Sleeping Beauty - Act III pdd - *repeated, September 17*

19 SACKVILLE, NB - Convocation Hall: Serenade; Trapdance; Sleeping Beauty - Act III pdd

21 HALIFAX, NS - Rebecca Cohn Aud: Serenade; Trapdance; Sleeping Beauty - Act III pdd - *repeated, September 22★★ (without Trapdance), 22*

23 La Bayadère - Act II; Four Temperaments; Concerto - *repeated, September 24*

26 CORNER BROOK, NF - Arts & Culture Centre: Concerto Barocco; Concerto pdd; Trapdance; Sleeping Beauty - Act III pdd; Death of a Lady's Man; Etc!

28★★ ST JOHN'S, NF - Arts & Culture Centre: Serenade; Sleeping Beauty - Act III pdd - *repeated, September 28 (with Trapdance added), 29 (with Trapdance added)*

30★★ La Bayadère - Act II; Concerto - *repeated, September 30 (with Four Temperaments added)*

OCTOBER, 1988:

1 ST JOHN'S, NF - Arts & Culture Centre: La Bayadère - Act II; Four Temperaments; Concerto

6 MONTREAL, QC - Place des Arts: La Ronde; Blue Snake - *repeated, October 7, 8*

NOVEMBER, 1988:

9 TORONTO, ON - O'Keefe Centre: Sleeping Beauty - *repeated, November 10★★, 10, 11, 12★, 12, 13★*

16 Serenade; Alice - *repeated, November 17, 18, 19★, 19, 20★*

23 Symphony in C; Have Steps Will Travel; Blue Snake - *repeated, November 24★★, 24, 25, 26★, 26, 27★, 27*

29 Kain Gala; Proust pdd†: Echo†; Sleeping Beauty - Act III

30 Sleeping Beauty

DECEMBER, 1988:

1★★ TORONTO, ON - O'Keefe Centre: Sleeping Beauty - *repeated, December 1, 2★, 2*

13 Nutcracker - *repeated, December 14, 15★★, 15, 16, 17★, 17, 18★, 18, 20★, 20, 21, 22★, 22, 23, 24★, 27★, 27, 28*

FEBRUARY, 1989:

8 TORONTO, ON - O'Keefe Centre: Romeo & Juliet - *repeated, February 9★★, 9, 10, 11★, 11, 12★, 12*

15 Four Temperaments; Daphnis & Chloe - *repeated, February 16, 17, 18★, 18, 19★, 19*

22 Concerto Barocco; Diana & Acteon Pas de Deux; Steptext; Etudes - *repeated, February 23★★ (without Barocco, Diana & Acteon), 23, 24, 25★, 25, 26★, 26*

MARCH, 1989:

15 TAMPA, FL - Festival Hall: La Ronde; Blue Snake - *repeated, March 16*

17 Merry Widow - *repeated, March 18★, 18, 19*

APRIL, 1989:

19 OTTAWA, ON - National Arts Centre: Steptext; La Ronde; Etudes - *repeated, April 20, 21*

27 TORONTO, ON - O'Keefe Centre: Dream; Tagore - *repeated, April 28, 29★, 29, 30★*

MAY, 1989:

2 TORONTO, ON - O'Keefe Centre: Merry Widow - *repeated, May 3, 4★★, 4, 5, 6★, 6, 7★, 7, 9★, 9, 10*

11 Dream; Tagore - *repeated, May 12*

13 Bruhn Competition; Le Corsaire pdd (National Ballet of Canada); Agon pdd† (Royal Danish Ballet); Le Corsaire pdd† (Royal Ballet); Sphinx - Second Movement (National Ballet of Canada); Hommage a Bournonville pdd† (Royal Danish Ballet); Allegri Diversi† (Royal Ballet); La Ronde

14 Merry Widow

31 LEVERKUSEN, GERMANY - Forum: Four Temperaments; Alice

JUNE, 1989:

1 LEVERKUSEN, GERMANY - Forum: Serenade; Blue-Eyed Trek; La Ronde

3 BERLIN, W. GERMANY - Theater des Westens: Serenade; Blue-Eyed Trek; La Ronde - *repeated, June 4★, 4*

6 FRIEDRICHSHAFEN, GERMANY - Graf Zeppelin Haus: Serenade; Blue-Eyed Trek; La Ronde - *repeated, June 7*

10 DUSSELDORF, GERMANY - Deutsche Oper Am Rhein: Four Temperaments; Alice

11 Serenade; Blue-Eyed Trek; La Ronde

13 FRANKFURT, GERMANY - Jahrhunderthalle Höchst: Four Temperaments; Alice

15 HAMBURG, GERMANY - Hamburgische Staatsoper: Alice; La Ronde - *repeated, June 16*

18 KIEL, GERMANY - Opernhaus: Four Temperaments; Alice

19 Serenade; Blue-Eyed Trek; La Ronde

22 LUDWIGSBURG, GERMANY - Forum am Schlosspark: Serenade; Blue-Eyed Trek; La Ronde

23 Four Temperaments; Alice

SEASON: 1989-90; **PERFORMANCES:** 121 (20 outside Toronto); **PREMIERES:** Dream Dances (Kylián); The Envelope (Parsons); Gloria (MacMillan); The Need (Parsons); Pastorale (Kudelka); Sleep Study (Parsons); Split House Geometric (Alleyne).

AUGUST, 1989:

10 TORONTO, ON - Ontario Place: Serenade; Giselle - Peasant pas de quatre; Sleep Study; Le Corsaire pdd; Etc! - *repeated, August 11★, 11, 12★, 12*

SEPTEMBER, 1989:

23 SASKATOON, SK - Saskatoon Centennial Aud: La Bayadère - Act II; La Ronde; Napoli - Act III - *repeated, September 24*

29 CALGARY, AB - Southern Alberta Jubilee Aud: La Bayadère - Act II; La Ronde; Napoli - Act III - *repeated, September 30*

OCTOBER, 1989:

1 CALGARY, AB - Southern Alberta Jubilee Aud: La Bayadère - Act II; La Ronde; Napoli - Act III

4 EDMONTON, AB - Northern Alberta Jubilee Aud: La Bayadère - Act II; La Ronde; Napoli - Act III - *repeated, October 5*

6 WINNIPEG, MB - Manitoba Centennial Concert Hall: With Royal Winnipeg Ballet; Seventh Symphony† (RWB); Blue-Eyed Trek; Symphony in C (NBC & RWB) - *repeated, October 7★, 7, 8★*

10 VANCOUVER, BC - Queen Elizabeth Theatre: La Bayadère - Act II; La Ronde; Napoli - Act III - *repeated, October 11, 12, 13, 14*

NOVEMBER, 1989:

1 TORONTO, ON - O'Keefe Centre: Giselle - *repeated, November 2★★, 2, 3, 4★, 4, 5★*

8 La Bayadère - Act II; La Ronde; Dream Dances - *repeated, November 9, 10, 11★, 11, 12★, 12*

15 Napoli - *repeated, November 16★★ (Acts I & III only), 16, 17, 18★, 18, 19★*

21 Tennant Farewell Gala; Giselle - Act II pdd; Mad Shadows - excerpts; Washington Square - excerpts; Canciones - Nino Lullaby; Masada - Scene II, The Final Night - excerpts; Khatchaturian Pas de Deux; Taming of the Shrew - Act I pdd† ; Onegin - Act III

22 Giselle - *repeated, November 23★★, 23, 24★, 24*

30 With Royal Winnipeg Ballet; Seventh Symphony† (RWB); Blue-Eyed Trek; Symphony in C (NBC & RWB)

DECEMBER, 1989:

1★★ TORONTO, ON - O'Keefe Centre: With Royal Winnipeg Ballet; Piano Variations† (RWB); Envelope; Tarantella† (RWB); Symphony in C (NBC & RWB)

1 With Royal Winnipeg Ballet; Seventh Symphony† (RWB); Blue-Eyed Trek; Symphony in C (NBC & RWB) - *repeated, December 2*

19 Nutcracker - *repeated, December 20, 21★★, 21, 22, 23★, 23, 24★, 26, 27★, 27, 28, 29, 30★, 30*

31 Nutty Nutcracker

JANUARY, 1990:

3★ TORONTO, ON - O'Keefe Centre: Nutcracker - *repeated, January 3, 4, 5, 6★, 6, 7★, 7*

FEBRUARY, 1990:

14 TORONTO, ON - O'Keefe Centre: La Fille Mal Gardée - *repeated, February 15★★, 15, 16, 17★, 17, 18★*

21 Concerto; Transfigured Night; Gloria - *repeated, February 22, 23, 24★, 24, 25★*

28 Serenade; Need; Elite Syncopations

MARCH, 1990:

1★★ TORONTO, ON - O'Keefe Centre: Serenade; Elite Syncopations

1 Serenade; Need; Elite Syncopations - *repeated, March 2, 3★, 3, 4★, 4*

MAY, 1990:

2 TORONTO, ON - O'Keefe Centre: Swan Lake - *repeated, May 3**, 3, 4, 5*, 5, 6**

9 Les Sylphides; Pastorale; Voluntaries - *repeated, May 10, 11, 12*, 12, 13**

15 Swan Lake - *repeated, May 15**, 16, 17, 18*, 18, 19*

23 OTTAWA, ON - National Arts Centre: Swan Lake - *repeated, May 24, 25, 26*

SEASON: 1990-1; **PERFORMANCES:** 128 (25 outside Toronto); **PREMIERES:** Concerto for Flute and Harp (Cranko); The Leaves Are Fading (Tudor); Paquita (Makarova after Petipa); the second detail (Forsythe); Time Out With Lola (Alleyne); Troy Game (North).

AUGUST, 1990:

9 TORONTO, ON - Ontario Place: Dream Dances; Swan Lake - White Swan pdd; Don Quixote pdd; Troy Game - *repeated, August 10*, 10, 11*, 11*

21 LEWISTON, NY - Artpark: Don Quixote - *repeated, August 22, 23*, 23*

24 Dream Dances; Steptext; Etudes - *repeated, August 25, 26**

SEPTEMBER, 1990:

21 FREDERICTON, NB - Playhouse Theatre: Concerto for Flute and Harp; Steptext; Don Quixote pdd; Dream Dances - *repeated, September 22*

23 SACKVILLE, NB - Convocation Hall: Concerto for Flute and Harp; Steptext; Don Quixote pdd; Dream Dances

25 HALIFAX, NS - Rebecca Cohn Aud: Concerto for Flute and Harp; Steptext; Don Quixote pdd; Dream Dances - *repeated, September 26*

OCTOBER, 1990:

1 OTTAWA, ON - National Arts Centre: Concerto for Flute and Harp; Need; Dream Dances - *repeated, October 2, 3*

6 QUEBEC CITY, QC - Le Grand Théâtre de Québec: Concerto for Flute and Harp; Need; Dream Dances

11 MONTREAL, QC - Place des Arts: Onegin - *repeated, October 12, 13*

31 TORONTO, ON - O'Keefe Centre: Onegin

NOVEMBER, 1990:

1** TORONTO, ON - O'Keefe Centre: Onegin - *repeated, November 1, 2, 3*, 3, 4*, 4*

7 Don Quixote - *repeated, November 8, 8**, 9, 10*, 10, 11*, 11*

14 Leaves Are Fading; Steptext; Etudes - *repeated, November 15, 16, 17*, 17, 18**

20 Onegin - *repeated, November 21, 22**, 22, 23*, 23*

DECEMBER, 1990:

11 OTTAWA, ON - National Arts Centre: Nutcracker - *repeated, December 12, 13, 14, 15*, 15*

18** TORONTO, ON - O'Keefe Centre: Nutcracker - *repeated, December 18, 19, 20*, 20, 21, 22*, 22, 23*, 23, 26, 27*, 27, 28, 29*, 29, 30*, 30*

JANUARY, 1991:

2 TORONTO, ON - O'Keefe Centre: Nutcracker - *repeated, January 3*, 3, 4, 5*, 5, 6*, 6*

FEBRUARY, 1991:

13 TORONTO, ON - O'Keefe Centre: Coppélia - *repeated, February 14**, 14, 15, 16*, 16, 17**

20 Concerto Barocco; Sphinx; second detail - *repeated, February 21, 22, 23*, 23, 24*, 24*

27 Paquita; Song of the Earth - *repeated, February 28*

MARCH, 1991:

1 TORONTO, ON - O'Keefe Centre: Paquita; Song of the Earth - *repeated, March 2* 2, 3*, 3*

5 Paquita; Greek Dances†; Romeo & Juliet pdd; Hommage au Bolshoi†; Giselle - Act II pdd; In the Middle, Somewhat Elevated pdd†; Top Hat†; Défilé†

6 Coppélia - *repeated, March 7***

MAY, 1991:

1 TORONTO, ON - O'Keefe Centre: Time Out With Lola; Daphnis & Chloe - *repeated, May 2** (without Time Out), 2, 3, 4*, 4, 5**

9 Sleeping Beauty - *repeated, May 10, 11*, 11, 12*, 14*, 14, 15, 16** (Prologue, Act I, Awakening, & Act III only), 16, 17, 18, 19**

Appendix B
Concert Group Itinerary 1966–67 to 1990–91

SEASONS: 1966-7 to 1990-1; **PERFORMANCES:** 103 (101 outside Toronto); **WORKS PERFORMED BY CONCERT GROUPS ONLY:** Solo (Franca [1966-7]); The Arena (Strate [1968-9]); Célébrations (Poll [1968-9]); Pas de Deux (David Gordon [1968-9]); Tango from Façade (Ashton [1969-70]); Autumn Song (Jean-Paul Comelin [1971-2]); Grand Pas Classique (Gsovsky [1989-90]).

MAY, 1967:

8 OSHAWA, ON - Eastdale Collegiate Aud: One in Five; Concerto Barocco; Death and the Maiden; ‡Solo; Rondo Giocoso; EH!

9 ORILLIA, ON - Orillia Opera House: One in Five; Concerto Barocco; Death and the Maiden; ‡Solo; Rondo Giocoso; EH!

10 OAKVILLE, ON - White Oaks S.S. Aud: One in Five; Concerto Barocco; Death and the Maiden; ‡Solo; Rondo Giocoso; EH!

11 OWEN SOUND, ON - Owen Sound Collegiate Aud: One in Five; Concerto Barocco; Death and the Maiden; ‡Solo; Rondo Giocoso; EH!

17 GALT, ON - Galt Collegiate Institute, Tassie Hall: One in Five; Concerto Barocco; Death and the Maiden; ‡Solo; Rondo Giocoso; EH!

18 SARNIA, ON - Sarnia Collegiate Institute of Technology: One in Five; Concerto Barocco; Death and the Maiden; ‡Solo; Rondo Giocoso; EH!

19 SIMCOE, ON - Simcoe District Composite School: One in Five; Concerto Barocco; Death and the Maiden; ‡Solo; Rondo Giocoso; EH!

23 NIAGARA FALLS, ON - Niagara Falls Coll. Vocational Institute: One in Five; Concerto Barocco; Death and the Maiden; ‡Solo; Rondo Giocoso; EH!

26 OTTAWA, ON - Capitol Theatre: One in Five; Concerto Barocco; Death and the Maiden; ‡Solo; Rondo Giocoso; EH!

27 PEMBROKE, ON - Champlain High School Aud: One in Five; Concerto Barocco; Death and the Maiden; ‡Solo; Rondo Giocoso; EH!

SEPTEMBER, 1967:

12* HAILEYBURY, ON - St Mary's Academy Aud: One in Five; Studies in White; Death and the Maiden; ‡Solo; Rondo Giocoso; EH! - *repeated, September 12*

14* KIRKLAND LAKE, ON - Strand Theatre: One in Five; Studies in White; Rondo Giocoso; EH!

15* TIMMINS, ON - Timmins High School Aud: One in Five; Studies in White; Death and the Maiden; ‡Solo; Rondo Giocoso; EH!

15 KIRKLAND LAKE, ON - Strand Theatre: One in Five; Studies in White; Death and the Maiden; ‡Solo; Rondo Giocoso; EH!

16 KAPUSKASING, ON - Civic Centre: One in Five; Studies in White; Death and the Maiden; ‡Solo; Rondo Giocoso; EH!

18 GERALDTON, ON - Geraldton Composite High School Aud: One in Five; Studies in White; Death and the Maiden; ‡Solo; Rondo Giocoso; EH!

19 MANITOUWADGE, ON - Manitouwadge High School Aud: One in Five; Studies in White; Death and the Maiden; ‡Solo; Rondo Giocoso; EH!

20 WAWA, ON - Michipicoten High School Aud: One in Five; Studies in White; Death and the Maiden; ‡Solo; Rondo Giocoso; EH!

21 SAULT STE MARIE, ON - Sault Collegiate Aud: One in Five; Studies in White; Death and the Maiden; ‡Solo; Rondo Giocoso; EH! - *repeated, September 22*

23 SUDBURY, ON - Sudbury High School Aud: One in Five; Studies in White; Death and the Maiden; ‡Solo; Rondo Giocoso; EH! - *repeated, September 24**

OCTOBER, 1967:

11 NORTH BAY, ON - Capitol Theatre: One in Five; Studies in White; Death and the Maiden; ‡Solo; Rondo Giocoso; EH!

SEPTEMBER, 1968:

23* OSHAWA, ON - Eastdale Collegiate: One in Five; ‡Célébrations; ‡Arena; ‡Pas de Deux (Gordon); EH! - *repeated, September 23*

24 WEST HILL, ON - Sir Wilfrid Laurier S.S. Aud: One in Five; ‡Célébrations; ‡Arena; ‡Pas de Deux (Gordon); EH!

25 VALLEYFIELD, QC - L'Auditorium du Séminaire: Studies in White; ‡Pas de Deux (Gordon); ‡Arena; ‡Célébrations; EH!

26 MONTREAL, QC - Théâtre Port-Royal: One in Five; ‡Célébrations; ‡Arena; ‡Pas de Deux (Gordon); EH! - *repeated, September 27 (Studies in White substituted for One in Five)*

28 CORNWALL, ON - General Vanier Aud: One in Five; ‡Célébrations; ‡Arena; ‡Pas de Deux (Gordon); EH!

30 PEMBROKE, ON - Champlain S.S. Aud: Studies in White; ‡Pas de Deux (Gordon); ‡Arena; ‡Célébrations; EH!

OCTOBER, 1968:

1 HAILEYBURY, ON - St Mary's Academy: Studies in White; ‡Pas de Deux (Gordon); ‡Arena; ‡Célébrations; EH!

2 KIRKLAND LAKE, ON - Strand Theatre: One in Five; ‡Célébrations; ‡Arena; ‡Pas de Deux (Gordon); EH!

3 TIMMINS, ON - Timmins High School Aud: One in Five; ‡Célébrations; ‡Arena; ‡Pas de Deux (Gordon); EH!

4 SUDBURY, ON - Sudbury High School Aud: One in Five; ‡Célébrations; ‡Arena; ‡Pas de Deux (Gordon); EH!

5 PARRY SOUND, ON - Parry Sound High School Aud: One in Five; ‡Célébrations; ‡Arena; ‡Pas de Deux (Gordon); EH!

7 NORTH BAY, ON - Algonquin Composite Aud: Studies in White; ‡Pas de Deux (Gordon); ‡Arena; ‡Célébrations; EH!

8 LINDSAY, ON - Academy Theatre: One in Five; ‡Célébrations; ‡Arena; ‡Pas de Deux (Gordon); EH!

9 KITCHENER, ON - Lyric Theatre: Studies in White; ‡Pas de Deux (Gordon); ‡Arena; ‡Célébrations; EH!

10 NIAGARA FALLS, ON - Niagara Falls High School Aud: Studies in White; ‡Pas de Deux (Gordon); ‡Arena; ‡Célébrations; EH!

11 STRATFORD, ON - Avon Theatre: One in Five; ‡Célébrations; ‡Arena; ‡Pas de Deux (Gordon); EH!

12★ OAKVILLE, ON - White Oaks High School Aud: Studies in White; ‡Pas de Deux (Gordon); ‡Arena; ‡Célébrations; EH!
12 EAST YORK, ON - East York Collegiate Aud: Studies in White; ‡Pas de Deux (Gordon); ‡Arena; ‡Célébrations; EH!

JANUARY, 1969:
19★ VICTORIA, BC - Royal Theatre: One in Five; ‡Célébrations; ‡Pas de Deux (Gordon); Studies in White; EH! **(Group A)** - *repeated, January 20*
20 WEYBURN, SK - Collegiate Aud: One in Five; Rondo Giocoso; ‡Célébrations; Studies in White **(Group B)**
21 NANAIMO, BC - Woodlands Jr. S.S. Aud: One in Five; ‡Célébrations; ‡Pas de Deux (Gordon); Studies in White; EH! **(Group A)**
21 MINOT, ND - McFarland Aud, Minot State College: One in Five; Rondo Giocoso; ‡Célébrations; Studies in White **(Group B)**
22 PORT ALBERNI, BC - A.D.S.S. Aud: One in Five; ‡Célébrations; ‡Pas de Deux (Gordon); Studies in White; EH! **(Group A)**
22 MOOSE JAW, SK - Peacock Aud: One in Five; Rondo Giocoso; ‡Célébrations; Studies in White **(Group B)**
23 CHILLIWACK, BC - Evergreen Hall: One in Five; ‡Célébrations; ‡Pas de Deux (Gordon); Studies in White; EH! **(Group A)**
23 YORKTON, SK - Yorkton Regional High School Aud: One in Five; Rondo Giocoso; ‡Célébrations; Studies in White **(Group B)**
24 KELOWNA, BC - Kelowna Community Theatre: One in Five; ‡Célébrations; ‡Pas de Deux (Gordon); Studies in White; EH! **(Group A)**
24 NORTH BATTLEFORD, SK - Sharp Aud: One in Five; Rondo Giocoso; ‡Célébrations; Studies in White **(Group B)**
25 KIMBERLEY, BC - McKim Aud: One in Five; ‡Célébrations; ‡Pas de Deux (Gordon); Studies in White; EH! **(Group A)**
25 RED DEER, AB - Red Deer Memorial Centre: One in Five; Rondo Giocoso; ‡Célébrations; Studies in White **(Group B)**
26 MEDICINE HAT, AB - Towne Theatre: One in Five; Rondo Giocoso; ‡Célébrations; Studies in White **(Group B)**

FEBRUARY, 1969:
3 REGINA, SK - Sheldon Williams Collegiate Aud: One in Five; Rondo Giocoso; ‡Célébrations; Studies in White **(Group B)**

JANUARY, 1970:
20 KINGSTON, ON - Grand Theatre: Nutcracker pdd; ‡Façade - Tango; Lesson
21 BELLEVILLE, ON - Vocational School Aud: Nutcracker pdd; ‡Façade - Tango; Lesson
22 BURLINGTON, ON - Central High School Aud: Nutcracker pdd; ‡Façade - Tango; Lesson

OCTOBER, 1971:
1 TORONTO, ON - East York Collegiate Aud: Giselle - Peasant pdd; Sleeping Beauty - dances from; Swan Lake - Black Swan pdd; Fandango; ‡Autumn Song; EH!
3 SUDBURY, ON - High School Aud: Giselle - Peasant pdd; Sleeping Beauty - dances from; Swan Lake - Black Swan pdd; Fandango; ‡Autumn Song; EH!
6 NORTH BAY, ON - Capitol Theatre: Giselle - Peasant pdd; Sleeping Beauty - dances from; Swan Lake - Black Swan pdd; Fandango; ‡Autumn Song; EH!
7 KIRKLAND LAKE, ON - Northern College Aud: Giselle - Peasant pdd; Sleeping Beauty - dances from; Swan Lake - Black Swan pdd; Fandango; ‡Autumn Song; EH!
12 WINDSOR, ON - Centennial High School Aud: Giselle - Peasant pdd; Sleeping Beauty - dances from; Swan Lake - Black Swan pdd; Fandango; ‡Autumn Song; EH!
14 LONDON, ON - Grand Theatre: Giselle - Peasant pdd; Sleeping Beauty - dances from; Swan Lake - Black Swan pdd; Fandango; ‡Autumn Song; EH!
15 TORONTO, ON - Burton Aud, York University: Giselle - Peasant pdd; Sleeping Beauty - dances from; Swan Lake - Black Swan pdd; Fandango; ‡Autumn Song; EH!
16★ HAMILTON, ON - Mohawk College Theatre: Giselle - Peasant pdd; Sleeping Beauty - dances from; Swan Lake - Black Swan pdd; Fandango; ‡Autumn Song; EH! - *repeated, October 16*
18 KINGSTON, ON - Grand Theatre: Giselle - Peasant pdd; Sleeping Beauty - dances from; Swan Lake - Black Swan pdd; Fandango; ‡Autumn Song; EH!
19 BELLEVILLE, ON - Centennial School Aud: Giselle - Peasant pdd; Sleeping Beauty - dances from; Swan Lake - Black Swan pdd; Fandango; ‡Autumn Song; EH!
21 PETERBOROUGH, ON - Thomas A. Stewart S.S. Aud: Swan Lake - Black Swan pdd; Giselle - Peasant pdd; Sleeping Beauty - dances from; Fandango; ‡Autumn Song; EH!
22 ORILLIA, ON - Orillia Opera House: Giselle - Peasant pdd; Sleeping Beauty - dances from; Swan Lake - Black Swan pdd; Fandango; ‡Autumn Song; EH!
23 DEEP RIVER, ON - C.J. MacKenzie High School Aud: Giselle - Peasant pdd; Sleeping Beauty - dances from; Swan Lake - Black Swan pdd; Fandango; ‡Autumn Song; EH!

APRIL, 1988:
7 NORTH BAY, ON - Arts Centre: Concerto Barocco; Sleeping Beauty - Bluebird pdd; Trapdance; Don Quixote pdd; Death of a Lady's Man; Etc!
8 BARRIE, ON - Fisher Aud: Concerto Barocco; Sleeping Beauty - Bluebird pdd; Trapdance; Don Quixote pdd; Death of a Lady's Man; Etc!
9 MARKHAM, ON - Markham Theatre: Concerto Barocco; Sleeping Beauty - Bluebird pdd; Trapdance; Don Quixote pdd; Death of a Lady's Man; Etc! - *repeated, April 10 (without Death of a Lady's Man)*

JANUARY, 1989:
20 GUELPH, ON - Ross Hall, John F. Ross High School: Concerto Barocco; Trapdance; Sleeping Beauty - Act III pdd; Concerto pdd; Etc!
21 WATERLOO, ON - University of Waterloo Theatre: Concerto Barocco; Trapdance; Sleeping Beauty - Act III pdd; Concerto pdd; Etc!

MARCH, 1989:
22 LONDON, ON - Alumni Hall: Concerto Barocco; Concerto pdd; Trapdance; Sleeping Beauty - Act III pdd; Death of a Lady's Man; Etc!
23 ST CATHARINES, ON - Playhouse, Brock Centre for the Arts: Concerto Barocco; Concerto pdd; Trapdance; Sleeping Beauty - Act II pdd; Death of a Lady's Man; Etc!
31 MARKHAM, ON - Markham Theatre for Performing Arts: Giselle - Peasant pdd; Sleep Study; Song of a Wayfarer; Dream pdd; Sleeping Beauty - Act III pdd; Envelope

APRIL, 1989:
1 MARKHAM, ON - Markham Theatre for Performing Arts: Giselle - Peasant pdd; Sleep Study; Song of a Wayfarer; Dream pdd; Sleeping Beauty - Act III pdd; Envelope
MAY, 1989:
15 ORILLIA, ON - Orillia Opera House: Giselle - Peasant pas de quatre; Song of a Wayfarer; Concerto pdd; Le Corsaire pdd; Envelope
16 KINGSTON, ON - Grand Theatre: Giselle - Peasant pas de quatre; Sleep Study; Song of a Wayfarer; Concerto pdd; Le Corsaire pdd; Envelope
SEPTEMBER, 1989:
27 LETHBRIDGE, AB - University Theatre for the Performing Arts: Giselle - Peasant pas de quatre; Concerto pdd; Sleep Study; Blue-Eyed Trek; Le Corsaire pdd; Envelope
OCTOBER, 1989:
16 SAULT STE MARIE, ON - White Pines Theatre: Giselle - Peasant pas de quatre; Concerto pdd; Sleep Study; Blue-Eyed Trek; ‡Grand Pas Classique; Envelope - *repeated, October 17*
MARCH, 1990:
29 NORTH BAY, ON - Arts Centre: Giselle - Peasant pas de quatre; Concerto pdd; Sleep Study; Blue-Eyed Trek; Le Corsaire pdd; Envelope
30 SUDBURY, ON - Grad Theatre: Giselle - Peasant pas de quatre; Concerto pdd; Sleep Study; Blue-Eyed Trek; Le Corsaire pdd; Envelope - *repeated, March 31*
MAY, 1990:
31 LONDON, ON - Grand Theatre: Split House Geometric; Napoli - Flower Festival pdd; Sleep Study; Transfigured Night; Le Corsaire pdd; Envelope
JUNE, 1990:
1 LONDON, ON - Grand Theatre: Split House Geometric; Napoli - Flower Festival pdd; Sleep Study; Transfigured Night; Le Corsaire pdd; Envelope
2 HAMILTON, ON - Sir John A. MacDonald S.S.: Split House Geometric; Napoli - Flower Festival pdd; Sleep Study; Transfigured Night; Le Corsaire pdd; Envelope
3 LEWISTON, NY - Artpark: Split House Geometric; Napoli - Flower Festival pdd; Sleep Study; Transfigured Night; Le Corsaire pdd; Envelope
OCTOBER, 1990:
15 NEPEAN, ON - Centrepointe Theatre: Concerto for Flute and Harp; Steptext; Troy Game
JANUARY, 1991:
17 GUELPH, ON - E.L. Fox Aud: Concerto for Flute and Harp; Steptext; Concerto pdd; Troy Game
19 OAKVILLE, ON - Oakville Centre for the Performing Arts: Concerto for Flute and Harp; Steptext; Concerto pdd; Troy Game
MAY, 1991:
22 LONDON, ON - Grand Theatre: Concerto Barocco; Sleeping Beauty - Grand pdd; Troy Game - *repeated, May 23*

Appendix C
Choreographic Workshops 1968–69 to 1989–90

SEASONS: 1968-9 to 1989-90; **PERFORMANCES:** 66 (2 outside Toronto); **PREMIERES:** all works are Workshop first performances; most were created for the Workshops; choreographers are indicated in parentheses following the first listing of each work.

APRIL, 1969:
16 TORONTO, ON - Edward Johnson Building, University of Toronto: Eleven for Now (Charles Kirby); Labyrinth (Ann Ditchburn); Electre• (Grant Strate); Status (Ross McKim) - *repeated, April 17, 18, 19, 23, 24, 25, 26*

NOVEMBER, 1970:
20 TORONTO, ON - Ryerson Theatre: Valses Nobles et Sentimentales (Earl Kraul); To Magick Pan with Love, Three Chestnuts, and Rothman's Cigarettes (Ann Ditchburn); Sister-Mother (Ross McKim); Dedicated to My Friend Emily (Ann Ditchburn); Hermatess (Patricia Oney); Song for Song My (Karen Bowes) - *repeated, November 21 (Pas de Trois [Timothy Spain] substituted for To Magick Pan)*
24 TORONTO, ON - Ryerson Theatre: Silent Harmony (Angela Leigh); Allone (Vanessa Harwood); Pas de Trois (Timothy Spain); To Magick Pan with Love, Three Chestnuts, and Rothman's Cigarettes; Poses (Christopher Bannerman); Summerset (Charles Kirby) - *repeated, November 25*

NOVEMBER, 1971:
22 TORONTO, ON - Theatre-in-Camera, Bathurst Street United Church: Moonlight Sonata (Sergiu Stefanschi); Battle Hymn of The Republic (Stephanie Leigh); Mirage (Veronica Tennant); The Next Piece (Gillian Hannant); Untitled (Howard Marcus); Untitled (Garry Semeniuk); A Man and A Dove (Ann Ditchburn); Off by Heart (Timothy Spain); And If by Chance We Find Each Other, It's Beautiful (Tomas Schramek); Epilogue (Christopher Bannerman); Rachmaninoff Pas de Trois (Hazaros Surmeyan); Easy (Karen Bowes) - *repeated, November 23, 25 (with Kate [choreographer unknown] added), 26 (with Kate added)*

NOVEMBER, 1973:
27 TORONTO, ON - Bathurst Street United Church: Contessa (Gloria Luoma); Monique (Stephen Greenston); Memoriae (Maria Barrios); Inventions• (Constantin Patsalas); Sonata (James Kudelka); Buffon's Curse (Hazaros Surmeyan); Pas de Deux (Daniel Capouch); Je N'ai Pas de Nom (Constantin Patsalas); Pilgrimage (Ann Ditchburn) - *repeated, November 28, 29, 30*

DECEMBER, 1973:
1 TORONTO, ON - Bathurst Street United Church: Contessa; Monique; Memoriae; Inventions•; Sonata; Buffon's Curse; Pas de Deux (Capouch); Je N'ai Pas de Nom; Pilgrimage

NOVEMBER, 1974:
27 TORONTO, ON - Bayview Theatre: After Hours (Ann Ditchburn); Sonata (James Kudelka); Kisses• (Ann Ditchburn); A Work in Progress (Part of The Rite of Spring - Constantin Patsalas) - *repeated, November 28, 29, 30*

APRIL, 1976:
9 TORONTO, ON - St Paul's Centre: Burleske (John Aubrey); Moonsigns (Ann Ditchburn); A Party• (James Kudelka); Klee Wyck (Gloria Luoma); Listen #2 (Ann Ditchburn); Black Angels• (Constantin Patsalas) - *repeated, April 10, 12, 13, 14*

APRIL, 1977:
7 TORONTO, ON - Bathurst Street Theatre: Corelli Variations (John Aubrey); Bits and Pieces (Rashna Homji and Stephen Jefferies); Circe (Ann Ditchburn); The Rite of Spring• (Constantin Patsalas) - *repeated, April 8, 9*
11 TORONTO, ON - O'Keefe Centre: Heat Wave (David Gornik); Elegie (Clinton Rothwell); Grande Polonaise Brillante (Charles Kirby); Washington Square• (James Kudelka); Circe
12 TORONTO, ON - Bathurst Street Theatre: Heat Wave; Elegie; Grande Polonaise Brillante; Washington Square•; Circe - *repeated, April 13*

APRIL, 1979:
2 TORONTO, ON - Bathurst Street Theatre: The Comedians (Clinton Rothwell); Pas de Deux (James Kudelka); Bored of the Lies (Gloria Luoma); Excerpt from The Cosmic Messenger (David Gornik); Speakeasy (Judith Marcuse §); Parranda Criolla (Constantin Patsalas) - *repeated, April 3, 4*
6 NIAGARA-ON-THE-LAKE, ON - Shaw Festival Theatre: The Comedians; Pas de Deux (Kudelka); Bored of the Lies; Excerpt from The Cosmic Messenger; Speakeasy; Parranda Criolla - *repeated, April 7*

APRIL, 1980:
15 TORONTO, ON - NDWT Theatre: Ebb and Flow (David Nixon); Obelisk (Gloria Luoma); Recital (Constantin Patsalas); Plus One (Clinton Rothwell); Inflections (Larry McKinnon §); The Rape of Lucrece (James Kudelka); Venus Pas de Deux (Larry McKinnon §); Canciones• (Constantin Patsalas) - *repeated, April 16, 17 (without Obelisk, Plus One), 18 (without Obelisk, Plus One), 19 (without Obelisk, Plus One)*

APRIL, 1983:
7 TORONTO, ON - Young People's Theatre: Please Hear What I Am Not Saying (Gretchen Newburger); Jeune Amour (Mark Raab); Eve (Sheri-Ann Silberg); Daphnis & Chloe pdd (R.W. Amatto §); Pax, It's No Game (Donald Dawson); Tierra de las Hadas (Richard Sugarman §); Lento (David Allan); Butterfly (David Nixon) - *repeated, April 8, 9*

APRIL, 1984:
5 TORONTO, ON - Bathurst Street Theatre: Saturn Return (Gloria Luoma); Just a Pas de Deux (Yuri Ng); The Journey to Here (Ingrid Filewood); Shelter (Bengt Jörgen); Reminiscence• (Luc Amyôt); Pastel• (David Allan) - *repeated, April 6** (without Saturn Return), 6, 7*

MARCH, 1985:

28 TORONTO, ON - Bathurst Street Theatre: One Light Night (Ingrid Filewood); Piano Trio (John Alleyne); Reminiscence II (Luc Amyôt); Elegy for a Lost Friend (Eva Robertson); Thoughts of Light (Donald Dawson); In Transition (Amalia Schelhorn); Rough Sketch (Yuri Ng); Circle (Bengt Jörgen); Allure - Taffeta Ballgowns (Matthew Nash §); Aphasia (Kim Nielson); On Occasion• (David Allan) - *repeated, March 29*** *(without One Light Night, Reminiscence II, Elegy for a Lost Friend, Thoughts of Light, In Transition, Aphasia), 29, 30*

MAY, 1986:

29 TORONTO, ON - Joey and Toby Tanenbaum Opera Centre : The Painted Wall (Chen Min §); Ophelia Dreaming (Manuela Cezanne); Whimsicelle (Richard Sugarman §); Ecstasis Fortis (Kim Nielson); Inner Drop• (Donald Dawson); Madrigals of Love and War (Jacqueline Dupuis); Visions Fugitives (Donald Dawson); Still Life (Yuri Ng); Tuwat• (Bengt Jörgen); Age of Reason (Donald Dawson); Self-Portrait (Luc Amyôt); Impulse (John Alleyne) - *repeated, May 30, 31*

MAY, 1989:

18 TORONTO, ON - Betty Oliphant Theatre: Variations on a Familiar Theme (Assis Carreiro); Symbiosis (Jean Grand-Maitre §); As Ever (Terrill Maguire §); Sleep Study (1987)• (David Parsons §); Dedication (Mark Raab); R.I.P. Jack (Yuri Ng); Untangle (Yuri Ng); Odin (Jean Grand-Maitre §); The Envelope• (David Parsons §) - *repeated, May 19, 20*

JUNE, 1990:

7 TORONTO, ON - Betty Oliphant Theatre: Kara (Yuri Ng and Catherine Margaret); Converging Solitude (Evann Siebens §); The Seven Deadly Sins (Liza Kovacs); are one (Michael Downing); Rain Season (Yuri Ng); 0 : 2 : 57 (John Alleyne); Lights Edge (Donald Dawson); Parallel (Dominique Dumais) - *repeated, June 8, 9*

Appendix D

Dancers of the National Ballet of Canada 1951–52 to 1990–91

The roster of dancers in the company is based on the listings published annually in the company's Souvenir Program. However, since these listings do not record changes (either departures or arrivals) which took place after the Souvenir Program went to print, these records have been supplemented from internal company sources. Guest artists, apprentices and non-dancing supernumeraries have not been included, nor have special appearances by the artistic director of the company if he or she was not listed as a regular company member for the year in question.

Each dancer's name is followed by his or her continuous seasons with the company and the highest rank attained in his or her final season. Until the 1977–8 Souvenir Program, the company's practice was to indicate differences in rank not with titles, but simply by different sizes of typeface. No consistency was observed from year to year as to the number of ranks in the company. For the seasons until 1977–8, therefore, rank is indicated by two roman numerals, the first indicating the level achieved by the individual in his or her final season of employment and the second the number of levels into which the company was divided for that season. For example, '55-60 (II/III); 63-69 (I/III)' following a dancer's name indicates an individual who served continuously from the 1955–6 to the 1959–60 seasons, finally attaining the second ranking in a year in which three ranks were used. The same dancer returned to the company for the 1963–4 to the 1968–9 seasons, finally attaining the first ranking in a year in which three rankings were used.

From 1977–8 on, abbreviations for the various company ranks are used, as explained in 'Abbreviations' (below). Chevrons « beside dancers' names indicate graduates of the National Ballet School. Where a dancer appeared with the company under two different names, the principal listing is under the name most frequently used while dancing with the company, with the alternate name cross-referenced to it. While every effort has been made to ensure the accuracy and completeness of this information, errors and omissions may yet exist. I apologize for these, and particularly to any company member whose name may inadvertently have been left out.

Abbreviations

c indicates rank of corps member
fs indicates rank of first soloist
pc indicates rank of principal dancer
pca indicates rank of principal character artist
ss indicates rank of second soloist
« graduate of National Ballet School

- A -

AARON, Myrna - 51-55 (III/III); 59-61 (III/III)
ABBEY, Susan - 58-61 (III/III)
ACEVEDO «, Donald - 80-82 (c)
ADAM «, Julie - 84-88 (c)
ADAM «, Mark - 88-90 (c)
ADAMS, David - 51-64 (I/IV)
ADAMS, Lawrence - 55-60 (II/III); 63-69 (I/III)
ALEXANDER, Ronald - 74-76 (IV/IV)
ALLAN «, David - 74-88 (ss)
ALLEMANN «, Sabina - 80-89 (p)
ALLEYNE «, John - 84-90 (fs)
AMOS, Ian - 71-73 (III/III)
AMYÔT «, Luc - 75-79 (p); 83-85 (fs)
ANDROSE, Edward - 64-65 (II/II)
APINÉ, Irene - 51-55 (I/III)
ARMSTRONG «, Amber - 85-91 (c)
ARMSTRONG, Brian - 71-75 (III/III)
ARNETT, Charles - 57-58 (III/III)
ASH, Taryn - 88-91 (c)
ASHWORTH, Corinne - 55-58 (III/III)
AUBREY, John - 73-80 (c)
AUGER «, Yolande - 72-88 (c)
AUGUSTYN «, Frank - 70-88 (p)
AULD «, Alexandra - 77-85 (ss)

- B -

BAIN «, Joy - 79-80 (c); 81-82 (c)
BANFIELD, Beverley - 56-60 (III/III)
BANKS, Joanna - 68-69 (III/III)
BANNERMAN, Christopher - 69-72 (III/III)
BARRIOS, Maria - 72-74 (III/III)
BAUER, Ellen - 84-86 (c)
BAURAC, Josephine - 72-74 (III/III); 77-79 (c)
BAYER, Marijan - 69-70 (I/III)
BECKER, Douglas - 79-80 (c)
BEESEMYER, Karla - 77-79 (c)
BEEVERS, Lawrence - 67-71 (III/III)
BELIVEAU, Bernadette - 57-59 (III/III)
BERTRAM «, Victoria - 63-91 (pca)
BLANTON, Jeremy - 62-71 (I/III)
BLOUIN «, Lorraine - 81-88 (ss)
BODIE, Susan - 74-85 (c)
BOMERS «, Carina - 73-76 (IV/IV)
BONNELL, Gloria - 56-59 (III/III)
BORNHAUSEN, Angelica - 69-71 (I/III)
BOUTILIER «, Sean - 76-83 (ss)
BOWEN, Richard - 73-75 (III/III)
BOWES «, Karen - 66-72 (I/III)
BRANDT, Edelayne - 54-57 (III/III)
BRAYLEY, Sally - 56-62 (IV/IV)
BROWN «, Suzanne - 80-84 (c)
BROWNLOW, Audrey - 81-84 (c)
BRYAN, Rebecca - 62-66 (I/II)
BURGESS, Walter - 53-55 (III/III)
BURK, Susan - 80-88 (c)
BURKE, Charles - 64-68 (III/III)
BURNE, Gary - 67-68 (I/III)
BUTKO, Natalia - 51-54 (II/II)
BYRNES, Anne - 75-76 (IV/IV)

- C -

CADRIN, Thérèse - 65-67 (II/II)
CAHILL, Tom - 58-59 (III/III)
CAMPBELL, Connie - 51-52 (II/II)
CAPOUCH, Daniel - 71-76 (III/IV); 77-79 (ss)
CAREF, Benjamin - 72-73 (III/III)
CARHART, Glenda - 75-76 (IV/IV)
CARMAN, Phillip - 72-73 (III/III)
CARR, Catherine - 56-59 (III/III); 61-64 (II/II)
CARRELL, John - see AUBREY, John
CARRUTHERS, Catherine - see CARR, Catherine
CARTER «, Todd - 77-89 (c)
CASSELS, Jeanette - 57-62 (IV/IV)
CASTELLAN «, Deborah - 72-75 (III/III)
CAUSEY, Maurice - 88-91 (c)
CHALMER «, Paul - 79-81 (c)

CHILDERHOSE, Diane - 51-55 (III/III)
CHOJNACKI, Marcel - 55-59 (III/III)
CHRISTIE, Robert - 54-55 (III/III)
CIMINO, Gerre - 69-75 (III/III)
COLE, Robert - 79-83 (c)
COLLINGWOOD, Katherine - 73-74 (III/III)
COLLINS «, Brendan - 86-88 (c); 89-90 (c)
COLLINS, Susan - see BODIE, Susan
COLPMAN, Judie - 51-62 (III/IV)
CONSOLATI, Maureen - see WEBSTER, Maureen
COOL «, Colleen - 66-73 (II/III); 74-83 (fs)
COREY, Winthrop - 72-75 (I/III)
COUSINEAU, Yves - 54-62 (III/IV); 63-72 (I/III)
CRAWFORD «, Elaine - 61-70 (II/III)
CRAWFORD, Susan - 54-57 (III/III)
CUMBERLAND «, Christy - 68-75 (III/III)
CYOPIK, Ainslie - 82-83 (c)
CZYZEWSKI «, Christopher - 70-71 (III/III)

- D -

DA SILVA, Harold - 55-59 (II/III)
DABIN, Joel - 76-80 (fs)
DARLING, Christopher - 64-66 (II/II)
DAVIDSON «, Andrea - 71-75 (II/III)
DAVIS, Robert - 63-64 (I/II)
DAWSON, Donald - 79-88 (ss); 90-91 (fs)
DE LICHTENBERG, Maryann - 59-63 (IV/IV)
DE LUCA, Norma - 72-73 (III/III)
DEININGER, Eric - 82-83 (c)
DENVERS, Robert - 73-74 (II/III)
DESROSIERS «, Robert - 71-72 (III/III)
DITCHBURN «, Ann - 68-72 (III/III); 73-79 (ss)
DORNIS, Judith - 54-56 (II/II)
DOUGLAS, Jennifer - 78-88 (c)
DOWNING, Michael - 88-91 (c)
DROMISKY «, Susan - 81-85 (c); 86-91 (ss)
DUBUC «, Philippe - 85-91 (c)
DUFRESNE, André - 51-55 (III/III)
DUMAIS «, Dominique - 87-91 (c)
DUPUIS, Jacqueline - 85-87 (c)
DUQUIS, Janine - 54-55 (III/III)
DYNOWSKA, Maria - see DYNOWSKA, Oldyna
DYNOWSKA, Oldyna - 51-57 (II/III)

- E -

EDWARDS «, Victor - 71-78 (ss)
ELLIOTT, Jane - see MCELLIGOTT, Jane
ENGLUND, Richard - 55-57 (II/III)
ESMONDE «, Miranda - 68-69 (III/III)
EVANGELISTA, Anne - 63-67 (II/II)
EVANOVA, Katrina - 57-59 (III/III)

- F -

FAIRCLOUGH, Dewi - 85-87 (c)
FEIN, Richard - 72-73
FERGUSON «, Nancy - 72-73 (III/III)
FERRARO, Edilio - 58-59 (III/III)
FISHER «, Norma - 72-75 (III/III); 76-77 (IV/IV)
FLETCHER «, Linda - 64-72 (II/III)
FOLEY, Alexandra - 88-91 (c)
FOOSE, Richard - 64-65 (II/II)
FORISTER, Albert - 75-83 (ss)
FOSTER, Walter - 51-53 (II/II)
FOURNIER «, Jennifer - 86-91 (ss)
FRANCA, Celia - 51-59 (I/III)
FRANCIS, Sandra - 52-54 (II/II)
FRENCH, Loretta - 72-74 (III/III)
FUJINO, Koichi - 72-73 (III/III)

- G -

GALETTO, Miguel - 68-69 (III/III)
GARCIA, Miguel - 74-82 (ss)
GEDDES, Lorna - 59-84 (c)
GEORGE, William - 71-73 (II/III)
GESELLE, Davina - 58-60 (III/III)
GIBSON, Glenn - 52-57 (II/III)
GIBSON, Roberta - 59-62 (IV/IV)
GILMOUR, Glenn - 58-64 (I/II); 65-70 (I/III)
GLASCO «, Kimberly - 79-82 (ss); 84-91 (p)
GOCHNAUER, Lois - 64-66 (II/II)
GOH, Chan Hon - 88-91 (ss)
GOLDMAN, Nina - 83-89 (c)
GORDON «, David - 68-70 (III/III); 71-72 (III/III)
GORNIK «, David - 73-84 (ss)
GORRISSEN, Jacques - 68-91 (pca)
GORTER, Uko - 87-89 (c)
GOTSHALKS, Jury - 51-52 (I/II); 53-55 (I/III)
GRANGER «, Leeyan - 63-68 (II/III)
GRAVELLE «, Elizabeth - 71-73 (III/III)
GREEN, Janet - 58-60 (III/III)
GREEN, Lydia - 87-91 (c)
GREEN, Sarah - 87-91 (ss)
GREENSTON, Stephen - 72-76 (III/IV)
GREENWOOD, Frances - 56-62 (IV/IV)
GREYEYES «, Michael - 87-90 (c)

- H -

HACQUOIL «, Andrea - 81-82 (c)
HADER «, Catherine - 82-84 (c)
HAIDER, Lawrence - 65-67 (I/II)
HALL, Elizabeth - 78-80 (c)
HANGAUER, Paul - 62-63 (IV/IV)
HANNANT «, Gillian - 70-72 (III/III)
HARRINGTON «, Rex - 83-91 (p)
HARRIS, Joey - 54-55 (I/III)
HARWOOD «, Vanessa - 64-86 (p)
HAYES, Muriel - 55-56 (II/II)
HELENA «, Mairi - 62-64 (II/II)
HERR, Sharon - 64-65 (II/II)
HICKIN «, Sally-Anne - 83-91 (c)
HILFERINK, Nicolas - 72-74 (III/III)
HILL, Joyce - 51-53 (II/II)
HINES «, Patricia - 85-88 (c)
HODGKINSON «, Greta - 90-91 (c)
HOMJI, Rashna - 76-77 (II/IV)
HOULE «, Julie - 83-87 (c)
HOWARD, David - 63-64 (I/II)
HUNTER, Fergus - 51-54 (II/II)
HURDE, Patrick - 59-63 (III/IV)
HUTTER, Victoria - 78-79 (c)

- I -

ICHINO, Yoko - 82-90 (p)
ILES «, Valerie - 75-77 (IV/IV)
ILLMAN, Margaret - 89-91 (fs)
INTINI, Vanda - 54-57 (III/III)
IRELAND, Dianne - 54-59 (III/III)
ITO, Robert - 51-55 (III/III); 56-58 (III/III)
IVINGS, Jacqueline - 53-61 (II/III); 62-67 (I/II)

- J -

JAGO, Mary - 66-84 (p)
JAGO, Paul - 75-79 (c)
JARVIS, Lilian - 51-60 (I/III); 61-63 (II/IV)
JARVIS, Lillian - see JARVIS, Lilian
JEANES, Rosemary - 68-72 (III/III)
JEFFERIES, Stephen - 76-77 (I/IV)
JOHNSON «, Jill - 87-91 (c)
JÖRGEN, Bengt - 82-85 (c)
JOYNER «, Kathryn - 72-75 (III/III)
JUST, Ole - 88-89 (c)

- K -

KABAYAMA «, Maki - 70-73 (III/III)
KAIN «, Karen - 69-91 (p)
KAISER, Gregory - 76-77 (IV/IV)
KALOCZY, Anton - 74-81 (c)
KASH, Shirley - 54-55 (III/III)
KATZ, Ruth - 84-85 (c)
KEEBLE «, Elizabeth - 64-68 (II/III)
KEEN «, Susan - 75-80 (c)
KEISS, Vera - 51-53 (II/II)
KENNEY, Colleen - 51-57 (II/III)
KENT, Louise - 67-69 (III/III)
KERVAL, David - 55-58 (III/III)
KHAN «, Nicholas - 89-91 (c)
KILGOUR, Murray - 67-71 (II/III)
KILLORAN, Joan - 61-66 (II/II)
KING, Gregory - see KAISER, Gregory
KIRBY, Charles - 65-71 (III/III); 72-91 (pca)
KLAMPFER «, John - 64-68 (II/III)
KNIAZEFF, Youra - 71-72 (I/III)
KNOBBS, Christopher - 66-70 (III/III)

KOFF, Gillian - 80-83 (c)
KOLZOVA, Mimi - 52-54 (II/II)
KOVACS «, Liza - 85-89 (c)
KRAUL, Earl - 51-70 (I/III)
KUDELKA «, James - 71-81 (fs)

- L -

LAERKESEN, Anna - 67-68 (I/III)
LAIDLAW, Susan - 67-69 (III/III)
LAING, Simon - 79-80 (c)
LAIRD «, Jennifer - 73-77 (IV/IV)
LAMBROS «, Annette - 77-80 (c)
LAMY «, Martine - 83-91 (p)
LANDRY «, Stephanie - 76-91 (c)
LARSON, Kenneth - 81-85 (c)
LAURENCE, James - 68-69 (III/III)
LAVOIE «, Serge - 81-86 (ss); 87-91 (p)
LAY «, Deanne - 76-77 (IV/IV)
LEAHY, Leonie - 60-61 (III/III)
LEGATE «, Stephen - 86-91 (ss)
LEIGH, Angela - 51-63 (II/IV); 64-66 (I/II)
LEIGH «, Stephanie - 69-72 (III/III)
LEIGH, Victoria - 70-71 (II/III)
LENDVAI, Yseult - 89-91 (c)
LEWIS, Maria - 60-63 (IV/IV)
LIGHTHEART «, Kim - 80-91 (p)
LIPITZ, Kenneth - 71-73 (II/III)
LOGVINOVA, Mimi - 53-56 (II/II)
LOOMIS «, Daphne - 73-79 (c)
LUCAS, Cynthia - 73-89 (fs)
LUCKETT, Clinton - 87-91 (c)
LUOMA «, Gloria - 71-83 (fs)
LYON, Valerie - 57-61 (III/III)

- M -

MACCARTHY, Jerome - 72-73 (III/III)
MACDONALD, Brian - 51-53 (II/II)
MACDONALD, Diane - 60-63 (IV/IV)
MACEDO «, Cynthia - 82-91 (ss)
MACGILLIVRAY, David - 90-91 (ss)
MACKINTOSH, Laird - 90-91 (c)
MADONIA «, Valerie - 79-81 (c)
MAGGS, Caitlan - 76-80 (c)
MAHLER, Donald - 56-61 (II/III)
MALAN, Angela - 89-91 (c)
MALINOWSKI «, Barbara - 69-71 (III/III)
MANN, Teresa - 56-61 (III/III)
MARCUS «, Howard - 64-69 (II/III); 71-72 (II/III)
MARKS, Dianna - 71-73 (III/III)
MARNI, Guido - 85-86 (c)
MARRIÉ, William - 90-91 (c)
MARTIN, Nicholas - see HILFERINK, Nicolas
MASON, Sylvia - 53-63 (III/IV)
MATINZI, Michael - 73-75 (III/III)
MATTHEWS, Brenda - 82-91 (c)
MAWSON «, Karin - 75-85 (ss)
MAYBARDUK «, Linda - 69-84 (fs)
MCCARTHY, JoAnn - 79-81 (ss)
MCCORMACK, Moira - 77-78 (c)
MCCULLAGH, Pauline - 54-56 (II/II)
MCELLIGOTT, Jane - 81-85 (c)
MCKAY, Suzanne - 88-91 (c)
MCKIM «, Michael - 73-74 (III/III)
MCKIM, Ross - 67-68 (III/III); 70-71 (III/III)
MCLEAN «, Laura - 78-80 (c)
MCNAMARA, Joseph - 88-89 (c)
MEADOWS, Howard - 51-64 (II/II)
MEADOWS, William - 73-75 (III/III)
MEARS «, Graeme - 90-91 (c)
MEINKE, David - 85-90 (c)
MEISTER, Hans - 57-62 (III/IV)
MEISTER, Ronald - 71-72 (III/III)
MEJIA, Mark - 72-73 (III/III)
MELOCHE, Katherine - 73-74 (III/III)
MELVILLE, Kenneth - 60-63 (III/IV)
MELVIN, Sheila - 62-63 (III/IV)
MENG, Martin - 85-86 (c)
MEUNIER, Francesca - 62-64 (II/II)
MILES, Maralyn - 62-66 (II/II)
MILES, Rosemary - 66-67 (II/II)
MILTON, Anthony - 66-68 (III/III)
MITCHELL, Gregory - 72-73 (III/III)
MOLLER, Ray - 53-58 (II/III)
MOLNAR «, Emily - 90-91 (c)
MONTAGUE «, Owen - 82-90 (p)
MONTY, Barbara - 55-56 (II/II)
MOORE «, Claudia - 71-73 (III/III)
MORGAN, Anthea - 86-91 (c)
MOSES, Samuel - 64-66 (II/II)
MUNRO, Alastair - 64-70 (III/III)
MURILLO «, Esther - 73-81 (fs)
MURPHY, Gwendolyn - 66-69 (III/III)

- N -

NEARY, Patricia - 57-60 (III/III)
NEEDHAMMER, Andrew - 84-91 (c)
NELSON, Daniel - 85-88 (c)
NEVILLE, Anne - 59-61 (III/III)
NEWBURGER, Gretchen - 80-85 (ss)
NG «, Yuri - 83-90 (c)
NICHOLS, Edward - 59-62 (IV/IV); 66-67 (II/II)
NICHOLSON, Dido - 79-80 (c)
NICHOLSON, Thomas - 73-77 (IV/IV)
NISBET, Joanne - 59-61 (III/III)
NIXON «, David - 78-84 (fs); 88-90 (p)
NORMAN «, Bardi - 64-67 (II/II); 68-70 (III/III)
NORMAN, Gary - 74-76 (I/IV)
NUSSBAUMER, Cathy - 81-82 (c)
NYCHKA «, Ronda - 84-89 (ss)
NYLAND, Diane - 61-62 (IV/IV)

- O -

O'CONNOR, James - 90-91 (c)
O'ROURKE, Kevyn - 68-70 (III/III)
ONEY «, Patricia - 68-83 (ss)
ORLANDO «, Simone - 90-91 (c)
ORR «, Jennifer - 74-77 (IV/IV)
OSBORNE, Gregory - 83-89 (p)
OTTER, Elizabeth - 88-90 (c)
OTTMANN «, Peter - 76-91 (fs)
OXENHAM «, Andrew - 64-70 (II/III); 73-75 (II/III)

- P -

PADVORAC, Theresa - 76-78 (c)
PAGE, Frances - 61-63 (IV/IV)
PAIGE, Cecily - 57-59 (III/III)
PAIGE, Frances - see PAGE, Frances
PALMER, Sylvia - 60-66 (II/II)
PATSALAS, Constantin - 72-84 (fs)
PAULK, Terrell - 72-73 (III/III)
PAUZÉ «, Alain - 70-72 (III/III)
PEDEN, David - 87-90 (fs)
PEGLIASCO, René - 67-69 (III/III)
PERSSON «, Johan - 90-91 (c)
PERUSSE «, Sonia - 72-76 (II/IV); 77-78 (fs)
PICK, Gunter - 66-67 (II/II)
PIERIN, Marco - 83-84 (p)
PLACE «, Pamela - 84-91 (c)
POOLE, Robert - 81-82 (c)
POPE, Betty - 54-59 (II/III)
POTTS «, Nadia - 64-65 (II/II); 66-70 (I/III); 71-86 (p)
POWERS, Patricia - 61-66 (II/II); 67-68 (III/III)
PROULX «, Michelle - 78-79 (c)
PUGH «, Kevin - 78-91 (p)

- Q -

QUINN «, Pierre - 83-91 (fs)

- R -

RAAB, Mark - 81-90 (c)
RAIMONDI, Letizia - 67-69 (III/III)
RANDAZZO «, Anthony - 81-87 (c)
RANDOLPH «, Craig - 78-84 (ss)
RANSOM «, Jeremy - 80-86 (fs); 87-91 (p)
RATHBUN «, Catherine - 61-62 (IV/IV)
REISER «, Wendy - 71-78 (fs)
RHATIGAN, Summer Lee - 86-88 (ss)
RICHARDSON «, Caroline - 85-91 (c)
RIMSAY «, Rebekah - 90-91 (c)
RITTER «, Alexander - 88-91 (c)
ROBERTS, Chester - 74-76 (IV/IV)
ROBERTSON «, Eva - 84-85 (c)
ROBERTSON, Ian - 58-61 (III/III)
ROCHMAN, Linda - 73-74 (III/III)
RODRIGUEZ, Sonia - 90-91 (c)
RODWELL, Frank - 52-56 (II/II)
ROLLO, Marilyn - 51-56 (II/II)
ROME, Gilbert - 63-66 (II/II)
RONALD «, Heather - 74-81 (c)

RONALDSON, James - 53-56 (II/II)
ROSELLI, Maria - 89-90 (c)
ROTHWELL, Clinton - 67-71 (I/III); 75-81 (p)
ROTHWELL, Maureen - 67-68 (III/III); 69-71 (II/III)
ROUSSEAU «, Hélène - 79-87 (c)
ROXANDER, David - 72-88 (fs)
ROY, Danielle - 66-69 (III/III)
RUBIN, Donna - 84-88 (c)
RUDNICK, Lesley - 86-87 (c)
RUDNICK, Lia - 68-69 (III/III)

- S -

SACKLEN, Per - 87-88 (c)
SAMSOVA, Galina - 61-64 (I/II)
SAMTSOVA, Galina - see SAMSOVA, Galina
SANDONATO, Barbara - 72-73 (I/III)
SAUNDERS, Gillian - 85-90 (c)
SAUNDERS «, Jane - 71-72 (III/III)
SCHAUFUSS, Peter - 67-69 (II/III); 77-84 (p)
SCHEIDEGGER, Katherine - 74-78 (c)
SCHELHORN «, Amalia - 78-86 (fs)
SCHMIDT, Hans - 61-63 (IV/IV)
SCHRAMEK, Tomas - 69-91 (pca)
SCHWENKER, Nancy - 61-62 (IV/IV); 63-64 (II/II)
SCOTT, Brian - 61-70 (III/III)
SCOTT, Bryan - see SCOTT, Brian
SCOTT, David - 59-63 (III/IV)
SEALANDER «, Kristina - 66-68 (II/III)
SEGARRA, Ramón - 64-65 (I/II)
SEMENIUK «, Garry - 70-72 (III/III)
SEWELL, Marilyn - 52-54 (II/II)
SHERVAL, Barbara - 66-70 (III/III)
SIDIMUS, Joysanne - 63-68 (I/III)
SILBERG, Sheri - 80-82 (c)
SIMPSON, Colin - 75-79 (c)
SMIDT, Christopher - 90-91 (c)
SMITH «, Barbara - 82-90 (c)
SMITH, Lois - 51-69 (I/III)
SMITH «, Raymond - 75-91 (p)
SNOW, Mark - 89-91 (c)
SOLERI, Kristine - 71-74 (III/III)
SOLLÈRE, Pearl - 53-55 (III/III)
SPAIN «, Timothy - 68-72 (II/III)
SPIRA, Phyllis - 67-68 (I/III)
STAINES «, Mavis - 73-78 (fs)
STEELE, Anne - see STEELE, Kathryn
STEELE «, Kathryn - 63-67 (II/II)
STEFANSCHI, Sergiu - 71-78 (p)
STEPANICK, Leonard - 60-72 (III/III)
STEWART, Joan - see STUART, Joan
STEWART, Katharine - 51-56 (II/II)
STEWART, Manard - 84-87 (c)
STIKEMAN «, Naomi - 89-91 (c)
STOCK, Gailene - 74-76 (II/IV)
STOLAR «, William - 78-82 (ss)
STRATE, Grant - 51-62 (III/IV); 63-64 (I/II)
STUART, Clive - 68-69 (III/III)
STUART, Joan - 52-56 (II/II)
SURMEJAN, Hazaros - see SURMEYAN, Hazaros
SURMEYAN, Hazaros - 66-91 (pca)
SZABLOWSKI «, Barbara - 72-81 (c)

- T -

TAYLOR, James - 88-91 (c)
TENNANT «, Veronica - 64-90 (p)
TERELL, Jocelyn - see TERELLE, Jocelyn
TERELLE, Jocelyn - 56-64 (I/II)
TESSMER, Karen - see TESSMER, Karyn
TESSMER, Karyn - 74-81 (fs); 83-90 (fs)
TEWSLEY, Robert - 90-91 (c)
THOMAS «, Sarah - 62-64 (I/II)
TODD «, Deborah - 78-88 (c)
TOOCHINA, Mary - 51-52 (II/II)
TRICK, Kathleen - 72-75 (III/III)
TRIESTE, Elena - 51-52 (II/II)
TURNER, Charmain - 58-64 (II/II); 65-84 (c)
TURNER, Charmaine - see TURNER, Charmain

- U -

ULLATE, Victor - 77-78 (fs)
URSULIAK, Alex - 63-65 (I/II)

- V -

VALENT, Renée - 67-68 (III/III)
VALTAT, Muriel - 88-90 (c)
VAN HAMEL «, Martine - 63-69 (I/III)
VAUGHAN, Amanda - 64-70 (III/III)
VILEN «, Julia - 87-91 (c)
VINCE, Claire - 89-91 (c)

- W -

WALKER, David - see KERVAL, David
WALKER «, Wendy - 67-69 (III/III)
WALLIN, Nils-Bertil - 90-91 (c)
WARMBRODT, Stanley - 63-64 (II/II)
WATKIN «, Aaron - 89-91 (c)
WEBSTER, Maureen - 63-67 (II/II)
WEICHARDT, Eric - 72-74 (III/III)
WEINSTEIN «, Miriam - 63-69 (III/III)
WERNER «, Elaine - 64-67 (II/II)
WHITE, Barbara - 62-63 (IV/IV)
WHITE, David - see ROXANDER, David
WILDER, Valerie - 70-78 (c)
WILKINSON, Barrie - 63-64 (I/II)
WINSTON «, Paul - 89-91 (c)
WINTER, Penelope - 56-61 (III/III)
WISEMAN, Morley - 59-63 (IV/IV)
WITHAM «, Marquita - 64-65 (II/II); 66-67 (II/II)
WITKOWSKY «, Gizella - 75-91 (p)
WOODING «, Jane - 72-78 (c)
WORTH, Colin - 57-64 (I/II)
WRIGHT, Gerald - 61-62 (IV/IV)
WYATT, Olivia - 51-53 (II/II)

- Y -

YEIGH «, Elizabeth - 72-73 (III/III)
YUDENICH, Alexei - 72-73 (I/III)

- Z -

ZANNE, Eugénie - 66-69 (III/III)
ZORINA, Leila - 57-61 (III/III)
ZUROWSKI, Diane - 90-91 (c)

Appendix E
Members of the Board, the National Ballet of Canada 1951–52 to 1990–91

The board membership lists were compiled from the annual Souvenir Programs and double-checked against the company's internal annual listings. Members are listed alphabetically by surname, using the form preferred at the time of publication in the Souvenir Program, followed by years of active membership on the board, with city of origin indicated in square brackets. Honorary members have not been included. Certain staff members of the company serve on the board ex officio and, since 1970, dancers have elected representatives to the board. All of these have been included, without special designation. Presidents of the board have been indicated within the general listing in boldface, upper case type, with their term of office as president stated separately.

- A -

Thomas P. **Abel**, 1961-7 [Toronto]
Mrs H.R. **Agnew**, 1957-61 [Toronto]
Donald C. **Aitken**, 1965-9 [St Catharines]
Michael O. **Alexander**, 1986 91[Toronto]
J.C.L. **Allen**, 1951-5 [Toronto]
John M. **Allen**, 1975-7 [Toronto]
Reid **Anderson**, 1989-91 [Toronto]
William A.B. **Anderson**, 1978-84 [Toronto/Ottawa]
Kenneth B. **Andras**, 1961-6 [Toronto]
Mrs Brook **Angus**, 1969-70 [Toronto]
Mrs G. **Armstrong**, 1970-2 [Toronto]
Judith **Aspinall**, 1987-91 [Toronto]
Philip **Aspinall**, 1966-8 [Montreal]
David **Atkins**, 1986-90 [Toronto]
Maria **Augimeri**, 1988-91 [Toronto]
Julian **AvRutick**, 1961-4 [Toronto]

- B -

André **Bachand**, 1952-61 [Montreal]
Martin **Baldwin**, 1951-8 [Toronto]
Mrs St Clair **Balfour, Jr**, 1961-9 [Toronto]
C.S. **Band**, 1952-4 [Toronto]
Mona **Bandeen**, 1985-91 [Toronto]
Mrs D.C. **Barber**, 1957-8 [Hamilton]
William S. **Barnard**, 1985-9 [Toronto]
R.V. **Barnett**, 1951-66 [Toronto]
J. Flavelle **Barrett**, 1968-77 [Toronto]
June **Barrett**, 1976-9 [Toronto]
Douglas G. **Bassett**, 1978-85 [Toronto]
Thomas J. **Bata**, 1963-74 [Batawa]
Hon. Justice Harry **Batshaw**, 1955-7 [Montreal]
Peter G. **Beattie**, 1976-88 [Toronto]
Roger L. **Beaulieu**, 1967-74 [Montreal]
Mrs Paul **Bedard**, 1962-3 [Quebec City]
Mary Grace **Bell**, 1979-81 [London]
Maxwell G. **Bell**, 1969-71 [Calgary]
Avie J. **Bennett**, 1984-91 [Toronto]
J.W. **Bennett**, 1957-9 [Toronto]
James E. **Bennett**, 1978-82 [Toronto]
Mrs Donald S. **Bethune**, 1970-2 [Hamilton]
Arthur **Bishop**, 1965-6 [Toronto]
Susan **Bissett**, 1986-91 [Toronto]
Mrs Walter **Blackburn**, 1961-4 [London]
Dr Vincent **Bladen**, 1969-72 [Toronto]
J.D.W. **Blythe**, 1961-3 [Toronto]
William B. **Boggs**, 1979-82 [Toronto]
D. Strachan **Bongard, Jr**, 1964-71 [Toronto]
Dr E.H. **Botterell**, 1956-7 [Toronto]
Gerard **Boudrias**, 1952-4 [Montreal]
T. Larry **Bourk**, 1988-90 [Toronto/Kitchener]
EDMUND C. BOVEY, 1981-90 [Toronto], **President 1985-7**
Walter **Bowen**, 1967-70 [Toronto]
Mrs Ronald G. **Brand**, 1970-2 [Windsor]
Paul D. **Break**, 1974-80 [Toronto]
George E.M. **Brickwood**, 1966-7 [Belleville]
Dr Joan **Bronskill**, 1960-2 [Belleville]
Peter **Brophy**, 1986-7 [Toronto]
David G.R. **Brown**, 1963-4 [Toronto]
Erik **Bruhn**, 1983-6 [Toronto]
Pierce **Bunting**, 1965-6 [Toronto]
Dr Gerald N. **Burrow**, 1983-8 [Montreal]
Thomas B. **Burrows**, 1975-9 [Toronto]

- C -

Michael B. **Callaghan**, 1966-70 [Toronto]
Elaine **Campbell**, 1970-89 [Toronto]
John D. **Campbell**, 1962-8 [Hamilton]
Pat **Campbell**, 1975-6 [Toronto]
Lynn **Cantor**, 1990-1 [Toronto]
Paul **Carder**, 1983-9 [Toronto]
William J. **Carradine**, 1979-84 [Toronto]
Mrs Owen **Carter**, 1959-60 [Sillery]
Mrs Patrick **Cassels**, 1959-61 [Toronto]
HAMILTON CASSELS, JR, 1960-72 [Toronto], **President 1965-6**
Mrs Hamilton **Cassels, Jr**, 1955-60 [Toronto]
Diana **Chant**, 1987-91 [Toronto]
Mrs J.K. **Chasty**, 1966-8 [Hamilton/Oakville]
William J. **Cheesman**, 1969-72 [Hamilton]
Mrs Robert F. **Chisholm**, 1966-71 [Toronto]
Yvonne **Chiu**, 1990-1 [Toronto]
Minnette **Church**, 1981-3 [London]
Mrs A.G. **Clark**, 1970-1 [Toronto]
Gavin C. **Clark**, 1963-72 [Toronto]
W. Edmund **Clark**, 1987-91 [Toronto]
Irena **Cohen**, 1977-80 [Winnipeg]
JUDITH LOEB COHEN, 1985-91 [Toronto], **President 1987-90**
J. Gordon **Coleman**, 1982-7 [Toronto]
Russell **Collier**, 1965-7 [Toronto]
Mrs Cecil **Collins-Williams**, 1966-7 [Toronto]
Charles F. **Comfort**, 1960-4 [Ottawa]
Dr John **Conway**, 1968-71 [Toronto]
Marvin **Corber**, 1977-9 [Montreal]
Tom F. **Corcoran**, 1990-1 [Toronto]
C.R. **Corey**, 1963-8 [London]
Harold **Corrigan**, 1977-83 [Montreal]
J.S. **Corrigan**, 1962-6 [Toronto]
James E. **Coutts**, 1974-5 [Toronto]
John **Cowperthwaite**, 1985-6 [Toronto]
Norman A. **Cox**, 1962-6 [Toronto]
G.H. **Craig**, 1951-3 [Toronto]
James **Cran**, 1966-70 [Toronto]
Mrs L.G. **Crawford**, 1963-7 [Montreal]
Mrs T. **Cristall**, 1951-8 [Edmonton]

- D -

Mrs D.N. **Dalley**, 1966-8 [Hamilton]
Mrs S.G. **Dalley**, 1962-4 [Ancaster]
Nancy **Davidson**, 1986-7 [London]
Jeannie **Davis**, 1980-9 [Mississauga]
Jean **de Brabant**, 1972-85 [Montreal]
PAUL S. DEACON, 1969-90 [Toronto/Ottawa], **President 1975-8**
Jean-Claude **Delorme**, 1979-82 [Montreal]
David L. **Dennis, Q.C.**, 1972-3; 89-91 [Toronto]
John D. **dePencier**, 1965-72 [Toronto]
Joan **Dewis**, 1972-7 [London]
Richard W. **Dodds**, 1978-90 [Toronto]
Mrs C.R. **Douglas**, 1965-71 [Toronto]
Mrs M.G. **Dover**, 1951-3 [Calgary]

Mrs Paulette **Drouin**, 1964-7 [Quebec City]
Nancy **Dunlap**, 1984-7 [Toronto]
Mrs Gilles **Dupuis**, 1963-4 [Quebec City]

- E -

Dr Arthur **Earle**, 1982-5 [Toronto]
M.G. **Eaton**, 1975-8 [Toronto/Montreal]
Sherry Taylor **Eaton**, 1986-91 [Toronto]
Gerry **Eldred**, 1972-9 [Toronto]
John F. **Ellis**, 1964-8 [Toronto]
Mrs E.C. **Elwood**, 1958-61 [London]
Arthur **Erickson**, 1972-5 [Vancouver]

- F -

Robert A. **Ferchat**, 1989-91 [Toronto]
D. Morgan **Firestone**, 1970-4 [Hamilton/Oakville]
Mrs Edouard **Fiset**, 1960-1 [Quebec City]
Dr James **Fleck**, 1966-74; 75-86 [Toronto]
Bernard **Flexer**, 1962-3 [Montreal]
David Glen **Fountain**, 1987-91 [Toronto]
Robert M. **Fowler**, 1952-3 [Montreal]
Joan **Fox-Revett**, 1968-79 [Toronto]
Miss Celia **Franca**, 1952-74 [Toronto]
Dr Murray **Frum**, 1985-91 [Toronto]
Dorinda **Fuller**, 1977-9 [London]

- G -

Charles **Gagnon**, 1972-3 [Montreal]
ANDRÉ J. GALIPEAULT, 1976-91 [Toronto], **President 1980-2**
Bruce C. **Galloway**, 1986-91 [Toronto]
Kay **Gardner**, 1985-9 [Toronto]
S. James **Gaston**, 1976-86 [Toronto]
ARTHUR E. GELBER, 1951-69; 85-91 [Toronto], **President 1961-3**
Gordon **Gibson**, 1958-64 [Toronto]
J. Douglas **Gibson**, 1971-3 [Toronto]
R.C. **Gibson**, 1962-4 [Toronto]
Philip G. **Givens**, 1967-71 [Toronto]
Ogden **Glass**, 1961-5 [Sherbrooke]
Ted A. **Glista**, 1972-3 [Mississauga]
John F. **Godfrey**, 1987-8 [Toronto]
JOHN M. GODFREY, 1961-70 [Toronto], **President 1967-9**
EDWIN A. GOODMAN, 1951-65; 69-73 [Toronto], **President 1958-60**
Kamala-Jean **Gopie**, 1990-1 [Toronto]
Jacques **Gorrissen**, 1975-81; 82-3 [Toronto]
Alexander **Grant,** 1975-83 [Toronto]
Peter **Grant**, 1980-2 [Toronto]
Louis J.M. **Gravel**, 1961-2 [Montreal]
A.G.S. GRIFFIN, 1953-61; 69-72 [Toronto], **President 1954-7**
Mrs Eric **Griffin**, 1956-7 [Hamilton]
Peter **Griffin**, 1958-62 [Galt]
Alfred A. **Guglielmin**, 1979-82 [Toronto]

- H -

Max **Haas**, 1954-9 [Toronto]
Mrs Max **Haas**, 1953-5; 58-60 [Toronto]
David **Haber**, 1973-5 [Toronto]
Janice **Haeberlin**, 1976-7 [Toronto]
Mrs O. **Hall**, 1972-3 [Vancouver]
John W. **Hamilton**, 1961-4 [Toronto]
Col C.M. **Harding**, 1963-5 [Brantford]
Mrs P. **Harris**, 1968-9 [Toronto]
Peter D. **Harris**, 1962-6 [Toronto]
William B. **Harris**, 1978-90 [Toronto]
M.C. **Hawkins**, 1954-5 [Toronto]
Neville **Hawthorne**, 1961-5 [Toronto]
Frank **Hay**, 1958-64 [Toronto]
Mrs George **Hees**, 1951-7 [Toronto]
Mrs Daniel **Heilig**, 1965-6 [Sherbrooke]
B.C. **Heintzman, Jr**, 1951-3 [Toronto]
W. Lawrence **Heisey**, 1988-91 [Toronto]
The Hon. Paul **Hellyer**, 1970-5 [Ottawa]
Ann **Henderson**, 1982-8 [Woodbridge]
LYMAN G. HENDERSON, 1963-78 [Toronto], **President 1969-72**
William R. **Herridge**, 1970-3; 85-91 [Toronto]
A.E. **Hetherington**, 1966-73 [London]
E. Bruce **Heyland**, 1985-91 [Toronto]
D.C. **Higginbotham**, 1956-9; 70-2 [Toronto]
John **Hirsch**, 1975-8 [Toronto]
H. Peter **Holland**, 1971-2 [Toronto]
Mrs Luther **Holton**, 1960-74 [Waterdown]
Mrs Mark **Holton**, 1953-5; 56-62 [Hamilton]
Ying **Hope**, 1982-6 [Toronto]
Tony **Houghton**, 1990-1 [Toronto]
JOHN D. HOULDING, 1976-88 [Toronto], **President 1982-5**
The Hon. Samuel H. **Hughes**, 1960-4 [Ottawa/Toronto]
W.S. **Hulton**, 1961-72 [Toronto]
Mrs Tuija **Hunnakko**, 1972-87 [Toronto]
Mrs Keith **Hutchison**, 1952-3; 64-71 [Montreal]

- I -

Dan **Iannuzzi, Jr**, 1972-3 [Toronto]
Joan **Ivory**, 1989-91 [Montreal]

- J -

Karl **Jaffary**, 1972-5 [Toronto]
Mary **Jago**, 1973-83 [Toronto]
Alan **Jarvis**, 1960-4 [Toronto]
Thomas **Jarvis**, 1967-74 [Toronto]
Robert D. **Johnston**, 1979-91 [Toronto]
Prof. E.M. **Jones**, 1951-5 [Saskatoon]
M.F. **Jones**, 1962-4 [Niagara Falls]
Bengt **Jörgen**, 1983-5 [Toronto]
Dr Robert C. **Joyner**, 1971-2 [Toronto]
Paul **Jurist**, 1986-91 [Toronto]

- K -

Karen **Kain**, 1979-80; 83-4; 89-91 [Toronto]
F.G. **Kellam**, 1961-2 [Kitchener]
Helen **Kelly**, 1974-7 [Belleville]
Derrick F. **Kershaw**, 1977-86 [Toronto/Port Hope]
G. Edmund **King**, 1978-86 [Toronto]
Leo **Knowlton**, 1958-61 [Toronto]
Michael **Koerner**, 1962-74 [Toronto]
Joyce **Kofman**, 1979-88 [Toronto]
Mrs R.J. **Kraszewski**, 1972-4 [Belleville]

- L -

Mrs Hugh **Labatt**, 1951-8 [London]
Stephanie **Landry**, 1985-9 [Toronto]
The Hon. Daniel **Lang**, 1969-75 [Toronto]
John E. **Lang**, 1979-81; 84-5 [Toronto/Calgary]
Z.R.B. LASH, 1951-4 [Toronto], **President 1952-4**
Jean **Leahy**, 1961-5 [Quebec City]
Mrs Jean **Leahy**, 1961-2; 64-70 [Quebec City]
H.H. **Leather**, 1956-7 [Hamilton]
Gordon H. **Lennard**, 1963-70 [Toronto]
Pearce **Lettner**, 1963-70 [Windsor]
Rosabel **Levitt**, 1974-9 [Toronto]
Dr Léon **Lortie**, 1957-61 [Montreal]
Pierre **Lortie**, 1987-90 [Montreal]
Jeanne E. **Loughheed**, 1976-85 [Edmonton]
Phillips **Lounsbery**, 1970-2 [Toronto]
Jolianne **Lowrie**, 1984-8 [Toronto]
Dr Frederick **Lowy**, 1989-91 [Toronto]

- M -

His Hon. Judge Bruce J. **Macdonald**, 1965-8 [Windsor]
Mrs C.D. **Macdonald**, 1974-5 [Toronto]
W.L. **Macdonald**, 1955-7 [Toronto]
Mrs W.B. **Macdonald, Jr**, 1955-6 [Toronto]
Eve **MacDougall**, 1985-91 [Toronto]
Mrs Bruce **MacGowan**, 1967-8 [Toronto]
J.P.S. **Mackenzie**, 1971-3 [Toronto]
Mrs D.I. **MacKinnon**, 1962-6; 67-72 [Belleville]
Peter **MacLachlin**, 1967-72 [Toronto]
Duncan K. **MacTavish**, 1957-8 [Ottawa]
Kay **Manderville**, 1969-70; 77-9 [Belleville]
André **Marcil**, 1958-69 [Montreal]
Allen **Marple**, 1989-91 [Toronto]
Carol **Marshall**, 1988-91 [Toronto]
R.K. **Martin**, 1960-2 [Toronto]
Bryn C. **Matthews**, 1963-8 [Toronto]
Mrs J.H. **Maudsley**, 1965-9 [Montreal]
Linda **Maybarduk**, 1978-9 [Toronto]

Mrs W. Stanley **McBean**, 1972-4 [Windsor]
Mrs S.K. **McBirnie**, 1956-7 [Toronto]
Mrs P.C. **McCabe**, 1959-61 [Tecumseh]
Brenda **McCarthy**, 1984-90 [Toronto]
Leighton **McCarthy**, 1969-72 [Toronto]
Barbara **McDermott**, 1985-6 [London]
Barbara **McDiarmid**, 1985-6 [Toronto]
H.J. **McDonald**, 1964-7 [Toronto]
Mrs Ross **McDonald**, 1968-70 [Toronto]
Robert J. **McGavin**, 1986-91 [Toronto]
The Hon. Frank C. **McGee**, 1965-8 [Toronto]
George V. **McGough**, 1987-90 [Scarborough]
IAN H. MCLEOD, 1970-9; 85-7 [Toronto/London], **President 1972-5**
Miles **McMenemy**, 1986-91 [Toronto]
Duncan **McTavish**, 1956-7 [Ottawa]
Julie **Medland**, 1989-91 [Toronto]
David **Meen**, 1982-91 [Toronto]
Senator Michael A. **Meighen**, 1986-91 [Toronto]
Mrs C.J. **Menendez**, 1963-5 [Ottawa]
Murray **Menkes**, 1988-91 [Toronto]
E.A. **Meredith**, 1975-6 [Toronto]
William B. **Merrick**, 1971-3 [Toronto]
Arthur **Minden**, 1958-9 [Toronto]
Mary **Mingie**, 1978-82 [Toronto]
Clive **Minto**, 1990-1 [Toronto]
William T. **Mitchell**, 1982-91 [Toronto]
P.T. **Molson**, 1964-6 [Toronto]
Mrs W.O. **Moore-Ede**, 1952-3 [Toronto]
Mrs R.T. **Morgan**, 1963-9 [Toronto]
D.W. **Morison**, 1963-8; 70-3 [Toronto]
Mrs F.J. **Mulqueen**, 1951-5 [Toronto]

- N -

MARK NAPIER, 1955-62 [Toronto], **President 1958**
Knowlton **Nash**, 1988-90 [Toronto]
J.H.B. **Nederpelt**, 1986-91 [Toronto]
Carol **Nesker**, 1988-91 [Toronto]
R. George **Ness**, 1969-73 [Toronto]
E.W. **Newell**, 1963-9 [Toronto]
Mrs Douglas M. **Norman**, 1973-4 [Toronto]
Henry G. **Norman**, 1956-8 [Montreal]
M.R. **Norman**, 1965-8 [Toronto]

- O -

Paul H. **O'Donoghue**, 1984-90 [Toronto]
Wanda **O'Hagan**, 1989-91 [Toronto]
Gwen **O'Loughlin**, 1958-61 [St Catharines]
June **Ogden**, 1975-7 [Hamilton]
Betty **Oliphant**, 1969-89 [Toronto]
Peter **Oliphant**, 1963-70 [Toronto]
Christopher **Ondaatje**, 1987-90 [Toronto]
The Hon. Mr Justice John H. **Osler**, 1957-66; 69-72 [Toronto]
Nina **Overbury**, 1971-2; 75-8; 79-80; 83-6 [Toronto]
David S. **Owen**, 1969-70 [Toronto]

- P -

William M. **Pape**, 1970-2; 79-81 [Belleville]
Lynne **Paton**, 1980-2 [Hamilton]
David P. **Payne**, 1981-4; 88-9; 90-1 [Toronto]
Robert E. **Peel**, 1961-70 [Toronto]
Miss Vida H. **Peene**, 1954-8 [Toronto]
P. Wayne **Penny**, 1968-72 [Toronto]
H.E.E. **Pepler**, 1974-7 [Toronto]
Mrs H.E.E. **Pepler**, 1972-4 [Toronto]
John C. **Perlin**, 1972-90 [St John's]
Mrs Richard **Perry**, 1968-9 [Toronto]
James **Peterson**, 1975-80; 86-9 [Toronto]
JAMES B. PITBLADO, 1988-91 [Toronto], **President 1990-1**
I.C. **Pollack**, 1957-62 [Quebec City]
C.A. **Pollock**, 1959-64 [Kitchener]
Jack **Pollock**, 1972-3 [Toronto]
R.F. **Porter, Jr**, 1953-5 [Toronto]
Mme. Omer **Pouliot**, 1957-9 [Quebec City]
Shirley **Powis**, 1975-8 [Toronto]
Bernard **Protter**, 1968-73 [Toronto]
Mrs Bernard **Protter**, 1970-2 [Toronto]

- R -

S.J. **Randall**, 1959-60 [Toronto]
E.V. **Rechnitzer**, 1962-4 [Toronto]
Mrs J.K. **Reid**, 1954-5; 56-9 [Windsor]
Dr J.K. **Reynolds**, 1981-9 [Toronto]
Victor **Rice**, 1983-7 [Toronto]
Leona **Riggs**, 1958-60 [Belleville]
Marion **Roberts**, 1983-5 [London]
Mrs John **Robertson**, 1962-5 [St Catharines]
E. Jane **Rogers**, 1978-81 [Vancouver]
Lucien **Rolland**, 1961-70 [Montreal]
Judy **Romanchuk**, 1986-91 [Calgary]
Barrie D. **Rose**, 1966-80 [Toronto]
Sandra **Rotman**, 1987-91 [Toronto]
Alex J. **Rubin**, 1964-70 [Toronto]
Wallace A. **Russell**, 1969-72 [Toronto]
Peter K. **Ryan**, 1966-8 [Windsor]

- S -

R. MCCARTNEY SAMPLES, 1971-89 [Toronto], **President 1978-80**
Jean Paul **Savard**, 1965-6 [Sherbrooke]
Norman H. **Schipper**, 1962-6 [Toronto]
Tomas **Schramek**, 1981-2; 85-91 [Toronto]
S.C. **Scobell**, 1954-62 [Montreal]
Mrs Douglas **Scott**, 1966-70 [Toronto]
Eric **Scott**, 1956-7 [Toronto]
Norman O. **Seagram, Jr**, 1952-6 [Toronto]
Lawrence F. **Sefton**, 1962-8 [Toronto]
Gordon **Sharwood**, 1965-9 [Toronto]
Mrs Terence **Sheard**, 1961-2 [Toronto]
E.J. **Shoniker**, 1959-63 [Toronto]
Guy **Sicotte**, 1965-6 [Montreal]
Heather **Sifton**, 1987-91 [Markham]
LT GEN. GUY G. SIMONDS, 1960-7; 68-9 [Toronto], **President 1963-5**
Bruce **Sinclair**, 1981-2 [Toronto]
Henry J. **Sissons**, 1962-6 [Toronto]
Dr H. Alan **Skinner**, 1951-67 [London]
James **Slater**, 1977-80 [Toronto]
Mrs Gordon **Small**, 1955-63 [Montreal]
Mrs Bruce **Smith**, 1958-9 [Edmonton]
Mrs Gerald E. **Smith**, 1968-70 [Windsor]
Ronald S. **Smith**, 1987-91 [Toronto]
Sam **Sorbara**, 1965-6 [Toronto]
Audrey **Southam**, 1977-80 [Hamilton]
D. Cargill **Southam**, 1953-4 [Montreal]
Mrs G.R. **Sparrow**, 1961-2 [St Catharines]
Nicholas **Speke**, 1972-3 [Toronto]
Mrs J.G. **Spragge**, 1953-4 [Toronto]
Renault **St Laurent**, 1957-70 [Sillery]
John G. **Staiger**, 1970-3 [Toronto]
Mavis **Staines**, 1989-91 [Toronto]
Paul F. **Starita**, 1986-91 [Toronto]
Marshal **Stearns**, 1955-6 [Toronto]
Mrs Robert N. **Steiner**, 1968-70 [Hamilton]
Timothy **Stewart**, 1976-88 [Caledon East]
H. Heward **Stikeman**, 1954-7 [Montreal]
Mary Alice **Stuart**, 1979-86 [Toronto]
Humphrey B. **Style**, 1958-9 [Toronto]
W.J. **Sutton**, 1967-70 [Toronto]
S.G. **Svensson**, 1972-4 [Toronto]
Terrance **Sweeney**, 1972-4 [Toronto]
Thecla **Sweeney**, 1972-3; 82-6 [Toronto]
John H. **Switzer**, 1990-1 [Toronto]

- T -

Burton **Tait**, 1971-80 [Toronto]
Judith **Tait**, 1970-1; 74-9 [Toronto]
Mrs Robert **Tanner**, 1956-8 [Belleville]
Mrs Paul D. **Taylor**, 1972-5 [Hamilton]
Veronica **Tennant**, 1970-3; 84-5 [Toronto]
Claude **Thibault**, 1966-70 [Sherbrooke/Lennoxville]
Mrs J.K. **Thomas**, 1963-70 [Toronto]
David Y. **Timbrell**, 1959-65; 70-2 [Toronto]
Philip **Torno**, 1961-4 [Toronto]
F.G. **Townsend**, 1962-9 [Toronto]
Joyce **Trimmer**, 1977-9 [Toronto]
Robert L. **Turnbull**, 1968-71 [London]
John N. **Turner**, 1990-1 [Toronto]
Murray **Turner**, 1965-7 [Toronto]
Edward S. **Tyityan**, 1988-91 [Toronto]

- U -

Mrs P.L. **Underwood**, 1963-8 [Toronto]

- V -

Robin **Vaile**, 1988-91 [Toronto]
Harry A.C. **Van Beurden**, 1965-71 [Toronto]
H.P. **van Gelder**, 1953-4 [Toronto]
Stanley **Vineberg**, 1952-5 [Montreal]
A. Hans **Vorster**, 1972-3 [Toronto]

- W -

A.H. **Wait**, 1964-6; 68-9 [Toronto]
Mrs A.H. **Wait**, 1959-69 [Toronto]
Hugh P. **Walker**, 1958-74 [Toronto]
W.P. WALKER, 1959-68 [Toronto], **President 1960-1**
Lynn **Wallis**, 1986-9 [Toronto]
Lenore **Walters**, 1986-90 [Toronto]
Mrs Michael **Walters**, 1962-5 [Kitchener]
Alexander **Walton**, 1952-5; 62-79 [Vancouver]
J.P. **Walwyn**, 1952-3 [Toronto]
J.F.W. **Weatherill**, 1966-73 [Toronto]
Donald C. **Webster**, 1966-9 [Toronto]
Leon E. **Weinstein**, 1966-7 [Toronto]
Col Douglas B. **Weldon**, 1965-70 [London]
William **Weldon**, 1989-91 [Toronto]
Denis **Whitaker**, 1962-4 [Toronto]
Mrs W.D. **Whitaker**, 1964-6 [Hamilton]
Peter G. **White**, 1978-84 [London]
Mrs R.B. **Whitehead**, 1951-8 [Toronto]
Roderick J. **Whitehead**, 1972-3 [Calgary]
Mrs John **Whiteside**, 1961-6 [Windsor]
T.F. WHITLEY, 1956-64 [Toronto/Vancouver], **President 1957-8**
Joseph. A. **Whitmore**, 1951-4; 61-2 [Toronto]
Fred **Whittall**, 1960-1 [Montreal]
Miss Mildred **Wickson**, 1954-61 [Toronto]
Valerie **Wilder**, 1976-8; 86-9 [Toronto]
W.P. **Wilder**, 1958-61 [Toronto]
Mrs C.I. **Wilson**, 1967-8; 72-3 [Belleville]
Gordon **Wilson**, 1988-91 [Toronto]
Graham **Wilson**, 1986-8 [Hamilton]
John **Wimbs**, 1979-81 [Toronto]
Jonathan A. **Wolfe**, 1990-1 [Toronto]
Mrs R.D. **Wolfe**, 1972-4 [Toronto]
Ray D. **Wolfe**, 1964-5; 71-2; 89-90 [Toronto]
Carolyn I. **Woodard**, 1988-90 [Toronto]
Mrs J.D. **Woods**, 1951-8 [Toronto]
Michael E. **Wright**, 1972-3 [Toronto]

- Y -

Mrs David **Young**, 1958-60 [Ancaster]
Robert G. **Young**, 1970-3 [London]

- Z -

Mrs Myron **Zandmer**, 1956-9 [Calgary]

Notes

Verification for the essential facts of the company's history comes primarily from three sources: the company's Archives; the National Archives of Canada, which house Celia Franca's personal papers and the records of the Canada Council; and interviews with dancers and others associated with the company throughout its development. The notes to the text try to document clearly all sources for statements about the company, indicating the locations of those sources, so that students may examine them for themselves, as necessary. I wish to acknowledge here, with thanks, the National Ballet of Canada, for permission to quote from documents in its Archives, and Celia Franca, for permission to quote from her papers in the National Archives of Canada.

Those whose names are listed below consented to speak with me about their involvement with the company. Conversations with them are cited in the individual endnotes, along with the date on which the conversation took place.

Lawrence Adams, David Adams, Miriam Adams, David Allan, Jocelyn Allen, John Alleyne, Reid Anderson, Frank Augustyn, James Austin, Larry Beevers, Carol Beevers, Victoria Bertram, Natalia Butko, Assis Carreiro, Lou Anne Cassels, Stephen Chadwick, Judie Colpman, George Crum, Dame Ninette de Valois, John de Pencier, Ann Ditchburn, Walter Foster, Celia Franca, Lorna Geddes, Arthur Gelber, Alexander Grant, Tony Griffin, David Haber, Lyman Henderson, Mary Jago, Robert Johnston, Karen Kain, Charles Kirby, Earl Kraul, James Kudelka, Charles Lester, Marquita Lester, Beth Lockhart, Linda Maybarduk, Mary McDonald, Howard Meadows, Joanne Nisbet, Rudolf Nureyev, Betty Oliphant, Dieter Penzhorn, Magdalena Popa, Timothy Porteous, Kevin Pugh, Wendy Reid, Galina Samsova, Peter Schaufuss, Georg Schlögl, Tomas Schramek, Patricia Scott, David Scott, Lois Smith, Grant Strate, Veronica Tennant, Glen Tetley, Martine van Hamel, David Walker, Lynn Wallis, Valerie Wilder, Gizella Witkowsky.

CHAPTER 1

1. For a contemporary expression of this point of view, see Harry Warlaw, 'Ballet in Canada Is Here to Stay,' *Saturday Night*, Vol. 64, No. 20 (22 February 1949), and *Mayfair* magazine, December 1951, p. 112.
2. Max Wyman, *The Royal Winnipeg Ballet: The First Forty Years* (Toronto and Garden City, New York: Doubleday, 1978), p. 52.
3. David Adams in conversation with the author, 11 April 1988.
4. Lois Smith in conversation with the author, 24 May 1988.
5. Martha Bremser, ed., *International Dictionary of Ballet* (Detroit, London, Washington: St James Press, 1977), entry under 'Wilde'; Celia Franca in conversation with the author, 14 October 1987.
6. Rasa Gustaitis, *Melissa Hayden, Ballerina* (London, New York, Toronto: Thomas Nelson & Sons, 1967), pp. 27, 28–9, and 41.
7. Franca, Celia, and Ken Bell, *The National Ballet of Canada: A Celebration* (Toronto, Buffalo, London: University of Toronto Press, 1978), p. 221.
8. Guy Glover, 'Reflections on Canadian Ballet, 1950,' *Canadian Art*, VIII, 3 (Spring, 1951), p. 127. Glover's article provides a detailed description of the Third Annual Canadian Ballet Festival.
9. Kathrine Sorley Walker, *De Basil's Ballets Russes* (London: Hutchinson, 1982), p. 190. See also Leland Windreich, 'Vancouver Dancers in the Ballet Russe: Three "Canadian Exotics,"' *Vandance*, May 1978.
10. Lois Smith in conversation with the author, 24 May 1988.
11. Lillian Leonora Mitchell, *Boris Volkoff: Dancer, Teacher, Choreographer* (Ann Arbor, Michigan: University Microfilms International, 1982), pp. 22–40.
12. Wyman, *The Royal Winnipeg Ballet*, p. 17.
13. Betty Oliphant in conversation with the author, 17 August 1988. See also 'Brief to the Royal Commission, Submitted on Behalf of the Canadian Ballet Festival Association,' 4 November 1949, p. 9, Dance Collection Danse.
14. 'Exile-Inspired Ballet: Halifax Group Organized by Latvians,' Toronto *Telegram*, 13 October 1950; Herbert Whittaker, 'Latvian Dancers Highlight Ballet Panorama at Eaton Auditorium, Saturday,' Toronto *Globe and Mail*, 16 October 1950.
15. Wyman, *The Royal Winnipeg Ballet*, pp. 76, 79, 265.
16. NBOC Archives, notes from Boris Volkoff to Aileen Woods, 28 April 1964, Aileen Woods File, #73. See also Herbert Whittaker, *Canada's National Ballet* (Toronto and Montreal: McClelland and Stewart, 1967), p. 8 and Mitchell, *Boris Volkoff*, pp. 71–85.
17. Mitchell, *Boris Volkoff*, p. 215.
18. Natalia Butko in conversation with the author, 7 July 1988.
19. For fuller descriptions of these festivals, see Wyman, *The Royal Winnipeg Ballet*, pp. 58–63, 66–7, 73, 76, and 230; see also Max Wyman, *Dance Canada: An Illustrated History* (Vancouver, Toronto: Douglas & McIntyre, 1989), pp. 38–41.
20. Wyman, *The Royal Winnipeg Ballet*, p. 76. Celia Franca acknowledges as well that Gweneth Lloyd had been involved in the consultation process (conversation with the author, 14 October 1987).
21. Metropolitan Toronto Reference Library, Special Collections Centre, Boris Volkoff Papers, Scrapbook #11.
22. NBOC Archives, notes from Boris Volkoff to Aileen Woods, 28 April 1964, Aileen Woods File, #73.
23. Metropolitan Toronto Reference Library, Special Collections Centre, Volkoff to James, 5 January 1949, Boris Volkoff Papers, Box #1, Envelope #3.
24. Whittaker, *Canada's National Ballet*, p. 15.
25. Stewart James to the *Globe and Mail*, 18 June 1977; National Archives of Canada, 'Ballet – Guy Glover,' Franca Papers (21-12).
26. Natalia Butko in conversation with the author, 7 July 1988.
27. Dame Ninette de Valois in conversation with the author, 16 March 1988.
28. Celia Franca in conversation with the author, 14 October 1987.
29. NBOC Archives, Aileen Woods File, #73.
30. NBOC Archives, Woods to Franca, 19 October 1950, 'Founding of Nat. Ballet – 1950–52' File, #500.
31. Brian Macdonald, 'The Impact of British Ballet on the Canadian Dance Scene,' *Dancing Times*, April 1963, p. 419.
32. Wyman, *The Royal Winnipeg Ballet*, pp. 74–6. Natalia Butko, in conversation with the author, 7 July 1988, believes that both Lloyd and Volkoff may have had their eyes on the artistic directorship and that some form of compromise was necessary to avoid offending one or the other of them.
33. Celia Franca in conversation with the author, 14 October 1987.
34. NBOC Archives, Aileen Woods File, #73.

35. NBOC Archives, notes from Boris Volkoff to Aileen Woods, 28 April 1964, Aileen Woods File, #73.

36. Celia Franca in conversation with the author, 14 October 1987.

37. NBOC Archives, handwritten notes dated 27 October, Aileen Woods File, #73.

38. NBOC Archives, 'Founding of Nat. Ballet – 1950–52' File, #500.

39. National Archives of Canada, notes by Sydney Mulqueen, 15 May 1963, Franca Papers (20-2).

40. NBOC Archives, Bernadette Carpenter to Aileen Woods, 29 March [1964?], Aileen Woods File, #73.

41. David Adams in conversation with the author, 11 April 1988; Celia Franca in conversation with the author, 14 October 1987. See also notes by Celia Franca for a lecture to the Ballet Circle, 24 April 1949, p. 6, which give an account of David Adams' dancing with the Metropolitan Ballet, National Archives of Canada, Franca Papers (9-1).

42. Celia Franca in conversation with the author, 19 August 1988.

43. Dame Ninette de Valois in conversation with the author, 16 March 1988.

44. Whittaker, *Canada's National Ballet*, p. 16, enshrines the comment, which can be found in numerous early press releases and publicity biographies.

45. Celia Franca in conversation with the author, 19 August 1988.

46. Ballet Rambert Archives, notes by Patricia Clogstoun on preparation of *Dark Elegies*; opening night program. Although the opening night program is dated 15 February 1937, Clogstoun's notes indicate that the first performance had to be postponed to 19 February.

47. Franca, *The National Ballet: A Celebration* , p. 8.

48. Alexander Grant in conversation with the author, 22 March 1988.

49. David Adams in conversation with the author, 11 April 1988.

50. Alexander Bland, *The Royal Ballet: The First Fifty Years* (Garden City, New York: Doubleday & Company, 1981), p. 296.

51. Celia Franca in conversation with the author, 14 October 1987.

52. See John Percival in the London *Times*, 16 May 1972.

53. National Archives of Canada, notes for a lecture to the Ballet Circle, 24 April 1949, Franca Papers (9-1).

54. John Gruen, *Erik Bruhn: Danseur Noble* (New York: Viking Press, 1979), p. 38.

55. In addition to the works and individuals already cited in notes to this paragraph, I have consulted the following sources in reconstructing the London period of Celia Franca's career: NBOC Archives, draft listing for *Creative Canada: A Biographical Dictionary of Twentieth-Century Canadians in Literature and the Arts*, dated 1967, Franca Files, Box #1; Ferdinand Reyna, trans. André Gâteau, *Concise Encyclopedia of Ballet* (London and Glasgow: Collins, 1974), entries under 'Franca' and 'Metropolitan Ballet'; Mary Clarke and David Vaughan, eds, *The Encyclopedia of Dance and Ballet* (London: Peerage Books, 1977), entries under 'Franca' and 'Metropolitan Ballet'; Bremser, *International Dictionary of Ballet*, entry under 'Franca.'

56. Wyman, *The Royal Winnipeg Ballet*, pp. 11–15.

57. Reyna, *Concise Encyclopedia of Ballet*, entry under 'Volkov.' See also Mitchell, *Boris Volkoff*, pp. 20–7.

58. Celia Franca in conversation with the author, 14 October 1987.

59. Mitchell, *Boris Volkoff*, p. 333.

60. Betty Oliphant in conversation with the author, 17 August 1988.

61. Celia Franca in conversation with the author, 19 August 1988.

62. NBOC Archives, Board Minutes for 21 May 1952, p. 3, #109-A. See also Whittaker, *Canada's National Ballet*, p. 40.

63. NBOC Archives, Board Minutes for 31 October 1951, Aileen Woods File, #73.

64. Lois Smith in conversation with the author, 24 May 1988; Galina Samsova in conversation with the author, 14 March 1988; Lawrence Adams in conversation with the author, 17 November 1989.

65. Mitchell, *Boris Volkoff*, pp. 291–2; a program for Toronto Theatre Ballet's appearance at a Promenade Concert on 17 July 1952 is in the Boris Volkoff Papers, Box #1, Envelope #7B, in the Metropolitan Toronto Reference Library, Special Collections Centre.

66. Celia Franca in conversation with the author, 14 October 1987; see also Whittaker, *Canada's National Ballet*, pp. 20–1.

67. Betty Oliphant in conversation with the author, 17 August 1988; Celia Franca in conversation with the author, 14 October 1987. See also Franca, *The National Ballet of Canada*, p. 14.

68. Celia Franca in conversation with the author, 14 October 1987.

69. Celia Franca in conversation with the author, 19 August 1988; Betty Oliphant in conversation with the author, 17 August 1988.

70. Betty Oliphant in conversation with the author, 17 August 1988.

71. Betty Oliphant in conversation with the author, 17 August 1988.

72. Betty Oliphant in conversation with the author, 17 August 1988.

73. Whittaker, *Canada's National Ballet*, pp. 28–9; Betty Oliphant in conversation with the author, 17 August 1988.

74. Celia Franca in conversation with the author, 14 October 1987; see also Whittaker, *Canada's National Ballet*, p. 20.

75. Natalia Butko in conversation with the author, 7 July 1988.

76. Whittaker, *Canada's National Ballet*, p. 27; NBOC Archives, Aileen Woods File, #73; Betty Oliphant in conversation with the author, 17 August 1988.

77. National Archives of Canada, publicity pamphlet for first summer session, Franca Papers (19-11).

78. Whittaker, *Canada's National Ballet*, p. 28.

79. Celia Franca in conversation with the author, 14 October 1987.

80. Celia Franca in conversation with the author, 19 August 1988.

81. Betty Oliphant in conversation with the author, 17 August 1988.

82. Betty Oliphant in conversation with the author, 17 August 1988.

83. Bernard Taper, *Balanchine: A Biography* (New York: Times Books, 1984), p. 151.

84. Celia Franca in conversation with the author, 19 August 1988.

85. Betty Oliphant in conversation with the author, 17 August 1988.

86. Judie Colpman in conversation with the author, 20 January 1988.

87. Howard Meadows in conversation with the author, 3 May 1988.

88. David Adams in conversation with the author, 11 April 1988.

89. Lois Smith in conversation with the author, 24 May 1988; Celia Franca in conversation with the author, 14 October 1987.

90. For accounts of these performances, see Franca, *The National Ballet of Canada*, p. 18 and Whittaker, *Canada's National Ballet*, pp. 23–6.

91. Metropolitan Toronto Reference Library, Special Collections Centre, Boris Volkoff Papers, Programmes 1940–53, Box #1, Envelope #7B.

92. Betty Oliphant in conversation with the author, 17 August 1988.

93. Franca, *The National Ballet of Canada*, p. 20; see also NBOC Archives, 'Pearl's Condensed Minutes II,' Minutes for 14th Meeting (August 22 [1951]), Aileen Woods File, #73, thanking Franca for financing audition tour with proceeds of summer school.

94. NBOC Archives, Board Minutes for 19 September 1951, Aileen Woods File, #73.

95. NBOC Archives, Board Minutes for 5 September 1951, Aileen Woods File, #73; for a sample of editorial reaction in the Winnipeg press of the time, see Wyman, *The Royal Winnipeg Ballet*, p. 77.

96. *Winnipeg Free Press*, 30 August 1951.

97. Celia Franca, quoted in Whittaker, *Canada's National Ballet*, p. 29. See also 'Artistic Director's Address to New Directors,' 20 January 1972, NBOC Archives, Ballet Production Files, 'Miscellaneous.' 'By this time the Winnipeg Ballet had decided to open up again and also turn professional, so I was preceded in every town by Arnold Spohr, at that time the Winnipeg's ballet master, who cleaned up the best dancers.'

98. Whittaker, *Canada's National Ballet*, p. 29.

99. Wyman, *The Royal Winnipeg Ballet*, pp. 79, 93.

100. Celia Franca in conversation with the author, 19 August 1988.

101. Wyman, *The Royal Winnipeg Ballet*, p. 79.

102. Grant Strate in conversation with the author, 15 April 1988.

103. Betty Oliphant in conversation with the author, 17 August 1988.

104. Earl Kraul in conversation with the author, 15 April 1988.

105. Judie Colpman in conversation with the author, 20 January 1988.

106. Natalia Butko in conversation with the author, 7 July 1988.

107. David Adams in conversation with the author, 11 April 1988.

108. Natalia Butko in conversation with the author, 7 July 1988.

CHAPTER 2

1. Celia Franca in conversation with the author, 14 October 1987.

2. Judie Colpman in conversation with the author, 20 January 1988.

3. Celia Franca in conversation with the author, 14 October 1987.

4. Natalia Butko in conversation with the author, 7 July 1988.

5. Celia Franca in conversation with the author, 14 October 1987.

6. Celia Franca in conversation with the author, 14 October 1987.

7. Betty Oliphant in conversation with the author, 17 August 1988.

8. Earl Kraul in conversation with the author, 15 April 1988.

9. *Royal Academy of Dancing Gazette*, [1951?], p. 49, Dance Collection Danse.

10. Betty Oliphant in conversation with the author, 17 August 1988.

11. NBOC Archives, Artistic Director's Report to the Fifth Annual Meeting of the Guild, 14 June 1956, #109-A.

12. Celia Franca in conversation with the author, 14 October 1987.

13. Lois Smith in conversation with the author, 24 May 1988.

14. NBOC Archives, Board Minutes for 16 January 1952, Aileen Woods File, #73.

15. See Franca's report on the Canadian Ballet Festival, 1950, in the *Royal Academy of Dancing Gazette*, [1951?], p. 49, Dance Collection Danse, and Anatole Chujoy's review of the Festival in the *Globe and Mail*, 22 November 1950.

16. Mitchell, *Boris Volkoff*, pp. 108–9, 127. See also programs for the period 1940–53 in the Boris Volkoff Papers, Metropolitan Toronto Reference Library, Special Collections Centre, Box #1, Envelope #7B.

17. Howard Meadows in conversation with the author, 3 May 1988.

18. Earl Kraul in conversation with the author, 15 April 1988.

19. 'Franca's Perfect Ballet Art Lifts Company to Stardom,' Toronto *Telegram*, 13 November 1951.

20. 'National Ballet Opens with Rousing Program,' Toronto *Globe and Mail*, 13 November 1951.

21. Betty Oliphant in conversation with the author, 17 August 1988.

22. Mitchell, *Boris Volkoff*, p. 285.

23. NBOC Archives, Board Minutes for 19 March 1952, #109-A.

24. NBOC Archives, Board Minutes for 1 October 1952, #109-A.

25. NBOC Archives, Notes dated 27 October, Aileen Woods File, #73.

26. National Archives of Canada, Board Minutes for 17 October 1951, Franca Papers (13-7); George Crum in conversation with the author, 13 December 1989; NBOC Archives, Board Minutes for 5 April 1984, #113.

27. NBOC Archives, Souvenir Program, 1958–9.

28. NBOC Archives, notes by David Haber for Board Meeting, 21 November 1974, David Haber Correspondence, #70-DH1.

29. NBOC Archives, Bob Osborne to NBOC, January 1963, Administration Files 1962–3, #70-B.

30. Joanne Nisbet and David Scott in conversation with the author, 13 May 1988.

31. NBOC Archives, Board Minutes for 21 May 1952 and 1 March 1956, #109-A.

32. NBOC Archives, transcript of Press Conference held 30 November 1972, David Haber Correspondence, #70-DH1.

33. Franca, *The National Ballet of Canada*, p. 55. For resignation date, see NBOC Archives, Board Minutes for 6 April 1955, #109-A.

34. Dates from annual Souvenir Programs.

35. NBOC Archives, Board Minutes for 9 September 1952, #109-A.

36. Betty Oliphant in conversation with the author, 17 August 1988.

37. NBOC Archives, Artistic Director's Report to the Fifth Annual Meeting of the Guild, 14 June 1956, #109-A.

38. Lois Smith in conversation with the author, 24 May 1988; David Adams in conversation with the author, 11 April 1988.

39. Betty Oliphant in conversation with the author, 17 August 1988.

40. Celia Franca in conversation with the author, 14 October 1987 and 19 August 1988. Franca's Cecchetti examination results are in the National Archives of Canada, Franca Papers (5-13). Margaret Saul was the examiner for both.

41. Lois Smith in conversation with the author, 24 May 1988.

42. Celia Franca in conversation with the author, 14 October 1987.

43. Celia Franca in conversation with the author, 14 October 1987.

44. National Archives of Canada, 'Report of the National Ballet Company's Visit to Vancouver,' Franca Papers (8-17).

45. Howard Meadows in conversation with the author, 3 May 1988; Judie Colpman in conversation with the author, 20 January 1988.

46. National Archives of Canada, 'Report of the National Ballet Company's Visit to Vancouver,' Franca Papers (8-17).

47. Judie Colpman in conversation with the author, 20 January 1988; Howard Meadows in conversation with the author, 3 May 1988.

48. Celia Franca in conversation with the author, 14 October 1987.

49. Judie Colpman in conversation with the author, 20 January 1988; Howard Meadows in conversation with the author, 3 May 1988.

50. Celia Franca in conversation with the author, 14 October 1987.

51. Celia Franca in conversation with the author, 14 October 1988.

52. Celia Franca in conversation with the author, 14 October 1988; Judie Colpman in conversation with the author, 20 January 1988.

53. Betty Oliphant in conversation with the author, 17 August 1988.

54. NBOC Archives, Board Minutes for 9 September 1952, #109-A.

55. Celia Franca in conversation with the author, 14 October 1987.

56. Judie Colpman in conversation with the author, 20 January 1988.
57. Rubin, Don, 'Celia Franca: Tartar in a Tutu,' *Chatelaine*, March 1974.
58. Celia Franca in conversation with the author, 14 October 1987.
59. NBOC Archives, Board Minutes for 23 March 1962, #109-C.
60. NBOC Archives, Franca Files, Box #2.
61. Grant Strate in conversation with the author, 15 April 1988.
62. NBOC Archives, President's Report to the Twelfth Annual Meeting of the Guild, 1963, #109-C.
63. Grant Strate in conversation with the author, 15 April 1988. Strate himself places the number of his works choreographed for the National at sixteen, not including the curtain-raiser he choreographed for the opening of the National Arts Centre in 1969.
64. Grant Strate in conversation with the author, 15 April 1988.
65. Victoria Bertram in conversation with the author, 10 May 1988; Grant Strate in conversation with the author, 15 April 1988.
66. NBOC Archives, Grant Strate to John Paterson, [n.d.], Personal Files, Strate.
67. Grant Strate in conversation with the author, 15 April 1988.

CHAPTER 3

1. Franca, *The National Ballet of Canada*, p. 22.
2. Lois Smith in conversation with the author, 24 May 1988.
3. NBOC Archives, Executive Committee Minutes for 20 May 1959, #109-B, suggest that the City contemplated a year-round lease as early as 1959, but a letter from Hamilton Cassels, Jr, to George H. Bates, 9 September 1966, Hamilton Cassels, Jr, Correspondence, #3-A, indicates that the company was still using the Orange Lodge as late as that date.
4. NBOC Archives, Board Minutes for 1 October 1952, #109-A.
5. NBOC Archives, Hamilton Cassels, Jr, to George H. Bates, 9 September 1966, Hamilton Cassels, Jr, Correspondence, #3-A.
6. National Archives of Canada, 'Notes on the Canadian Tour of November 1969,' by André Dufresne, Franca Papers (19-7).
7. Lois Smith in conversation with the author, 24 May 1988.
8. NBOC Archives, Artistic Director's Report to the Annual Meeting (October 15, 1959), p. 1, #109-A.
9. NBOC Archives, submission to the Canada Council, 3 May 1963, p. 8, Canada Council Files, #105-H.
10. National Archives of Canada, Celia Franca to Alan Skinner, 28 March 1953, p. 5, Franca Papers (14-22).
11. NBOC Archives, Antony Tudor to Carman Guild, 5 June 1962, Ballet Production Files, *Judgment of Paris*.
12. NBOC Archives, handwritten notes, 'Organization to Date,' [n.d.], Aileen Woods File, #73.
13. NBOC Archives, Board Minutes for 7 April 1952, #109-A.
14. NBOC Archives, Aileen Woods File, #73.
15. NBOC Archives, 'Artistic Director's Address to New Directors,' 20 January 1972, Ballet Production Files, 'Miscellaneous.'
16. National Archives of Canada, lecture by Celia Franca to the Ballet Circle on Sunday, 24 April 1949, p. 8, Franca Papers (9-1).
17. NBOC Archives, Board Minutes for 3 April 1951, Aileen Woods File, #73.
18. National Archives of Canada, Celia Franca to Alan Skinner, 21 January 1954, Franca Papers (15-11).
19. Toronto *Evening Telegram*, 25 January 1954. See also Wyman, *The Royal Winnipeg Ballet*, p. 87.
20. Walter O'Hearn, 'Ballet Squabbles Fast Becoming a Headache,' *Montreal Star*, 30 January 1954.
21. NBOC Archives, Board Minutes for 18 March 1954, #109-A; Executive Committee Minutes for 1 February 1954, #109-B.
22. National Archives of Canada, notes to Draft Policy Report, [n.d.], p. 7, #4, Franca Papers (18-7).
23. Celia Franca in conversation with the author, 14 October 1987.
24. See entry under 'Sergeyev, Nicholas' in Bremser, *International Dictionary of Ballet*.
25. Celia Franca in conversation with the author, 19 August 1988.
26. See also Erik Bruhn's analysis of the Sergeyev influence with respect to *Giselle* in his essay 'Restaging the Classics,' in Charles Payne, *American Ballet Theatre* (New York: Alfred A. Knopf, 1979), p. 327.
27. Celia Franca in conversation with the author, 14 October 1987.
28. National Archives of Canada, summary of press comments, [n.d.], Franca Papers (15-9). 'Lois Smith's costume, unfortunately, was in such bad taste that each of her entrances provoked laughter.' (trans. J.N.)
29. Karen Kain in conversation with the author, 18 May 1988.
30. Lois Smith in conversation with the author, 24 May 1988.
31. National Archives of Canada, Celia Franca to Alan Skinner, 21 November 1951, Franca Papers (14-22).
32. Celia Franca in conversation with the author, 14 October 1987.
33. Howard Meadows in conversation with Lynn Neufeld, 1989.
34. Janice Ross and Stephen Corbett Steinberg, comps, *Why a Swan? Essays, Interviews, & Conversations on 'Swan Lake'* (San Francisco: San Francisco Performing Arts Library and Museum, 1989), p. 65.
35. Jack Anderson, *The Nutcracker Ballet* (London: Bison Books, 1979), p. 108. The Ottawa Ballet Company's 1947 production was thus not the first North American *Nutcracker*, as its program claimed. See Wyman, *Dance Canada*, p. 41.
36. Payne, *American Ballet Theatre*, pp. 360, 362.
37. Leslie George Katz, Nancy Lasalle, and Harvey Simmonds, comps, *Choreography by George Balanchine: A Catalogue of Works* (New York: Viking Penguin, 1984), pp. 210–11.
38. Ross and Steinberg, *Why a Swan?*, pp. 65–6, 70.
39. Katz, *Choreography by George Balanchine*, pp. 202–3.
40. Celia Franca in conversation with the author, 14 October 1987.
41. Sydney Johnson, '*Giselle* Illuminated,' *Montreal Star*, 22 January 1954.
42. John Martin, 'Young Canadian Ballet Pays a Brief Visit,' *New York Times*, 3 April 1955.
43. NBOC Archives, Board Minutes for 3 December 1952, #109-A.
44. Celia Franca in conversation with the author, 14 October 1987; NBOC Archives, Ballet Production Files, *Offenbach in the Underworld*.
45. The National performed *Offenbach in the Underworld* at the Brooklyn Academy of Music on 26 March 1955; ABT premièred its production at the Metropolitan Opera House on 18 April 1956 (Payne, *American Ballet Theatre*, p. 364).
46. Grant Strate in conversation with the author, 15 April 1988.
47. Celia Franca in conversation with the author, 14 October 1987.
48. See reviews in *Dance and Dancers* for July 1950 and March 1962.
49. Marie Rambert, 'Andrée Howard: An Appreciation,' *Dancing Times*, March 1943.
50. NBOC Archives, Franca to Cyril Frankel, 8 February 1959, Ballet Production Files, *The Mermaid*.

51. NBOC Archives, Howard to Franca, 3 February 1959, Ballet Production Files, *The Mermaid*.

52. Celia Franca in conversation with the author, 14 October 1987.

53. NBOC Archives, Lenore Crawford, *London Free Press*, [exact date unknown] 1959, Personal Files, Kraul.

54. Celia Franca in conversation with the author, 14 October 1987.

55. Celia Franca in conversation with the author, 19 August 1988.

56. John Percival, *Theatre in My Blood* (London: Herbert Press, 1983), pp. 107, 124, and 126.

57. Percival, *Theatre in My Blood*, p. 125.

58. Grant Strate in conversation with the author, 15 April 1988. See also Franca, *The National Ballet of Canada*, p. 192.

59. NBOC Archives, Franca to Michael Wood, Royal Opera House, Covent Garden, 5 September 1963, Franca Files, Box #1.

60. National Archives of Canada, Franca to Ashton, 11 January 1967, Franca Papers (3-8).

61. NBOC Archives, Artistic Director's Report to the Fifth Annual Meeting of the Guild, 14 June 1956, #109-A.

62. NBOC Archives, Franca to Michael Wood, Royal Opera House, Covent Garden, September 5, 1963, Franca Files, Box #1.

63. Dame Ninette de Valois in conversation with the author, 16 March 1988.

64. Wyman, *The Royal Winnipeg Ballet*, p. 255.

65. David Adams in conversation with the author, 11 April 1988.

66. Lois Smith in conversation with the author, 24 May 1988.

67. David Adams in conversation with the author, 11 April 1988.

68. National Archives of Canada, Walter Homburger to Alan Skinner, 8 January 1955, Franca Papers (15-14); NBOC Archives, Ballet Production Files, *Dark of the Moon*; Celia Franca in conversation with the author, 14 October 1987.

69. David Adams in conversation with the author, 11 April 1988.

70. Celia Franca in conversation with the author, 14 October 1987.

71. David Adams in conversation with the author, 11 April 1988.

72. National Archives of Canada, Franca to Cranko, 2 March 1964, Franca Papers (6-3).

73. Grant Strate in conversation with the author, 15 April 1988.

74. NBOC Archives, Address by Grant Strate to the Toronto Committee of the National Ballet Guild, 20 February 1964, Aileen Woods File, #73.

75. Grant Strate in conversation with the author, 15 April 1988.

76. NBOC Archives, as quoted by Don Rubin in an unidentified clipping, Personal Files, Strate.

77. Grant Strate in conversation with the author, 15 April 1988.

78. NBOC Archives, Address by Grant Strate to the Toronto Committee of the National Ballet Guild, 20 February 1964, Aileen Woods File, #73; Grant Strate in conversation with the author, 15 April 1988.

79. NBOC Archives, Board Minutes for 29 June 1966, #109-C.

80. Grant Strate in conversation with the author, 15 April 1988.

81. NBOC Archives, report by Grant Strate to the Canada Council on Senior Arts Fellowship Grant, 7 March 1963, Canada Council Files, #105-H.

82. NBOC Archives, Strate to John Paterson, 25 November 1962, Personal Files, Strate.

83. NBOC Archives, report by Grant Strate to the Canada Council on Senior Arts Fellowship Grant, 7 March 1963, Canada Council Files, #105-H.

84. Allen Hughes, *New York Times*, 3 February 1964.

85. Grant Strate in conversation with the author, 15 April 1988.

86. Celia Franca in conversation with the author, 14 October 1987.

87. Paul Roussel, *Le Canada*, 14 February 1953. 'A few lively variations, some good solos, and the elimination of its folklore inspiration would convert *Le Pommier* into a pretty divertissement.' (Trans. J.N.) For Franca's account of *Le Pommier* and its Montreal reception, see *The National Ballet of Canada*, p. 85.

88. David Adams in conversation with the author, 11 April 1988; see also Wyman, *Dance Canada*, p. 73.

89. Celia Franca in conversation with the author, 19 August 1988.

90. Celia Franca in conversation with the author, 14 October 1987.

91. Nathan Cohen, *Toronto Star*, 31 January 1961.

92. Lois Smith in conversation with the author, 24 May 1988.

93. Galina Samsova in conversation with the author, 14 March 1988.

94. Martine van Hamel in conversation with the author, 15 December 1989.

CHAPTER 4

1. National Archives of Canada, Draft Report by Celia Franca to the Annual General Meeting, October 1961, Franca Papers (11-9).

2. Natalia Butko in conversation with the author, 7 July 1988.

3. P. B. Waite, *Lord of Point Grey: Larry Mackenzie of UBC* (Vancouver: University of British Columbia Press, 1987), p. 180.

4. Wyman, *Dance Canada*, p. 79.

5. NBOC Archives, Board Minutes for 2 February 1956, p. 3, #109-A; President's Report to the Fifth Annual Meeting of the Guild, 14 June 1956, p. 3, #109-A. National Archives of Canada, Peter Dwyer to E.P. Taylor, 28 August 1959, Canada Council Files (RG 63 Vol. 224).

6. Grant Strate in conversation with the author, 15 April 1988.

7. Miss Kai's position in the company as indicated in NYCB program for 1966, in the author's private collection. NBOC Archives, correspondence between Franca and Una Kai, April and May 1961, and letter from Joseph Martinson to Franca, 17 May 1961, Ballet Production Files, *Concerto Barocco*.

8. Franca, *The National Ballet of Canada*, p. 221; Lorna Geddes in conversation with the author, 15 July 1988.

9. NBOC Archives, Betty Cage to Carman Guild, 12 July 1962, Ballet Production Files, *Serenade*.

10. National Archives of Canada, Notice of Award, 29 January 1963, Canada Council Files (RG 63 Vol. 225).

11. Galina Samsova in conversation with the author, 14 March 1988.

12. The National premièred the work on 19 October 1962. The Royal Ballet gave its first performance on 3 November 1962 (Bland, *The Royal Ballet*, p. 287).

13. Betty Oliphant in conversation with the author, 17 August 1988; NBOC Archives, Carman Guild to A.C. Smith, Department of External Affairs, 29 December 1962, Administration Files, 1962–3.

14. Figures for the Royal Alexandra Theatre from *The Canadian Encyclopedia*; for the O'Keefe Centre from Baillie, Joan Parkhill, *Look at the Record: An Album of Toronto's Lyric Theatres, 1825–1984* (Oakville: Mosaic Press, 1985).

15. NBOC Archives, Board Minutes for 4 February 1959, #109-A.

16. NBOC Archives, Board Minutes for 17 April 1963, #109-C.

17. NBOC Archives, Board Minutes for 17 April 1963, #109-C.

18. Bland, *The Royal Ballet*, p. 272.

19. NBOC Archives, Celia Franca to Michael Wood, Royal Opera House, 5 September 1963, Franca Files, Box #1.

20. Franca, *The National Ballet of Canada*, pp. 192–3.

21. Grant Strate in conversation with the author, 15 April 1988.
22. National Archives of Canada, Peter Dwyer to Guy Glover, 7 April 1964, Canada Council Files (RG 63 Vol. 715).
23. Grant Strate in conversation with the author, 15 April 1988.
24. NBOC Archives, Carman Guild to John Cranko, 21 April 1964, Ballet Production Files, *Romeo and Juliet*.
25. NBOC Archives, Wallace A. Russell to Hamilton Southam, 1 September 1967, Hamilton Cassels, Jr, Correspondence, #3-D; Celia Franca in conversation with the author, 19 August 1988.
26. Grant Strate in conversation with the author, 15 April 1988.
27. Grant Strate in conversation with the author, 15 April 1988; NBOC Archives, report by Grant Strate to the Artistic Council, 28 June 1969, Personal Files, Strate.
28. NBOC Archives, Dieter Gräfe to Wallace Russell, 28 April 1970, Ballet Production Files, *Romeo and Juliet*.
29. National Archives of Canada, Celia Franca to John Cranko, 8 May 1970, Franca Papers (6-3).
30. National Archives of Canada, John Cranko to National Ballet Guild, [n.d.], Franca Papers (6-3).
31. NBOC Archives, Jürgen Rose to Celia Franca, 1 September 1965, Personal Files, Rose and Franca. 'Hat sich viel in Eurer Kompanie verändert? – Irgendwie hänge ich sehr an all den Kindern. Es ist schon ein sehr lieber Haufen. Ärger gibt es überall einmal, aber bei Euch kommt man schnell darüber hinweg, weil alle so begeistert bei der Sache sind, jeder gibt sein Bestes, und das ist ein sehr schönes Gefühl!' (Trans. J.N.)
32. Earl Kraul in conversation with the author, 15 April 1988.
33. Galina Samsova in conversation with the author, 14 March 1988.
34. David Adams in conversation with the author, 11 April 1988.
35. National Archives of Canada, [Celia Franca] to John Cranko, 2 March 1964, Franca Papers (6-3).
36. Lois Smith in conversation with the author, 24 May 1988.
37. Veronica Tennant in conversation with the author, 9 May 1988.
38. Celia Franca in conversation with the author, 19 August 1988.
39. *Ballet Notes*, 'Romeo and Juliet,' compiled by Assis Carriero for the National Ballet of Canada, author's private collection.
40. Joanne Nisbet in conversation with the author, 13 May 1988.
41. Galina Samsova in conversation with the author, 14 March 1988.
42. NBOC Archives, Lilian [Jarvis] to John [Paterson], 5 December [1963], Personal Files, Samsova.
43. Galina Samsova in conversation with the author, 14 March 1988.
44. Martine van Hamel in conversation with the author, 15 December 1989.
45. Galina Samsova in conversation with the author, 14 March 1988; Martine van Hamel in conversation with the author, 15 December 1989.
46. National Archives of Canada, Artistic Director's Report to the Eighth Annual Meeting, September 1959, Franca Papers (13-4).
47. NBOC Archives, Minutes of the Annual General Meeting, 25 September 1958, #109-A.
48. NBOC Archives, Celia Franca to Niels Bjørn Larsen, 27 August 1962, Franca Files, Box #1.
49. Rudolf Nureyev in conversation with the author, 30 August 1989.
50. See, for example, Ralph Hicklin, 'Toronto Thanks Bruhn for Gift with 25 Cheering Curtain Calls,' Toronto *Globe and Mail*, 7 January 1965.
51. Earl Kraul in conversation with the author, 15 April 1988.
52. Rudolf Nureyev in conversation with the author, 30 August 1989.
53. Lois Smith in conversation with the author, 24 May 1988.
54. Nathan Cohen, 'Honorable, but Unsuccessful,' *Toronto Daily Star*, 6 January 1965; Ralph Hicklin, 'Toronto Thanks Bruhn for Gift with 25 Cheering Curtain Calls,' Toronto *Globe and Mail*, 7 January 1965; Nathan Cohen, '25 Curtain Calls for Bruhn – All Earned,' *Toronto Daily Star*, 7 January 1965.
55. Nathan Cohen, '25 Curtain Calls for Bruhn – All Earned,' *Toronto Daily Star*, 7 January 1965. For Cohen's review of *Romeo and Juliet*, see 'Opulent – but Spiritless,' *Toronto Daily Star*, 8 January 1965.
56. Peter Schaufuss in conversation with the author, 17 November 1989.
57. Payne, *American Ballet Theatre*, p. 367.
58. Gruen, *Erik Bruhn*, pp. 150–1.
59. Earl Kraul in conversation with the author, 15 April 1988.
60. Bland, *The Royal Ballet*, p. 285; Rudolf Nureyev in conversation with the author, 30 August 1989.
61. Rudolf Nureyev in conversation with the author, 30 August 1989.
62. NBOC Archives, Notes by Grant Strate, 'Discussion with Erik Bruhn – Montreal – October 15, 1965,' Ballet Production Files, *Swan Lake*.
63. Rudolf Nureyev in conversation with the author, 30 August 1989.
64. Martin Bernheimer, 'Nureyev at the Crossroads,' *Los Angeles Times*, 4 September 1977.
65. NBOC Archives, George Crum, Notes on Music, [n.d.], Ballet Production Files, *Swan Lake*; Celia Franca to Erik Bruhn, [n.d.] (in response to his letter of 13 January 1966), Franca Files, Box #1.
66. Rudolf Nureyev in conversation with the author, 30 August 1989.
67. Grant Strate in conversation with the author, 15 April 1988.
68. Celia Franca in conversation with the author, 19 August 1988.
69. Grant Strate in conversation with the author, 15 April 1988.
70. Celia Franca in conversation with the author, 19 August 1988.
71. Victoria Bertram in conversation with the author, 10 May 1988.
72. Lois Smith in conversation with the author, 24 May 1988.
73. Victoria Bertram in conversation with the author, 10 May 1988.
74. William Littler, 'Celia: First Lady of Canadian Ballet,' *Toronto Star*, 6 April 1968.
75. National Archives of Canada, Gerry Eldred to Celia Franca, 29 December 1976, Franca Papers (11-4).
76. NBOC Archives, Executive Committee Minutes for 19 January 1968 and 19 March 1968, #109-D.
77. NBOC Archives, Board Minutes for 21 June 1967, #109-C.
78. NBOC Archives, Executive Committee Minutes for 27 February 1968, #109-D.
79. Clive Barnes, 'Canada's National Ballet Stages "Cinderella,"' *New York Times*, 22 April 1968.
80. Ralph Hicklin, 'A Decorous Cinderella,' Toronto *Telegram*, 16 April 1968.
81. Clive Barnes, 'Canada's National Ballet Stages "Cinderella,"' *New York Times*, 22 April 1968.
82. Wendy Michener, 'Celia's Cinderella Suggests Embalmer's Loving Care,' Toronto *Globe and Mail*, 16 April 1968.
83. NBOC Archives, Celia Franca to Gerald Arpino, 6 November 1973 and 20 November 1973, Ballet Production Files, *Kettentanz*.
84. For her own account of the *Cinderella* taping, see Franca, *The National Ballet of Canada*, pp. 148, 152.
85. NBOC Archives, Erik Bruhn to Celia Franca, 13 January 1969, Bruhn Files.
86. Ralph Hicklin, 'Small Group Best of Strate Night in Performance Lacking Subtlety,' Toronto *Globe and Mail*, 5 January 1965.
87. Lois Smith in conversation with the author, 24 May 1988.

88. NBOC Archives, André Fortier to John Godfrey, 21 February 1968, Hamilton Cassels, Jr, Correspondence, #3-D.

89. As quoted by Nathan Cohen, 'Celia Franca Says She Isn't Wanted and Quits the National Ballet,' *Toronto Star*, 16 November 1968.

CHAPTER 5

1. As quoted by Nathan Cohen, 'Celia Franca Says She Isn't Wanted and Quits the National Ballet,' *Toronto Star*, 16 November 1968.

2. NBOC Archives, notes by Hamilton Cassels, Jr, 22 November 1968, Hamilton Cassels, Jr, Correspondence, #3-D.

3. Lawrence Adams in conversation with the author, 17 November 1989.

4. Dancers' Council to John Godfrey, 25 November 1968, Dance Collection Danse.

5. Dancers' Council to John Godfrey, 25 November 1968, Dance Collection Danse.

6. Lawrence Adams in conversation with the author, 17 November 1989.

7. National Archives of Canada, Memo to File from Peter Dwyer, 18 November 1968, Canada Council Files (RG 63 Vol. 788).

8. NBOC Archives, Notes by Hamilton Cassels, Jr, 15 November, 16 November, 17 November, 24 November, 3 December, 12 December 1968, Hamilton Cassels, Jr, Correspondence, #3-D.

9. NBOC Archives, Executive Committee Minutes for 15 December 1966, #109-B, and for 16 December 1968, #109-D.

10. NBOC Archives, Board Minutes for 3 December 1968, #109-C.

11. NBOC Archives, Press Release, 20 December 1968, Franca Files, Box #1.

12. Dieter Penzhorn in conversation with the author, 2 May 1988.

13. NBOC Archives, Board Minutes for 20 December 1968, #109-C.

14. NBOC Archives, Celia Franca to Aileen Woods, 18 November 1968, Franca Files, Box #1.

15. NBOC Archives, Board Minutes for 9 October 1968, #109-C.

16. NBOC Archives, Board Minutes for 9 October 1968, #109-C.

17. NBOC Archives, Petit-Franca correspondence, 11 and 19 June 1968, Ballet Production Files, Petit Administrative Correspondence; W.A. Russell to Roland Petit, 31 May 1968 and 4 April 1968; Ballet Production Files, *Kraanerg*.

18. NBOC Archives, Executive Committee Minutes for 31 July 1967, #109-D.

19. David Haber in conversation with the author, 14 December 1989.

20. NBOC Archives, Peter Dwyer to Lyman Henderson, 30 October 1969, Canada Council Files, #105-C. See also NBOC Archives, 'Special Dress Rehearsal (*Kraanerg*) 1969,' Canada Council Files, #105-C.

21. Sid Adilman, 'National Ballet Won't Perform *Kraanerg* in Paris,' *Toronto Star*, 2 June 1972; NBOC Archives, Artistic Management Committee Minutes, 23 November 1971, Franca Files, Box #2.

22. NBOC Archives, notes by Grant Strate and Louis Applebaum, Ballet Production Files (Curtain-Raiser File).

23. David Haber in conversation with the author, 14 December 1989.

24. Grant Strate in conversation with the author, 15 April 1988.

25. Victoria Bertram in conversation with the author, 10 May 1988.

26. NBOC Archives, Artistic Director's Report to the Annual General Meeting, 12 November 1971, #109-E.

27. NBOC Archives, Artistic Director's Report to the Annual General Meeting, 12 November 1971, #109-E.

28. Victoria Bertram in conversation with the author, 10 May 1988.

29. NBOC Archives, presentation by Franca to the Board Meeting of 7 August 1969, National Ballet Guild of Canada – Season 1969–70, #109-D.

30. NBOC Archives, Artistic Management Committee Minutes, 11 November 1969, Administration Files 1969–70, #70-H.

31. John Percival, 'Promising Canadians,' London *Times*, 4 April 1975.

32. Richard Buckle, 'Worthy of a Prince,' London *Sunday Times*, 13 April 1975.

33. National Archives of Canada, Klaus Kolmar to Carman Guild, 2 December 1955, Franca Papers (18-6).

34. NBOC Archives, Artistic Director's Report to the Annual General Meeting, 12 November 1971, #109-E.

35. NBOC Archives, W.P. Walker to Arthur Gelber, 3 June 1964, Administration Files 1964–5, #70-D.

36. Wyman, *The Royal Winnipeg Ballet*, pp. 124–5; NBOC Archives, Executive Committee Minutes, 20 October 1965, #109-B.

37. David Haber in conversation with the author, 14 December 1989.

38. NBOC Archives, Board Minutes for 10 December 1969, #109-C.

39. NBOC Archives, Wallace Russell to Christopher Allan (for Erik Bruhn), 6 December 1971, Bruhn Files.

40. Gruen, *Erik Bruhn*, pp. 169–75.

41. NBOC Archives, Christopher Allan (for Erik Bruhn) to Celia Franca, 4 January 1972, Bruhn Files.

42. David Haber in conversation with the author, 14 December 1989.

43. Ann Ditchburn in conversation with the author, 19 March 1990.

44. Veronica Tennant in conversation with the author, 9 May 1988.

45. *Dance and Dancers*, Vol. 23, No. 7, Issue 271 (July 1972).

46. James Monahan, 'The National Ballet of Canada,' *Dancing Times*, July 1972, p. 519.

47. Dieter Penzhorn in conversation with the author, 2 May 1988.

48. Celia Franca in conversation with the author, 19 August 1988.

49. Celia Franca in conversation with the author, 19 August 1988.

50. Lyman Henderson in conversation with the author, 13 July 1988.

51. Veronica Tennant in conversation with the author, 9 May 1988.

52. Celia Franca in conversation with the author, 19 August 1988. See also NBOC Archives, 'National Ballet Guild 4 March, 1972,' Hamilton Cassels, Jr, Correspondence, #3-E.

53. Betty Oliphant in conversation with the author, 17 August 1988.

54. NBOC Archives, Executive Committee Minutes for 19 January 1972, #109-D, and for 15 March 1972, #109-D.

55. Celia Franca in conversation with the author, 19 August 1988.

56. David Haber in conversation with the author, 14 December 1989.

57. Celia Franca in conversation with the author, 19 August 1988.

58. Betty Oliphant in conversation with the author, 17 August 1988.

59. Betty Oliphant in conversation with the author, 17 August 1988.

60. NBOC Archives, David Haber to Betty Oliphant, 14 August 1972, David Haber Correspondence, #70-DH1.

61. David Haber in conversation with the author, 14 December 1989.

62. Celia Franca in conversation with the author, 19 August 1988.

CHAPTER 6

1. National Archives of Canada, Celia Franca, Appointment Book for 1972–3, Franca Papers (12-12).

2. Rudolf Nureyev in conversation with the author, 30 August 1989.

3. NBOC Archives, Artistic Director's report to the Annual General Meeting, 11 September 1973, #109-E. For Franca's further account of the production, see *The National Ballet of Canada*, pp. 244–52.
4. Rudolf Nureyev in conversation with the author, 30 August 1989.
5. Mary Jago in conversation with the author, 14 July 1988.
6. Karen Kain in conversation with the author, 18 May 1988.
7. Veronica Tennant in conversation with the author, 9 May 1988.
8. Tomas Schramek in conversation with the author, 20 May 1988.
9. Victoria Bertram in conversation with the author, 10 May 1988.
10. Celia Franca in conversation with the author, 19 August 1988.
11. Rudolf Nureyev in conversation with the author, 30 August 1989.
12. See Bremser, *International Dictionary of Ballet*, entry under 'Franca.'
13. Celia Franca in conversation with the author, 19 August 1988.
14. Dieter Penzhorn in conversation with the author, 2 May 1988; Larry Beevers in conversation with the author, 21 April 1988.
15. Larry Beevers in conversation with the author, 21 April 1988.
16. Dieter Penzhorn in conversation with the author, 2 May 1988.
17. Dieter Penzhorn in conversation with the author, 2 May 1988.
18. Veronica Tennant in conversation with the author, 9 May 1988.
19. Clive Barnes, 'To Play the Met, Get Nureyev,' *New York Times*, 6 May 1973.
20. Robert J. Landry, 'Canada Comes On Strong in Met Debut; Well-Staged, New *Sleeping Beauty*,' *Variety*, 2 May 1973.
21. Veronica Tennant in conversation with the author, 9 May 1988.
22. NBOC Archives, Board Minutes for 19 June 1973, #109-E.
23. NBOC Archives, Brief accompanying the 1975–6 submission to the Canada Council, Canada Council Files, 'Submissions 1975-76.'
24. NBOC Archives, draft Brief to the Canada Council, 5 January 1972, Canada Council Files, 'Briefs 1972.'
25. Celia Franca in conversation with the author, 19 August 1988.
26. Dieter Penzhorn in conversation with the author, 2 May 1988.
27. Betty Oliphant in conversation with the author, 17 August 1988.
28. Karen Kain in conversation with the author, 18 May 1988.
29. Franca, *The National Ballet of Canada*, p. 248.
30. Karen Kain in conversation with the author, 18 May 1988.
31. National Archives of Canada, Celia Franca, Report on Varna Competition, 1970, Franca Papers (10-10).
32. Karen Kain in conversation with the author, 18 May 1988.
33. NBOC Archives, transcript of Press Conference held 30 November 1972, David Haber Correspondence, #70-DH1.
34. NBOC Archives, Celia Franca to John Neumeier, 4 July 1973, Ballet Production Files, *Don Juan*.
35. NBOC Archives, *Coppélia* contract, Ballet Production Files, *Coppélia*.
36. Angela Warnick, 'It's Hard to Argue with Her Record,' *Hamilton Spectator*, 15 November 1973.
37. National Archives of Canada, Lawrence Schafer to Celia Franca, 2 December 1972, Franca Papers (1-14).
38. Gruen, *Erik Bruhn*, pp. 187–8.
39. NBOC Archives, Celia Franca to Erik Bruhn, 30 January 1974, Ballet Production Files, *Coppélia*.
40. NBOC Archives, Ian H. McLeod to Robert A. Laidlaw, 15 October 1974, Administration Files 1973, #70-N.
41. NBOC Archives, Johnson Ashley to Gerry Eldred, 21 February 1975, Bruhn Files.
42. David Haber in conversation with the author, 14 December 1989.
43. Gruen, *Erik Bruhn*, pp. 189–90.
44. Michael Iachetta, 'Rudi Makes Bruhn's Role His Own,' *New York Daily News*, 9 August 1974.
45. Notes by David Haber for Board Meeting of 7 October 1974, David Haber Correspondence, #70-DH1.
46. Gruen, *Erik Bruhn*, p. 190.
47. NBOC Archives, Ian H. McLeod to Board of Directors, 11 January 1974, #109-E. Press Release, 11 January 1974, Franca Files, Box #1.
48. Bland, *The Royal Ballet*, pp. 137–8.
49. NBOC Archives, Minutes of the Annual General Meeting, 9 September 1974, #109-E.
50. Celia Franca in conversation with the author, 19 August 1988.
51. John Fraser, 'Oliphant Resigns from National Ballet,' Toronto *Globe and Mail*, 4 March 1975.
52. Celia Franca in conversation with the author, 19 August 1988.
53. David Haber in conversation with the author, 14 December 1989.
54. David Haber in conversation with the author, 14 December 1989.
55. Details regarding the production of *Mad Shadows* provided by David Haber in conversation with the author, 14 December 1989, and by Ann Ditchburn in conversation with the author, 19 March 1990.
56. David Haber in conversation with the author, 14 December 1989.
57. David Haber in conversation with the author, 14 December 1989; see also NBOC Archives, David Haber to Monique Michaud, 4 March 1975, Canada Council Files, 'Meetings 1975'.
58. NBOC Archives, David Haber to John Neumeier, 27 January 1975, Ballet Production Files, *Don Juan* Lighting Plot.
59. NBOC Archives, Ballet Production Files, *Le Coq d'Or*, passim.
60. David Haber in conversation with the author, 14 December 1989.
61. NBOC Archives, Nicholas Beriosoff to Celia Franca, 14 January 1974, Ballet Production Files, *Le Coq d'Or*; David Haber in conversation with the author, 14 December 1989.
62. David Haber in conversation with the author, 14 December 1989.
63. NBOC Archives, Nicholas Beriosoff to Gerry Eldred, 18 August 1975, Ballet Production Files, *Le Coq d'Or*.
64. John Fraser, 'Oliphant Resigns from National Ballet,' Toronto *Globe and Mail*, 4 March 1975.
65. NBOC Archives, David Haber to the Board, 26 March 1975, Haber Correspondence, #70-DH1.
66. Lyman Henderson in conversation with the author, 13 July 1988.
67. NBOC Archives, Haber to Beriosoff, 20 May 1975, Ballet Production Files, *Le Coq d'Or*.
68. NBOC Archives, Executive Committee Minutes for 7 October 1975, #109-E.
69. National Archives of Canada, notation in Appointment Book for 3 June 1975, Franca Papers (12-14).
70. NBOC Archives, Press Release, 7 June 1975, Administration Files 1975–6, #70-O_2.
71. Lyman Henderson in conversation with the author, 13 July 1988.
72. NBOC Archives, Press Release, 7 June 1975, Administration Files 1975–6, #70-O_2.
73. See Sid Adilman's column, *Toronto Star*, 26 September 1975.
74. National Archives of Canada, Celia Franca to Jock McLeod, 18 September 1975, Franca Papers (21-9).

CHAPTER 7

1. National Archives of Canada, Erik Bruhn to Celia Franca, 1 October 1964, Franca Papers (20-2).

2. David Haber in conversation with the author, 14 December 1989.
3. NBOC Archives, Gerry Eldred to Erik Bruhn, 20 June 1975, Bruhn Files.
4. Rudolf Nureyev in conversation with the author, 30 August 1989.
5. Veronica Tennant in conversation with the author, 9 May 1988.
6. Rudolf Nureyev in conversation with the author, 30 August 1989.
7. NBOC Archives, Gerry Eldred to David Haber, 25 November 1974, Ballet Production Files, *Coppélia*.
8. Gruen, *Erik Bruhn*, pp. 157–8, 193–5.
9. John Fraser, 'Nureyev, Leave Canadian Ballet Alone,' *New York Times*, 27 July 1975.
10. Clive Barnes, 'Nureyev – The Canadians' Passport,' *New York Times*, 17 August 1975.
11. 'Letters,' *New York Times*, 3 August 1975.
12. NBOC Archives, Artistic Director's Report to the Annual General Meeting, 11 September 1973, #109-E.
13. NBOC Archives, I.H. McLeod to Gerry Eldred, 14 March 1973, Administration Files 1972–3, #70-M_1.
14. Payne, *American Ballet Theatre*, pp. 129ff.
15. Edward Thorpe, *Kenneth MacMillan: The Man and His Ballets* (London: Hamish Hamilton, 1985), p. 84; Richard Austin, *Lynn Seymour: An Authorised Biography* (London: Angus & Robertson, 1980), p. 132.
16. NBOC Archives, Board Minutes for 18 July 1972, #109-E; Executive Committee Minutes for 25 April 1974, #109-D.
17. Alexander Grant in conversation with the author, 22 March 1988. For the rights to *Fille*, see Alexander Grant, letter to the *Globe and Mail*, 28 September 1988.
18. Alexander Grant in conversation with the author, 22 March 1988.
19. Bland, *The Royal Ballet*, p. 248.
20. Alexander Grant in conversation with the author, 22 March 1988.
21. Alexander Grant in conversation with the author, 22 March 1988.
22. Lauretta Thistle, 'Appointment Raises Questions,' *Ottawa Citizen*, 1 November 1975.
23. Alexander Grant in conversation with the author, 22 March 1988.
24. NBOC Archives, Erik Bruhn to Gerry Eldred, 29 June 1976, Bruhn Files.
25. Alexander Grant in conversation with the author, 22 March 1988.
26. NBOC Archives, David Allport (for Erik Bruhn) to Gerry Eldred, 12 July 1976, Bruhn Files. By 4 January 1977, Bruhn had once again granted permission for his name to appear on the credits of *Swan Lake*. See NBOC Archives, Gerry Eldred to Mary Jolliffe, 4 January 1977, Ballet Production Files, *Swan Lake*.
27. NBOC Archives, Board Minutes for 7 October 1975, #109-E; see also *Toronto Star*, 29 November 1975.
28. NBOC Archives, Celia Franca to Michael M. Koerner, 25 June 1971, Administration Files 1971–2, #70-L; Gerry Eldred to Peter Sever, 14 July 1976, Administration Files 1975–6, 1976–7, #70-P.
29. Alexander Grant in conversation with the author, 22 March 1988.
30. David Vaughan, *Frederick Ashton and His Ballets* (London: Adam and Charles Black, 1977), pp. 493–4.
31. Alexander Grant, note to the author, November 1994.
32. Vaughan, *Frederick Ashton*, p. 322.
33. NBOC Archives, Board Minutes for 25 April 1978, #109-E.
34. Alexander Grant in conversation with the author, 22 March 1988.
35. Details regarding Ballet Revue from Ann Ditchburn in conversation with the author, 19 March 1990, and Tomas Schramek in conversation with the author, 20 May 1988. Statistics regarding ticket sales courtesy Mr Schramek, who functioned as business manager for the group.
36. Doug Hughes, 'National's Grant Takes Sour Milk with Ice Cream,' *Vancouver Province*, October 1979.
37. Ann Ditchburn in conversation with the author, 19 March 1990. NBOC Archives, Ann Ditchburn to Erik Bruhn, 1 November 1985, Bruhn Files.
38. William Littler, 'Ballet Takes On a Life of Its Own,' *Toronto Star*, 12 April 1977; Gina Mallet, 'No Sign of Skimping in New Ballet,' Toronto *Sunday Star*, 18 February 1979.
39. As quoted by Paula Citron in 'James Kudelka: Profile of an Enigma,' *Dance in Canada*, Spring 1985, p. 14.
40. NBOC Archives, Souvenir Programs, 1980–1 and 1981–2.
41. Gruen, *Erik Bruhn*, p. 156; Wyman, *Dance Canada*, p. 145.
42. NBOC Archives, Board Minutes for 18 January 1979, #109-E; Letter of Agreement between Imperial Oil and the National Ballet of Canada, Ballet Production Files, *Newcomers*.
43. Walter Terry, 'Making It to Ballet's "Big Time,"' *Saturday Review*, 3 September 1977, p. 41.
44. Alexander Grant in conversation with the author, 22 March 1988.
45. Peter Schaufuss in conversation with the author, 17 November 1989.
46. NBOC Archives, Executive Committee Minutes for 16 April 1973, #109-D.
47. NBOC Archives, Board Minutes for 20 June 1978, #109-E.
48. Alexander Grant in conversation with the author, 22 March 1988.
49. Galina Samsova in conversation with the author, 14 March 1988.
50. Alexander Grant in conversation with the author, 22 March 1988.
51. Alexander Bland, 'A Case of Taking Colas to Newcastle,' *Observer*, 12 August 1979.
52. Mary Clarke, 'Triple Bill,' *Guardian*, 8 August 1979.
53. Clement Crisp, 'Swan Lake,' *Financial Times*, 7 August 1979.
54. Mary Clarke, 'Swan Lake,' *Guardian*, 7 August 1979.
55. Fernau Hall, 'Brave Try with a Masterpiece,' *Daily Telegraph*, 7 August 1979.
56. Alexander Bland, 'A Case of Taking Colas to Newcastle,' *Observer*, 12 August 1979.
57. Mary Clarke, 'Triple Bill,' *Guardian*, 8 August 1979.
58. Clement Crisp, 'Jago and Schaufuss,' *Financial Times*, 8 August 1979.
59. Fernau Hall, *Daily Telegraph*, 8 August 1979.
60. Clement Crisp, 'La Fille Mal Gardée,' *Financial Times*, 9 August 1979.
61. Alexander Grant, note to the author, November 1994.
62. Nicholas Dromgoole, 'Born to Dance,' *Sunday Telegraph*, 12 August 1979.
63. John Percival, 'Something Old, Something New, Something Borrowed ...,' *Dance and Dancers*, September 1979, pp. 28–41.
64. Both Grant and Oliphant as quoted in 'Grant's Remarks Anger Oliphant,' Toronto *Globe and Mail*, 17 August 1979.
65. See *Performing Arts Magazine*, August 1982.
66. Alexander Grant in conversation with the author, 22 March 1988; Michael Crabb, 'Alexander Grant's Dismissal from the Complex National Ballet: An Artistic Director's Lot,' *Performing Arts*, Winter/Spring 1983, p. 37.
67. NBOC Archives, Board Minutes for 19 April 1979, #109-E.
68. Karen Kain in conversation with the author, 18 May 1988; Frank Augustyn in conversation with the author, 15 July 1988.
69. Stephen Godfrey, 'Karen Kain Strikes Back at the National Ballet,' Toronto *Globe and Mail*, 26 May 1982; 'National "Needs New Ballets,"' Toronto *Globe and Mail*, 29 May 1982. For Kain's own account of these

events see Karen Kain, *Movement Never Lies: An Autobiography* (Toronto McClelland & Stewart, 1994), pp. 147–51.

70. Betty Oliphant in conversation with the author, 17 August 1988.

71. Helen Bullock, 'National Ballet Drops Grant,' *Toronto Star*, 30 June 1982.

72. Karen Kain in conversation with the author, 18 May 1988.

73. NBOC Archives, Board Minutes for 17 June 1970, #109-C.

74. Karen Kain in conversation with the author, 18 May 1988.

75. Helen Bullock, 'National Ballet Drops Grant,' *Toronto Star*, 30 June 1982.

76. Robert Johnston in conversation with the author, 2 May 1988.

77. Peter Schaufuss in conversation with the author, 17 November 1989.

78. NBOC Archives, photocopy of playbill for the Scottish Ballet, 1978, Ballet Production Files, *Napoli*.

79. NBOC Archives, Board Minutes for 26 November 1981, #109-E.

80. NBOC Archives, Monique Michaud to R. McCartney Samples, 29 May 1980, Canada Council Files 1980–1.

81. See Karen Kain in Stephen Godfrey, 'Karen Kain Strikes Back at the National Ballet,' Toronto *Globe and Mail*, 26 May 1982, and Frank Augustyn in Stephen Godfrey, 'National "Needs New Ballets,"' Toronto *Globe and Mail*, 29 May 1982.

82. NBOC Archives, Board Minutes for 25 June 1980, #109-E.

83. NBOC Archives, Board Minutes for 18 September 1980, #109-E.

84. Peter Schaufuss in conversation with the author, 17 November 1989.

85. Peter Schaufuss in conversation with the author, 17 November 1989.

86. Alexander Grant in conversation with the author, 22 March 1988.

87. Alexander Grant in conversation with the author, 22 March 1988.

88. Lois Smith in conversation with the author, 24 May 1988.

89. Alexander Grant in conversation with the author, 22 March 1988.

CHAPTER 8

1. Lina Fattah, Interview with Erik Bruhn, *Dance and Dancers*, December 1983; Celia Franca in conversation with the author, 19 August 1988. The invitation could have been issued during the run of American Ballet Theatre at the Royal Alexandra Theatre in 1952. The program for 4 February 1952 (Metropolitan Toronto Reference Library, Special Collections Centre, Boris Volkoff Papers, Scrapbook #11) lists Bruhn among the dancers for that engagement. That date falls between the National's tour engagements in Montreal (2 February) and London (7 February).

2. Helen Bullock, 'National Ballet Drops Grant,' *Toronto Star*, 30 June 1982.

3. Robert Johnston in conversation with the author, 2 May 1988.

4. NBOC Archives, Board Minutes for 29 September 1982, #109-E.

5. Lyman Henderson in conversation with the author, 13 July 1988.

6. Valerie Wilder in conversation with the author, 17 August 1988.

7. Betty Oliphant in conversation with the author, 17 August 1988.

8. Lina Fattah, Interview with Erik Bruhn, *Dance and Dancers*, December 1983.

9. David Adams in conversation with the author, 11 April 1988.

10. Details regarding search procedures with respect to immigration regulations from Lyman Henderson in conversation with the author, 13 July 1988.

11. Valerie Wilder in conversation with the author, 17 August 1988.

12. Lynn Wallis in conversation with the author, 17 August 1988.

13. Valerie Wilder in conversation with the author, 17 August 1988.

14. NBOC Archives, 'Observations and Thoughts on Our First Completed Tour of Europe 85,' Copenhagen, June 1985, Bruhn Files.

15. Veronica Tennant in conversation with the author, 9 May 1988.

16. Lina Fattah, Interview with Erik Bruhn, *Dance and Dancers*, December 1983.

17. Gary Smith, 'Custodians or Creators?,' *Hamilton Spectator*, 10 October 1987.

18. Mary Jago in conversation with the author, 14 July 1988.

19. NBOC Archives, Executive Minutes for 15 December 1966, #109-B; Board Minutes for 13 January 1971, #109-E.

20. Valerie Wilder in conversation with the author, 17 August 1988.

21. Wendy Reid in conversation with the author, 6 May 1988.

22. Frank Augustyn in conversation with the author, 15 July 1988; Robert Johnston in conversation with the author, 2 May 1988.

23. Robert Johnston in conversation with the author, 2 May 1988.

24. NBOC Archives, Board Minutes for 25 September 1984, #113; Wendy Reid in conversation with the author, 6 May 1988.

25. NBOC Archives, Erik Bruhn to Pierre Wyss, 8 December 1985 and Valerie Wilder to Robert Trinchero, 26 August 1985, Bruhn Files.

26. NBOC Archives, Erik Bruhn to Artistic Staff, 23 July 1985, Bruhn Files.

27. Valerie Wilder in conversation with the author, 17 August 1988.

28. Details regarding Allan's repertoire and the development of *Masada* from David Allan in conversation with the author, 9 May 1988.

29. David Allan in conversation with the author, 9 May 1988.

30. Details concerning Alleyne's Stuttgart background and choreographic ambitions from John Alleyne in conversation with the author, 13 May 1988.

31. Paula Citron, 'Patsalas Comes Back to Ballet,' *Toronto Star*, 23 October 1987.

32. Gruen, *Erik Bruhn*, p. 212; NBOC Archives, Board Minutes for 26 March 1975, #109-E.

33. NBOC Archives, Souvenir Programs, 1980–1 and 1982–3.

34. NBOC Archives, Wallace Russell to Erik Bruhn, 25 July 1968, Bruhn Files.

35. NBOC Archives, Erik Bruhn, undated draft of letter, Bruhn Files.

36. William Littler, 'World Veteran Bruhn Takes Helm of National,' *Toronto Star*, 9 December 1982.

37. Valerie Wilder in conversation with the author, 17 August 1988.

38. Details on Tetley's views of the company and background to the acquisition of *Sphinx* and *Alice* from Glen Tetley in conversation with the author, 14 July 1988.

39. Glen Tetley in conversation with the author, 14 July 1988.

40. NBOC Archives, Board Minutes for 18 March 1986, #109-E; Valerie Wilder in conversation with the author, 17 August 1988.

41. NBOC Archives, Alexander Grant–Natalia Makarova correspondence, 30 October 1981 to 18 November 1981, Ballet Production Files, *La Bayadère*.

42. Payne, *American Ballet Theatre*, p. 365.

43. NBOC Archives, Program Note, O'Keee Centre House Program of 1–5 May 1985.

44. NBOC Archives, ms., by Erik Bruhn, of tribute to Terry Westmoreland, [n.d.], Bruhn Files.

45. Gruen, *Erik Bruhn*, pp. 86–91, 138–40.

46. NBOC Archives, Sir Robert Helpmann to Robert Johnston, 16 April 1986, Bruhn Files.

47. NBOC Archives, Erik Bruhn to Sir Robert Helpmann, 1 October 1985, Bruhn Files.

48. NBOC Archives, Erik Bruhn to Maina [Gielgud], [n.d.], Bruhn Files.

49. Gruen, *Erik Bruhn*, pp. 36, 44.

50. Veronica Tennant in conversation with the author, 9 May 1988.
51. Karen Kain in conversation with the author, 18 May 1988.
52. Veronica Tennant in conversation with the author, 9 May 1988.
53. John Alleyne in conversation with the author, 13 May 1988.
54. Karen Kain in conversation with the author, 18 May 1988.
55. Frank Augustyn in conversation with the author, 15 July 1988.
56. John Alleyne in conversation with the author, 13 May 1988.
57. NBOC Archives, draft ms., by Erik Bruhn, of Artistic Director's Report on 1984–5 season, Bruhn Files.
58. Robert Johnston in conversation with the author, 2 May 1988.
59. Veronica Tennant in conversation with the author, 9 May 1988.
60. Veronica Tennant in conversation with the author, 9 May 1988; Donn Downey, 'Danish Dancer Fostered New Canadian Ballets,' Toronto *Globe and Mail*, 2 April 1986; William Littler, 'Erik Bruhn Helped Ballet Soar,' *Toronto Star*, 2 April 1986.
61. Lynn Wallis in conversation with the author, 17 August 1988.
62. NBOC Archives, Erik Bruhn to all the National Ballet of Canada, 19 March 1986, Bruhn Files.

CHAPTER 9

1. *The Canadian Encyclopedia*, entry under 'National Development in the Arts, Letters and Sciences, Royal Commission on.'
2. Dance Collection Danse, 'Brief to the Royal Commission, Submitted on Behalf of the Canadian Ballet Festival Association,' 4 November 1949.
3. NBOC Archives, Executive Committee Minutes for 20 September 1972, #109-D.
4. NBOC Archives, Audited Statement for 1951–2 season, Founding of the Nat. Ballet – 1950–52, #500; Franca, *The National Ballet of Canada*, p. 62.
5. NBOC Archives, Minutes for the Annual General Meeting of 21 October 1980, #109-E.
6. National Archives of Canada, Report by Alan Skinner on New York Trip, 1954, Franca Papers (15-12). These figures are comparable to Chase's contributions to Ballet Theatre's 1948 season at the Metropolitan, as reported in Payne, *American Ballet Theatre*, p. 159.
7. A.G.S. Griffin in conversation with the author, 6 May 1996; Judie Colpman in conversation with the author, 20 January 1988; Jocelyn Terelle in conversation with the author, 8 June 1990. On personal guarantees for bank loans, see Franca's anecdote about George Hees in *The National Ballet of Canada*, p. 17.
8. NBOC Archives, W.P. Walker to the Canada Council, 15 May 1961, Canada Council Files, #105-H.
9. National Archives of Canada, Mabel Hees to Trevor Moore, 25 August 1954, Franca Papers (15-13).
10. National Archives of Canada, Sydney Mulqueen to the Right Honourable Louis St Laurent, 19 May 1952, Franca Papers (13-8).
11. NBOC Archives, Board Minutes for 25 February 1953, #109-A.
12. NBOC Archives, Board Minutes for 23 April 1956 and for 26 June 1956, #109-B.
13. NBOC Archives, Invoice, 25 March 1963, Administration Files 1962–3, #70-B.
14. Waite, *Lord of Point Grey*, pp. 154–5, 180; J.L. Granatstein, *Canada, 1957–1967: The Years of Uncertainty and Innovation* (Toronto: McClelland and Stewart, 1986), p. 140.
15. National Archives of Canada, A.G.S. Griffin to A.W. Trueman, 29 April 1957, Canada Council Files (RG 63 Vol. 223).
16. Granatstein, *Canada, 1957–1967*, p. 146.
17. National Archives of Canada, A.W. Trueman to A.G.S. Griffin, 2 May 1957, Canada Council Files (RG 63 Vol. 223).
18. National Archives of Canada, A.G.S. Griffin to the Chairman and members of the Canada Council, 26 July 1957, Canada Council Files (RG 63 Vol. 223).
19. Waite, *Lord of Point Grey*, pp. 180–1.
20. National Archives of Canada, Memo from A.W.T. [A.W. Trueman] to Council, 20 February 1961, Canada Council Files (RG 63 Vol. 224). See also the Canada Council's First Annual Report to 31 March 1958. The Stratford and Vancouver Festivals, at $50,000 each, were the closest competitors; the Montreal and Toronto Symphonies each received $25,000.
21. Granatstein, *Canada, 1957–1967*, pp. 145, 147. Timothy Porteous in conversation with the author, 21 February 1990.
22. Timothy Porteous in conversation with the author, 21 February 1990.
23. National Archives of Canada, Memo from A.W.T. [A.W. Trueman] to Council, 30 May 1960, Canada Council Files (RG 63 Vol. 224).
24. National Archives of Canada, Peter Dwyer to Carman Guild, 19 February 1959, Canada Council Files (RG 63 Vol. 224).
25. National Archives of Canada, Press Release, 26 September 1961, Canada Council Files (RG 63 Vol. 1348).
26. National Archives of Canada, Peter Dwyer to Guy Glover, 17 January 1961, Canada Council Files (RG 63 Vol. 224); Lincoln Kirstein to Peter Dwyer, 16 August 1961 (RG 63 Vol. 1348).
27. National Archives of Canada, Press Release, 22 November 1961, Canada Council Files (RG 63 Vol. 1348).
28. National Archives of Canada, Lincoln Kirstein to Peter Dwyer, 16 August 1961, Canada Council Files (RG 63 Vol. 1348); Peter Dwyer to Guy Glover, 20 September 1961, Canada Council Files (RG 63 Vol. 1348).
29. National Archives of Canada, Lincoln Kirstein and Richard Buckle, A Report on Ballet in Canada, 1962, Canada Council Files (RG 63 Vol. 1348).
30. National Archives of Canada, Lincoln Kirstein, A Report on Ballet in Canada, Canada Council Files, (RG 63 Vol. 1348).
31. Lincoln Kirstein, as quoted in John Fraser, 'Praise for National Ballet School from the Frank and Mighty Kirstein,' Toronto *Globe and Mail*, 11 May 1974.
32. National Archives of Canada, Richard Buckle, A Report on Ballet in Canada, 1962, Canada Council Files (RG 63 Vol. 1348).
33. National Archives of Canada, D. Park Jamieson to D.B. Weldon (Chairman of the Canada Council), 18 June 1962, Canada Council Files (RG 63 Vol. 1376).
34. University of British Columbia Archives, Memo by A.W.T. [A.W. Trueman] attached to summary of survey, N.A.M. Mackenzie Papers (Canada Council Working Papers, #140 8/1).
35. *Annual Report*, the Canada Council, 29 June 1963.
36. All percentages based on figures supplied in the Council's *Annual Reports*. Where grants to ballet schools are reported separately, they have been excluded from the comparisons.
37. National Archives of Canada, A.W. Trueman to Arthur Gelber, 16 May 1962, Canada Council Files (RG 63 Vol. 224).
38. National Archives of Canada, Notes by P.M.D. [Peter M. Dwyer], 19 November 1962, Canada Council Files (RG 63 Vol. 1376).
39. National Archives of Canada, Brooke Claxton to Kenneth LeMay Carter, 17 October 1958, Canada Council Files (RG 63 Vol. 1351).
40. Lyman Henderson in conversation with the author, 13 July 1988.
41. NBOC Archives, Lyman Henderson to Robert Elie, 6 May 1970, Canada Council Files, #105-C.

42. NBOC Archives, Executive Committee Minutes for 10 June 1970, #109-D.

43. NBOC Archives, Minutes of the Annual General Meeting of 29 September 1975, #109-E.

44. NBOC Archives, Monique Aupy [Michaud] to Lyman Henderson, 13 December 1971, Canada Council Files, #105-F.

45. Lyman Henderson in conversation with the author, 13 July 1988.

46. Robert Johnston in conversation with the author, 2 May 1988.

47. *Annual Report*, the Canada Council, 1986, 1987, and 1988. Robert Johnston in conversation with the author, 2 May 1988.

48. Comparisons based on financial statements released in the company's Annual Reports, 1986–7 to 1991–2. For 1995 cut, see Deirdre Kelly, 'Anderson quits National, blames government cutbacks,' Toronto *Globe and Mail*, 11 November 1995.

49. National Archives of Canada, Celia Franca to Alan Skinner, 17 February 1953, Franca Papers (14-22).

50. NBOC Archives, Memorandum, 4 November 1970, Franca Files, Box #2.

51. NBOC Archives, Notes by Alan Skinner, Aileen Woods File, #73.

52. National Archives of Canada, Alan Skinner to Angela Labatt, 15 December 1953, Franca Papers (15-11).

53. NBOC Archives, Notes by Joan Tanner, 29 February 1964, Aileen Woods File, #73.

54. NBOC Archives, Notes by Maggie Reid, 4 January 1964, Aileen Woods File, #73.

55. NBOC Archives, Board Minutes for 12 January 1955, #109-A.

56. NBOC Archives, Board Minutes for 7 October 1970, #109-C.

57. NBOC, Finance and Operating Committee Minutes for 17 and 26 February 1964, #109-F.

58. NBOC Archives, Memo from Carman Guild to Lt.-Gen. Guy Simonds, 5 June 1963, Finance and Operating Committee Files, #109-F.

59. NBOC Archives, Marg Morgan to Aileen Woods, 1 March 1964, Aileen Woods File, #73.

60. NBOC Archives, Board Minutes for 12 April 1972, #109-E.

61. NBOC Archives, Notes by Maggie Reid, 4 January 1964, Aileen Woods File, #73.

62. NBOC Archives, Kraul Biography, Personal Files, Kraul.

63. NBOC Archives, Chairman's Agenda Script for Annual General Meeting of 21 October 1987, #113.

64. NBOC Archives, Board Minutes for 12 September 1978, #109-E.

65. NBOC Archives, National Ballet of Canada Annual Report for 1988–9 and for 1991–2.

66. Wendy Reid in conversation with the author, 6 May 1988; see also Board Minutes for 22 April 1985, #113.

67. NBOC Archives, Minutes of the Annual General Meeting of 15 November 1968, #109-C.

68. NBOC Archives, Board Minutes for 13 September 1979, #109-E.

69. NBOC Archives, Minutes of the Annual General Meeting of 26 October 1982, #109-E.

70. NBOC Archives, National Ballet of Canada Annual Report for 1991–2.

71. John Pettigrew and Jamie Portman, *Stratford* (Toronto: Macmillan, 1985), vol. 2, p. 247.

72. NBOC Archives, Mary Jolliffe to Paul Robin, 30 July 1976, Canada Council Files, Marketing and Public Relations 1976.

73. Robert Johnston in conversation with the author, 2 May 1988.

74. NBOC Archives, Board Minutes for 21 June 1979, #109-E.

75. Robert Johnston in conversation with the author, 2 May 1988.

CHAPTER 10

1. Valerie Wilder in conversation with the author, 7 June 1990.

2. NBOC Archives, Erik Bruhn to Edmund C. Bovey, 18 March 1986, Personal Files, Patsalas. See also Deirdre Kelly, 'National Ballet Appoints Team to Carry on Bruhn's Work,' Toronto *Globe and Mail*, 9 April 1986.

3. NBOC Archives, Board Minutes for 7 April 1986, #109-E.

4. Valerie Wilder in conversation with the author, 7 June 1990.

5. Constantin Patsalas, letter to the editor of the Toronto *Globe and Mail*, 21 November 1986; Donn Downey, 'Concerto Goes to Court,' Toronto *Globe and Mail*, 6 November 1986.

6. Thomas Claridge and Deirdre Kelly, 'Patsalas Fails in Bid to Bar Ballet,' Toronto *Globe and Mail*, 8 November 1986.

7. Valerie Wilder in conversation with the author, 17 August 1988.

8. Program Notes for 'A Program of Dance Works by Constantin Patsalas,' 27-31 October 1987, author's private collection.

9. Death notice, Toronto *Globe and Mail*, 22 May 1989.

10. Valerie Wilder in conversation with the author, 7 June 1990.

11. Paul Taylor, 'Legal, Medical, Social Work Advice Available at Innovative AIDS Clinic,' Toronto *Globe and Mail*, 20 July 1989.

12. Glen Tetley in conversation with the author, 14 July 1988.

13. NBOC Archives, Press Release #27/36.

14. Valerie Wilder in conversation with the author, 7 June 1990.

15. NBOC Archives, Submission to the Canada Council for 1976–7, Canada Council Files 1976.

16. Bremser, *International Dictionary of Ballet*, entry under 'Tetley.'

17. Glen Tetley in conversation with the author, 14 July 1988.

18. Valerie Wilder in conversation with the author, 17 August 1988.

19. NBOC Archives, Board Minutes for 20 December 1977, #109-E.

20. NBOC Archives, Press Release #48/43.

21. NBOC Archives, Erik Bruhn to Sonia Arova, 12 September 1985, Bruhn Files; Gruen, *Erik Bruhn*, pp. 38–40ff.

22. NBOC Archives, Program Note to Program for First Annual Erik Bruhn Prize, 14 May 1988.

23. NBOC Archives, Press Release #24/37.

24. Lyman Henderson in telephone conversation with the author, 15 July 1993.

25. NBOC Archives, Program for 14–17 June 1984.

26. Details on Anderson's background and career from Reid Anderson in conversation with the author, 8 June 1990.

27. NBOC Archives, Press Release #5/42.

28. NBOC Archives, Press Release #7/42.

29. James Kudelka in conversation with the author, 10 May 1996.

30. NBOC Archives, Media Release #27/45.

31. Sid Adilman, 'Harris says sorry for Kain snub,' *Toronto Star*, January 16, 1996.

32. Deirdre Kelly, 'Anderson quits National, blames government cutbacks,' Toronto *Globe and Mail*, November 11, 1995.

33. NBOC Media Release, #15/45.

34. NBOC Media Release, #16/45.

35. 'Augustyn or Tennant may follow Anderson,' Toronto *Globe and Mail*, 9 January 1996.

36. James Kudelka in conversation with the author, 10 May 1996.

37. NBOC Media Release, #38/45.

Select Bibliography

The select bibliography lists all books cited in the text as well as those consulted in its preparation. It does not attempt comprehensiveness on the subject of ballet in general. For such detail, interested readers are referred to the general reference works cited below, particularly Bremser, *International Dictionary of Ballet*, and Getz, *Dancers and Choreographers*. Full bibliographical information for articles in journals, newspapers, and periodicals cited in the text is provided in the appropriate endnote; these references are not included in the select bibliography.

Ambrose, Kay. *The Ballet-Lover's Companion*. London: Adam and Charles Black, 1949.

–*The Ballet-Lover's Pocket-Book*. New York: Alfred A. Knopf, 1984 (first published 1945).

–*Beginners, Please!* London: Adam and Charles Black, 1953.

Anderson, Jack. *The Nutcracker Ballet*. London: Bison Books, 1979.

Austin, Richard. *Lynn Seymour: An Authorised Biography*. London: Angus & Robertson, 1980.

Baillie, Joan Parkhill, comp. and annotator, with an introduction by William Kilbourn. *Look at the Record: An Album of Toronto's Lyric Theatres, 1825–1984*. Oakville: Mosaic Press, 1985.

Bland, Alexander. *The Royal Ballet: The First Fifty Years*. Garden City, New York: Doubleday & Company, 1981.

Bremser, Martha, ed. *International Dictionary of Ballet*. 2 vols. Detroit, London, Washington: St James Press, 1993.

Bruhn, Erik, and Lillian Moore. *Bournonville and Ballet Technique: Studies and Comments on August Bournonville's Etudes Chorégraphiques*. London: Adam and Charles Black, 1961.

Clarke, Mary, and David Vaughan, eds. *The Encyclopedia of Dance and Ballet*. London: Peerage Books, 1977.

Crabb, Michael, ed. *Visions: Ballet and Its Future: Proceedings of the National Ballet of Canada's 25th Anniversary Conference held in Toronto, 15–16 November, 1976*. Toronto: Simon & Pierre, 1978.

Franca, Celia, and Ken Bell. *The National Ballet of Canada: A Celebration*. Toronto, Buffalo, London: University of Toronto Press, 1978.

Getz, Leslie. *Dancers and Choreographers: A Selected Bibliography*. Wakefield, Rhode Island, and London: Asphodel Press, 1995.

Goodman, Edwin A. *Life of the Party: The Memoirs of Eddie Goodman*. Toronto: Key Porter Books, 1988.

Granatstein, J.L. *Canada, 1957–1967: The Years of Uncertainty and Innovation*. Toronto: McClelland and Stewart, 1986.

Gustaitis, Rasa. *Melissa Hayden, Ballerina*. London, New York, Toronto: Thomas Nelson & Sons, 1967.

Kain, Karen, with Stephen Godfrey and Penelope Reed Doob. *Movement Never Lies: An Autobiography*. Toronto: McClelland & Stewart, 1994.

Katz, Leslie George, Nancy Lasalle, and Harvey Simmonds, comps. *Choreography by George Balanchine: A Catalogue of Works*. New York: Viking Penguin, 1984.

Marsh, James H., ed. *The Canadian Encyclopedia: Second Edition*. 4 vols. Edmonton: Hurtig, 1988.

McKinsey and Company, Management Consultants. *Directions for the Dance in Canada*. Ottawa: Canada Council Information Services, 1973.

Mitchell, Lillian Leonora. *Boris Volkoff: Dancer, Teacher, Choreographer*. Ann Arbor, Michigan: University Microfilms International, 1982.

Oxenham, Andrew, with Michael Crabb. *Dance Today in Canada*. Toronto: Simon & Pierre, 1977.

Payne, Charles. *American Ballet Theatre*. New York: Alfred A. Knopf, 1979.

Percival, John. *Theatre in My Blood*. London: Herbert Press, 1983.

Perlmutter, Donna. *Shadowplay: The Life of Antony Tudor*. New York: Viking, 1991.

Pettigrew, John, and Jamie Portman. *Stratford*. 2 vols. Toronto: Macmillan, 1985.

Reyna, Ferdinand, trans. by André Gâteau. *Concise Encyclopedia of Ballet*. London and Glasgow: Collins, 1974.

Ross, Janice, and Stephen Corbett Steinberg, comps. *Why a Swan? Essays, Interviews, & Conversations on 'Swan Lake.'* San Francisco: San Francisco Performing Arts Library and Museum, 1989.

Sparshott, Francis. *A Measured Pace: Towards a Philosophical Understanding of the Arts of Dance*. Toronto, Buffalo, London: University of Toronto Press, 1995.

–*Off the Ground: First Steps to a Philosophical Consideration of the Dance*. Princeton: Princeton University Press, 1988.

Stuart, Otis. *Perpetual Motion: The Public and Private Lives of Rudolf Nureyev*. New York: Simon & Schuster, 1995.

Taper, Bernard. *Balanchine: A Biography*. New York: Times Books, 1984.

Thorpe, Edward. *Kenneth MacMillan: The Man and His Ballets*. London: Hamish Hamilton, 1985.

Trueman, Albert W. *A Second View of Things: A Memoir*. Toronto: McClelland and Stewart, 1982.

Vaughan, David. *Frederick Ashton and His Ballets*. London: Adam and Charles Black, 1977.

Waite, P.B. *Lord of Point Grey: Larry Mackenzie of UBC*. Vancouver: University of British Columbia Press, 1987.

Walker, Hugh. *The O'Keefe Centre: Thirty Years of Theatre History*. Toronto: Key Porter Books, 1991.

Walker, Kathrine Sorley. *De Basil's Ballets Russes*. London: Hutchinson, 1982.

Watson, Peter. *Nureyev: A Biography*. London, Sydney, Auckland: Hodder & Stoughton, 1994.

Whittaker, Herbert. *Canada's National Ballet*. Toronto and Montreal: McClelland and Stewart, 1967.

Wyman, Max. *Dance Canada: An Illustrated History*. Vancouver, Toronto: Douglas & McIntyre, 1989.

–*The Royal Winnipeg Ballet: The First Forty Years*. Toronto and Garden City, New York: Doubleday, 1978.

Photo Credits

All photos are courtesy the National Ballet of Canada archives, unless otherwise indicated.

Chapter One
2, Elizabeth C. Frey; 3, Ken Bell; 5, W.H. Stephan; 6, John Lindquist; 8, *Evening Standard* (London); 14, Fednews; 18, Tom Davenport; 21, Basil Zarov; 23, (upper left), unidentified; (lower right), John Grange; 26, June Stichbury

Chapter Two
28, *Spectator* (Hamilton); 29, Ken Bell; 30, unidentified; 32, Ken Bell; 36, John Grange; 38, Andrew Oxenham; 41, unidentified; 43, *Globe and Mail*; 46, unidentified; 47, Time Life Syndicate (Martha Swope); 48, (upper) unidentified; (lower) Janine; (left and centre) Anthony Crickmay; (right) Barry Gray

Chapter Three
50, unidentified (photo courtesy Jocelyn Allen); 51, Ken Bell; 52, John Lindquist; 57, unidentified (photo courtesy Hugh Anson-Cartwright); 59, 60, 61, unidentified; 65, Fednews; 66, Jack Blake; 68, Ballard and Jarrett; 69, unidentified; 71, Alex Gray; 73, unidentified; 75, Ken Bell

Chapter Four
78, Erik Christenson; 79, Ken Bell; 80, unidentified; 83, 84, Ken Bell; 87, Erik Christenson; 90, Courtney G. McMahon; 93, Alex Gray; 94 (left) Courtney G. McMahon; (right) Andrew Oxenham; 98, (all photos) A & A Photographers; 100, (left) Ken Bell; (centre) *Telegram* (Toronto); (right) *Toronto Star* (Reg Innell); 103, MIRA (Myra Armstrong); 108, Harold Whyte

Chapter Five
112, Anthony Crickmay; 113, 119, Ken Bell; 120 (upper), Courtney G. McMahon; (lower), Andrew Oxenham; 122, 125, Anthony Crickmay; 129, unidentified; 132, Zoë Dominic; 134, Anthony Crickmay

Chapter Six
140, 141, Anthony Crickmay; 143, *Toronto Star*; 147, Anthony Crickmay; 149, Judy Cameron; 153, MIRA (Myra Armstrong); 155, Andrew Oxenham; 156–7 (all photos), MIRA (Myra Armstrong); 159, Ontario Place Forum (Franz Maier); 161, Andrew Oxenham; 166, Anthony Crickmay

Chapter Seven
168, Andrew Oxenham; 169, Deborah Shackleton; 170, unidentified; 173, Anthony Crickmay; 178, Andrew Oxenham; 181, Barry Gray; 182, Andrew Oxenham; 184, David Street; 187, 189, 192, Andrew Oxenham; 197, Barry Gray; 198, Andrew Oxenham

Chapter Eight
202, 203, Andrew Oxenham; 204, Courtney G. McMahon; 207, 211, 213 (left), Andrew Oxenham; 213 (right), Leslie Spatt; 216, 218, Andrew Oxenham; 221, David Street; 223 Royal Winnipeg Ballet (Bruce Monk); 225, unidentified

Chapter Nine
230, Andrew Oxenham; 231 (left and centre) unidentified; (right) unidentified (photo courtesy Lou Anne Cassels); 234, Ken Bell; 238 (left), Erik Christenson; (right), Paul Smith; 240, Time Life Syndicate (Martha Swope); 243 (upper) Ken Bell; (lower) Courtney G. McMahon; 247, unidentified; 250, Quebec City Official Photographer; 253, Anthony Crickmay; 254, Ken Bell; 257, Andrew Oxenham; 258, *Toronto Star* (P. Power)

Chapter Ten
260, Andrew Oxenham; 261, David Street; 262 (left) Cylla von Tiedemann; (centre and right) David Street; 264, 267, Andrew Oxenham; 270, Maya Wallach; 274, Lydia Pawelak; 276, Cylla von Tiedemann; 275, David Street; 277, Cylla von Tiedemann; 279, unidentified; 281, Andrew Oxenham; 284, *Globe and Mail* (Toronto) (Tibor Kolley); 286, Andrew Oxenham

Index

Numerals in italic type indicate a reference to the text of a photo caption.

Aaron, Myrna, *21*
Abramsky, Jules, 251
The Actress (Kudelka), 275, 280
Adams, David, 6, 13, 15, 16, 17, 18, 23, 24, 25, 26, 33, 34, 35, 40, 57, 58, 59, 68–9, 72, 73, 82, 94–5, 114, 131, 205–6, ch1n41, *5, 29*
Adams, Lawrence, 17, 93, 114, 115, *60*
Adolph Bolm Ballet, 17
Afternoon of a Faun (Robbins), 177
AIDS (Acquired Immune Deficiency Syndrome), 264, 265, *216*
Albrechtsen, Henning, 271
Alice (Tetley), 220–1, 266, 267, 280, *221*
Allan, David, 123, 179, 215–7, 265, 268
Allemann, Sabina, 191, 220, *120*
Alleyne, John, 98, 210, 217, 225, 226, 268, 269, 272, 278, 281, *261, 264*; as resident choreographer NBOC, 274–5
Ambrose, Kay, 18, 42–5, 48, 62, 90, 251, *43*; as author and illustrator, 42; as designer, 44, 52, 57–8, 69, 70, 82, 102, 242, ch3n28, *57, 243*; background and experience, 42–4; death (1971), 45; relationship with Franca, 42, 44–5
American Ballet Theatre (ABT), 60, 63, 95, 128, 158, 171, 174, 184, 192, 193, 209, 213, 220, 221, 222, 234, 270, 284; *see also* Ballet Theatre
American School of Ballet, 242
Amyôt, Luc, *198*
Anderson, Bert, 136
Anderson, Reid, 262, 269, 285, *247, 261, 276, 281*; as artistic director NBOC, 273–83; background and experience, 271–3; resignation from NBOC, 283–4
Angali (Patsalas), 180, 183, *264*
Anne, Princess, *113*
Antonijevic, Aleksandar, 281, *281*
Apiné, Irene, 6, 7, 24, 34, 85, *6, 32*
Applebaum, Louis, 68
L'Après-midi d'un Faune (Woizikowsky/Nijinsky), 15
The Arena (Strate), 70
Armstrong, Kay, 34, 36, 72
Arova, Sonia, 270, 281
Arpino, Gerald, 186
Artistic Management Committee. *See* National Ballet of Canada; Artistic Management Committee
Artistic Management Council. *See* National Ballet of Canada; Artistic Management Council
Ashton, Frederick, 36, 48, 56, 66–7, 106, 107, 146, 161, 175, 177–9, 182, 184, 185, 193, 278, 280, 285, *178, 182, 198, 286*; choreographic style, 177–8
Auger, Yolande, *211*
Augustyn, Frank, 58, 126, 131, 134, 145, 148, 151, 152–4, 178, 184, 186, 193–4, 199, 211, 220, 226, 281, 284, *94, 153, 270*
Australian Ballet, 15, 41, 195, 223–4, 271

Bach, Johann Sebastian, 70, 82
Bailemos (Franca), 15
Bain, Joy, *120*
Baker, Michael Conway, 181
Balanchine, George, 4, 5, 6, 22, 46, 47, 53, 61, 70, 76, 81–4, 85, 87, 88, 120, 165, 185, 222–3, 241, 244, 273, 276, 285, *223, 240*; influence on North American ballet, 36, 177
Baldwin, Janet, 9, 11, 13
Balfour, Mrs St Clair, 115
Ballet; corporate sponsorship, 53, 54, 150, 163, 183, 256; in Canada, prior to 1950, 5–8; on television, 16, 122; — (*Cinderella*), 108, *108*; — (*Dance of Salomé*), 33; — (*La Sylphide*), 158; — (*Mad Shadows*), 161; — (*Romeo and Juliet*), *94*; — (*The Sleeping Beauty*), 148; private philanthropic support for, 232, 234–5, 256; state support for, 4, 53, 232, 234, 235–6, 248, 255, 256, 283–4, *258*
Ballet B.C., 217, 273, 274;
Ballet Behind Us (Adams), *68*
Ballet Composite (Adams), 68
Ballet Concert. *See* National Ballet of Canada, Ballet Concert
Ballet de Wallonie (Charlevoi), 162
Ballet for All. *See* Royal Ballet; Ballet for All
Ballet Jooss, 15
The Ballet Lover's Companion, 42
The Ballet-Lover's Pocket Book, 42
Ballet Opera House (Toronto), 51, 269
Ballet Opera House Foundation, 269
Ballet Rambert, 4, 15, 33, 254
Ballet Revue, 180
The Ballet Student's Primer, 42
Ballet Theatre, 6, 7, ch9n6; *see also* American Ballet Theatre
Les Ballets Chiriaeff, 81; *see also* Les Grands Ballets Canadiens
Ballets Russes of Colonel de Basil, 7, 34, 59, 161
Ballets Russes of Serge Diaghilev, 128–9
Banff School of Fine Arts, 272
Barbara Allen (Adams), 68
Barnes, Clive, 107–8, 150, 172
Barra, Ray, 95
Baryshnikov, Mikhail, 158–9, 209, 210, 211, *159*
Batsheva Dance Company, 183
Battle of the ballets, 55
La Bayadère, Act II (Petipa/Makarova), 96, 190, 221
Bayaderka, Act IV (Petipa/Valukin), 86, 96, 97, 186–9, 190, 221, *187*
Beauty and the Beast (Menken), 98
Beecroft, Norma, 181
Beethoven, Ludwig van, 183
Beevers, Carol, 80, *80*
Beevers, Larry, 147
Beginners, Please!, 42
Béjart, Maurice, 179, 217
Bennathan, Serge, 269
Benson, Susan, *90, 276*
Beriosoff, Nicholas, 16, 161–2, 163, 164, 198, 222
Beriosova, Svetlana, 16, 60, 85, *3*
Berlin Opera Ballet, *122*
Berlioz, Hector, 218
Bertram, Victoria, 98, 106, 121, 122, 145, 179, *169*
Black Angels (Patsalas), 177, 180
Blais, Marie-Claire (*La Belle Bête*), 160
Bland, Alexander, 187, 188
Blanton, Jeremy, *79*
Blatch, Cecilia, 54
Blue-Eyed Trek (Alleyne), 274
Blue Snake (Desrosiers), 215
Board of directors, NBOC. *See* National Ballet of Canada, board of directors
Bolsby, James. *See* James, Stewart
Bolshoi Ballet, 85–6, 187, 286
Bolshoi ballet school, 42, 152
Bolshoi Theatre (Moscow), 153, 154
Boston Ballet choreographic competition (1979), 218
Bournonville, August, 99, 195, 197
Bournonville style, 99, 101, 158–9, 197
Boutilier, Sean, *38*
Bovey, Edmund C., 262
Bowes, Karen, 121, *75, 83, 119*
BPI Financial Corporation, 256
Brahms, Johannes, 181
Brinson, Peter, 122, 186
Brooklyn Academy of Music, 62, 71, 150
Brown Earth (Ditchburn), 122
Bruhn, Erik, 16, 42, 107, 109, 127–8, 129, 165, 169–71, 174, 179, 180, 183, 194, 199, 200, 203, 213, 231, 242, 255, 257, 258, 262, 266, 268, 271, 274, 278, 279, 280, 281, 284–5, ch8n1, *100, 169, 170, 203, 204, 225, 247, 262*; and artistic exchanges, 209, 224, 269–71; and Canadian modern dance, 206, 209, 210–11, 214–15; and long-range planning, 209, 214; and team approach to administration, 207–8, 213, 222, 269, 273, 285; as artistic director NBOC, 133–4, 136–7, 197, 203–28, 263; as choreographer, 170, 188, 207–8, 219, *207*; as coach, 209–10, 224–7; as

producer of ballets, 46, 95, 99–106, 155–7, *61*; as resident producer, NBOC, 154, 170, 176, ch7n26; death (1986), 227, 261; farewell letter to NBOC, 228; landed immigrant status, 170, 206–7, 210; last public appearance, 227; retirement from dancing (1971), 128, 158; return to stage in character roles, 155, 157, 158, 198, *155, 157, 197*
Buckle, Richard, 125, 241–2; *see also* Canada Council; survey of ballet in Canada (1962)
Build-a-Ballet Fund. *See* Volunteer Committee Build-a-Ballet Fund
Bujones, Fernando, 184
Butko, Natalia, 18, 26, 31, 35, 80, *36*
Byers, Bettina, 23

Cafe Dances (House), 269
Cage, Betty, 83
Camelot (Lerner and Loewe), 86
Campbell, Norman, 122, *108*
Canada Council, 80, 81, 89, 107, 110, 115, 118, 122, 150, 165, 174, 196, 232, 235, 236, 247–8, 252; and deficit reduction, 245–6; creation (1957), 233, 236; financial support for dance, 239–40, 243–4; financial support for NBOC, 83–4, 236–8, 243–4; survey of ballet in Canada (1962), 240–5, 255; touring office, 127, 136, 254
Canadian Ballet Festival Association, 8, 233
Canadian Ballet Festivals, 8, 10, 233; fourth annual (1952), 8; second annual (1949), 7; third annual (1950), 6, 8, 10, 13, 18, 31, 33, ch1n8
Canadian Broadcasting Corporation (CBC), 37, 81, 122
Canadian Dance Teachers Association (CDTA), 7, 8, 11, 18–19, 20, 39–40
Canadian National Ballet Company (original name of NBOC), 33, 125
Canadian Opera Company, 37, 116, 232, 246, 269
Canciones (Patsalas), 180, 183; Lullaby 265
Carmen (Petit), 174
Le Carnaval (Fokine), 15, 129; (Fokine/Franca), *51*
Carpenter, Bernadette, 13
Carr, Mary, 256
Carreiro, Assis, 282
Carroll, Lewis, 220
Carse, Ruth, 80
Carsen Centre. *See* Walter Carsen Centre for the National Ballet of Canada
Carsen, Walter, 51, 256, 278
Carter Barron Amphitheatre (Washington DC), 91, 92, 98
Casse-Noisette. *See The Nutcracker*
Cassels, Jr, Hamilton, 115
Cecchetti, Enrico, 5, 16, 17, 20, 267
Cecchetti movement syllabus, 5, 19, 21–2, 63
Chabukiani, Vakhtang, 85
Chalmer, Paul, 192, 193, 281
Chase, Lucia, 209, 234
Chatelaine, 44
La Chatte (Balanchine), 165
Chicago Black Hawks, 80
Chicago Festival (1979), 195
Chiriaeff, Ludmilla, 81
Christensen, Lew, 60
Christensen, William, 60–1
Christian Culture series (Windsor), 252
Chujoy, Anatole, 13
Cinderella (Ashton), 106, 108; (Franca), 96, 106–8, 110, *108*, Emmy award for (1970), 108; (Orlikovsky), 96–7; (Konstantin Sergeyev), 106; (Stevenson), 108, 278
Clarke, Anthony, *87*
Clarke, Mary, 187, 188
Claxton, Brooke, 237, 245
Cleary Auditorium (Windsor), 252
Clemens, Margaret, 37
Cohen, Judith Loeb, 231
Cohen, Nathan, 74–5, 102
Cohen, Selma Jeanne, 122
Coliseum (London), 125, 126, 128–30, 136–7, 157, 186, *129*
Colpman, Judie, 23, 26, 30, 31, 44, *21, 26, 30*
Commonwealth Arts Festival, 126
Concerto (MacMillan), 268
Concerto Barocco (Balanchine), 76, 82–3, 84, 126, *83*
Concerto for Flute and Harp (Cranko), 276
Concerto for the Elements (Patsalas), 218, *264*; application for injunction to prevent performance, 263–4; *see also Piano Concerto* (Patsalas)
Conn, Robert, 281
Cool, Colleen, *182, 253*
Coppélia (Saint Léon/Bruhn), 3, 154–8, 278, *155, 157*; (Saint Léon/Christensen), 60; (Saint Léon/Franca), 23, 26, 45, 56, 57, 155, *3, 23*; (Saint Léon/Semenoff), 60
Le Coq d'Or (Fokine/Beriosoff), 161–5, 198
Coralli, Jean, 123
Corey, Winthrop, *149*
Le Corsaire, pas de deux (Klavin/Samsova), 81, 85, 97, 100, 101, *98*
Cousineau, Yves, 96, 198, *79, 90*
Covent Garden. *See* Royal Opera House, Covent Garden
Cragun, Richard, 128, 277, *257*
Cranko, John, 15, 16, 46, 65–6, 88–90, 91–4, 95, 107, 127, 199, 271–3, 274, 276, 277–8, *66, 93, 257, 261, 277*
Cranks (Cranko), 66
Craske, Margaret, 17, 267
Crevier, Gerald, 23
Crisp, Clement, 188
Cronyn, Hume, 250
Crum, George, 37–8, 48, 62, 72, 117, 212, 252, *29, 182*
Cunningham, Merce, 70
Curious Schools of Theatrical Dancing: Part I – 1977 (Grossman), 210
Cyclus (Strate), 70–1, *75*

da Silva, Harold, *60*
Daily Express (London), 65
Daily Telegraph (London), 188
Dance and Dancers, 129, 189, 205, 207
Dance Collection Danse Archives, 233
Dance of Salomé (Franca), 33, 34, 35
Dance Perspectives, 122
Dancers' Council. *See* National Ballet of Canada, Dancers' Council
Dances from the Classics (Petipa/Ivanoff/Franca), 59
Dances from the Sleeping Beauty (Petipa/Franca), 59
Dancing Times, 10, 129
Daphnis and Chloe (Tetley), 267
Dark Elegies (Tudor), 63, 76, 97, 199, *14*; first performance, 15, ch1n41
Dark of the Moon (Harris), 68–9
Dawson, Donald, *129*
de Valois, Ninette, 4, 5, 9, 14, 15, 36, 56, 59, 66–7, 87, 88, 128, 146, 175, 200, 241, 285, *134*; advice to NBOC founders, 11–12, 19, 37, 53–4
de Vos, Audrey, 68
Death and the Maiden (Howard), 64, *51*
Deidre (Franca), 54
del Tredici, David, 220
Delfau, André, 162
Desrosiers, Robert, 210, 214–5
Desrosiers Dance Theatre, 210
Deveson, Rosemary, 7
Diaghilev, Serge, 17, 53, 59, 161, 165; influence on western ballet, 4, 5, 16, 20
Diana and Acteon, pas de deux (Vaganova/Bujones), 268
Ditchburn, Ann, 106, 121, 122, 123, 128, 160–1, 177, 179, 180–1, 182, 189, 217, 265, *122, 161*
Divertimento No. 15 (Balanchine), 273, 276
Dolin, Anton, 61
Don Juan (Neumeier), 145, 154, 199, 276
Don Quixote (Petipa/Beriosoff), 198–9, 222, 228, 278; pas de deux (Petipa), 34, *6*; — (Petipa/Beriosoff), *213*; — (Petipa/Beriosova), 85
Donna Inez de Castro, 219
Dowell, Anthony, 178, 191, 199, 284
Drabinsky, Garth, 280
Drake, Julia, 257
The Dream (Ashton), 175, 177, 178, 180, 182
Dream Dances (Kylián), 219
Dromgoole, Nicholas, 189
Dromisky, Susan, *120*
Drylie, Patricia, 6
Dufresne, André, *21*
Dunn, Sir James, 236
Dwyer, Peter, 83, 89, 115, 238, 241, 245
Dynowska, Oldyna, *36, 68*
Earle, David, 210, 214, 215

Eaton Auditorium, 16, 17, 30, 33, 37, 42, 57, 58, 121
The Ecstasy of Rita Joe (Vesak), 161
Edinburgh, Duke of, 25
Education, Department of (Ontario), 236
Edward Johnson Building (University of Toronto), 121
Eldred, Gerry, 39, 135, 160, 170, 176, 204
Electre (Strate), 70, 121
Elite Syncopations (MacMillan), 179, 180, 268; Calliope Rag, 179
Elizabeth, Princess, 25
Employment and Immigration, Department of, 206
Endangered Species (Grossman), 210, 214, 215, *211*
English National Ballet, 185, 192, 197, 285; *see also* London Festival Ballet
Enigma Variations (Ashton), 179
Erik Bruhn Competition, 269–71
Etude (Armstrong), 33, 35–6, *36*
Etudes (Lander), 179
Exit, Nightfall Miserere (Earle), 210
Expo 67 (Montreal), 103, 127, 256
Expo 70 (Osaka), 92, 126, 127
Expo 86 (Vancouver), 219
External Affairs, Department of, 127

Fandango (Tudor), 127, 149, 254, *253*
Farrally, Betty, 7, 25, 272
Feld, Eliot, 127
Fielman, Judy, *120*
La Fille Mal Gardée (Ashton), 66, 161, 175, 177, 178, 187, 189, 227, *189*
Financial Times (London), 188
The Fisherman and His Soul (Strate), 69
Fleck, James, 115
Fletcher, Linda, *120*
Flindt, Flemming, 120
Fokine, Michel, 16, 33, 60, 82, 161, 162, 163, 164–5
Fonteyn, Margot, 15, 59, 85, 146, 150, 151, 169, 174, 223, *234*
For Internal Use Only (Spain), 122
Forgotten Land (Kylián), 219
Forsythe, William, 217, 268, 272, 273, 278
Forum (Ontario Place), 158–9, 215, 218, *159*
Foss, Lukas, 118
Four Schumann Pieces (van Manen), 177
The Four Temperaments (Balanchine), 120, 126, 222
Fournier, Jennifer, 267–8, 279
Frames of Mind (Grand-Maître), 269
Franca, Celia, xi, 8, 9, 17, 18, 19, 22, 23, 25, 26, 34, 37–45, 46, 51, 52, 55, 62, 66, 67–8, 69, 70, 72, 74, 79–80, 81, 82, 83, 84, 85, 86, 88, 89, 91, 92, 95, 96, 97–8, 99, 100, 105, 109, 121–4, 128, 130, 132, 136–8, 144, 151, 152, 154, 155, 159–60, 161, 162, 163, 165–6, 170, 171, 175–6, 186, 198, 199, 203, 209, 211, 217, 222, 242, 247, 248, 249, 250, 252, 268, 272, 279, 285, ch8n1, *8, 14, 46, 47, 48, 66, 93, 134, 166, 234, 250*; and Cecchetti tradition, 5, 20, 21–2, 40–1, ch2n40; as choreographer, 14, 33–4, 35, 36, 45, 72–3, 96, 106–8, *73, 108*; as dancer, 35, 48, 57, 58, 90, 96, 105–6, 123, 145–6, *3, 23, 52, 113, 173*; as producer of ballets, 56–9, 61, 63–4, 82, 102; as teacher and coach, 20–1, 30–3, 36; authority as artistic director, 39, 52–4, 74, 113–17, 133–5, 164, 257; background and training, 15–16, 29–30; final resignation from NBOC (1975), 3, 165; initial invitation to Canada, 3–4, 9–13; musicality, 31; resignation as artistic director (1968), 41, 110, 113–17, 255; retirement as dancer (1959), 57
Fraser, John, 154, 171–3, 174
Freedman, Harry, 218
Frey, Frank, *122*
Frost, Leslie, 235

Gable, Christopher, 174
Gagnon, André, 161
Gala Performance (Tudor), 63, *243*
Galipeault, André, 195
Geddes, Lorna, 179
Gelber, Arthur, 231
Georgiadis, Nicholas, 132, 142, 143, 146, 148, *132*
Gielgud, Maina, 224
Gillies, Don, 72
Gilmour, Glenn, 254, *79, 254*
Ginastera, Alberto, 71, 218
Giselle (Coralli/Perrot/Blair), 158; (Coralli/Perrot/Dolin), 60; (Coralli/Perrot/Franca), 56, 57–8, 61–2, 123, 199, *57*; peasant pas de deux, 24, 33; (Coralli/Perrot/Wright), 123–6, 278, *203*; peasant pas de quatre, 124, *125*
Glasco, Kimberly, 179, 191, 193, 220, 280, *221*
Globe and Mail (Toronto), 35, 108, 154, 171, 172, 190, 193
Gloria (MacMillan), 268
Glory of Mozart festival (1991), 273
Glover, Guy, 6, 89
Gnatt, Poul, 195
Godfrey, John M., 113–14, 115
Goh, Chan Hon, 273, 279–80, *286*
Goldman, Nina, 269, *261*
Gontcharova, Nathalie, 162
Goodman, Eddie, 231
Gopal, Ram, 44
Gordon, David, 121, *113*
Gordon, Gavin, 87
Gore, Walter, 64
Gorrissen, Jacques, 179
Gotshalks, Jury, 6, 7, 24, 34, 85, *6, 32*
Gould, Morton, 219
Gräfe, Dieter, 91, 92
Graham, Martha, 221, 267
Grain (Lloyd), 17
Grand-Maître, Jean, 269
Les Grands Ballets Canadiens, 81, 119, 165, 181, 182, 183, 210, 212, 219, 239, 241, 243–4, 245, 248, 252, 284
Grant, Alexander, 15, 164, 165, 185, 186, 190, 191, 198, 199–200, 207, 208, 210, 217, 218, 219–20, 221–2, 226, 257, 268, 280, *169, 184*; and Canadian choreography, 179–84; and Erik Bruhn, 176, *197*; and Frederick Ashton, 175, 177–9, 278, *182*; appointment as artistic director NBOC, 176–7; background and experience, 174–5; casting policies, 192–3, *192*; dismissal (1982), 193–5, 203, 206
Gratton, Hector, 72
Gray, Mr Justice W. Gibson, 264
Gray, Roz, 257
Griffin, A.G.S., 234–5, 237
Grossman, Danny, 210, 214, *211*
Gruber, Caroline, *223*
Guardian, 187
Guild, Carman, 39, 83, 88, 91, 233, 251

Haber, David, 39, 118, 119, 121, 127, 136–8, 155, 170, 175, 217, *113, 159, 166*; as artistic director NBOC, 159–65; as co-artistic director NBOC, 154; resignation as artistic director NBOC (1975), 164–5
Haider, Lawrence, *79*
Halifax Ballet, 24
Hall, Fernau, 188, 189
Harkness Ballet, 183
Harrington, Rex, 98, 220, 280, 281, *218, 221, 258, 264*
Harris, Joey, 68–9, 72
Harris, Mike, *258*
Hart, Evelyn, 125–6, 210, *221*
Harwood, Vanessa, 86, 98, 131, 149, 155, 178, 198, 212, *103, 143, 192, 253*
Haskell, Arnold, 152
Hatch-Walker, David, 121
Have Steps Will Travel (Alleyne), 269, 274, *261*
Haydée, Marcia, 93–4, 95, 128, 217, 272, *257*
Hayden, Melissa, 6, 83
Hedda (Kudelka), 180, 181
Heeley, Desmond, 102–3, 106, 124, 199, 222, 223–4, *125*
Hees, George, 235, ch9n7
Hees, Mabel, 235–6
Heiden, Heino, 109–10
Heisey, Ann, 256
Heisey, Lawrence, 256
Helpmann, Robert, 15, 106, 223
Henderson, Lyman, 115, 133, 163, 164, 204–5, 206, 246, 247, 271, 284, *247*
Her Majesty's Theatre (Montreal), 62
Here We Come (Bruhn), 207–8, 219, *207*
Herman, Mildred. *See* Hayden, Melissa
Hermann, Jane, 221
Hersey, David, 146, 147, 149

Hickin, Sally-Ann, 269, *261*
Hicklin, Ralph, 102, 109
Hodgkinson, Greta, *281*
Hoffmann, E.T.A, 155
Hogarth, William, 87
Holm, Hanya, 221, 267
Homburger, Walter, 17, 39, 249
Hot House: Thriving on a Riff (Grossman), 214, 215
L'Hôtel perdu (Desrosiers), 210
House, Christopher, 269
The House of Atreus (Strate), 70, 71–2, 126, *71*
The Houston Ballet, 108
Howard, Andrée, 64–5, *51*
Hughes, Allen, 71, 72
Humphrey, Doris, 71
Hunter, Ian, 126
Hurok, Sol, 130–1, 141–2, 147, 150, 173–4, 221, *173*
Hurok Concerts, 130, 141, 148, 149, 151, 154, 170, 173, 174, 212, 221
Hynd, Ronald, 223–4

Ibsen, Henrik (*Hedda Gabler*), 181
Ichino, Yoko, *213*
Idzikowski, Stanislas, 5, 15, 16, 40, 128, 129, 254
L'Ile Inconnue (Patsalas), 218, 265, 266, *203*, *218*
Illmann, Margaret, 273, 279
Imperial Oil Company sponsorship of *Newcomers*, 183
In Paradisum (Kudelka), 210
Inglesby, Mona, 15
Intermezzo (Feld), 127
International Alliance of Stage and Theatrical Employees (IATSE), 44
International Artists Concert Agency, 39
International Ballet, 15
Interrogating Slam (Alleyne), 274
Ito, Robert, *21*
Ivings, Jacqueline, *21*

Jackson International Ballet Competition (1982), 195
Jacob's Pillow dance festival, 63, *6*
Jago, Mary, 131, 144, 155, 178, 182, 184, 188, 190, 198, 199, 210, 212, *119*, *125*, *149*, *173*, *187*, *192*, *203*
James, Henry (*Washington Square*), 181
James, Stewart, 8, 9, 11, 18, 37
Jarvis, Lilian, 96–7, *3*, *32*, *51*, *59*, *60*
Jefferies, Stephen, 191–2, *181*
Jeune Pas de Deux (Strate), 69
Joffrey Ballet, 63, 164–5, 284
John Cranko Prize, 283
Johnson, Sydney, 61
Johnston, Robert H., 39, 204, 256, 257–8, 285
Jolliffe, Mary, 256
Jonson, Ben, xi
Judgment of Paris (Tudor), 63, 127

Juilliard School of Music, 71
Kai, Una, 82
Kain, Karen, xi, 58, 98, 131, 134, 144, 148, 151, 152–4, 178, 179, 184, 186, 193–4, 198, 199, 211, 220, 224, 226, 272, 275, 280, 283, 284, *94*, *143*, *153*, *169*, *192*, *198*, *223*, *253*, *258*, *261*, *270*, *277*, *284*
Kash, Shirley, 40
Kehlet, Niels, 128
Kenney, Colleen, 18, *32*
Kerval, David. *See* Walker, David
Kettentanz (Arpino), 186, 187
Khachaturian Pas de Deux (Allan), 215
Khadra (Franca), 15, 175
Kiev Ballet, 84
Killam, Izaak Walton, 236
Killoran, Joan, *90*
Kilowatt Magic (Lloyd), 17
Kim, Willa, *231*
King, Jack, 161, 181
Kirby, Charles, 121, 179, *87*
Kirkwood, Dolores, 272
Kirov Ballet, 22, 143, 146, 152, 187, 190, 221, 286
Kirov Ballet School, 242
Kirstein, Lincoln, 22, 241–2, *240*; *see also* Canada Council; survey of ballet in Canada (1962)
Kisses (Ditchburn), *122*
Knobbs, Christopher, 115
Kolpakova, Irina, 152, 153
Kraanerg (Petit), 118–21, 127, 128, *113*, *119*
Kraul, Earl, 26, 31, 34, 58, 59, 64, 93, 95, 100–2, 103, 131, 254, *21*, *36*, *51*, *60*, *93*, *94*, *98*, *100*, *204*
Kudelka, James, 123, 161, 177, 179, 180, 181–3, 189, 210, 217, 265, 278, 280, *161*, *181*, *182*, *247*, *275*, *281*; appointment as artistic director NBOC, 284–5, *284*; as artist in residence NBOC, 183, 275–6; as company choreographer NBOC, 182, 218
Kudo, Elaine, 209
Kylián, Jirí, 217, 219, 268, 272, 273, 278

Laidlaw, Robert A., 155, 234–5
Lamy, Martine, 280, *274*, *286*
Lanchbery, John, 16, 223–4
Lander, Harald, 102, 128, 179
Larsen, Niels Bjørn, 99, 196, 198
Laurencia, pas de six (Chabukiani/Samsova), 81, 85, *84*
Lavoie, Serge, 192, 280, 281, *207*, *277*
Lavrovsky, Leonid, 85–6
Lawless, Anthony B., 39
Leese, Elizabeth, 72
Legate, Stephen, 280
Legende (Cranko), 128, *257*
Leigh, Angela, 18, *21*, *59*
Lendvai, Yseult, 273, 279, *286*
The Lesson (Flindt), 120, 126
Lightheart, Kim, 191, 215, 273, *120*, *216*
Lilac Garden (Tudor), 15, 52, 63, 76, 89, *52*

Limón, José, 71, 174, *149*
Littler, William, *113*
The Littlest One (Adams), 68
Livent Inc., 280
Lloyd, Gweneth, 7, 8, 10–12, 13, 18, 19, 21, 25, 211, 272, ch1n32; and notice concerning state of Canadian ballet, 54–5; as choreographer, 17, 45, 67; background and training, 16–17
Lois Smith Night, 106
London Festival Ballet, 69, 94–5, 162, 164, 185, 195, 198, 222; *see also* English National Ballet
Loquasto, Santo, 98, *275*
Lost in Twilight (Patsalas), 218
Le Loup (Petit), 120, 126, 149, 153
The Lovers' Gallery (Staff), 16
Lucas, Cynthia, 179, *161*, *181*, *216*

Macdonald, Brian, 11, 34, 72, 183–4, 203, 272, *68*; article in *Dancing Times,* 10, 183
Mack, Paul, 256
Mackenzie, Larry, 237
MacMillan, Kenneth, 15, 121, 146, 174, 179, 266, 268
Mad Shadows (Ditchburn), 160–1, 177, 180, 181, 186, 187, 188, 190, *161*
Madsen, Egon, 124
Majocchi, Gilda, 142
Makarova, Natalia, 96, 158, 190, 221, 272, 279, *279*
Malakhov, Vladimir, 281
Marcil, André, 252
Marcus, Howard, *87*
Margaret, Princess, 186
Mariinsky Theatre (St Petersburg), 56
Markova, Alicia, 61
Martin, John, 62
Martins, Peter, 185
Masada (Allan), 215–16, *216*
Mason, Sylvia, *21*
Massey Commission, 80, 232–3, 236, 237
Massey, Vincent, 236
Massine, Leonid, 165
Maybarduk, Linda, 179, *125*, *253*
McAllister, David, 271
McClung, Marcia, 257
McDonald, Mary, 38, *87*, *182*
McDowall, Wendy, 256
McEachren, Frank, 246
McGill Chamber Orchestra, 218
McKim, Ross, 121
McLeod, Ian H., 159, 165, 172
Meadows, Howard, 23, 34, *21*, *23*
Menck, Susa, *143*
Mercury Theatre (London), 4, 15
The Mermaid (Howard), 64
The Merry Widow (Hynd/Helpmann), 223–4, 278
Mess, Suzanne, 37, 68
Messerer, Asaf, 85–6
Messiaen, Olivier, 266

Metropolitan Ballet, 6, 13, 15–16, 33, 54, 85, 99, 124, 161, ch1n41
Metropolitan Opera House (New York), 130, 142, 149, 150, 158, 161, 171, 173, 184, 185, 215, 221
Mets, Laine, 45
Michaud, Monique, 122, 247
Michener, Wendy, 108
Minkus, Ludwig, 187
The Miraculous Mandarin (Kudelka), 275, 280
The Mirror Walkers (Wright), 120, 127
Mirvish, Ed, 86
Miss Julie (Cullberg), 171
Mobile (Ruud), 210
Moller, Ray, 72, *3*, *60*
Monahan, James, 129
Monotones (Ashton), 36, 207
Monotones II (Ashton), 177
Montague, Owen, 98, 192, 220, 273, 280, 281, *203*, *207*, *216*, *218*
A Month in the Country (Ashton), 175, 177, 179, 280
Montreal Festival (1957), 81
Montreal Star, 61
Montreal Symphony, 126–7, 232, 252, ch9n20
Monument for a Dead Boy (van Dantzig), 177
The Moor's Pavane (Limón), 143, 149, 174, *149*
Morton, James, 136
Moscow International Ballet Competition (1973), 151, 152–4
Mozart, Wolfgang Amadeus, 276
Mulqueen, Sydney, 4, 8, 9, 12, 53, 155, 231, 233, 235, *231*
Munch, Edvard, 181
Munro, Alastair, *75*
Murphy, Father Stanley, 252
Musings (Kudelka), 275, 280

Napoli (Bournonville/Gnatt), 195; (Bournonville/Schaufuss), 195–6, 198, *169*, *192*, *197*; Toronto opening, 196–7
Nataraja (Patsalas), 180, 183, *264*
National Archives of Canada, 64
National Arts Centre (Ottawa), 39, 118–21, 127, 133, 136, 143, 146–7, 148, 256
National Arts Centre Orchestra, 136
National Ballet Guild of Canada, 17, 21, 24, 37, 110, 233, 235, 244, 245; regional branches, 233, 248–55; summer school, 20–1, 22–3, 24, 37; *see also* National Ballet of Canada; board of directors
National Ballet of Canada; and Canadian choreography, 34, 36, 56, 67–74, 122–3, 127, 161, 179–84, 210–11, 215–19; and guest artists, 6, 83, 127–8, *257*; and rivalry with Royal Winnipeg Ballet, 17, 24–5, 55; and touring, 52, 54, 55, 57, 58, 59–61, 132, 143, 214, 234, 235, 248–52, 254, 268–9, 273; archives, xi, 9, 11, 91, 224; Artistic Management Committee, 117, 163; Artistic Management Council, 117, 123; audition tour (1951), 20, 24–6; Ballet Concert, 109, 269; Belleville engagement (1956), 250–2; board of directors, 42, 53, 54, 55, 58, 87, 107, 113–16, 117, 118, 123, 133, 135, 159–60, 161, 162, 163–4, 193–5, 196, 207, 231–2, 255, 258, 261, 263, 266, 269, 271, 274; choreographic workshops, 46, 121–3, 177, 180, 215, 217; concert group, 268–9, 274, 275; Covent Garden début (1979), 185–7, 193, 195, 198; Covent Garden début (1979) critical reception, 186–91; Creating Dances in the Schools, 282; Dancers' Council, 114–15, 118, 121; dancers' representation on board of directors, 133, 194; early press coverage, 62, 239–40; European tour (1972), 126–30, 131–2, 135–6, 186, 187, 217, *113*, *134*, *257*; European tour (1975), 157, 186, 190; European tour (1985), 208, 214; European tour (1987), *129*; European tour (1989), 274; expansion during *Romeo and Juliet*, 94–5, 123; expansion during *Sleeping Beauty*, 131–3, 152; financial affairs, 52–3, 54, 55, 79, 81, 107, 114, 133, 141–2, 150, 196, 213, 232, 233–5, 237, 246, 255, 273; first performance (1951), 33–4; first performance (1951), critical response to, 34–6; gala (1984), 209–11, 214; marketing, fundraising, and development, 81, 209, 212–14, 248, 255–6, 270, *234*; national scope of, 12, 19; palace revolution (1972), 133–5, 136, 247, 256, 258; Prologue to the Performing Arts, 115, 282; set painting, *238*; Shell student matinees, 282; Stepping Out, 282–3; subscription ticket sales, 115, 212–13, 268; Townsend report, 117; *A Tribute to George Balanchine*, *222–3*, wardrobe, *238* orchestra, 37–8, 136
National Ballet School, 7, 21, 22, 85–6, 97–8, 122, 152, 153, 171, 178, 180, 191, 192, 197, 207–8, 210, 217, 219, 220, 242, 254, 264, 272, 274, 280–2, 284, *120*, *161*, *204*, *207*, *254*, *281*
National Gallery of Canada, 235
Negin, Mark, 70
Netherlands Dance Theatre, 219, 266, 273
Neumeier, John, 154, 161, 170, 199, 217, 276
New York City Ballet, 5, 6, 82, 83, 171, 185, 222, 241, 285
New York Times, 71, 107, 171, 172
Newburger, Gretchen, *38*
Newcomers (Macdonald), 183–4; Fantasmes, 184
Nielsen, Kim, *261*
Nijinsky, Vaslav, 15, 165
Nisbet, Joanne, 38, 48, 63, 96, *38*, *47*
Nixon, David, 192, 220, *141*, *192*, *218*, *231*
Norman, Gary, 155
Now and Then (Neumeier), 276
Nureyev, Rudolf, 38, 84, 85, 99–102, 103–4, 105, 118, 130–3, 136–7, 141–4, 148, 149, 150, 153, 154, 157, 158, 169–70, 184, 185, 187, 196, 199, 209, 222, *100*, *141*, *143*, *147*, *149*, *169*, *170*; influence on NBOC, 144–6, 151–2, 171–4
The Nutcracker (Petipa/Ivanoff), 26; (Petipa/Ivanoff/Balanchine), 60; (Petipa/Ivanoff/Christensen), 60; (Petipa/Ivanoff/Franca), 56, 58, 96, 98–9, 102, 107, 123, 148, 149, *258*; (Petipa/Ivanoff/Kudelka), 98, 256, 275, 285, *275*, *281*; (Petipa/Ivanoff/Toumine), 60, ch3n35
Nychka, Ronda, 267, *264*, *267*

Observer, 187
Odeon Palace Theatre (Hamilton), 58
Offenbach in the Underworld (Tudor), 63, 76, 199
Oiseaux Exotiques (Patsalas), 218, *213*
O'Keefe Centre (Toronto), 70, 71, 76, 86–7, 89, 107, 109, 123, 126, 128, 131, 155, 196, 213, 215, 269, 271, 278, 282, 283, *79*, *203*
Olds, Elizabeth, *223*
Oliphant, Betty, 8, 17, 18–20, 21, 22–3, 26, 31, 32, 39–42, 48, 99, 115, 117, 121, 136–7, 159, 164, 170, 190, 193–4, 205, 281; and Cecchetti tradition, 5, 19–20, 22, 40–1, *18*; and the National Ballet School, 40, 42, 97, 134, 242, 282, *41*, *204*; as associate artistic director NBOC, 42, 116, 134; as ballet mistress NBOC, 40, 134, *21*; as dance educator, 7, 42, 86, 152; resignation as associate artistic director NBOC (1975), 42, 162–3; response to palace revolution (1972), 134–5
Onegin (Cranko), 88, 89, 199, 271–2, 276, *261*
Ontario Arts Council, 236, 246, 247, 283, 284
Oracle (Tetley), 179, 267, 269
Orange Lodge, 51, ch3n3
Osborne, Gregory, 215, *216*
Ottawa Ballet Company, 60, ch3n35
Ottawa Citizen, 176
Ottmann, Peter, 98, 179, 220
Oxenham, Andrew, *113*

Pape, James, 37
Paper Things, 253
Paquita (Petipa/Makarova), 279
Paris Opéra Ballet, 105, 123, 209
Parsons, David, 268
A Party (Kudelka), 177, 180
Pas de Chance (Adams), 68
Pas de Deux Romantique (Adams), 68
Pas de Six (Adams), 68
Pastorale (Kudelka), 182–3, 275, *274*
Les Patineurs (Ashton), 66, 177, 178, 207

Patsalas, Constantin, 123, 177, 179, 180, 183, 189, 217–19, *203, 218, 264*; and suit for constructive dismissal, 218, 263–4; as artistic advisor NBOC, 262–3, 266, *262*; as company choreographer NBOC, 182, 217–18; as resident choreographer NBOC, 210, 217, 218, 264; death (1989), 264–5
Patterson, Gregory, 257
Pavlova, Anna, 85, 151; Franca's dancing compared to, 35
Penzhorn, Dieter, 132, 152
Percival, John, 124, 189, 190
Perrot, Jules, 123
Persson, Johann, 281
Petipa, Marius, 22, 34, 48, 59, 123, 141, 142, 151, 162, 187, 222, 279
Petit, Roland, 118, 120, 174, *113*
Petrushka (Fokine), 162, 165
Phantom of the Opera (Webber), 98
Phases (Strate), 126
Philadelphia Ballet Guild, 63
Piano Concerto (Patsalas), 218; *see also Concerto for the Elements* (Patsalas)
Picasso, Pablo, 4
Piletta, Georges, 118, 128
Pineapple Poll (Cranko), 65–6, 89, *65, 66*
Pitblado, Jim, 256
Pitblado, Sandra, 256
Place des Arts (Montreal), 89, 147, 269
Playhouse (Kudelka), 180
Poll, Heinz, 109
Polovetsian Dances (Prince Igor) (Fokine/Beriosoff), 16; (Fokine/Franca), 33, 35; (Fokine/Volkoff), 34
Le Pommier (Franca), 72–3, *73*
Poole, William, 256
Popa, Magdalena, *129, 279*
Porteous, Timothy, 238
Post Script (Macdonald), 183
Potts, Nadia, 98, 131, 134, 149, 153, 178, 198, 212, 227, *192, 253*
Premiere Dance Theatre (Toronto), 264
Pride and Prejudice (Lloyd), 17
La Prima Ballerina (Heiden), 109–10
Prince of the Pagodas (Cranko), 65
Princess Aurora (Petipa/Franca), 59
Prokofiev, Serge, 89, 106
Prologue to the Performing Arts. *See* National Ballet of Canada; Prologue to the Performing Arts
Promenade Concerts, Varsity Arena, 23
Pugh, Kevin, 98, 179, 192, 220, 265, 273, 281, *192, 213*

Quinn, Pierre, 98, 280, *207*
Quinte Dance Centre, 252
Raab, Mark, *211*
Rachmaninoff, Sergei, 64, 215
Radio City Music Hall Rockettes, 6
The Rake's Progress (de Valois), 66, 87–8, 95, 96, *79, 87*
Rambert, Marie, 4, 5, 7, 16, 19, 53, 54, 64, 128
Randazzo, Anthony, 192, 281, *207*
Ransom, Jeremy, 98, 104, 192, 271, 280, 281, *275*
Ransom, Kay, 8–9, 233
Raymonda, Act III (Petipa/Westmoreland), 222
Realm (Earle), 215
The Red Shoes, 4
Reid, Maggie, 252
Reid, Wendy, 212, 256
Les Rendezvous (Ashton), 66
Rimsky-Korsakov, Nikolai, 161
Riopelle, Jean-Paul, 118
The Rite of Spring (Tetley), 267, 276; (Nijinsky), 165; (Patsalas), 180, 183, 266
Ritter, Alexander, 271, 280
Robarts, John, 246
Robbins, Jerome, 152, 177
Roberts, Jean, 115, 247
Romeo and Juliet (Ashton), 185; (Cranko), xi, 88–96, 98–9, 102, 106, 108, 121, 126, 127, 131, 152, 177, 198, 252–3, 276–7, *90, 93, 94, 243, 276*; negotiations for rights, 66, 89, 90–3; (MacMillan), 132, 174; (Nureyev), 185
Ronaldson, James, 39, 133, *52*
La Ronde (Tetley), 267, *267, 270*
Roper, June, 7
Rose Latulippe (Macdonald), 183
Rose, Jürgen, 90, 93, 96, 107, *90, 243, 276*
Rothwell, Clinton, 153, 184, *119*
Roussel, Paul, 72
Roxander, David, *192*
Royal Academy of Dancing, 21, 272
Royal Academy of Dancing Gazette, 31
Royal Alexandra Theatre (Toronto), 60, 76, 128, *29, 57, 65*
Royal Ballet, 4, 14–15, 16, 66–7, 69, 85, 87, 88, 99, 103, 106, 108, 122, 125, 130, 146, 150, 171, 174–6, 178, 179, 186, 187, 189, 191–2, 196, 199, 268, 270, 280, 284, 285, *187, 286*; Ballet for All, 69, 122, 175, 186; *see also* Sadler's Wells Ballet
Royal Ballet School, 207, 208, 242, 272, *281*
Royal Commission on National Development in the Arts, Letters, and Sciences (1951). *See* Massey Commission
Royal Danish Ballet, 16, 99, 102, 128, 184, 195, 209, 224, 264, 270, 271
Royal Flemish Ballet, 71
Royal Opera Ballet (London), 272
Royal Opera House Covent Garden (London), 15, 59, 65, 73, 118, 128, 132, 161, 174–5, 176, 186, 187
Royal Swedish Ballet, 42, 109, 171, 183, 222
Royal Winnipeg Ballet, 7, 11, 25, 55, 66, 76, 81, 126, 154, 161, 178, 183, 210, 219, 239, 241, 243–4, 245, 248, 272, *223*; *see also* Winnipeg Ballet
Rusk, Dean, 236
Russell, Wallace A., 39, 116, 133–6, 137; resignation as general manager NBOC (1972), 135
Ruud, Tomm, 210
Ryerson Theatre (Toronto), 121

S'Agapo (Patsalas), 210
Sadler's Wells Ballet, 4–5, 8, 15, 16, 33, 56, 59, 61, 65, 73–4, 99, 146, 174–5, 191; *see also* Royal Ballet
Sadler's Wells Theatre (London), 128
Sadler's Wells Theatre Ballet, 6, 13, 14, 15, 106
St Laurent, Louis, 235, 236
St Lawrence Hall, 21, 23, 51, 269, ch3n3, *46, 98*; fire (1973), 92, 108, 177
St Margaret's Church, Eglinton, 51
Samsova, Galina, 18, 76, 82, 84–5, 93–4, 95, 96–7, 131, 186, 242, *84, 93*
San Francisco Ballet, 60, 192, 210, 284
Satie, Erik, 177
Saturday Review, 184
La Scala (Milan), 142, 143, 150, 209
Schafer, Lawrence, 87
Schaufuss, Frank, 102
Schaufuss, Peter, 102, 178, 184–5, 189, 195–8, 203, *169, 184, 187, 189, 192*
Schéhérazade (Fokine), 162
Schelhorn, Amalia, 191
Schramek, Tomas, 96, 131, 145, 155, 178, 180, *125*
Schubert, Franz, 64
Scott, Brian, *79*
Scott, David, 38, 48, 212, *38*
Scottish Ballet, 195
Seillier, Daniel, 109
Semenoff, Simon, *173*
Sequel (Strate), 70
Serenade (Balanchine), 76, 82, 83–4, 222, 244, *79*
Sergeyev, Konstantin, 106, 107
Sergeyev, Nicholas, 56, 61, ch3n26
Seymour, Lynn, 87, 88, 99–102, 118–19, 124, 174, 185, *100, 122*
Shaw Festival, 246
Shearer, Moira, 4
Shubert theatres (New York), 234
Sinatra Suite (Tharp), 209
Sinfonia (Patsalas), 218
Skinner, Dr Alan, 234, 252
The Sleeping Beauty (Petipa), 59, 73–4, 174–5, *60*; (Petipa/Nureyev), 130–3, 151, 153, 154, 170, 173, 198, 209, 211, 278, *132, 141, 143, 147, 173*; New York opening, critical response to, 149–50; preparations and rehearsal period for, 141–6; production and touring problems of, 146–9; Bluebird pas de deux (Petipa), 146; — (Petipa/Nureyev), 145, 148, 153, *153*
Smith, Barbara, 269, *203, 211, 261*
Smith, Lois, 6, 7, 17, 23, 24, 25, 33, 34, 57, 58–9, 62, 68, 76, 95, 98, 101–2, 106, 131, 198, 199, ch3n28, *3, 5, 21, 29, 59, 79, 87, 100, 250*
Smith, Raymond, 98, 220, 280, *178, 192, 216, 261*
Sokolow, Anna, 70, 71
Soldiers' Mass (Kylián), 219

Soleri, Kristine, *147*
Solitaire (MacMillan), 97, 121, 268, *120*
Solov, Zachary, 109
Somers, Harry, 70, 71
Song of a Wayfarer (Béjart), 179
Song of the Earth (MacMillan), 179, 266, 268
Southam, Hamilton, 118
Spain, Timothy, 121, 122, *119*
Sphinx (Tetley), 179, 199, 220, *231*
Split House Geometric (Alleyne), 269, 274
Spohr, Arnold, 25, 272
Sports committee for Canada, 7
Spring Awakening (Kudelka), 275
Staff, Frank, 16
Stannus, Edris. *See* de Valois, Ninette
Stefanschi, Sergiu, 131, *103*, *125*, *159*
Le Stelle e Solisti Balletto Canadese, 215
Stevenson, Ben, 108, 278
Stewart, Katharine, *36*
Stolar, William, 192, 193
Stone, Paddy, 6
The Strangeness of a Kiss (Bennathan), 269
Strate, Grant, 25–6, 35, 45–8, 63, 64, 65–6, 68, 69–72, 73, 81, 82, 83, 88–9, 91–2, 104, 105, 117, 118, 120, 180, 218, 265, *21*, *66*; as assistant to Franca, 46, *46*; as choreographer, 47, 109, ch2n63; as resident choreographer NBOC, 46, 121; evaluation of English and American ballet, 46–7; influence of American choreography on, 70
Stratford Festival (Ontario), 70, 81, 103, 109, 121, 183, 232, 246, 256, ch9n20
Stravinsky, Igor, 4
Strike, Maurice, 155
The Stuttgart Ballet, 88–9, 91–3, 95, 124, 184, 189, 210, 217, 266, 268, 271–3, 276, 277, 282, 284
Subscription ticket sales. *See* National Ballet of Canada; subscription ticket sales
Sunday Telegraph (London), 189
Surmeyan, Hazaros, 155, 179
Swan Lake (Petipa/Ivanof), 68; (Petipa/Ivanof/Balanchine), 61; (Petipa/Ivanof/Bruhn), 95, 96, 102–6, 108, 121, 123, 126, 127, 148, 149, 176, 185, 186, 187, 188, 278, 280, *103*; Bruhn's Act I solo for Prince, 103–4, 188; Bruhn/Nureyev collaboration on, 104; compression into two acts, 104–5, 129, 155; von Rothbart as woman in, 105–6; pas de trois, 176, 186; (Petipa/Ivanof/Christensen), 60–1; (Petipa/Ivanoff/Franca), 56, 58–9, 61, 62, 102, *5*, *59*, *61*
La Sylphide (Bournonville/Bruhn), 95, 96, 127, 128, 129, 145, 146, 149, 158, 170, 176, 194, 197, 224, *113*, *204*; Toronto première, 99–102, 157, *100*; (Bournonville/Lander), 102, 128; (Bournonville/Schaufuss), 195
Les Sylphides (Fokine), 34; (Fokine/Bruhn/Franca), 154; (Fokine/Franca), 30, 33, 121, 144, *29*, *30*, *32*
Symphonic Variations (Ashton), 66, *286*
Symphony in C (Balanchine), 222, *223*

T. Eaton Company, 18
Taglioni, Marie, 110
Tagore (Tetley), 267
The Taming of the Shrew (Cranko), 88, 89, 256, 277–8, *276*, *277*
Tanner, Bob, 250, 251
Tanner, Joan, 250
Taylor, E.P., 81
Taylor, Paul, 70
Tchaikovsky, Peter Ilich, 84, 103
Teatro San Carlo (Naples), 197
Telegram (Toronto), 35, 36, 107, *55*
Tennant, Veronica, 58, 84, 86, 95, 98, 128, 129, 131, 133, 134, 144, 148, 149, 155, 170, 178, 181, 198, 203, 208, 210, 215, 216, 224, 225, 272, 280, 284, *79*, *87*, *94*, *108*, *113*, *119*, *141*, *143*, *147*, *192*, *216*, *277*; farewell performance (1989), 265, 277–8; retirement from dancing, 276–7
Ter-Arutunian, Rouben, *231*
Terelle, Jocelyn, 82, *51*
Terry, Walter, 184, 185
Tessmer, Karyn, 179, *178*
Tetley, Glen, 179, 199, 219–21, 269, 271, 272, 276, 278, 280, *221*, *225*, *231*, *270*; as artistic associate NBOC, 266–9
Tewsley, Robert, 281, *274*, *281*, *286*
Tharp, Twyla, 209
Theatre under the Stars, 6
Thistle, Lauretta, 176
Thomas, Don, 251
The Three-Cornered Hat (Massine), 165
Time Cycle (Strate), 70
Times (London), 124
Toronto Dance Theatre, 210
Toronto International Festival (1984), 199, 271
Toronto Star, 74, 195, *113*
Toronto Symphony, 39, 232, 246, ch9n20
Toronto Theatre Ballet, 18
Toumine, Nesta, 60
Town, Harold, 70, 71, *71*
Townsend report. *See* National Ballet of Canada; Townsend report
Transfigured Night (Kylián), 219
Trapdance (Alleyne), 269, 274
Triptych (Strate), 102, 109
Trueman, A.W., 236, 238, 239
Tudor, Antony, 5, 15, 16, 19, 36, 52, 56, 63–4, 65, 68, 71, 76, 82, 127, 199, 253, 267, *253*
The Two Pigeons (Ashton), 177, 178, 207, *178*, *182*

Ulanova, Galina, 85–6
Ursuliak, Alexander, 84, 242

Vaganova Academy (St Petersburg), 279
Vaganova technique, 22
Valukin, Eugen, 86, 221, *187*
van Hamel, Martine, 76, 82, 86, 95, 97–8, 102, 131, 153, 220, *79*, *98*, *120*
van Manen, Hans, 177
van Praagh, Peggy, 41, 66
Vancouver Festival, ch9n20
Vangsaae, Mona, 184
Variety, 150
Varna International Ballet Competition (1966), 97, 153; (1970), 153; (1980), 125
Varsity Arena (University of Toronto), 57
Vasarely, Victor, 118, *119*
Vesak, Norbert, 161
Volkoff, Boris, 7–8, 9, 10–12, 13, 16, 18, 19, 21, 23, 26, 34, 37, 211, ch1,n32; as teacher, 6, 17–18, 41, 85; at Berlin Olympics (1936), 7; background and training, 17
Volkoff, Janet. *See* Baldwin, Janet
Volkoff Canadian Ballet, 8
Voluntaries (Tetley), 267
Volunteer Committee Build-a-Ballet Fund, 254, 255, 273, *231*
von Gencsy, Eva, 272
Vousden, Sydney, *23*

Walker, David, 39
Wallis, Lynn, 207–8, 265, 266, 274, 285, *262*; as artistic co-ordinator NBOC, 207; as co-artistic director NBOC, 261–3, 268–71
Walpurgis Night, pas de deux (Lavrovsky), 85
Walter Carsen Centre for the National Ballet of Canada, 52
Washington Square (Kudelka), 180, 181, *181*
Welffens, Peter, 71
Wendrup-Schandorff, Silja, 271
Westmoreland, Terry, 222
Whispers of Darkness (Vesak), 161, 163
Whistler, Rex, 87
Whitehead, Pearl, 4, 8, 9, 37, 155, 231, *231*
Whitley, Tom, *234*
Whitmore, Joseph A., 233
Whittaker, Herbert, 35, 36, *71*
Les Whoops-de-Doo (Macdonald), 183
Wickson, Mildred, 7, 13
Wigman, Mary, 45
Wilde, Patricia, 6
Wilder, Valerie, 205, 207, 212, 265–6, 274, 285, *262*; appointment as executive director NBOC, 285; as associate director NBOC, 273; as co-artistic director NBOC, 261–3, 268–71; as artistic administrator NBOC, 207
William Morris Concert Agency, 39, 127
Wilson, John H., 39, 116
Winnipeg Ballet, 7, 24, 25, 68; royal command performance (1951), 25; *see also* Royal Winnipeg Ballet
Winnipeg Ballet Club, 7
Winnipeg Free Press, 24–5
Winter Night (Gore), 64

Witkowsky, Gizella, 179, 181, 220, *218*, *223*, *231*
Woods, Aileen, 4, 8, 9–10, 11, 115, 116, 117, 155, 231, *231*
Wright, Peter, 120, 124, 125, *125*
Wyman, Max, 8, 11
Xenakis, Iannis, 118

Yeddeau, David, 8, 10, 11, 25
York University dance department, 46, 72
Yvaral, 118

Zeffirelli, Franco, 219

The text of this book has been composed in Bembo, with the margin headings set in Frutiger.

DESIGN AND LAYOUT BY
V. JOHN LEE COMMUNICATION GRAPHICS INC.

EDITORIAL DIRECTION BY RAMSAY DERRY